The Riddle of the Bamboo Annals

竹書紀年解謎

© David S. Nivison (倪德衛)

2009

airiti press.

The Riddle of the Bamboo Annals
竹 書 紀 年 解 謎

ISBN-Paperback: 978-986-85182-1-6
ISBN-Hardcover: 978-986-85182-5-4
Publishing Date: May 20, 2009
Price: Paperback USD$37
Hardcover USD$75 (Direct order from distributor)

Author: David S. Nivison 倪德衛
Consultant: Shao Dongfang
Publisher: Airiti Press Inc.
Editor in Chief: Eliza Chang
Editorial Team: Peggy Shih, Hwanyan Lu, Karen Yen
Production: David Lai
Cover Design: Hsin-ling Lin

Distributor: Airiti Inc.
10Fl-3, No. 880 Zhongzheng Rd., Zhonghe City, Taipei 23586, Taiwan, ROC
Tel: +886 2 8228 7701 Fax: +886 2 8228 7702
press@airiti.com

Subject (LC): Zhu shu ji nian (竹書紀年), China - History - Chronology

In Memory of

Wilbur Knorr

Wilbur Knorr was a Stanford professor of Classics and Philosophy, a scholar devoted to the history of Greek, Arabic and medieval Latin mathematics, whose brilliant career was cut short by early death in 1997. We had long shared an interest in ancient astronomy and chronology. The day before he died, I told him I wished to dedicate to him the book I was then writing. This is that book, already preceded by several monographs, also dedicated to Knorr. In the autumn of 1993, we taught together a "continuing education" course on world archaeoastronomy, which we called "Time and the Stars." I took responsibility for ancient China and pre-Columbian Mexico, leaving the rest of the world to Wilbur and a third participant, Vladimir S. Tuman. (Tuman was a retired professor of physics; I had retired as a Stanford professor of Chinese and Philosophy in 1988.)

-- DSN, June 2008

Scholars Recommending This Book

Ying-shih Yü　余英時
Professor Emeritus, Princeton University
美國普林斯頓大學榮休教授

Chen Li　陳力
Deputy Director, National Library of the PRC
中華人民共和國國家圖書館副館長

Victor H. Mair
Professor of Chinese Language and Literature,
Department of East Asian Languages and Civilizations,
University of Pennsylvania

David N. Keightley
Professor Emeritus, University of California, Berkeley

Shao Dongfang　邵東方
Director, East Asia Library, Stanford University
美國史丹佛大學東亞圖書館館長

Equally versed in early classical texts, oracle bone and bronze inscriptions, archaeology as well as astronomy, Professor Nivison has devoted the last 30 years to a reconstruction of Chinese chronology in high antiquity. Taking as his point of departure the authenticity of the "Modern Text" *Bamboo Annals*, an assumption diametrically opposite to the long received view, his approach had not only been revolutionary but also proved to be methodologically more fruitful in riddle-solving. The present volume, written almost wholly from 2000 to 2007, therefore represents what is called "the final conclusions arrived at late in life" (wannian dinglun 晚年定論) in the Chinese scholarly tradition. This book is also a vivid testimonial to its author's moral and intellectual integrity as a scholar in defense of historical truth. In questioning the validity of the Chinese state-sponsored "Three Dynasties Chronology Project" in a most serious manner, Professor Nivison has exercised the critical power of a historian to its highest possible degree. As a result his courageous fight for the purity of scholarship has not only won the support of many leading specialists of the field but also evoked, through Chinese translation, a widespread sympathetic response from the general reading public in China.

Ying-Shih Yü, Professor Emeritus, Princeton University
美國普林斯頓大學榮休教授　**余英時**

倪德衛先生為美國著名漢學家，研究中國上古史有年，著作等身，尤其是對於《竹書紀年》及夏商周年代學的研究，在學術界自成一派，具有很大影響。我非常敬佩倪德衛先生年逾八十仍筆耕不輟，並多有創見，也非常盼望早日見到倪德衛先生的新作出版。

《竹書紀年》為先秦重要史籍，圍繞該書，前人作了大量的研究，它不僅關乎先秦史及先秦年代學，同時它也是中國古代文獻學尤其是辨偽學的重要研究對象。近年來，夏商周年代學已然成為全世界漢學界關注的一個焦點，其中許多問題都涉及到了《竹書紀年》。相信隨著倪德衛先生新著的出版，一定會給學術界帶來新的話題，同時也會使先秦史及先秦年代學的研究進一步深入。特此推薦。

Chen Li, Deputy Director, National Library of the PRC
中華人民共和國國家圖書館副館長　**陳力**

Since 1979, a full thirty years and more, Professor David S. Nivison has been dissecting the "Modern Text" of the *Bamboo Annals* (*Jinben Zhushu Jinian*). He has applied a broad battery of analytical techniques to the data in the text, and he has been relentless in his efforts to correlate the dates in the *Bamboo Annals* with materials from historical, inscriptional, and astronomical sources. Nivison's decades-long dedication to this task has resulted in a succession of publications that have been carefully scrutinized by scholars around the world. Their criticisms have resulted in increasing refinements by Nivison. The entire process of discovery, discussion, and elaboration is now assembled in *The Riddle of the Bamboo Annals*, which constitutes a major contribution to the dating of events before 841 BC.

Victor H. Mair, Professor of Chinese Language and Literature,
Department of East Asian Languages and Civilizations,
University of Pennsylvania

Contents

Tables and Diagrams

Preface

0. There is one thing above all else that anyone beginning to read this book must recognize: The reader is going to be required to consider fairly and with an open mind argument after argument that a very widely held belief among Chinese scholars is a complete mistake. That belief is that the so-called "Modern Text" *Bamboo Annals* (*Jinben Zhushu jinian* 今本竹書紀年) is a fake, or at best a crude attempt to reconstruct the authentic original text of the ancient chronicle. This brief (2 *juan*) chronicle begins with Huang Di (implied date probably 2402 BCE) and continues to the end of the fourth century BCE. When finished it was buried (in a tomb or cache of treasures in what is now Henan), and was discovered around 280 CE. Its subsequent bibliographical record peters out with the Yuan Dynasty. There was a flurry of printings of it in late Ming. And high Qing scholars noticed that quotations from it in early encyclopedias and commentaries often differed from the received printed text. This is especially true for the last fourth of it, which is, I admit, a mess. This part will not occupy my attention. Part Three of my book will put before you my recovery of what I claim is the actual bamboo strip arrangement of (probably) the first five-sevenths of the original. Part One reprints two monographs of mine that use the *Bamboo Annals* to reconstruct the entire chronology of Ancient China down to the end of Western Zhou. (Attachments are new.) The object of my attention in Part Two is the work of the "Three Dynasties Chronology Project" (Xia-Shang-Zhou Duandai Gongcheng) in the PRC, active from 1996 through 2000 when it published its initial "brief report."

Professor Edward L. Shaughnessy opens his celebrated article "On the Authenticity of the *Bamboo Annals*" (*HJAS* 46, 1986) with a discussion of method, with my work in focus:

> Nivison's arguments for the authenticity of the data that he has utilized in one fashion or another in his chronological reconstruction are open to suspicions of circularity. His chronology must be correct for his interpretation of a multi-stage editorial process in the making of the *Bamboo Annals* to be correct, and the same is true, to some extent, in reverse. But, it is never acceptable methodology to prove one unknown with another unknown.

In fairness to both of us I should point out that Professor Shaughnessy is talking about work I did a long time ago. We have both come a long way since then. Further, his point is the need for as much hard data as possible in doing the sort of work we do. I readily agree that I need all the help I can get. But there is an idea in what I have just quoted that needs mending.

There is not just the "suspicion" of circularity in what I do. The circularity is there, and it is unavoidable. Typically, I assemble a mass of material, some of it well established data but perhaps of debatable relevance, some of it even more debatable hypothesis. Then, treating all of this as "given" (that is one point where the "circularity" comes in), I try to show that it fits together in a surprising and to me convincing way. Absolutely essential to this procedure, the massing of material must be fearless; everything, both what would favor the picture I am building and what would count against it, must be accounted for. There must be no "cherry-picking" of evidence. The aim is to end up with the best possible explanation of everything. Counter-evidence must be "explained away"; and if you can't, you are wrong.

0.1 Now consider again Shaughnessy's last sentence: "But it is never acceptable methodology to prove one unknown with another unknown." History is an inductive enterprise. We do not have two bins, for the "known" and the "unknown.' What we have are propositions with different degrees of probability. So let us translate: "It is never acceptable methodology to use a proposition with very low probability to show that another proposition with very low probability really ought to be seen as having very high probability." Or biconditionally (for that is where Shaughnessy sees "circularity" in my work), it is never allowable to put together a bunch of very low probability propositions in such a way as to try to show that they all actually have very high probability.

At this point a flood of counter-examples ought to stream into one's mind. Here is a thought experiment from one of my articles: There has been a bank robbery. The robbers have escaped in a get-away car. There are three witnesses to the escape. All three are known to the police as inveterate liars. But the police think that there could have been no collusion among them or with the robbers. They are questioned separately, and all three give the same license plate number for the car. Finish this story yourself.

Let's do it with some numbers. You have a die-like object with ten faces instead of six, the faces having the numbers 0 through 9. Testing your suspicion that the die is not "fair," you throw it and it turns up 3: one chance in ten. You throw again and get 1: again one chance in ten, but taken together, for 31, one chance in ten times ten; and so on. As you keep on, the chance that you will, just by accident, continue throw by throw to get the next number of the decimal extension of the ratio of the diameter of a perfect circle to its circumference becomes progressively infinitely small. Just for this reason, if you keep on and do actually continue to get the decimal extension of this ratio, the chance that all this has been just by accident becomes itself infinitely small. So some organizing "story" (sc. historical narrative) is ordering the "evidence": instead of having an *a priori* probability of 0.1, each throw had a probability of 1.0.

0.2 A good live example is always better than a mere thought experiment; so let me develop a historical argument that plays a large role in this book. We all know how debatable the Xia Dynasty is. Its reality is taken for granted usually in China, but is usually dismissed by Westerners. In the *Bamboo Annals*, also usually doubted (in both China and the West), there are seventeen reigns, precisely dated. Professor David W. Pankenier is an expert seen by some of us as having a hyper-active imagination that often misfires. In *Early China* 9-10 (1983-85) he sees an obscure account in *Mozi* 19 as referring to a celestial event marking the passing of heaven's approval to Yu of Xia, who in the *Annals* is received by Shun in Shun's 14th year counting from Yao''s abdication in his favor; and on this occasion Yu is given a "dark baton" which we can interpret as conveying authority. This in turn we should correlate with Shun's conveying authority to Yu in Shun's *de jure* 14th year (2029 in the *Annals*), which is treated in the *Annals* as the *de facto* beginning of Xia. The "dark baton" is the imagined shape of a spectacular conjunction in February, 1953 BCE. So that, we are invited to think, is when Xia began.

This is obviously *prima facie* highly doubtable, but I found it tempting, noting that the interval 2029 to 1953 is 76 years, one *bu*,[1] probably not an accident. Accidentally I learned in December 1988 that Kevin

---

[1] The ancient *zhang-bu* intercalation cycle assumes 365.25 days per solar year. The winter solstice coincides approximately with the first day of a lunar month every 19 years, therefore 19 years is taken as a basic unit of time, called a *zhang*, of 6939.75 days, rounded to 6940. In this period there are approximately 235 lunar months, = (12 x 19) + 7, therefore there must be seven intercalary months in one *zhang*. 4 *zhang* = 1 *bu*, = (4 x 6940) minus 1, = 27759 days. 27759 divided by 60 (the *ganzhi* cycle of 60 days) is 462 with a remainder of 39. 39 x 20 = 780, = 60 x 13. Therefore the *ganzhi* for the first day of a *bu* is unique in a period of 20 x 4 x 19 years, = 1520 years, called one *ji*. So counting backward or forward 1520 years (= 555,180 days) from a given *ganzhi* date will theoretically give the same *ganzhi* in the 60-day cycle; and counting back 5 *bu* will require counting back 15 days in the cycle of 60. Thus, knowing that *yihai* (12) was the first day of the (*jian yin*) 7th lunar month of 453 (the date of the victory of Zhao, Han and Wei over Zhi Bo), the compilers of the *Bamboo Annals* concluded that in 2353 (Huang Di 50), = 100 zhang (= 20 + 5 *bu*) before 453, the *ganzhi* for the first of the *jian yin* 7th lunar month must be *yihai* (12, = 60 + 12 = 72) minus 15 = *gengshen* (57) – as in strip *002 (pp. 126-127) below. Actually a calculation in the system is one day short for about every three centuries backward or forward. (A skeptic who thinks the *Jinben Annals* a Ming Dynasty creation must account for the foregoing, and in doing so – in order to get Huang Di 50 = 2353 -- must know of a datum not in the *Jinben* but found only in Luo Bi's *Lu shi*, saying that there was a seven-year period of mourning after Huang Di's death. The skeptic must suppose his Ming inventor knew about this and deliberately left it out of his creation, in order to fool gullible people like me.) On the intercalation cycle, see Sivin 1969 p. 14.

The zhang-bu rule for intercalation is explicit in Liu Xin's San Tong Li system. See Christopher Cullen, "The Birthday of the Old Man of Jiang County and Other Puzzles: Work in Progress on Liu Xin's Canon of the Ages," Asia Major (third series) 14.2 (2001), p. 33 and note 10. (I am indebted to Howard L. Goodman of Asia Major for calling my attention to this material.) Cullen cites work by Yabuuchi Kiyoshi expressing a common view that systematic placing of an intra-year intercalary month did not begin until the 6th century BCE. I would argue that in much earlier times the division of the tropical year into equal 24ths had been devised, and its existence indicates already a focus on the problem of how to determine when an intra-year intercalation was due: that is precisely what it was for. (There could be non-astronomical

Pang (a consultant at the Jet Propulsion Laboratory in Pasadena) had been using his computer to ferret out ancient dates, and had put his finger on the solar eclipse of October 16, 1876 BCE, as the eclipse of Zhong Kang 5th year 9th month in the *Annals*. One would need to consider also the story of an eclipse in the *Zuo zhuan*, mentioning another eclipse in "the books of Xia," possibly this one, when the sun had been in Fang (on one much debated interpretation of the *Zuo* text). Pang's eclipse was visible no nearer than Mongolia, and was ring-form, unspectacular and of low magnitude, not even considered as a possibility by Zhang Peiyu (*Early China* 15, 1990). To all this I added tentatively theories of my own that almost no one accepts: that reign lengths in the *Annals* were usually accurate; and that reigns of record usually began with the year after completion of mourning for the king's predecessor, a practice that I guessed was reflected in the Xia chronicle by gaps of one, more often two, or at times three or four years between reigns; theoretically they should all be two years.

Every item in this list was doubtable, and the cumulative doubtability of all of them just happening to be right was consequently enormous. But when I dared to write down "1953" followed by *Annals* reign lengths with two-year gaps, and calculated the exact date of the first day of the Xia-calendar 9th month of the 5th year of Zhong Kang, I got October 16, 1876. And the sun was in fact in lunar lodge Fang on this day. I concluded that the possibility of this result being accidental was so small I must accept it as correct. And this meant that *every* item, in the initially highly doubtable list, was also correct.

0.3 There were two flies in this ointment. The *Annals* account of the eclipse gave the day as *gengxu* (47), but it was really *bingchen* (53), and the year given, equivalent to 1948, was only 72 years off, not 76 years. I had to "explain away" these discordant data. I found I could do so by assuming that the author of this sentence was indeed using the *zhang-bu* intercalation cycle, as I had suspected, but was using it together with contemporary observations (late 400's) to get a date (counting back 20 *bu*) when he thought the sun would be in Fang.*

So everything fits, and the fit is the proof. If you agree, I urge you to keep on reading my book. I have just demonstrated the kind of reasoning I use in it all the time.

I owe various acknowledgements. To CSLI Stanford, for permitting my use of my article appearing here as Chapter Two. To David N. Keightley, for having pushed me into the Fufeng bronzes (and for informal instruction and encouragement for almost a decade before that, enabling me to read them). To Edward L. Shaughnessy and David W. Pankenier, for discoveries that have made this book possible. To Zhang Peiyu, Xu Fengxian, and Chang Yuzhi, for patiently reading and criticizing some of the monographs presenting the basics of my thinking. To Li Xueqin, for kind words early in my odyssey giving me the courage to go on with it. To all of these Chinese scholars for work which I have used constantly (and probably not enough). To various people unnamed, not necessarily excluding some of the above, for criticism, sometimes not gentle, provoking me into doing more work. To my friend Jiang Zudi of Intel for keeping my computer working and for sharing with me news from China and criticisms of recent archaeology. And especially to my colleague and friend Shao Dongfang, Director of Stanford's East Asia Library, for provocative scholarship, for translating much of what I have done, and for finding publishers for even more of it. Obviously I alone must answer for the results. Now that I have put it all together, *qing zhizheng*.

Others have been very important in making this book possible. Electronic editors "Peggy" Shih, "Hwanyan" Lu, "Karen" Yen and "David" Lai of Airiti Press Inc have been extraordinarily patient with their trans-Pacific author. And the book itself owes its being indirectly to the Chiang Jing-kuo Foundation, which financed my colleague Shao Dongfang for two years as we began work on our "New Translation and Study" of all texts of the Bamboo Annals, now being considered for publication by an American university

reasons for not heeding this rule, of course. An administrative decision to change the first month of the year, or mere carelessness, could result in a 13th month "year end" intercalation, or even a 14th month.) I think I have shown that the 24-fold division of the year was a feature of calendar astronomy even before Shang; and in Appendix 4 of this book I identify and analyze late Shang instances of intra-year intercalation that accord with the qi-center rule. (For the early existence of the system of 24 weather periods, see D. Nivison, "The Origin of the Chinese Lunar Lodge System," in A. Aveni, editor, World Archaeoastronomy, Cambridge, 1989.

press. Several years ago I came to see that our joint venture was not the place to publish theories about the Bamboo Annals which were my own, and which were not necessarily shared by Shao; but the Nivison-Shao book was going to have to refer to those theories; so "The Riddle" had to be written and published first.

D.S.N. 7 July, 2008

* Zhang Peiyu has pointed out to me a difficulty showing that I must assume something more here. I suppose an investigator who believed (1) that the Zhong Kang eclipse was in Fang; and (2) that counting back one whole cycle (20 *bu* = 1 *ji*, i.e., 1520 years) from a date in his own time when the sun was in Fang in Xia month 9 would get him to an ancient date when this would be true. He is trying to stretch back the received chronology so as to get Yao 1 be the numerologically required date 2145 (instead of 2026, my own calculation of the exact date for Yao 1). Toward this objective, he sets 1953 back one *bu* (76 years) to 2029, and sets 1876 (for the eclipse) back one *bu*, getting 1952. This he tests by subtracting one *ji* (1520 years) getting 432, and finds that the sun was not in Fang on the *shuo* of the Xia 9th month of that year, or the next. He keeps on trying, and 428 seems to work: the first day of the *zi* month (Xia 11th month) of 427 was *jiyou* (46); 59 days earlier, *gengxu* (47), should therefore be the first of the Xia 9th month of 428; the sun was in Fang; and 428 + 1520 = 1948 (Nivison and Pang, *Early China* 15 (1990) pp. 87-95). But 428, *zi*-calendar, was a 13-month year, and the winter solstice was the first day of 427. Applying intercalation rules, one finds that the identified month (which did in fact begin with *gengxu*) was the *intercalary* (Xia) 9th month. This may be irrelevant; but in each of the classical "Six Calendars" based on the *zhang-bu* system this month is taken as beginning with *jiyou* (46), not *gengxu* (47). So I must assume that the investigator is ignoring this (if he knew about it at all), and is simply applying the *zhang-bu* system abstractly.

(I use two ugly but conventional transcriptions. The seventh Western Zhou king I call "Yih Wang," rather than "Yi Wang," the ninth king. The ancient state which was the fief of Kangshu I call "Wey." The later state which was the major fragment of the ancient Jin state, and which gave us the *Bamboo Annals*, I call "Wei.")

The Riddle of the *Bamboo Annals*

Introduction

0.4 This book presents the results of my work, since 1979, on the *"Modern Text" Bamboo Annals*, *Jinben Zhushu jinian*. That is far too many words, so from here on I will call it simply "the BA." The BA is a short book in two *juan* (chapters? – of about 16,000 characters in all), in the form of a chronicle of the early rulers of and in north China, from the supposed first one, Huang Di (the "Yellow Emperor" – supposedly 2402-2303, as I will show) down to 299 BCE, near or at the end of the reign of the second "king" (*wang*) of the state of Wei. The BA has been called "modern" at first disparagingly, to distinguish it from an "ancient text" (*guben*) which appeared to be different, surviving now only in quoted fragments collected from sources such as old encyclopedias and historical commentaries. In other words "modern" meant fake, the firm judgment of the greatest scholars of eighteenth century China.[1] Thirty years ago I would have agreed. Fake it is not; but "modern" it has come to be named.

The original text that became the BA was discovered around 280 CE in a royal tomb or underground royal storehouse in Jixian, in the part of Henan which is north of the Yellow River. (The date given in the *Jin shu* "Annals of the Emperors" is 279.) This tomb or storehouse must have been tunneled into a hillside, because the peasant woodcutter who stumbled on it was able to walk in. He probably found treasures of obvious value, perhaps such as bronze ritual objects, and also convenient bundles of sticks which he was able to use as torches to light his way. Before he had used up too many torches, fortunately his discovery came to the attention of local officials, and then to the imperial court of what we call the Western Jin Dynasty. The bundles of sticks were of course books, written on bundles of carefully prepared strips of bamboo. These books had been lying hidden safely underground for almost six centuries. One of them, still relatively intact, was the book that became, after non-significant editing, what I am now calling the BA.

This claim is disputed. The judgment of the Qian Long scholars was not absurd. Tang bibliographies record a text in 12, or 13, or 14 *juan*. There is little in Song and Yuan, and nothing after that, until late Ming, when many editions of the two-*juan* text appear. And it is true that there are many quotations or paraphrases of a "Bamboo Annals" or "Annals from Jixian" that differ from the BA, especially from the last third of the second *juan* of it. It seemed that the original was much longer, and had disappeared by Yuan times, and that either someone in the Ming Dynasty had tried to reconstitute a text from quoted fragments and other material, guessing at reign lengths, and the result had gotten accepted as authentic; or else someone less scrupulous had simply put together a deliberate fake, passing it off as the authentic original.

But the difference between 2 and 12 or 13 or 14 could be simply different ways of organizing the same text, And it could well be that two texts were produced by Jin Dynasty court scholars that were almost the same for the most part, but differed considerably otherwise. It is known that there were two teams of Jin scholars working on the discovered original, one including Xun Xu and He Qiao for several years beginning probably in 281, and another including Shu Xi working more carefully on remaining difficulties beginning about 290. It is my opinion that the early bibliographies record the work of the second group, which has not survived except in quoted fragments, and that the first group's work has survived, and indeed is what accounts for a lot of the quotations, though still a lot of the quotations are from the lost work of the second group. I also think that anyone looking at the BA would have to agree that even at best we must assume that the last part of the discovered original was in very bad shape when it reached the Jin court, the bamboo strips at that point unbound and scattered, many damaged, and some lost entirely. I will be dealing with this last part almost not at all.

---

[1] One of the strongest condemnations is in the account (*tiyao*) in the published catalog of the Imperial Manuscript Library *Siku quanshu zongmu*. For the concurring opinion of the historical critic Zhang Xuecheng see his "Notes of 1795" ("Yimao Zhaji"), *Zhang shi yishu* (Jiayetang edition), "Waibian" 2, pp. 16b-17a.

Opinion among Chinese scholars in China since the eighteenth century has been divided. By the twentieth century the majority of scholars in China and almost all Western scholars had come to accept the judgment of Wang Guowei (d. 1927). (This is what I myself was taught in graduate school at Harvard.) Wang believed the BA to be an outright forgery. He published a text of it with notes trying to show how every item in it could have been obtained or derived by the forger from previously known material – except, significantly, for lengths of reigns, i.e., for claimed absolute dates. For these he has to suppose that the forger relied heavily on his own imagination. I will be arguing that this is exactly where the forgery hypothesis – or the reconstitution hypothesis, for that matter -- can be shown to be simply impossible.

0.5 The twentieth century has witnessed a wealth of archaeological discovery, tempting many scholars to try to extend back into time our knowledge of Chinese history, especially of datable history. (The earliest generally accepted date is 841 BCE, the first year of the "Gong He" Regency after the flight into exile of the tenth Western Zhou king Li Wang. The *Shiji*, the first general history of China in the early 1st century BCE, gives us that date, carefully matched with dates of rulers of contemporary regional states.) Much of the newly discovered material contains dates, but dates that are frustratingly incomplete. The many thousands of oracle bone inscriptions almost always have day dates in the 60-day cycle, sometimes also lunar month dates (in an unknown lunar calendar), very rarely the reign year of the current king (unnamed), and even more rarely referring to an eclipse. Ritual bronze vessels of the Western Zhou often have inscriptions, and over sixty of these have "complete" dates of hotly disputed meaning: typically the year of the king's reign (almost never naming the king), the lunar month (four possible first months), a technical term probably naming the quarter (much dispute there), and the cycle for the day. With this in hand you use a good lunar calendar (the best is by Zhang Peiyu) and do some educated guessing. I have spent many hours playing this game. One also draws on similar material in ancient literature.

Sooner or later someone was bound to think of bringing the scorned BA into this mix. I was that person, one Sunday night in November 1979, as I was preparing a seminar lecture for the next evening, facing a handful of professors (including David N. Keightley) and graduate students from Berkeley and Stanford. The subject was to be (at Professor Keightley's request) the recently discovered cache of bronzes from Fufeng, Shaanxi. From recent excavation reports and from published collections of bronze inscriptions I selected some "fully dated" ones that had to be related, four of them describing royal audiences in a building called the "Shilu Palace" and with the same named officer, "Sima Gong," introducing to the king the guest and maker of the vessel. The year dates were low, so I was probably looking for a short reign, the style of the characters telling me it should be somewhere around 870-850. So why not check the BA? After all, no one was watching me. Guiltily I reached for Legge's text in his translation of the *Shang shu*. The BA dates Xiao Wang 870-862, Yi Wang 861-854, and Li Wang 853-842.

Within five minutes I realized that I was staring in disbelief at my major work for the rest of my life. The dates in the BA didn't work, but three of the dates in the inscriptions implied the same *yuan* year, and all were so close to what the *Shiji* "*shijia*" chapters implied that the BA dates though wrong had to be based in some way on the real dates, and I had to find out how and why. The BA thus was not a fake but a priceless historical source. The seminar the next evening was exciting, and shaped the careers of two of the graduate students, Ed Shaughnessy and David W. Pankenier.

0.6 I had decided that the four "Shilu Palace" inscriptions belonged to the reign of Yi Wang. This created a puzzle, because three of them probably implied 867 as first year, but one implied a date two years later.[2] The same problem confronted me in two inscriptions naming Gong Wang as reigning king: the later one implied a first year two years later than the other. Soon I found more examples of this, in inscriptions with high year numbers requiring assignment to the reign of Xuan Wang, whose first year 827 was not in dispute; yet several from 809 on required 825 as *yuan*. Examples mounted up: The BA gives Wen Wang of Zhou a reign of 52 years; but in the *Shiji* it is 50.

---

[2] I am assuming that Yi Wang's father Yih Wang was still alive during the irregular king Xiao Wang's first five years and died in 868; and that a Xiao Wang court continued until 864, when Prince Hu (later Li Wang) was born.

The explanation is revealed in the BA itself: the chronicle for the Xia Dynasty begins with Yu, and at his death his hand-picked successor was ignored. "After the three years of mourning the world turned to Qi," Yu's son. From then on, after the death of almost every king there is a gap of a few years, most often two, which have to be for completion of mourning. After Xia, mourning for the deceased king did not demand an interregnum but did get reflected in the calendar, the post-mourning "accession" date being observed later in a reign, as Shaughnessy pointed out to me, perhaps after the deceased king's chief officers had retired, been dismissed, or died, I reasoned.[3]

Shaughnessy alone has accepted this idea. Without exception, as far as I know, scholars in China have rejected it, often emphatically, if they have considered the matter at all.[4] But I have found it to be the primary key explaining how and why the dates in the BA differ from the real ones. For chronicles in the book after the Xia, editing of the original text during Warring States in the fourth century BCE forgot or resisted this principle. First years of reigns got pushed forward or backward as a result. In one case two reigns (Tai Wu and Yong Ji of Shang) actually got reversed. In another case, a whole reign was invented, the reign of the infamous "bad last emperor" Jie (Di Gui) of Xia. There were, of course, other factors involved. I have worked all this out in Chapter Two, which republishes my paper in a conference volume (2000) for a small conference (1998) at Stanford in memory of my late friend Wilbur Knorr. Chapter One is devoted to an ancient vexing problem, the disputed date of the Zhou conquest of Shang. This chapter is the previously unpublished English original of an article I published in China in 1997.

These opening chapters, recovering historical information with the help of the BA, owe much to discoveries in 1982-1984 made by Shaughnessy and Pankenier. In fact the second chapter would have been impossible without them; for I doubt that I would ever have hit on the essential insights myself. In *Early China* 7 (1981-1982, appearing in 1983) -- Pankenier had beaten me into print: I published as quickly as I could (too quickly in fact) in the *Harvard Journal of Asiatic Studies* at the end of 1983 -- Pankenier explained puzzling astronomical data in the Xia Di Gui chronicle (dated 1580, but actually late 1576); and in 1984 (publishing in *EC* 9-10) he identified a spectacular conjunction of the five visible planets in February of 1953 BCE, convincingly linking it to Shun's transfer of authority to Yu, thus beginning the Xia Dynasty.

Alerted by a phone call in December of 1988, from Ashley Dunn, a science writer for the *Los Angeles Times*, I looked at work on an ancient early Xia solar eclipse by Kevin Pang, an investigator working for the Pasadena Jet Propulsion Laboratory. I thereby discovered another proof of Pankenier's discovery. (Pang and I published in *EC* 15, in 1990. I had invited Pankenier to be a co-author but he declined.) This soon led me on to an exact chronology of reigns, to the day, for all of Xia and all of Shang. By 1995 (up-dated 1997) I had in hand the draft of a book, now already rendered as a whole obsolete by more discoveries; but two chapters of that are in print (1997 and 1998) in China, one being the Chinese version of Chapter One of the present book, solving (so I claim) the problem of the date of the Zhou conquest. Otherwise the 1995-1997 book draft will probably remain unpublished, but I condensed the essence of it into a long monograph published in Victor Mair's *Sino-Platonic Papers* in 1999. My friend and collaborator Shao Dongfang, now head of Stanford's East Asia Library, translated this for me and arranged publication in Taipei in 2002.

0.7 The mourning-completion idea is probably the major stumbling block to acceptance of my work in the PRC. It is probably true that one will accept it if and only if one also accepts the BA as authentic, and the leading mainland Chinese scholars reject both.[5] In 1995 (the year of my book draft!), at the urging of State Councilor Song Jian, the PRC government decided to finance an enormous five-year project to involve two hundred or more scholars and scientists in various fields, to work out scientifically an exact chronology of Chinese history as far back as possible before 841. This "Three Dynasties Project" (Xia-Shang-Zhou Duandai Gongcheng) was to report in 2000. I knew that the Project would simply ignore the BA, and I knew by this time that the BA was essential to working out a chronology (having already done it myself).

---

[3] 809 was the year following completion of mourning for Gong He, who had been Regent during Li Wang's exile. (The *Shiji* mixes up Gong He and his probably much younger brother Gong Yu.)

[4] Actually, Wang Guowei refers to the idea, in guessing why his supposed forger handled Xia chronology as he did. Wang treats the theory as so familiar as not to require a reference. (*Jinben Zhushu jinian shuzheng*, at the end of Xia; he might have cited Lei Xueqi, *Yizheng* at Wen Ding 12, who cites *Han shi nei zhuan and Zheng Xuan*)

[5] Pankenier is an exception. He rejects the Nivison-Shaughnessy hypothesis but does accept the BA as for the most part authentic, though (he thinks) badly deformed in its present account of conquest era events. Chen Li is another exception, if he still believes the three years mourning is a late invention.

This challenge accounts for the next four chapters. For the 1998 annual meeting of the Association for Asian Studies I organized (with D. N. Keightley) a "roundtable" to discuss the PRC Project and its prospects, as sympathetically as we could. My notes on that meeting, prepared with Keightley's help, constitutes Chapter Three. Chapter Four is a paper of mine for the 2002 AAS meeting in Washington DC. Four of the leading Project scholars were in the panel with me with papers of their own, and Shao Dongfang too had a paper. A week later most of us met again at the University of Chicago, where (April 12) I gave the annual H. G. Creel Lecture, invited by Shaughnessy, who had long been a professor there. That lecture's focus by no accident was the ancient Chinese three-years mourning institution and its importance for the study of Chinese chronology, with three of the four PRC guests listening. You have it now as Chapter Five. Chapter Six is a paper for another conference, now postponed indefinitely, which was to be held in Beijing in October of 2003. As a preface to Chapter Five, and in introducing Part Two, I recount the extraordinary sequence of events in Beijing in spring and summer 2002, which led up to the decision to hold such a conference, and to my being invited to contribute a paper for it, presented here. At the end of the paper I propose that the PRC table its work on chronology and instead hold an international conference on the BA.

0.8 Not being able to say everything at once, I have been neglecting Edward Shaughnessy. In 1986 he published a now famous paper in *HJAS* on the BA, which led step by step to the work I now publish in Chapters Seven and Eight. What Shaughnessy did was to notice and put together two things: (1) The most credible sources have the first Zhou king Wu Wang dying two years after the victory over Shang; but the BA gives him five years, the last three numbered 15, 16, and 17. (2) The BA chronicle for the next king Cheng Wang starts with entries for every year, up to year 14; then there is a gap, to year 18. Why are years 15, 16 and 17 missing? Shaughnessy found a note by one of the Jin Dynasty editors of the discovered texts, saying that the text of another book, the *Mu Tianzi zhuan*, was written on bamboo strips of 40 spaces. So Shaughnessy went back to the Wu Wang chronicle, and found an exact 40-space sequence that fitted into the Cheng chronicle gap, making perfect sense there, and leaving perfect sense if cut out of the Wu Wang chronicle. Furthermore counting back from the beginning of the gap to the beginning of the Cheng Wang chronicle one gets a text of exactly 10 x 40 spaces.[6]

So apparently the BA is not merely an adaptation or rough copy of the original. This part of it, at least, was an exact copy, word for word, except (perhaps) that a bamboo strip had been lifted from the Cheng chronicle and inserted into the Wu chronicle – by the Jin editors, Shaughnessy thought, either by accident or deliberately. (He eventually decided they did it deliberately, and thinks he knows their reason. I will be proving that it was done before the text was buried in Wei, for a quite different reason.[7])

The challenge now was to see how much more of the BA might turn out to be an exact copy of the original strip text. I worked through the rest of the Cheng Wang chronicle, and also the chronicle of the next king Kang Wang (making one small correction[8]), but I could go no farther without sheer guesswork. Looking back at Xia, however, I found that the whole of the chronicle for the last king Di Gui (not counting a long subtext) was exactly eight strips' worth. By 1989 I had worked out the exact chronology for Xia, and knew that the Di Gui chronicle was an invention, hence a later addition to the BA, but still done long before the text was buried. Pankenier had dated the puzzling astronomical events of Di Gui 10 (1580) to 1576. I now knew that 1576 was originally year 2 of the reign of the 14th Xia king Kong Jia. So at the time the Di Gui chronicle was invented, the Kong Jia chronicle must have been rewritten, so as not to have this astronomical detail. Perhaps its form would reveal this.

Sure enough, the opening main text of the Kong Jia chronicle is exactly 40 spaces; and after that there is a long subtext, obviously fiction, of 135 characters. 136 would be 4 x 34. Perhaps, then, these subtexts, or most of them, were on strips marked as subtext by leaving the top three and the bottom three spaces blank. The first half of the BA has many such subtexts, usually rich in mythological details. I began counting characters and quickly found so many cases that worked out as I expected that I knew my guess must be right, at least for most of this material. (I later found that long subtexts in the Huang Di and Yao chronicles

---

[6] As my colleague Shao Dongfang has noted, this count does not include the mandatory words "*Cheng Wang, ming Song*" (King Cheng, personal name Song) (Shao 2002 (1) pp. 104-105). For this see Chapter Seven.

[7] "Shaughnessy's Strip" was a virtual strip, not an actual one. See demonstration, Chapters Seven and Nine.

[8] The BA has Bo Qin, first duke of Lu, dying in Kang 19; the actual date is Kang 16.

had simply been broken up by the Jin editors, who distributed the pieces where they seemed to fit according to sense. When reassembled, these counted out as expected.) This result I presented in March of 2004, in a paper for the annual meeting of the Society for the Study of Early China, which was a side meeting at the annual convention of AAS in San Diego. (Robin Yates of McGill University handled my illustrations while I talked.)

The rest of the story for the whole of the BA, main texts and subtexts, required more detective work, but the detective work was getting easier. I was able to present the explanation given here in Chapter Seven, at the annual spring meeting of AAS in San Francisco in 2006, at that time distributing the whole of the original text I had recovered. An artistically refined form of that is included here as Chapter Eight, exhibited vertically in strip form, with matching translations strip by strip. I got 300 strips, with three strips of summaries for the Three Dynasties. Xia had 60 strips, Shang had 60, and Western Zhou 100. The total of 300 was obviously in bundles of 60. There must have been two more bundles, which I couldn't reconstruct. Before November of 1979 I still believed with everyone that the BA was a fake. Now I know exactly what the first five-sevenths of the original looked like, 303 strips, word after word. (For more details see my introduction to Part Three.)

There is one more chapter. I have there found it enlightening to try to write down everything I find myself thinking about the history of the text that became the BA, from perhaps 450 BCE when it may not yet have been distorted, down to ca. 280-300 CE, after it was worked on, maybe twice, by the Jin Dynasty court scholars. I add a short essay that came to me as I was working this out, on that quaint story about the loss of the fabled Nine Cauldrons of Zhou, in the River Si in Song, said in the BA to have happened in 327 BCE but almost certainly an invented myth, at first bearing a different date. From my analysis of this colorful problem I even obtain one more proof of my date (1040 BCE) for the Zhou conquest of Shang. There are twelve others in Chapter One.

There are four "Appendices." The first assembles astronomical information needed if one is to follow arguments about the BA and related inscriptions. I wrote it intending to offer it to Erik Eckholm, a science writer who was planning a major article in the Tuesday Science Section of the *New York Times*. (Eckholm had interviewed me in preparing a short article in the *Times* for October 10, 2000.) That article didn't get written, but the material is just as useful here. Appendix 2 is the material I distributed with my AAS presentation April 5, 2002, "Two Approaches to Dating" (Chapter Four here), criticizing the work of the "Three Dynasties Project" in the PRC. Next is the data for 66 Western Zhou bronze inscriptions having full dates; here I am merely correcting and adding to my previously published work. (Any analysis of chronology must be consistent with such material.)

Appendix 4 is my most recent work, done in April-May 2008. Here I attempt to match *jiagu* texts from the last reigns of Shang with absolute dates, making use of their references to sacrifices in the ritual cycle, especially those in the huge set of inscriptions made during the campaign against the Yi Fang in the Huai valley in Di Xin's 10th and 11th years. This is a challenge addressed by all major scholars, Dong Zuobin, Chen Mengjia, Chang Yuzhi, Li Xueqin and Xu Fengxian. It is especially important for me, because I attempt to give a complete chronology from Huang Di through Western Zhou, using the BA. For Xia and Shang, in Chapter Two I both work down from Yu of Xia, and also work back from Di Xin of Shang. I do the latter more thoroughly in my monographs of 1999 (English) and 2002 (Chinese). These two approaches have to be consistent, and to this end I must get the dates for Di Xin right. (The dates for Yu are guaranteed by a planetary conjunction and a solar eclipse.) But the Three Dynasties Project, together with Li Xueqin and Xu Fengxian, has Di Xin dates differing completely from mine. In Appendix Four, Supplement 3, I will argue that the trouble begins with a surprising error made by the esteemed Japanese scholar Shima Kunio, followed by Xu and Li. Moreover, all fail to see that one must recognize a second calendar in Di Xin's reign.

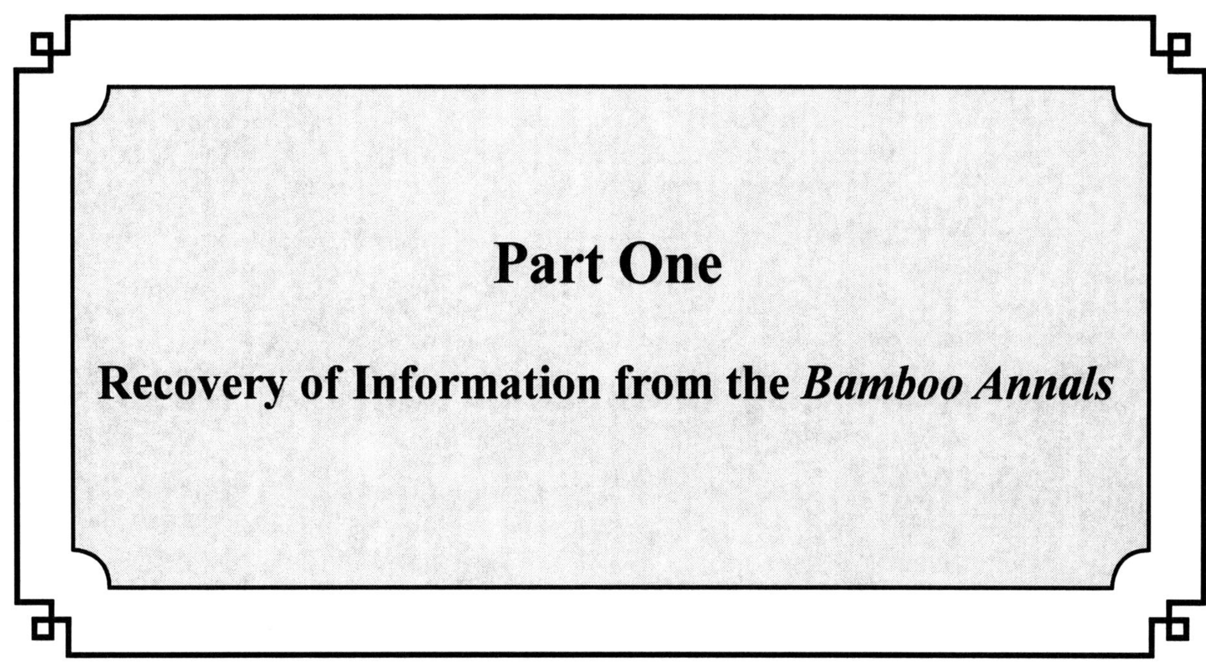

Part One

Recovery of Information from the *Bamboo Annals*

Chapter One

1. I offer here the previously unpublished English text of Chapter Eight of my draft book *The Riddle of the Bamboo Annals*, written in 1995 and revised in 1997. A Chinese translation was published in 1997, in *Wu Wang ke Shang zhi nian yanjiu*, compiled by Beijing Shifan Daxue, Guoxue Yanjiusuo. (My paper, pp. 513-525, is titled "Wu Wang Ke Shang zhi Riqi"; I added (pp. 525-532) a chronology from Huang Di to You Wang, as in the *Zhushu jinian*, with my proposed correct chronology; my analysis of the dates in fifty-six Western Zhou bronze inscriptions, and a bibliography. These things I omit here; they are covered elsewhere in the present book.) I no longer plan to publish this draft book as a whole. My research in the past ten years has gone far beyond it. But this chapter of it remains substantially what I have to say about the famous problem of the date of the Zhou conquest. I give here the 1997 text with essential revisions (duly noted), with supplements for needed comments.

The Date of the Zhou Conquest of Shang

1.0 In Chapter Two [1], I have attempted to fix the chronology of the Shang kings from Wu Ding's death (in 1189, I believe) to the end of the dynasty 150 years later. Fraternal succession disappeared, as kings became increasingly anxious about fraternal usurpation. As kings tried to set up their heirs before their own deaths, chronology becomes tangled. Although the Wenwu Ding calendar begins in 1118, Wu Yi actually died in 1109, on a royal hunt "in the He-Wei area." This hunt, conventionally capping a successful campaign (against the "Lord of the Yu Fang") must in part have been intended as a warning to the rising Zhou power. The warlike Zhou chief Ji Li (1127-1102) had been winning victory after victory. Finally, when he came to court (probably in 1102) the Shang king (who was perhaps Wenwu Ding renamed Di Yi) threw him in prison, where he soon died. After that peace between the two powers was never more than pretense. The "Duo Yi" chapter of *Yi Zhou shu* has Wu Wang after his victory (in 1040) saying to Zhou Gong that "Heaven's withholding its favor from Yin has been going on for sixty years, since before I was born"; i.e., from Ji Li's death on, Zhou had not regarded Shang's rule as sanctioned by Heaven.

In 1086 Di Xin became king of Shang. We read in the *Annals* that eleven years before the conjunction (of 1059, dated back 12 years), hence in 1070, Wen Wang ("Chang, Lord of the West") held a conclave of lords in his own court, an obvious threatening move. The Shang king (says the *Annals*) staged a hunt in the Wei valley the following year, clearly a response to the threat, for this was the Zhou homeland. The next year was 1068, when Di Xin's second calendar begins, and there must have been at that time a great assembly of lords in the Shang capital, from which Wen Wang would not dare to stay away. In any case it is stated in the *Annals* (which is quite silent about a calendar or an assembly) that in this year (that is, two years after the assembly in Zhou) Wen Wang was imprisoned in Youli, where he remained for the next seven years. (This is where he must have been, then, when he addressed his sons (by letter?) about "planning for the succession" on the occasion of the lunar eclipse of March, 1065, recorded in *Yi Zhou shu* #23 "Xiao Kai.") On Wen Wang's release in 1062 he found increasing support among the other lords. In 1058 Di Xin is said to have recognized him as having the authority "to conduct punitive expeditions of his own," seen by the Zhou as the "mandate," an authority Wen Wang was certain to exercise anyway. In 1056 he declared himself king, with a new calendar. In 1055 he held another convocation of regional lords. It would seem that Di Xin ignored the threat, choosing at this time to march east again against the Eastern Yi, perennial enemies (there had been a great campaign against them earlier, in 1077-76).[2] Wu Wang succeeded in 1049, and we continue to argue how long it took him to mount the final campaign.

---

[1] All references to parts of the original book draft are deleted or changed here to refer to the present book, unless otherwise noted.

[2] I argued here that the famous rhinoceros-shaped Xiao Chen Yu *zun*, dated 15th year *yong* day, on the occasion of the Shang king's return from campaigning against the Yi Fang, should probably be dated 25 April 1054. In the *Zuo zhuan* (Zhao 11.4) we read "Zhou [Xin] defeated the Eastern Yi and brought ruin on himself." The campaign of 1077-1076 can be dated from 70 or more oracle inscriptions made along the route. [For dispute about the date see pp. 251-2.]

1.0.1 Summary of the argument: I have published three articles concerning the problem of the date of the Conquest, in 1983, 1984, and 1985. Each is partly right and partly wrong. I explain this matter first, in 1.1. In 1.2, I set out the basic assumptions I am using. In 1.3, I present the analysis of the *Annals* that leads me to the date 1040. In 1.4, I offer twelve arguments of confirmation. In 1.5, I tabulate the main events, with dates, during the century concluding with Zhou Gong's surrendering full royal power to Cheng Wang, effective 1030.

1.1. Brief critique of relevant published articles by DSN:

1983: *Harvard Journal of Asiatic Studies* 43, 481-580: "The Dates of Western Chou".[3]

Right: (1) Each Western Zhou king had two calendars, a calendar counting from his succession year; and a calendar counting from the year after completion of mourning, i.e., two years later, the accession year. The *Bamboo Annals* normally uses the latter in dating a king's death. (But as Shaughnessy (1991 p. 155 n. 60) has noticed, the succession calendar was used early in a reign, and the accession calendar only later. For example, in Xuan Wang's reign, the succession date 827 governs the calendar through 810, and dates are counted from 825 only after completion of mourning for Gong He in 809.)

(2) Wen Wang named 1058 his "mandate" year, and proclaimed himself universal king with a royal "Zhou" calendar beginning 1056. The reason for this two-year delay (explained in Nivison 1983, pp. 530-531) was probably to allow all mourning obligations among the people to expire before they were required to recognize the new government by using the new calendar.

(3) Wen Wang died in 1050, at the end of a reign of 2 + 50 years. The *Annals* dates for Wen Wang are 1113-1062, displaced backward twelve years (together with other pre-Conquest Zhou dates) by re-dating of the conjunction of 1059 to 1071. [See p. 120.]

(4) Lunar phase terms in Western Zhou dates should be interpreted approximately as did Wang Guowei: They name lunar quarters, or the first days of quarters. (The proof, in brief: the prefatory statement in the "Kang Gao" chapter of the *Shang shu*, long recognized as out of place, is actually an alternative preface to the "Shao Gao" chapter. A comparison of the two texts shows that the term *zaishengbo* must name a day that is either the 6th or 7th of the month; therefore *jishengbo*, which should be the next day, must be the first day of the second quarter. Examination of Xuan Wang inscriptions then shows that Wang's schema is right.

Wrong: The date of the Conquest was not 1045, it was 1040. I had misread the *Shiji*: The *shijia* chapters say that the Conquest was in Wu Wang's 11th year; the "Zhou Benji" says that the Zhou army had crossed the Yellow River by the 12th month of the 11th year, and that the victory was won on *jiazi* in the 2nd month. The historian was actually following standard Western Han practice, taking "12th month" to be the name of the post-winter-solstice month, as it is in the Xia calendar. Thus he understood "12th month" as the name of the first month of the Shang calendar, so for him "2nd month" was two months later in the same year. In doing this he was misreading his own source (which as I explain below was in error anyway); so the *Shiji* is worthless as evidence for a "12th year" date. (I also gave incorrect dates for Gong Wang, Yih Wang and Xiao Wang; and I gave an incorrect argument for the (correct) date 1105 for Di Yi.)

1984: *Early China* 8 (1982-1983), 76-78: "1040 as the Date of the Chou Conquest"

Right: 1040 is the correct date for the Conquest.

Wrong: I argued for this by supposing that Wen Wang's reign was just 50 years, 1101-1052, so that 1040 was Wu Wang's 12th year. Actually, Wen Wang did die in 1050, and (as I realized later) the Conquest was not in a "12th year." Seeing that this argument was unsatisfactory, I returned to 1045 as Conquest date in my publications from 1985 through 1989. I had resolved the problem by 1990 (see below), by discovering how to explain "12th year" as an ancient error, and by discovering an unnoticed feature of the Zhou calendar, namely, that it took as winter solstice day a day that was two (or three) days late.

[3] This article developed papers presented in New York (1980) and Taiyuan (1981).

1985: *Guwenzi Yanjiu* 12, October, 445-461: "*Guoyu* 'Wu Wang fa Yin' tian xiang bian wei"

Right: The astrological description of the sky at the time of the launching of the Conquest campaign, as given in the *Guoyu*, "Zhou Yu" 3, is not a true report but an incorrect calculation made centuries later.

Wrong: I argued that this calculation was inserted into the *Guoyu* in the 1st century BCE, and was presumably made at this time. (Hence Sima Qian does not use it, and Liu Xin does.)[4] Furthermore, I was again assuming that the Conquest was in 1045. Therefore my reconstruction of the incorrect calculation was completely wrong. I now am sure that the calculation was based on observations in the early or middle 5th century BCE, and must have been made by a historian who knew that the date was 1040, 2nd month, *jiazi*; but in analyzing this date he used bad science: (1) he accepted the "standard" 76-year intercalation cycle (the *zhang-bu* system) as completely accurate; and (2) he believed that Jupiter circled the zodiac in exactly 12 years. Actually, the *zhang-bu* system gives a *ganzhi* day date a day early for each three centuries back, and the Jupiter cycle is about 11.86 years. Therefore (1) he reasoned that a Xia-calendar *jiazi* victory day would have been the 1st of the 3rd month. He was thus led to believe that the intended calendar must be the Zhou [i.e., *jian zi*] calendar, not the Xia [*jian yin*] calendar, so that the campaign must have started late in 1041, i.e., not in the winter solstice month (as it in fact did), but 30 + 29 days earlier; and he calculated (2) that in that year Jupiter must have been in Chun Huo (Quail Fire), as it would seem to be if one counted by twelves back from any observed Quail Fire year in the first half of the 5th century.

1.2. Basic premises:

(a) Reconstruction of chronology must use, or explain, the dates in the "modern text" *Bamboo Annals*. Shaughnessy's discovery (1986) that a strip's worth of text was moved from the Cheng Wang chronicle to the end of the Wu Wang chronicle shows that the text is genuine. (But the strip-text was moved before the text was buried in ca. 300 BCE. The *Zuo zhuan* assumes that events mentioned in the strip-text occurred in Wu Wang's reign; and the "Jin Teng" chapter of the *Shang shu* assumes that Wu Wang lived longer, as in the strip-text. See Chapter Nine.[5])

(b) In the *Bamboo Annals*, the 5-planet conjunction put in Di Xin 32 = 1071, and said to be in Fang, must be read as referring to the conjunction in Jing in 1059 BCE, as suggested by Needham (1959 p. 408 n. c) and confirmed by Pankenier (*EC* 7 p. 4). (And the erroneous date and location must be explained and due allowance made for the error; i.e., one must not simply dismiss the text because it is in error.) The Conquest cannot be earlier than 9 + 5 years later (actually it was 9 + 10 years later), because Wen Wang died nine years later.

(c) The month and day dates in the "Wu Cheng" chapter of the *Shang shu*, as quoted by Liu Xin, are valid (but misinterpreted by Liu): The only years in the possible time range that satisfy these data are 1045 and 1040.

1.3. Basic argument for 1040: The calendars for Cheng Wang through Mu Wang in the *Bamboo Annals*, when Mu Wang's first year is corrected (by using bronze inscriptions) from 962 to 956, and when allowance is made for 2-year mourning intervals, show that Cheng Wang's succession year must be 1037 BCE (and that the first year of Wen Wang's royal Zhou calendar must have been 1056 BCE, 100 years before Mu Wang 1). An editor who knew Cheng Wang's first year, but did not admit mourning intervals, would have dated Kang Wang two years early, to 1007, which is the *Annals'* date, instead of 1005 (succession) and 1003 (accession). The Xiao Yu *ding* inscription, 25th year, shows that 1003 is correct as accession date. Therefore the editor was correct in believing 1037 to be Cheng Wang's "first year." But this editor dates the Regency 1044-1038, making Wu Wang die in 1045; and this is impossible. So putting the Regency before the beginning of Cheng

---

[4] Li Xueqin (*Zhaji* p. 210) has pointed out that the *Shiji* does use another part of this paragraph in the *Guoyu*; therefore my assumption that this paragraph was invented and inserted in the *Guoyu* after Sima Qian and before Liu Xin cannot be right. (Perhaps Professor Li was here gently correcting me, without naming me.)

[5] In 1997 I held that an actual strip was moved, and that this must have been done as early as 425. I now think that there may have been an alteration of chronology as early as 425, but without moving a strip. I examine this matter in Chapters Seven and Nine.

Wang's reign was a mistake. The Regency must have begun in 1037, which must be Cheng Wang's succession year. Wu Wang died two years after the victory (Chapter Eight, strips 204-206 and comment; also *Shiji* "Feng Shan Shu"), so the Conquest date must be 1040.

1.3.1 Objection: The *Lu shi Chunqiu* and the *Bamboo Annals* say that the victory was in Wu Wang's 12th year (and the *Shiji* seems to be misusing a source that said the same). This implies that the date must be 1045.

14. Reply: This is what I supposed in *HJAS* 43; But "12th year" is an error.
(a) A calculation (as above) made ca. 475-450 BC would have concluded that the campaign started in late 1041, with Jupiter in Chun Huo. If the calculator knew that Jupiter was in Chun Huo also in the Mandate year (the year after the conjunction), and that Wen Wang died in the 9th year of the Mandate, he would have to suppose that the Mandate year was 2 x 12 years before 1041, i.e., 1065, so he would suppose that the 1056 calendar was Wu Wang's. His received [true] information must have been that Wu Wang's death was in the 12th year (sc. of his own calendar) and the Conquest was in the 17th year (sc. of the royal calendar). Not knowing that two different calendars were involved, he would suppose that the two dates had gotten reversed, and would try to correct them. This could be done in two steps: (1) One might suppose that Zhou Gong's 7-year Regency was the seven years (1042-1036) prior to Cheng Wang's accession year 1035, rather than the seven years beginning with Cheng Wang's succession year (1037-1031, the correct dating). This would put the Conquest in the 12th year, i.e., 1045, if Wu died two years later. (2) Wu Wang's death could then be moved from his 14th year to his 17th year.[6]
(b) A different error made later also produces the date 12th year (see Chapter Nine). In Wei after Huicheng declares himself king in 335, it becomes necessary to anticipate him by dating the grant to Tangshu Yu [the grant founding Jin] to 1035, calling the year a year when Jupiter was in Da Huo [as in *Guoyu*, "Jin Yu" 4]. This forced choosing 1050 as conquest year and moving the conjunction back 12 years, which made 1050 Wu Wang's 12th year.

1.4.1 Confirmation of 1040, #1: Oracle inscriptions for Di Xin's campaign against the Ren Fang (or Yi Fang), in his 10th and 11th years, fit the years 1077-76, and these years only. (See Appendix 4.) These inscriptions taken together require (1) that the "10th year" end with day *jiawu* (31), *yiwei* (32), or *bingshen* (33); and that this year had a "9th month" followed by a lunar month lacking a "*qi*-center," therefore being intercalary. 1077 is the only possibility.) Therefore Di Xin 1 = 1086. But the *Bamboo Annals* date for Di Xin 1 is 1102, 16 years earlier. The best explanation of this is that at some time in early Warring States the *de facto* first year of Zhou 1040, as Wu Wang 1, was confused with the *de jure* first year 1056, which also came to be seen as Wu Wang 1. This would make Di Xin's 46th year appear to be 1057 rather than 1041. This 16-year shift is seen in earlier Shang reigns in the *Annals*; e.g., Wu Yi's reign, actually 1145/43-1109, is made to be 1159-1125; and Zu Geng's reign, actually 1188-1178, is made to be 11 + 16 years earlier. (It was supposed that his 11 years must precede Zu Jia's 33 years, instead of being the first 11 years of Zu Jia's "33 years." See Chapter Two.)

1.4.2. Confirmation of 1040, #2: Oracle inscriptions show that Di Yi 1 = 1105. (See Chapter Two, Appendix 4 End Note, and Nivison 1999 and 2002, Appendix 2. The "8th year" inscription set consisting of *Ku-fang* 1661 and other fragments requires an intercalary 3rd month, and it fits only the year 1098, a date confirmed by several other inscriptions.) A frequently quoted or paraphrased line from an unknown source, sometimes said to be the *Da Dai li ji*, says that "Wen Wang in (the/his) 15th year produced Wu Wang." The meaning probably is the 15th year of Di Yi, i.e., 1091. The *Bamboo Annals* says that Wu Wang died in his 54th year, which would have to be 1038. If this was two years after the Conquest, the Conquest date must be 1040.

1.4.3. Confirmation of 1040, #3: In the *Bamboo Annals* the enfeoffment of Cheng Wang's younger brother Yu as lord of Tang, later Jin, is dated to 1035. The compilers must have believed that Jupiter was in station

---

[6] The effect would have been to push dates after this forward three years, later corrected. There are two bits of possible evidence; see Nivison 1999 and 2002, Appendix 1. [I thought in 1997 that "Shaughnessy's strip" had been moved at this stage, effecting this three year change. I have now proved that there was no such strip. See pp. 189-192.]

Da Huo, Great Fire, in that year, which was 3 x 12 years after the conjunction, said to be in Fang (the middle lunar lodge of Da Huo) and in 1071. The *Guoyu*, "Jin Yu" 4, says explicitly that when Jin began Jupiter was in Great Fire. But Jupiter actually was in Great Fire in 1043 and 1031. If in 1043, Wu Wang was still alive (even if the Conquest was in 1045; he is said to have died at the very end of the year of his death); and the story of the event in the *Shiji* shows that it was Cheng Wang's action, when he was still a minor but *de jure* king, hence during the Regency. So it must have been in 1031. This is confirmed by *Zuo zhuan*, Xi Gong 15.14, which implies that the shy Shang prince Ji Zi, enfeoffed in Korea, was present at the ceremony. Ji Zi almost never came to court, but would have attended the great convocation recorded in the *Annals* in the summer of the last Regency year, the probable occasion of Tang-shu's enfeoffment. This can only be so if the Regency was 1037-1031, and the Conquest was in 1040.

1.4.4. Confirmation of 1040, #4: The "Lu Shijia" in the *Shiji* says that Wu Wang granted Lu to Zhou Gong right after the Conquest, and that Zhou Gong gave it to his son Bo Qin soon after Cheng Wang's succession. Only then does the account take up the revolt of Lu Fu and the royal uncles. Liu Xin as quoted in the *Han shu* says that Bo Qin's reign in Lu was 46 years; and that it began in the first year of Cheng Wang's 30-year calendar (i.e., for me, his accession calendar). The *Shiji*, "Lu Shijia," has a chronology of Lu dukes that implies that Bo Qin's death was in 999; so his first year would be 1044 (the first year of Cheng Wang's 37 years, in the *Annals*), but this is impossible. The difficulty is resolved by careful analysis of the *Bamboo Annals*, which reveals that Bo Qin's actual death date must have been 990. (The date given, 989, is due to distortions in the text, generated by (1) mourning intervals; and (2) a displacement of three-years. By (1), Bo Qin's first year was backed from 1035 to 1037; and by (2) his whole tenure was at first moved down three years, making his death date 990 + 2 – 3 = 989. Later, most other 3-year displacements of dates were reversed, but Bo Qin's death date was not.) The wrong date 999 can be traced to the reign of Lu duke Xian Gong, who died in 856. The *Shiji* gives him a reign of 32 years; the *Annals* account implies a reign of 23 years. Thus Cheng Wang's dates are 1037/35-1006, 2 + 30 years; therefore the Conquest was in 1040. (See Nivison 1999 and 2002, Appendix 1.)

1.4.5. Confirmation of 1040, #5: *Yi Zhou shu* 45, "Wu Jing" (Wu Wang warned) begins, "12th year, 4th month. The king reported a dream. On day *bingchen* (53) it was divined...." (We are supposed to understand that this dream was an omen portending the king's imminent death.) "An order then was given for Dan, Duke of Zhou, to appoint the successor, and to give Prince Song the text (of the order), and a copy of the "Bao Dian" (Treasured Document)." When a date is thus incomplete, normally the first of the month is meant, which should be *yimao* (52). The 12th year (of Wu Wang, counting from his succession in 1049) was 1038, and the 4th month begins with *yimao* if one supposes that the day counted as winter solstice was two days late. Shang oracle inscriptions suggest that this was the practice, i.e., the autumn equinox day was determined by observation, and the interval to the winter solstice (89 days) was assumed to be 91 days. The "Bao Dian," which is *Yi Zhou shu* 29, opens with a complete date: "It was the King's 3rd cult-year, 2nd month, day *bingchen* (53), first of the month...." This should be the same year, for if the 2nd month began with *bingchen* (53), the 4th month (30 + 29 days later) should begin with *yimao* (52). The only year that could be *both* "the King's 3rd year" and *also*, in another calendar (counting from the year following his father's death) his 12th year, is 1038, and 1038 only if the Conquest was in 1040.[7]

1.4.6. Confirmation of 1040, #6: The "Luo Gao" chapter of the *Shang shu* ends with an account of a sacrifice by Cheng Wang, called *zheng ji sui*, on day *wuchen* (5), said in the pseudo- Kong Anguo commentary to be the last day of the month; and the "Luo Gao" dates the event in the 12th month of the 7th year of the Regency. Two dates must be considered: 1036 and 1031. 1036 requires that the 12th month be the second month before the solstice month (possibly followed by an intercalary 12th month), the date being 27 November. 1031 requires that the date be 31 December, and that the next month begin one day earlier than indicated in Zhang Peiyu's tables (the syzygy was at 03:20, so this is likely). The solstice

---

[7] In Zhang Peiyu the year 1038 had day *yiyou* (22) as winter solstice. If the day two days later was understood, the recognized solstice was *dinghai* (24), so Zhang's second month (first day *bingxu* (23)) becomes (*jian zi*) first month. The fourth month counting from there Zhang begins with *jiayin* (51), but the syzygy was 22:49, almost *yimao* (52). The second month (Zhang's third) begins with bingchen (53). So *bingchen* in month 2 was the date of the "Bao Dian," and 59 days later, on the night of *yimao* (52), the king had the dream, divined the next morning. [On autumn equinox as base date, see p. 250, note 36. – added Oct 5, 2008.]

was on *dingmao* (4), 30 December, and one may assume as before that a 91-day count from the equinox specified *jisi* (6), 1 January. Thus if 1031 was the date, Cheng Wang thought he was sacrificing on the eve of the solstice, giving a plausible meaning for *ji sui*, "sacrifice for [the end of] the year," as well as a more satisfactory meaning for *zheng*, supposed to be a "winter sacrifice for royal ancestors." In 1036, the date could not be at the end of the year, unless the next year were taken as beginning with the pre-solstice month, making the date the last day of autumn, rather than any date in "winter." So 1031 seems to be the date, requiring that the Regency be 1037-1031, and that the Conquest be in 1040.

1.4.7. Confirmation of 1040, #7: The fact that the astrological text in the *Guoyu* can be best explained as calculated in the early fifth century BC, during the last years of Confucius' life, by someone who believed the Conquest to have been in 1040 BC, is itself a confirmation that 1040 is probably the correct date.

1.4.8. Confirmation of 1040, #8: Pankenier (1983 p. 241) has noted another text giving the location of Jupiter at the time of the launching of the Conquest campaign. A commentary to the "Ru Xiao" chapter of *Xunzi* says that at that time Jupiter was in the "north." Chun Huo would be due south, on an astrologer's chart. Having explained "Chun Huo" as a calculator's error, one must consider the alternative "north." If the campaign started in January of 1040, as would be required if one interpret the "Zhou Benji" data as in the Xia calendar, one finds that at that time Jupiter was in lunar lodge Xu, the middle lodge of station Xuan Xiao, due "north" on an astrologer's chart.

1.4.9. Confirmation of 1040, #9: Zheng Xuan (see Kong Yingda's commentary to the Odes of Bin in the *Shi jing*) said that Cheng Wang was born in Wu Wang's succession year. We should expect that Zhou Gong would return full royal authority to the young king effective in the king's 20th year. Thus Cheng Wang was born in 1049, was 13 *sui* at his succession in 1037, and was 20 *sui* in 1030. The Regency therefore was 1037-1031, and this requires that the Conquest was in 1040. (Zheng Xuan does not derive his date of Cheng Wang's birth from his date for Cheng Wang's assuming full power, which he puts in Cheng Wang's 22nd year; and his absolute dates are quite different; so this is independent evidence.)

1.4.10. Confirmation of 1040, #10: As Liu Xin quotes the "Wu Cheng" chapter of the *Shang shu* (in Ban Gu's *Han shu*, 21B), the Conquest campaign is said to start in the first month.. But if I take the *Shiji* to be using a source that dated the events in the Xia calendar, that source must have made the campaign begin in the 11th month, because the Yellow River had been crossed by day *wuwu* in the 12th month. As Liu quotes it, the "Wu Cheng" continues: "*yue ruo lai er yue ... jiazi ...*" This is normally misinterpreted by supposing a break (or punctuation) after "*lai*." But "*lai er yue*" is a single phrase, and it seems to mean "the second month in the next year." Compare, for example, "*lai dingmao*," in the "Shi Fu" chapter (#37) of *Yi Zhou shu*, which has to mean (though this too is usually misinterpreted) "on day *dingmao* (4) of the next month," i.e., the 3rd month, since *jiazi*, the victory day, was the next to last day of the 2nd month. (In oracle inscriptions, "*lai dingmao*" would normally mean "day *dingmao* in the next *xun*," or in a future *xun*.) This shows that the "Wu Cheng" text is a modification of a text that originally did have the campaign beginning in the Xia 11th month. This is just what my analysis requires, if the date is 1040.

1.4.11. Confirmation of 1040, #11: One might expect that astrologically weighted days would be preferred for the performance of important ceremonies or the inauguration of great events: the first day of the year, for major appointments; full moon day, for a holocaust sacrifice; the first day of a month and/or season, for the start of a campaign. Similarly, the first days of the twenty-four weather periods could be expected to be thus favored. If one starts with the true winter solstice day, and counts off the weather periods (*qi jie*) taking that day as the first day of Dong Zhi, the major events of the Conquest campaign fall on such days, if the year was 1045. But if one supposes that the true autumn equinox was taken as Qiu Fen day (making the observed winter solstice day two days late, if one divides the year into equal fourths), then it is 1040 that satisfies this test:

Qiu Fen	2 Oct 1041	JD 134 1473 +16
Han Lu	18 Oct	1489 15
Shuang Jiang	2 Nov	1504 15
Li Dong	17 Nov	1519 15
Xiao Xue	2 Dec	1534 15
Da Xue	17 Dec	1549 15
Dong Zhi	1 Jan 1040	1564 16
Xiao Han	17 Jan	1580 15 *Guisi* (30)
Da Han	1 Feb	1595 15
Li Chun	16 Feb	1610 15
Yu Shui	3 Mar	1625 15
Jing Zhi	18 Mar	1640 15
Chun Fen	2 Apr	1655 16
Qing Ming	18 Apr	1671 15 *Jiazi* (1)
Gu Yu	3 May	1686 15
Li Xia	18 May	1701 16
Xiao Man	3 Jun	1717 15 *Gengxu* (47)
Mang Zhong	18 Jun	1732 15
Xia Zhi	3 Jul	1747 16
Xiao Shu	19 Jul	1763 15
Da Shu	3 Aug	1778 15
Li Qiu	18 Aug	1793 15
Chu Shu	2 Sep	1808 15
Bai Lu	17 Sep	1823 15
Qiu Fen	2 Oct	1838 16

The key events:

Zhou month 1 / Xia month 11, day *guisi* (30) = 17 January, Campaign begins, first day of Xiao Han (Lesser Cold)

Zhou month 4 / Xia month 2, day *jiazi* (1) = 18 April, Victory at Muye, first day of Qing Ming (Clear Brightness)

Zhou month 6 / Xia month 4, day *gengxu* (47) = 3 June, Celebration in Zhou on full moon, first day of Xiao Man (Grain Ripening)

The sequence of solar periods (*qi jie*) here follows *Huainanzi*, "Tian Wen," 12th paragraph. Ideally all periods are 15 days, but there must be five more days in a normal year; so the text says that there are 46 days from Dong Zhi through Da Han, from Chun Fen through Gu Yu, from Li Xia through Mang Zhong, from Xia Zhi through Da Shu, and from Qiu Fen through Shuang Jiang. I interpret this as meaning in effect that the days Dong Zhi, Chun Fen, Li Xia, Xia Zhi, and Qiu Fen are extra days, so that beginning with each of these one counts 16 days.

1.4.11.1 Lunar months as given by Zhang Peiyu for 1040 begin on the following *ganzhi*; at three points, I propose months beginning one day later, to avoid having two short (29-day) months in sequence, and two pairs of long (30-day) months in the same year. (In each case, the syzygy given by Zhang is late in the 24-hour day.) I give Zhang's data first, with my regularizations below:

(a) 1040:	05	34	03	33	02	32	01	31	01	30	60	30
			04		03		02					
Xia month	11	12	1	2	3	4	5	6	7	8	9	10
Zhou month	1	2	3	4	5	6	7	8	9	10	11	12

The major events occur in Xia months 11, 2, and 4. The "Wu Cheng," as quoted by Liu Xin in *Han shu* 21B, says that the victory day *jiazi* (in Xia month 2) is five days (inclusive) after *jisibo*.[8] Therefore I take *jisibo* (Jsi below, beginning the fourth "quarter") as the 24th, in a month following a long (30-day) month, and as the 25th, in a month following a short (29-day) month (as does Xia month 2). The victory day is the 29th, next-to-last (the month is a long month).

In the following diagram, *fei* (F) is new moon day, standardized as the 2nd after a long (30-day) month and the 3rd after a short (29-day) month. The day *zaishengbo* (ZSh) is five days (inclusive) later, as in the introductory narrative at the beginning of the "Shao Gao" combined with the one at the beginning of the "Kang Gao" (1.1 (1983) (4) above). *Jishengbo* (JSh) must be the next day, and *jiwang* (JW), full moon day, is standardized as always nine days later *Jipangshengbo* (JPSh), must be "[the day] after PSh."

(b) Xia months 11 to 4, 23 December 1041 through 17 June 1040 (first days of *qi* periods are underlined)

	Month 11	Month 12	Month 1	Month 2	Month 3	Month 4
1	(05) 23 Dec	(34) 21 Jan	(04) 20 Feb	(33) 21 Mar	(03) 20 Apr	(32) 19 May
2	(06) Fei	(35)	(05) F	(34)	(04) F	(33)
3	(07)	(36) F	(06)	(35) F	(05)	(34) F
4	(08)	(37)	(07)	(36)	(06)	(35)
5	(09)	(38)	(08)	(37)	(07)	(36)
6	(10) ZSh	(39)	(09) ZSh	(38)	(08) ZSh	(37)
7	(11) JSh	(40) ZSh	(10) JSh	(39) ZSh	(09) JSh	(38) ZSh
8	(12)	(41) JSh	(11)	(40) JSh	(10)	(39) JSh
9	(13) PSh	(42)	(12) PSh	(41)	(11) PSh	(40)
10	(14) Dong Zhi	(43) PSh	(13)	(42) PSh	(12)	(41) Psh
11	(15)	(44) JPSh	(14)	(43) JPSh	(13)	(42)JPSh 1
12	(16)	(45)	(15)	(44)	(14)	(43) 2
13	(17)	(46)	(16)	(45) Chun Fen	(15)	(44) 3
14	(18)	(47)	(17)	(46)	(16)	(45) 4
15	(19)	(48)	(18)	(47)	(17)	(46) 5
16	(20) Jiwang	(49)	(19) JW	(48)	(18) JW	(47) 6
17	(21)	(50) JW	(20)	(49) JW	(19)	(48) JW
18	(22)	(51)	(21)	(50)	(20)	(49)
19	(23)	(52)	(22)	(51)	(21)	(50)
20	(24)	(53)	(23)	(52)	(22)	(51)
21	(25)	(54)	(24)	(53)	(23)	(52)
22	(26)	(55) Ford He	(25)	(54)	(24)	(53)
23	(27)	(56)	(26)	(55)	(25)	(54)
24	(28) JSi	(57)	(27) JSi	(56)	(26) JSi	(55)
25	(29) PSi	(58) JSi	(28) PSi	(57) JSh 1	(27) PSi	(56) JSi
26	(30) Start	(59)	(29)	(58) 2	(28)	(57)
27	(31)	(60) Li Chun	(30)	(59) 3	(29)	(58)
28	(32)	(01)	(31)	(60) 4	(30)	(59)
29	(33)	(02)	(32)	(01) Muye 5	(31) Li Xia	(60)
30		(03)		(02)		(01)

[8] On the element '*-bo*' in many *yuexiang* (lunar phase) terms, see note at the end of this chapter.

One must reconcile several accounts, some of them garbled by passing through hands of persons who did not understand the dates. The "Wu Cheng" as quoted by Liu Xin says that Wu Wang started from his capital on *guisi* (30), the day after *pangsibo* (PSi), in the "1st month." Using the "Zhou Benji," we can correct this to "11th month." *Yi Zhou shu*, "Shi Fu," dates this action to *dingwei* (44), the day after *pangshengbo* (PSh), in the "1st month." Here "1st month" together with the statement that Wu Wang was beginning his march repeats the quoted "Wu Cheng" error; but the rest of this date is meaningful, because Liu (not giving his source) says that on *bingwu* (43) Wu Wang "rejoined his army" (or reached his army), which must have been already in the field ahead of him; and my analysis shows that *pangshengbo* in my (i.e., Xia) "12th month" was in fact day *bingwu*. This can be known from more of what Liu Xin quotes from the "Wu Cheng": "In the 4th month, six days (inclusive) after *jipangshengbo* (JPSh), day *gengxu* (47), Wu Wang offered a holocaust in the Zhou ancestral temple," i.e., after the victory and back in his capital. *Jipangshengbo*, "the expansion of the birth of the (*bo* =) gibbous moon having occurred," ought to be the next day after *pangshengbo*. (The fact that *gengxu* (47) in month 4 is dated on *jipangshengbo* shows that in a long month the 16th is the last day of the second quarter, which is thus nine days long. I assume that in the 2nd "quarter," which is nine days, "*pang*" is two days after "*ji*," whereas in the "4th quarter," only six days long, it is the next day in a short month, but absent in a long month, as is required by the date of the victory at Muye, "five days (inclusive) after *jisibo*" near the end of the "2nd month.") The "Shi Fu" confirms that the 4th month begins with *yiwei* (32), because it starts "4th month, *yiwei* day: Wu Wang had completed his mastery of the world," etc.; and there can be no reason for "*yiwei*" other than to date the beginning of the 4th month, in which the victory rites were performed.

1.4.11.2 But the victory was on Qing Ming day. This is confirmed by the last line of the "Da Ming" ode in the "Da Ya" part of the *Shi jing* (Ode #236). That ode narrates Heaven's favor to Zhou through Wang Ji, Wen Wang and Wu Wang, down to Wu Wang's victory. The last line reads, "*Si fa da shang, hui zhao qing ming*." The meaning has escaped all translators and commentators known to me: the line says, "He (Wu Wang) then attacked Great Shang; this occurred in the morning, Qing Ming (Day)." Thus the "Da Ming" ode is a Qing Ming Day hymn.

(It is true that names of other *qi* periods are not known in texts as early as this. But Qing Ming, the occasion of annual sacrifices to ancestors, is likely to be a very ancient name. And the existence, even earlier than this, of the concept of *qi* periods (however named) can be demonstrated by an analysis of the earliest known system of 28 lunar *xiu*. See my article in Aveni 1989.)

1.4.12 Confirmation of 1040, #12: Professor D. N. Keightley has attempted to estimate the date of the Zhou Conquest by using an interesting probability argument, in his book *Sources of Shang History* (1978), and he reached exactly the dates that I am defending (p. 175): Estimating an average of 20 years per reign, he counts back from 841 (the first year of the Gong He regency), getting 1041. Then, counting forward from 1180, which is the last year he gives Wu Ding (I would have said 1189), and not counting Feng Xin (nor would I), he gets 1040. I am arguing that the campaign began in late 1041 (in the Chinese calendar, i.e. 17 January 1040), and was concluded on 18 April, 1040.[9]

15 The victory was apparently indecisive. The battle was bloody, with great numbers of "ears taken"; the Shang king Di Xin was captured and killed. But Wu Wang found it necessary to confirm Di Xin's son Lu Fu as the new Shang king, known as Wu Geng, in reality dividing authority with him, while at the same time naming three of his own brothers as "overseers" of the remaining Shang realm. Shang dependent lords were accepted as Zhou vassals. Much too soon after this, late in 1038, Wu Wang suddenly died. His brother Dan, "Duke of Zhou," assumed authority as regent. Dan persuaded another brother, Shi (Shao Gong) to support him; but the other brothers abroad, suspecting usurpation, rebelled, joining forces with Wu Geng. Dan's suppression of the rebellion in two years, defeating and executing Wu Geng, was the real conquest. After

---

[9] The *Shiji* says that the Zhou army completed its crossing of the Yellow River at Mengjin on day *wuwu* (55) in the 12th month, which was 11 February. Yet Wu Wang waited 66 days before joining battle. The river crossing was the most dangerous part of the campaign, and had to be done in late winter at maximum low water. The day of battle, both a *jiazi* day and Qing Ming Day, had probably been picked long in advance, maybe even years in advance. (Note added 22 Aug 2007)

more military consolidation, a great assembly of lords was convoked in the summer of 1031, and at the end of the year Dan surrendered his authority to the young king, Cheng Wang, who was now of age, at 20 *sui*.

1.5.1 I add here a resume [amended 2007] of the main events, with my dates, of the century ending in Cheng Wang's assuming full royal authority in 1030. *Annals* dates are on the left, my own on the right:

Birth of Chang (= Wen Wang)		1129 ?
Death of Dan Fu	1139	1127
Ji Li (= Wang Ji)	1138	1126
Zhou victory	1135	1123
Wenwu Ding given calendar by his father Wu Yi		1118
Zhou victory	1129	1117
Ji Li at court, given gifts	1125	1113
Zhou defeat	1123	1111
Zhou victory	1121	1109
Death of Wu Yi	1125	1109
Wenwu Ding 1	1124	1108 (also 1118)
Zhou victory	1118	1106
Di Yi reign, year 1	1111	1105
Zhou victory	1114	1102
Probable Di Yi accession celebration		1102
Ji Li at court, imprisoned, dies	1114	1102
Wen Wang succeeds	1113	1101
Wenwu Ding dies	1112	?
Wen Wang accession year		1099
Earthquake in Zhou capital	1109 (3rd year)	1093 (13th year)
Wu Wang Fa born		1091 (15th year)
Di Xin 1	1102	1086
Yi Fang (Ren Fang) campaign, years	10-11	1077-1076
Lords assemble in Zhou	1082	1070 (Wen Wang 60 *sui*?)
Royal hunt in Wei valley	1081	1069
New Shang calendar, probable court celebration		1068
Wen Wang at court, imprisoned	1080	1068
Lunar eclipse; Wen Wang writes sons		1065
Wen Wang released	1074	1062
Conjunction	1071	1059
"Mandate"; Zhou defeats Mi	1070	1058
Zhou victories, Ji, Yu, Cong	1069	1057
Zhou capital moved to Feng	1068	1056
Zhou promulgates royal calendar		1056
Lords assemble in Zhou capital	1067	1055
Shang campaign against Eastern Yi		1055-1054 ?
Zhou plans new capital at Hao	1067	1055
Wen Wang dies	1062	1050
Wu Wang succeeds	1061	1049
Cheng Wang born		1049

Zhou show of force at Mengjin	1052	?
Ji Zi imprisoned in Shang	1052	1044 ?
Di Xin kills Bi Gan	1052	1043 ?
Wei Zi fees from Shang	1052	1042 ?
Zhou campaign begins	1051	1041
Zhou victory at Muye	1050 (12th year)	1040 (17th year, from 1056)
Lu Fu made Shang king by Wu Wang	1050	1040
"Yin" overseers appointed	1050	1040
Lords received, enfeoffed	1049	1039
Wu Wang ill	1048	1038
Wu Wang dies, age 54 *sui*	1045 (17th year)	1038 (12th year, from 1049)
Cheng Wang succeeds; Regency	1044	1037
Lu Fu (Wu Geng), overseers rebel	1044	1037
Cheng Wang accession		1035
Rebellion put down	1042	1035
Lords assemble in Zhou capital	1038	1031
Tangshu Yu enfeoffed	1035	1031
Zhou Gong resigns regency	1038	1031
Cheng Wang, 20 *sui*		1030
Cheng Wang has full power	1037	1030

A note on '-*bo*' 霸:

The character 'bo' 霸 is usually transcribed '*ba*'; but this is the transcription proper when this character is used in the political-verbal sense "to be or become the dominant lord *bo* 伯 in a region (e.g., "*Xi Bo*" Lord of the West" said of Chang=Wen Wang) or in the whole of China (e.g., Qi Huan Gong by the year 679). By careless custom we use '*ba*' also in the nominal sense when we mean '*bo*'; but (adapting an idea of Pulleyblank) I assume there was an *ablaut* change distinguishing the two senses.

The character 霸 in a Western Zhou bronze inscription lunar phase term, such as "*jishengbo*," "*jisibo*," etc., appears to me to mean "light of the moon when dominant in the lunar disk." The political meaning 伯 is derivative; the primitive graph was egg-shaped, a pictograph of a gibbous moon, becoming the modern 白 ("white"). So I take '-*bo*' in such a lunar phase term in Western Zhou usage to mean in effect "gibbous moon." (I am, granted, not completely sure of this; but the reader is entitled to know what I have been thinking.)

It is essential to specify "Western Zhou." This use of 霸 in a date becomes dead by Warring States times. It is reborn in a way in Han mis-readings of ancient texts, when (as Pankenier points out) it came to be realized that the moon shines by reflected sunlight, and not by essential "moon-light." At that point the character 魄 '*po*' ("animal soul") was appropriated as a synonym for what 霸 had been thought to be, and was taken as referring to what was thought to be true "moonlight," the unlit part of the lunar disk (sometimes faintly glowing , with what we now see as "earthshine," actually doubly reflected sunlight). Thus (I think) '-*po*' would not be an appropriate reading for 霸 in a Western Zhou lunar phase term.

Consequently I cannot agree with Pankenier (1986 and 2002) that the Chinese had no concept of the lunar cycle as divided into quarters until after this change in meaning. The graph 霸 in a Western Zhou date (as now shown by many inscriptions) means "the moon when half or more than half full," the appropriate modern reading being '-*bo*,' not '–*po*,' and not '-*ba*.'

Attachment 1: The Myth of the Preliminary Campaign

The *Shiji* and the *Shang shu da zhuan* have Wen Wang dying in the seventh year of his Mandate. The *Yi Zhou shu* "Wen Zhuan" and the BA have him dying in the ninth year. We know that he died in 1050, nine years after the conjunction, so "ninth year" is right. To see that "seventh year" is also right, notice that in Di Xin 33 = 1070 = 1058 (strip 175 on strip page 12) Wen Wang was given authority to take military action at his own discretion (this Zhou would interpret as a conferral of the "mandate" to rule), and two years later in Di Xin 35 = 1068 = 1056 (strip 176) he moved his capital from Cheng 程 (Zhou capital since 1108) to Feng 豐 (and in the next year hosted an assembly of regional lords).

This move of capital marked in effect a second "Mandate" year, the first year of a year-count (otherwise not revealed in the BA). So also with Cheng Tang of Shang (strip 113, strip page 8): in Di Gui 15 = 1575 he moved his capital to Bo. (This date is probably accurate; but that is a separate problem.) For the BA, this marked the beginning of his royal year count, because (strip 131 on strip page 9) his first year as world ruler, BA date 1558, is called "year 18." Likewise with Zhou, the first year (the conquest year) in the BA is "year 12," continuing an unexpressed year count beginning (in this case) with the *pro forma* unrecorded succession year of Wu Wang, BA date Di Xin 42 = 1061. (In reality Wu Wang's succession year was 1049; but this too is a separate problem.)

As I will explain in Chapter Nine, there were two different ways of getting the conquest year to be "12th year": one (probably due to Wei chronological propaganda ca. 335-300) counted from the supposed succession year of Wu Wang, the other (probably much earlier, due to chronological thinking in Lu) counted from the second Mandate year, through the death of Wen Wang in year seven and on to Wu Wang's fifth year. Once "12th year" became entrenched, one would expect that there would be instances of someone counting 12 from the earlier Mandate year, which had made Wen Wang die in year nine. This would generate two different supposed dates for Wu Wang's campaign against Shang, namely Wu Wang's fifth year 1045, and his third year, which we must read as 1047. (For this latter count to give the same date as the former would require the date to be "14th year"; but there is no such tradition.) Perhaps we see the residue of this conception in the first *liezhuan* chapter of the *Shiji*, where Bo Yi and Shu Qi scold Wu Wang for engaging in military action while still in mourning.

Two different campaign dates two years apart would have to be reconciled. It would not do for the first one to be a failed attempt. So it is conceived to have been a mere show of force and military exercise to test the troops and the loyalty of the allies – a "*guan bing* 觀兵" campaign. But a different more colorful suggestion is advanced by Pankenier, who holds that the conquest was (and was planned to be) in a year when Jupiter was in Chun Huo. (Jupiter was actually in Chun Huo in 1046; so Pankenier has to argue that "12th year" is a mistake for "13th year, counted from 1058.) He argues that this supposed first campaign was intended as a conquest campaign, but was aborted when Jupiter, slowly moving toward Chun Huo, unexpectedly started retrograde motion, thereby terrifying the invading Zhou army; so Wu Wang announced (as he does, in the *Shiji*) that it was not yet "the will of Heaven" to press the attack. This theory forgets that if Jupiter were seen as this important, the ancients would have known in advance that it would not be in Chun Huo in this year, and they would also not have been surprised by retrograde motion, which occurs every year just when Jupiter is in opposition, and therefore most prominent in the night sky.

But the real question is whether there was an earlier "campaign" at all. The controlling difference must be two years, if the explanation is to be counting twelve from the two mandate dates (two years apart) to the putative conquest date. The *Shiji* "Zhou Benji" seems to make the difference three years: the *guan bing* campaign is in year 9, the Yellow River is crossed in the final campaign in year 11, month 12, and the victory is in month 2 (year not stated). But this month 2 is in the *Shiji* assumed to be still in year 11, because "month 12" here just means the last month of winter, and the historian is assuming that in the governing calendar at the time of the events the year began earlier than this. (This is the way the Han civil calendar named months most of the time from Gao Zu to Wu Di: In the *Shiji* for most of this era the civil year began with the first month of winter, called "10th month"; "*zheng yue*" (which means first month) was the name of the fourth month.) The Simas made a mistake in not seeing that contemporary Han practice could not be read back into ancient dates, as the BA reveals: It puts the conquest in Wu Wang year 12 = 1050, and the first campaign in Di Xin year 51 = 1052, which for the BA is Wu Wang year 10. The *Shiji* authors put the *guan bing* campaign in year 9 only because the authors thought the final campaign was in year 11 rather than in year 12.

It became necessary to have two events, for two dates, which were not recognized as two different names for the same year, and so the first campaign is in fact imaginary. This conclusion is confirmed when we examine carefully how the descriptions of the imaginary event and the real event match up. The BA says that in Di Xin 51, winter, 11th month, day *wuzi* (25), the Zhou army crossed [the Yellow River] at Mengjin and returned (*du Mengjin er huan* 渡盟津而還), i.e., having made a daring show of force but no more. But Liu Xin as quoted in *Han shu* 21B (quoting the lost *Shang shu* "Wu Cheng") says of the *final* campaign that the [Zhou] army first set out five days ahead of the king "on day *wuzi* (25) of the Shang 11th month." Further on, Liu gives us this: "On day *bingwu* (43), [Wu Wang] rejoined his army" (*bingwu huan shi* 丙午還師). The word *huan* is shifting its meaning: return, cause to go back, withdraw; but also return to, rejoin. We should expect somewhere to find a statement that in the supposed preliminary campaign Wu Wang *withdrew* his army on day *bingwu*. The expected statement is found in Jiang Sheng's reconstruction of the original "Tai Shi" chapter of the *Shang shu*: "On day *bingwu* the king withdrew his army" – again, "*huan shi.*" (Legge *Shoo King* p. 298,) We find the words "*huan shi*" on this occasion also in the *Shiji* "Zhou Benji." But the telling detail is the exact date "11th month day *wuzi*" in both accounts.

More interesting are the adventures of the term "Qing Ming," which names the day of the victory at Muye in the last line of *Shi* 236, the "Da Ming" Ode, "*hui zhao qing ming*" 會朝清明, "This happened in the morning of Qing Ming [Day]." The correct meaning of this line was probably already lost in philological prehistory. (Retaining this knowledge would have required not only knowing the correct date of the conquest but also knowing that in early Zhou times the winter solstice was normally identified by counting 91 days from the autumn equinox.) Karlgren is probably about right in taking its supposed meaning in Warring States to have been "the morning of the encounter was clear and bright."

So understood, the line makes us wonder what the point of it could be. Stories are invented to answer questions like this. The story is in *Lü shi chunqiu* 15 Lan 3: The Shang king sends a messenger, Jiao Li, to Wu Wang to inquire his intentions. Wu Wang replies that the Zhou army is headed for the outskirts of the Shang capital and will arrive for battle on *jiazi* day. Jiao Li departs to make his report. The weather turns bad. The troops are struggling in the mud. Wu Wang's officers entreat him to stop and rest but he refuses. He has given his word, and he fears that the Shang king will kill Jiao Li if the Zhou forces do not arrive on *jiazi*. Part of this story is echoed in *Guoyu* "Zhou Yu" 3.7, recounting the conquest campaign from beginning to end, when on arrival at Muye the Zhou army "marshaled in the rain" the night before. So, good weather in the morning was a sign of Heaven's favor.

But several readings of the basic "Da Ming" text do not fit the final campaign at all. One could read the text "the morning when we met was clear and bright." This would require a different clarifying story, if "the morning when we met" was the gathering at Mengjin rather than the last minute marshalling at the battlefield. Instead, the text was altered: In the *Chu ci* "Tian Wen" we find this: "*hui zhao zheng meng, he jian wu qi*" 會鼂爭盟,何踐吾期 but also "*qing meng*" 請盟. Here "*qing ming*" 清明 has become "*zheng meng*" 爭盟 or "*qing meng*" 請盟 by a simple modification of the characters but with a complete change in meaning: not "clear and bright" but "competed in oath-taking," i.e., "eagerly pledged allegiance," or "requested oath-taking." Hawkes translates this, "On the morning of the first day we took our oath. How did we all arrive in time?" "First day?" Perhaps Hawkes is thinking of the "Tai Shi" address, staged on three consecutive days in the *Shang shu*. But for which event? The final real campaign, or the supposed preliminary one? The *Shiji* ("Qi Shijia" "*that* Tai Shi") has it that there was a "Great Address" on each occasion – another instance of a detail in the earlier mythical event being copied from the later real one.

And there was a problem of getting there on time in each. The *Shiji* "Zhou Benji" says that at the *guan bing* event eight hundred regional lords assembled miraculously at the same time, without that time being set in advance. So how did they know when to come? Obviously this is what the "Tian Wen" text is talking about. But in the final real event there really must have been an "appointed time" problem. Having crossed the Yellow River in force in February, with the plan of doing battle in April on *jiazi*- Qing Ming Day, the army could not camp for two months close to Muye. It would have to secure the river-crossing site, moving up to the battlefield in the last few days, making sure to get there, in battle formation, exactly at the right time to take advantage of the luck of the date.

Seen as myth, other aspects of the *guan bing* event are what one would expect. Miracles abound, not only the amazing spontaneous assembly of eight hundred lords and their forces. At the crossing of the Yellow River a white fish jumps into the king's boat, and when he offers it in sacrifice red fire descends on his lodge and takes the form of a red bird. (This is the story in the *Shiji*. But in the BA these marvels occur in the final campaign. See strips 200-202 in Chapter Eight.)

The Twelve Chronograms, the Twelve Jupiter Stations and the Lunar and Solar months: the Astrology behind the Battle of Muye, 18 April 1040 BCE

Here I give you a diagram which I will try to explain:

			7 Wu 7			
		8 Si 6		6 Wei 8		
	9 Chen 5		S		5 Shen 9	
10 Mao 4	Left	E		W	Right	10 You 4
	3 Yin 11		N		11 Xu 3	
		2 Chou 12		12 Hai 2		
			1 Zi 1			

The twelve chronograms (*chen* 辰) are *zi, chou, yin, mao, chen, si, wu, wei, shen, you, xu, hai.* They are used in three systems: to name the twelve two-hour segments of the 24-hour day, to name lunar and solar months, and to name years in a once-supposed Jupiter calendar. (That use continues in the use of the cycle of 60 *ganzhi* as *sui*-names.) Herewith I give my understanding of what the systems are, and how they are related to each other and to the standard diagram of the zodiac. Please imagine my simplified diagram made up of squares as if it were a set of concentric circles: the outside has the numbers 1 (due north: at bottom) through 12 in counter-clockwise order, for the zodiac spaces and Jupiter stations, and the lunar months; the next inside has the names of the twelve chronograms, numbered, in clockwise order, for the solar months and for the twelve two-hour divisions of the day; the innermost has the first letters of the cardinal directions.

Beyond what is shown in my diagram, we must imagine the lunar zodiac of 28 lodges grouped into the 12-space zodiac of 12 Jupiter stations: they start with station 9. And imagine the whole as projected onto the horizon. Jupiter stations #1, #4, #7, and #10 have three lodges each; all other have two each. Think of

Xu, lodge #11 and middle lodge in Jupiter station #1, Xuan Xiao, at north. It will (as intended here) be at the bottom of a circular diagram of the system; i.e., like a Chinese king, one is viewing the universe facing south. Due east (left) will have lodge #4, Fang, in the middle of Jupiter station #10, Da Huo; and so on.

Thus the lodges and stations are arranged counter-clockwise, which is the direction of the apparent movement of the sun, Moon and planets through the zodiac band of constellations. The chronograms, on the contrary, are arranged clockwise. Why? The answer is that the Handle of the Big Dipper is seen as the dial of a heavenly clock, pointing to the chronograms in succession.

First, hours. The sun rises in the east and appears to move west through the day, being (in our hemisphere) slightly south of the zenith at ideal noon. Translated onto our diagram, this movement is clockwise. This is caused by the diurnal rotation of the earth, so everything else in the heavens also moves clockwise through the 24-hour day, whether seen or not. This includes the Big Dipper, so its Handle, as celestial clock-dial, also moves clockwise. Where it will be pointing at a fixed time of the 24-hour day, say midnight, will depend on the time of year, because actually the Handle is thought always to be pointing at Da Huo; thus the Handle will point due north at midnight, when the (unseen) sun is due north, only at the time of year when the sun is in Da Huo. (The sun's location in the zodiac can be determined by noting the asterisms on the meridian just before dawn and just after dusk; the sun must be east of the former and west of the latter, ideally midway between.)

Next, months: In the classical system – think back about 4500 years – the sun was in Xu (the 11th lunar lodge 虛, not the 11th chronogram 戌), due north, at the winter solstice. The month when this occurs was called the *zi* month. Therefore at this time, with the sun at due north at midnight, at the same time the Handle must point (at Da Huo) due east, three spaces clockwise from the sun. It will be useful to think of these times as the middle days of the solar months, called "*qi*-center" days. (Ideally a lunar month has the number and name of the solar month whose *qi*-center it contains; and if it contains no *qi*-center, it is intercalary, without change of number.)[10] If the Handle is pointing due east at midnight, it will have pointed due north at the preceding ideal 6:00 pm. Thus at the beginning of the *zi* month, when the sun and moon are in the same place, i.e., in Zi, but due west at ideal dusk, the Handle will point north at dusk, at Zi. At the beginning of the next lunar month the sun-moon conjunction will be approximately 1/12 counter-clockwise from north, so the Handle, always pointing at Da Huo in fact, will be pointing four spaces clockwise from the sun, and at an ideal 6:00 pm when the sun and moon are due west the Handle will thus be pointing at Chou, chronogram #2. And so on, around the zodiac and through the year. Thus in the Lunar Calendar, "Yin Li" (*yin* as in *yin* and *yang*), the successive lunar months are named for the chronograms in clockwise order, whereas the successive shuo (sun-moon conjunctions beginning the lunar months) are in counter-clockwise order.

Finally, Jupiter. Jupiter is called the "year star," because traditionally it was thought to move through the zodiac one space a year, having a period of 12 years[11]. (Actually the mean period is about 11.86 years.) The lunar system had to be analyzed so that the *zi* month will be the month containing the winter solstice. The guiding criterion for the Jupiter system is what we read in the *Shiji*,."Tian Guan Shu." There Sima Qian says that as the planet Jupiter, the "year star" *sui xing*, moves right (i.e., counter-clockwise; he is thinking of a diagram like ours, and is looking at the bottom of it), what he calls "the *yin* of the year" *sui yin* (again *yin* as in *yin* and *yang*, not the chronogram *yin*) moves left (i.e., clockwise). Perhaps the term *yin* is transferred from the conceptual lunar calendar, thought of as the analog of a Jupiter calendar. But now, the Dipper Handle is conceived as pointing at an imaginary "planet" moving around the zodiac in the opposite direction

[10] Solar months, 12 to a year, were either 30 or 31 days long. The mean length of a synodic (apparent) lunar month (from new moon to new moon) is slightly more than 29.5 days. (The Chinese practice was to alternate 30 and 29 days, with an extra 30-day month as needed.) A sidereal month (the time taken for the moon to round the 28-lodge lunar zodiac) is about 27 1/3 days.

[11] The names of the Jupiter stations are numbered in counter-clockwise order (the outside numbers in my diagram, starting at the bottom, due north. This is the actual order of the transit of the planet in its theoretical 12-year cycle): 1, Xuan Xiao; 2, Qu Zi; 3, Jiang Lou; 4, Da Liang; 5, Shi Shen; 6, Chun Shou; 7, Chun Huo; 8, Chun Wei; 9, Shou Xing; 10, Da Huo; 11, Xi Mu; 12, Xing Ji. Compare Needham vol. 3: p. 243, Fig. 91, and p. 403, Table 34.

from Jupiter. The two cross, the *Shiji* says, at *chou* and *yin*: as the "year star" (*sui xing*) moves right from *yin* to *chou*, the "*yin* of the year" (*sui yin*) moves left from *chou* to *yin*. It follows that when Jupiter *sui xing* (or *sui*) is at due north, its imaginary correlate (we often find it called "counter-Jupiter") called *sui yin*, or elsewhere *tai sui*, must be due east.

How must the Dipper Handle be observed for this to be the way of it? Consider the situation when Jupiter and the sun are in conjunction, about 30 days during which Jupiter cannot be seen; immediately after this is the heliacal rising of Jupiter, clockwise from the sun at dawn because the sun moves counter-clockwise through the zodiac twelve times as fast as Jupiter. If the Handle is then pointing east, the conjunction and rising must be in Da Huo, and at the preceding midnight the Handle will have pointed due north. Now consider the next year's conjunction and rising. This must occur (ideally) when Jupiter and the sun are in the next station, Xi Mu, Split Wood, corresponding to Yin. The handle at dawn must point (at Da Huo always) not due east but one space south of east . At the preceding midnight it will have therefore been pointing not due north at Zi, but one space east of north at Chou. And the next year, by the same reasoning, the conjunction and rising must be in Xing Ji, at Chou, while the Dipper pointing the preceding midnight must be at Yin.

The year after that the conjunction and rising must be due north, in Xuan Xiao, at Zi, and the pointing of the Handle the preceding midnight, hence the location of *sui yin* or *tai sui*, must be due east. This was the situation when the *Xunzi*, "Ru Xiao" chapter, says that "Wu Wang was marching east to meet *tai sui*," and (according to Yang Liang's commentary) Wu Wang's astrologer Yu Xin advised him not to attack northward, because Jupiter (*sui*) was then in the north. The advice would have been relevant only when the Zhou army after marching east to Meng Jin from the Zhou homeland made its crossing of the Yellow River, turning north to attack the Shang capital. But Wu Wang was now most of the way to his long planned objective, so naturally he rejected the warning.

The respect he might ordinarily have had for astrological advice would in this case be outweighed by his desire to do battle on the doubly lucky day *jiazi*-Qing Ming.[12] The Li *gui* inscription dated soon after the victory opens with the words,

> Wu Wang campaigned against Shang. It was *jiazi* morning. In the annual cauldron (*ding*) rite,
> [we] were able to inform [the royal ancestors] that we had quickly routed the Shang [forces].

Here I make use of Shaughnessy 1991 pp. 87-105, but I choose the interpretation of Yu Xingwu (p. 94), modifying it in the light of my discovery that the day was Qing Ming Day, the annual celebration of the favor of the ancestors.. This indicates that the *ding* rite was the major annual address to the ancestors (not to Shang Di), and was a report rather than an inquiry. So this inscription not only confirms the day *jiazi*, but also is consistent with the date Qing Ming. We can count this as another supporting proof that the conquest was in 1040, the victory being on April 18th exactly.

---

[12] Qing Ming Day will only rarely be a *jiazi* day. This means that probably the year too must have been chosen long in advance. See my argument at the end of Appendix 4.

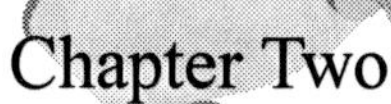

Chapter Two

The Chronology of The Three Dynasties

Published in Suppes, Moravcsik and Mendell, *Ancient and Medieval Traditions in the Exact Sciences*, Stanford: CSLI, 2000*

This is a digest of a much longer monograph, "The Key to the Chronology of the Three Dynasties: the "Modern Text" *Bamboo Annals*," *Sino-Platonic Papers* 93, January 1999, pp. 1-68. In 2002 a revised version was published in Chinese in Taipei in *Jingxue Yanjiu Luncong* 10. That monograph was a reduction of a yet unpublished book, like this one titled *The Riddle of the Bamboo Annals*. The monograph, and the book, were dedicated to the memory of Wilbur Knorr. Two chapters of the book [here, Chapter One; and another on Western Zhou] were published in Chinese (in 1997-1998).

What follows is an argument in outline for the authenticity of the *Jinben Zhushu jinian*, together with a demonstration of the use of this text to deduce the exact chronology of all of pre-771 Chinese history.

The "Modern Text" *Bamboo Annals* (*Jinben Zhushu jinian*, hereafter BA), usually held to be a modern fake, contains the earliest existing chronology of the Three Dynasties Xia, Shang and Zhou, and is not later than about 299 BCE. I use it to deduce or infer Chinese dates prior to 841 BCE (This date, the first year of the "Gong He" era that terminated the effective reign of tenth Western Zhou king Li Wang, has been the earliest generally accepted date).

The authenticity of the text was shown by Shaughnessy's discovery (1986) that a slip's worth of text has been moved from the Cheng chronicle to the Wu chronicle. This alteration was made prior to the book's burial in 299 BCE -- contra Shaughnessy, who thinks the transposition was a mistake of scholars restoring the book after its discovery ca 280 CE, in a royal tomb or subterranean repository in North China. The slip text gives Wu Wang three more years of life after his illness (actually fatal) two years after the Conquest of Shang; and just before the slip text the BA refers to the "Jin Teng" chapter of the Sha*ng shu*, which also implies incorrectly that Wu survived this illness. Moreover, the *Zuo zhuan*, a history virtually all now agree was written before 300 BCE, assigns to Wu Wang's reign events mentioned in the transposed slip text.

Some have objected that the slips must have been scattered, probably water-soaked, the thongs binding them into a book rotted away, so that it would be quite likely that the restorers might have gotten a slip in the wrong place. But the tomb (or whatever it was) was located in hill country, and must have been hollowed into a hillside, for the thieves who discovered the treasure were able to walk in, and used bundled books as torches. They were therefore dry, and most of them were still whole (*Jin shu j.* 51, on Shu Xi).

Another objection sometimes made is that my analysis, as well as Shaughnessy's, must assume that the text of the BA was inscribed on bamboo slips of a standard length, 2 *chi* 4 *cun*; with a standard number of graph spaces per slip, namely 40 (accepting the testimony of Xun Xu; see Shaughnessy 1986, p. 166). The objection is that this must be only a mean figure, because all bamboo texts so far discovered have slip texts of varying lengths, and individual characters taking up varying amounts of space. But Du Yu, third century author of the commentary on the *Zuo zhuan*, has said that there were different kinds of documents, on different materials, the most important official texts being on *ce*, defined (see Pines 1997 p. 82 and n. 18) as 2 *chi* 4 *cun*. One could expect that the inscription of important state documents like the BA would adhere to strict formal rules. Until archaeologists encounter other documents of this character and provenance, the objection has to be tabled. If our assumption leads to implications that survive independent testing, this should settle the matter.[1]

---

* I am grateful to CSLI for permission to republish this essay.

[1] "Chinese Bookmaking an Ancient Craft" (Los Angeles: *The Free China Journal* vol xiii no. 1, Jan 6, 1996, p. 5): The article shows illustrations ("Photos courtesy of National Palace Museum") of two Warring States era bamboo pieces modeled in bronze with text inlaid in gold; the characters are of uniform size and the columns are of uniform length.

Parts of the BA chronology can be shown to be correct, or systematically correctable. Therefore we should be at worst open minded about the rest of it, and should judge a datum in it to be wrong only with good reason, *which normally should include an exact explanation for the error*, as well as the correct information. Dates are more vulnerable than reign lengths: if a date is wrong, it follows that all other dates are wrong unless some reign length is wrong. But this is not true of reign lengths. On the contrary, if some reign lengths can be shown to be right, this justifies a presumption that others are right, unless they can be shown to be wrong.

Two chronicles were joined together to form the BA: an earlier chronicle down to 785 BCE, near the end of the reign of Xuan Wang, the next-to-last king of Western Zhou; and a later one, chronicling the lords of Jin, from 784 BCE,[2] and the princes of Wei, probably from 396 or 395 BCE. This joining was done in the court of Xiang Wang of Wei, 318-296 BCE, with modifications glorifying Jin-Wei history, and partly overwriting earlier features exalting Zhou history. After the text was exhumed, ca 280 CE, Jin Dynasty court scholars including He Qiao and Xun Xu worked on it at once. Jin and Wei dates were rewritten as Zhou dates, presumably to facilitate reconstitution of the text. In a few years, the work was interrupted and personal copies were made which became the *Jinben* text. Around 290 CE, work was resumed by other court scholars including Shu Xi. Jin and Wei dates were restored from 770 BCE on, and much more material was added from the recovered slips, many of which were damaged or out of order. The resulting "*Guben*" text was kept in the north after the end of Western Jin. The full text was available to Li Daoyuan (6th century), but in the south Pei Yin had to rely on quotations, and Shen Yue probably had at most an incomplete copy of the *Jinben* text. After the Sui reunification scholars could use the full text, but it must have remained in manuscript and was later lost. The shorter *Jinben* did get printed. It began to come to the attention of serious scholars in late Ming.

My method will be to get started by fixing the date of an event in the BA by astronomical evidence. I then will use this to frame a hypothesis consisting of one or more plausible premises, and will deduce tentative conclusions from them. Then I will verify one or more of these conclusions by other evidence, ideally astronomical. (Astronomical data includes not only dramatic events like eclipses and conjunctions, but also syzygies and lunar quarters.) I will count this verification as confirmation that the hypothetical premises are very probably true. I will then use these results, heuristically, as a basis for positing more hypothetical premises, and will proceed in the same way, confirming them in turn.

I. The dates of Wen Wang

The BA records a conjunction of the five visible planets in "Di Xin 32," i.e., in 1071, and in Fang, "mansion" 4 (of 28) in the Chinese lunar zodiac, near Antares. The importance of conjunctions in early political thought, and their great rarity, justifies the assumption that this is an incorrect record of the actual conjunction in 1059 -- 12 years later -- in Chun Shou, sixth of the twelve "Jupiter stations" comprising the Chinese zodiac, in the region of Cancer. (See Pankenier 1981-82 p. 5. The BA's error will be explained later [in Chapter Nine].) Jupiter was thought to move approximately from one station to the next each year, completing a full cycle in twelve years. (The actual mean time is 11.86 years.) The conjunction was thought to be a heralding of the passing of the "Mandate of Heaven" from Shang to Zhou; so other early Zhou dates are likely to be related to this date. Therefore:

Hypothesis: All late pre-Conquest Zhou dates in the BA are set back 12 years.

Argument: The BA's dates for Wen Wang are 1113-1062. Tentatively I infer 1101-1050, 52 years. But other texts, e.g., the "Wu Yi" chapter of the *Shang shu*, give Wen Wang 50 years. Nivison (1983, pp. 524-535) and Shaughnessy (1991, pp. 148-155) have shown that Zhou kings had two "first year" dates, a succession date, and after two years for completion of mourning an accession date. Therefore,

(Added 2007)

[2] Probably exact Jin dating was indicated from 784 but the royal Zhou calendar continued through 771. (Added 2007)

Hypothesis: Wen Wang's dates are 1101/1099-1050, 2 + 50 years.

Confirmation: Yi Zhou shu 23, "Xiao Kai," describes a lunar eclipse in the 35th year of [a king who can only be] Wen Wang, interrupting a "*bai wang*" (veneration of the full moon) rite in the night after day *bingzi* (13), in the first month.[3] One can assume that the conventional "Xia" calendar is intended, taking the first month as the pre-spring-equinox month, and beginning the day at dawn. There was such an eclipse in the longitude of Zhou, shortly after midnight following 12 March, day *bingzi*, in 1065 BCE. (For reasons for doubt about this text and identification, see Shaughnessy 1991, pp. 222-23. I consider its systematic relation to my entire construction to be decisive in its favor.)

If 1099 was a first year for Wen Wang, his 35th year was 1065. That he died in 1050 is attested by *Yi Zhou shu* 25 "Wen Chuan," showing that Wen Wang died in the 9th year of his "Mandate." A fragment of Huangfu Mi's *Di wang shi ji* says that "in Wen Wang's 42nd year Jupiter was in Chun Huo. Wen Wang thereupon renamed this year the "first year" of his receiving the Mandate [of Heaven]." The 42nd year would be 1058; the conjunction, including Jupiter, was in 1059 in Chun Shou; therefore Jupiter was in Chun Huo in year 42. The 9th year was 1050.

II. The Zhou calendar of 1056

Some texts say Wen Wang died 9 years after the conjunction (BA), or in 9 years counting from the year when he first called himself king (*Yi Zhou shu*, "Wen Zhuan"); some say he died in the 7th year of his kingship (*Shiji*, *Shang shu da zhuan*).

Hypothesis: as argued in Nivison (1983, pp. 530-531), Wen Wang delayed promulgating a calendar for two years, respecting mourning obligations among the people. (To use a calendar implied recognizing the ruler issuing it; one could not do this if one's unmourned father had acknowledged the preceding ruler.) Thus 1056 should count as Wen Wang's first "royal" year, i.e., "first year" for the Zhou Dynasty. 1056 also counted as first year for Wu Wang, the reason perhaps being that Wen Wang in that year named Wu "expectant king" (following late Shang practice; see below [p. 46, p. 93 note 35]).

Confirmation: The BA (with other texts) says that the first year of Mu Wang (the fifth king) was 100 years after Wu Wang or the beginning of Zhou. The "four quarters" interpretation of lunar phase terms in Zhou inscriptions and in early Zhou written texts is correct (as shown in Nivison 1983, pp. 485-492; Nivison 1999, pp. 49-50; and Shaughnessy 1991, pp. 136-145). If one uses this interpretation of the phase terms, the Shi Ju *gui* inscription, "3rd year," requires the date 954; and the Qiu Wei *gui* inscription, "27th year," requires the date 930 (Nivison 1999, pp. 5-6).

Therefore 956 is Mu 1, and 1056 is Zhou year 1 in a new Zhou royal calendar.[4]

---

[3] [Li Xueqin (2001 (1999)) has shown convincingly that there was no "*bai wang*" rite. The verb bai 拜"show due respect" for something, takes as object here not the single word *wang* 望, but the embedded sentence *wang shi wu shi* 望食無時, "the fact that a lunar eclipse occurred unscheduled." (An eclipse at wang "full moon" must of course be lunar.)]

[4] [This theory is rejected by Pankenier (1992, *BSOAS*), who sees it (correctly) as blocking his theory that the Zhou conquest was in 1046, year 13 (rather than year 12, the *Annals* year number) counting from 1058. (The preliminary report of the Three Dynasties Project pp. 46-49 accepts 1046, without crediting Pankenier.) In the *Annals* there is nothing, but this is to be expected. It has Tang of Shang's reign beginning in year 18, and Wu Wang's reign beginning in year 12, with nothing said about when these calendars began. We can deduce that it is assumed that Wu Wang's pre-conquest calendar begins with his succession year, and that Tang's pre-conquest calendar begins with his moving his capital to Bo. Similarly, I assume that in an earlier *Annals* text, before Wei editing moved the conjunction back 12 years, thus generating a "12th year" date for the conquest, it was the move of the Zhou capital to Feng in 1056 which counted as royal calendar year 1. See my argument in "The Myth of the Preliminary Campaign" on p. 27 of this book.]

III. Dates of the first four Zhou kings

Shaughnessy (1991 p. 155 n. 60) has argued convincingly that normally a king's accession calendar is used only late in his reign. (This is quite clear, e.g., in Xuan Wang's reign, first years 827/825; the accession calendar begins to be used in the middle of 809; Nivison 1999, p 47.) Therefore 956 (assumed as first year in the early inscription Shi Ju *gui*) is Mu Wang's succession year. But the BA's date is 962, six years early. Therefore

Hypothesis: Mu Wang's first year has been back-dated six years because three earlier mourning periods are omitted. The BA gives Zhao Wang 19 years, from 981, which must be 4 years early; so his dates are 977/975-957 (2 + 19); and it gives Kang Wang 26 years, from 1007, which must be 2 years early; so his dates are 1005/1003-978 (2 + 26).

Confirmation: The date "25th year" in the text of the Xiao Yu *ding* inscription (which refers to Cheng Wang as predecessor), requires 979, confirming 1003. The date "12th year" in the reference to the "Bi Ming" (lost) chapter of the *Shang shu* as quoted in *Han shu* 21B requires 994, confirming 1005 (Nivison 1999, pp. 7, 46; Shaughnessy 1991, p. 284). [See Appendix 2, Part IV "The 2-*yuan* Hypothesis"]

Hypothesis: The BA gives Cheng Wang 37 years, 1044-1008, i.e., 7 years for the Regency of Zhou Gong, and 30 years (1037-1008) for Cheng Wang's majority. There are three errors in this: (1) the 30 years are Cheng Wang's accession calendar (there was no majority calendar); (2) like other kings, Cheng Wang had two years of mourning completion, which were 1037-36; and (3) the Regency coincided with the first 7 years of Cheng's 2 + 30 years, i.e., 1037-31, and did not precede his 30 years.

Confirmation: The BA date for the appointment of Tang-shu Yu as lord of Tang (which became Jin, ancestor-state to Wei which created the BA) is 1035. (This is three Jupiter periods after 1071, the BA date for the conjunction, put in Fang; and seven centuries before 335, the date given for the self-coronation of King Huicheng of Wei.) And the *Guoyu* ("Jin Yu" 4) says that in the year of this appointment Jupiter was in the 10th Jupiter station Da Huo (middle mansion being Fang). The nearest Da Huo year was 1031; and the *Shiji* account makes clear that the event was in the Regency. The only explanation that would have this event in the Regency is to date the Regency 1037-1031. This implies that Wu Wang died in 1038, and therefore 1037-36 must have been mourning years. If the BA reigns for Zhao and Kang were 4 and 2 years early, except that the stated reigns (19 and 26 years) were their accession reigns, then the BA date for the first year of Cheng must be 0 years early, except that the implied reign, 30 years in the BA, must really be the accession reign. One can therefore infer that the actual 30 years was 1035-1006, preceded by two years for completion of mourning, and that 1037 was Cheng Wang's succession year. Wu Wang therefore must have died in 1038 BCE, 12th year in his own succession calendar.

Hypothesis: The Conquest was in 1040, 17th year of the (or Wu's) royal calendar.

Confirmation: (I give one among many; for others, see Nivison 1997 [and Chapter One].) There is inscription and old text evidence (a) that first days of years, of lunar months, and of *qi*-periods were favored as lucky days for important events; and (b) that the calendar of 24 *qi*-periods (of 15 or 16 days each, used in determining intercalation) was fixed from a relatively easily observed autumn equinox (the first day of *qi*-period Qiu Fen), rather than from a difficult-to-ascertain winter solstice. This made the recognized winter solstice two days late. (See Nivison 1999, pp. 8, 28, 49; for evidence of the early use of the *qi*-period system, see Nivison 1989.) If the Conquest year was 1040, and the campaign events are dated using information in the *Shiji*, interpreted as being in the Xia calendar, then the day was 18 April, *jiazi*, and was the first day of Qing Ming, the major annual ancestor celebration. The "Da Ming" ode in the "Da Ya" part of the *Shi jing* is a paean of the glories of the Zhou ancestors, ending with Wu Wang's conquest of Shang. The last line reads, "*si fa Da Shang; hui zhao, Qing Ming*" -- "Then he attacked Great Shang; this happened in the morning, Qing Ming [Day]." (Obviously, a confirmation of this date reconfirms Cheng Wang's dates.)

In taking these positions on the debated issue of the dates of Conquest era events, I am specifically rejecting as errors (1) the BA's location of the slip-text in the Wu chronicle; and (2) the BA's choice of conquest-era dates. I am committed to explaining these errors.

Explanation of the slip[-text] transposition[5]: When (a) conquest in year 17, and (b) Wu's death in year 12, came both to be seen as Wu calendar dates, it must have been supposed that they were reversed. Two changes "corrected" this "reversal": (1) taking Cheng's 30-year reign beginning 1035 as his majority tenure, and making the 7-year Regency precede it, while keeping the 1056 calendar fixed (as beginning 100 years before Mu 1) put the Conquest in year 12, and Wu's death in year 14, = 1043; (2) transposing the slip's worth of text then added three years to Wu's life, making him die in year 17, = 1040. This must have required moving later dates down three years, in a penultimate stage of the BA. Two residues betray this effect: (1) The shift had to stop with Mu 1 (100 years after Zhou 1), making Zhao's reign 2 + 16 years; the present text has two Zhao campaigns against Chu, in years 16 and 19. (2) The present text has Bo Qin of Lu dying in 989, instead of 992 (correctable to 990). (Nivison 1999, pp. 25-26.)

Explanation of BA Conquest era dates: The Wei editors in Xiang Wang's reign (beginning 318) accepted a chronology with the slip's worth of text moved, but without mourning intervals, i.e., taking 962 as Mu 1, with the Regency's 7 years preceding Cheng's 30, the 30 years beginning with Cheng Wang's actual succession year 1037; and they accepted "12th year" as the conquest date, but counted from what they took to be Wu Wang's succession year, 1061. This put the conquest year, believed incorrectly to be a year when Jupiter was in its 7th station Chun Huo (as in *Guoyu*, "Zhou Yu" 3.7), at 1050, and put Wu Wang's death in 1045. The year of Tangshu Yu's appointment, necessarily a Da Huo year (as in *Guoyu*, "Jin Yu" 4) therefore had to be 1035. This matched Huicheng's *yuan* as king: He declared himself king in 335, so that his *yuan* would be 100 years after his grandfather Wei Si's *yuan* 434 as *hou*. (The Jin scholars were led by confusion in the *Shiji* to make 335 the *yuan* year; see Nivison 1999, pp. 55-56, corrected here in Chapter Nine.).[6] At the same time they took Wen Wang's nine "Mandate" years as preceding Wu Wang, thus setting the conjunction at 1071 (one Jupiter cycle before the correct date 1059), which had to be a Da Huo year (being 3 x 12 years before 1035). It was therefore taken to be in Fang, in the middle of Da Huo.

[Further explanation of the BA's conquest era dates: In taking 1050 as the date of the conquest, the "Modern Text" calls the preceding year the 52nd year of Di Xin of Shang; and an earlier version of the "modern Text" (quoted by the Tang monk Yixing) calls it "Year *gengyin* (27), 11th year of Wu Wang." The Yixing quote contains a *sui* name, and thus reveals an earlier version of the "Modern Text" that began the Zhou chronicle with 1051 when the victorious campaign is said to have begun (consistently with the end-of Zhou summary), rather than with 1050. The explanation for "52nd year" is probably as follows:

When the earlier Zhou version moved the conquest date from 1040 to 1045, there had to be an adjustment in the reign of Di Xin, which could no longer extend through 1041. The date of Di Xin's last year was probably changed from the year before the conquest, i.e., before *de facto* Zhou 1 (= 1040), to the year before the Zhou royal calendar, i.e., before *de jure* Zhou 1 (= 1056). This would be a shift of 16 years back. The present text makes Di Xin 1 be 1102. Therefore Di Xin's calendar must originally have begun in 1086.

Confirmation of 1086 as Di Xin 1 (a): The 1059 conjunction was in Chun Shou (Station 6). Call this year Di Xin n. Changing the location to Da Huo (Station 10) meant changing the year to Di Xin n+4. But in the present text the date is called Di Xin 32. If n+4 = 32, then n = 28, so 1059 must be Di Xin 28. Therefore, Di Xin 1 = 1086. (The conjunction date was moved back a Jupiter cycle to 1071, because leaving it at 1059 would have made 1050 both the date of Wen Wang;'s death and the date (by Wei reasoning) of the conquest. Thus Wei reasoning, like earlier Zhou-Lu reasoning, moved Di Xin 1 back a total of 16 years.)

---

[5] I am now certain that there was no actual slip transposition but merely a moving of text, which was just enough to constitute a slip. It must have been done well before the text was buried, because the effects on chronology are seen in other fourth century BCE texts; see Chapter Nine. (Added 2008)

[6] Shaughnessy has convinced me that I had been in error here. Du Yu saw the text a year or two after its discovery, and he says explicitly that according to the text Huicheng died in his 16th year as king. So setting 335 as *yuan* year was the work of post-discovery editors. What really must have happened was that Huicheng *declared* himself king in 335, announcing that the *next* year would be his new "year 1." See Chapter Nine. (Added 2007)

Confirmation of 1086 as Di Xin 1 (b): Oracle inscriptions (Chen Mengjia 1956 pp. 301-304) for a Shang eastern campaign in years 10-11, almost certainly in Di Xin's reign, require that year 10 have an intercalary 9th month (a lunar month lacking a *qi*-center*, following the regular 9th lunar month), and also that the year end with day *jiawu* (31), *yiwei* (32) or *bingshen* (33). The only possible year is 1077. If 1077 was year 10, then year 1 was 1086.

When Di Xin 1 was set at 1102, and the conquest was set at 1050, Di Xin's 46-year reign had to be extended six years to 52 years. "52 years" is a feature of the Wei calculation only. It has no other significance.

* *Qi*-center days were the middle days of conventional solar months of 30 or 31 days. The supposed winter solstice day was the middle day in solar month 1. The probably correctly observed equinox days were the *qi*-center days (middle days) of solar months four and ten. The autumn equinox in 1077 BCE was 2 Oct, JD 132 8324, *dingyou* (34). In 1077, a lunar month containing only 29 days began on the next day, *wuxu* (35); thus there could be no *qi*-center day in that month. The preceding month, i.e., the lunar month containing the autumn equinox, was the 9th lunar month, if we assume that the civil calendar for that year began with the *chou* month (lunar month after the lunar month containing the winter solstice), as was normal during much of Shang.]

(The foregoing bracketed text differs from my original article – see my note on p. 44. Further, when I wrote my original article I had not read the serious argument by Xu Fengxian and Li Xueqin dating the Yi Fang campaign to 1066 and Di Xin 1 to 1075. My refutation is in Appendix 4 Supplement 3.)

IV. The date of the beginning of Shang.

The BA [as explained above] is a synthesis of two chronicles, an earlier one for Zhou, and a later one for Jin-Wei (whose rulers set the calendar used in the BA (text as discovered) from the date 784 on).[7]

Hypothesis: The 7 + 30-year reign given Cheng continues an error that was in the earlier Zhou chronicle, which did recognize 2-year mourning completion periods (and therefore took Mu 1 as 956, and Zhou 1 as 1056). This Zhou chronicle's dates for Cheng Wang therefore were 1042-1036, 1035-1006, 7 + 30 years, making the Regency precede the 30 years, and therefore taking the 30 years as a majority calendar. Even independently of the slip-move, then, the Zhou-favored conquest date was 1045.

Confirmation: This date 1045 reflects the date of the Shang king's recognition of Wen Wang's grandfather Dan Fu as lord of Zhou: the BA date is now 1157, twelve years back-dated, therefore originally 1145, 100 years earlier. Likewise, the first year of Yao -- whose minister of agriculture was supposed to have been the Zhou founding ancestor Hou Ji -- is even now in the BA 2145, which is 1000 years before 1145. It is likely then that 1145 is correct. Further argument will show that 1145 was the succession year of the 27th Shang king Wu Yi. This recognition of Dan Fu in that year was thus appropriate, Dan Fu being the leader of the major (at times threatening) power in the west.

Another chronological scheme, perhaps dating from the fourth century BCE, was the Yin Li. Its date for the Conquest was 1070, i.e., 25 years earlier than the Zhou-oriented date. The Yin Li also had dates for the beginnings of Shang (Yin). Its date for Tang's conquest of Xia (end of year) was 1580, and for Shang 1 (Tang 1) 1579 (see Chen Mengjia p. 212). I assume that these two dates are also 25 years earlier; therefore

Hypothesis: the Zhou-oriented earlier stage of the BA was the basis for the Yin Li scheme, and had correct dates for Shang, even if its Conquest date was five years early; the Yin Li simply moved these dates back 25 years. Therefore Shang began in 1554.

---

7 Probably from 770 on; see Chapter Eight, strips 275 and 277 and comment. (Added 2007)

Confirmation: As Pankenier (1981-82) points out, the BA and the Han apocrypha say that Shang lasted 496 years. So if the year after the conjunction of 1059 counts as the *de jure* beginning of Zhou, Shang's beginning date must be 1554. This conclusion is further confirmed, as Pankenier further points out, by the fact that the BA dates Shang 1 to 1558, and it also dates the *cuo xing* movement of the planets to 1580. But in fact this phenomenon (heliacal risings in rapid succession) occurred in late 1576. Therefore (again) the first year of Shang must be 1554, four years later than 1558.

Comment: Pankenier is right. But his confirmations are not conclusive, for three reasons: (1) 1058 and 1056 both can be regarded as first years for Zhou. (Pankenier does not recognize post-mourning dates, so he would not admit this.) (2) Pankenier's explanation for the 4-year shift 1554 back to 1558 is wrong, and so that shift cannot yet be confidently tied to the back-dating of the planet display. (See pp.48 and 51-52.) He thinks the shift applies to all dates from late Xia to middle Zhou, and results from re-dating the Zhou conquest to 1050 from a supposed 1046. This is impossible; [the Shang calendar was still being used in 1046, as in Yi Zhou shu "Feng Bao." See p. 254 in this book.] Thus, he is forced to date Mu 1 to 958, and therefore to reject the "four-quarters" interpretation of lunar phase terms, and to reject the mourning period hypothesis, and consequently to ignore without explanation the BA's 52-year reign for Wen Wang.(e.g., Pankenier 1995 in *EC* 20 p. 130 note 10). (3) Many would distrust his sources for "496 years." (Further, my own assumption that the Yin Li's dates for Shang are 25 years early is only a careful guess.) So more confirmation of 1554 is needed. I provide it by exploiting another astonishing discovery of Pankenier's, which enables me to date the whole of Xia, showing that Xia ended in 1555 BCE.

V. The dates of Xia

Hypothesis: Pankenier's argument (1983-85), taking the date of the conjunction of February 1953 BCE in lunar zodiac space Ying Shi as marking the transfer of power from Shun to Yu, first Xia ruler (dated in the BA 2029), is correct.

Confirmation: There are interregnums between Xia reigns in the BA, about a third of them 2 years; and some are explicitly said to be for mourning. Therefore

(*sub-hypothesis*) it is reasonable to suppose that all of them ought to be just two years; further, since I have found BA reign lengths in early Zhou to be accurate, therefore

(*sub-hypothesis*) it is reasonable to suppose that Xia reign lengths in the BA are accurate.

Confirmation: The BA records a solar eclipse at the beginning of the ninth month of the fifth year of the fourth Xia king Zhong Kang. Other texts (e.g., *Zuo zhuan*), apparently referring to the same eclipse, say that the sun at the time was in lunar lodge Fang. When these premises are combined, they imply that the eclipse occurred on 16 October 1876 BCE, in Fang. In fact,

(*First result*) a ring-form eclipse did occur on that day, in the morning in the longitude of the Xia domain (north of Xia, but near enough to have been reported); and the sun was in Fang. (See Nivison and Pang, *EC* 1990.) The unlikelihood of this result being accidental is so great that the result confirms the foregoing hypotheses. Further,

(*Second result*) the year 1555 turns out to be the last year of Fa, the next-to-last Xia king. The unlikelihood of this being accidental justifies another hypothesis:

Hypothesis: Di Gui (usually called Jie), the BA's (and Chinese tradition's) last ruler of Xia, is a fiction. There was no such king.

Confirmation: (1) Texts in the BA for most Xia kings are short and irregular in length. But the chronicle for Di Gui is long, and can be counted out into exactly 8 slips' worth of text (at 40 spaces per slip; see Shaughnessy 1986). This indicates that it was composed and inserted later. (2) The BA chronicle for Xia as a whole has 17 kings; the (*de jure*) first year of the first king Yu is given as 1989, the ninth king 1789, and the 17th king (Di Gui) 1589. This indicates that an earlier stage of the BA gave Xia 16 reigns, the first eight being 200 years and the second eight being 200 years, followed by 1589 as the first year of Shang. More analysis (p. 51 and in Nivison 1999, pp. 34-37) shows that this is what the BA once said. Meanwhile,

(*Third result*) the dates deduced for the 14th king Kong Jia are 1577-1569. The name suggests that the first day of his reign ought to be a *jia* day in the 60-day cycle and the *gan* ten-day "week." Actually, in the Xia calendar this day (first of the pre-spring-equinox month) was 17 February, Julian Day 114 5471, *jiazi* (01), first day of the cycle. This is so surprising as to warrant another hypothesis:

Hypothesis: When a king has a name terminating in a *gan* term, the *gan* is determined by a day that counts as the first day of his reign.

Partial confirmation: The name "Di Gui" ends in a *gan*. This king did not exist; but there was a last king, namely Fa. The two-year interregnum preceding his reign in the BA begins with 1563, which would be his succession year. The first day was 12 February, JD 115 0580, a *guiyou* (10) day. (There are a few other Xia cases; see Nivison 1999, pp. 13-14.)

VI. The dates of Shang

A fuller confirmation of the last hypothesis will greatly strengthen my deduction of the dates of Xia and the first year of Shang. Only a few Xia kings had *gan* names (all satisfy my *gan* hypothesis), but all thirty of the Shang kings had such names. My deduction of their dates, using BA reign lengths and tables of first days of lunar months (astronomical evidence), will show that every Shang king's name was determined in this way.

I proceed by assuming the *gan* hypothesis, refined to fit the Shang case; and assuming that BA reign lengths for Shang are accurate, except for five kings (Tai Wu, Pan Geng, Zu Jia, Di Yi, Di Xin) where I can show that they are not, and can show why. I will assume also that as in Xia and Western Zhou, so also in Shang a king had a succession year and an accession year after completion of mourning; except that in the Shang the mourning-completion period could be three years, if one counted the predecessor's year of death as year 1. [This would often have to be done in order to make the king's sacrifice day, determined by his *gan*, be in proper generational order. Perhaps whether the deceased king died early or late in the year was also a factor.] Partial evidence for this variable treatment of a Shang king's death year is found in Liu Xin's treatment of Tang's death year in *Han shu* 21B, pp. 48b-49a. It was both Tang's death year and his successor Tai Jia's first year.

A refinement of the *gan* hypothesis for Shang is required by the facts (1) that a king never had the same *gan* as his predecessor; and (2) that no king had *gui* as a *gan* (probably because it was the *gan* of the founder's father). Therefore

Hypothesis: In Shang, a king's *gan* is the *gan* of the first day of his succession year, unless this was the *gan* of his predecessor; in that case, his *gan* is the *gan* of the first day of his accession year; if the indicated *gan* is *gui*, the next day, *jia*, is used instead. This rule, with BA reign lengths, yields the complete chronology for Shang.

Confirmation: See Table V for confirming data. I obtain the data (using Zhang Peiyu) by finding the most probable years having the right first days, and by assuming that the reign lengths in the BA are accession reigns, i.e., that initial mourning periods are no longer assumed, as in the BA chronicle for Western Zhou. The chronology that I obtain is confirmed in several ways:

(1) It successfully explains the complex series of events at the beginning of the dynasty, as recorded in the BA. (See Tables II and V and their explanations. I argue that Wai Bing and Zhong Ren were Yi Yin's

puppets, as he tried to unseat Tai Jia, whom he placed in confinement in 1541. In 1536 Tai Jia escaped from confinement, in his 7th year (BA), i.e. his 4th accession year, killing Yi Yin.)

(2) It explains the impossible 75 years given to the fifth generation king Tai Wu. (His reign was long, actually 3 + 60 years.) Tai Wu's first year was fixed at 1475 (100 years after 1575, Tang's claimed first year); so when mourning periods were denied, a 12-year gap opened before Tai Wu, filled by reversing the order of Tai Wu and Yong Ji, and extending Tai Wu's reign through what had been Yong Ji's reign.

(3) It thus explains the fact that the BA and all other received chronologies make Yong Ji precede Tai Wu, whereas ritual inscriptions in the oracle corpus show that Tai Wu came first. (As in Keightley 1978, p. 186 note d; Keightley reads Yong Ji as "Lü Ji," and takes Tai Wu and Yong Ji (Lü Ji) to be brothers. The chronology that I reconstruct indicates that they probably were "brothers" in the broad Chinese sense, i.e., first cousins, since Tai Wu was born not later than 1498, and Yong Ji died in 1401; see Table II.)

It also yields as dates for Wu Ding 1250/1247-1189, i.e., 3 + 59 years, whereas the BA has 1274-1216, i.e., 59 years. The 27-year set-back of Wu Ding's death validates the correct dates: it results from 16 years, being the set-back of Di Xin's reign from 1086-1041 to 1102-1057 (later changed to 1051), i.e., taking 1056 as Zhou 1 rather than 1040; and 11 years, making Zu Geng's reign precede Zu Jia's, rather than (correctly, I would argue) coinciding with the first 11 years of Zu Jia's claimed 33 years. It also shows that Pan Geng really had only 24 years; his claimed 28 years actually included Yang Jia's 4 years, whereas the BA makes Yang Jia's 4 years precede the 28 years, increasing the set-back of earlier dates to 31 years. And it shows that Zhong Ren's 4 years actually coincided with Tai Jia's 1-4 of 12 years, whereas the BA makes the 4 years precede the 12 years, thereby increasing the set-back to 35 years. The true date of Shang 1, i.e., 1554, set back 35 years, became 1589, as expected first year for Shang in an earlier BA (see "dates of Xia" above). This date disappeared when the invented 31-year reign of "Di Gui" was inserted, pushing Shang 1 down to 1558, as in the present BA. (See Tables IV, V, VI and Nivison 1999 pp. 36-37.)

The *gan* hypothesis has to be modified for Shang reigns after Zu Jia: I conjecture that the reason for the Shang practice of having two kings in each generation was to fend off the danger of ministerial usurpation during mourning (attempted by Yi Yin, almost successfully). Eventually the greater danger was perceived to be fraternal usurpation. To prevent this Zu Jia (a successful usurper) started the practice of giving his heir royal status immediately, and the effective year of this act determined the heir's *gan*. After that, fraternal succession ceased, and father-son succession was the rule. I confirm these hypotheses by using oracle inscriptions to reconstruct the late Shang ritual cycle, precisely dated from 1111 through 1041. (See the table on pp. 239-40.) This reconstruction is confirmed dramatically by my success in explaining and validating the BA account of the death of Wu Yi, said in the BA to have been in 1125, but actually 16 years later, in 1109, as oracle inscriptions show; and during a hunt in the territory of the Yu Fang, i.e., "in the He-Wei area," as the BA says; oracle inscriptions verify the hunt, the location and the year (see Nivison 1999, p. 29).

VII. Western Zhou kings from Gong Wang to 771 BCE

Shaughnessy (1991, pp 253-4 n) has reasonably argued that Mu Wang's 55 year reign in the BA was (at least partly) caused by taking his life-span as his reign-length: An omen in Zhao 6 in the BA, actually 972, marked Mu's birth, on Shaughnessy's theory; this would make his death date 918, and so 917 must be Gong Wang's succession year.

Confirmation: There were five kings after Mu Wang who succeeded on the deaths of their fathers, and would originally have had reigns beginning with two-year mourning completion periods, which were originally dropped in the chronology adapted in the BA, while 771 was kept as the last year of Western Zhou. (Hence the BA has 853 as first year for Li Wang; see Nivison 1983, p. 528.) Therefore Gong Wang's succession year, given as 907 in the BA, must be 917. And if this 10-year reduction were extended back to the proposed birth date of Mu Wang, that date would become 962. But 962 is the date for the beginning of Mu's *reign* after deleting mourning periods for the three preceding kings. This coincidence would be taken as evidence that 55 years was the length of Mu's reign rather than the length of his life.

So Gong Wang's beginning dates are 917/915--, validated by bronze inscription dates; further, the BA record in Yih Wang's first year that "Heaven dawned twice in Zheng" may refer to the dimming of first light in the Hua Mountains caused by a sunrise solar eclipse farther east, on 21 April 899; in any case, inscriptions verify 899/897 as beginning dates for Yih Wang [see Appendix 3 p.220 #15-22].

Hypothesis: I amend Shaughnessy's dates for Xiao, Yi and Li. Yi Wang's dates, 861-854 in the BA (and 865-858 according to Shaughnessy 1991, pp. 259-286) must be 867-860, with Xiao 872-868, and Li 859/857-828 (and Yih 899/97-873).

Confirmation: An "original note" in the Xiao chronicle dates the birth of Yi Wang's son, later Li Wang, to 864, and this date (as Lei Xueqi argued two centuries ago) is correct. (It gives Li Wang a 37-year life, instead of a 37-year reign before his exile.) The events of this year and the next ought therefore to be in the Yi Wang chronicle, but in the BA they are in the Xiao chronicle, while there are events in every year of Yi Wang except years 4 and 5, which must therefore be 864-863. [see Diagram 3 in Appendix 2, p.218]

This accounting gives Xiao Wang, a usurping king, only 5 years, 872-868, whereas the BA gives him 9 years. The probable explanation is that Xiao Wang hung on in one of the two Zhou capitals (near Luoyang and Xi'an) and did not withdraw until Yi Wang's heir was born, in Yi 4. When the BA makes these four years precede Yi's eight years, giving them to Xiao and thus making his reign nine years, earlier dates were pushed back four years, to Gong Wang. His reign thus is reduced in the BA from (2 +) 16 years to 12 years. I contend that no other explanation for this reduction of Gong Wang to 12 years is possible, and this confirms my dates for Yih, Xiao, Yi and Li. [see Appendix 2, pp. 210-215.]

Hypothesis: Xuan Wang's received dates are 827-782, 46 years. The dates should be 827/825-784, 2 + 42 years. You Wang's dates are not 781-771, i.e., 11 years, but 783/781-771, 2 + 11 years.

Confirmation: The original BA (testimony of Du Yu in "*Zuo zhuan* Hou Xu") changed from Zhou dates to Jin dates in 784, first year of Shang-shu of Jin. An entry "Xuan Wang died" at 784 as *yuan nian*, "first year" (for Shang-shu) would have been incongruous, if at the same time You Wang's first year were recognized as 781 (= Shang-shu 4). So the date of Xuan's death would have to be changed from [Shang-shu] "*yuan nian*" to [Shang-shu] "*san nian*." (The graphs *yuan* and *san* are similar.) That Xuan's death year was 784 seems to be required by the Shi Hong *gui* inscription (very similar to the Mao Gong *ding* inscription, which must be in You Wang's first year; both resemble the text of the *Shang shu* chapter "Wen Hou zhi Ming," probable date 770). It has a first year date requiring 783. (See my note on bronze inscription 63 on p. 226.)

NOTE [This theory is, of course, possible only if Jin dating did begin in 784 in some text like the BA. I have not tried to construct such a text. My reconstruction of strip text from strips 275 through 282 assumes that the BA as received is the buried text, except (1) that in the buried text there were no *sui*-names, and (2) that the buried text did have the *yuan* dates for Shangshu and for Wen Hou, presented as subtext in full size characters (and not as small-character in-text notes, as does the Fan Qin text). Note on Wei revision of conquest-era chronology (p. 40): In my original article in the Knorr volume, I had supposed that Huicheng Wang had picked the date 335 to declare himself king, so that the date would be 700 years after the date of Tangshu Yu's being granted the fief of Tang. I assumed that Wu 12 as conquest date was received information for the Wei editors. The *Guoyu* had made the conquest year a Chun Huo (Jupiter station 7) year (incorrect), thus requiring for the BA that the fief year (a Da Huo = station 10 year) be 1035. (It was 1031 in fact.) I further held that making 335 be Huicheng's *yuan* (as well as his declaration year) was a mistake made by the Wei editors. I now think that Huicheng picked 335 to declare himself king, so that 334 could be his royal *yuan* year, 100 years after his grandfather's *yuan* year as *hou*; that prefixing 700 to 335 determined that 1035 be Tangshu's fief year, known to be a Da Huo year; that this in turn determined that 1050 must be the conquest year; that "12th year" as conquest year is the result of Warring States calculation (the result of moving the conjunction of 1059 back one Jupiter cycle) and has no validity; and (with Shaughnessy) that it was the Jin scholars who misdated Huicheng Wang's reign. – added October 2008]

TABLES OF DATES

(left: *Bamboo Annals* dates; right: proposed correct dates)

I XIA DYNASTY

	Bamboo Annals	Proposed
1. Yu (= Shun 14)	2029-	1953-
Shun 14, conjunction		*1953*
(mourning (Shun)	1992-90, 3	1916-15, 2
Yu (*de jure*)	1989-82, 8	1914-07, 8
(mourning)	1981-79, 3	1906-05, 2
2. Qi	1978-63, 16	1904-89, 16
(mourning)	1962-59, 4	1888-87, 2
3. Tai Kang	1958-55, 4	1886-83, 4
(mourning)	1954-53, 2	1882-81, 2
4. Zhong Kang	1952-46, 7	1880-74, 7
Year 5, eclipse	*1948*	*1876*
(mourning)	1945-44, 2	1873-72, 2
5. Xiang	1943-16, 28	1871-44, 28
(usurpation)	1915-76, 40	
(mourning)		1843-42, 2
6. Shao Kang	1875-55, 21	1841-21, 21
(mourning)	1854-53, 2	1820-19, 2
7. Zhu	1852-36, 17	1818-02, 17
(mourning)	1835-34, 2	1801-00, 2
8. Fen	1833-90, 44	1799-56, 44
(mourning)	(none) 0	1755-54, 2
9. Mang	1789-32, 58	1753-96, 58
(mourning)	1731, 1	1695-94, 2
10. Xie	1730-06, 25	1693-69, 25
(mourning)	1705-03, 3	1668-67, 2
11. Bu Jiang	1702-44, 59	1666-08, 59
(retires; no interregnum; dies in Qiong 10 but no calendar break)		
12. Jiong	1643-26, 18	1607-90, 18
(mourning)	1625-23, 3	1589-88, 2
13. Jin	1622-15, 8	1587-80, 8
(mourning)	1614-13, 2	1579-78, 2
14. Kong Jia	1612-04, 9	1577-69, 9
First day = jiazi		*17 Feb 1577*
(mourning)	1603-02, 2	1568-67, 2
15. Hao	1601-99, 3	1566-64, 3
(mourning)	1598-97, 2	1563-62, 2
16. Fa	1596-90, 7	1561-55, 7
(no interregnum)		
17. Di Gui	1589-59, 31 (imaginary)	

II SHANG DYNASTY

	Bamboo Annals	Proposed
Planet display	1580	1576
Tang, year 1	1575	1575
Conquest of Xia	1559	1555

1.	Tang	1558-47,	12	1554-43,	12
	(Mourning)			1542-40,	3
[2.	Wai Bing	1546-45,	2	1541-40,	2]
[3.	Zhong Ren	1544-41,	4	1542/39-36,	3 + 4]
4.	Tai Jia	1540-29,	12	1542/39-28,	3 + 12
Yi Yin usurpation		1540-34,	7	1542-1536,	7
Yi Yin killed		1534		1536	

(The *Annals* says that Yi Yin actually made himself king. I think that he was trying to do this, but got no farther than setting up Wai Bing and Zhong Ren as his puppets, while he had Tai Jia in detention; that is probably why those two are omitted in some chronologies.)

5.	Wo Ding	1528-10,	19	1527/24-06,	3 + 19
6.	Xiao Geng	1509-05,	5	1505/02-98,	3 + 5
7.	Xiao Jia	1504-88,	17	1497/94-78,	3 + 17
8.	Tai Wu	1475-01,	75	1477/74-15,	3 + 60
9.	Yong Ji	1487-76,	12	1414/12-01,	2 + 12
10.	Zhong Ding	1400-92,	9	1400/97-89,	3 + 9
11.	Wai Ren	1391-82,	10	1388/87-78,	1 + 10
12.	Hedan Jia	1381-73,	9	1377/74-66,	3 + 9
13.	Zu Yi	1372-54,	19	1365/63-45,	2 + 19
14.	Zu Xin	1353-40,	14	1344/41-28,	3 + 14
15.	Kai Jia	1339-35,	5	1327/24-20,	3 + 5
16.	Zu Ding	1334-26,	9	1319/16-08,	3 + 9
17.	Nan Geng	1325-20,	6	1307/04-99,	3 + 6
18.	Yang Jia	1319-16,	4	1298/96-93,	2 + 4
19.	Pan Geng	1315-88,	28	1292-69,	24
20.	Xiao Xin	1287-85,	3	1268/66-64,	2 + 3
21.	Xiao Yi	1284-75,	10	1263/60-51,	3 + 10
22.	Wu Ding	1274-16,	59	1250/47-89,	3 + 59
23.	Zu Geng	1215-05,	11	1188/85-78,	3 + 8
24.	Zu Jia	1204-72,	33	1177/75-56,	2 + 20
25.	Feng Xin	1171-68,	4	[1175-72,	4]
26.	Kang Ding	1167-60,	8	[1171-56],	
				1155/53-46,	2 + 8
27.	Wu Yi	1159-25,	35	1145/43-09,	2 + 35
28.	Wenwu Ding	1124-12,	13	1118-08/06,	10 + 3
29.	Di Yi	1111-03,	9	1105-87,	19
				[-69,	37]
30.	Di Xin	1102-51,	52	1086-69,	
				1068-41,	46

(Pan Geng probably counted Yang Jia's 4 years as part of his "28"; Zu Jia must have counted Zu Geng's 11 years as part of his own "33." Both moves were attempts at usurpation, Zu Jia's being successful. Wu Ding's intended heir was probably Zu Ji, named in inscriptions as *xiao wang*; I assume that he was chief mourner during part or all of Zu Geng's tenure. Zu Jia guaranteed the succession in his own line by appointing Feng Xin to royal status in 1175, and (on Feng Xin's death) Kang Ding in 1171. Kang Ding continued this policy, as did Wu Yi, actually giving his son Wenwu Ding a calendar of his own in 1118. (The same benefit was accorded Zhou Xin in 1086.) Wenwu Ding may be identical with Di Yi, taking that title (as "Wenwu Di Yi") in 1105. He may have died in 1082 (p.257 note 45); his son Zhou Xin probably took the title Di Xin in 1068, appointing his heir Lu Fu to royal status (as "Wu Geng"), with a new calendar.)

III WESTERN ZHOU DYNASTY

	Wen Wang	1113-62, 52	1101/99-50,2 + 50
	Conjunction	*1071*	*1059*
	Mandate	1070	1058
	Royal calendar		1056
1.	Wu Wang	1061-45, 17	1049-38, 12
	Conquest	1050 (1061=50=12)	1040 (1056=40=17)

(Probably the "Royal Calendar" was a "junior king" calendar for Wu Wang. It then seemed that Wu Wang, with a 12-year reign, conquered in year 17. The anomaly was resolved by shifting Zhou Gong's Regency back five years (making it the 7 years preceding Cheng Wang's 30), and transposing text from Cheng Wang's chronicle to the end of Wu Wang's (as discovered by Shaughnessy) to give Wu Wang three more years of life. The effect was to switch "12" and "17.")

	Wu as king	1050-45, 6	1040-38, 3
2.	Cheng Wang	1044-08, 7 + 30	1037/35-06, 2 + 30
	Zhou Gong, Regent	1044-38, 7	1037-31, 7
3.	Kang Wang	1007-82, 26	1005/03-78,2 + 26
4.	Zhao Wang	981-63, 19	977/75-57, 2 + 19
5.	Mu Wang	962-08, 55	956/54-18, 2 + 37
6.	Gong Wang	907-86, 12	917/15-00, 2 + 16
7.	Yih Wang	895-71, 25	899/97-73, 2 + 25
8.	Xiao Wang	870-62, 9	872-68, 5

(Li Wang was born in 864, and Yi Wang's lack of an heir before that time was probably one justification for Xiao Wang's usurpation. So Xiao Wang's claimed tenure, presumably disputed by Yi Wang, probably continued through 864, and this gave him 9 years in effect. Yi Wang's father Yih Wang may have been in forced retirement, living to 868.)

9.	Yi Wang	861-54, 8	867/65-60, 2 + 6
10.	Li Wang	853-42, 12	859/57-28, 2 + 30
	Gong He Regent	841-828, 14	841-828, 14
11.	Xuan Wang	827-82, 46	827/25-84, 2 + 42
12.	You Wang	781-71, 11	783/81-71, 2 + 11

(Li Wang 1 = 853 in the BA probably is a residue of an earlier chronology that dropped mourning periods, giving Li 30 years, Xuan 42 years, and You 11 years. There seem to be no believable events ascribable to Xuan 45-46. The calendar of Shang-shu of Jin, which continued the *Annals* beginning in 784, would not have been able to recognize 781 as year 1 for You Wang (his actual accession year, I assume) without treating 782 as Xuan Wang's last year. The Shi Hong *gui* inscription, which must be a first year inscription in You Wang's calendar, requires 783 as "1st year.") [But see my note on the Shi Hong *gui* (bronze #63) in Appendix 3.]

IV DEVELOPMENT OF PRE-ZHOU CHRONOLOGY

In the earliest stage Shun 14 = 1953 = *de facto* beginning of Xia. In Yao 58 Shun forced the banishment of Yao's heir and imprisoned Yao; and there were two-year mourning periods after deaths of rulers. This made Huang Di 1 = 2287, a date apparently chosen for calendar convenience (see below). In the next stage time intervals are lengthened so as to make Yao 1 = 2145; as a result 2287 has to be saved as the first year of a supposed Zhuan Xu Calendar. (The date is confirmed by a quotation from Liu Xiang's *Hong Fan zhuan,* in the middle chapter of the "Monograph on the Calendar" in the *Xin Tang shu*. [See Nivison, "Response," in *Early China* 15 (1990), pp. 169-170.]) In this stage Shang 1 = 1589 (see Nivison 1999, pp. 36-37). In the final stage mourning periods are dropped (and "2287" disappears). 2353 and 2104 are two dates important for Wei: 2353 is 100 *zhang* (19-year cycles) before 453, when Wei came into existence; 2104 is two conjunction intervals (2 x 516 1/2 years) before the conjunction date 1071 (as altered by Wei), recording "a celestial display (*jing xing)* in Yi."

	Present Text	Earlier	Earliest
Huang Di 100	2402	2406	2287
HD 50 (rite)	2353		
Zuo Che 7*	2302	2306	2187
Zhuan Xu 78	2295	2299	2180
ZX 13		2287	
Mourning		2221 (2)	2102 (2)
Di Ku 63	2217	2219	2100
Mourning		2156 (2)	2037 (2)
Zhi 9	2154	2154	2035
Yao 1	2145 (100)	2145 (100)	2026 (58)
Yao 42 (*jing xing*)	2104		
Yao 58			1969
Yao dies	2046	2046	
Mourning	2045 (3)	2045 (3)	
Shun 1	2042 (50)	2042 (50)	1968
Yao dies (Shun 9)			1960
Mourning (calendar break)			1959 (2)
Shun 14 (conjunction)	2029	2029	1953
Shun, death	1993	1993	1917
Mourning	1992 (3)	1992 (3)	1916 (2)
Yu 1 (Xia)	1989	1989	1914
Zhong Kang eclipse	1948	1948	1876
Mang (9th king)	1789	1789	1753
Di Gui (31 years)	1589		
Shang, first year	1558	1589	1554

The re-dating of the eclipse of 1876 back to 1948 appears to be based on observed sun locations, 432-428, and on 427 as the first year of a *jiyou bu.* 428 is one *ji* (20 *bu*, 1520 years) after 1948. (See Nivison and Pang, *EC* 15.) 2287 is 60 x 31 years before 427: *ganzhi* for first days repeat at 31-year intervals, and increase by 12 at 60-year intervals. Therefore the "earliest" column appears to be a chronology accepted at a time when 427 could be conceived as a base date; and the "earlier" column appears to be a modified chronology worked out later, but while a record of sun locations 432-428 was still available. The "present text" chronology implies Zhuan Xu's death in 2218. His death date is said in the *Zuo zhuan* (Zhao 8) to be a year when Jupiter was in Chun Huo. This reveals that this chronology in most of its details (as well as the compilation of the *Zuo zhuan*) is tied to a calculation from an observed Jupiter position made in some year between 400 and 330. E.g., Jupiter was in Chun Huo in 370 BCE; 2218 - 370 = 1848 = 12 x 154 (12 years was the supposed period of Jupiter). (See *MH* vol. 3, Appendix 3, p. 659. Chavannes infers from this that the BA must be an authentic ancient text.) For 1558 as Shang first year see pp. 51-52.

[* Seven years of mourning after Huang Di; see p. 113.]

V SHANG KINGS: HOW DATES DETERMINE GAN NAMES

(*gan* = last digit of cycle number: 1 = jia, 2 = yi, 3 = bing, 4 = ding, 5 = wu, 6 = ji, 7 = geng, 8 = xin, 9 = ren, 10 = gui (= jia))

	King	*Annals* dates (lengths)	Nivison dates (lengths)	First days (cycle #)	Generation
2.	Wai Bing	1546 (2)	1541-40 (2)	1/11(33)	2(?)
3.	Zhong Ren	1544 (4)	1542 (3+4)	1/22(39)	2(?)
			/1539		
4.	Tai Jia	1540 (12)	1542 (3+12)		3
			/1539	1/18(51)	
5.	Wo Ding	1528 (19)	1527 (3+19)	2/4(11)	3
			/1524	2/1(24)	
6.	Xiao Geng	1509 (5)	1505 (3+5)	1/3(34)	4
			/1502	12/31'03(47)	
7.	Xiao Jia	1504 (17)	1497 (3+17)	2/3(47)	4
			/1494	1/31(60)	
8.	Tai Wu	1475 (75)	1477 (3+60)	1/23(21)	5
			/1474	11/22'75(55)	
9.	Yong Ji	1487 (12)	1414 (2+12)	12/18'15(16)	5
			/1412		
10.	Zhong Ding	1400 (9)	1400 (3+9)	1/13(54)	6
			/1397		
11.	Wai Ren	1391 (10)	1388 (1+10)	1/28(14)	6
			/1387	12/19'88(39)	
12.	Hedan Jia	1381 (9)	1377 (3+9)	12/29'78(41)	7
			/1374		
13.	Zu Yi	1372 (19)	1365 (2+19)	1/16(02)	7
			/1363		
14.	Zu Xin	1353 (14)	1344 (3+14	1/21(58)	8
			/1341		
15.	Kai Jia	1339 (5)	1327 (3+5)	1/15(21)	8
			/1324		
16.	Zu Ding	1334 (9)	1319 (3+9)	1/16(04)	9
			/1316		
17.	Nan Geng	1325 (6)	1307 (3+6)	1/3(54)	9
			/1304	1/30(37)	
18.	Yang Jia	1319 (4)	1298 (2+4)	1/23(01)	10
			/1296		
19.	Pan Geng*	1315 (28)	1292 (24)*	1/17(27)	10
20.	Xiao Xin	1287 (3)	1268 (2+3)	1/22(38)	10
			/1266		
21.	Xiao Yi	1284 (10)	1263 (3+10)	1/26(08)	10
			/1260	1/24(22)	
22.	Wu Ding	1274 (59)	1250 (3+59)	1/4(54)	11
			/1247		
23.	Zu Geng	1215 (11)	1188 (3+8)	1/8(24)	12
			/1185	12/7'86(07)	
24.	Zu Jia*	1204 (33)	1177 (2+20)	1/7(20)	12
			/1175		
25.	Feng Xin	1171 (4)	1175 (4)	1/14(38)	13
26.	Kang Ding	1167 (8)	1171 ((16+))	1/29(14)	13
			1155/53 (2+8)		
27.	Wu Yi	1159 (35)	1155 ((10+))	1/3(12)	14
			1145/43 (2+35)		
28.	Wenwu Ding	1124 (13)	1145 ((27+))	1/13(14)	15
			1118-1109 (10		
			1108-1106 +3)		
29.	Di Yi	1111 (9)	1105 (19)	1/21(52)	16?
30.	Di Xin	1102 (52)	1106 ((20+))	1/2(28)	17?
			1086-1069 (18		
			1068-1041 +28)		

*There were four kings in generation 10. This must indicate that something unusual was happening. In working out the *gan* sequence, I have found it necessary to assume that Pan Geng, traditionally 28 years, properly had only 24, and claimed his brother Yang Jia's four post-mourning years as his own, i.e., he was attempting to usurp the succession for his own heir, intending that Xiao Xin would merely hold the throne in trust. This kept on until there wee no brothers left. Similarly Zu Jia, traditionally with a reign of 33 years, must have counted his own reign (which came to 2+20) as continuing Zu Geng's years (3+8). (The actual legitimate heir of Wu Ding was Zu Ji (or Zu Ji's heir).) Another instance is Wu Gong of Jin (Quwo line): when in 679 he replaced the rival line of Jin lords, he took *hou* Min's calendar as his own (see p. 166).

The first king, Tang or "Tai Yi," declared himself king in 1575, the year after the *cuo xing* celestial display of late 1576 (the planets' heliacal risings occurring in quick succession). 1572 (allowing three years for mourning-completion in the populace) could have given his *gan*: the post-solstice lunar month began 22 Jan, *yichou*. (In 1542 Yi Yin offered a sacrifice to Tang on an *yichou* day.)

In the table above, if the succession year determines the *gan*, only one first-day date is entered in the fourth column. (Tai Jia is a special case: his succession date was preempted by Zhong Ren.) If the *gan* of the succession-year first-day is the same as the *gan* of the predeceased king, then the post-mourning year (accession year) determines the *gan*; its first day is then entered in the next line.

Events in reigns 2-3-4 appear to be as follows: Tang's chief minister Yi Yin was trying to make himself king. Tang died early in 1542. His grandson Tai Jia succeeded in that year, 1542-1-0 being mourning years. In 1542 (beginning with a *ren* day) Yi Yin named Zhong Ren acting king while Tai Jia did mourning. Then in 1541 Yi Yin exiled Tai Jia and replaced him by Wai Bing for two years as chief mourner. In 1539-36, four years, Zhong Ren was nominal king, but in 1536, Tai Jia's seventh year *de jure*, Tai Jia escaped from confinement and killed Yi Yin.

There is a way to avoid assuming the anomalous single year of mourning at the beginning of the reign of Wai Ren, 11th king: Assume that Zhong Ding's reign is 2 + 9, and that the intercalation due in 1389 is at the end of 1390. Wai Ren succeeds in 1389 (rather than 1388), beginning with the actual third month counting from the solstice month. Assume then that first days of lunar months were chosen so as to make 29- and 30-day months alternate. Wai Ren's dates then are 2 + 10, 1389/1387-1378. (Take 1389 first day as *renwu* (19), 8 Feb, rather than *guiwei* (20), 9 Feb.)

Beginning with Kang Ding (also called Geng Ding) and Feng Xin (also called Lin Xin), the *gan*-name was (I think) determined by the date when as a prince the future king was named heir. (Feng Xin died before his father, so another prince, who became Kang Ding, had to be appointed.) Apparently also both Wenwu Ding and Di Xin were given reign-calendars while their fathers were still living.

"Di Yi" may simply be a title claimed by Wenwu Ding in 1105 (some later inscriptions mention sacrifices to "Wenwu Di Yi"). Wenwu Ding's accession year was 1106, perhaps giving Di Xin his *gan*. Wu Yi gave Wenwu Ding his own calendar in 1118. Similarly, I assume that "Di Yi" gave his heir ("Zhou Xin") a calendar in 1086, dying some years later. A new calendar apparently began in 1068, beginning with a *geng* day, and perhaps that year marked both the effective king's assumption of the title "Di Xin," and the naming of the heir, Prince Lu Fu, as expectant king "Wu Geng." The interval 1105-1068 is 37 years, the reign-length assigned to Di Yi in other chronologies.

VI SHANG DATE SHIFTS EXPLAINED

Here I attempt to assist readers in understanding the complex but important table on p. 52.

First, an example with a minimum of explanation. Consider the 18th king, Yang Jia: his reign was 1296-93, preceded by mourning, 1298-97, indicated by '(2+4)'. Column 1 is empty for kings later than Tai Wu. Column (2) has '+31', meaning that Yang Jia's dates are moved back 31 years to 1329-28, 1327-24, by eliminating the accumulated overlapping of 16+11+4 years. But in column (3) mourning periods are eliminated for kings 10, Zhong Ding, through 22, Wu Ding, and this operation includes Yang Jia. (After Wu Ding mourning years are absorbed in other ways.) But since the elimination of mourning years is cumulative, the reduction for Yang Jia is 8, not 31. After column (3), we have *Annals* reign dates and lengths. These are obtained by subtracting the proper number, 8, from the accession reign dates in column (2), i.e. from 1327-1324, getting 1319-1316, and taking '4' as the reign rather than 2+4.

Column numbered (1): 1575 is the date picked (probably retro-actively) by Tang as year 1 for his calendar as king, 1575 being the next year after the *cuo xing* celestial display (firmly dated to 1576 by Pankenier). The Song state probably kept accurate records of dates of Shang kings; in any case this date would be remembered. Exactly 1000 years later was 575, which was the first year of Song Ping Gong. Sometime in Warring States, experts working on the text that later became the *Bamboo Annals* noticed that 1474 was the accession year for the main sequence king in the fifth generation, Tai Wu. Since the fifth Western Zhou king Mu Wang's first year is exactly 100 years after the first year of the first Zhou royal calendar, they thought this ought to be true for Shang also; so they replaced the 3-year mourning period for Tang by the 2-year tenure of Wai Bing, whom Yi Yin had put in Tai Jia's place as mourner when Tai Jia was exiled. The data in column (1) show the effects of this from Wai Bing to Tai Wu. (The earlier dates are accurate.)

Column numbered (2): This column shows the effects of the undoing of overlaps: Di Xin was moved back 16 years. Zu Geng, whose years were claimed by Zu Jia as part of his claimed reign of 33 years, was moved back 11 years, for a total of 27 years. Similarly Pan Geng claimed his predecessor Yang Jia's four post-mourning years as part of his claimed 28, so at this point there is a 4-year set-back, the total from here back being 16+11+4=31. 31 years is the back-dating back to Zhong Ren, whose four years were the first four of Tai Jia's post-mourning 12 years, so from here back the total is 35, with one exception: Tai Wu had been moved back 31 years to (accession) 1506, so Tang's royal year one, 1575, could only be moved back 31 years, to 1606. (So it henceforth is 1+4 years after the *cuo xing* instead of being only 1 year after.) A notable effect was that the first year of Shang *de facto*, 1554, moved back 35 years to 1589.

Column (3) shows the calculation of the elimination of mourning periods at the beginnings of reigns. The motive was probably to restore the absolute date 1575 for Tang. This required moving the Tang date and what the Tai Wu date had become down 31 years. To do this, the Warring States experts eliminated mourning periods after Tai Wu, until the 31 years were used up; after that, mourning periods were absorbed in other ways. But before Tai Wu, from Tai Jia back mourning periods were already absorbed in other ways, so the elimination of mourning applied just to the four kings after Tai Jia down to and including Tai Wu, in each case 3 years; thus a 12-year gap opened before Tai Wu. The king after Tai Wu was Yong Ji, who happened to have a 2+12 year reign; this was cut to 12 years, which were moved back into the gap, reversing the order of these two kings (the reversal persists in all chronologies, but *jiagu* material shows it to be wrong). Tai Wu's years were then extended down through what had been Yong Ji's last year, to an impossible total of 75 years; so the first reign to which the 31-year reduction is applied is Zhong Ding; and since mourning is being eliminated, we must first reduce Zhong Ding from 3+9 years to 9, i.e., to 1428-1420, and then subtract 31 minus 3, i.e., 28, to get the *Annals* dates 1400-1392 (*not* 1400/97-1389). Reigns later than Wu Ding are unaffected, because the 31 years were used up.

I take this accounting as a confirmation of my recovery of Shang dates using the principle that a Shang king's *gan* name is determined by the *gan* of his first reign day. But there is more to be said. The undoing of overlaps, at the column (2) stage, had been part of a program of moving dates *back*, in order to get Yao's first year back from 2026 to 2145, which had been picked earlier as 1000 years before 1145, the actual first year of Wu Yi, and the year when "Old Duke" Dan Fu of Zhou had been accorded court status by Wu Yi. There could be no retreat. 1590 had become the last year of the last Xia king Fa, and could not be moved down again. The only solution was to make 1589 (resulting from adding the overlaps 16+11+4+4 = 35 to 1554) be the first year of another "last" Xia reign; so Di Gui was invented, and the reason his reign is 31 years exactly is because 31 years was the total of overlaps back to Tai Wu, 16+11+4.

None of this argument would remain standing if the Pankenier-Shaughnessy-Nivison calculation of 1086 as the actual first year of Di Xin were wrong: because the initial set-back has to be 16 years, with effects all the way back to Yao. The Three Dynasties Project scholars have determined the date to be 1075, not 1086; and their reasons are impressive. I will return to this matter at the end of this book.

SHANG DATE SHIFTS, TRUE DATES TO ANNALS DATES

King	*True Dates*	*(Reign)*	*(1)*	*(2)*	*(3)*	*Annals*	*(Reign)*
"Di Gui" (Jie of Xia, imaginary)						*1589*	(*31*)
cuo xing	1576		1576	+35 1611	-31	1580	
1. Tang 1	*1575*-43	(33)	*1575*	+*31* 1606	-31	*1575*	(29)
Shang 1	1554	(12)	1554	+35 *1589*	-31	1558-47	(12)
Mourning (replaced by Wai Bing)	1542-40	(3)	----				
2. Wai Bing (= mourning)	1541-40	(2)	3-2=+1 1542-41	+35 1577-76	-31	1546-45	(2)
3. Zhong Ren	1539-36	(4)	+1 1540-37	31+4=35 1575-72	-31	1544-41	(4)
4. Tai Jia	1539-28	(12)	+1 1540-29	+31 1571-60	-31	1540-29	(12)
5. Wo Ding	1527/24-06	(3+19)	+1 1528/25-07	+31 1559/56-38	-31, +3	1528-10	(19)
6. Xiao Geng	1505/02-98	(3+5)	+1 1506/03-99	+31 1537/34-30	(-31+3=)-28, +3	1509-05	(5)
7. Xiao Jia	1497/94-78	(3+17)	+1 1498/95-79	+31 1529/26-10	(-28+3=)-25, +3	1504-88	(17)
Yong Ji				(+3+3+3, +3=12, inserted)		1487-76	(12)
8. Tai Wu	1477/*74*-15	(3+60)	+1 1478/*1475*-15	+31 1509/*1506*-46	-31	*1475*-01	(75)
			(3+60, +1)	(-3; 60+1, +2+12, =75)			
9. Yong Ji	1414/12-01	(2+12)		(2+12 given to Tai Wu: -14, -31= -45)			
10. Zhong Ding	1400/97-89	(3+9)		+31 1431/28-20	-31, +3	1400-92	(9)
11. Wai Ren	1388/87-78	(1+10)		+31 1419/18-09	(-31+3=)-28, +1	1391-82	(10)
12. Hedan Jia	1377/74-66	(3+9)		+31 1408/05-97	(-28+1=)-27, +3	1381-73	(9)
13. Zu Yi	1365/63-45	(2+19)		+31 1396/94-76	(-27+3=)-24, +2	1372-54	(19)
14. Zu Xin	1344/41-28	(3+14)		+31 1375-72-59	(-24+2=)-22, +3	1353-40	(14)
15. Kai Jia	1327/24-20	(3+5)		+31 1358/55-51	(-22+3=)-19, +3	1339-35	(5)
16. Zu Ding	1319/16-08	(3+9)		+31 1350/47-39	(-19+3=)-16, +3	1334-26	(9)
17. Nan Geng	1307/04-99	(3+6)		+31 1338/35-30	(-16+3=)-13, +3	1325-20	(6)
18. Yang Jia	1298/96-93	(2+4)		+31 1329/27-24	(-13+3=)-10, +2	1319-16	(4)
19. Pan Geng	1292	(24)	24+4=28: +27+4=	+31 1323	(-10+2=) -8	1315	
	-69			+27 -96	-8	-88	(28)
20. Xiao Xin	1268/66-64	(2+3)		+27 1295/93-91	-8, +2	1287-85	(3)
21. Xiao Yi	1263/60-51	(3+10)		+27 1290/87-78	(-8+2=) -6, +3	1284-75	(10)
22. Wu Ding	1250/47-89	(3+59)		+27 1277/74-16	(-6+3=) -3, +3	1274-16	(59)
23. Zu Geng	1188/85-78	(3+8, =11)		+27 1215/12-05	(-3+3=) 0	1215-05	(11)
24. Zu Jia	1177/75	(2+20, +11=33)		16+11=27 1204/02		1204-72	(33)
	-56			+16 -1172			
25. Feng Xin	1175-1172	(4)		[-4] 1171-68		1171-68	(4)
26. Kang Ding	1155/53-46	(2+8)		+16 1169/67-1160		1167-60	(8)
27. Wu Yi	1145/43-09	(2+35)		+16 1161/59-1125		1159-25	(35)
28. Wen Ding	[1118-09], 1108-06	([10+]3)		+16 [1134-1125],1124-22[-12]		1124-12	(13)
29. Di Yi	1105-1087	(19)		-10+16 1111-1103	(19-10=9)	1111-03	(9)
30. Di Xin	1086			+16 1102		1102	

Attachment: The 853 Problem

In Section VII, "Western Zhou kings from Gong Wang to 771 BCE," I "amend" a few of Shaughnessy's dates. We agree that Xiao 1 was 872, and it is generally agreed that the Gong He Regency began in 841. The BA dates Yi Wang to 861-854, eight years. I make the eight years 867-860, but Shaughnessy's dates are 865-858. This looks trivial. But it is not trivial, and it demands close attention.

One way of describing the difference is that whereas we both recognize a 30-year reign for Li Wang (including his years of exile), I posit an initial two years of formal mourning completion and Shaughnessy does not. Those two years are part of my explanation for the BA's date Li Wang 1 = 853: I am proposing that in an earlier deformed chronology two years of mourning completion had been omitted for the last two Western Zhou kings, Xuan Wang and You Wang (Nivison 1983 p. 528). Shaughnessy of course could do the same. (I reduce 859 to 853 by subtracting 2 x 3; Shaughnessy would be reducing 857 to 853 by subtracting 2 x 2.) But Shaughnessy does not do this. Instead, he argues that 853 is a valid date. He points out that the BA has the death of Qi Xian Gong as Li 3 = 851; and the death of Yan, *zi* of Chu, as Li 6 = 848. These dates – 851 and 848, but expressed differently -- are also the dates given in the *Shiji*, so they must be right. But this, he thinks, implies that 853 as *yuan* date must also in some sense be right. The impression of circularity in this reasoning reveals a suppressed premise: Shaughnessy in effect is assuming that when we correct BA dates we are limited to correcting *yuan* dates; dates of events within reigns, as expressed in the BA, are untouchable, because (as he has explained to me) he believes the ancient Chinese had no concept of absolute time other than as given by stacked up reign lengths, and therefore had no independent way of determining the date of an intra-reign event. I would object that sometimes this might be true, but not always, if only because there were other available state chronicles.

I have argued with him that this way of thinking often leads him into error in other matters. But aside from that, he is in trouble right here: He now has to find some sense in which 853 could be valid (a problem that I, of course, do not have). It can not be a post-mourning *yuan*. The only other possibility is that it must be a coming-of-age *yuan*, i.e., Li Wang succeeded as a minor (this much I agree with), and by 853 had gotten old enough to assume royal power. But how old? Shaughnessy accepts (as do I) the in-text note in the BA dating Li Wang's birth to Xiao 7, which in the BA system is 864, since in the BA Xiao's *yuan* year is 870. But we both agree that Xiao's actual *yuan* was 872. For Shaughnessy, this means that Xiao 7 (which for him can't be amended, and for him has to be counted from the actual *yuan*) has to be 866; so in 853 he was 14 *sui*. In this way, Shaughnessy thinks, he has shown that a young teen-ager can be a fully functioning king. (864 as birth date makes Li Wang only 12 *sui* in 853, patently absurd for a royal coming-of-age.) Shaughnessy therefore sees no difficulty in accepting the inference he wants, that Cheng Wang at the beginning of Zhou became "of age" in 1035, even though (as we both agree) he was born in 1049, and so was only 15 *sui* in 1035. (This too is a problem that I do not have, since I date the conquest to 1040 rather than to 1045, and therefore make 1031 the last year of the Zhou Gong Regency.)

Shaughnessy's line of analysis shores up his case for 1045 as conquest date, but deprives him of two other reasonable explanations in later Zhou history: (1) As Lei Xueqi pointed out two hundred years ago, the traditional 37 years of reign accorded Li Wang is probably due to confusion with the length of his life, actually 864-828. (2) One would think that Shaughnessy's program of analysis of the BA would require him to explain why the BA gives Gong Wang a reign of only 12 years, if the actual reign was 2 + 16 years. (The *Wenxian tongkao* (j. 250) also gives Gong Wang 12 years; so "12 years" is not a mere accident.) Shaughnessy has no explanation for this, and never faces the problem. My account is given in Section VII above (and in more detail in my AAS 2002 handout in Appendix 2, Parts II, III, and VII Diagram Three). My account requires that Li Wang was born in 864, and that 864 be recognized as the fourth year of Yi Wang, as well as (in a sense) the last year of Xiao Wang. Chronology could not recognize four years (867-864) with two kings at once, and gave Xiao Wang nine years rather than five, pushing earlier dates back and reducing Gong Wang from 16 to 12. So Yi Wang's *yuan* must be 867, not 865. Thus the basic principle of sufficient explanation is at issue in this detail that seemed merely trivial. (Bronze inscriptions indicate that 865 was Yi Wang's accession year, implying that his father the exiled Yih Wang lived until 868. But Yi Wang's eight years in the BA seem to be his entire reign. Perhaps this is so because Xiao Wang, the king immediately before Yi Wang, was not Yi Wang's father.)

Shaughnessy's error here is so important, and so damaging to other parts of his very valuable work (and so difficult to identify and scotch), that I need to do more than merely to refer here to published work of mine that in effect refutes him. The most obvious work is my analysis of the chronology of Lu, in Appendix 1 of Nivison 1999 and 2002. There are three chronologies available, in the *Shiji shijia* chapter for Lu, in the *Han shu* (21B), and in the BA. I will compare the *Shiji* and the BA carefully, referring to the *Han shu* when I need to. (The *Han shu* chronology, due to Liu Xin, is enormously distorted to conform to Liu's error in dating the conquest of Shang to 1122.) Here are the two chronologies:

Lu Dukes	*Shiji* death date	Reign	BA death date	(Implied reign)	DSN
1..Bo Qin	(999)		989		990, 46 years
2 Kao Gong	(995)	4 years	988	(1 year)	986, 4 years
3 Yang Gong	(989)	6	(982)	(6)	980, 6 years
4 You Gong	(975)	14	968	(14)	966, 14 years
5 Wei Gong	(925)	50	918	(50)	916, 50 years
6 Li Gong	(888)	37	879	(39)	879, 37 years
7 Xian Gong	856	32	(856)	(23)	856, 23 years
8 Shen Gong[8]	826	30	826	(30)	826, 30 years

(Implied data are in parentheses.)

One salient detail of the above chronology in the BA is the death date for #5 Wei Gong. The BA puts this in Mu Wang 45, i.e., 918 in the BA system counting from the BA's *yuan* which is 962. The result is an impossible problem for Shaughnessy, who believes (1) that event dates in the BA must be accepted as given, and counted from correct *yuan* dates; and (2) that Mu Wang's correct *yuan* was 956 (I agree), and that his reign was only 39 years (again I agree). Thus Shaughnessy's belief (1) simply must be wrong.

Li Gong is another problem for Shaughnessy. The BA puts his death in Yih Wang year 17 = 879, counting from 895, the BA's incorrect *yuan* year for Yih Wang. Shaughnessy would count from 899, the correct *yuan*, which would give him 883. But as my analysis shows, the correct death date is 879, as given in the BA. As Lei Xueqi noticed, the *Shiji* has reversed the digits in Xian Gong's reign length: it should be 23 years, not 32 years. The result is that all earlier dates in the *Shiji* are exactly nine years too early. This confirms the dates I have deduced.

Other details in my analysis are explained in Appendix 1 of Nivison 1999 and 2002: Something has pushed Bo Qin's death date down three years (from Kang Wang 16 to Kang 19: I offer a tentative explanation), crushing Kao Gong from four years to one year. The two-year differences for the next three dukes are the result of an unexpressed error in the succession year for Li Gong. It was the same as the first year of Gong Wang, but the first year in the wrong sense, not the succession year 917 but the accession year 915. (Therefore Wei Gong not only did not die in a non-existent 45th year of Mu Wang; he didn't die in Mu Wang's reign at all.)

989 as death year for Bo Qin is corrected by raising the year by 3 and reducing it by 2. Bo Qin's 46 years comes from Liu Xin *via* the *Han shu*, the proper count being from Cheng Wang's accession year 1035, first of 30. Without the two-year correction the count would have been from Cheng Wang's succession date; but *Han shu* 21B, giving us Liu Xin's information, says explicitly that Bo Qin began his reign in Lu in the same year Cheng Wang began his reign of 30 years, and that Bo Qin's reign was 46 years.

Other examples disproving Shaughnessy's theory are to be found in the BA for Mu Wang. Mu Wang 9 has the "Spring Palace" being built. The Shi Ju *gui gai* is dated "3rd year" and has Mu Wang visiting the "new palace" in mid-spring. To interpret the BA so as to get the correct date, one must count 9 from the BA's *yuan* 962 for Mu Wang, not from the correct *yuan* 956. (Counting 3 from 956 does give the correct year 954, but

[8] Fan Qin's BA at Xuan Wang 2 has 慎; *Shiji* "Lu Shijia" has 眞 (properly Zhen) with a *Suoyin* note "pronounced 慎 (*shen*)." Legge (corrected to *pinyin*) would give us "Zhen."

"3rd year" is not in the BA.)

This will not always work. To get the correct date 1876 for the Xia Zhong Kang 5 solar eclipse, one must count 5 from the correct *yuan* 1880, not from the BA *yuan* 1952. Each case must be examined separately. (In this case what was done was to step up the date 1876 by 76 years = 1 *bu*, then reduce it by 4 years, and call the result "Zhong Kang 5.") But often the BA simply translates into its system an absolute date from another source.

An especially sticky problem is the dating of the Ji Li – Xi Bo Chang succession. There, what the BA does is to backdate pre-conquest Zhou events 12 years (with the backdating of the conjunction of 1059 to 1071). The reign of Chang (i.e., Wen Wang) was 2 + 50 years, 1101/1099-1050. This becomes 52 years, 1113-1062. The result is translated into the BA system, Wen Ding 1124-1112, Di Yi 1111-1103, Di Xin 1102-1051. So Ji Li is made to die in 1114 = Wen Ding 11, with Chang succeeding in Wen Ding 12, whereas actually the succession was in year 5 in the reign of Di Yi, by my analysis 1105-1087 (certain to be controversial; but see my comment on strips 168-169 in Chapter Eight, and my table in section 8 of Chapter Nine). If one insisted on Wen Ding 12 as the *yuan* for Wen Wang Chang, and simply corrected the BA by reducing Shang reign dates by 16 (which works for Di Xin), one would have Wen Ding reigning 1108-1096. Wen Ding 12 would then be 1097. But we know from multiple evidence (including astronomical evidence) that Wen Wang died in 1050 at the end of a reign of 50 years, counting from 1099; and there is good evidence, e.g., from *Lü shi chunqiu*, that his reign was 2 + 50 years = 52 years, as the BA implies.

The *Lü shi chunqiu* material is in 6 "Ji Xia" 4 "Zhi Yue" (see Nivison 1999 and 2002, 2.3 and note 3): "*Zhou Wen Wang li guo ba nian, sui liu yue, Wen Wang qin ji wu ri er di dong*" 周文王立國八年, 歲六月, 文王寢疾五日而地動. "Wen Wang had ruled the state for eight years. A year [later], in the sixth month, Wen Wang went to bed sick, and in five days there was an earthquake." The story continues: Wen Wang's ministers ask him to take action to avert the portended evil; he does various acts of benevolence, and soon his illness was cured. Then the account closes: "*Wen Wang ji wei ba nian er di dong. Yi dong zhi hou sishi san nian, fan Wen Wang li guo wushi yi nian er zhong....*" 文王即位八年而地動. 已動之後四十三年, 凡文王立國五十一年而終. "An earthquake occurred when Wen Wang had been ruling for eight years. Forty-three years after the earthquake, when Wen Wang had been ruling for a total of fifty-one years, he died."

But actually the earthquake occurred in Wen Wang's ninth year. The author of this part of the *Lü shi chunqiu* text does not understand this rare use of the word *sui* 歲 in a date. (I have analyzed other examples in an unpublished paper "A Telltale Mistake in the *Lü shi chunqiu*[9].) The meaning is not "in the 6th month of the [same] year," but "in a year's time," i.e., "a year later." (Riegel *Lü shi chunqiu* p. 164 gives the sense intended by the author, but it needs a note. The author's original source must have had some intervening event recorded before 歲六月; hence the repetition of "Wen Wang" immediately following.) Consequently the author gets the total reign one year short; the implied length originally was 52 years.

The date of the quake accordingly was Wen Wang 9, = 1093. In my note (Chapter Eight) on strips 168-169, I show (with the help of Shaughnessy and Ma Chengyuan) that an original "13th year" (of Di Yi) has been reduced to "3rd year." This adds to my proofs (Nivison 1999 and 2002, Appendix 2) that Di Yi 1 was 1105.

I began these comments with the problem of the date 853 as *yuan* for Li Wang in the BA. My own explanation in Nivison 1983 p. 528, that in an earlier BA the reigns for Xuan Wang and You Wang had been two years less than the correct lengths, concludes, "evidently they have been corrected from standard sources" such as the *Shiji*. My reconstruction of the strip text in Chapter Eight in this book persuades me that the buried text as discovered must have had the reign lengths now accepted. It follows that the corrections must have been done in pre-burial editing (when there was no *Shiji*). I have also suggested in the present chapter that the reigns may have been Xuan 2 + 42 and You 2 + 11. I am far from sure of this. The analysis of several bronze inscriptions is involved (see Appendix 3, bronzes 61-63). The matter needs more

[9] Paper "A Tell-tale Mistake in the *Lü shi chunqiu*" presented at the annual meeting of the Western Branch of the American Oriental Society, Boulder, Colorado, October 1989.

study. Shaughnessy has firm views about this matter already, which I am weighing.

It is only fair here to note another firm view of his that I weighed doubtfully for years, eventually finding it valid. The problem is the incorrect dating in the BA of events in the reign of the Wei ruler Wei Ying, who eventually declared himself King, with a second reign and "royal" calendar beginning in 334, dying in 319 as Huicheng Wang. The *Shiji* makes a big mistake and gives this reign to Huicheng's successor Xiang Wang. The BA doesn't make this mistake, but it does share another mistake with the *Shiji*, by taking the year 335 as "year 36," so that Wei Ying's succession year becomes 370 rather than 369, both in the *Shiji* and in the BA. Shaughnessy's work on this problem is for the most part excellent, and will be found in his recent book (*RECT*, 2006), pp. 233-239, "The Chronology of Wei Huicheng Wang."

The BA makes 335 not only "year 36" but also (a) the year when Ying declared himself king, and (b) the year he took as year 1 of his royal calendar (implying that he died in "year 17" rather than in "year 16"). For a long time I thought that this error was a feature of the buried text, because I was (and remain) convinced that he did declare himself king in 335, for a compelling political reason; and I regard the original text as political propaganda.[10]

[10] I will return to this matter in Chapter Nine. See pp. 181, and 187n.

Part Two

The Challenge of the Three Dynasties Project
(1996-2000)

Introduction to Part Two

Chapter Three consists of my record of the Roundtable discussion of the Three Dynasties Project in the PRC, held at the annual convention of the Association for Asian Studies in Washington D.C. 28 March 1998. Professor David N. Keightley and I organized this event, and this record was written at the time by me with his advice and help. It is as accurate as I could make it, and I accept full responsibility for it. One participant, Professor Sarah Allan, was obviously the best informed: she had just published a translation of an official description of the Project in *Early China News*. Sarah was probably the person most sympathetic with the Project's aims and procedures. I was probably the most uneasy, as the following chapters show. I will let those chapters speak for themselves. All are in a sense documents, public addresses or intended as public statements. I want to indicate here why I selected them, by explaining their context.

The Project's genesis is itself cause for anxiety. It began when the PRC accepted a proposal by State Councilor Song Jian, a physicist, who in his international travels noticed that museums of Near Eastern ancient materials were able to date their exhibits much more precisely that could similar museums in China. China should and could, he thought, do better. The government accepted the idea, and a decision was made to finance, liberally, a five-year project, to bring together all the scientific and academic talent China could organize. Scholars in Chinese universities were understandably delighted, with the prospect of government financing for the latest equipment, for organized excavations, and for training advanced students. But the PRC government's interest from the start was getting results which would bring China international prestige; and this meant fixing "scientifically" an exact chronology as far back as possible, and if necessary farther back than possible. It was inevitable that this prospect would draw criticism from international scholars, and it was inevitable also that such criticism would be perceived – accurately – by involved Chinese scholars as detrimental to the prospect of getting more government support in the future.

The tension has strained to the limit friendships among the small community of scholars in this country who work in the areas that have been the Project's focus. All of us value our amicable relationships with Chinese scholars in the PRC. Some of us, like me, are excited by discoveries we think we have made that open up opportunities for truly astonishing results. Others, for whom smooth relations with Chinese scholars in the PRC have been very important, are uninterested in chronology and believe that straightening it out is going to be forever impossible anyway. So, from this point of view it will be asked, why don't I agree that "what the Chinese do with their own history" is their own business, and simply keep quiet? And, of course, for me this would be too high a price to pay for amity. Chinese history, like any history, is the business of any scholar who takes an interest in it. I will be as polite as I can be, but I must say what I think is both true and important.

Especially sensitive is the question of political influence on scholarship. I do not believe there has been any pressure on Project scholars to endorse a preconceived story of the past. But the Project was started in order to get a set of precise dates that could be pinned on museum exhibits. My critics are in effect telling me, "Yes, the Chinese scholars are being required to do something we believe impossible, so what they will do – to be broadcast to the world as a great achievement of Chinese science and as at last a standard set of dates – will, we have to admit, be bad work. But so what? It doesn't matter." And I do not see how I can be fairly expected to agree that it doesn't matter, or to behave as if I agreed. Reports have reached me that at the Project's beginning a committee of scholars addressed a plea to their government, saying that much valuable work can indeed be done, but it will not be possible to reach agreement on an exact set of dates. I was told that word came back that they were to get on with their work, and produce the expected chronology. This they have tried to do, sometimes (I am told) shouting at one another in anger. Peter Hessler has reported in his book *Oracle Bones* that when a consensus could not be reached on a date, a vote was taken, and the date with the most votes was declared correct.[1] Voting is a political institution. Votes are

[1] Hessler 2006, p. 387. Hessler says this in a ten-page chapter centered on his interview with Project Leader Li Xueqin, climaxing his account throughout the book about the career and suicide of the major oracle bone scholar Chen Mengjia (1911-1966). A story (perhaps invented) had circulated that Chen had killed himself because of an alleged affair with a

held to decide what to do, not to decide what is true.

Hessler is often reporting what people have told him, information of a kind that will not appear in official documents, and I must do the same. To do this is irresponsible, unless you admit it frankly. I know that much of what my Chinese friends have told me they have learned by telephone, from their friends in China who are highly critical of the Project; and of course one must be wary of bias. A prominent informant has been the late Professor Zou Heng, and I have been warned that his relationship with the Project director Professor Li Xueqin has been notoriously unfriendly. From my own regrettable troubles (probably well known) over many years with one younger American scholar, I think I can appreciate this danger. But there are matters involved that are too important to be ignored; and at crucial points I myself am both witness and participant.

John Major, chairing the Roundtable, urged us quickly to make our views known in China, obviously good advice. To that end I condensed the book I had completed in 1995 after twenty-five years of work, into a monograph published informally in Victor Mair's *Sino-Platonic Papers* in January 1999, and soon thereafter distributed at the AAS meeting in Boston, and in China. (More formal publication in Chinese had to wait until 2002.) Shaughnessy and I wrote a paper on the Jin Hou Su Bell Set, refuting the line of analysis of chronology we knew by that time the Project would employ, circulating it in China in 1999 but not being able to get it published until 2001. In mid-2000 I obtained a copy "not for distribution" of the May 2000 Preliminary Report of the Project. I distributed a criticism of it in September, which I reproduce here. Immediately after that a slightly revised Report became available, and in early October I was interviewed by phone by Erik Eckholm of the New York Times, whose article appeared October 10th. I am not used to being interviewed and I did not measure my words. Innocently thinking I was harmlessly saying what was obvious, I predicted that the Report would be "torn to pieces." Some American critics at once charged me with being "irresponsible." I learned later that many Chinese had been shocked. I regret having caused discomfort, but the important question has to be whether I was right.

On July 9th 2001, I met for lunch at the Harvard Faculty Club with Professors Sarah Allan of Dartmouth and Yunkuen Lee (李潤權) from Harvard, to plan a panel of papers discussing the Project's work, for the spring 2002 meeting of AAS. The details were left to Prof. Lee, who would be chair. I was to appear as critic, with my Stanford colleague Shao Dongfang (邵東方) offering an informative but neutral account. Ultimately four Project scholars were invited, to speak on aspects in which they were experts, including Professor Li Xueqin (李學勤), the Director, who would speak first. My paper "Two Approaches to Dating," with handouts, is Chapter Four, together with Appendix 2. I distributed the paper in advance to the other panelists. This version of the paper was explicit about government pressure to produce a detailed chronology. The day before I flew to Washington I received phone calls from Professors Allan and Lee pleading with me to delete this. I agreed to review what I had written, and made some revisions, but not enough to meet objections. For what happened next, see the two opening pages of Chapter Five, which presents the text of my H. G. Creel Lecture at the University of Chicago on 12 April, a week after the AAS panel in Washington.

Professor Li had obligations in China and had to return at once after the Washington meeting, but the remaining Chinese guests went on to Chicago for my lecture Friday April 12th and an all-day seminar Saturday April 13th. These three attended the Chicago events. I had planned the Chicago lecture realizing that the Nivison-Shaughnessy 2-*yuan* hypothesis was the main cause of our work not being heeded in China; so I talked for an hour on the high antiquity of the three-years mourning institution and its effect on the dating of kings. There was a day-long seminar on the 13th, featuring a paper since published in China by Jiang Zudi 蔣祖棣, computer engineer at Intel Corporation near Stanford, criticizing the Project's c14 work. Mr. Jiang had a PhD in archaeology from Beijing University and had participated in historically important

Beijing opera actress, but Li said explicitly that Chen had been driven to suicide because he was attacked as a Rightist during the Cultural Revolution. In a very minor way Li (age 24 and vulnerable) had been driven earlier to participate in this attack himself, and he expressed deep regret about the matter. I must be a decade older than Li, and I have wanted to think of him as a friend. I am grateful for Hessler's story, and I was impressed by Prof. Li's obvious sincerity. The Cultural Revolution was a horrible time, for which China's rulers, not its unwilling participants, should be ashamed.

field work. He had been one of my main sources of information on what was going on in Beijing. Present throughout taking notes and taping important sessions was a Chicago graduate student who was a friend of Jiang's, named Zhang Lidong 張立東.

When Jiang Zudi's paper was presented and discussed on Saturday, to our astonishment two of the Chinese guests admitted the justice of his criticisms. Zhang Lidong was quietly taking notes and taping everything, in Washington and in Chicago. By May he was back in Beijing, and on May 24th he published his account, in *Zhongguo Wenwubao*, an archaeological newsprint weekly, whose editors had a collection of articles critical of the Project ready to publish. Three days later a meeting was announced in a Beijing hotel for the first week in June, with a hundred scholars invited. (About sixty came.) Jiang's paper was to be discussed, together with mine presented in Washington, translated for the occasion. The editor who had published Zhang Lidong, we learned, was ordered to return all other critical papers to their authors, and to publish nothing critical of the Project in the future.

The two American travelers who had accepted Jiang Zudi's criticisms in Chicago were asked to account for themselves. Both denied agreeing with Jiang, and maintained that they had merely "instructed" us there. At the end of the meeting it was announced that the Project's multi-volume final report would soon be published without change.

As the summer passed, somehow the wind shifted. On August 16th *Zhongguo Wenwubao* published an article in which the four visitors to America answered questions giving them the opportunity to respond to Zhang Lidong's article in May. But in early July I received a letter from Zhang Lidong, surprisingly now in the Project's office in Beijing, asking me many questions about my work on chronology and on the *Bamboo Annals*. He queried me about my role in organizing meetings in the United States, and indicated he was gathering similar information from other critics like me – obviously, I had to assume, doing this at the request of the Project directors. Some serious rethinking must have been going on.

Later in August, as I learned from Chinese friends near Stanford, there was a meeting of a committee of twenty-one Project "scholars" – in effect, I later realized, the Project's Central Committee. The purpose of the meeting was to decide whether to authorize publication of the final report. It was reported to me that all who spoke were critical. Publication was postponed indefinitely.

The matter of an international conference was brought up – this had been a part of the Project's plans from the start, to cap and review the Project's work, but (as I had learned indirectly in Washington) it had been vetoed by responsible officials. The committee of twenty-one decided to revive the plan, and scheduled the event for October, 2003. All critics were to be invited. Subsequently I received an invitation and at once accepted. My paper is included in this book as Chapter Six. (My paper closes with a formal proposal for an international conference specifically on all texts of the *Bamboo Annals*, especially the supposedly fake "modern text.")

But early in 2003 the SARS epidemic erupted, and first the invited Japanese scholars, then many others, decided not to attend. (My wife was begging me not to go.) As a result, the conference was postponed indefinitely, and now one never hears of it. Meanwhile in January of 2003 another cache of bronzes was discovered (the so-called "Meixian Bronzes"), containing dated vessels[2] which show (again) that the Nivison-Shaughnessy hypothesis is correct. There are two cauldron texts, one of them in many copies, for years 42 and 43, numbers so high they must be dated in the reign of Xuan Wang. Neither will accept 827 as *yuan*. Both accept 825.

I was more recently (October 2007) told by Mr. Chen Li, Deputy Director of the National Library of China in Beijing, that publication of the Project's final report was imminent. (I am uneasy about this. It should be obvious that there first should be that international conference originally scheduled for October 2003.) Meanwhile it appears to me that the Project's actions have in effect rendered its preliminary report null, as far as chronology is concerned.

---

[2] Appendix 3, #61 and #62. (See Xia Hanyi 2003.5.)

Chapter Three

Getting the Dates Right: the Xia-Shang-Zhou Chronology Project

AAS Session 113 Roundtable, 28 March 1998, Washington D. C.

John Major (Book of the Month Club), Chair;
organizers and editors, David S. Nivison, with David N. Keightley

(Partcipants, wherever seated, are listed alphabetically at the end. I have thought it wise not to identify speakers by name. Identities of the main speakers will probably be obvious, but opinions change, and one's sense of what one would wish to say in this or that situation can also change. It has seemed to me best to accord to all formal if not actual "deniability." To this end, all have been promoted to the professorate (even graduate students). The chairman and the editors have been left exposed. --DSN)

John Major: I will serve as time policeman, primarily. Please be succinct, germane, structured, focused. Prof. K will begin, describing the project going on in the PRC. There will then be briefer comments by the other members. Following this, I will attempt a brief summary. Open discussion will follow.

Prof. K: There was a prospectus of the "Sandai" (Three Dynasties) Project in *Early China News* last year. (A longer version is available.) The introductory account is based on conversations with Li Xueqin and Li Boqian, in the Chinese Academy of Social Sciences. What I am saying now represents an informal understanding, and is also based on recent conversations with Li Xueqin, and a recent (non-official) lecture by Li.

The Project resulted from an initiative by Song Jian, State Councillor and space scientist, who is interested in archaeology. Song in his travels noticed that datings of exhibits in museums around the world were more precise than those in China, and he hoped Chinese museums could do better. His urging prompted the PRC government to action. This is the first time the government has put serious money into an early history project. It involves four directors, and several hundred other people. Furthermore, it is meant to be interdisciplinary -- an important and unusual development in itself for China. Thus it includes both the Academy of Social Sciences (Shehui Kexueyuan) and the Academy of Sciences (Kexueyuan). Thus it crosses new lines, and there are many strong disagreements among such a wide group. The project is designed to provide a chronological framework, not necessarily an exact calendar (this would be a secondary aim). There will be many planned site testings for carbon 14 data, so that the sheer quantity of it should put approximate dating on a firmer basis. This will concentrate on the central plain -- perhaps unfortunately. The directors insist that the project is not designed to establish early dates for Chinese civilization. This one can see from the fact that they are starting with Xia, and not with Huang Di. The goal is to get relatively accurate reign dates for pre- Gong He Western Zhou kings back to late Shang, and only a relatively secure "framework" for early Shang and for Xia (Xia being taken to mean Erlitou).

There are eight task forces, individually chaired, plus a ninth -- the directors' committee. Everything will be published, not just the conclusions -- eight different volumes plus one synthesis volume. No unified account is implied. Thus there will be many disagreements in the published material.

The project is proceeding in several stages:
First: Collecting previous work. Two books have already been published, including one collecting studies of the problem of dating the Zhou conquest of Shang (*Wu Wang ke Shang zhi nian yanjiu*). (The speaker displayed a copy.)
Second: Getting good C-14 data from selected sites (including some new excavations). Combined with this effort will be a program of bringing all laboratories up to international standards in both C-14 and AMS technology -- an additional dividend of great importance.
Third: There was a 1997 conference on Western Zhou, with a focus on the problem of separating late Shang and early Zhou material and sites. The site H18 at Feng was taken as standard for the last Shang sites before Zhou. Standards were adopted for representative materials.

Fourth: Attention is being given to astronomy, notably the problem of the double dawn recorded in the *Bamboo Annals* for the first year of Yih Wang (7th Western Zhou king): "the day dawned twice in Zheng" (in the Hua Shan area). This is thought to be a reference to the sunrise solar eclipse of 21 April, 899 BCE, claimed to have been visible in Zhou. A dawn eclipse in Sichuan has been observed to test this idea, and it was found that there was indeed a "double dawn" effect.
Fifth: A lot of new Western Zhou bronze inscriptions are being collected; e.g., the Jin Hou Su bells, and materials from the Jin Hou tombs, from the third through the tenth dukes in sequence, and their inscriptions.
Sixth: More Shang materials are being collected. At Yin-xu, they have selected 500 tombs, the artifacts and skeletal remains to be examined. For the oracle bone inscriptions with eclipse records, they plan to get AMS dating (accelerated mass spectography: less material required) from those or similar bones; several hundred bones have been selected. Archaeological. inscriptional and textual materials will be combined.

John Major: We proceed to comments from the other roundtable members, in turn. Please keep your comments to four minutes.

Prof. Nivison: Many of the people engaged in this project in China are personal friends of several of us. And in an important sense all of them are friends of all of us; we all, they and we together, being members of the ancient and universal company of scholars. So let's try a thought experiment: Suppose it were the other way around. We are the ones conducting a grandiose project, and somewhere in Beijing there is a conference going on, with a roundtable trying to assess what we are doing. What would we want them to be saying about us?

First: I think we would hope that they would not jump at conclusions, and would be open-minded as to what we might achieve. For our part, let's not jump at conclusions, and let's be open-minded about what they may achieve.
Second: We would expect them to be curious, and I think we would want them to be. For our part, we are indeed curious.
Third: I think we would hope that if they had ideas they thought would be helpful, they would offer them now, and not wait until we were done, and then tell the world, in testy reviews, what we ought to have been doing. For our part, I think we should keep in touch with them, and if we have suggestions we could make we should make them now, trying always to do it diplomatically.
Fourth: If the shoe were on the other foot, I suspect we would go farther, and actually ask them to give us suggestions and ideas. So the question arises: Have they done this? Yes, to a degree they have. One volume came out in December -- Prof. K showed it to you -- containing scholarship not just by Chinese in China but also by Japanese and American scholars (some of them here in this room), on the problem of the date of the Zhou conquest; and another is already being readied on the exact dates of all the Western Zhou kings. I hope that there will be other similar volumes, on problems in earlier periods; and that for these too scholars outside China will be asked for contributions.

I now turn to a different matter. I see two kinds of approaches to the problems of Three Dynasties chronology.
First: There is what I will call the "parameters" approach: trying to estimate approximate dates of periods or of reigns, by typing and periodizing artifacts like bronzes and inscriptions on the basis of style, etc; or seeking approximations by C-14 and AMS testing of any discoveries containing organic material. These methods are getting better, yielding less imprecise results. But by their very nature they can't reach exactitude, only at best close estimates.
Second: There are what I will call (misusing the word a little) "deductive" approaches. Usually this will involve starting with explicit or implied references to astronomical events in old texts or inscriptions -- though the chain of reasoning from there may be long, and the starting point very ordinary, for example a lunar month date naming a day in the sixty-day cycle. One may then turn to a table of sidereal events, or compute the exact time of such an event. In this way one is trying to fix not a good estimate, but an exact date. A good example is the problem of the supposed dawn eclipse in the first year of Yih Wang of Zhou (the seventh king). There are two that might be suggested: one occurred on 21 April 899 BCE; and another, apparently a bit late, on 3 July 903 BCE. These are only four years apart; and no technique of approximation is going to get as close as four years plus or minus. But if you deduce 903 as the right date, and it should be 899, you cannot say that you got it about right; you are just plain wrong. If someone says,

of the "deductivist's" work, that one would feel easier if the result were offered as (e.g.) about 899, rather than exactly 899, this objector just doesn't understand the distinction I am making.

The point I want to make -- to people right here -- is that both these approaches have their place, sometimes applicable to the same problem; and both should be pursued, now and in the future, neither waiting on the other. Each scholar would do well to think of his or her chosen approach as experimental, at this stage.

Prof. M: I want to take up Prof. Nivison's points about method. First, consider the problem of dating the reign of Hammurabi in Near Eastern history. Dating him is crucial, because tied to his dates is the dating of much else, before and after, for centuries. There had been three competing hypotheses, long, short, and in between. At the time this was being argued, C-14's were too imprecise to be useful (+ / - 100 years). Astronomical data was repetitious every 130 years. King lists were tried; but they were not compiled from lists of kings, but from lists of people who had held office under this or that king, and so using them required much guessing. Building foundation inscriptions were tried, with the same difficulty. Finally scholars turned to interstate relations; the data in these records, compared with material from other states, could determine when the people involved were alive. All of this, with some guess-work, led to the consensus that 1750 (validating the "in between" chronology) must be the date, approximately, of Hammurabi, but obviously it remains uncertain and only approximate. The kind of problem, the type of materials, and the reasoning, seem not unlike Prof. Nivison's "deductive" methodology, yet the result was imprecise and uncertain. I suspect the same is going to be true for China -- where we have fewer records, all in a single language, with no interstate correlations.

Now consider the "double dawn" problem, cited by Prof. Nivison. F. R. Stephenson has been working on this, and there is a publication by him and Houlden on the matter. The trouble is that there is great difficulty in attaining the kind of precision needed to establish the occurrence of a solar eclipse at a certain place exactly at sunrise at that place, because the earth's rotation has been slowing down. The slowing may be slight, no more than one or two seconds per year, but over almost three thousand years it will add up to hours. There are eclipse records -- e.g., one in England in 1230, and one in Russia in 1472 -- exact enough to give some indication of the rate of slowing; and from the estimated rate, one can deduce that the eclipse of 899 BCE, as a dawn eclipse, must have occurred far to the east of Zhou, perhaps as far as Korea or Japan. Exactitude seems impossible. So here again, use of "deductive" methods yields uncertainty, albeit of a different kind: one gets a precise figure, but with very good reasons for doubting it. Scientific precision may not be possible.

Prof. N: The "Three Dynasties" project is one of five (? or ten?) national level initiatives by the State Council, to be completed over the next five-year period. This says a lot about its perceived cultural significance. Turning from the prospectus and Prof. K's analysis to Song Jian's article in *Henan Ribao*, June 1996 -- the first publication on the "Sandai Gongcheng" -- one can see cause for concern. He does think of Huang Di as the beginning of Chinese civilization. A rationale and guiding principles are set out: "surpassing the *yi-gu* ("doubt antiquity") program but staying out of superstition." There will be a tension between the needs of the state bureaucracy and the expectations of the academic experts. Li Xueqin and others are doing their best to rein in unrealistic expectations about the date of the Yellow Emperor, the Shang kings, etc. But Song Jian urges majority rule, using "democratic centralism" to make every effort to reach consensus. He wants to publish the conclusions as the national standard, arguing that even if we cannot assume that the results are the absolute truth, they can be used as a relatively reliable scheme for research and teaching, at home and abroad; if new discoveries are made later, these results can be revised, he maintains, in the same manner.

But I doubt that this will work, once the official chronology has been published. And there is going to be strong pressure on the academics to come up with definitive conclusions. Song Jian talks about getting rid of the "approximately's".

On the other hand, I am much less pessimistic than Prof. M about using astronomical data. For the double-dawn eclipse, as Stephenson has demonstrated, the diminution of the light of the sun (the eclipse was annular) would have been much too slight for a double dawn to have been observed on that date. But our prospects for refining the Delta T figure are better than Prof. M suggests. We have 4th and 5th century BCE eclipse data that can be used. Stephenson and Houlden published their atlas of historical eclipses on this basis; it seems quite reliable. But we must do better than the 899 date.

Prof. O: I had misunderstood what was expected of me. I was ready to talk about chronology, not methodology. There is a long study of Western Zhou chronology in Prof. Shaughnessy's 1991 book *Sources of Wsestern Zhou History*. He said then that it was by no means the final word, though it was his last word, and I think it was as close to being right as was possible at that time. The most significant contributions the West has made come from astronomy. This is particularly true of two events of kinds that occur so infrequently that if we can match them with the historical record they carry much conviction. One is the 1059 planetary conjunction. Pankenier has shown that conjunctions like this occur no more often than once in 517 years. The *Bamboo Annals* record of a conjunction not many years prior to the conquest (though it is mis-described) is therefore compelling. The conquest, accordingly, has to be after 1059, probably between ten and twenty years after.

As to the 899 eclipse recorded in the *Bamboo Annals* (both texts), of course you can discount the *Bamboo Annals*, but that would be a serious mistake, given recent archaeological discoveries that confirm *Annals* entries (including the usually suspected "modern text"). As to the line, "Heaven twice dawned in Zheng" in the chronicle for the first year of Yih Wang, a Korean scholar (Pang Sunjoo) had published the date 899 earlier. But a February news article said that Chinese scientists had just discovered it. The Project has said that they couldn't cite Pang, because they didn't know where he lived today (!). We need better cooperation than that. The 899 eclipse has been accepted by the Project as dating Yih Wang's first year. Contra Prof. M, we can fix some problems with precision. (Should we use scientific precision to discount precision?)

The discovery of new materials is also important. The Jin lord tombs at Qü Cun have excited much debate. The bell inscriptions (16 bells) with their 350 characters include one year date, with four other full dates. These dates taken together prove that Wang Guowei was correct in arguing that lunar phase terms assume a four-quarter system. But the calendar doesn't seem to fit the historical records. The bells record a "33rd year"; and the *Shiben* verifies the name given; but the *Shiji* does not give this lord a 33rd year. We must presume the *Shiji* is wrong (it has the chronology of Jin mixed up, and probably omits a lord). Unfortunately the *Bamboo Annals* does not give death dates for lords of Jin until after Jin Hou Su -- unlike the death dates of lords of other states. Anyway, the *Shiji* cannot be trusted for Jin dates. But perhaps "33rd year" is in the royal calendar, not the Jin ducal calendar.

On this assumption, given the "33rd year" date in the inscription, scholars have debated whether the bells are to be dated in the reign of Li Wang, supposing it to have been 37 years long, or in the reign of Xuan Wang, accepted as 46 years in length. But if the 899 eclipse does date the first year of Yih Wang, it follows that a 37 year reign for Li Wang is impossible: his first year cannot have been 878 (as suggested by some readings of the *Shiji*) Therefore the bells must date to Xuan 33. That is where the archaeologists had put it anyway. If Xuan Wang's reign began in 827, year 33 must (one would think) be 795. But the month and day dates don't fit 795, but do fit 794. The solution: the text reads, "It was the 33rd year. [The king] went on procession in the southern and eastern lands. In the first month ... he went from the capital to the Eastern Capital ..." We must take "in the first month" as referring to the next year, 794, and the dates do fit 794 perfectly. There are many other examples of Western Zhou bronze inscriptions having to be read in this way.

The inscription describes a campaign in Western Shandong. The *Bamboo Annals* tells us that in the 32nd (note: not 34th) year of Xuan Wang he went on campaign in Lu (we find this only in the *jinben*, not in the *guben*!*). The two-year discrepancy is accounted for by the Nivison-Shaughnessy hypothesis that two calendars were used in a king's reign, one counting from his succession year, and the other counting from the third year, after the king had completed mourning for his predecessor. So the *Annals*, too is consistent with the date 794.

---

*I added this parenthesis -- DSN

John Major (summarizing): There appears to be a great investment of national pride in this project, as well as of financial and human resources. We can be sure that they will "finalize" dates for all of us. As with the universal acceptance of pinyin, the list of dates that results when this project is over -- love them or hate them -- will be standard the world over. And of course the trouble is that we are not sure that they will get it right. What can we do to help? We should start listening to one another. There has been too much contention in the past. We should avoid arguments that generate more heat than light. We should get results out quickly, and communicate them to our Chinese colleagues.

General discussion followed, for the final hour:

Prof. P (University of Pennsylvania): There is a long tradition of trying to establish an exact chronology. Sima Tan and Sima Qian tried it, and failed. The State Council won't get the dates right either. Sombody will have to correct the project's conclusions later.

Prof. K: Establishing an exact calendar is a very small part of the project. It is a mistake to think of it as primarily about getting dates right. I myself doubt the usefulness of astronomical data. But in any case, this is not the China of twenty years ago. All material will be published and available; there will be no "unified account." (I probably have more doubts about being able to get such exact dates than anyone else here.) The results may well be conflicting; what if AMS results do not match the eclipse records? The Project is also translating much Mesopotamian and Western evidence into Chinese, to learn the methodology. And top astronomers are involved. That's new.

Prof. N: Prof. K., what you say is informed by your contacts with the academic experts, but I am less than sanguine. Read Song Jian's essay. He insists that the project stick to the "main issue"; everything else is to be ancillary to "the Three Dynasties chronology." There is no doubt that the State Council expects this.

Prof. K: True; but everything will be out. The C-14 results will all be published.

Prof. M: Let me respond to the original statement by Prof. N. I am not pessimistic about the use of astronomy, but about our interpretation of what the texts say. "Double dawn" is all the *Annals* text says. But if this refers to an eclipse, then astronomy cannot solve the problem, because the eclipses are all annular for this time period. Perhaps this is not a real record at all. Perhaps it was fabricated for some other purpose.

Prof. Q (CASS, Institute of World History): I have been involved with this project, and I prepared the English translation of Song Jian's proposal. His first article, in *Guangming Ribao*, shocked all of us. It was thought ridiculous that a physicist could tell us what to do. But then people saw the prospect of funding. Li Xueqin saw it as an opportunity to improve our scholarship, to learn from other countries, an opportunity to do comparative studies, improve our C-14 technology. This is how things work in China: we have the "will of the government" vs the "will of the scholars," and they differ.

I have taught early Chinese history in America, and I encounter the problem of the Xia: All U.S. textbooks deny its existence; all Chinese textbooks affirm it; and half the students of the class are Chinese! Xia is deeply rooted for us. I have lived in southern Shanxi for several years. There are many Xia place names there. It is not easy to wipe it out.

Prof. R (University of Chicago): Let's think about the nature of the whole project. For many Chinese it is much bigger than a chronology project. It is fundamentally really about archaeological sites. Chinese scholars will not change their research programs, but they will get extra funding. There are two levels: one about chronology and dates; another about sites, materials, and close reading of texts. Let the archaeology come first. Dates perhaps will come later.

Prof. S: I have tried to use material culture to prove the existence of the Xia. I agree with Prof. R. Friends in China see this as a way to understand the Xia, Shang and Zhou, a broader archaeological question. Archaeology has until now not been a priority, as my experience with research on the Three Gorges has shown me. Technical methods being used in the project are new, and this is great for archaeology.

Prof. T (University of Pennsylvania): We must bear in mind that C-14 dating, even with its plus or minus confidence intervals, still has only a 2/3 chance of being right.

Prof. K: True; and for this reason it is important that wood sources are being used for tree-ring dating. Extensive samples are now being used. It is important that the project have some success -- not in the sense of getting exact dates but there must be an intelligible write-up. Success will lead to other scholarly projects. But that doesn't necessarily mean that precise dates will be arrived at.

Prof. U (McGill University): It is very interesting that the money is going into this project rather than into surveys in the Three Gorges area. It seems to me that Gorges sites should be exploited before they are flooded. This says something about the State Council's political interests. So I have a question for Prof. K.: How widespread are these sites they will examine? Will they include Sanxingdui? Chu sites? Jiangsu sites? There is no true central state at this stage, but a city-state system. Are they going as far as Yan in the Northeast? It would be good to expand, to get more comparative data.

Prof. K: It really is a central plains project. But the hope is that if successful it could then be expanded.

Prof. V (Harvard): There are two narratives, as Prof. R. said: one, very pluralistic and scholarly, no hard dates, just an array of evidence; the other, a very political project, dedicated to getting a hard, fixed chronology -- a new *He Tu* (River Chart), to keep among the regalia in Beijing. These two projects can exist in the same person at the same time. But we should remain open-minded: the end result will fall in between. Is there any procedure for involving Taiwan scholars?

Prof. K: I'm not sure ...

Prof. N: They have been solicited, as have we, for the volumes being published. But (to Prof. V.) the hoped for result is not as esoteric as a revealed document, a "River Chart"; They want a table at the back of Cihai, that everyone can rely on.

Prof. V: That's the idea of a *He Tu*!

Prof. W (University of Arizona): In tomb reports, grave goods are dated by typologies, very sophisticated, to broad periods -- "Spring and Autumn," "Zhanguo," etc.; and one can have sequences across such periods in the same graveyard. Perhaps we have nothing better to go on, and that's all we'll ever get. We need closer dating of texts. (I'm guessing at this -- DSN)

Prof. X: Egyptian chronology was based on pottery sequences. The basic method was worked out by Flinders Petrie. The method, applied to sequences in the agora at Athens, now has attained an accuracy down to ten years. The relative chronology is good.

Prof. O: Remember the Fu Hao debate: The archaeologists based their dating on the pottery sample, and they were right. The historians got it wrong, and wanted to date Fu Hao to late Shang. For the tombs of the Jin lords, archaeologists have a convincing sequence. I would trust the archaeologists more than the historians.

Prof. S: Archaeology is based on stratigraphy. There was not much pottery in the Fu Hao tomb, and the bronze typology was complicated.

Prof. W: A graveyard is in use for hundreds of years ....

John Major: But one can get benchmarks via C-14 dating ....

Prof. K: In the project, they have worked on the dividing line between Shang and Zhou, studying intrusive tombs. This will be very useful. They are picking tombs with useful stratigraphies.

Prof. S: What does "Central Plains" mean?

Prof. K: The Yellow River area. I.e., Xia-Shang-Zhou; Erlitou for the Xia.

Prof. S: There has been no list of sites to be included....

Prof. Y: What is K. C. Chang's role? His hypothesis that the Three Dynasties were not sequential has been very influential. Does his illness prevent consultation?

Prof. K: Yes, he has been consulted.

Prof Y: We should note the potential usefulness of this project for comparative study. At Dongbei Shida there is an ancient world civilizations group. Has that group been involved? How well have Mesopotamian scholars been involved? There is a Beida dissertation comparing Maya and Shang.* The work of Higham and Bellwood in Southeast Asia should also be related. I know Dongbei Shida has been involved. [* The dissertation is by Jiang Zudi. He gave me a copy. – DSN]

Prof. K: Dongbei Shida has been involved in the translation of methodologies.

John Major: I want to invite a comment from Prof. Z. Do you have any comment on the impact of the Three Dynasties Project?

Prof. Z: They are working on prompt use and publication of discoveries, and are trying to introduce new techniques. But C-14 dates give you a scatter. People know what they want to find, and C-14 data held to be contaminated are thrown out. Are all data to be reported?

Prof. K: I don't know; but they are trying to report everything.

Prof. Q: They try to insure the right data.

Prof. A (University of Massachusetts): Prof. Z.'s comment provides the missing piece. There is the latent suggestion that this is a top down initiative to remove the "*ca.*" from museum labels. If we have comments to make, earlier will be better than later. The present panel should constitute itself a corresponding committee -- with a letter-head. Could the Society for the Study of Early China set this up?

Prof. W: If anyone wants to volunteer ....

Prof. U: I have a question for Prof. K. We have been presented with the leaders. To what extent are younger scholars involved? To what extent is the project an educational program to train them? And what will happen, after the five years pass, to all this new technology, and to the upgraded laboratories? Will these things change the face of Chinese archaeology entirely? Regardless of what may be achieved in establishing date sequences?

Prof. K: These are among the stated aims of the project. Young people have assignments. The spin-off from the labs, computers, etc., may be one of the most important results of the project. It may provide the inertia to keep the project going five years from now. It may be a mixed bag -- I'm less interested in dates -- but it would be silly for the Chinese not to take advantage of the opportunities offered.

Prof. O: I want to make a general comment on Prof. Nivison's distinction between plus-or-minus approximation and 899-type precision, i.e., C-14 vs. the historian. There are two different programs, as several people have pointed out, viz., the archaeological and the historical. The latter endeavor is not futile. Getting the dates right is important. It really makes a difference in Western Zhou. Archaeology requires committees; history is done by crazy individuals. But if you don't get the dates right you won't get history right. What I fear is that the new orthodox dates will render other dates -- perhaps the right ones -- unacceptable. We seem to be saying that archaeology, etc., is respectable scholarship, and that the quest for exact dates is irresponsible and politically motivated. But we should not be skeptical about the general worth of chronological studies -- of careful work seeking to fix on exact dates.

John Major: The casting of dates in stone may be the least important thing that happens, but it may be the most visible. Every textbook in the world will be obliged to use those new dates! If you think you have the date right, publish it now and send it immediately to the Sandai Project!

Prof. B (University of Virginia): To what extent is the project interested in looking at new sites? Do we have enough archaeological evidence now, or do we need more?

Prof. K: There is new excavation in old sites, but not new sites. Attention has been paid, for example, to new Shang tombs (i.e., in sites where many tombs are known to exist), with an eye to their chronological importance. There will be minor new excavations, maybe. As to eclipse records, it is of some interest that there are very few eclipse records for an unimportant political year in China. The eclipse record putatively assigned to 899 does not convince me that the eclipse actually occurred. Approximate dates established archaeologically can be very important; thus we are going to know the approximate dates of Erlitou; this will be useful for triangulation, comparison with other cultures, etc. Of course, debate continues as to whether Erlitou is Xia. My own views about this, and my questions about dating, have been well published, and I won't repeat them here. But it will be useful to compare different chronologies (sc. of the approximate kind that archaeology can establish).

Prof. Nivison: I would like to suggest, and underline the suggestion, that as we pursue different programs of investigation, for example falling into the two broad categories that I have sketched, we regard all programs, including our own, as experimental. We don't know what is going to work out best yet, and all reasonable programs should be pursued concurrently. We shouldn't say that one approach should wait until others are "finished," because nothing is ever going to be finished.

Prof. Keightley: What precision can AMS dating provide?

Prof. N: Plus or minus 20 years.

Prof. Keightley: But the eclipse bones (assuming AMS testing) are not in the PRC but in Taiwan.

Prof. O: They will use bones of a similar period.

Prof. K: Yes; they can now take very small samples, for AMS testing.

John Major: We have seen a good demonstration of the possibilities involved in discussion like this. Let us use the pages of *Early China* to keep in touch.

David Nivison: Keightley and I have been taking notes. We will communicate with you, asking your help in getting the record of this session accurate. We have in mind writing it up for publication and possibly sending it to Beijing.

[I assured members of the Roundtable that there would be no formal "Report" issued in the name of the Roundtable unless all members agreed to it. I came to perceive a few months later that no such agreement was going to be possible. If the tone of such a report was going to be at all critical, some of us would be sure to object. On the other hand, I realized that I could not honestly be the author of a report purged of any suggestion of criticism; and given my own prominence in chronological research, even a suggestion of a critical tone would carry weight. So I did nothing with this at the time. But much has happened since 1998. My notes on this meeting have historical value. As they are these are my own, and mine only.
--- DSN]

Participants:

Allan, Sarah
Bradford, Rosalind
Brooks, E. Bruce
Childs-Johnson, Elizabeth
Harper, Donald
James, Jean M.
Keightley, David N.
Kinney, Anne B.
Knoblock, John
Liu, Xinru
Mair, Victor H.
Major, John
Meyer, Andrew
Nivison, David S.
Pankenier, David W.
Qing, Ren
Shaughnessy, Edward L.
Wu, Hung
Weld, Susan,
Yates, Robin D. S.

Xia-Shang-Zhou Chronology Project (San-Dai Gongcheng), May 2000 Draft Report:
D. S. Nivison's comment, 15 September 2000

The copy of the Draft Report that has come to my attention is 74 pages. It is designated "brief draft," and "second editing," and dated "May 2000"; and also "for internal use only," in effect what we would call "classified." I will return to these aspects of the document. But first I will criticize what it contains. I address specifically the intention to announce a date for the Zhou conquest of Shang, i.e., section 3, pp. 31-40. (The date to be endorsed is 1046 BCE (#3.6.2, p. 40).) The date of the conquest has been a storm-center of controversy for thousands of years, and one can expect that the Project's "solution" is to be the centerpiece of its results, after five years of heavily financed work involving hundreds of scholars. My main point is not that I object to the date chosen, though I do, and I will explain why. I object to the Project endorsing a set of fixed dates, whatever they may be. These are my reasons:

Anyone familiar with arguments in this area in recent decades knows that controversy is going to continue. The Project has been brought into existence by the government of the PRC. If the evident intention goes forward, Project-endorsed dates are going to be seen as the dates pronounced to be correct by the PRC. Inevitably this will be the attitude of the PRC itself. What happens, then, when and if the consensus of world scholarship comes to be that one or many of these officially endorsed dates are wrong? It is difficult enough for an individual scholar to admit a mistake, and many never do, no matter how obvious the error. For the government of China to be in this position, on a matter that is obviously one involving much national prestige, would poison scholarship for generations. It can be predicted that government sponsors would insistently defend Project "results," and leading PRC scholars in the Project would feel under extreme pressure to do the same, no matter what. Publications world-wide would take sides, many editors insisting that articles submitted must use the "official" chronology. Politics would taint research, smothering intellectual honesty. Specific issues might even become entangled in cross-Strait relations. Scholars everywhere in the world would start laughing at the spectacle. No one needs this. This is not the way responsible scholarship is done. The ancient and universal company of scholars -- which is a world community, not a Chinese community --must always be left completely free to pursue the truth, wherever that pursuit may lead. And they will pursue it, no matter what the PRC thinks it can say.

Now I will show how far from certainty is the Project's main conclusion.

There are not many of us in the West who work on the intersection of inscriptions, old texts and astronomy, that pre-771 chronology demands. But among the conquest dates actively debated among us, the one the Project has chosen to affirm -- 1046 -- is defended without reserve by only one of us, and is not merely doubted but is thought absurd by several of us, including me. The case depends on accepting the highly controversial premise that in the conquest year Jupiter was in station 7, Chun Huo ("Quail Fire"). Once Wen Wang's death has been pinned to 1050 (by *Yi Zhou shu*, "Xiao Kai," lunar eclipse of 1065 in Wen's 35th year, and other compelling evidence), the only possible subsequent Chun Huo year is 1046.

The Project appeals to two pieces of evidence. The recently discovered Li *Gui* inscription, with the conquest as event date, is read as saying "Jupiter was in the right place" (*sui ding*, = *sui dang*), and this it is held must mean "in Chun Huo," because Chun Huo was the celestial correlate (*fenye*) of Zhou. The late Yu Xingwu is said to have agreed with this interpretation. This is incorrect. Yu actually took the words as context demands, as *sui zhen*, "annual divination rite" -- no mention of Jupiter. (I will omit my own analysis, that shows exactly why the fixed date of an "annual divination rite" happened to coincide with the exact day of the victory.) Furthermore the *fenye* concept is a Warring States concept, belonging to an era 500 years or more after the inscription.

The other supposed evidence is the text in *Guoyu*, "Zhou Yu" 3.7, dated to 522 in the *Guoyu* narrative, saying that at the start of Wu Wang's campaign late in the pre-conquest year "Jupiter was in Chun Huo," with much other celestial detail about the sun, moon, zodiac and calendar. That this much precise detail could have been in a contemporary record that then somehow survived invisibly more than 500 years is at once cause for suspicion. Further, the text implies a contradiction, namely that the partly lost "Wu Cheng" chapter of the *Shang shu*, in its account of the conquest campaign, both is and is not consistent with the

"4-quarters" understanding of lunar phases (which those who accept 1046 must reject). But, worse, the argument commits the fatal error of ignoring counter-evidence. There is a conflicting account, simple and therefore more credible, of Jupiter's position at the time. One finds it in Yang Liang's commentary, quoting "Shizi," to the "Ru Xiao" chapter of the Xunzi, and according to it Jupiter was "in the north."[1] The existence of this conflicting account must be explained, before one can use the *Guoyu* account to prove anything. A "north" location for Jupiter is half the zodiac (= six years) away from any "Chun Huo year."

Trying this out, one finds that if one then counts forward six years, from ((1046 + 1 =) 1047 to 1041 (as the year when the conquest campaign began), then counting on by 12-year intervals -- the supposed (but erroneous) period of Jupiter -- one gets to dates in the half-century after 522 that are times when Jupiter actually was in Chun Huo. The reasoning of the person who invented the text with its Chun Huo date then becomes obvious. Other details in the text are explainable once one sees that he must have been using the (also erroneous) 76-year intercalation cycle to calculate exact days. (This will show that he started with an account like that in the Shiji, "Zhou Benji," that has the campaign starting in the 11th month rather than the 1st month, concluding three months later rather than one month later; and that this account must have been in the Xia calendar rather than in the Zhou calendar.) If I am right here, the celebrated *Guoyu* text is simply a clever fake. Jupiter thus would not be in Chun Huo at the time of the conquest, and its date therefore could not possibly be 1046. I do not represent this as certain (for at present nothing is); but surely 1046 is far too unlikely for the Project to be announcing it as the solution, at long last, to the problem of the date of the conquest.

This is only one of many doubtful things in the chronology of the Draft Report. Why did the Project not probe these problems more adequately? Let us look at recent history. In 1997-1998, when we in North America began watching the Project, we learned (by word of mouth) that there would be an international conference in China in the spring of the last year, to assess the Project's work. Nothing happened. Instead, news leaked out that there was so much conflict among scholars in China that they were shouting at one another. More silence. Then last fall a one-page schedule of tentative Three Dynasties dates slipped out through the internet; and there was an occasional "trial balloon" article in a newspaper or periodical. I sent a critique of one of these to the Project Director last February, adding that present disagreements, certain to continue, made it highly advisable not to endorse any exact chronology. I received no reply.

Now, only a week ago, I found myself for the first time looking at a copy of a "Draft Report" dated back in May 2000 (already a second editing), that had gone only to a highly restricted list of insiders in China. At the same time, I was warned not to reveal how I had seen it, lest the scholar in China who had let it out get into trouble. And more reports reached us, that many scholars in China have been vigorously but helplessly protesting the high-handed way the Project is being run. Further, I am told that the final Report, three times as long and not open to change, is to be published immediately.

What should have happened? Plans for an international conference should have been in place, scheduled for July or August, for the specific purpose of criticizing the Report. And as soon as the second Draft was issued in May, it should have been made available as widely as possible among the international community of scholars, who all, whether able to attend or not, should have been asked to prepare criticisms for presentation and publication. Had this been done, problems such as the one I discuss would have boiled to the surface. Some problems would perhaps have been resolved. But the whole picture would have become clear -- that any attempt to issue a definitive chronology at this time could only result in embarrassment for China later on. Of course our Chinese friends have the right to do what they think best. But if they intended their work to impress the world of scholarship, then in their own interest, and in China's interest, they should have sought to find out what the international reaction to their work would be.

[The passionate tone of this statement is, I suppose, itself a part of history. I think it accurately reflects many persons' attitudes eight years ago. I hope it is no longer appropriate, but that remains to be seen.]

---

[1] See pp. 20, 33, and 205

Chapter Four

The Three Dynasties Chronology Project: Two Approaches to Dating[*]

D. S. Nivison, (AAS 2002, Washington, D.C.; Panel 79, 5 April)

Today's meeting is for me an occasion for greeting old friends again. Zhang Changshou and I have both taken part in previous conferences. Li Xueqin and I, on one of his many visits to us, spent a pleasant sunny afternoon exploring Point Lobos in California. My meeting Zhang Peiyu today perhaps for the first time gives me the opportunity to thank him for his critical attention to a draft paper of mine, in which I had boldly attempted to refute a published article of his on the "modern text" *Bamboo Annals*, *"Jinben" Zhushu jinian* ("今本" 竹書紀年). While disagreeing with me he nonetheless recommended my paper to his own publishers, the editors of *Lishi Yanjiu* 歷史研究, who accepted it, pending translation. His example of open-mindedness should be a model for all of us.

But I must say what I honestly think. My focus is the chronology of Western Zhou prior to Gong He, especially the 9th century part of it, in the *Brief Report* of the Xia-Shang-Zhou Chronology Project, published in October 2000. I reject all but two of the exact dates in the whole *Report*, but I will deal here only with middle and late Western Zhou. I omit its ample data from site work and radio-carbon testing, which is Qiu Shihua's subject. I lack the competence to criticize this, and even if the methodology can be questioned (as some colleagues tell me), the parameters it sets for exact chronology seem to be acceptable.[1]

On November 10, 2000, I was quoted -- accurately -- by Erik Eckholm in the *New York Times*, using severe language: I said that the *Brief Report* would be "torn to pieces" by critics. Response in the Chinese press has been understandably agitated. I will try today to explain what moved me to say this.

I turn my attention to the Project's dates for the 10th Western Zhou king Li Wang prior to his exile, i.e., 877-841, 37 years. There has long been disagreement about this. There is conflicting evidence in the same book, the *Shiji*. In its chronicle for Zhou, "Zhou Benji," the account of Li Wang begins "*Li Wang ji wei sanshi nian*" 厲王即位三十年, understood as a date, "[When] Li Wang had reigned for 30 years," he was fond of profit and was close to Duke Yi of Jong, etc. We later find the date "in the 34th year," and further on "three years later," he was driven into exile, giving a total of 37 years (or 36, if "three" is inclusive).[2]

But in other parts of the *Shiji*, the year of exile is carefully fixed as 842, not 841, by comparison with the chronologies of nine regional states. The chapter on Qi ("Qi Shijia") is most precise. It says that Li Wang fled into exile in the 9th year of Wu Gong, and that the 10th year was the first year of the Regency; and further that the 24th year was the first year of Zhou king Xuan Wang, known to be 827; so Wu Gong 1 = 850, and Wu Gong 9 = 842.

---

* I am grateful to the *Journal of East Asian Archaeology* for permission to re-publish this article.

[1] One criticism is that in using previous work establishing pottery sequences in approximately equal time periods (Pre-Zhou and Early Western Zhou; Early to Middle Zhou; etc.), the sequences have been renamed referring to historical reigns or parts thereof, resulting in periods ranging from 11 years to 108 years, thus improperly making previous work support the Project's dating of reigns. Another is that the range of uncertainty of 14-C results has been speciously reduced by a process of "nihe"擬合, i.e., adjusting the results to the Project's periodization and reign dates (unpublished paper by Jiang Zudi 蔣祖棣, Stanford Research Fellow).

[2] My own analysis of the "modern text" *Bamboo Annals* leads me to conclude that Li Wang's post-mourning reign (including the Gong He Regency) was exactly 30 years. I therefore suspect that this is what the *Shiji* source meant. If so, that source must have read "*shi si nian*" (14th year) rather than "*san shi si nian*" (34th year). (Perhaps "*san*" 三 is a misreading of an old form of "*qi*" 乞 = 迄 "reaching to.") The 14th year was significant: counting from the first of 30 years (857) it would be 844, when Li Wang -- if he was born in 864 -- would have assumed control as *wang*. The following "*san nian*" then would mean "in the 3rd year" [of his reign as king in his own right], which would be 842. (The "1st-year" and "3rd-year" Shi Dui 師兌 *gui* fit the years 857 and 842. In the 3rd-year *gui* the king quotes his own words in the 1st-year *gui*, but the dates do not fit the same calendar.)

The precision of the Qi chapter goes farther back: before Wu Gong was Xian Gong, who had a reign of 9 years, thus formally beginning in 859. Xian Gong became duke of Qi by a military coup, which would be in 860, killing his half-brother Hu Gong. Furthermore, immediately before this account, and after the brief account of how Hu Gong became duke of Qi, are the words "*Hu Gong xi du Pugu, er dang Zhou Yi Wang zhi shi*" 胡公徙都蒲姑，而當周夷王之時, "Hu Gong moved the capital to Pugu, and was a contemporary of King Yi of Zhou." Thus it is likely that Yi Wang was still king in 860, and that Li Wang's pre-exile reign was at most 18 years.

Another quite independent bit of evidence in favor of a pre-exile reign for Li Wang of much less than 37 years is the received length of the reign of Li Wang's grandfather Yih Wang 懿王; the few sources we have (mostly late) agree that it was 25 years (in one case 20 years); and the Project's date for the first year of Yih Wang, marked by an eclipse, is 899. If 899 is right Yih Wang's 25th year was not earlier than 875; and after him came the irregular reign of Yih Wang's uncle Pifang, as Xiao Wang, and then the reign of Yih Wang's son Yi Wang, and only after that could Li Wang have become king.

The Project rejects "25 years" for Yih Wang, of course. But in the face of such obviously contradictory evidence, one must ask which evidence can be "explained away." I see no way of explaining away the 25 years for Yih Wang. And attempts to escape the dating in the "Qi Shijia" seem to me to be indefensible.[3]

More evidence can be found in the "modern text" *Bamboo Annals* (as noticed by Lei Xueqi two centuries ago): it says (in a note he takes as original) that Li Wang was born in 864, making 37 years his life-span. So it would seem that Li Wang's pre-exile reign-length may have gotten confused with his life span. There are other bits of supporting evidence for the shorter reign-length: The "Wey 衛 Shijia" seems to indicate a pre-exile reign-length of not more than 25 years; and the story of Shao Gong exchanging his own infant son for the infant son of Li Wang (the later Xuan Wang, thus saving the prince's life) suggests that Li Wang was still a very young man when driven into exile.[4] Likewise the account of his suddenly becoming a tyrant; why now, if he has already been reigning for decades? But if he is an adolescent, and then has just taken the reins of government from a regent in 844 -- as must be the case if he was born in 864 -- there is no puzzle about it. These arguments are perhaps not tight. The 25 years given Yih Wang and the precise dating in the "Qi Shijia" are the real challenge. How are these things to be explained, if "37 years" is right?

What about the "modern text" *Bamboo Annals*? It is reported that the Project solicited a research paper on it by Prof. Chen Li 陳力 of Sichuan University, i.e., the paper he published in 1997.[5] Prof. Chen finds the text's first year for Yao, 2145 BC, given correctly in a Six Dynasties Daoist book; so the "modern text" is not so "modern" after all. Apparently it really is an ancient text. But the *Report* ignores this, and almost never even mentions the "modern text" *Bamboo Annals*, obviously relying on the widespread persuasion that it is a fake.[6] By dismissing it the *Report* commits what I have elsewhere called the "safe evidence" fallacy,[7] i.e., the idea that only "safe," highly probable or untainted or unchallenged evidence merits attention, either as supporting one's hypothesis or as counting against it. In arguing for one's hypothesis, putting together

---

[3] Some interpreters have taken the words "*dang ... shi*" as dating Hu Gong's moving of the capital to Pugu. But this move is not a significant event in Qi history, but merely describes Hu Gong's reign (the move was immediately reversed by his successor); and the words "Ruler A *dang* Ruler B *shi*" is the standard way of saying that Ruler A was contemporary with Ruler B. (See examples in the "Chen Qii 陳杞 Shijia" and the "Chu Shijia.")

[4] For these ideas see Lei Xueqi 雷學淇, *Zhushu jinian yizheng* 竹書紀年義證 j. 23,under Xiao 7.

[5] Chen Li 陳力, "Jinben Zhushu jinian zhi San dai ji nian ji xiangguan wenti" 今本竹書紀年之三代積年及相關問題, *Sichuan Daxue Xuebao* 四川大學學報 1997 no. 4, pp. 79-85.

[6] The book is the *Zhen gao*, 真誥, by Tao Hongjing 陶弘景, Liang Dynasty. This indifference is in spite of the fact that Chen Li's work has a summary in the Project's internal *Bulletin*, no. 26 (10 July 1997, pp. 2-3), including the startling discovery about the date 2145 BC. If the text Tao saw had this date, the rest of its dates were almost certainly the same as those in the "modern text." (Different chronologies are more likely to diverge in earlier dates than in later ones; furthermore, the earlier the "modern text" chronology can be attested, the more likely it is to be a faithful reproduction of the tomb text's chronology.) If the Project scholars had been alert, they would have seen at once that Prof. Chen's discovery implies that the Project's dating for Li Wang is very unlikely. (The "modern text" gives Li Wang only 12 years before his exile.)

[7] D. Nivison, "Response," in *Early China* 15 (1990) p. 151 ff.

pieces of evidence that individually have low probable worth can sometimes result in a combination that has high probability. On the other hand, even if counter-evidence seems weak, it may still be that if it turns out to be true it would destroy your hypothesis; and in that case you cannot reason that since it isn't generally considered "safe" you can ignore it. On the contrary, you must either refute it, or shrink its probability by offering a reasonable explanation of it, or grant that the probability of your own hypothesis is at most no higher than the probability that the unwelcome evidence is invalid. [And this probability may always turn out not to be low – if the "weak" datum when combined with other unnoticed data forms a coherent whole with high probability.]

This is the predicament of the Project and its *Report*, in relation to the "modern text" *Bamboo Annals*. Among other things, the *Annals* too gives Yih Wang 25 years; and if it is authentic it has by far the earliest chronology available. I have put in your hands my analysis of it that presents the case for its authenticity, by showing diagrammatically for Western Zhou how its dates appear to have been derived from the true dates of all reigns. If this book is authentic -- not necessarily true, but close enough -- then the entire chronology of the *Report* is wrong.

Let us see just what is at stake in the "37 years" controversy. First of all, if Li Wang's pre-exile reign was less than 37 years, then the Shanfu Shan *ding*, with its "37th year" date, must be a late Xuan Wang vessel, not a Li Wang vessel as the *Report* has it. But the rest of the date, "1st month, *chuji*, day *gengxu* (47)" does not fit 791, the 37th year counting from 827, for in 791 the day *gengxu* would be the 18th, impossible for *chuji*; the year required is 789, when a *yin* calendar would begin with *gengxu*, and 789 is the 37th year counting from 825.

Therefore if the 37 years theory for Li Wang is wrong, then the Nivison-Shaughnessy "two *yuan*" hypothesis is true: normally the reign-length of record for a king omits years at the beginning when the king is completing mourning for his father, with the result that he has, in a sense, two "first years," the succession year and the year two years later (the "accession year") when he formally claims all the regalia and ritual of kingship. And it should be obvious that any exact chronology that accepts the two-*yuan* theory is going to be completely different from any -- like the *Report's* -- that ignores or rejects it.

But Shaughnessy had already presented proof of the two-*yuan* theory that the Project *Report* ignores. He shows, simply by counting, that there are two Kang Wang dates that cannot be handled in the same reign, no matter how that reign is dated, unless the two-*yuan* theory is accepted. The two are the date in the "Bi Ming" chapter of the *Shang shu* as quoted by Liu Xin, and the date in the Xiao Yu *ding* inscription.[8]

The *Report* (p. 28) does discuss the Xiao Yu *ding* inscription, but does not list it in its six-page table of Western Zhou dates in inscriptions and old texts. The inscription is dismissed, one must suppose, because (1) the vessel was lost in the Taiping Rebellion, so all we have is a bad rubbing; and (2) the day-date is effaced and has to be inferred from the text. We have here an egregious example of the "safe evidence" fallacy.

The damage does not stop here, once "37 years" for Li Wang is rejected. The Project has rejected Wang Guowei's "4-quarters" analysis of lunar phase terms, in favor of a modified "2 halves" theory, and it requires this theory in dating the Zhou conquest. (Look at my handout for details.) But the "2 halves" theory was worked out in order to handle within the reign of the sixth king Gong Wang two inscriptions that name Gong Wang as king; and the two-*yuan* theory takes care of the problem without requiring giving up Wang Guowei.

Further, the rejection of "37 years" leads to a proof of Wang Guowei: All late Western Zhou inscriptions with dates higher than 18 years that the Project has given to Li Wang must now be returned to Xuan Wang, among them the much discussed Jin Hou Su Bell Set inscription, with its 33rd year date. Nivison and Shaughnessy have a brief article in *Zhongguoshi Yanjiu* last year (expanded in the current issue of *Early China*), that shows *conclusively* just how this inscription must be dated.

---

[8] E.L.Shaughnessy, *Sources of Western Zhou History* (Berkeley: University of California Press, 1991), pp. 242-245.

Conclusively? We find reasons to suspect that the reigns of Jin Hou Su (Xian Hou) and Mu Hou are out of order. When the two reigns are switched, Jin Hou Su's reign starts in 795, Xuan 33, the date of the inscription. The proof: dates of battles given in the "Jin Shijia" then match dates given in the "modern text" *Bamboo Annals* and in the *Hou Han shu*, probably quoting the "ancient text." [9] When the inscription is dated correctly -- see my handout -- it becomes clear that the lunar phase dates in it require Wang Guowei's theory. Here again is enough to shake apart virtually the entire Western Zhou chronology in the *Report*.

Defenders of the *Report* have offered one counter-argument, echoed by Prof. Li Xueqin: "*Nihe*"-adjusted C-14 dating yields dates 814-794 that are closer to the *Shiji* dates for Jin Hou Su's death and burial --812 -- than are ours, which is 785. The "*nihe*" adjustment procedure is vulnerable to methodological criticism. But let us waive that. What such an argument forgets is that C-14 dating is performed not on events but on physical objects associated with those events -- objects such as fragments of coffin wood, or pieces of human or animal bone. The C-14 content of a sacrifice is not fixed at the moment its throat is slit. A human bone will have been formed decades earlier. And probably the coffin will not only have been made of well-seasoned wood, but the coffin itself would probably have been made many years earlier than the burial. None of these things can be known. But obviously an upper limiting date 814 for a death dated 812 is not nearly early enough. So the numbers actually support us rather than the Project.

There has been a storm of criticism of the Project's work in China. Some scholars have published their objections. (Others have not dared to.) The exact chronology for Western Zhou in the *Report* is at the very least so shaky that one would not want it to have appeared under auspices -- of the PRC, no less -- that must encourage busy and uninformed persons -- students, professors in other fields, editors, curators of museums, reporters -- to accept it uncritically. But that is exactly what has happened. It need not have happened, and it would not have happened, had the Project leaders not worked in relative secrecy.[10] Thus they were not pushed hard enough by critics to look carefully at difficulties. The unresolved difficulties ought to have persuaded them that it is much too soon to promulgate a definitive chronology.

When using C-14 technology, etc., to get closer and closer *approximations* to correct absolute dates, it can make sense -- if the work is sound -- to claim, after five years of work on a massive scale, "These are the best results at present obtainable. We hope they can be improved with more work." But the detective work for ascertaining exact dates isn't like that, and it is a mistake to forget the difference, in the claims one makes. *Exact* dates are either right or wrong, and if they are wrong you throw them away, try to find the point in your reasoning where you went wrong, and start over. Further, "democracy" has no place in this kind of work. One does not settle a dispute over a date by calling for a show of hands.[11]

No one can object to an individual scholar -- who is going to be doubted anyway -- publishing his own set of dates, clearly representing it as his own, and his (probably debatable) arguments for them. The problem is an insufficiently cautious publication of a set of exact dates that claims to be the latest and best, having the authority and prestige of the Chinese government. Most of the crucial background questions have scarcely been addressed by the world community of scholars.

---

[9] [DSN 2007: I now believe that there is an error here in our article. Fan Ye must have been loosely paraphrasing the *jinben* text. I do not think this error damages our complete argument. See Appendix 2, p. 216.]

[10] The preliminary version of the Project's report issued in May 2000 is labeled "*neibu*," i.e., for "internal" distribution only. The short "Bulletins" keeping Project participants informed of all Project work are unrestricted, apparently, for the first half year. Beginning in October of 1996 one finds at the end of each issue publication information in Chinese and in English, concluding (harmlessly) 版權所有, "All rights reserved." But beginning with issue 51, dated 25 February 1999, the Chinese for "All rights reserved" is changed to 內部資料, 不得引用與轉發, "Internal material, not to be quoted or disseminated."

[11] [DSN addition 2007: Resolving a dispute by calling for a show of hands? Peter Hessler (*Oracle Bones*, New York: HarperCollins 2006 p. 387): "Some say that the project was motivated primarily by a sense of competition with the West, which has earlier recorded dates for cultures such as ancient Egypt. During the Chronology Project, academic differences about ancient dates were sometimes resolved by voting – Chinese scholars gave their opinions, and the year with the most votes won."]

Foremost among these is the question, is the "modern text" of the *Bamboo Annals* authentic, that is, does it give us dates that were represented as being true by chronologists in the 4th century BC? If the answer to that question is yes, then whether they were right or wrong they must have had reasons; and probably that will mean that almost every date the Project has published is wrong. As my colleague Mr. Shao Dongfang will show, that question about the *Annals* is still wide open.[12]

[12] Li Xueqin's book *Xia-Shang-Zhou niadaixue zhaji* (李學勤, 夏商周年代學札記, Liaoning Daxue Chubanshe, 1999), republishes articles by him on chronological problems raised by the Project's work With few exceptions the articles originally appeared between 1997 and 1999, and most of them are arranged in chronological order. One of the outstanding virtues of this book is the author's candor. Li makes no attempt to conceal points where he has changed his mind. [.... I.e., even if not calling attention to such a change, he lets both the earlier and the later argument stand, so one can readily trace the evolutiion of his thinking.] But of course I have to make my own appraisal of these shifts in his thinking, and in some very important matters Li has repudiated positions that I think were correct. Li's thinking has quite obviously guided the Project's thinking on exact chronology. Li's book thus shows me how Li and the other Project scholars reasoned their way into their worst mistakes. Li at first accepted Wang Guowei's "four-quarters" analysis of lunar phase (*yuexiang*) terms, and in particular he accepted "*chuji*" as one of those terms But later, struggling with the problem of dating the 37th-year Shanfu Shan *ding* and the 33rd-year Jin Hou Su *bianzhong*, he decides that although they are stylistically very late Western Zhou, they cannot be in Xuan Wang's reign. -- [There are obvious difficulties: In the former, the date information does not fit Xuan Wang's 827 calendar; and as to the latter, according to the *Shiji* Jin Xian Hou Su's reign was 812-822, Xuan 6-16.] Work by Nivison and Shaughnessy resolves both of these difficulties, the former by our "two-*yuan*" hypothesis, and the latter by our argument for switching the reigns of Xian Hou and Mu Hou of Jin. But Li had either forgotten or rejected the two-*yuan* theory (though he had publicly praised me for proposing it in 1981); and the implications of our article on the Jin *bianzhong* inscription apparently escaped the attention of the busy administrator Li had become. (We published in 2001; but the Chinese manuscript was available in China in the spring of 1999.) So Li decided that these had to be Li Wang inscriptions, and that regardless of arguments to the contrary Li Wang just had to have had 37 years before his exile. Thereafter, the resulting problems of dating other late Western Zhou inscriptions with high year numbers forced him [apparently] to abandon Wang Guowei's system, including his own former analysis of the term "*chuji*"; it now appeared to him not to be a phase term at all, but an intrusion of a different kind of dating into the apparatus of phase terms.

Readers should notice that the two-*yuan* theory is fully as important as the question of the authenticity of the "modern text" *Bamboo Annals*. The diagrammatic analysis of the *Annals* in my handout (pp. 8-9 of the handout, but in this book at the end of Appendix 2) uses the two-*yuan* theory at every step. Without it, I would have to agree with the doubters that the *Annals* text is either a late invention, or is at best almost useless for chronological studies.

[In this chapter and in several others I am reproducing what are in effect documents. Here, the paper has been translated (by Xu Fengxian) and published both in Taipei and in the PRC. Now using it as a chapter in a book, I face the danger of unnecessarily confusing the reader. I have used square brackets when I am adding or changing something.]

Chapter Five

The Three-Years Mourning Institution and the Chronology of Ancient China

The Herrlee G. Creel Lecture at the University of Chicago, 12 April 2002

David S. Nivison,

Stanford University (emeritus)

My lecture (as written), "The Three Years Mourning Institution and the Chronology of Ancient China," assumes as "handout" the full text (as written) for my AAS paper in Washington, 5 April 2002, "The Three Dynasties Chronology Project: Two Approaches to Dating," plus "Supporting Material."

5.1 This lecture followed by one week a brief presentation by me at the AAS meeting in Washington DC. What I say is a continuation of my argument in that presentation. I have distributed an expanded version of that presentation, tacking on a one-page summary. I review those events now, briefly, in order to show the significance of what I wish now to say.

My Washington paper was a criticism of the tentative chronology of Western Zhou, ca. 1050 BCE to 771 BCE, as recently published by the five-year "Xia-Shang-Zhou Chronology Project" in China. There was a preliminary dinner meeting with the Chinese guests representing and supporting the Project. I had argued that the exact dates published by the Project are almost completely wrong. Discussion centered on previous written work of mine that those present had seen, as well as on a distributed text of my paper. I had observed that the size and length of the Project, and its enormous financial backing by the Chinese government, together with the mode of publication and wide publicity about it, carried the implication that its work was intended to be accepted by the world as the definitive solution to the problems it addressed in ancient Chinese chronology.

(Anyone doubting that this was the intention -- and that it was the government's intention -- must reckon with known facts and plain evidence in the Project's periodic internal bulletins. The Project was initiated by the government in 1996, in order to achieve a definitive set of dates, so as to put Chinese history on a par with that of other ancient civilizations. Since February of 1999 its *Brief Bulletin* ("Jian Bao") has borne an official governmental classification as "internal material (*neibu ziliao*) not to be disseminated," indicating that it was being treated as government work. Repeatedly this bulletin shows persons at the highest level of government, watching the Project's proceedings with intense interest, and characterizing its results as the achievements of organized socialist science.)

On the contrary, I argued that the Project has failed to address threshold problems that must be settled before any such work deserves attention, and has proceeded to publish claimed results in exact dating only because its leaders had perceived that they must, and that any other course was politically unacceptable. (Instead, I said, it should have admitted that issuing definitive results which world scholarship would accept is not yet possible.) The Chinese guests understandably were unhappy with the suggestion that they had yielded to political influence. I was pressed to delete all references to government connections from my presentation. I remained silent. The Director, Li Xueqin, broke the impasse by saying that he would preface his distributed paper with an explicit assertion of the Project's complete independence. I thus had to decide whether I would read my paper as written. I decided instead to stress and embrace the implication of his claim, namely that the Project's work must stand on its own, and should not be accepted by the world unless and until it had survived the most rigorous criticism by the world community of scholars, like any other piece of research. This I did, as eloquently as I could, the next day.

5.1.1 I chose as the focus of my substantive criticism the Project's dates for the tenth Western Zhou king Li Wang, as having had 37 years of reign before being driven into exile in 842. (The Project had said 841.) I pointed to a combination of nearly conclusive evidence that Li Wang's pre-exile reign had been no more than 18 years. I then noted that this required (1) re-dating several bronze inscriptions from Li Wang to the end of the reign of the eleventh king Xuan Wang, in turn requiring accepting the truth of the Nivison-Shaughnessy hypothesis that normally a Western Zhou king had two years of mourning-completion before the reign of record as given by historians; and (2) re-dating the Jin Hou Su bell-set inscription (on which Nivison and Shaughnessy had just published, in English and in Chinese) from 845 to 795. The last also shows the Project's interpretation of bronze inscription date formulas to be systematically mistaken (this alone being enough to upset the Project's entire chronology).

In discussion, it developed (as I expected) that the crucial issue was the Nivison-Shaughnessy hypothesis. This at least one of the Chinese guests found impossible to accept (The others remained silent.). This hypothesis in turn requires accepting the high antiquity of the institution of three years (actually 25 months) of severe ritual mourning for a deceased parent, especially one's father. On the contrary the prevailing view in contemporary China has been that this practice was the invention of Confucius or early Confucian ritualists, ca. 500-300 BCE.

I

5.2 Am I about to give two mini-lectures within one hour -- one on mourning and the other on chronology?

No. Then what do these two subjects have to do with each other? In talking about institutions of mourning, I am talking about traditional behaviors and obligatory attitudes a person must adopt on the death of someone who has been close to and important to him (or her) in life, the closest and most important (in the kind of society that China has had) being one's father. The regularization of such matters in a society featuring a ritualized cult of the dead implies keeping track of earlier relationships, one's father's father, and so on, i.e., of ancestors; and this is going to mean that the focus of my attention must be family lines having status and with it power -- the higher status and the more power the closer my attention. (It is sometimes said that the peasants had no ancestors.)

So generational order is important. But as important, the pairing of one order with another, notably that of the person at the head of the social-political order, the king. Thus, in the Shi Qiang *pan* inscription, we find two paired lists, with short characterizations: the kings of Zhou, and the ancestors of Shi Qiang. There is order only, here, not measure. But one wants measure (for generations are of no fixed length), and this is naturally given by counting the years of tenure of the kings, who are in this way the creators of political time for the whole social-political order of things.

5.2.1 Two matters now demand attention. Nothing lasts forever, not a human life, and not even the primacy of a line of kings. So attention is required the problem of continuing the year count when one line is replaced by another, which is to be recognized as the "next" one. This is the problem of legitimate succession, *zheng tong*. But fully as demanding, one would think, is the problem of what happens when one ruler succeeds another. There are two possibilities. When the King of England dies, the herald announces, "The King is dead. Long live the King." The concept here is that the instant the passing monarch breathes his last, the ritually authorized successor is king. In contrast, in the Renaissance stage of the late *ancien regime* in France (which passed into history in 1789), close examination of the rites of passage attending the death of the monarch shows that in a ritual sense the deceased king was conceived to be *still there*, until his body was laid to its rest in the tomb, and meanwhile the successor existed in a sort of ritual limbo.[1]

Both these concepts existed in ancient China, in sometimes visible tension; and this is true both for kings and for lesser heads of state, the various *zhu hou*. The first is seen in situations where close study requires us to assume that the year count for the successor must take as first year the very year of his predecessor's death. (I will argue that this was often the case in the Shang Dynasty; but often too it was the year following the death that counted as first year; and there must have been a system that determined which way it would go.) The second, however, the idea that the deceased was for a time not yet departed, was (I will argue) the rule. Here the rites of burial and prolonged mourning for the deceased ruler -- supposedly three years -- were (probably) much more important for the status of the successor than was true in France.

By Warring States times there seems to be only a dimming memory of this. But the three years mourning (usually defined as 25 lunar months) was attested and defended in Warring States texts, and it became general throughout elite social classes in later dynastic times. In early modern times when one can examine it most easily, it required suspension of normal activity. This was to be both personal (e.g., sexual), and political: enforced temporary retirement if one were an official; denial of access to the civil service examinations for the prescribed duration of mourning, if one were at an earlier career stage.

---

[1] Metcalf, Peter, and Richard Huntington, *Celebrations of death: the anthropology of mortuary ritual.* Second edition, Cambridge: Cambridge University Press, 1991, pp. 173-179. I am indebted to Prof. D. N. Keightley for calling my attention to this material.

5.3 This aspect of mourning, as temporary suspension of or delay in normal activity, becomes especially serious for one whose normal and proper activity would be the control and direction of the governmental power over the whole social-political order. In relatively modern times this was not allowed to be a problem. But in antiquity it was a problem, and it was more of a problem the farther back one probes. Grasping this point -- that the essence of mourning is the suspension of normal activity -- is the key to understanding a little short story -- probably true, for all of its being a story -- which has been the focus of endless controversy.

The story is told in the third "book" of the *Mengzi*, 3A1-2. In the first short bit, we see Mengzi talking in the state of Song with the heir (later Wen Gong) to the dukedom of the tiny state of Teng, on the Lu-Song border, advising him that a ruler must follow the moral example of Yao and Shun. This is the familiar Mengzi, revivalist. The continuation of the story requires me to quote it entire. With minor but important changes, I follow D. C. Lau:[2]

II

5.3.1 Duke Ding 定 of Teng 滕 died. The crown prince (*shizi*) said to [his assistant] Ran You 然友, "I have never been able to forget what Mengzi once said to me in Song. Now that I have had the misfortune to lose my father, I want you to go and ask Mengzi's advice before making funeral arrangements."

Ran You went to Zou to ask Mengzi's advice.

"Splendid," said Mengzi. The funeral of a parent is an occasion for giving of one's utmost. Zengzi has said, 'Serve your parents in accordance with the rites during their lifetime; bury them in accordance with the rites when they die; offer sacrifices to them in accordance with the rites; and you deserve to be called a good son.' I am afraid I am not conversant with the rites observed by the feudal lords (*zhu hou*) [such as your prince]. Still, I have heard something about funeral rites. Three years as the mourning period, mourning dress made of rough hemp with a hem, the eating of nothing but rice gruel -- these were observed in the Three Dynasties [i.e., Xia, Shang, Western Zhou] by men of all conditions alike, from Emperor to Commoner."

Ran You reported this to the crown prince, and it was decided to observe the three-years mourning period. The elders and all the officials were opposed to this and said, "The ancestral rulers of the eldest branch of our house in Lu[3] never observed this; neither did our own ancestral rulers. When it comes to you, you go against our accepted practice. This is perhaps ill-advised. Furthermore, the *Records say*, 'In funeral and sacrifice, one follows the practice of one's ancestors.'" [But the crown prince] said, "I have authority for what I do."

The crown prince [then] said to Ran You, "In the past I have never paid much attention to studies, caring only for riding and fencing. Now the elders and all my officials do not think too highly of me, and I am afraid they may not give of their best in this matter. Go and consult Mengzi for me."

Ran You went once again to Zou to ask Mengzi for advice.

---

[2] *Mencius*; Translated and with an introduction by D. C. Lau. Harmondsworth: Penguin Books, Ltd., 1970 (rpr. 1983), pp.95-97.

[3] This does not mean that the rulers of Teng were descendants of the rulers of Lu. The meaning is that the first rulers of both Lu and Teng were sons of Wen Wang, with Zhou Gong Dan, the first fief-holder of Lu, having priority of age over other *zhu hou* having a similar relation to the Zhou royal house.

"I see," said Mengzi. "But in this matter the solution cannot be sought elsewhere. Confucius said, 'When the ruler dies the heir entrusts his affairs to the steward [of the tomb] (*zhong zai* 冢宰) and sips rice gruel, showing a deep inky color on his face. He then takes his place [as sovereign] (*ji wei* 即位) and weeps, and none of his numerous officials dare show a lack of grief. This is because he sets the example. When someone above shows a preference for anything, there is certain to be someone below who will outdo him. The gentleman's virtue is like wind; the virtue of the common people is like grass. Let the wind sweep over the grass, and the grass is sure to bend.'[4] It rests with the crown prince."

Ran You reported on his mission.

"That is so," said the crown prince. "It does, indeed, rest with me."

For five months he stayed in his mourning hut, issuing no orders or prohibitions. The officials and his kinsmen approved of his actions and thought him well-versed [in the rites]. When it was time for the burial ceremony, people came from all quarters to watch. He showed such a grief-stricken countenance and wept so bitterly that the mourners were greatly delighted.

III

5.4 So the story ends. A common twentieth-century appraisal of this story in the *Mengzi* -- probably the dominant one -- has been to argue that it refutes the traditionalist claim that the three-years mourning institution is extremely ancient. On the contrary, it is claimed, the *Mengzi* text, much prized by the Confucians, inadvertently reveals that the institution must be a warring states invention, almost certainly an invention by the Confucians themselves. How could it be otherwise, if the practice was unknown among earlier ducal generations in, of all places, the state of Lu, home of Confucius? Perhaps Mengzi himself believed in its antiquity. But why should we?

We find this criticism as early as 1919, in an early article by Hu Shi 胡適[5]. This was, of course, at the time when many young Chinese were expressing exasperation with traditionalist Confucian mores. Hu later (1936) changed his view, adopting the analysis of Fu Sinian 傅斯年.[6] Fu argues from early texts, e.g., in the *Lun yu*, describing mourning as observed by Gao Zong 高宗 (Wu Ding 武丁) of Shang (see below), that the three-years mourning, with extraordinary austerities, was a Shang practice. But Fu believed it was not followed in Western Zhou, or in Lu, which could be expected to preserve and continue Zhou customs.

The more extreme theory that it was all a Warring States Ru-ist invention has flourished more recently, both in the Peoples' Republic and among recent American scholars. Keith N. Knapp, exploring the history of the ideal of *xiao* (孝"filial piety") in *Early China* 20 (1995), both supports the theory of late invention and gives a useful summary of earlier argument.[7] And a year ago the argument emerged again in the on-line "Warring States Group" started by E. Bruce Brooks, in which many of us participate, myself included. (I interposed objections that were quickly dismissed by others.) A rare defense of the view that Mengzi's statements can be accepted as true is made by an older scholar, Yang Ximei 楊希枚 (1977 and 1995)[8] Yang's analysis is valuable, but I find that I cannot accept all of it.

---

[4] *Lun yu*, XII.19

[5] Hu Shi, *Zhongguo zhexueshi dagang* 中國哲學史大綱, Commercial Press, 1919, pp. 125-133; also "San nian sang-fu di zhujian tuixing 三年喪服的逐漸推行," in *Wuhan Daxue Wenzhe Jikan* vol. 1, no. 2 (1930), pp. 405-414.

[6] Hu Shi, "Shuo Ru 說儒," *Zhongyang Yanjiuyuan Lishi Yuyan Yanjiusuo Jikan* vol. 4,no. 3 (1936), pp. 244-246; Fu Sinian, "Zhou dong-feng yu Yin yi-min 周東封與殷遺民," same publication and issue, pp. 233-239.

[7] Knapp, Keith N., "The *Ru* Reinterpretation of *Xiao*," *Early China* 20 (1995), pp. 195-222, especially pp. 209-213.

[8] Yang Ximei, "Mengzi Teng Wen-Gong Pian San-nian Sang Gushi di Fenxi" 孟子滕文公篇三年喪故事 的分析, *Shihuo Yuekan* 1.3 (June 1977), pp. 135-152; also Yang Ximei, *Xian-Qin wenhuashi lunji* 先秦文化史論集 (Beijing: Zhongguo Shehui Kexue Chubanshe, 1995) pp. 402-433.

5.4.1 Nobody is thinking carefully enough. The Teng heir-prince consults Mengzi, and then announces that three years of mourning will be observed, and everyone is dreadfully upset. But what, exactly, could have caused such distress among his officials and kinsmen? We read the story, and think, "*Three* years! Who could endure all that?" But surely, *mere time was not the problem*. The problem was the required abnormal activity, and the *suspension of normal activity* during that time. Suppose the heir-prince, become Wen Gong 文公 of Teng, had said nothing to anybody, and had simply opened every court session with the statement, "We are now in mourning, and will start the day with a moment of silence," following this by bowing his head and in silence counting slowly to twenty before continuing with the day's business. Doing nothing more, he could have kept this up for ten years, and nobody would have batted an eye.

Furthermore, one can put one's finger on one particular detail that must be what caused the objecting. Much of Mengzi's prescriptions affect only the heir -- uncomfortable hemp garments, disagreeable food, painful sleeping arrangements. One detail stands out as involving the government, and as dangerous: the idea that the heir is, in effect, to suspend his functioning as prince for the duration of the three years, turning over the direction of public business to his chief minister. Everyone would, of course, soon tire of mandatory weeping, but it would not harm the public interest. So it must have been this -- that the heir-prince was to turn over government functions to his chief minister -- that the "officials and kinsmen" were primarily objecting to, insisting that this had not been the practice of ancestral dukes of Lu and Teng.

So it is quite possible that the objectors in Teng were right. What was actually being proposed was rules of mourning behavior, binding on the whole court, that indeed had not been observed -- at least for a long time back and perhaps never -- by the ancestral dukes of Lu and Teng. And it can still be true that Mengzi was right: he was describing truly an ideal that was the ideal for all of past time called "the Tree Dynasties." Then what, exactly and in detail, was the Teng heir-prince, as guided by Mengzi, proposing to the Teng court?

5.4.2 Yang Ximei suggests that Mengzi's initial disclaimer, "I am not conversant with the rites observed by the feudal lords" (*zhu hou zhi li, wu wei zhi xue ye* 諸侯之禮, 吾未之學也) is edged. Mengzi (Yang guesses) perceives that the heir-prince wants to use rites appropriate for a universal king, *tianzi*, and is subtly putting him down. This misses the point, and assigns to Mengzi an anxiety that belongs to an earlier age. (Moral-philosophical objection to ritual presumptiveness is prominent in the *Lun yu*, in words ascribed to Confucius.[9]) But I see no reason in the present story to think that this is what the heir-prince wants. It seems to have been true, as the ritual classics say, that the *wang* or "son of heaven" was laid to rest in seven months counting from the month of death. Thus, in the "modern text" *Bamboo Annals* (*Jinben Zhushu jinian* 今本竹書紀年) Wu Wang dies in the 12th month, and is interred in the following 6th month. And Yang gives many examples from the *Chunqiu* and *Zuo zhuan* of *zhu hou* who are buried in 5 months (inclusive).[10] There is no reason not to assume that the heir-prince takes his *zhu hou* status for granted. In due course, his father's burial occurs just five months (inclusive) later.

IV

What Mengzi proposes, and the heir-prince accepts, can be seen from Mengzi's prescriptions -- rough hemp with a hem, rice gruel -- from his quotation from Confucius -- the heir entrusts his affairs to the steward of the tomb (*zhong zai*), takes his position as lord (*ji wei*) and weeps - and from what the prince is described as doing: "for five months he stayed in his mourning hut, issuing no orders or prohibitions." We thus may suppose that Mengzi has given the heir the whole of Confucius' supposed statement on this (*Lun yu* 14.40, translation adapted from Brooks and Brooks, *The Original Analects*):[11]

---

[9] E.g., Confucius on Guan Zhong's misuse of the rites, *Lun yu* 3.22.

[10] Yang, 1995, p. 412.

[11] Brooks, E. Bruce, and A. Taeko Brooks, *The Original Analects: Saayings of Confucius and His Successors*. New York: Columbia University Press, 1998, p. 123. The text: 子張曰, 書云, 高宗諒陰, 三年不言, 何謂也? 子曰, 何必高宗? 古之人皆然. 君薨, 百官總己以聽於冢宰, 三年. Others accept 大 as the meaning of 冢 and translate 冢宰 "prime

Zi Zhang said, "The *Shu* says, 'When Gao Zong was in the mourning hut, for three years he did not speak.' What does it mean?" (The quotation is from the *Shang shu* chapter "Wu Yi 無逸," ascribed to Zhou Gong but probably 4th century BCE; Gao Zong is the 22nd Shang king Wu Ding, my dates 1250/47-1189.)

The Master said, "Why just Gao Zong? All the men of old were like this. When the ruler passed away, the hundred officials continued in office, and took orders from the steward of the tomb (*zhong zai*), for three years."

5.5 Are the 4th century authors of these texts making this up? Echoing pseudo-Confucius here, I have to reply, Why just Gao Zong? And why just the Shang Dynasty? There is at the moment a hubbub of debate about whether there really was a Xia Dynasty, the supposed first of the classical "Three Dynasties," Xia, Shang (or Yin) and Western Zhou. I will make no apologies. There was, and you will see in a moment why I think there is no room for doubt about the matter. It is to the Xia, not the Shang, that we must first look for tight evidence about the early form of the three-years mourning institution. (Shang will have its turn soon enough. Zhou will soon follow.)

V

A few minutes ago I dropped in place the title of a much debated book, the "modern text" *Bamboo Annals*, *Jinben Zhushu jinian*. Most of the great scholars of the high Qing, the Qian Long era -- such as Cui Shu 崔述, Wang Mingsheng 王鳴盛, and Zhang Xuecheng 章學誠 -- agreed that this two-*juan* text in chronicle form is a fake, put together by some ambitious antiquarian in the Ming Dynasty, or perhaps earlier. This is usually supposed to have been done after disappearance of the original text of the book, discovered around 280 CE in what seems to have been the tomb of the Wei king Xiang Wang (318-299 or 296 BCE[12]). Zhu Youzeng 朱右曾 in the 19th century and Wang Guowei 王國維 in the 20th have been the main proponents of this view more recently, and apparently most scholars still agree with them. There have always been dissenters -- notably Lei Xueqi 雷學淇 two centuries ago in China, and the missionary and Oxford professor-translator James Legge. Recent work by Shaughnessy (1986) and in China by Chen Li 陳力 (1997) require accepting the book as at least in some degree authentic. Shaughnessy showed that a bamboo slip that belongs in the chronicle for Cheng Wang of Zhou has gotten moved to the end of the chronicle for Wu Wang.[13] This establishes the authenticity, word for word, of a key part of the *text*, thus shifting the burden of proof, defeating the standing presumption of fakery for the whole of the *text*. Chen has demonstrated beyond reasonable doubt that a key part of the *chronology* informing the "modern text" was known in the pre-Tang Six Dynasties, thus defeating the presumption that the rest of the *chronology*

minister." Translators admit the phrase 總己 to be difficult. D. C. Lau has "all the officials joined together and placed themselves under the prime minister" (*Confucius: The Analects*, Penguin Books, Harmondsworth, 1984 (1979), p. 131).

12 Sima Zhen 司馬貞 of Tang, *Shiji Suoyin* 史記索隱 at the words "23rd year ... King Ai died," in the "Wei Shijia"魏世家 chapter (*Shiji* 44): "The *Annals* from the Ji Tomb 汲冢紀年 ends with the 20th year of Ai Wang. [This is because the next king] Zhao Wang announced his "first year" only after completing the three-years mourning." The last Wei king in the *Annals* text is actually Xiang Wang, misunderstood as "Ai Wang" in the *Shiji* (and by Sima Zhen also). There is an unresolved dispute whether the *Annals* text "jin wang zhong er shi nian"今王終二十年 means "The present king ended [his life and reign] in the 20th year," or "[The chronicle for] the present king ends in the 20th year." Sima Zhen apparently is taking the latter interpretation, but is assuming that the date is nonetheless the date of the death of "the present king."

13 Shaughnessy, E. L., "On the Authenticity of the *Bamboo Annals*," *Harvard Journal of Asiatic Studies* 46.1 (1986), pp. 149-180. Shaughnessy thinks the slip was incorrectly located by the Jin court restorers ca. 280 CE; I argue that it was deliberately relocated sometime in the 4th century BCE. [Note: I now believe that only text, not an actual strip, was moved, and that this was done before 300 BCE. See Chapter Nine, especially pp. 189-191.] (Shaughnessy's article, translated into Chinese, is included in Shao Dongfang 邵東方 and Ni Dewei 倪德衛, eds., *Jinben Zhushu Jinian Lunji* 今本竹書紀年論集, Taipei: Tonsan Press, 2002 (hereafter *Jinben Lunji*).)

must be invented.[14]

The problem with this "modern text" is that there are many quotations in early historical commentaries and encyclopedias that differ from the text we have in book form. Adherents of the fakery thesis therefore consider that only quoted fragments are authentic. They have made very useful collections of these fragments, collectively called the "ancient text" (*Guben Zhushu jinian*). The differences between the two texts have to be explained. So even the defenders of authenticity usually argue that the "modern text" is to some extent a post-discovery rewriting. Most defenders argue that this rewriting is extensive enough so that one cannot use it for reconstructing chronology, at least earlier than Zhou.[15]

5.5.1 My own view is this: After the discovery of the cache of books from which we have the *Annals*, the bundles and piles of bamboo slips containing the writings were rescued and taken to the Western Jin court, and worked on by court scholars. This took time, and someone participating or with access to the work got impatient and made a copy, before the work of sorting slips and reconstitution in current script was finished. This copy was significantly shorter than what finally resulted from the court scholars' labors. It may have been the only version that got taken south to Jiankang ca. 315-317 CE at the end of Western Jin, and it was the only version that eventually got printed, probably in early Song. The last part of it, chronicling the Wei 魏 state, especially shows incomplete work. This does not mean that the rest can be accepted as it stands. Almost all of the "Three Dynasties" part shows politically motivated manipulation of the chronology by pre-imperial hands. I see a major reworking of the chronology done in the reign of Xiang Wang of Wei at the end of the fourth century BCE, on top of an earlier recasting done from a Zhou court viewpoint, maybe a century earlier. I have spent more than two decades trying to discover exactly what was done, thus working back to a true chronology of the entire Three Dynasties. I find no evidence of any arbitrary rewriting of the dates after the discovery of the text.

VI

The account begins with Huang Di, and I do not know at what point myth gives way to history. But with Xia at the latest there is solid material. Exact dates are indicated now by *ganzhi* 干支 *sui*-歲 names that are of course inserted by the Jin editors. These *sui*-name dates start with Yao, dated 2145. (If Yao is real, I find that the date should be 2026.) There is a brief chronological summary at the end of the account of each of the "Three Dynasties." Xia is said to be 471 years long, with 1559 as terminal date; so we are meant to take 2029 as Xia year one. In the text this is the 14th year of Shun, and the narrative says that in this year Shun handed over control of his government to Yu, who (later) becomes the first Xia king.

In a brilliant piece of detective work, David W. Pankenier has shown, in an article in *Early China* 9-10 (1983-85), that this event coincided with (and may well have been in response to) a spectacular conjunction of the five visible planets in February, 1953 BCE. Few believed him. (I did, right off.)[16] (So the *Annals* dates that event 76 years early -- 2029 minus 1953. Remember that number 76.)

5.6 Xia is important for my subject today, because the Xia chronicle exhibits interregnums between reigns, and the most frequent length of these is two years.[17] Further, internal notes (of uncertain origin) in the text

---

[14] Chen Li, "Jin- Guben Zhushu Jinian zhi San Dai Jinian ji Xiangguan Wenti"今古本竹書紀年之三代積年及相關問題, *Sichuan Daxue Xuebao* 1997 no. 4, p. 80. (Included in *Jinben Lunji*).

[15] For discussion, pointing out the error in this judgment, see D. S. Nivison, "The Key to the Chronology of the Three Dynasties: The "Modern Text" *Bamboo Annals*," *Sino-Platonic Papers* 93 (January 1999), p. 52, and N 2002 p. 299.

[16] D. W. Pankenier, "*Mozi* and the Dates of Xia,Shang and Zhou: A Research Note." *Early China* 9-10 (1983-85), pp. 175-183. (A Chinese translation of Pankenier's article is included in *Jinben lunji.*)

[17] The frequencies: zero years, 3; one year, 1; two years, 7; three years, 4; four years, 1. (There is also a fictitious insert of a 40 years interregnum after the 5th king Xiang, telling a story that came to be generally accepted.)

say that the first two, both of three years, are for completion of mourning for the royal predecessor. These interregnums vary from one to four years, showing signs of editorial pushing and pulling. I reasoned that originally all should be just two years: the year of death would be the last year of the predecessor-king, the death date being followed by 25 (or 27) lunar months of mourning -- the actual meaning of "three years."[18] So the three years would not be complete until the second year after the succession year.

5.6.1 By accident, in December, 1988, I learned that Kevin Pang, a consultant in the Pasadena Jet-Propulsion Laboratory, had been pursuing an avocation, using computer technology to try to pin down dates in early Chinese history. He thought he had identified the solar eclipse mentioned in the *Zuo zhuan* (Zhao 17) as recorded in "the Books of Xia," as located "in Fang." And (assuming it was the same one) we find it in the *Bamboo Annals* as being on day *gengxu* (47) in the 9th month of the 5th year of Zhong Kang of Xia. I put this guess together with Pankenier's discovery and my own guess that the Xia interregnums were all two years, but I assumed that reign lengths were otherwise as in the *Annals*. In minutes I had an exact fit: Pang's eclipse was annular, its path of totality north of the probable Xia domain but not so far north that it could not have been reported, and the sun's location was exactly in Fang, a narrow space in the lunar zodiac of only 7 degrees. The date was 16 October 1876 BCE, the 1st of the 9th month (Xia calendar) in Zhong Kang 5, if Shun 14 were 1953 BCE. This was something to publish -- which we did, after meeting a bit of resistance. (Some people seem to distrust (or dislike?) this way of doing history.)[19]

It was also something to follow up. The first challenge (included in our publication) was the *Annals'* day *gengxu*, which was wrong; and the *Annals'* year, which was 1948, not 1876. These errors had to be explained (because you can't simply ignore apparent evidence that you don't accept; you have to account for it). The date for the beginning of Xia had been moved back one *bu*, 76 years, 1953 to 2029 in the *Annals*. So I saw reason to think that the manipulation of the chronology back-dating the eclipse, which probably would have been done in the late 5th century BCE, had involved using a system like the so-called "Yin Li" system. But 1948 is not 76 years earlier than 1876; the interval is only 72 years. Why?

5.6.2 The calculator would have had the information that got into the *Zuo zhuan*, so he thought the sun had to be in Fang, and that it would also be in Fang 20 x 76 years later. After 20 x 76 years, one "*ji*" of 1520 years, the occurrence of winter solstices on the first days of their months, and the *ganzhi* of first days of lunar months, were supposed to be repeated exactly. Further (this was before the Chinese had discovered the precession of the equinoxes) the sun's zodiac location on any date in the cycle would also be the same as in the preceding *ji*. So the calculator counted back 76 years from 1876 to 1952, then counted down 1520 years to 432, and found that in that year the sun was not in Fang on the 1st of the Xia 9th month. He tried the next year, and the next, and the next. No luck. But finally 428 worked, perfectly. This forced him to select a date four years later, i.e., 1948, a year only 72 years back from 1876.[20]

What would the *ganzhi* be for the first day of the Xia 9th month of 1948? The same as for 428, which was the year before 427; and in the Yin Li system 427 begins a 76-year *bu*, with jiyou (46) as winter solstice first-of-month day. The winter solstice month is the 11th month in the Xia calendar; so the 9th month of 428, hence 1948, begins 30 + 29 days earlier, i.e. gengxu (47). It is inconceivable that a post-discovery faker would have been using this system, and would also have known the true date of the eclipse; nor would such a person have any reason to try to go through the reasoning that I have reconstructed. (The Chinese had discovered precession by 400 CE.) So here is another proof that the chronology in the "modern text" *Bamboo Annals* is authentic -- authentic, furthermore, not just for Zhou but all the way back through Xia.

---

[18] The sources and data on the length of the three-years mourning have been conveniently drawn together by Gu Yanwu 顧炎武 (1613-82), *Rizhi lu* 日知錄 j. 5, 28th section (out of 49 sections in the chapter). The section is an unusually long one.

[19] Nivison, D. S., and K. D. Pang, "Astronomical Evidence for the *Bamboo Annals'* Chronicle of Early Xia." *Early China* 15 (1990), pp. 87-95.

[20] A *bu* is named for its supposed first day, in a year starting with the winter solstice month (Xia calendar 11th month), in which the winter solstice day is the 1st of the month. First days of *bu*, in the *ganzhi* system of naming days, recur in a cycle of 20 *bu*, i.e., in one "*ji*," of 1520 years. One *ji* before 427 is 1947. If this *ji* begins with day *jiyou* (46), then the preceding Xia 9th month must begin with day *gengxu* (47). [For an important caution see the note at the end of my Preface, p. 6.] (But this system has a cumulative error, of one day early over about 300 years back.)

But of course, "authentic" does not mean correct.

The next move: what would show up if I continued the method, using *Annals* reign lengths but with all interregnums the same, just two years? In earlier work, Pankenier had fixed 1554 as the first year of Shang. He reasoned that 496 years as the length of Shang, given in the *Annals* and also in one of the *chan-wei* texts, should be counted back from the "Mandate Year" of Zhou, i.e., the year after the brilliant conjunction of May 1059 BCE. This gave him 1555 as the last year of Xia.[21] I now applied my method to see if I got another fit. The result was amazing: 1555 turned out to be not the last year of the infamous bad last Xia king Jie = Di Gui, but the last year -- exactly -- of the preceding king in the Xia list, Fa.

5.6.3 So Jie must be a fiction![22]

Proof of this immediately jumped out. Three items (but the list could be longer): (1) The *Annals* has 1989 as *de jure* year 1 of the first king Yu; 1789 as year 1 of the ninth king Mang, and 1589 as year 1 of the 17th king Jie. So apparently at some earlier time it was thought that Xia must have 8 kings = 200 years plus 8 kings = 200 years; and the interregnum lengths had been juggled (and other adjustments made) to make this be so. So at this stage Jie wasn't there, and 1589 had been the first year of Shang. (2) Shaughnessy's proof of the transposed bamboo slip had involved accepting the statement in Xun Xu's preface to the *Mu Tianzi zhuan*, that the slips in the recovered texts were just 40 graph spaces long. I counted the graphs in the (unusually long) chronicle for Jie, and got eight slips. But other reign accounts for Xia were of irregular lengths, usually quite short. So the Jie chronicle text must have been composed and inserted later. (But still early, when books were still being made of bundles of bamboo slips of exactly 40 spaces each.) (3) Pankenier had put his finger on an actual celestial event in the *Annals* account of Di Gui. In his supposed 10th year, *Annals* date 1580, "the five planets moved in succession (*wu xing cuo xing* 五星錯行), and at night stars fell like rain." This happened in late 1576: the planets had their heliacal risings in rapid succession, and at about the same time there was an annual meteor shower. The date turns out to be the second year of Kong Jia (below). So the account of Kong Jia must have been rewritten when the account of Di Gui was inserted. Sure enough: the present account of Kong Jia begins with exactly one slip's worth of text, in part obviously fiction, followed by a long set of equally invented stories (about the king's fondness for dragons, etc.) exhibited as commentary, probably being four slips of 34 spaces each (spaced three down from the top and three up from the bottom, to distinguish it from main text).

5.6.4 Backtracking, I next looked at this Kong Jia, the 14th Xia king -- interesting, because he had a *gan* as second syllable of his name; and there has been an ocean of speculation about the meaning of such *gan* names, found in every king of the next dynasty Shang. Could it be that these names were determined simply by the first day of the king's reign? I now had the date: it was 17 February 1577 BCE, and it is a simple matter to deduce the *ganzhi* equivalent; here it is *jiazi*, first day in the 60-day cycle.[23]

I suspected something. The preceding king was Jin, also known by a second name, Yin Jia; and his succession year (the first year of the interregnum preceding Jin's reign) begins with *jiaxu* (11). There is a still earlier date that can be checked, namely the succession year of Shang Jia Wei, the Shang founding ancestor, given in the *Annals* as the equivalent of 1718.[24] Maybe this date was obtained from an accurate

---

[21] Pankenier first developed this argument in his article "Astronomical Dates in Shang and Western Zhou, *Early China* 7 (1981-2; actually published 1983), pp. 2-37. Much of this article I cannot accept, but the date 1554 for the beginning of Shang I believe is correct.

[22] The insertion of the 31-year account of Di Gui is probably connected with the padding of the chronology that shifted the date of the 1876 eclipse back to 1948. If so, it occurred around 400 BCE. My claim that Di Gui (Jie) is fictitious requires an account of two texts that are perhaps earlier than this: *Shi*, Ode 304;and *Shang shu*, "Li Zheng." In the Ode, "Xia jie" should be "the champion of Xia," rather than "Jie of Xia"; and in the "Li Zheng," 桀德惟乃弗作,往任是惟暴德,罔後, "jie de" should be "[men] of noble virtue [will then not be caused to appear, while it will only be men of cruel temper who come forward for office" etc.].

[23] To get the *ganzhi*, consult a table that gives Julian Day numbers for the date in question. Divide the JD number by 60, and subtract 10 from the remainder; if the remainder is less than 10, add 50 instead.

[24] 1718 BCE is apparently a valid date, preserved in the records of the Song state, whose rulers claimed to be of the Shang royal lineage. The lord of Song chose 318 BCE, i.e., 2 x 700 years later, to announce his claim to the title *wang*.

Shang chronology preserved in the descendant state Song. The first day of that year in the Shang calendar was *jiaxu*. It might just be that the *ganzhi* system had originated with the inauguration of Shang Jia Wei, and then certainly the day chosen ought to be *jiazi*, not *jiaxu*.

Could it be that originally those two dates had been *jiazi*, with the impending first day for Kong Jia being merely *jiayin* (50)? One could imagine Kong Jia finding this distasteful, and accordingly decreeing that the day count must be jumped forward ten days. Jin and Shang Jia, of course, would be relegated to *jiaxu* oblivion. (Jin was not Kong Jia's father but merely his first cousin, so this would not be diminished parricide; and the indignity to Shang Jia, far in the past, would be less obvious, and in any case of no concern to the Xia king.) Thus he, Kong Jia, would be inaugurated on a *jiazi* day. The *Annals* records a celestial marvel in the last year of Jin (maybe right after the king's passing?): *shi ri bing chu* 十日並出, "Ten suns arose at once." Or perhaps -- the rising of the sun being the beginning of a day -- "Ten days occurred at once." May one then conjecture that the 60-day cycle is an *ur*-Shang creation?[25]

5.7 I am probably going to be told that with that last suggestion I am merely playing. But a *gan* name as determined by the first day in a reign is serious; and there are four Xia era examples, and no counter-examples.[26] So one must now consider the whole of Shang. I will omit here most of the details, inviting critical attention to my published work, and admitting that it represents several years of trial and error. I thought at first that I could never get results that either I or anyone else could accept with confidence. But my final results have seemed to solve some very puzzling problems.

VII

Again, my program must be to suppose that the mourning institution structures the chronology. But in the *Bamboo Annals* for Shang, there are no interregnums indicated. Perhaps then they are really there, but have been deleted. I think this is not quite true. The factor that might have created interregnums is still at work, but with a different effect: I assume that initial mourning-completion periods (not actual interregnums) were in each king's calendar, and no longer appear there. The king's reign of record is the reign beginning with the first year after mourning is finished. Further, in Shang it seems that a king's year of death counts as his last year only if he lived through most of it. E.g., Tang died early in the 13th year of his reign as universal king, but this same year counts as the first year of his grandson-successor Tai Jia[27]. The result is that often the initial mourning-completion period for a Shang king appears under analysis to be three years rather than two.

5.7.1 There are more peculiarities about the Shang king list that must require special accommodation in any system that one tries to reconstruct. One is that never does a king have the same *gan* as the preceding king. Another is that no king ever has *gui* as a *gan*. (A probably related phenomenon, as I will show, is the prevalence of fraternal succession; in the first two-thirds of the dynasty normally there were two brothers in each generation.) Yet another restriction: the *gan* determines the ruler's posthumous cult day, which cannot precede that of his father in the same ten day period. To make the *gan* institution work, there has to be a set of rules, and I think a basic rule is this. If the first day of the succession year gives a *gan* that is the same as that of the predecessor, then the first day of the post-mourning year (let us call it the "accession year") is used

---

(Similarly the lord of Wei had chosen 335 BCE to announce his claim, although his "royal" calendar started in 334. 335 is 700 years after 1035, the (invented) date in the *Annals* for the first year of the ancestral founder Tangshu Yu.

[25] It is perhaps worth noting that Shang Jia's father did not have a *gan* name, but a *zhi* name: he was Zi Hai, or Wang Hai, *hai* being the last of the twelve *zhi*. So perhaps the *gan* naming convention, and maybe even the *ganzhi* day-cycle, began with Shang Jia.

[26] The fourth is Di Gui. If he didn't exist, we must consider the possibility that the name "Di Gui" belongs to the true last Xia king Fa, whose succession year began with the day *guiyou* (10).

[27] On the death year of Tang and the first calendar year of Tai Jia, see *Han shu* 21B, quoting Liu Xin 劉歆(pp. 48b-49a in Wang Xianqian 王先謙, *Han shu bu zhu* 漢書補注 (Guangxu 26 = 1900), Taipei Yiwen Yinshuguan photolith).

instead; and if *gui* is determined as a *gan*, it defaults to *jia*. (This system could misfire; but it never does.[28]) The first month of the year varies (probably allowing some choice) but is usually the last month of winter.

You can see that the reconstruction of Shang chronology is going to be too complicated to deal with in a lecture; I must ask you instead to examine critically my publications.[29] But there are details during the first century of it that are worth trying to look at now. The following is my reconstruction based on the "modern text" *Bamboo Annals* account together with my *gan* theory. Tang died in his 13th year counting from 1554, i.e., 1542, which counts as Tai Jia year 1, of 3 + 12. During the first seven of these years Tang's first minister Yi Yin ran the government and was trying to eliminate Tai Jia. To this end he banished Tai Jia and used two uncles of Tai Jia as puppets, first Wai Bing, for the second and third of Tai Jia's three mourning years (thus replacing Tai Jia as chief mourner), then Zhong Ren for the first four of Tai Jia's 12-year "accession" reign. Thereupon, in his actual 7th year according to the *Annals*, Tai Jia escaped from confinement (of six years duration, as in *Mengzi* 5A6) and killed Yi Yin. The system sketched above then continues.

VIII

5.7.2 In due course we get to the two kings in generation 5, being in all received chronologies Yong Ji,[30] 12 years in the *Annals*, and Tai Wu, 75 years. There are two errors here: 75 years is impossible; and oracle inscriptions show that actually Yong Ji followed Tai Wu.[31] So, what happened? The chronology of Shang was being perfected in the 4th century BCE by experts who had straightened out Zhou chronology; and for them numerology and astrology were part of chronological science. They knew that the fifth Zhou king Mu Wang had succeeded in the 100th anniversary of the beginning of Zhou.[32] Tai Wu, the first (and "main line") king in Shang generation 5, actually had 1474 as accession year (so my *gan* theory tells me), and 1575 had been Tang's first year in his own domain (according to the *Annals*, and I think correctly), probably because 1575 followed the *cuo-xing* celestial event of 1576. The pre-Qin chronologists would think that this was too close to be accidental. The indicated one-year "correction" of 1474 to 1475 was made, and held fixed.

Then all mourning-completion periods were disallowed. There were four, of three years each, after Tai Jia and before 1475, so a 12-year gap appeared. Yong Ji's reign as I have deduced it was 2 + 12 years, so his reign (as 12 years) was shifted into the 12-year gap before Tai Wu, and Tai Wu's already very long reign was extended down through what had been Yong Ji's years, thus stretching his reign to 75 years. (This hypothesis is exactly consistent with the *gan* names of the kings.)[33]

---

[28] If the interval is two years, the predecessor was a *jia* king, and the first day of the succession year is a *jia* day, the first day of the accession year could be a *gui* day, defaulting to *jia*.

[29] The major publication that tries to reconstruct the Shang chronology in all of its complexity is my monograph "The Key to the Chronology of the Three Dynasties: The "Modern Text" *Bamboo Annals*," *Sino-Platonic Papers* 93 (January 1999) pp. 1-68. A revised version of this in Chinese has been published in *Jing xue yanjiu luncong* 經學研究論叢 10.

[30] Yong Ji: others, using oracle inscriptions take the name to be Lü Ji. The confusion is (I believe) due to a misreading of the *hewen* 己 with two 口 tucked inside for the name. It should be resolved as 邕己 (邕 with two 口 at bottom, not 巴), not as 呂己.

[31] Keightley, D.N., *Sources of Shang History*, Berkeley: University of California Press (1978) pp. 185-186, and note d.

[32] The "modern text" *Annals* has Mu Wang 1 = 962, and the end-of-Zhou summary takes 1062 as Wu Wang 1, although the chronicle text has 1062 as Wen Wang's year of death (in the 3rd month: i.e., early in the year). In my reconstruction, Mu Wang 1 = 956, and 1056 is the first year of a "mandate" calendar beginning in the third year of Wen Wang's last nine years following the conjunction of 1059; 1056 may also have counted as the first year of a Wu Wang calendar. The biography of Shu Xi 束晳 in the *Jin shu* says that Mu Wang's first year was 100 years "after the receipt of the Mandate," and scholars have disagreed about what this means, some holding that this must be regarded as the correct "*gu-wen*" text, differing from the "modern text." I argue that the Shu Xi biography "receipt of the Mandate" is a paraphrase, its intended meaning being just what the "modern text" says. This disagreement leads others to the view that the "modern text" is a radical rewriting of the chronology at this point, making it useless for chronological analysis.

[33] We find "75 years" also in the "Wu Yi" chapter of the *Shang shu* (where Tai Wu, temple name Tai Zong in the *Annals*, is called "Zhong Zong," as also in the *Shiji*); so this chapter must be a 4th century BCE invention, though probably containing authentic earlier material.

5.7.3 During the first three centuries of Shang there were two kings in each generation, and this calls for explanation. I can offer only a guess. In the crisis of the first succession, after the reign of the founder, Yi Yin had tried to treat the legitimate successor's mourning-completion years as an interregnum, by banishing Tai Jia and wedging a royal uncle into position as puppet, maneuvering to make himself king. Thus was exposed a major danger. During the mourning period the heir-prince was supposed to turn over real exercise of the royal power to his predecessor's prime minister. But that gentleman could not be counted on to play by the rules, and might try to usurp the succession for himself.

To guard against this danger king A would designate a younger brother to succeed himself as interim king B, while his own son and heir went through the very arduous and for a time incapacitating mandatory mourning rites. (King B would have to mourn his brother, but this would be less demanding.) With king B's passing, the true heir would succeed as king C (mourning his uncle, a less demanding duty than mourning his father, which he had already done). King C would then repeat the process. Thus turning over the government to the *zhong zai* was avoided, interregnums were avoided, and it would be assured that the succession would remain in the royal family main line. In the ducal line of Lu during Western Zhou, we find the same thing, Shang-style fraternal succession with two brothers in each generation.[34] So the Teng heir-prince's critics seem to be right: this dangerous mourning requirement, temporary abdication to the prime minister, had *not* been observed by the early dukes of Lu.

5.7.4 This worked well for centuries. But in generation 10 it broke down, for then we find four brothers in succession, with the last, Xiao Yi, getting himself succeeded by his own son, as Wu Ding. So fraternal usurpation now became the danger instead of ministerial usurpation. This led soon to father-son succession as the norm for the rest of Shang, with the son protected against the dangers of the mourning period by being given royal status as a "king in waiting" at once, at his father's inauguration. (Thus we have Lin Xin (or Feng Xin) following Zu Jia recognized as a king, even though he predeceased his father.)[35]

IX

This change in the succession institution complicates the work of chronologists like me. For example, I think I have proved that Wu Yi took the further step of giving his son and chosen heir Wenwu Ding a calendar of his own in 1118, ten years before Wu Yi died, at the end of 1109, and his example was probably followed by the remaining Shang kings. But for the last 80 years of the dynasty we have the help of oracle inscriptions on sequences of events such as scheduled sacrifices and the movement of troops, which make possible fixing exact dates. Using these, twenty years ago Shaughnessy and I established 1086 as the first year of the last king Di Xin. We have both published our reasoning, ignored (of course) by the Xia-Shang-Zhou Chronology Project. (Recently I have found two other independent ways of fixing the same date. There can be no doubt that it is right.)[36]

---

[34] Li Xueqin 李學勤, *Xia Shang Zhou niandaixue zhaji* 夏商周年代學札記, Liaoning Daxue Chubanshe (1999) p. 141. Circumstances for these fraternal successions vary, however, so the pattern may be coincidental.

[35] See Keightley 1978, pp. 186 and 187 note h. My analysis based on *gan* names leads me to conclude that Lin Xin or Feng Xin (as in the *Annals*) was given royal status by his father Zu Jia but soon died, and that Zu Jia then appointed Kang Ding in his place. Zu Jia himself must be judged a usurper; his eldest brother Zu Ji was probably the designated heir of Wu Ding. Oracle inscriptions apparently in Kang Ding's reign refer to a "Fu Ji" 父己 as "*xiao wang*"小王. (Shima Kunio 島邦男 (*In-kyo bokuji sorui* 殷墟卜辭綜類 (Tokyo: Kyuko shoin 1977 (1967) 496.4) lists 11 inscriptions with the term *xiao wang*; the one identifying Fu Ji ("Father Ji") as *xiao wang* occurs together with an inscription appealing to "Fu Jia," who must be Zu Jia.) I assume that this Fu Ji is Zu Ji 祖己, functioning as chief mourner for Wu Ding during the reign of Zu Geng, but dying before Zu Geng, with Zu Jia then displacing Zu Ji's heir, if he had one. This Fu Ji is probably the Zu Ji in the *Shang shu* chapter "Gao Zong Yong Ri" (which must mean "The Day of the *Yong* Sacrifice *to* Gao Zong" (= Wu Ding; the standard view is that the sacrifice is *by* Gao Zong, but oracle inscription idiom shows that this is a mistake).

[36] Our proof: Oracle inscriptions for the Ren Fang (or Yi Fang) campaign in Di Xin's 10th and 11th years contain enough information to require (so we think) that year 10 had an intercalary 9th month (i.e., the month after the 9th, lacking a *qi*-

5.8 I will pass over the vexing problem of the date of the Zhou conquest. I note only that the Project's date depends on three inadmissible assumptions: one, that the account in the *Guoyu* putting Jupiter in Chun Huo is authentic; two, that Wang Guowei's theory of lunar phase terms is wrong; and three, that the account by Shizi 尸子 (*Xunzi*, "Ru Xiao," commentary by Yang Liang) putting Jupiter in the astrological "north" can be dismissed without explanation. (The Project has also misinterpreted the Li *gui* inscription so as to make it seem to support the *Guoyu* on Jupiter's location, and has wrongly claimed the support of Yu Xingwu 于省吾 for this incorrect interpretation.[37])

X

5.8.1 Important for my subject is the question whether Western Zhou kings too observed the three-years mourning institution. Here the evidence is rich, and solid. What we look for is evidence that a king's reign can be described as having a certain number of years, and also as having two plus that number of years. I.e., for Western Zhou, like Xia and unlike Shang, a king's year of death never counted as the first year of the reign of his successor. In Western Zhou history from the Conquest on, this is true for every Western Zhou king whose predecessor was his own father, i.e., excepting only the 8th king Xiao Wang, whose predecessor was his nephew, and the 9th king Yi Wang, whose predecessor was his great uncle. It also holds for Wen Wang, the *de jure* founder and father of the first king. Independent sources firmly imply that Wen Wang died in 1050, in the last year of a 50-year calendar. One text (*Yi Zhou shu* 逸周書 23 "Xiao Kai"小開) identifies precisely a lunar eclipse on a *bingzi* day in the first month of spring in his 35th year, which has to be 1065 BCE, the year when the lunar eclipse so described actually occurred. Two others together identify his 42nd year as being the first year of his last nine, when he claimed to be universal king, the year being when Jupiter was in Chun Huo, and also being the next year after a conjunction marking the transfer of heaven's Mandate to Zhou. That year thus can be exactly identified, as 1058, making his first year 1099 and his last 1050. Two other sources say he reigned for 50 years. Yet two others say or imply that he reigned for 52 years. One of these, the *Bamboo Annals*, places his first year in a narrative reaching back to the time of his grandfather. This one gives exact dates, 1113-1062; but it also dates the conjunction to 1071, twelve years early, and the conjunction date is tied to Zhou chronology (Wen Wang had just nine more years); so Wen Wang's dates in the *Annals* must be corrected to 1101-1050.[38] This is 2 + 50 years, not just 50.

For Wu Wang, probably because of the brevity of his reign and because of the turbulence of the time I find no direct calendar evidence, but traditions are rich implying that he was in mourning at the beginning of

---

center), and that the year ended with day *jiawu*, *yiwei*, or *bingshen*. The only such year in the possible time range was 1077. One other proof: The enfeoffment of Tangshu Yu as first lord of Jin is dated (incorrectly) in the *Annals* 1035, and the *Guoyu* ("Jin Yu" 4.1) says that in the year Tangshu got his appointment Jupiter was in Da Huo, its middle lunar lodge being Fang. This required that the conjunction of 1059, containing Jupiter, had to be considered to be in Da Huo (since 1059 is 2 x 12 years earlier than 1035, and 12 years was thought to be one Jupiter cycle), i.e., in Jupiter station 10; whereas its actual location was in Chun Shou, station 6. The date in Di Xin's reign therefore got raised by 4; and also this implied that 1050 was a Chun Huo (station 7) year for Jupiter, and thus (following the *Guo yu* "Zhou Yu" 3.7) must (it was thought) be the year of the Zhou conquest of Shang. But Wen Wang was known to have had nine more years of life after the conjunction. To resolve this difficulty, the date of the conjunction had to be moved back one Jupiter cycle to 1071, still with the (altered) year number in Di Xin's reign. His first year thus got moved back a total of 4 + 12 = 16 years, to its present location in the *Annals*, which is 1102. So the original date for Di Xin 1 must have been 1086.

[37] *Xia-Shang-Zhou duandai gongcheng: 1996-2000 nian jieduan chengguo baogao (jian ben)* 夏商周斷代工程：1996－2000 年階段成果報告 (簡本) (Beijing: Shijie Tushu Chuban Gongsi, 2000) p. 44; For Yu Xingwu's actual view, that *sui* means "year" in this inscription, see Yu Xingwu, "Li gui Mingwen Kaoshi"利簋銘文考釋, *Wenwu* 1977.8 pp. 10-12. (Prof. Yu, now deceased, was one of the most distinguished scholars working on ancient inscriptions.)

[38] For sources and analysis, see D. Nivison, "The Key to the Chronology of the three dynasties," pp. 3-5; D. Nivison, "The Chronology of the Three Dynasties," in Suppes, Moravcsik, and Mendell, eds. *Ancient and Medieval Traditions in the Exact Sciences* (Stanford: CSLI Publications, 2000) pp. 206-207; and D. Nivison, "The Dates of Western Chou," *Harvard Journal of Asiatic Studies* 43 (1983) pp. 518-524.

his reign (e.g., the chapter on Bo Yi and Shu Qi, first of the biographical chapters in the *Shiji*). From there on the most impressive evidence is the overarching analysis one must make to account for precise dates in old texts and in bronze inscriptions. The picture that results is given you in four diagrams explaining how *Bamboo Annals* dates were got from true dates. This (I argue) was done by deleting mourning periods from the reigns of the three kings between Wu Wang and Mu Wang, and from the reigns of the five kings after Mu Wang who succeeded their fathers. The implication is that Mu Wang's reign, 55 years in all sources but one (one giving 50, accepted by Karlgren, must be a garble) -- 962-908 in the *Annals* -- represents a stretching, (2 x 3 =) 6 years back and (2 x 5 =) 10 years down. So his actual reign must have been 2 + 37 years, 956/954-918. This can be confirmed by bronze inscription dates.[39]

5.8.2 In my handout I give you more evidence, most of it from Western Zhou bronze inscription dates, for this institution of a two-year period at the beginning of a reign that is normally not included in the reign of record. What we find is that most Western Zhou kings had two *yuan* years two years apart, required by different documents: the actual succession year and the actual third year. The most important evidence (because the most intractable for anyone rejecting this Nivison-Shaughnessy "two *yuan*" hypothesis) comes from the reigns of Cheng Wang, Kang Wang, Mu Wang, Gong Wang, and Xuan Wang. To summarize material in my handout: (1) In Cheng Wang's reign, the *Annals* gives both the 5th year and the 7th year for the founding of Luoyang; and while the "Luo Gao" in the *Shang shu* clearly dates the last year of the Zhou Gong Regency to his 7th year, hence to Cheng Wang's 7th year, the He *zun* inscription, which appears to belong to the same year, is dated "5th year." (2) In Kang Wang's reign, dates in the "Bi Ming" chapter of the *Shang shu* and in the Xiao Yu *ding* inscription require *yuan* years two years apart. (3) In Mu Wang's reign (e.g.) the 27th year Qiu Wei *gui* and the 34th year Xian *gui* require *yuan* years two years apart. (4) In Gong Wang's reign, two bronze inscriptions that actually name Gong Wang require *yuan* years two years apart. (5) In Xuan Wang's reign, all bronze inscriptions prior to the middle of 809 require the *yuan* year 827, and all after that, except for two provincial inscriptions, require as *yuan* year 825.

There is much more evidence for Xuan Wang's reign. Especially interesting is the Bo Ke *hu* inscription, unfortunately on a lost bronze vessel. No king is mentioned. It says that Bo Ke, the maker, received a gift of thirty servants (or slaves) from a high government official, "Bo Da-shi"白大師. The expression of gratitude then refers to this dignitary as *Tian you wang bo* 天右王白. Obviously, if these phrases refer to the same person, 白 cannot be a name; it must be 伯. The meaning of the longer phrase must be "the lord functioning as king, with Heaven's help." No one but Gong He could be so addressed. The date, "16th year, 7th month, *jishengbo* (2nd quarter), day *yiwei* (32)" is satisfied by the date 5 June or 4 August 826, assuming 841 as year 1, and 826 as beginning with the pre- or post-solstice month. If this is right, Gong He was still functioning as regent in the last year of mourning for Li Wang, with his calendar still continuing.[40] This shouldn't be surprising: Xuan Wang probably had been far away in the Fen Valley with his father, and organizing a new administration would take much time.

5.8.3 Another piece of information also concerns Gong He, still later in the reign of Xuan Wang. Gong was a domain in Wey (Wey was then a major state) apparently belonging to the ruling line, and thus "Gong" was their surname. In the 13th year of Xi 釐 Hou of Wey King Li of Zhou fled into exile. Xi Hou died in his 42nd year, 813. The *Shiji* ("Wey Shijia," *Shiji* 37) says that the heir-prince was Gong Bo Yu 共伯餘, who was displaced by a younger brother named Gong Bo He 共伯和 in 812, this younger brother then succeeding as Wu 武 Hou, reigning for 55 years. (After 771, as a reward for loyal service, Ping Wang raised his status, so that history knows him as Wu Gong.)

Sima Qian has obviously mixed up Gong Bo Yu and Gong Bo He. It must have been the latter, our Gong He, who was the legitimate heir. (It is unlikely that there would be two such prominent men of Wey with exactly the same name, so close together in time. Sima Qian was unaware that "the Gong He Regency"

---

[39] See pp. 217-218; also Nivison, "Key" (1999) and N 2002 sections 3 and 8.

[40] Shaughnessy 1991 (p. 285) dates the Bo Ke *hu* in 842, 16th year counting from 857, which I recognize as the accession year of Li Wang. To do this, I think one would have to see Gong He as having already assumed power in the middle of 842, continuing the Li Wang calendar, and not starting his own calendar until the next year. Perhaps this is possible. But it requires supposing that already by the middle of 842 the tumult of the king's expulsion has passed completely, and that Gong He is comfortably established, his new position taken for granted.

was the regency of a man named Gong He.) He's younger brother Gong Yu, with his followers, attacked Gong He at their father's tomb, and forced Gong He to retreat into the tunnel entrance, where he committed suicide. (Therefore mourning for Gong He was complete in 809; this must be why 809 is the year when the royal court started using Xuan Wang's accession calendar.) What is interesting is that Gong He, the heir, and therefore chief mourner for their father, was in lonely vigil at the tomb, and unprotected, even though he must have been a very old man. The attack on him was in the second year of mourning for Xi Hou. It seems evident that the three-years mourning institution was alive and well at this time, both at the royal court and in at least one of the major regional states.[41]

XI

5.9 Now, what next? What happens after the destruction of the Western Zhou state in 771 and the feeble survival of the Zhou line of kings thereafter in Luoyang? I find no evidence of the two-*yuan* institution after 771. But we do have the following, from the backward-looking *Gongyang zhuan* after the end of "Eastern Zhou" and the "Warring States" era that was the setting of Mengzi's consultations with the heir-prince of Teng. I quote from the Nivison-Shaughnessy article in the current issue of *Early China*:[42]

5.9.1 First, the *Chunqiu* text, for the 9th year of Wen Gong of Lu, 618 BCE:

9th year, spring: Lord Mao came seeking money.

Then the *Gongyang* commentary:[43]

Q: Who was Lord Mao?
A: He was a grand officer of the Son of Heaven
Q: Why is he not called a [royal] emissary?
A: Because this happened during mourning. [The king] had not yet become ruler (*jun*). It was only the succession year.
Q: Why does one say that the king had not yet become ruler?
A: He had taken his position (*ji wei*), but he did not yet call himself king (*cheng wang*)....

The Nivison-Shaughnessy article continues, paraphrasing: The *Gongyang zhuan* text goes on to explain why these things are so: The concept of being a subject requires that one cannot be without a ruler for a single day; but the concept of continuity requires not only that there cannot be two rulers in one year, but also that there cannot be a blank year without a ruler; and the ideal of filiality requires that for three years one cannot bear to supplant one's parent.

What can be inferred from this? Notice the obvious tension between the value of due ritual respect for the defunct ruler, and the anxiety about the necessity of there being absolutely no hiatus between reigns: "One must never be without a ruler." It appears that by now the idea of having the new ruler delay picking up the reins of government until after the required months of mourning is an idea that has been deliberately dropped. So the *Gongyang zhuan* does not contradict my interpretation of the Teng story. On the contrary, it supports that interpretation.

---

[41] *Shiji* (4.23a in Qing court Wuying Dian edition in Taipei Yiwen Yinshuguan photolith) "Zhou Benji," has a long note by Zhang Shoujie 張守節 (Tang Dynasty, i.e., *Shiji Zhengyi*) after the text on the Gong He Regency. Zhang of course knows what the *Annals* account is, but he decides it must be wrong, and assumes that the *Shiji* is right in identifying Gong He as Wu Gong. The account of the suicide at the tomb is in *Shiji* ("Wey Shijia") 37.2b.

[42] Nivison, David S., and Edward L. Shaughnessy, The Jin Hou Su Bells Inscription and Its Implications for the Chronology of Early China," *Early China* 25 (2000: actually 2002, pp. 29-48), p. 39.

[43] Prof. David W. Pankenier called my attention to this *Gongyang* material.

5.9.2 I have had to reject Yang Ximei's thesis that the Teng heir-prince wanted to honor his father with rites proper for a *tianzi*. This idea reads into Mengzi a concern belonging to an earlier time. The *Lun yu* is loaded with the Master's criticisms of prominent persons in recent history (such as Guan Zhong) for grasping for ritual display to which they were not entitled; but in Mengzi's time it was taken for granted that sooner or later, and probably sooner, some state ruler would unite the world and replace the Zhou king. But Yang was right in seeing that it was something about the character of the proposed mourning revival, and not its mere length, which the prince's critics were resisting.

XII

He is, I think, right about something else, which stands out at the end of the story in the *Mengzi*. The people, attracted from far and wide by the report of the prince's filiality, were "delighted" with his apparently genuine display of grief. The officials and kinsmen had been won over. Even for his withdrawal from government functioning (at least during the five months culminating in the burial), he was praised as one who knew the rites. Yang's suggestion is that the mourning program had the function of reassuring the populace and officers in place: their new ruler was a person with a character that made him fit to rule, and would rule not arbitrarily but always with restraint, and with a due regard for hallowed custom.

If it is right to see the three years mourning as a regimen qualifying the new ruler-designate on such psychological-moral grounds, this suggests another more interesting question. It is often observed -- reasonably, I think -- that religious beliefs and forms gradually evolve. In early times we see literal belief, peoples even virtually convinced that they see and hear their gods and spirits, to whom they appeal with genuine dread. There follows a falling off of literal belief, replaced with psychological and moralistic justification for religious discipline. In China Confucius perhaps is transitional. By the third century Xunzi is clearly "enlightened," almost a Santayana-like atheist. The value of rite is how it displays and what it does to human character. So we can ask, if Yang is right about mourning as a moral-psychological qualifying discipline for Warring States rulers (at least minor ones), what then had been the way in which it filled this qualifying role in earlier ages? In ages when the gods were all too real, and rituals and sacrifices were accorded them out of genuine dread?

5.9.3 My guess -- it's a guess -- is this. The king, or lord, or lineage head, was the mediator in relations between the human world and the world of spirit powers. He alone could perform the most important sacrifices. Shang oracle inscriptions show that the archaic Chinese king was the chief diviner, in this role both ascertaining the will of the spirits and securing their favor for the community, their aid in war, their granting of rain, of success in the hunt. It was he and his staff of diviners who determined which offended ancestor spirit was causing sickness. When the sick person was someone other than himself, apparently, shaman-like, he could effect a cure by offering himself to the irate spirit as a surrogate victim, then using his ritual powers to protect himself.[44]

I have used the controversial word "shaman" here, but I will not argue that the archaic Chinese king was essentially a shaman. This kind of essentialism magnifies a concept when we should be looking at details. Some of the details fit the concept, and some do not. The king is cool. He doesn't go into trances, display what some students have called "arctic hysteria." (Though he does have weird dreams, which must be interpreted. There was even a technical literature for the purpose.[45]) But he does have very striking numinous powers. Do these powers flow to him simply because of his position? This probably is a

---

[44] This curing capacity of the Shang king is analyzed in D. S. Nivison, ""Virtue" in Bone and Bronze," included in Nivison (edited by Bryan Van Norden), *The Ways of Confucianism: Investigations in Chinese Philosophy,* (Chicago and La Salle: Open Court, 1996) pp. 17-23.

[45] Such dream-interpretation texts appear to be listed in *Yi Zhou shu* #45 "Wu Jing."

necessary condition, but it is not likely to be a sufficient one.

My suggestion is that when the time came for him to assume this position, he had to submit to a disciplined ordeal that had the function of an initiation; and that this ordeal was the three-years mourning for his predecessor, usually his father. If this is right, the three-years mourning as observed by his new subjects assured them that he was indeed "the one man," a fully qualified ruler. And it also assured the ancestor spirits that the dynastic line was in good hands, and that he was fully qualified for his ritual-sacrificial role. But over and above this, the ordeal itself created in him the power to approach spiritual beings. The ascetic details alone suggest this. And the requirement of ritual silence, especially, suggests it.

XIII

5.10 It is now possible to review the history of the three-years mourning institution and its interaction with power, and consequently with chronology. As far back as I can reach toward its beginnings, I see it as an absolute religious obligation to very real, even dreadful spirit powers (powers, we should remember, that demanded that kings offer human sacrifices). The requirements were at this early time so severe that they took all of the time and energy of the king-to-be. At this stage the new king was not quite king, and the deceased king was not quite gone. There was, therefore, not the danger we might suppose to dynastic continuity. To take advantage of the new king's incapacity so as to displace him would be to incur the quite dreadful wrath of the spirits. Therefore the mourning interval could with relative safety be a period when there was "no king," a genuine interregnum. So it was in the Xia era.

Tang, in displacing the Xia king, had to deal with the dangers of religious transgression. The defunct king was carefully mourned by the whole people, but still there ensued years of drought, ended only by Tang offering himself as a victim. Moreover, the beginning of a new dynastic power was a time of vulnerability, especially for the first successor to the founder. Even in the Xia this had been true. Qi, Yu's son and successor, had finally to kill his father's minister Yi.[46] At the beginning of Shang, Yi Yin took advantage of this vulnerability, and almost succeeded.

The power of the spirits was weakening, enough to make interregnum-at-succession impossible. Yi Yin's stratagem of using uncles as stand-in kings actually provided the precedent for a solution: fraternal succession, i.e., an interval of rule by a junior uncle to the heir. The heir was thus able to discharge his mourning obligations without danger to the succession. But the superseded interregnum institution had an echo in the handling of the calendar: a king's reign -- even the reign of a royal brother, which did require some mourning -- could not formally begin with a new royal calendar until mourning was complete. Eventually, as I have explained, regular fraternal succession stopped working for political reasons: the opportunity for usurpation that had been denied the prime minister was available to the stand-in younger brother, and sooner or later a younger brother was bound to use it, by having his own son succeed himself. Even so, Wu Ding, son of younger brother Xiao Yi, must have had a credibility problem, both with the ancestors and with his subjects. It is therefore perhaps not by accident that he was remembered above others for his rigorous observance of the mourning rites.[47]

This background helps to explain the suspicions entertained by the Zhou royal uncles, of the Duke of Zhou, paradigmatic prime minister and younger brother, at an especially vulnerable time for the new Zhou

[46] The "modern text" *Bamboo Annals* has perhaps been cleansed at this point. The information is found in an "ancient text" fragment, variously quoted in the biography of Shu Xi in the *Jin shu*, and in Liu Zhiji 劉知幾, *Shi Tong* 史通, chapters "Yi Gu" and "Za Shuo." [But Lei Xueqi disagrees, pointing out that the text seen by Du Yu in 280 could not have had this account. (*Kaoding Zhushu jinian: Jinian bian wu*, "Bian Jin shu zhi Wu."辨晉書之誤) Perhaps the account comes from the *Suoyu* 瑣語, another bamboo tomb text.]

[47] In the circumstances, if Xiao Yi was to secure the succession for his son, he could not use another younger brother as stand-in, even if there was yet another surviving younger brother. Wu Ding had to do it all himself, as king.

Dynasty. His actions -- dramatically surrendering his power to the heir-prince -- insured the stability of father-son succession. The mourning obligation continued, probably with much less pressure on the heir, and with it there continued the Shang precedent of post-mourning calendars. The post-mourning calendar both expressed the piety of the heir, and allowed the ordinary man who happened to have his own mourning obligation to avoid ritually departing from his father's ways until that obligation was discharged.[48]

With the destruction of the Western Zhou power in 771 and the powerless regimes in Luoyang propped up by the more powerful regional lords, the double-*yuan* system disappeared altogether. Even before 771, regional states had been ignoring it (as the Jin Hou Su bell set inscription shows). Religious sanctions were still further weakening. And for most purposes, people were no longer using the royal calendar anyway. But as the *Gongyang zhuan* shows, the echo of mourning in required political language died slowly, and probably was still detectable in Chunqiu times.

5.10.1 What, then, was Mengzi up to in his advice to the heir-prince of Teng? He was reviving not inventing. Even if perhaps the reviving was creative in detail, it was the reviving of a religious institution in moral garments . In Teng it went amusingly far: the young prince was even persuaded to keep his hands off government business. There was little of that that mattered, in tiny Teng, a sub-marginal political entity.[49] But the story did matter. True or not, it is a story that China never forgot.

So on the one hand one cannot say that Mengzi is not sometimes embroidering history. [50] The institution of three-years mourning as he idealizes it may no longer have existed anywhere; and what its exact form was earlier is arguable. On the other hand, when one follows chronology as a clue, to trace the institution back into its past, the indications are that the farther back one goes, the stronger the institution was, and the more severe were its demands on kings. Its beginnings are forever lost in prehistory.

The value of an institution, we want to say, is a matter completely separate from its history; but we always find it difficult to keep history and value distinct. (In ordinary life perhaps we shouldn't necessarily separate them; but in doing history we should never assume something couldn't have been so simply because we don't like it.) Wang Guowei thought the Xia interregnums in the *Bamboo Annals* were supposed to be mourning-completion periods. He rejects them as invented.[51] But Wang, actually a traditionalist himself, rejects them because he thinks that everything in the book that he cannot find a source for is invented. On the other hand, Chen Li, who is my ally in recognizing a measure of authenticity in the *Annals*, nevertheless also thinks that these interregnums are invention. They must be, because the antiquity of the three-years mourning institution was what everyone assumed since Warring States China, but that's all wrong: he adds, "We now know that three years of mourning was not practiced during the Xia." For him, the matter does not even merit a footnote.[52]

---

[48] This principle accounts for an apparent "post-mourning" calendar [perhaps in Wu Wang's name: Chapter Nine, sections 1 and 4] beginning in 1056, two years after Wen Wang had proclaimed a change of the Mandate to Zhou in 1058. The matter is analyzed, with appropriate text, in Nivison, "The Dates of Western Chou," pp. 530-531.

[49] The *Jinben Zhushu jinian* ("modern text" *Bamboo Annals*) dates an ending of Teng by the Yue state in 415. Apparently this was not final.

[50] This aspect of Mengzi's thinking is explored in D. S. Nivison, "Mengzi as Philosopher of History," in Alan K. L. Chan, ed., *Mencius: Contexts and Interpretations*, Honolulu: University of Hawai'i Press, 2002, pp. 282-304.

[51] See Wang's long note at the end of the chronicle for Xia, in his Jinben Zhushu jinian shuzheng 今本竹書紀年疏證.

[52] Chen Li, "Fresh Evidence for the Authenticity of *Jinben Zhushu Jinian*," (*Social Sciences in China* 1993.3, October, vol. 14 no. 3;. (This is a partial translation of Chen Li, "Jinben *Zhushu jinian* Yanjiu," *Sichuan Daxue Xuebao Congkan* no. 28) p. 107. For the Chinese original text of Chen's article, see *Jinben lunji* pp. 143-171), p. 160. (The translator's name is given as Chen Tifang.)

Chapter Six

"Zai Tan Jinben *Zhushu Jinian* yu Sandai Niandaixue"

再談"今本"竹書記年與三代年代學

The International Symposium on the Chronology of Xia, Shang and Zhou Beijing, October 2003
(apparently cancelled)

Outline of Nivison's argument in "Zai Tan" paper for Beijing conference originally scheduled Oct 2003

First:

It is a mistake to "standardize" a chronology (or any set of statements of fact). At most, it is reasonable to publish a set of dates describing it as what most scholars accept, if there actually is a consensus. It is especially dangerous for an institution or government enjoying or needing public trust to try to promote a "standard" chronology. If advances in scholarship show that what was published as "standard" is wrong, many people will have been misled, and the institution's reputation will have been needlessly damaged. In particular, the PRC government risks misleading the public and damaging its own prestige, if at the present time it endorses a chronology of the Three Dynasties. At the very least, a consensus must first be reached as to the authenticity of the "Modern Text" *Bamboo Annals*, and as to the usability of this text for ascertaining correct dates. (The Xia-Shang-Zhou Project has ignored this text.)

Second:

This risk is not trivial, because (1) there is a reasonable probability that all of the dates in the "Modern Text" are the dates in the original, i.e., they are authentic; and (2) there is also a reasonable probability that if they are authentic, they can be used to infer correct dates that are very different from or other than dates published by the PRC's Xia-Shang-Zhou Project.

As for (1), consider the date in the *Annals* of rites on day *gengshen* (57), 7th month, year 50, of Huang Di. A date as precise and as far back as this must be a calculation (i.e., neither a record nor an arbitrary invention). I work out the calculation, following *Annals* usage indicating the date should be the first day of the month:

a) The "Modern Text" and "Ancient Text" taken together date Huang Di's rites on *gengshen* (57) to 2353 BCE.
b) 2353 is 100 *zhang* (1900 years) before 453, when the "Three Jin" defeated Zhi Bo, gaining independence.
c) In the *zhang-bu* system, to get the cycle-day 20 zhang earlier than a given date, one counts back 15 days.
d) The 1st of the Xia 7th month of 453 was *yihai* (12); so the 1st of the 7th month of 2353 must be *gengshen.*

My precise calculation is almost certainly correct, and if correct it almost certainly shows that all of the "Modern Text" dates are authentic.

As for (2), as an example I use data in the "Modern Text" to get a complete chronology (to the exact day) for Xia reigns, with four astronomical confirmations (conjunctions, an eclipse, and first days of lunar months):

a) Pankenier has shown that the conjunction of 1953 dates Shun's transfer of power to Yu in Shun 14.
b) The *Annals* says that on the 1st of the 9th month of the 5th year of Zhong Kang the sun was eclipsed.
c) The *Zuo zhuan* puts the eclipse in Fang. and implies it was not in Xia but near enough to be reported.
d) Using *Annals* reign lengths and making interregnums (for mourning) 2 years, the date is 16 Oct 1876.
e) On that date there was a solar eclipse, north of Xia but reportable. The sun was in Fang at the time.
f) The same calculation shows that the first day of the reign of the 14th king Kong Jia was 17 Feb 1577.
g) This day was a *jiazi* day (1st in the 60-day cycle), explaining why the king was called "Kong Jia."
h) Pankenier has shown that the last year of Xia was 496 years before the conjunction of 1059, i.e., 1555.
i) The same count (*Annals* reign lengths, 2-year gaps) gives 1555 as the last year of Fa, next-to-last king.
j) So Di Gui (= "Jie") must be an invention. There is abundant evidence for this judgment.

The Project merely offers approximate dates for the beginning and end of Xia, without dates of reigns.

I then show how two implications from (2) can be applied to *Annals* data for Shang and Western Zhou, to recover probably correct dates, very different from the Project's dates: (a) While the *Annals* doesn't indicate gaps between reigns in Shang and Western Zhou, gaps can be assumed, and must have been long enough for completion of mourning. (b) In Shang, first days of reigns determined *gan* names of kings.

Conclusion: Even my critics must see that fixing reign dates for the Three Dynasties is at best too risky at present. We should instead be trying to agree on how to evaluate and use the "Modern Text" *Bamboo Annals.*

The International Symposium on the Chronology of Xia, Shang and Zhou
Beijing, October 2003
(apparently cancelled)

"Zai Tan Jinben *Zhushu Jinian* yu Sandai Niandaixue"

再談"今本"竹書紀年與三代年代學

(Further Remarks on the "Modern Text" *Bamboo Annals* and Three Dynasties Chronology; June 2003, revised September and October 2003)[1]

A few decades ago Chinese in the PRC adopted the "Pinyin" system of transcribing the pronunciations of Chinese characters into Roman letters. This system has been adopted by most of the world. It was needed; many systems and non-systems had come into use throughout the world, with attendant confusion. World scholars could not have straightened out the mess by themselves. Most of us were grateful.

One might think that the same could be said for ancient Chinese chronology. There has been a similar world-wide cacophony of different systems. Chinese scholars, in the Xia-Shang-Zhou ("Sandai, Three Dynasties") Project funded and organized by the PRC government, have worked out and (tentatively) published a chronology of the Three Dynasties, detailed back to late Shang. It seems that it is to be adopted as standard by Chinese schools and reference books in the PRC. So perhaps we all should gratefully adopt this too. We sense that this is expected of us.

But there is a difference between a system of transcription and a set of dates. A system of transcription becomes correct simply by being adopted. A set of dates does not "become" correct. It either is correct or it is not. A set of dates is a set of statements of fact, and it is correct only if those statements are true. The very notion of making such a set "standard" is a conceptual mistake. One could report a consensus, if there were one; but there is none.

The mistake is serious. One risks misleading millions of students, and many thousands of scholars and journalists worldwide with interests in China but with no specialization in chronology that would enable them to criticize what they are offered. A government endorsing such a set of dates takes a more unpleasant risk. Scholarship goes on, and will go on. New things will be discovered, and there is the possibility that this set of dates will soon be shown to be obviously and absurdly wrong. Any institution that has endorsed the set risks being made to look foolish. This is a risk that the Chinese government does not need to take. It is a risk that its leading scholars ought to be warning it not to take.

The work of American scholars on the "Modern" Text of the *Bamboo Annals* ("Jinben" *Zhushu jinian*) gives a measure of this risk. The Sandai Project has ignored this text. But this text has a set of dates reaching back to the late 2000's BCE. The dominant view has been that this is all the product of recent arbitrary invention, perhaps as late as the Ming Dynasty. But there is the possibility that it is the work of specialists in the 4th Century BCE. It is easily shown that many of the dates are wrong. But if they are the work of Warring States thinking it may be possible to work back through that thinking to find out what the real dates are. And it is also not hard to show that if this is the case, the work of the Sandai Project will probably have to be discarded.

---

[1] My studies leading to this article began in a sense as far back as 1979, in a seminar on bronze inscriptions led by me at Stanford University. Members of the seminar included David N. Keightley, David W. Pankenier, and Edward L. Shaughnessy. I am indebted to all three for stimulating criticism as well as for direct contributions to my research (especially to Pankenier, as my references to his discoveries will show). My work came to the attention of Prof. Li Xueqin in 1981, and I take this opportunity to thank Prof. Li for his encouragement and generous praise of my work, then and later. In the past three years, I have benefited especially from collaboration in *Annals* studies with my colleague Shao Dongfang, now Curator of the East Asia Library in the Stanford University Library system.

In ignoring this text, the Project's work exhibits what may be called the "safe evidence fallacy." True, in *building a case* for a theory, one naturally wants to base one's arguments primarily on the best evidence available. But in *defending one's theory against attack*, one must consider all of the evidence, and apparent evidence, that could be brought against it. And so, in building one's case, one must also anticipate criticism, by carefully weighing all the evidence, including conflicting evidence, discarding evidence only after giving an adequate explanation of it.[2] Wang Guowei tried to do this with the "Modern Text" *Annals*, by showing where a faker could have got his material. But Wang did not account for the dates in that text. This is something that the Project needed to do – or admit doubt if it could not -- because its primary concern was dates. To ignore conflicting material simply because you prefer material that supports your conclusion is to argue in a circle.

The Project has committed the same error in other ways (as have other scholars). Perhaps the most famous is the problem of the location of the planet Jupiter at the time of the Zhou conquest of Shang. The *Guoyu,* "Zhou Yu" , says that Jupiter was in station 7, Chun Huo (Quail Fire), perhaps implying the date 1046. But a note in Yang Liang's commentary to the *Xunzi*, "Ru Xiao" chapter, quotes an advisor to Wu Wang saying that Jupiter was "in the north," and this means that the planet was in station 12, 1 or 2, which would make 1046 impossible. The Project, and Professor Li Xueqin (and Professor Pankenier in the United States), accept the *Guoyu* account and ignore Yang Liang's material.[3] The task here is not just to argue that one account is more probable than the other, but to explain how the account you reject could have come into existence, and be believed and recorded, if it is not true. If you can't do this, you should admit that your conclusion is little better than a guess.

The Project commits the same error in other damaging ways. For example, in analyzing dates in bronze inscriptions, it ignores the Xiao Yu *ding*, which is explicitly a Kang Wang object because it identifies Cheng Wang as predecessor. It is true that the vessel is lost, and rubbings of the long text are very bad, so bad that the day date at the beginning is illegible. But the day is deducible from the text farther on. If one accepts this bad text as evidence and if one also accepts the explicit Kang Wang date (from the *Han shu*) in the otherwise lost "Bi Ming" chapter of the *Shang shu*, one must conclude that the Nivison-Shaughnessy double *yuan* hypothesis is true, and all of the chronology for Western Zhou must be redone. By eliminating the Xiao Yu *ding* as unsafe, the Project is able to avoid even mentioning Nivison-Shaughnesy.

I will now give two arguments that will show how real is the danger that the Project's conclusions will be shown to be wrong. The first argument shows that the dates in the "Modern Text" *Bamboo Annals* are almost certainly the dates in the original text. The second argument will show that if this is so then one cannot construct a Three Dynasties chronology if one ignores this material.

---

[2] The requirement that pseudo-evidence be explained can be seen by considering what a laboratory scientist would have to do if two tests – e.g., two C14 datings -- gave sharply conflicting results. If no more tests could be made, one could not simply accept one result and forget the other. One would want to find a reason why the rejected result ought not to be trusted, e.g., by finding a reason to believe there was contamination, or some procedural mistake. In the C14 case, one normally could perform more tests, perhaps finding that they all agreed with the result you believed to be right. But the historian cannot do this when evaluating conflicting testimony. A detective might generate more testimony by asking people questions; but a historian (like a detective in many ways, as Collingwood noticed) cannot generate more testimony from living people. If a historian rejects a statement in a text, he has to provide a plausible explanation why it's there. If he doesn't, he leaves open the possibility that he has made the wrong choice. And if he simply can't, he probably has made the wrong choice.

[3] Professor Pankenier does try to deal with the "north" problem in his Stanford doctoral dissertation. I think the attempt fails, and as far as I know he has ignored the problem in publications since then.

I

I turn first to the pre-dynastic chronicles at the very beginning of the *Modern Text Bamboo Annals*. By "pre-dynastic" I mean preceding the "Three Dynasties" Xia, Shang and Zhou, understanding Yao and Shun (treated separately) to be part of the story of Yu, the first ruler of the Xia. The rulers covered here are Huang Di, Di Zhi (Shao Hao), ZhuanXu, Di Ku, and Zhi (son of Di Ku). All of these may be completely mythical, but they would have been considered historical by the compilers of the *Zhushu jinian*.

Dates are not given in *Jinben* before the first year of Yao, dated year *bingzi* (13), which was (in effect) 2145 BCE. But reign lengths are given for Huang Di (100 years), Zhuan Xu (78 years) Di Ku (63 years) and Zhi (9 years). All these reign lengths are found also in *guben* fragments. There is a vitally important *Guben* fragment[4] with the information that there was a seven-year interval of mourning between Huang Di and Zhuan Xu under the leadership of an official named Zuo Che; and this information is not in the *Jinben*.

Di Zhi between Huang Di and Zhuan Xu is well-known as Shao Hao, but there is no chronicle for him here. He probably was not in the original text, but was added by Shen Yue (441-513, Liu Song, Qi and Liang Dynasties), or someone later. Shen is identified as the author of the brief commentary explaining the origin of Di Zhi. This commentary was probably at first simply a note by Shen Yue on the name Shao Hao in the commentary text on Zhuan Xu's origins. Shen Yue's interest in this mythical figure is explained by the fact that Shen claimed descent from "Shao Hao."[5]

Thus, the intended date of the beginning of Huang Di's reign is 2145 + 9 + 63 + 78 + 7 + 100, = 2402 BCE. This makes possible an inference that cannot be ignored by *Zhushu jinian* criticism. In the middle of the *Jinben* Huang Di chronicle, and exactly in the middle of his supposed reign, is a record of rites and following events (natural and human), dated Huang Di 50, month 7, day *gengshen* (57). There is no *guben* version of this line.[6] There is evidence in other parts of the book that in a date of this kind the named day is often to be understood as the first day of the lunar month. It is not conceivable that this is a record, nor is it conceivable that such precision is merely blind and arbitrary invention. The date was calculated; but how?

Huang Di 50 has to be 2353 BCE. Any calculation of a date in remote past time, done in the 4th century BCE, would use the *zhang-bu* system. One *zhang* is 19 years of 365 ¼ days each, rounded to 6940 days total (235 lunar months, 7 intercalary). One *bu* is 4 *zhang*, minus one day, = 76 years, 27759 days. A *bu* is named for its first day in the 60-day cycle, which is unique in a series of 20 *bu*, = 1520 years. The cycle of *zhang* and *bu* then begins again, with the same first days in the 60-day cycle for every lunar month therein. If one is figuring back only 20 *zhang* from a certain first-of-month date, one must move back through the cycle 15 days, so that in 80 *zhang* one gets back to where one started.

Suppose that the calculator was doing his work in Da Liang, the capital of the Wei state, in the late 4th century BCE. We must find the date where the calculator began counting. That date must have been the first day of the 7th lunar month, in the Xia calendar (taking the year as starting with the pre-spring-equinox month), of the year 453 BCE, when Zhao, Han and Wei defeated Xun Yao, lord of Zhi, thus gaining their *de facto* independence. The year 453 was thus *the most important year in the entire history of the state of Wei.* 2353 is 100 *zhang* back from 453, = 80 + 20 *zhang*. The day that began the Xia 7th month of 453 was *in fact* day *yihai* (12). We can disregard 80 *zhang*, because it brings us back to *yihai*. 20 *zhang* farther back requires moving the first day of the 7th month back 15 days, from *yihai* (12, = 60 + 12 = 72) to *gengshen* (57), the day named in the Huang Di chronicle.

---

[4] This Guben fragment is quoted in the *Lu shi* 路 史 ("Hou Ji" 後 紀 6) by Luo Bi 羅 泌 (12th century CE). (Fang Shiming 方 詩 銘 and Wang Xiuling 王 修 齡, *Guben Zhushu Jinian Jizheng* 古 本 竹 書 紀 年 輯 證 (Shanghai: Shanghai Guji Chubanshe, 1981, p. 170; 2005 edition p. 180.)

[5] See Shen's autobiography at the end of his *Song shu.*

[6] The line is repeated in the long mythic commentary text that immediately follows, and this commentary text, with other similar ones, appears in Shen Yue's *Song shu* "Fu Rui Zhi"; but these texts are not identified there as from the *Jinian*, nor have *Jinian* scholars claimed them as from the *Jinian* original text. On the contrary the claim has been that they were copied into the *Jinben* by its purported forger. If the *Jinian* is not a forgery, then presumably these texts, unless otherwise marked, were part of the original.

Have I reconstructed the reasoning of the compiler? It seems inconceivable that the exact and detailed calculation just given could be merely mine and not also his. A critic will properly object that one must guess why the 1st of the 7th month was important. Was it the date of the victory celebration? Or merely the exact middle day of the year. And why prefigure the event in the imaginary reign of Huang Di?

These are fair questions, but the need for guesswork in answering them does not much diminish the likelihood that my calculation is the calculation of the authors of the original text as buried. To work this out I needed both *Jinben* and *Guben*, and this ties *Jinben* and *Guben* together. Without the line in the *Jinben* chronicle dating the rites to day *gengshen*, there would have been no problem to discuss. Without the Zuo Che seven years supplied by the quotation from the *Lu shi*, the first year of Huang Di could not have been fixed at 2402, and the 50th year could not have been fixed at 2353. The *Jinben* does not even have an entry for the year 453. The restorers must have been aware of its importance, but they had not yet found a slip with the record of the allied victory. For that record we must look at another *Guben* text implied in the *Shiji suoyin* by Sima Zhen of Tang.

If we do accept this explanation for the date "50th year, 7th month, day *gengshen,*" it tends to confirm the authenticity (not the truth, of course) of the entire *Jinben* chronology. It might have been possible for some later hand to alter the dates in it locally, for example, by switching two reigns while leaving the set of two occupying the same time-span; or (as in the forty-year interregnum between Xiang and Shao Kang of Xia) to invent dates within a fixed interval. But the standing assumption has to be that the dates in the *Jinben*, however expressed, are the dates that were put there by the hands that finalized the text in 299 BCE. Those dates, all of them, must be dates that result in the 50th year of Huang Di being 2353 BCE. Anyone who thinks that they were different in any detail bears the burden of proof. One cannot simply assume that some dates were different, or that they were all invented, in order to make one's favorite argument work.[7]

My discussion thus far is designed to persuade you that there is a fair chance that the chronology in the *Bamboo Annals* as we now have it is authentic. By this I mean that there is a good chance that, true or not, it is the chronology that was in the buried text, as finalized in Warring States China. So any chronology that *depends* on assuming that the *Bamboo Annals* is not authentic had better not be published by the Chinese government as authoritative unless the possibility of the *Annals* being authentic has been eliminated.

But does the Project have to assume – as it in fact has done -- that the *Bamboo Annals* is not authentic, and can be safely disregarded? To show that this has to be the Project's precarious position, I move to my second argument.

II

I must now show that if the *Bamboo Annals* chronology is authentically a Warring States creation, then it can be used to obtain what is probably the true chronology of at least a substantial part of Three Dynasties history, different from or other than what the Project has done.

Paradoxically the easiest way to begin to do this is to examine the chronology of Xia in the *Bamboo Annals*. Xia is a time so early that the Project has not tried to offer any exact dates for it at all. It merely

---

7 If this recovery of past calculation is accepted, it does more: Du Yu, the Jin general and scholar who wrote the standard commentary on the *Zuo zhuan*, saw the *Zhushu jinian* only a year or so after its discovery, and he describes what he saw as beginning with Xia. There has been endless argument ever since about the pre-Xia part of it. Was it perhaps added later? The Liu Song historian Pei Yin in his *Shiji jijie*, who seems never to have seen the *Zhushu jinian* himself, quotes other historians' statements about it. Pei (*Shiji jijie* "Wei Shijia" at succession of "Ai Wang") says that "Xun Xu said, and He Qiao agrees, that the *Jinian* begins with Huang Di." So even as early as the Liu Song Dynasty (420-478) there were arguments about this. But now it seems that the Huang Di chronicle is mathematically tied to the rest. Furthermore, both the use of the *zhang-bu* system and the glorification of the state of Wei appear to tie the composition of this date in Huang Di 50 to the middle Warring States era.

tells us that the Xia lasted from about 2070 to about 1600. Many people -- but not I -- even doubt that there was a Xia Dynasty.

In the *Bamboo Annals* Xia is given 471 years, terminating with the victory of Tang of Shang in 1559. Therefore the *Bamboo Annals* is taking 2029 as the first year of Xia. In the *Bamboo Annals* 2029 is the 14th year of Shun, when Shun turned over to Yu the reins of government. (We can call this the *de facto* first year of Xia.) In a very important article published in 1985, David W. Pankenier argues persuasively that this political event must have coincided with a dramatic conjunction of the planets, in February of 1953 BCE. So, cross out 2029 and write in 1953. In due time Shun dies, and there is an interval of three years for mourning for him before Yu formally succeeds. After that, after the death of almost every Xia king, there is an interval when there was no king, apparently for mourning. The intervals vary, but the number of years most often found is two. This would be expected: a king dies, and there must be 25 months of royal inactivity. The mandatory 25 months will be complete some time in year two, counting the year after the predecessor's death as year one. So only in the year after that will the new king's calendar formally begin.

So let us try an experiment: Let's accept Pankenier's date 1953 for the 14th year of Shun. And let's accept the reign lengths after that in the *Bamboo Annals*, and let us suppose that the intervals between reigns were always two years. (After Bu Jiang, who didn't die but resigned, there will be no interval.) Several extraordinary things result from this experiment.

First: The text says that there was a solar eclipse on the first day of the ninth month of the fifth year of the fourth king Zhong Kang. A text in the *Zuo zhuan* says that at the time of the eclipse the sun was in Fang (the fourth lunar mansion); and various accounts have it that border lords who were supposed to report it did not do so, and were punished; thus it was not observable in the Xia capital, but was near enough to be reported.

All of these things are true. The eclipse was discovered by Kevin Pang, who published an article on it with me in 1990. The day given by my experiment turns out to be 16 October 1876 BCE, which is correct. The eclipse was ring-form, and occurred in the morning, north of the Xia domain, and the sun was in Fang at the time.

Second: When in my experiment I get to the 14th Xia king named Kong Jia, I can calculate the first day of his reign, assuming the Xia calendar, which begins the year with the lunar month preceding the month containing the spring equinox. The date was 17 February 1577 BCE. That day was a *jiazi* day, the first day in the 60-day cycle. It is a reasonable assumption that this is why he got the name "Kong Jia," "Great Jia."

Third, Pankenier has shown something else, which he first published in 1983. The *Bamboo Annals* gives the Shang Dynasty 496 years, from 1558, said to be the year following Tang's victory, to 1062, said to be the year of death of Wen Wang of Zhou in the third month, i.e., the first year of effective power of Wu Wang, the conqueror. Both dates are wrong, Pankenier argues, and I agree. The last year of Shang – *de jure*, we might say – ought to be 1059, which was the year of another dramatic conjunction taken as marking the change of Heaven's Mandate in favor of Zhou. (The date of this conjunction in the *Bamboo Annals* is 1071, which is an explainable error.)[8] i.e., 1058 was the year of the Zhou Mandate. Therefore the first year of Shang must have been not 1558 but 1554, which is 496 years back from 1058; and the date of Tang's victory must have been 1555, the last year of the last Xia king.

In the *Bamboo Annals* the last Xia king is Di Gui, better known as Jie. Continuing my experiment to the end, I find that I get to 1555, exactly, not as the last year of Di Gui or Jie, but as the last year of Jie's supposed predecessor Fa. The indicated conclusion is that Jie is imaginary. There was no such king. He

---

[8] My hypothesis: the Wei editors made the creation of Jin (Wei's ancestor state) be 700 years before 335, when the Wei ruler declared himself king. This date 1035 was supposed to be a year when Jupiter was in station 10, Da Huo. Therefore the Zhou conquest had to be in 1050, since it was supposed to have been in a year when Jupiter was in station 7, Chun Huo. But Wen Wang lived nine years after the conjunction. So the conjunction (containing Jupiter) was dated back one 12-year Jupiter cycle to 1071.

is a Warring States invention. I think this is true, and I think the evidence is good. For example (as others have noticed), the narrative for Jie is suspiciously similar to the narrative for the last Shang ruler Di Xin (i.e., Zhou Xin or Shou). But I will not pursue the matter further.[9] The numbers seem to me to be decisive.

Instead, let me sketch a strategy for using two suggested results so far, applying them to the chronology of Shang and of Zhou. The two results:
(1) It appears likely that when a ruler has a *gan* name ("Jia" in "Kong Jia") – as all of the kings of Shang had – the *gan* is the *gan* of the first day of his reign.
(2) Reigns of record did not include a preliminary period for mourning for the preceding king. In effect this will mean that reigns of Shang and Western Zhou kings were normally longer than the *Bamboo Annals* says, longer by just the number of years required for completing mourning.

Received chronologies for Shang and Western Zhou, including those in the *Bamboo Annals*, have the longest reign in the middle of each dynasty. In Shang it is the reign of Tai Wu, a king in the fifth generation; his reign is said to be 75 years. In Western Zhou it is the reign of the fifth king Mu Wang, a reign of 55 years. 75 years is of course impossible, and 55 years is less than likely. The *Bamboo Annals* has fixed dates for the beginning and end of Western Zhou. Perhaps when mourning periods were deleted or ignored for kings before and after Mu Wang, the result was to stretch Mu Wang's reign. Three kings before Mu Wang succeeded their fathers: Cheng Wang, Kang Wang and Zhao Wang. After the fifth king Mu Wang there were seven kings, but two (the eighth and ninth, Xiao Wang and Yi Wang) did not succeed their fathers. Therefore we should try the guess that the *Bamboo Annals* dates for Mu Wang, which are 962-908, should begin six years later and end ten years earlier, making the true dates 956-918. These dates satisfy bronze inscriptions, and solve a vexing problem. The first year of the 7th king Yih Wang is fixed by a solar eclipse in 899. If this is accepted, and one tries to fit in a supposed 55-year reign for Mu Wang, then there is no way to get reign lengths for some of the kings before Mu Wang except by making arbitrary guesses, which do not satisfy other evidence. But if Mu Wang's reign was only 39 years this problem disappears.

There are complications for reigns after Mu Wang, which I pass over now. You will find my solutions in recent articles of mine published (in Chinese) in Taiwan.[10] But it should be obvious that if there is reason to heed *Annals* dates at all, then *Annals* post-Mu Wang dates must be either accepted or explained. The seventh king Yih Wang is given 25 years. The Project gives Yih Wang only eight years. If "8 years" is accepted, "25 years" must be "explained away." I think it cannot be: the reign of record was 25 years (not including two years at the beginning for completion of mourning). If it was this long, then the Project's dates for the next three kings must be completely wrong.

Shang is more complicated, and there is less supporting evidence. (The Project doesn't attempt precise dates before 1250. My methods, using the *Annals*, do much more.) To use the *gan* hypothesis one must use *Bamboo Annals* reign lengths as far as one can, and hunt through Zhang Peiyu's *Zhongguo Xian Qin shili biao* for the most likely first days. One finds at once that the intervals between reigns of record are usually three years rather than two years, i.e., the first year in the mourning interval often has to be the succession year (year of the predecessor's death). Further, the "first day" can be either the first day of the actual reign, or the first day of the formal calendar following completion of mourning. This flexibility is required, probably because the *gan* was not only determined by the first day of the reign (in some sense), but also had to satisfy other requirements. The *gan* determined the king's sacrifice day, and this day had to conform to rules of lineage hierarchy. And a king's *gan* could not be the *gan* of his predecessor.

---

[9] Ni Dewei (David S. Nivison), "San Dai Nandaixue zhi Guanjian: 'Jinben' *Zhushu Jinan*" 三代年代學之關鍵: 今本竹書紀年, in *Jingxue Yanjiu Luncong* 經學研究論叢 no. 10 (2002, pp. 223-309), pp.244-245, 275-280. I think that apparent references to Jie in the pre-Han *Shang shu* and in the *Shi jing* are ancient misinterpretations.

[10] Ni Dewei 倪德衛, "Lun Jinben *Zhushu Jinian* di Lishi Jiazhi" 論今本竹書紀年的歷史價值 (On the Historical Value of the "Modern Text" of the *Bamboo Annals*), in Shao Dongfang 邵東方 and Ni Dewei, eds., *Jinben Zhushu Jinian Lun Ji* 今本竹書紀年論集 (Studies on the Modern Text of the *Bamboo Annals*), Taipei: Tonsan Press 唐山出版社, 2002, pp. 41-82, especially pp. 56-65; also Ni Dewei, "San Dai Nandaixue zhi Guanjian," pp. 256-262. The first article is drawn from the part of the second article dealing with Western Zhou. Both articles were translated into Chinese by Shao Dongfang.

Another complication for Shang is that in all received chronologies Tai Wu is preceded by Yong Ji; but oracle inscriptions show that Yong Ji must actually have followed Tai Wu. The application of my rules shows why the correct order has been changed. In Western Zhou the fifth king Mu Wang's reign began exactly 100 years after the formal first year of the dynasty. Chronologists tried to make Shang work the same way, and the *Bamboo Annals* has 1475 as Tai Wu's first year, 100 years after 1575, which was Tang's first year in his own domain. 1475 is close: the actual succession year was (I believe) 1477. But the point is that 1475 was fixed by the 100 years requirement, and the first year of Shang was also fixed. Therefore, when for other reigns initial mourning periods were disregarded, a gap opened up before Tai Wu, which was just enough to accommodate the reign of Yong Ji; so the two reigns were switched, and Tai Wu's already long reign was extended through the years that had been Yong Ji's, making Tai Wu's reign an impossible 75 years. One of my Taiwan articles shows how I worked out the rest of this complex story.[11]

I have not been trying to persuade you that my conclusions are true. I respect your need to examine my arguments with great care, taking much time. My point has been more modest. I have wanted to persuade you merely that there is a reasonable possibility that I am right; and that this question has to be fully explored before it is safe – for any institution or government valuing its prestige -- to offer to the world a chronology of the Three Dynasties or any significant part thereof.

I therefore close with a formal proposal: Attempts to agree on a chronology of the Three Dynasties should be set aside for the time being. We should address instead the problem of evaluating the "Modern Text" *Bamboo Annals*. This could be an international project, to be concluded several years hence with an international conference, followed by appropriate publication of full and careful criticism.

In September, 1981, I was able for the first time to visit the Peoples' Republic of China. The occasion was a meeting in Taiyuan, this being the Fourth Meeting of the Chinese Paleography Society (Zhongguo Guwenzi Yanjiuhui). I had two Stanford graduate students with me, Edward L. Shaughnessy and David W. Pankenier, who have since become distinguished professors. All of us presented papers, mine being an early statement of my work trying to use the "Modern Text" *Bamboo Annals* to recover exact dates in Chinese history before 841 BCE, using (albeit clumsily) some of the methods I use in this book. At one of the social gatherings, a senior Chinese scholar (who, I hope, will be grateful for my not identifying him) whispered in the ear of one of the students, (Shaughnessy, I think), "If Prof. Nivison wants to be taken seriously in China, he must stop talking about the *Bamboo Annals*."

I did not doubt this kind advice, but (of course) it merely sharpened my determination to be taken seriously, no matter what. This story does show that I was not being completely honest in my statements in the 1998 Roundtable. I knew then that my main problem with the "Three Dynasties Project" was that what I knew to be the only way of "getting the dates right" was a way the Chinese scholars would not dream of using. They would, therefore, get them wrong. It was also obvious to me that since the stated purpose of the Project was to recover an accurate chronology, and since the magnitude of the Project and the Chinese government's very generous funding of it gave a good measure of the government's determination to get what it wanted, the Project scholars were bound to be required to try to do something they would probably believe to be impossible – since they are, after all, very good scholars. I probably ought to have said exactly this.

Where are we now? Joined to the chapter on the Roundtable was my statement criticizing the initial report of the Project, and while perhaps historically interesting, this statement was too fierce. I failed to consider the possibility that the Project's initial report would come to be judged, by leading project scholars themselves, to be unacceptable. Apparently that has happened. It was announced in June 2002 that the

---

[11] Ni Dewei, "San Dai Niandaixue zhi Guanjian," pp. 246-256 and pp. 265-280.

much larger final report would soon be published, with conclusions unchanged. But at summer's end a meeting of the Project's central committee tabled it, and scheduled an international conference for October 2003, to which all critics would be invited. I was invited, and you have just read the paper I wrote. The October conference was postponed indefinitely because of the SARS epidemic, and in January of 2003 new material had come to light (the Meixian bronzes) making it obvious that the Project's work on dates would have to be done over.

Meanwhile, there is no final report. I was told in the fall of 2007 that it would be published "soon" (I kept my doubts to myself). More recently another writer wondered in print whether Nivison would have a different attitude toward the Project if its results "had gone his way." To this one must reply simply that there have not been any results. The Chinese press has not surprisingly been enthusiastic, hailing the Project's work as equal in importance to the *Yongle Dadian* and the *Siku Quanshu*, but this is as irrelevant as journalistic sensationalism usually is. Real scholars in China are keeping their own counsel. The hype in the papers (if remembered) will be embarrassing to China, and this does bother me a little, but it is not really my concern.

My remaining task, to which I now turn, is to show convincingly that the *Bamboo Annals* text we have (down to the end of Western Zhou at least) is authentic, and cannot be ignored by historians, least of all by historians who recognize the importance of "getting the dates right."

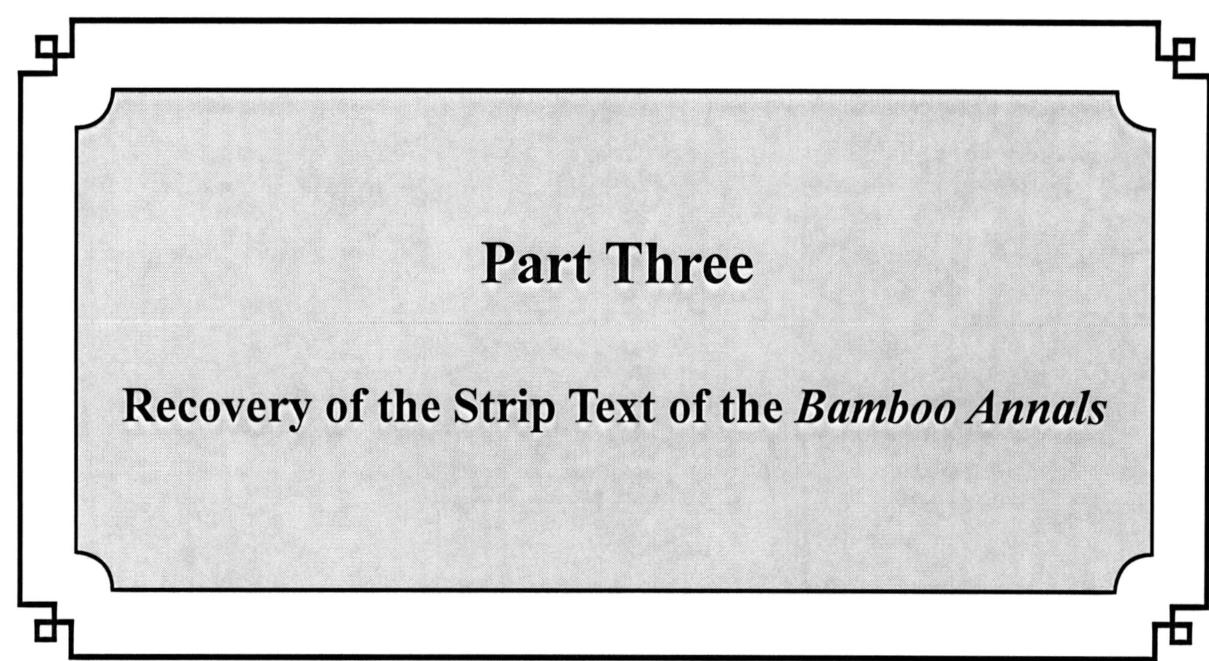

Part Three

Recovery of the Strip Text of the *Bamboo Annals*

Introduction to Part Three (2007)

By September of 2003 the "sound and fury" surrounding the Project was forgotten, and I was looking again at a puzzle touched on in one of my responses to friendly voices in a 1996 book in my honor edited by P. J. Ivanhoe, my former student. In closing my comment on the paper in this book by Prof. E. G. Pulleyblank (British Columbia), I mull over the surprisingly precise date in the BA chronicle for some rites performed by Huang Di: "50th year, 7th month, day *gengshen* (57)." One assumes the first of the month is intended. This precision required that the date either be a record, or a calculation, and not simply an arbitrary invention. I couldn't believe it was a record, but (I am a very slow thinker) I hadn't been able to think of a possible calculation. I did find it very soon after this.

I presented the solution (lifting it from my 1999 monograph in *SPP* 93, p. 35, but working out details exactly) in a very short paper for the annual meeting of the Western Branch of the American Oriental Society in Berkeley on October 10th. One must count back reign lengths before the earliest date in the BA, Yao 1 = 2145, adding a *guben* datum (from Luo Bi's *Lu shi*), that there had been a seven-year hiatus for prolonged mourning after Huang Di's death. One gets 2402 as Huang Di 1, and therefore 2353 as Huang Di 50. The calculator was using the *zhang-bu* intercalation cycle: 19 years at 365.25 days = 235 lunar months (including 7 intercalary months) = 1 *zhang*; 4 *zhang* = 1 *bu*, 20 *bu* = 1 *ji* = 1520 years, when *ganzhi* for first days of lunar months are repeated. One *bu* divided by 60 gives a remainder of 39 days; so in counting back by *bu* from a given first-of-month date one must reduce the *ganzhi* for the day by 39 for each *bu* back. 2353 is 100 *zhang* before 453, the date of the victory of Zhao, Han and Wei over Zhi Bo (Xun Yao), making Wei an independent state: so this is Warring States Wei work. The first day of the (Xia calendar) 7th month of 453 was *yihai* (12); therefore the first of the 7th month of 2353 was *gengshen* (57). (I leave the simple arithmetic as an exercise. The cycle isn't quite accurate, of course, but that doesn't matter.)

The chronicle for Huang Di 50 is followed by a very long subtext describing the rites and attending phenomena, causing me to focus my attention anew on what the original strip text had looked like. Look now at strip text page 1 in Chapter Eight. I found that the entries up through year 50 made up exactly one strip (with blanks between years), and that when I joined all of the pieces of subtext for Huang Di in the BA together I got a long stretch of 12 strips at 34 *zi* per strip. (In strip 014 I have doubled the name "Xian Yuan," but sense as well as count requires this.) This exercise confirmed that the whole of the tomb strip text was assembled following some simple rules, and I had most of them. What I did not know yet was how names of rulers used as titles of the rulers' chronicles were handled, in all possible cases, and how irregular pieces of subtext, not in multiples of 17 *zi*, were handled. The simplest assumption was that both ordinarily would be set off by blanks (except that names of rulers sometimes get more formal treatment, as Chapter Seven explains). A 34-*zi* sequence terminates the chronicle for Shang king Tai Wu, strip 142 on strip page 10. The next time this happens is in strips 159-160 on strip page 11, where a two-17's sequence terminates the chronicle for Zu Jia. In between, there is a short piece of subtext on strip 147; and there are fifteen kings, enough to test the proposed rule. Next, look at strip page 16: in the chronicle for Mu Wang of Zhou, there are two subtext sequences that can't be measured in 17's, in strips 235-236, and in strip 242; and in the last, the subtext exactly fills one 40-space strip, obviously designed to do so, because this strip both terminates a bundle of sixty and ends the first 100 years of Western Zhou, if as seems likely in an earlier stage of the text Western Zhou began in year 1045.

I concluded that I could be confident enough of these rules to justify in rare cases adjusting received text to fit them, giving readers fair warning. The most important example of this is in strips 250-251 on strip page 17, where I make up a subtext, *Li Wang sheng* ("[in this year] Li Wang was born"), taking the words out of a short double-column in-text note in the BA chronicle for Xiao Wang. In a sense I am also doing this on strip page 19, where I treat the first years of Jin Shangshu (strip 275) and Wen Hou (strips 276-277) as subtexts, while continuing royal Zhou dating to the end of the You Wang chronicle. I have argued that this is really what Du Yu meant, when he wrote in his postscript to his commentary on the *Chunqiu* and *Zuo zhuan* that Jin dates began with Shangshu in the tomb text *Zhushu jinian*.

By early summer of 2005 I had a complete text to the end of Western Zhou (which turned out to be 100 strips) and more tentatively to 679 (another 20 strips), when Wu Gong of Quwo eliminated the rival line of lords of Jin. This I presented at the April 2006 AAS meeting in San Francisco. The rest I leave to others.

Chapter Seven

Recovery of the *Bamboo Annals* Strip Texts for Shang and Western Zhou

Nov. '05, Stanford; April '06 AAS

The basic text rule, as argued by Shaughnessy (1986) based on Xun Xu, is that a full strip could hold 40 *zi*, and chronicle main text did have exactly 40 *zi* per strip, except that there must be a space between years. Subtext, which traditional editions exhibit in *zi* of the same size as main text, followed different rules, on which Shaughnessy is silent. A formally exhibited piece of subtext, I have found, could begin or end in the middle of a strip. So also could a piece of main text.

I first present an argument that (Rule 1) *Bamboo Annals* subtexts in reigns from Huang Di through Cheng Wang are usually in what I will call formal mode, exactly 17 *zi* per half-strip, the unit of 17-zi material being the only text in its half strip, starting four spaces down in a top half strip and ending with the fourth space up in a bottom half strip. This was to distinguish subtext from chronicle main text, which according to Xun Xu was in 40-*zi* strips – actually, I find, in strips of 2 x 20 *zi*-spaces. (I take a half-strip of *zi*-spaces to be either the top or the bottom half of a long strip of 40 *zi*-spaces separated in the middle.)

Then (Rule 2) I show that there is a formal mode for a king's royal name followed by his personal name when functioning as the title of a reign-chronicle: the names (not being events in the flow of time) are treated as subtext material. That is to say, in formal mode the names-as-title will be the only text in a whole half-strip. And in the special cases of the three most prominent pre-dynastic rulers, namely Huang Di, Zhuan Xu and Yao, for each the name as title is the only material in a whole strip.

Next (Rule 3), I show that there was an informal mode for a king's names, royal and personal, when functioning as the title of the chronicle for a reign. Especially in a long sequence of very short reigns, starting each reign with a new half-strip would waste a lot of space. In this case the names are marked as not themselves part of what happens, by being preceded and followed by blanks.

Last (Rule 4) when a piece of descriptive or background subtext material is of other than n x 17-*zi* length, it is marked – informal mode -- as subtext by leaving the space before and the space after blank, within the flow of 20-*zi* main text material.

Finally, I examine the problematic subtext of 10 half-strips in the chronicle for Cheng Wang of Zhou, showing it to be authentic tomb text. I solve several puzzles about it and point out the implications of this solution:

(a) The 40-*zi* piece of main text that Shaughnessy shows to have been moved from the Cheng chronicle to the Wu chronicle must have been moved in Warring States, not in Western Jin. And the motive must have been a Warring States motive.
(b) Doubt about the authenticity of the Cheng Wang subtext being removed, we can confidently count strips, getting 100 for Western Zhou (with a one-strip summary), and 60 for Shang (with a half strip summary). Thus the *Zhushu jinian* was a composition, not an accretion, and we can look for other evidence of this.

(Other evidence: e.g., the Shang count breaks in two, the second 30 strips beginning with the reign of Wu Ding, thought of as the most important king after Tang. And the Western Zhou count also breaks in two, the first 60 strips concluding with the exploits of Mu Wang in the West, and the last 40 beginning with a celebration in the Zhou court in 945 BCE, probably believed in early Warring States to be the 100th anniversary of the Zhou conquest of Shang. The Xia chronicle too appears to have been 60 strips, 30 + 30, the second bundle beginning appropriately with the restoration of Shao Kang. Thus my five bundles of 60 strips each perhaps were actually ten bundles of 30 each. Tang-Song era bibliographies suggest an original total of fourteen.)

So, Rule 1, here is an argument leading to the conclusion that subtexts usually ("formally") had 2 x 17 characters per strip:

a) Pankenier has shown that the conjunction of 1953 dates Shun's transfer of power to Yu in Shun 14.
b) The *Annals* says that on the 1st of the 9th month of the 5th year of Zhong Kang the sun was eclipsed.
c) The *Zuo zhuan* (Zhao 17) puts the eclipse in lunar lodge Fang. and *Shang shu* 9 "Yin Zheng" (a *guwen* chapter) implies it was not in the Xia home area but near enough to be reported to the Xia court.
d) Using *Annals* reign lengths and making interregnums (for mourning) 2 years, the date is 16 Oct 1876.
e) On that date there was a solar eclipse, north of Xia but reportable. The sun was in Fang at the time.
f) The same calculation shows that the first day of the reign of the 14th king Kong Jia was 17 Feb 1577.
g) This day was a *jiazi* day (1st in the 60-day cycle), explaining why the king was called "Kong Jia."
h) Pankenier has argued that the last year of Xia was 496 years before the conjunction of 1059, i.e., 1555.
i) The same count (*Annals* reign lengths, 2-year gaps) gives 1555 as the last year of Fa, next-to-last king.
j) So Di Gui (= "Jie") must be an early invention. There is abundant evidence for this judgment.[1]
k) If the Di Gui chronicle is fiction, it (and other factors) pushed earlier material back 35 years.[2]
l) But the astronomical events at Di Gui 10 = 1580 (identified by Pankenier, who shows the date should be Di Gui 14 = 1576) must have been at Kong Jia 2.
m) So the Kong Jia chronicle must have been rewritten at this time.
n) It has a main text of 40 spaces followed by a 135 space subtext, one short of 8 x 17.
o) This suggests that subtexts were normally n x 17 characters long, confirmed by counting other examples.
p) Notably the subtexts at the ends of Zu Jia and Wen Ding of Shang are each 34 *zi* long.[3]

So they can be, and were (if we adopt the best explanation of their length), formally exhibited as subtexts by being displayed 17 *zi* per half strip.

Now, Rule 2, the formal treatment of royal names as titles of reign-chronicles. A convenient example is the second Zhou king Cheng Wang. Accepting Shaughnessy's transposed strip-text argument, one can count back from the gap between years 14 and 18, to the point where the text was inserted in the Wu Wang chronicle, for at both places one can conclude exactly where strips begin and end. After the inserted text in the Wu Wang chronicle there is exactly one half strip of text in the Wu chronicle. And before the gap in the Cheng chronicle, there are exactly ten 40-space strips of main text. But the Cheng year sequence has to begin with the king's names. The only place for these names is the second half of the last Wu Wang strip, and no more text is available to fill the rest of the space in that half strip. So the formal treatment of a king's names as title is to put them in an otherwise empty half strip.

Next, Rule 3: The informal treatment of king's names as reign titles can be seen by looking at the Yin (Shang) main text between the 34-*zi* subtext terminating Zu Jia and the 34-*zi* subtext terminating Wen Ding. (I have relocated this Wen Ding subtext at the end of the Wen Ding chronicle, where it is as appropriate as it is where the Jin restorers put it, and where it can be made to fit without breaking a strip.) This stretch of text must all be made of 20-space half-strip text. The only way to make this count out right is to have each king's two names preceded and followed by single blank spaces. (Thus to have a consistent hypothesis we must assume that that kings' personal names were included in the tomb text for Shang. This turns out not to be true for post Western Zhou text.)

Last, Rule 4, the informal treatment of subtexts of irregular length was simply to mark them off by blanks. To see this, look at the chronicle for Zhou kings Kang Wang, Zhao Wang and Mu Wang as far as

[1] E.g., all traditional sources have 17 reigns in Xia. The BA makes Di Gui 1 be 1589. The first 8 begin with Yu 1 = 1989; the second 8 begin with Mang 1= 1789. This indicates that in an earlier version of the book Shang began at 1589 (for the full accounting see Nivison 1999 and 2002, section 7 and Appendix 3).

[2] "Other factors": Cumulative backdatings of Shang reigns to eliminate overlaps push Shang 1 back 35 years; then cancellation of initial mourning periods opens up a 31-year gap which is filled by inventing the Di Gui chronicle (main text being exactly 8 strips). The result is to date Shang 1 to 1558 rather than to 1554. (See Nivison *ibid.*)

[3] The subtext for Wen Ding must have been at the end of the 13-year Wen Ding chronicle, but was moved by the Jin editors of the BA to follow year 11, made to be the date of Zhou lord Ji Li's death. (See Chapter Eight, Strip Text p. 12.)

[Zhou] strip 60 (cumulative count, strip 242; see Chapter Eight Strip Text p. 16). Kang Wang gets formal treatment. Zhao Wang doesn't, because the Kang chronicle doesn't end with the end of a half strip.[4] Mu Wang doesn't (perhaps he might have) because there is no blank space at the end of the account of Zhao Wang. Reading on through Mu Wang from strip 53 as far as strip 60, we encounter two pieces of subtext. The first, 自武王至穆王享國百年穆王以下都于西鄭, has 18 *zi,* close, but not good enough, because it begins in the middle of a half strip, so it follows Rule 4. The example at strip 60 is especially interesting, because it has 39 *zi*, and so (introduced by a blank) exactly fills one 40-space strip, and surely was composed so as to do so, thus terminating the bundle of 60 strips. (It is still following rule 4, because rule 1 would apply only if it consisted of 2 x 17 *zi.*) I think the fact that this subtext happens to fit exactly into strip 242 strongly confirms my construction of Rule 4.

Let us return to Cheng Wang. His chronicle in *Jinben* contains one apparently formal subtext, which cannot be in the right place, because it would start in the middle of a half-strip. Why is it there? Also, it contains a phrase naming Qin and Han, obviously impossible for a Warring States text. Others would tell me that this plus that is more than enough to condemn it as forgery. So cross it out. (This is just what I did, mentally, when I touched on this problem in an article in 1995; see the note at the end of this chapter.)

But I can't shut my eyes to it unless I can find a plausible reason why, if forged, it is there at all, and I cannot do this. So I cannot dismiss this problematic text by crossing it out. Furthermore, I now can see that this text has the proper word count for it to be a proper formal subtext.

The Jin court restorers must have put this subtext where it is. So its location in the tomb text must have seemed obviously wrong. A subtext that counts out in 17's, as (I think) this one does,[5] must have been on its own half-strips; so it must have been located after a half-strip of 20-space chronicle text, or a whole strip of 40 spaces, that ended with the end of a sentence and the end of a subject. The appropriate subject matter must have been somewhere in the preceding text, but probably not in what immediately preceded, and so the location seemed wrong. The subtext is about Zhou Gong, emphasizing his importance in Zhou history. An adequate piece of justifying main text material is the sentence which is the last but one in Zhou strip number 36 (cumulative BA count 218):

王錫韓侯命。十三年王師會齊侯魯侯伐戎**<u>夏六月魯大禘于周公廟。</u>**十四年齊師圍曲城克之。

The year is the 13th year. I put the sentence we want with underline: "Summer, 6th month: in Lu there was a great *di* rite in Zhou Gong's ancestral temple." The ceremony befitted the decease of a king. Zhou Gong was being given the highest honor Zhou civilization could bestow.

So something has been done to the main text that prevents this sentence from ending strip 36. The trouble is not far to seek: According to the main text as it now reads, Zhou Gong was still alive. His death is given as being in the 21st year, and his burial in the 22nd year. Either the 13th year should be the 23rd year, or the 21st and 22nd years should be the 11th and 12th years. Trying each shows that the second is right.

I give the whole text below, as it was and as it is. At left is the original relevant part of the Cheng Wang main text, with the desired text to be "transposed" in its original place, in bold italics underlined. On the right is the same text still italicized, after repositioning of the Zhou Gong material, so as to get the desired text in strip position. One notices that when the original is restored the sequence of events is straightened out. With the strip text in the Wu chronicle, the Nine Cauldrons are moved to Luo before the new location had even been planned. The planning of "Cheng Zhou," the royal location in Luo Yi where the cauldrons would be, was back in Cheng Wang 5. Now we can see the sequence: year 5, planning stage; year 15,

---

[4] The Kang chronicle did once end with the end of a half strip. In strip 231 we read that "Lu Hou Qin Fu" died in year 19. Actually Qin Fu died in Kang 16, which was 990, i.e., 46 years after Cheng Wang's accession year 1035, this being the first year of Qin Fu's reign as lord of Lu. See Chapter Two, Attachment "The 853 Problem." There already is an entry at Kang 16, but there is nothing else at Kang 19; so if Qin Fu's death is correctly dated, four *zi* spaces are saved, and this makes the Kang chronicle end at the end of a half strip.

[5] This subtext ends with a song sung by King Cheng, of four 7-syllable lines. I have inserted blanks for pauses, thus treating it as one 34-space line.

physical relocation of the cauldrons to Luo; year 17, formal announcement that the new royal city was ready; year 18, formal rites placing the cauldrons in their new permanent location.

Here are strip-texts for years 11 through 22, not including the 5-strip subtext:

年春正月王如豐唐叔獻嘉禾王命唐叔歸禾于周文公王命周平公治東都***周文公薨于豐***。十二年	年春正月王如豐唐叔獻嘉禾王命唐叔歸禾于周文公王命周平公治東都。十二年王師燕師城韓
王師燕師城韓王錫韓侯命***葬周文公于畢***。十三年王師會齊侯魯侯伐戎***夏六月魯大禘于周公廟***	王錫韓侯命。十三年王師會齊侯魯侯伐戎***夏六月魯大禘于周公廟。***十四年齊師圍曲城克之。
The subtext was originally here. It is essentially an encomium for Zhou Gong, after the words 大禘于周公廟, not even mentioning the cauldrons.	The subtext remained here in the tomb text, but in the Jinben the Jin restorers have moved it down to follow the 18th year entry on the cauldron rituals.
。十四年齊師圍曲城克之。***十五年肅慎氏來賓初狩方岳誥于沬邑冬遷九鼎于洛。十六年箕子***	***十五年肅慎氏來賓初狩方岳誥于沬邑冬遷九鼎于洛。十六年箕子來朝秋王師滅蒲姑。十七年***
來朝秋王師滅蒲姑。十七年冬洛邑告成。十八年春正月王如洛邑定鼎鳳凰見遂有事于河。十	冬洛邑告成。十八年春正月王如洛邑定鼎鳳凰見遂有事于河。十九年王巡狩侯甸方岳召康公
九年王巡狩侯甸方岳召康公從歸于宗周遂正百官黜豐侯。二十一年除治象 [6]。二十	從歸于宗周遂正百官黜豐侯。二十一年除治象***周文公薨于豐。二十二年葬周文公于畢***。二十

Minimum recopying required recopying these strips. What the Wei experts started with is on the left, and what they ended with is on the right. Key sentences are in italics: A strip's worth of text was transposed, but not an actual strip; and it was done carefully: it could not have been an accident.

The subtext has nothing to do with the cauldrons. It is simply and appropriately a celebration of the achievements of Zhou Gong, entered immediately *after the strip which ended with the record of the last rites for him*: 夏六月魯大禘于周公廟, "Summer, 6th month: in Lu there was a great *di* rite in Zhou Gong's ancestral temple."

We must conclude, then, that the Cheng chronicle main text *was crudely altered in order to create the appearance of a strip that could be moved,* to make Wu Wang's reign three years longer. Actually there never was such a strip, and no physical object was moved. All that was needed was *text*, of the right length having the right words. The tinkering with the Cheng Wang text was done simply to cover the tinkerers' tracks, to create the possibility of a gap where (reporting to their king) they could claim there had been a strip, which they had then moved to its "proper" location in the Wu Wang chronicle. If this is (barely) conceivable in Warring-States Wei; it is not conceivable at all in post-Han Jin, after the triumph of Confucianism and centuries of a focus of attention on early death rituals. If there be any doubt that this must have been done before the *Annals* text was finalized and buried; just reflect that it mentions the "Jin Teng," undeniably a pre-Han text, in connection with Wu Wang's illness, and the "Jin Teng" suggests that Wu Wang survived that illness, just as the altered *Annals* says. But we know he did not. The altered *Annals* text assumes that he survived, and the "Jin Teng" story, without making a point of it, simply takes the assumption for granted. That story would not have been invented unless there were some reason to suppose it true. The altered *Annals* provided the reason.

---

6 Moving the death and burial required a new year, 二十二年, "22nd year" preceded by a space, i.e., five additional spaces of text. So whatever was there before under the date "twenty-first year" got over-written and is now unrecoverable. But why did the Wei tinkerers not simply leave whatever was there in place, and move the rest of the text down to make room for it? They wanted to have their changes be unnoticed, of course. And they surely wanted to avoid avoidable recopying. But we will see at the dynasty's end that a change that would alter the number of strips was forbidden.

But why was this done?

The root cause of these problems was, it seems to me, the editing project faced by the experts at the court of Warring States Wei. The beginning of Jin and Wei was the Zhou king Cheng Wang's grant of the fief of Tang to his younger brother Tangshu Yu. The Wei experts in Warring States wanted the granting to be in 1035 (wrong), because that was 700 years before *Hou* Ying's announcement in 335 of his claim to be a king, Huicheng Wang, his royal calendar to start in 334 – an even hundred years after the first year of Wei Wen Hou, 434. They thought they knew two things[7]: that the grant was made in a year when Jupiter was in Da Huo ("Great Fire"), Jupiter station 10 (probably right); and that in the year of the Zhou conquest Jupiter was in Chun Huo ("Quail Fire"), Jupiter station 7 (certainly wrong). Jupiter was supposed to have a 12-year period moving around the zodiac one station a year (near term, on average right). If 1035 was a Station 10 year, then so was 1047; so 1050 must be a station 7 year.

Thus, these two beliefs, plus their decision to make 1035 the beginning of Jin, drove them to the conclusion that the conquest must have been in 1050 (wrong). They knew that Cheng Wang had a 30-year reign (right) and they thought it began in 1037 (wrong: what began in 1037 was Cheng Wang's 2 + 30 years). They saw that to get close to solving their problem, they had to assume (wrongly) that Zhou Gong's 7-year regency had preceded Cheng Wang's 30 years, i.e. it was 1044 through 1038. They knew that the standard belief was that Wu Wang had died two years after his victory (right); indeed, this is surely what the *original* text of the *Zhushu jinian* had said, in early Warring States. And they accepted the by then received view (wrong) that the victory had been in Wu Wang's year 12. *So they had to produce an argument that Wu Wang had lived three years longer, viz., 1047-46-45, which would be Wu Wang's reign-years 15-16-17.*

It is sometimes claimed that the idea that Wu Wang lived more than two years after the conquest cannot be found in writings earlier than middle Han. So its presence in the *Bamboo Annals* must be the result of a strip move after the text's discovery in Western Jin. This is a mistake. There is explicit counter-evidence in the "Xiao Wen" chapter of the *Guanzi.* Duke Huan of Qi, guided by his astute advisers, has achieved the status of *bo*, first lord of the realm. So he tempts himself with the idea of making himself king. His advisers parry the suggestion skillfully, inducing Duke Huan to reflect. Zhou had had one sage ruler after another: Dan Fu, Ji Li, Wen Wang, and at last Wu Wang, who "attacked Shang and defeated it, then died in seven years" 武王伐殷克之七年而崩. But the task was still not done; only then was Zhou Gong, working with Cheng Wang, able to create the foundations of an enduring state.

It is sometimes argued that "in seven years" can be taken as "in his seventh year," counting from the year after Wen Wang's death, which would -- if you think the conquest was in 1045, Wu Wang's fifth year -- make Wu Wang's death be two years after the victory over Shang. But reading 七年 as an exact date here ignores the effect of 而; and it would be weird unless this text contained a statement that the conquest was in Wu Wang's 5th year, and it doesn't; in fact, there is no such statement anywhere. Further this reading ignores the thrust of the argument, which is that the task took a long, long time, even for sage rulers much abler than the lords of Qi. The seven years are Wu Wang years 11 (when the attack started), 12, 13, 14, 15, 16, and 17, just as in the *Jinben* text used by Yixing in the Tang Dynasty. The *Guanzi's* source was probably the *Zhushu jinian.*

My argument will meet resistance, so here is some indirect evidence. In *Lü shi chunqiu* 14.3.1 (Riegel pp. 311-312, chapter 3 "Awaiting the Right Time" "Yu Shi") we read of Wu Wang that he was justly nursing resentment for past injuries done by Shang. Then "in the 12th year of his reign he finished the matter with the deed of the *jiazi* day." In the *Shiji*, "*shijia*" chapters for Qi and for Lu, the victory is dated Wu's 11th year, but there is in fact no un-resolvable conflict as to the year number: the historian was following a source that gave him "11th year 12th month" as the date of the Zhou forces' crossing of the Yellow River ("Zhou Benji"), and he gave this an anachronistic early Han reading, taking "12th month" as the *name* – usable in any calendar -- of the post-winter-solstice month (as it was in the "Xia" calendar).[8] He assumed (probably)

[7] *Guoyu* "Jin Yu" 4, and "Zhou Yu" 3.7; critique of the latter in D. Nivison, "Sandai Niandaixue zhi Guanjian: Jinben *Zhushu jinian,*" Taibei: Taiwan Xuesheng Shuju, *Jingxue yanjiu luncong* 10 (2002.3) pp. 282-283.

[8] Anyone who finds this "unconvincing" should glance at the *Shiji*, *benji* chapters for the reigns of Gao Zu down to the

that in the applicable ("Zhou") calendar this "12th" month was the *second* month of the 11th year.[9]

The conquest is (in the *Lü shi chunqiu* and in the *Shiji's* source) being taken as in the 12th year of Wu Wang's own reign calendar (not in a continuing "Mandate" calendar, which does seem to be assumed in the "Zhou Benji"). This dating is generated by the same reasoning that forced three more years into the end of Wu Wang's life. If political propaganda demands that the Tang enfeoffment be in 1035, making the conquest 1050, the received chronology had to be given another "correction," for it said (if correct) that 1050 was Wen Wang's year of death. The problem was solved by moving the conjunction of 1059 back one Jupiter cycle to 1071. Wen Wang died nine years after the conjunction; so Wu Wang's succession year became 1061, and he conquered in year 12 of *his own* calendar, way past his calendar year 7. Thus (again) we must conclude that the strip-text move was Warring States work.

Before we can be sure that the subtext in Cheng Wang's chronicle is authentic, contributing its five strips to the total strip count for Western Zhou, we must deal with the phrase "down to Qin and Han," 迄于秦漢. We should look for something in four characters for which this phrase could have been substituted. The long subtext at the beginning of the Zhou chronicle is in part based on Ode 245, which begins with the story of the mythic birth of Hou Ji. The original composers of this early Zhou part of the subtext matter are following this ode's story. The ode ends with the words 以迄于今, "down to the present time"; so perhaps this is what the buried text said. The referential ambiguity of the word "present" (*jin*) might have seemed disturbing to the Jin restorers, causing them to substitute words with unambiguous reference. The original then (I suggest) was 以迄于今, not 迄于秦漢.

When the five strips in this subtext in the Cheng Wang chronicle are counted, the total count for Western Zhou becomes 100 strips. I venture that no one will suppose this to be an accident: those five strips were intended to be counted, intended by the Warring States composers of the whole book. That the whole book is a composition is evident from more detail. Look at the strip text for Shang. The total strip count is another "prestige" number, not 100 but 60, as in the *ganzhi* cycle. Now notice that it naturally divides in two. The second half, strips 31-60, begins with the reign of Wu Ding, said to be the most benevolent of Shang kings, viewed obviously as the most important king after "Pacifier" Tang. The set of 100 Western Zhou strips also can be seen as in two parts. Look at strip 60. It is a subtext of 0+39 *zi*, filling a strip, summarizing Mu Wang's exploits as traveler in the Western Regions. Next, beginning the next bundle of sixty, comes a strip recording an assembly of the regional lords in the Zhou capital in the year 945, just 100 years after 1045, which was probably widely believed in the 4th century BCE to be the date of the Zhou conquest. This, like Yao's first year 2145, must be a residue of the earlier chronicle used and altered by the Warring States Wei court. That chronicle must have had 1145 as the succession year of Wu Yi, who on that date first recognized the Zhou ruler Dan Fu as "Duke of Zhou. (The *Jinben* has year 1157, reflecting the 12-year shift in Zhou dates caused by moving the conjunction of 1059 back to 1071.[10])

The strip text restoration of the Xia chronicle requires some editing, duly noted, but it seems to be like the chronicle for Shang, exactly 60 strips (if one begins it after Shun's grant of authority to Yu in Shun's 14th year), and it breaks in the middle just where one would expect. The forty years of the (imaginary) Han Zhuo interregnum after the assassination of King Xiang has come to its fortunate end. The legitimate royal line of Xia is restored on strip 31, in the inauguration of Shao Kang, sixth king of Xia. Further, the text from the beginning, Huang Di, through Shun's 14th year is probably also 60 strips (this too requires some editing). Moreover, this requires the last four strips for Shun to be also the first four for Xia, as in a sense they were:

---

beginning of Wu Di. The Han official calendar during most of this time began the year with the beginning of "winter." So normally the *first* month of the year is called "10th month."

[9] Ironically, "11th year" is arguably correct, but not in the sense intended. Wu Wang's calendar year 1 in Zhou was 1049, but the significant date is sometimes taken to be the year of his father's death, in the 3rd month (e.g., *Zhushu jinian*, end-of-Western-Zhou summary, where the year is 1062). He died in his 12th year (*Yi Zhou shu* 45), which year was his 3rd year as king (*Yi Zhou shu* 29). The conquest was in 1040, year 11 counting from 1050.

[10] Late pre-conquest Shang dates are backed 16 years, so the BA first year for Wu Yi, 1159, represents the absolute date 1143, which was Wu Yi's accession (post mourning) year, taken here as Wu Yi's first year, because the BA Shang scheme does not recognize the succession-accession distinction, whereas the Zhou scheme does (Wen Wang is accorded a 52-year reign, i.e., 2+50).

From Yu's *de jure* first year (1989 in the *Jinben*) through the end of Xia (*Jinben*: 1559) is 431 years, but the end-of-Xia summary makes the Xia Dynasty last 471 years, thus counting from the beginning of Yu's *de facto* rule (Shun 14, *Jinben* system 2029).

I attach my tentative strip text restoration for the *Bamboo Annals*, from the beginning (Huang Di) through You Wang of Western Zhou, and on for another 20 strips.[11] The Shang and Western Zhou strip texts are preserved in the *Jinben* almost exactly. I obtain them by little more than direct copying from the *Jinben* text, following the rules that I have derived. Where I do more, I explain carefully.

--- David S. Nivison
20 August 2005, revised 16 November 2005, 17 July 2007, and 24 August 2007

Note added 30 July 2007:

The contradictory placing of statements about the death, burial and *di* rite for Zhou Gong has long been noticed. Shao Dongfang's article (2002 (2)) is especially important because it not only reviews the history of discussion but also links the problem with Shaughnessy's claim (rejected by Shao) that a strip of Cheng Wang text was moved to near the end of the Wu Wang chronicle: Shao notes that if the Zhou Gong material is put back into a defendable order Shaughnessy's strip ceases to be a strip. Reviewing my own previous work, I find that I discussed the problem incompletely at the end of my article in *EC* 20 (1995) "An Interpretation of the Shao Gao," p. 193, making the same point. There I like most earlier commentators took the position I am here rejecting, i.e., that the text for year 13, including the *di* rite, belongs in year 23.

I had two motives pushing me into making that mistake. First (as I admitted), I feared that a Warring States rewriting of the Cheng chronicle moving the death and burial from years 11-12 to years 21-22 would have torn the text up so much that my use of the *Annals* to reconstruct Zhou and pre-Zhou dates would have been impossible or at least very doubtful; and I was already quite sure of this reconstruction. Second, the guess that it was the record of the *di* rite that was moved from an original year 23 seemed the simplest assumption: it seemed simpler to move one entry rather than two; and what would have been "year 23" is now blank. These reasons are not good enough, because in either case six strips would have had to be rewritten, eleven minus the five for the subtext: altogether, strips for years 12 through 22, or strips for years 13 through 23. So actually it is just as simple to assume that the death and burial were re-dated. And in neither case do I have to fear that the rewriting "must have torn the text up" so as to make my chronological analysis more difficult or impossible.

Furthermore either way the same conclusion follows: the strip text was rewritten in Wei before the book was buried, in order to make it possible to move the strip text to the Wu chronicle. In my 1995 article I do not go on to try to reconstruct the Wei editors' reasoning, saying instead that this "will have to be my subject in a later publication." That "later" publication is this book, a full twelve years later, and I have worked this out in this chapter, summing it up in Chapter Nine. What has happened in the meantime, making me sure of my ground, is my recovery of the entire strip text down through Western Zhou and into Jin, and in particular my rescuing the various subtexts, notably the one in the Cheng chronicle, as parts of the original text. This work on the subtexts I didn't do until September 2003. Once one sees that this subtext has to be a

---

[11] The last 20 strips in the fifth bundle of 60 carry the chronicle to 679, ninety-two years beyond Western Zhou, and I admit uncertainty about what I have done here. The *Jinben* uses Zhou reign dates for this era and the tomb text did not. Restoring the tomb text requires guesswork, and this I try to explain. Another difficulty is knowing where and why to stop. One assumes that one must "come out even" at the end of a royal dynasty; but no royal dynasty end could be expected at the end of the last 60-strip bundle I was restoring. What I did find was that the 60th strip (strip 303) ended exactly with two momentous events, the rise of Huan of Qi as the first of the Five Hegemons, and the king's recognition of Wu Gong of Quwo as the *de jure* ruler of Jin, terminating the first series of Jin civil wars, and terminating the dynasty of Jin lords descended from Wen Hou Chou. The *Jinben* text begins to show signs of serious omissions after Jin Wen Gong (636). I doubt that restoring another bundle of 60 strips will be possible, but I leave this as a standing challenge to others. (I think there must have been seven bundles altogether.)

five-strip unit and has nothing to do with the placing of the cauldrons, it follows at once that the immediately preceding strip must have ended with the record of the *di* rite. Zhou Gong therefore died in year 11, which was 1027 BCE. He was probably a year or two over sixty.

Chapter Eight

The Strip Text of the *Bamboo Annals* Huang Di to Jin Wu Gong

(Worked out by D. S. Nivison September-October '05, revised July '06 and July-August '07)

The strip text, as far as I have gone with it, appears to have been in bundles of sixty strips:, as follows:

(1) Pre-dynastic regimes, Huang Di through Shun 14	Strip Pages 1-4
(2) Xia, from Shun 15	Strip Pages 5-8
(3) Shang	Strip Pages 9-12
(4) Zhou, through Mu Wang 17	Strip Pages 13-16
(5) Zhou Mu Wang 18 through Jin Wu Gong 27	Strip Pages 17-20

Western Zhou terminates with strip 40 in bundle 5, thus Western Zhou has exactly 100 strips.

There is an argument for seeing each bundle as having been divided into two half-bundles of 30 strips each. If so, I have recovered the first ten of possibly fourteen original half-bundles. Some early bibliographies say that the original consisted of twelve, or thirteen, or fourteen *juan.* This suggests that the last four half-bundles were damaged, disordered and incomplete. And this is the impression one gets from the surviving *Jinben.* I have gone as far as I can without pointless guesswork.

Each strip of forty characters or character-spaces appears to me to have been broken in the middle in some way, probably simply for the threading tying the strips together. This division was normally invisible in the flow of language, but it could have a function; for this reason, I have marked it by inserting a blank row. Main text (chronicle form) half lines have twenty characters or spaces (marked here by ◦ a space is required between year entries). Subtext (not in chronicle form) half lines have seventeen characters top half and seventeen bottom half, leaving three spaces at the top of the column (of 17 + 17) and three at the bottom. Combinations of 17 top half and 20 bottom half, or the reverse, often occur, at the transition from subtext to main text or from main text to subtext. Also sometimes a ruler's name(s) serving as the title to his chronicle occurs at the top of the top or bottom half of a strip with nothing else in that half strip. (See formal rules in Chapter Seven.)

In the buried text, it is also possible for a short piece of subtext to be embedded in main text, with a blank at the beginning and another at the end. (In printed editions the main text / subtext distinction is preserved: subtexts have characters the same size as main text but distinguished by being in columns of a standard length starting a small distance from the top. In Fan Qin, the subtexts are in columns of 17, but only one space down from the top.) In the strip restorations here, subtexts embedded in main text are distinguished by being in italics; but italics are not used for subtexts marked by their formal arrangement in 17's on their own half-strips. (In the accompanying translation, all subtexts are in italics.) Italics are not used in the Chinese for names of rulers used as titles of reigns. These are marked with underline.

Restoration of the strip text reveals aspects of design. Xia and Shang each have 60 strips, so probably the whole book is planned in 60's. (When *guben* material is used here, it is in italics.) The compilers controlled the word-counts for the parts of the book., and could use structure of the text to reflect important assumed stress points in history, the most obvious being dynastic transitions. (Note that text structure confirms the inference that the real beginning of Xia was Shun's action in his 14th year, the Xia 60 strips beginning with Shun 15.)

Not only 60's, but even mid-points of 60's are significant. The second 30 begins with the main text record of the death of Yao. The third 30 terminates with the Xia restoration after the (fictitious) 40-year interregnum between Xiang and Shao Kang. The sixth 30 begins with the succession of Wu Ding, celebrated in the subtext as the best king of Shang. The eighth 30 begins with the Duke of Zhou's returning the royal authority to Cheng Wang. The ninth 30 ends with the first appearance of Jin as a world power, giving military support to Xuan Wang; and the tenth begins with a Jin victory.

Western Zhou is given 100 strips rather than 60, but the way its first 60 ends is perhaps surprising. A traditional Confucian moralist might see Mu Wang's ostentatious western travels as slightly embarrassing, but there is no hint of such an attitude here. A subtext (embedded in main text rather than set off in 17's, but tailored to fill one 40-space strip) adds the travel account all up, apparently seeing it as glorious; and it is immediately followed (beginning of the fifth 60) by a court reception of the regional lords, which I think we can see as a centennial celebration of the Zhou conquest of Shang, in 945. Yao 1 is made to be exactly 1200 years earlier, showing that in the Zhou-oriented text which the Wei state used as basis for the *Zhushu jinian* the conquest had been dated (in effect) 1045. Careful analysis reveals a set of dates at centennial intervals: in effect, 2145, 1145, 1045, 945.

The one "45" date here that one can perhaps trust as history is 1145, from which the other dates appear to have been calculated. In Nivison's chronology 1145 was the succession year of Shang king Wu Yi, who (just as one should expect) at once received at court the "Old Duke" Dan Fu, probably the most powerful western border lord, giving him official recognition and status as "Zhou Gong." (He is conventionally called "the Old Duke" (Gu Gong) to distinguish him from the famous Zhou Gong Dan, brother of Wu Wang and regent for Cheng Wang. After Zhou claimed the "empire" (*tianxia*), by Zhou royal edict Dan Fu was retroactively given the title "Great King," Tai Wang).

Recovered Strip Text

Huang Di through Quwo (Jin) Wu Gong

(Strips 1 through 303)

Italics are used in the translation for all subtexts, formal or informal. In the Chinese, subtexts in formal mode are sufficiently indicated by strip lenghth and position, and are not put in italics. Italics are used in the Chinese (1) for all informal (embedded) subtexts; (2) in the translation (but not in the Chinese) for royal personal names; (3) in the Chinese and in the translation, for any text created by me out of *guben* material or required by theory; and (4) at other times, as explained in "Comments" (pp. 167-176). Underline is used for all kings' names when used as titles of reigns, both in the Chinese text and in the translation. Underline is used also for all dates on strip page 20 (Chinese and translation).

In Chapter Eight my objective is to present a demonstration of my discoveries as to how the *Bamboo Annals* text was arranged on bamboo strips – the implication being that the entire text is authentic. The translations on facing pages are offered merely for the convenience of readers who, I hope, will be interested in the reconstruction of the text but who may not be able to read Chinese easily or at all. The translation for the most part merely adapts Legge. For a properly careful and critical translation, readers should turn to the "new translation and study" by me and my colleague Shao Dongfang, soon to be published. Comments at the end are essentially comments on structure, not on translation.

001 **Huang Di [the "Yellow Emperor."]** ***Name Xian Yuan*****.**

002 First year: When [Huang] Di took his position as ruler he resided in You Xiong. He for the first time instituted court caps and robes. 20th year: Felicitous clouds appeared. He put his officers in order using [titles taken from the appearance of the] clouds. 50th year, Autumn, 7th month, [first day] *gengshen*: phoenixes came, and the emperor sacrificed by the Luo River.

003 *His mother's name was Fubao. She saw a flash of lightening around the star Shu in the Northern Dipper, its brilliance illuminating the countryside around her. Feeling it she became pregnant. In twenty-five [lunar] months she gave birth to [Huang] Di on Shouqiu {Longlife Hill}. While still a weak [baby] he was able to talk. Dragon-like*

004 *in appearance he had the virtue of a sage. He summoned the many spirits to his court and employed them, [having] Yinglong attack Chiyou, fighting with the strength of the Four Beasts, tigers, panthers, bears and grizzly bears. With [the help of] the [divine] lady Ba he stopped the pestilent rains. When the world*

005 *was pacified, his sage virtue brilliantly covered all. Many auspicious omens appeared. There was the quyi grass springing up in his courtyard; when a glib-tongued person came to court the grass pointed at him, so that such persons did not dare to approach. When the omens of the felicitous*

006 *clouds appeared, vapors from the Red Quarter (south) joined with vapors from the Azure Quarter (east). In the Red Quarter there were two stars, and in the Azure Quarter there was one star – three altogether, all yellow in color. When the sky was*

007 *clear and bright they appeared in [the constellation] Sheti, and were called the Felicitous Stars. The emperor in yellow robes fasted within the palace. As he sat [in a boat] on the Xuanhu above [its junction with] the Luo stream, some phoenixes gathered. They did not eat live insects; they did not tread*

008 *on live grass. Some of them stayed in the emperor's east garden; some of them nested in the corniced galleries; some sang in the courtyards. As the males sang, the females danced. There were qilin in the parks, and spirit-birds came with dignified grace. There were*

009 *lou as big as goats, big yin [colored] like rainbows. The emperor, seeing that the ether of earth was dominant, reigned by the virtue of earth. [Beginning with] day gengshen, the sky was misted over for three days and three nights, [so that] it was dark in the daytime. The emperor asked Tianlao, Limu and*

010 *Rongcheng, "Oh, gentlemen, what [do you make of this]?" Tianlao replied, "I have heard it said that when a country is at peace and its ruler is fond of culture, then phoenixes dwell in it. When a country is in disorder and its ruler is fond of war, then the phoenixes leave*

011 *it. Now phoenixes fly about in your eastern borders and are happy there. The sound of their singing is exactly in tune, in accord with Heaven. In view of this, [one sees that] Heaven is giving your majesty severe instructions, which you must not*

012 *disobey." The emperor ordered the diviner to divine about it, but the turtle shell was [only] scorched. The diviner said, "I am not able to divine it. You should ask a sage." The emperor said, "I have already asked Tianlao, Limu, and Rongcheng [about it]." The diviner, facing north*

013 *with a double reverence, said "The turtle does not contradict sage wisdom, [so] it was [only] scorched." After the mist had abated, [the emperor] was relaxing by the Luo stream, when he saw a great fish. When he had killed five victims in sacrifice to it, Heaven then rained heavily seven days*

014 *and seven nights. The fish floated off to the sea, and thereby were obtained the Diagram and the Book. The Dragon Diagram, came forth from the He, and the Turtle Book came forth from the Luo. Written in red, in seal characters, they were presented to Xian Yuan, who then received the many spirits in the Bright Court.*

015 59th year: The [chiefs of the] Guanxiong (Perforated Breasts) People came as guests (in submission). The [chiefs of the] Changgu (Long Legs) People came as guests (in submission). 77th year: Chang Yi was sent down [from the court] to dwell by the Ruo River. He begat Di Qian Huang. 100th year: The earth was rent. The emperor died. *When he was buried,*

1

	15	14	13	12	11	10	09	08	07	06	05	04	03	02	01	
01	五													元	**黃**	01
02	十													年	**帝**	02
03	九													帝	**軒**	03
04	年	七	再	犯	之	容	大	生	時	雲	定	顏	母	即	**轅**	04
05	貫	夜	拜	也	今	成	螻	草	見	之	聖	有	曰	位	**氏**	05
06	胸	魚	曰	召	鳳	曰	如	或	於	瑞	德	聖	附	居		06
07	氏	流	龜	史	凰	於	羊	止	攝	赤	光	德	寶	有		07
08	來	於	不	卜	翔	公	大	帝	提	方	被	劾	見	熊		08
09	賓	海	違	之	于	何	螾	之	名	氣	群	百	大	初		09
10	長	得	聖	龜	東	如	如	東	日	與	瑞	神	電	製		10
11	股	圖	智	燋	郊	天	虹	園	景	青	畢	朝	繞	冕		11
12	氏	書	故	史	而	老	帝	或	星	方	臻	而	北	服		12
13	來	焉	燋	曰	樂	曰	以	巢	帝	氣	有	使	斗	。		13
14	賓	龍	霧	臣	之	臣	土	於	黃	相	屈	之	樞	二		14
15	。	圖	既	不	其	聞	氣	阿	服	連	軼	應	星	十		15
16	七	出	降	能	鳴	之	勝	閣	齋	赤	之	龍	光	年		16
17	十	河	游	占	音	國	遂	或	于	方	草	攻	照	景		17
18	七	龜	于	也	中	安	以	鳴	中	中	生	蚩	郊	雲		18
19	年	書	洛	其	夷	其	土	於	宮	有	於	尤	野	見		19
20	昌	出	水	問	則	主	德	庭	坐	兩	庭	戰	感	以		20
21	意	洛	之	之	與	好	王	其	于	星	佞	虎	而	雲		21
22	降	赤	上	聖	天	文	庚	雄	玄	青	人	豹	孕	紀		22
23	居	文	見	人	相	則	申	自	扈	方	入	熊	二	官		23
24	弱	篆	大	帝	副	鳳	天	歌	洛	中	朝	羆	十	。		24
25	水	字	魚	曰	以	凰	霧	其	水	有	則	四	五	五		25
26	產	以	殺	已	是	居	三	雌	之	一	草	獸	月	十		26
27	帝	授	五	問	觀	之	日	自	上	星	指	之	而	年		27
28	乾	軒	牲	天	之	國	三	舞	有	凡	之	力	生	秋		28
29	荒	轅	以	老	天	亂	夜	麒	鳳	三	是	以	帝	七		29
30	。	軒	醮	力	有	其	晝	麟	凰	星	以	女	於	月		30
31	一	轅	之	牧	嚴	主	昏	在	集	皆	佞	魃	壽	庚		31
32	百	接	天	容	教	好	帝	囿	不	黃	人	止	丘	申		32
33	年	萬	乃	成	以	武	問	神	食	色	不	淫	弱	鳳		33
34	地	神	甚	矣	賜	則	天	鳥	生	以	敢	雨	而	鳥		34
35	裂	于	雨	史	帝	鳳	老	來	蟲	天	進	天	能	至		35
36	帝	明	七	北	帝	凰	力	儀	不	清	有	下	言	帝		36
37	陟	庭	日	面	勿	去	牧	有	履	明	景	既	龍	祭		37
38	。													于		38
39	既													洛		39
40	葬													水		40
	015	014	013	012	011	010	009	008	007	006	005	004	003	002	001	

016 *one of his ministers named Zuo Che, was moved and thought of the emperor's virtue, and took his cloak, cap, table and staff and in [Huang Di's] temple made offerings to them. Each year in each season the regional lords and the grand officers came to court there. Seven years after the death [of Huang Di], Zhuan Xu was established [as di].*

017 **The Emperor Zhuan Xu**, ***Name Gao Yang***.

018 *His mother's name was Nü Shu. She saw a star with the brilliance of a green gem pierce the moon like a rainbow, and felt [sexual contact] in herself in the Dark House Palace. She gave birth to Zhuan Xu by the Ruo Stream. On top of his head he had [the image of a] weapon; he had the virtue of a sage.*

019 *When he was ten years old he assisted Shao Hao. (As for* ***Di Zhi***, ***called Shao Hao****, his mother was called Nü Jie. She saw star(s) like a rainbow flow down to Huazhu (the Hua Isle), and then she dreamed that she met [the spirit] and imagined that she felt [sexual contact], and gave birth to Shao*

020 *Hao. When he rose to the position of emperor there were auspicious appearances of phoenixes.) When [Zhuan Xu] was twenty he rose to the position of emperor.* First year: The Emperor took his position as ruler and dwelt in Pu. 13th year: For the first time there was made a calendar with [sidereal] emblems. 21st year:

021 The "Welcoming the Clouds" music was made. 30th year: The Emperor begat Bo Gun; he dwelt by the south side of Tianmu. 78th year: The Emperor died. Shu Qi raised a revolt. Xin Hou destroyed him. **Di Ku**, ***Name Gao Xin***.

022 *He was born with double teeth; he had the virtue of a sage. He had been enfeoffed as Xin Hou, and succeeded Gao Yang as ruler of the world. He had blind musicians beat drums and strike bells and chime stones; phoenixes beat their wings and danced [to the music].* First year: The Emperor took his position [as ruler] and dwelt in

023 Bo. 16th year: The Emperor had Chong lead an army to put an end to You Kuai. 45th year: The Emperor conferred on [Yao], Lord of Tang, a charge. 63rd year: The Emperor died. *The Emperor's son Zhi was raised [to the throne, but] after nine years he was displaced.*

024 **The Emperor Yao, *Name Tao Tang***.

025 First year: The emperor took his position as ruler, and dwelt in Ji. He commanded Xi and He [to make] a calendar and [matching] zodiac. 5th year: He for the first time went on a tour of inspection of the Four [Sacred] Mountains. 7th year: A *lin* appeared. 12th year: He for the first time held a military review. 16th year: [The chief of] the Qusou people came

026 as guest [to make his submission]. 19th year: [Yao] ordered Gong Gong to regulate the yellow River. 29th year: Spring: [The chief of] the Jiaoyao (Pigmies) came to court [in homage], with tribute of sinking feathers. 42nd year: A lucky star appeared in Yi. 50th year: The emperor traveled for pleasure

027 to Mount Shou, riding in a plain carriage with dark horses. 53rd year: The emperor sacrificed at the Luo River. 58th year: The emperor ordered Hou Ji to banish the emperor's son Dan Zhu to the Dan River [area]. 61st year: He ordered

028 Gun, *bo* of Chong, to regulate the Yellow River. 69th year: Gun, *bo* of Chong, was degraded. 70th year: Spring, first month: The emperor had [the chiefs of] the Four [Sacred] Mountains convey to Shun of Yu an appointment. 71st year: The emperor ordered his two daughters to be married to

029 Shun. 73rd year: Spring, first month: Shun received the emperor's abdication in the ancestral [temple] of culture. 74th year: Shun of Yu for the first time made a tour of inspection to the Four [Sacred] Mountains. 75th year: Yu [of Xia], Superintendent of Works, regulated the Yellow River. 76th

030 year: The Superintendent of Works attacked the *rong* of Cao and Wei and defeated them. 86th year: The Superintendent of Works entered [the emperor's presence] for an audience, and received as a ceremonial gift a dark colored jade *gui*-tablet. 87th year: The division [of the empire] into twelve provinces was established for the first time. 89th year:

2

	30	29	28	27	26	25	24	23	22	21	20	19	18	17	16	
01	六	舜	崇	于	賓	元	**帝**	亳	生	作				**帝**		01
02	年	。	伯	首	。	年	**堯**	。	而	承				**顓**		02
03	司	七	鯀	山	十	帝	**陶**	十	駢	雲				**頊**		03
04	空	十	治	乘	九	即	**唐**	六	齒	之	昊	十	母	**高**	群	04
05	伐	三	河	素	年	位	**氏**	年	有	樂	登	年	曰	**陽**	臣	05
06	曹	年	。	車	命	居		帝	聖	。	帝	而	女	**氏**	有	06
07	魏	春	六	玄	共	冀		使	德	三	位	佐	樞		左	07
08	之	正	十	駒	工	命		重	初	十	有	少	見		徹	08
09	戎	月	九	。	治	羲		帥	封	年	鳳	昊	瑤		者	09
10	克	舜	年	五	河	和		師	辛	帝	皇	氏	光		感	10
11	之	受	黜	十	。	曆		滅	侯	產	之	。	之		思	11
12	。	終	崇	三	二	象		有	代	伯	瑞	**帝**	星		帝	12
13	八	于	伯	年	十	。		鄶	高	鯀	。	**摯**	貫		德	13
14	十	文	鯀	帝	九	五		。	陽	居	二	**少**	月		取	14
15	六	祖	。	祭	年	年		四	氏	天	十	**昊**	如		衣	15
16	年	。	七	于	春	初		十	王	穆	而	**氏**	虹		冠	16
17	司	七	十	洛	僬	巡		五	天	之	登	。	感		几	17
18	空	十	年	。	僥	狩		年	下	陽	帝	母	己		杖	18
19	入	四	春	五	氏	四		帝	使	。	位	曰	於		而	19
20	覲	年	正	十	來	岳		錫	瞽	七	。	女	幽		廟	20
21	贄	虞	月	八	朝	。		唐	人	十	元	節	房		饗	21
22	用	舜	帝	年	貢	七		侯	拊	八	年	見	之		之	22
23	玄	初	使	帝	沒	年		命	鞞	年	帝	星	宮		諸	23
24	圭	巡	四	使	羽	有		。	鼓	帝	即	如	生		侯	24
25	。	狩	岳	后	。	麟		六	擊	陟	位	虹	顓		大	25
26	八	四	錫	稷	四	。		十	鐘	術	居	下	頊		夫	26
27	十	岳	虞	放	十	十		三	磬	器	濮	流	於		歲	27
28	七	。	舜	帝	二	二		年	鳳	作	。	華	若		時	28
29	年	七	命	子	年	年		帝	皇	亂	十	渚	水		朝	29
30	初	十	。	丹	景	初		陟	鼓	辛	三	既	首		焉	30
31	建	五	七	朱	星	治		。	翼	侯	年	而	戴		死	31
32	十	年	十	于	見	兵		帝	而	滅	初	夢	干		七	32
33	有	司	一	丹	于	。		子	舞	之	作	接	戈		年	33
34	二	空	年	水	翼	十		摯	。	。	曆	意	有		乃	34
35	州	禹	帝	。	。	六		立	元	**帝**	象	感	聖		立	35
36	。	治	命	六	五	年		九	年	**嚳**	。	生	德		**顓**	36
37	八	河	二	十	十	渠		年	帝	**高**	二	少	生		**頊**	37
38	十	。	女	一	年	搜		而	即	**辛**	十					38
39	九	七	嬪	年	帝	氏		廢	位	**氏**	一					39
40	年	十	于	命	游	來		。	居	。	年					40
	030	029	028	027	026	025	024	023	022	021	020	019	018	017	016	

031 *Shun imprisoned Yao in Pingyang.* A pleasure palace was built [for Yao] in Tao. 90th year: The emperor went to live in retirement in Tao. 97th year: The Superintendent of Works made a tour of inspection of the twelve provinces. 100th year: The emperor passed away in Tao.

032 *His mother's name was Qingdu. She was born in the Dou-Wei country. There was always a yellow cloud covering her. After she grew up, whenever she looked into the Three Rivers, there was always a dragon following her. One morning a dragon bearing a picture*

033 *came. The substance of its text was this: "Red receives Heaven's favor." The eyebrows [of the figure in the picture] were varicolored and beautiful; the whiskers were more than a foot long; [the figure] was seven feet two inches tall; its face was pointed above and broad below; its feet were treading on the lunar constellation Yi. Thereupon cold and dark winds*

034 *blew from all directions, as the red dragon impregnated her. She was pregnant for fourteen months, and then gave birth to Yao in Danling ("red mound"). In appearance he was like the picture. He grew to be ten feet tall. He had the virtue of a sage. He was given Tang as a fief. He dreamed that he climbed*

035 *up to Heaven. In Gao Xin's declining years the world turned to Yao. In the emperor's 70th year of rule a lucky star appeared in the constellation Yi, and there were phoenixes in the [palace] courtyards. The red plant grew. The excellent grain flourished. Sweet dew moistened the ground,*

036 *and springs of sweet water came forth. The sun and moon were like joined jade discs, and the five planets were like a string of pearls. In the [emperor's] kitchens there appeared a piece of flesh as thin as a fan which when shaken produced a breeze that cooled foods so that they did not spoil. It was called*

037 *the meat fan (jiefu). Also there was a plant that grew along the [palace] stairs. On the first of the lunar month it produced one pod; half way through the month it had grown fifteen pods; from the 16th day on it dropped a pod each day, so that on the last day*

038 *there were none. In a short (29-day) month one pod would shrivel and not drop off. It was called the "auspicious bean," also the "calendar bean." When the surging waters had been calmed [the emperor] gave the credit to Shun, and was going to resign from [the rule of] the world in favor of Shun. So he purified himself*

039 *and fasted, and built altars near the He and the Luo River. Selecting a lucky day he then led Shun and others up Mount Shou. Along the islets of the He there were five old men taking their ease there. They were probably the essences of the five planets. They said to each other, "The River*

040 *Diagram will come forth, telling the emperor the appointed time. He who knows us is the double-pupilled yellow [one from] Yao." The five old men then flew away becoming flowing stars, ascending and entering the constellation Mao (the Pleiades). In the second month, on day xinchou (38), [beginning at] the first light of dawn, the rites were all performed. As the*

041 *day declined a glorious light came out of the He, and auspicious vapors filled the sky on all sides; white clouds rose up and whirlwinds shook [everything]. Then there was a dragon-horse holding in its mouth a shield, green in color with red markings; it climbed up the altar, laid down the shield-diagram, and*

042 *left. The shield resembled a turtle's carapace, the diagram was labeled in white jade, with a casing in red jade, immersed in yellow gold, and bound with an azure cord. The label read, "Graciously given to Emperor*

043 *Shun." It said that Yu and Xia were to be given Heaven's mandate [to rule]. The emperor then wrote down the words and put them away in the Eastern College of Elders. Two years later, on the second xin day of the second month, leading all his officers, he cast a jade disc into the Luo River. When this ceremony was finished,*

044 *he withdrew and waited. As the day was ebbing, a red brilliance arose; a prime turtle came forth [from the River] bearing writing: on its carapace were designs in red that formed words. It stopped at the altar. The writing said that [the emperor] must resign in favor of Shun. Subsequently, he yielded [the imperial position] to Shun. When*

045 *Yao's competence declined, Shun imprisoned him in Pingyang, and took his throne. he also restricted Yao's son Dan Zhu, and kept him away from seeing his father. [After Yao died], his son Dan Zhu avoided Shun, [staying] in Fangling. Shun tried to yield to him without*

3

	45	44	43	42	41	40	39	38	37	36	35	34	33	32	31	
01															舜	01
02															囚	02
03															帝	03
04	堯	退	舜	去	日	圖	齋	盡	曰	醴	天	四	至	母	于	04
05	德	侯	言	甲	昃	將	修	月	箑	泉	而	合	其	曰	平	05
06	衰	至	虞	似	榮	來	壇	小	脯	出	上	赤	文	慶	陽	06
07	舜	於	夏	龜	光	告	場	則	又	日	高	龍	要	都	作	07
08	囚	下	當	背	出	帝	於	一	有	月	辛	感	曰	生	游	08
09	之	昃	受	廣	河	以	河	莢	草	如	氏	之	赤	於	宮	09
10	于	赤	天	九	休	期	洛	焦	莢	合	衰	孕	受	斗	于	10
11	平	光	命	尺	氣	知	擇	而	階	璧	天	十	天	維	陶	11
12	陽	起	帝	其	四	我	良	不	而	五	下	四	祐	之	。	12
13	取	元	乃	圖	塞	者	日	落	生	星	歸	月	眉	野	九	13
14	帝	龜	寫	以	白	重	率	名	月	如	之	而	八	常	十	14
15	位	負	其	白	雲	瞳	舜	曰	朔	連	帝	生	彩	有	年	15
16	復	書	言	玉	起	黃	等	蓂	始	珠	在	堯	鬢	黃	帝	16
17	偃	而	藏	為	回	姚	升	莢	生	廚	位	於	髮	雲	游	17
18	塞	出	於	檢	風	五	首	一	一	中	七	丹	尺	覆	居	18
19	堯	背	東	赤	搖	老	山	曰	莢	自	十	陵	餘	其	于	19
20	子	甲	序	玉	乃	因	遵	曆	半	生	年	其	長	上	陶	20
21	丹	赤	後	為	有	飛	河	莢	而	肉	景	狀	七	及	。	21
22	朱	文	二	柙	龍	為	渚	洪	生	其	星	如	尺	長	九	22
23	使	成	年	泥	馬	流	有	水	十	薄	出	圖	二	觀	十	23
24	不	字	二	以	銜	星	五	既	五	如	翼	及	寸	於	七	24
25	與	止	月	黃	甲	上	老	平	莢	箑	鳳	長	面	三	年	25
26	父	于	仲	金	赤	入	游	歸	十	搖	皇	身	銳	河	司	26
27	相	壇	辛	約	文	昴	焉	功	六	動	在	長	上	常	空	27
28	見	其	率	以	綠	二	蓋	於	日	則	庭	十	豐	有	巡	28
29	朱	書	群	青	色	月	五	舜	以	風	朱	尺	下	龍	十	29
30	避	言	臣	繩	緣	辛	星	將	後	生	草	有	足	隨	有	30
31	舜	當	東	檢	壇	丑	之	以	日	食	生	聖	履	之	二	31
32	於	禪	沈	文	而	昧	精	天	落	物	嘉	德	翼	一	州	32
33	房	舜	壁	曰	上	明	也	下	一	寒	禾	封	宿	旦	。	33
34	陵	遂	於	闓	吐	禮	相	禪	莢	而	秀	於	既	龍	一	34
35	舜	讓	洛	色	甲	備	謂	之	及	不	甘	唐	而	負	百	35
36	讓	舜	禮	授	圖	至	曰	乃	晦	臭	露	夢	陰	圖	年	36
37	不	既	畢	帝	而	於	河	潔	而	名	潤	攀	風	而	帝	37
38															陟	38
39															于	39
40															陶	40
	045	044	043	042	041	040	039	038	037	036	035	034	033	032	031	

046 *success. Zhu subsequently was given Fang as a fief, and submitted to [the house of] Yu (= Shun). After three years [of mourning], Shun assumed the position of Son of Heaven.*

047 **The Emperor Shun**, ***Name You Yu***. First year: The emperor took the position [of emperor] and dwelt in Ji. He made the Great Shao music. 3rd year: Gao Yao was ordered to create a penal code.

048 9th year: Xiwangmu came to court. 14th year: Auspicious clouds appeared. Yu was ordered to take care of affairs [of state] for [the emperor]. *His mother's name was Wodeng. Seeing a large rainbow, she felt herself impregnated, and bore Shun in Yaoxu. His eyes had double (chong) pupils,*

049 *so he was named Chonghua (Double Brightness). He had the face of a dragon with a large mouth, a dark complexion, and a body six feet one inch tall. Shun's father and mother hated him. They had him plaster the granary, and set fire to it from below; but Shun was wearing bird*

050 *work clothes and flew away. They had him dig a well, and filled it with rocks from above, but he was wearing dragon work clothes and got out from the side. While he was plowing in Li, he dreamed that his eyebrows were as long as his hair. Subsequently*

051 *he was raised [to office] and employed [in important work, leading to becoming emperor]. When he took the imperial position, the calendar bean grew up on the stairs, and phoenixes nested in his courtyards. When chime-stones were struck or tapped as music for the nine-fold shao [performance], the many [kinds of] animals all danced. A lucky star appeared in Fang. The earth produced*

052 *the [spirit]-horse chenghuang. When Xiwangmu came to court, he/she presented white bracelets and jade thumb-rings for archers. When [the emperor] had been reigning for fourteen years there was a performance of bells, chimes, mouth organs and flutes. Before it was finished there was a great storm of rain and thunder with a violent*

053 *wind that uplifted houses and uprooted trees. Drumsticks and drums were scattered on the ground; [the sounds of the] bells and chimes were mixed up; the dancers fell to the ground; the music master lost his head and ran away. But Shun, keeping hold of the frames suspending the bells and chime-stones, laughed and said, "It is obvious that the empire*

054 *is not just one man's empire! Indeed, this is shown by these bells, chimes, organs and flutes." Accordingly he presented Yu to Heaven, [doing this by] having him perform the duties of the Son of Heaven. When this was done harmonious vapors responded on all sides and felicitous*

055 *clouds arose. They were like smoke yet not smoke, like clouds yet not clouds, beautiful yet confused, sighing and spiraling. All the officers joined in harmony and sang the "Felicitous Clouds" [music]. The emperor then sang it: The felicitous clouds*

056 *how bright! Slowly blending together! The brilliance of the sun and moon [shines] dawn after dawn! All the officers then advanced together and bowed their heads to the ground, singing, Shining, shining is High Heaven, Brightly the stars are ordered; The brilliance of the sun and moon Spreads*

057 *over [our] One Man. The emperor then sang again: Sun and moon have their constancy, Stars and chronograms their course. The four seasons follow their rule, The myriad peoples truly fulfilled! Ah! Our ordered music Matches the spirit of Heaven, Inspiring*

058 *sages and worthies; None but do fully savor it. Chang! Go its drums! Merrily we dance to it! Its spirit all expressed, We pick up our skirts and leave. Thereupon winds from whatever direction blew genially, and [more] felicitous clouds massed together; coiled dragons*

059 *bestirred themselves and quickly [came out of] their dens; flood-dragons and fish leaped up from their deeps; tortoises and turtles all came out of their holes: [all were] shifting from [allegiance to] Yu (虞=Shun) to serve Xia. Shun then set up an altar near the Yellow River following the precedent of Yao.*

060 *At day's end a glorious brilliance came forth betokening blessing. A yellow dragon came out onto the bank where the altar stood, bearing on its back a diagram thirty-two feet long and nine feet wide. It had a text in red with green ornament. The text said that [Shun] must abdicate in favor of Yu [of Xia].*

4

	60	59	58	57	56	55	54	53	52	51	50	49	48	47	46	
01													。	**帝**		01
02													九	**舜**		02
03													年	**有**		03
04	於	奮	聖	于	爛	雲	非	風	乘	登	工	瞳	西	**虞**	克	04
05	下	迅	賢	一	兮	興	一	發	黃	庸	衣	子	王	**氏**	朱	05
06	昃	於	莫	人	禮	焉	人	屋	之	即	服	故	母		遂	06
07	榮	其	不	帝	縵	若	之	拔	馬	帝	飛	名	來		封	07
08	光	藏	咸	乃	縵	煙	天	木	西	位	去	重	朝		於	08
09	休	蛟	聽	再	兮	非	下	桴	王	蓂	又	華	。		房	09
10	氣	魚	饕	歌	日	煙	也	鼓	母	莢	使	龍	十		為	10
11	至	踴	乎	曰	月	若	亦	播	之	生	浚	顏	四		虞	11
12	黃	躍	鼓	日	光	雲	乃	地	來	於	井	大	年		賓	12
13	龍	於	之	月	華	非	見	鐘	朝	階	自	口	卿		三	13
14	負	其	軒	有	旦	雲	於	磬	獻	鳳	上	黑	雲		年	14
15	圖	淵	乎	常	復	郁	鐘	亂	白	皇	填	色	見		舜	15
16	長	黿	舞	星	旦	郁	石	行	環	巢	之	身	命		即	16
17	三	鱉	之	辰	兮	紛	笙	舞	玉	於	以	長	禹		天	17
18	十	咸	精	有	群	紛	筦	人	玦	庭	石	六	代		子	18
19	二	出	華	行	臣	蕭	乎	頓	在	擊	舜	尺	虞		之	19
20	尺	其	已	四	咸	索	乃	伏	位	石	服	一	事		位	20
21	廣	穴	竭	時	進	輪	荐	樂	十	拊	龍	寸	母	元		21
22	九	遷	褰	從	頓	囷	禹	正	有	石	工	舜	曰	年		22
23	尺	虞	裳	經	首	百	於	狂	四	以	衣	父	握	帝		23
24	出	而	去	萬	曰	工	天	走	年	歌	自	母	登	即		24
25	於	事	之	姓	明	相	使	舜	奏	九	傍	憎	見	位		25
26	壇	夏	於	允	明	和	行	乃	鐘	韶	而	舜	大	居		26
27	畔	舜	是	誠	上	而	天	磬	石	百	出	使	虹	冀		27
28	赤	乃	八	於	天	歌	子	堵	笙	獸	耕	其	意	作		28
29	文	設	風	子	爛	卿	事	持	筦	率	於	塗	感	大		29
30	綠	壇	循	論	然	雲	也	衡	未	舞	歷	廩	而	韶		30
31	錯	於	通	樂	星	帝	於	而	罷	景	夢	自	生	之		31
32	其	河	慶	配	陳	乃	是	笑	而	星	眉	下	舜	樂		32
33	文	依	雲	天	日	倡	和	曰	天	出	長	焚	於	。		33
34	言	堯	叢	之	月	之	氣	明	大	於	與	之	姚	三		34
35	當	故	集	靈	光	曰	普	哉	雷	房	髮	舜	墟	年		35
36	禪	事	蟠	遷	華	慶	應	天	雨	地	等	服	目	命		36
37	禹	至	龍	于	弘	雲	慶	下	疾	出	遂	鳥	重	咎		37
38														陶		38
39														作		39
40														刑		40
	060	059	058	057	056	055	054	053	052	051	050	049	048	047	046	

061 15th year: The emperor commanded the Lord of Xia to sacrifice in the Great Hall. 17th year, spring, second month: [The Lord of Xia] entered the College, and for the first time performed the *wan* ("myriad") dance. 25th year: [The chief of] the Xishen [people] came to court, with tribute of bows and arrows.

062 29th year: The emperor commanded that his son Yijun be enfeoffed in Shang. 30th year: The empress Yu was buried in Wei. 32nd year: The emperor commanded that the *hou* of Xia should assume general direction of the army. He subsequently ascended the [sacred] peaks on the borders. 33rd year, Spring,

063 first month: The *hou* of Xia received [Shun's] appointment in the Spirit Temple [to be his successor as emperor]. Subsequently the nine-province [division of the empire] was restored. 35th year: The emperor ordered the *hou* of Xia to [lead the army to] punish the Miao. [The chief of] the Miao people came to court [in submission]. 42nd year: [The chief of] the Xuandu people came to court,

064 with tribute of precious jade. 47th year, winter: Hoarfrost descended, without killing plants and trees. 49th year: The emperor dwelt in Mingtiao. 50th year: The emperor died. *Mourning 3 years.* **The Emperor Yu**, ***Name Xiahou***.

065 *His mother's name was Xiuji. She went out walking and saw flowing stars penetrating the constellation Mao. She dreamed that she had intercourse, and imagined that she became pregnant. After that she swallowed a spirit-pearl. Xiuji's back split open and she gave birth to Yu in Shiniu. He had the nose of a tiger, and a big mouth;*

066 *both ears had three openings. On the top of his head were [the designs of] the constellations Kou ("the Hook") and Ling ('the Bell"). On his breast was [the design,] in gems, of the constellation Dou ("the Dipper"). On the soles of his feet were marks [forming the character] ji ("self"); accordingly he was named "Wenming" ("destiny indicated in marks"). When he grew up he had the virtue of a sage, and was nine feet nine inches tall. He dreamed that he was bathing in the Yellow River,*

067 *and took some water [in his hand] and drank it. Also, there was an auspicious sign of a white fox with nine tails. In the time of Yao, Shun employed him. Once when Yu was looking at the Yellow River, a tall man with a white face and the body of a fish came out and said, "I am the River [Spirit]-*

068 *Essence." He called out to Yu saying "Wenming will regulate the waters." When he had finished speaking he gave Yu the River Diagram explaining the problem of regulating waters, then withdrew and disappeared into the deep. When Yu's regulating of the waters [of the Yellow River] had been finished, Heaven gave him a black jade scepter,*

069 *to use in announcing the completion of his labors. When the Way of Xia was about to flourish, plants and trees grew luxuriantly; azure dragons tarried in the borders; the spirit Zhurong descended on Mount Chong. Thereupon [Yu] received the abdication of Shun, and took his position as Son of Heaven.*

070 *The Luo [River] produced the Turtle Book; this was the "Hong Fan" (the "Great Plan"). When the three-years mourning was finished, he made his capital at Yangcheng.* First year: The emperor took his position, and dwelt in Ji. He promulgated the "Seasons of Xia" among the regional states. 2nd year: Gao Yao died.

071 5th year: [Yu] went on a tour of inspection, and assembled the regional lords at Mount Tu. 8th year, Spring: [Yu] assembled the regional lords in Kuaiji, and executed [the chief of] the Fangfeng people. In summer, in the 6th month, it rained gold in the Xia [capital] city. In Autumn, 8th month, the emperor died in Kuaiji.

072 *On a tour of inspection to the south, while crossing the Yangzi, in mid-stream there were two yellow dragons that held up the boat on their backs. The boatmen were all terrified. Yu laughed and said, "I have received my appointment from Heaven, and I bend my strength to care for humanity. One lives and dies according to destiny.*

073 *Why should I worry about dragons? The dragons at this went away, dragging their tails behind them. Yu reigned for 45 years. Yu presented [his] chief minister] Yi to Heaven [for approval]. Seven years later Yu died. When the three-years mourning was completed, the empire gave its allegiance to [Yu's son] Qi.*

074 **The Emperor Qi**. First year: The emperor took his position as ruler in the City of Xia. He set a great feast for the regional lords in the Jun Tai ("Wheel Tower"). The regional lords followed the emperor back to his capital, Ji. He [there] set a great feast for the regional lords in the Xuan Tai ("JadeTower.") 2nd year: Bo Yi, *hou* of Bi,

075 left and went to his state. The king led an army to attack the [state of] You Hu, and there was a great battle in Gan. 6th year: Bo Yi died; a sacrifice was performed for him. 8th year: The emperor sent Meng Tu to Ba, to judge legal cases. 10th year: The emperor made a tour of inspection, and danced

5

	15	14	13	12	11	10	09	08	07	06	05	04	03	02	01	
01	益	。			五							貢	正	九	十	01
02	出	**帝**			年							寶	月	年	五	02
03	就	**啟**			巡							玉	夏	帝	年	03
04	國	。	奚	南	狩	洛	以	精	取	兩	母	。	后	命	帝	04
05	王	元	憂	巡	會	出	告	也	水	耳	曰	四	受	子	命	05
06	帥	年	龍	狩	諸	龜	成	呼	飲	參	修	十	命	義	夏	06
07	師	帝	哉	濟	侯	書	功	禹	之	鏤	己	七	于	鈞	后	07
08	伐	即	龍	江	于	是	夏	曰	又	首	出	年	神	封	有	08
09	有	位	於	中	涂	為	道	文	有	戴	行	冬	宗	于	事	09
10	扈	于	是	流	山	洪	將	命	白	鉤	見	隕	遂	商	于	10
11	大	夏	曳	有	。	范	興	治	狐	鈐	流	霜	復	。	太	11
12	戰	邑	尾	二	八	三	草	水	九	胸	星	不	九	三	室	12
13	于	大	而	黃	年	年	木	言	尾	有	貫	殺	州	十	。	13
14	甘	饗	逝	龍	春	喪	暢	訖	之	玉	昴	草	。	年	十	14
15	。	諸	禹	負	會	畢	茂	授	瑞	斗	夢	木	三	葬	七	15
16	六	侯	立	舟	諸	禹	青	禹	當	足	接	。	十	后	年	16
17	年	于	四	舟	侯	都	龍	河	堯	文	意	四	五	育	春	17
18	伯	鈞	十	人	于	於	止	圖	之	履	感	十	年	于	二	18
19	益	臺	五	皆	會	陽	於	言	時	已	既	九	帝	渭	月	19
20	薨	諸	年	懼	稽	城	郊	治	舜	故	而	年	命	。	入	20
21	祠	侯	禹	禹	殺	元	祝	水	舉	名	吞	帝	夏	三	學	21
22	之	從	荐	笑	防	年	融	之	之	文	神	居	后	十	初	22
23	。	帝	益	曰	風	帝	之	事	禹	命	珠	于	征	二	用	23
24	八	歸	於	吾	氏	即	神	乃	觀	長	修	鳴	有	年	萬	24
25	年	于	天	受	夏	位	降	退	於	有	己	條	苗	帝	。	25
26	帝	冀	七	命	六	居	於	入	河	聖	背	。	有	命	二	26
27	使	都	年	於	月	冀	崇	於	有	德	剖	五	苗	夏	十	27
28	孟	大	禹	天	雨	頒	山	淵	長	長	而	十	氏	后	五	28
29	涂	饗	崩	屈	金	夏	乃	禹	人	九	生	年	來	總	年	29
30	如	諸	三	力	于	時	受	治	白	尺	禹	帝	朝	師	息	30
31	巴	侯	年	以	夏	于	舜	水	面	九	於	陟	。	遂	慎	31
32	蒞	于	喪	養	邑	邦	禪	既	魚	寸	石	居	四	陟	氏	32
33	訟	璿	畢	人	秋	國	即	畢	身	夢	紐	三	十	方	來	33
34	。	臺	天	生	八	。	天	天	出	自	虎	年	二	岳	朝	34
35	十	。	下	死	月	二	子	錫	曰	洗	鼻	。	年	。	貢	35
36	年	二	歸	命	帝	年	之	玄	吾	於	大	**帝**	玄	三	弓	36
37	帝	年	啟	也	陟	咎	位	珪	河	河	口	**禹**	都	十	矢	37
38	巡	費			于	陶						**夏**	氏	三	。	38
39	狩	侯			會	薨						**后**	來	年	二	39
40	舞	伯			稽	。						**氏**	朝	春	十	40
	075	074	073	072	071	070	069	068	067	066	065	064	063	062	061	

076 [Shun's music,] the nine *shao*, in the wilds of Da Mu. 11th year: The junior prince Wu Guan was banished to Xihe. 15th year: Wu Guan led Xihe in rebellion. Peng *Bo* Shou led an army to punish Xihe. Wu Guan

077 returned to his allegiance. 16th year: [The emperor] died. *Mourning four years.* **The Emperor Tai Kang**. First year: The emperor took his position as ruler, and dwelt in Zhenxun. He went hunting beyond the Luo River. Yi entered [the court] and lived in Zhenxun [taking possession of it]. 4th year: [The emperor] died. *Mourning two years.*

078 **The Emperor Zhong Kang**. First year: The emperor took his position as ruler, and dwelt in Zhenxun. 5th year, autumn, 9th month, day *gengxu*: There was an eclipse of the sun. The *hou* of Yin was ordered to lead an army to punish Xi and He. 6th year: [The lord of] Kunwu was given an appointment

079 as *bo*. 7th year: [The emperor] died. *Mourning two years.* The heir, Xiang, left [the capital] and lived in Shangqiu, relying on the support of lords of the same surname in Zhenguan and Zhenxun. **The Emperor Xiang**. First year: The emperor took his position [as ruler], residing in Shang. He made a punitive expedition against the Huai Yi.

080 2nd year: He made a punitive expedition against the Yi [tribes] of Feng and Huang. 7th year: The Yi [tribes] of Yu came [to court] as guests [to submit]. 8th year: Han Zhuo killed Yi. He had his son Jiao reside in Guo. 9th year: Xiang resided in Zhenguan. 15th year: The Shang

081 lord Xiangtu created [an army of] chariots and horses. After that, [Xiang] returned to Shangqiu. 20th year: Han Zhuo destroyed [the state of] Ge. 26th year: Han Zhuo had his son lead an army to destroy [the state of] Zhenguan. 27th year: Jiao

082 attacked Zhenxun. There was a great battle in Wei. The boat [of the lord of Zhenxun] was overturned, [he was killed,] and [his state] was destroyed. 28th year: Han Zhuo had his son Jiao assassinate the emperor. Empress Min was just then pregnant, and returned to [her people] the Reng. Bo Mi fled to Ge. *Next*

083 *year*, the Xia heir Shao Kang was born. Shao Kang left the Rong people and fled to Yu. Bo Mi coming from Ge led armies of Zhenxun and Zhenguan attacking [Han] Zhuo. The heir Shao Kang had Ruyi attack Guo, killing Jiao.

084 Elder son Zhu led an army destroying Ge. Bo Mi killed Han Zhuo. Shao Kang left [the city of] Lun and returned to the City of Xia. *Empress Min gave birth to Shao Kang. When he grew to manhood he became chief shepherd of the Rong. Mindful of the evil designs of Jiao, he was able to take precautions. Jiao 澆*

085 *sent Jiao 椒 to hunt for him. As [Jiao 椒] was about to reach Rong, Shao Kang fled to the [lord of] Yu , and became his chief cook, in order to escape trouble. Si, [lord of] Yu, thereupon gave him two beautiful [daughters] as wives, and gave him Lun as his town,*

086 *with ten square li of farmland and a troop of 500 men. [Thus Shao Kang] was able to display his virtue, and give signs of his plans, so as to collect [under his lead] the multitudes [loyal to] Xia, and give assurance to the [former] officials [of Xia]. Bo Mi, a former official of Xia, [operating] from the Ge [state],*

087 *gathered [the forces of] the two Zhen [cities] to attack [Han] Zhuo. [Han] Zhuo, relying on [his son] Jiao, was always at ease, ever forgetful of the evil he had done and making no preparations [against revenge]. Shao Kang sent Ru Yi to spy on Jiao. Earlier, [Han] Zhuo had married a woman of the Shunhu people, by whom he had a son*

088 *who had died young. The son's wife was named Nuqi, living alone as a widow. Jiao while on the borders [of his domain] went to her house pretending he was looking for something. Nuqi mended his lower garments for him, and they spent the night together. Ru Yi sent a man at night*

089 *to surprise him and cut off his head, but it turned out to be Nuqi's. Jiao, being strong and a good runner [made good his escape]. So [Ru] Yi went hunting and released dogs to chase wild animals, and they bit Jiao and brought him down; so then Jiao's head was cut off*

090 *and presented to Shao Kang. When this happened, the multitudes [loyal to] Xia killed [Han] Zhuo, and raised up Shao Kang and returned him to the City of Xia. As soon as the regional lords heard about this they elevated [Shao Kang] to the position of Son of Heaven, to sacrifice to the Xia [ancestors] and do Heaven's work. Thus the former things [i.e., the authority of the House of Xia] were not lost.*

6

	30	29	28	27	26	25	24	23	22	21	20	19	18	17	16	
01							子	年	伐	侯	二	作	**帝**	來	九	01
02							杼	夏	斟	相	年	伯	**仲**	歸	韶	02
03							帥	世	鄩	土	征	。	**康**	。	于	03
04	歸	使	子	收	有	使	師	子	大	作	風	七	。	十	大	04
05	于	人	早	二	田	椒	滅	少	戰	乘	及	年	元	六	穆	05
06	少	襲	死	斟	一	求	戈	康	于	馬	黃	陟	年	年	之	06
07	康	斷	其	以	成	之	伯	生	濰	遂	夷	居	帝	陟	野	07
08	於	其	婦	伐	有	將	靡	少	覆	遷	。	二	即	居	。	08
09	是	首	曰	浞	眾	至	殺	康	其	于	七	年	位	四	十	09
10	夏	乃	女	浞	一	仍	寒	自	舟	商	年	世	居	年	一	10
11	眾	女	歧	恃	旅	少	浞	有	滅	丘	于	子	斟	。	年	11
12	滅	歧	寡	澆	能	康	少	仍	之	。	夷	相	鄩	**帝**	放	12
13	浞	也	居	皆	布	逃	康	奔	。	二	來	出	。	**太**	王	13
14	奉	澆	澆	康	其	奔	自	虞	二	十	賓	居	五	**康**	季	14
15	少	既	強	娛	德	有	綸	伯	十	年	。	商	年	。	子	15
16	康	多	圉	日	而	虞	歸	靡	八	寒	八	丘	秋	元	武	16
17	歸	力	往	忘	兆	為	于	自	年	浞	年	依	九	年	觀	17
18	於	又	至	其	其	之	夏	鬲	寒	滅	寒	同	月	帝	于	18
19	夏	善	其	惡	謀	庖	邑	帥	浞	戈	浞	姓	庚	即	西	19
20	邑	走	戶	而	以	正	。	斟	使	。	殺	諸	戌	位	河	20
21	諸	艾	陽	不	收	以	后	鄩	其	二	羿	侯	朔	居	。	21
22	侯	乃	有	為	夏	除	緡	斟	子	十	使	斟	日	斟	十	22
23	始	畋	所	備	眾	其	生	灌	澆	六	其	灌	有	鄩	五	23
24	聞	獵	求	少	撫	害	少	之	弒	年	子	斟	食	畋	年	24
25	之	放	女	康	其	虞	康	師	帝	寒	澆	鄩	之	于	武	25
26	立	犬	歧	使	官	思	既	以	后	浞	居	。	命	洛	觀	26
27	為	逐	為	汝	職	於	長	伐	緡	使	過	**帝**	胤	表	以	27
28	天	獸	之	艾	夏	是	為	浞	歸	其	。	**相**	侯	羿	西	28
29	子	因	縫	諜	之	妻	仍	世	于	子	九	。	帥	入	河	29
30	祀	嗾	裳	澆	遺	之	牧	子	有	帥	年	元	師	居	叛	30
31	夏	澆	共	初	臣	以	正	少	仍	師	相	年	征	斟	彭	31
32	配	顛	舍	浞	伯	二	惎	康	伯	滅	居	帝	羲	鄩	伯	32
33	天	隕	而	娶	靡	姚	澆	使	靡	斟	于	即	和	。	壽	33
34	不	乃	宿	純	自	而	能	汝	出	灌	斟	位	。	四	帥	34
35	失	斬	汝	狐	有	邑	戒	艾	奔	。	灌	居	六	年	師	35
36	舊	澆	艾	氏	鬲	諸	之	伐	有	二	。	商	年	陟	征	36
37	物	以	夜	有	氏	綸	澆	過	鬲	十	十	征	錫	居	西	37
38								殺	氏	七	五	淮	昆	二	河	38
39								澆	。	年	年	夷	吾	年	武	39
40								伯	明	澆	商	。	命	。	觀	40
	090	089	088	087	086	085	084	083	082	081	080	079	078	077	076	

091 **The Emperor Shao Kang**. First year: The emperor took his position as ruler. The regional lords came to his court. He received the Duke of Yu as a guest [offering service]. 2nd year: The Yi tribes of Fang came as guests [to submit]. 3rd year: The position of [Hou] Ji as Minister of Agriculture was restored [to his descendant]. *Pei Juo, descendant of Hou Ji, had lost the [hereditary] office,*

092 *and it was restored with this [action].* 11th year: Ming, *hou* of Shang, was employed to regulate the [Yellow] River. 18th year: [The emperor] moved to Yuan. 21st year: [The emperor] died. *Mourning two years.* **The Emperor Zhu**. *[The original] Zhu was an able commander for Yu [the Xia founder], so the Xia*

093 *imperial line rewarded him [by using his name].* First year: The emperor took his position as ruler. He resided in Yuan. 5th year: He moved from Yuan to Laoqiu. 8th year: He went on a punitive expedition toward the Eastern Sea, as far as Sanshou, and got a fox with nine-tails. 13th year:

094 Ming, lord of Shang, died [while doing his work] on the Yellow River. 17th year: [The emperor] died. *Mourning two years.* **The Emperor Fen**. First year: The emperor took his position as ruler. 3rd year: The nine Yi [tribes of the east] came [to court] to do service. 16th year: Yong, *bo* of Luo, fought with the *bo* of He

095 and the Yi [tribe] of Feng. 33rd year: A son of [the chief of] the Kunwu was given You Su as a fief. 36th year: A circular earth[work] was made. 44th year: [The emperor] died. **The Emperor Mang**. First year: The emperor took his position as ruler.

096 He went with the dark scepter to perform a *bin* [ritual of homage] to [the god of] the He (Yellow River). 13th year: [The emperor] went on a hunting tour eastward to the sea, and caught a big fish. 33rd year: The *hou* of Shang moved to Yin. 58th year: [The emperor] died. *Mourning one year.* **The Emperor Xie**. First

097 year: The emperor took his position as ruler. 12th year: Zi Hai, *hou* of Yin, was a guest of [the lord of] You Yi. [The lord of] You Yi killed him and banished [his followers]. 16th year: Wei, *hou* of Yin, attacked You Yi with the army of the *bo* of He, killing their lord Mian

098 Chen. *Zi Hai, hou of Yin, behaved licentiously as guest of You Yi. Mian Chen, lord of You Yi, killed him and banished [his followers]. Therefore Shang Jia Wei, [hou of] Yin, borrowed the army of the bo of He (the River),and attacked You Yi with it, destroying You Yi, and then killing*

099 *their lord Mian Chen. After an interval of decline, Shang Jia Wei caused [the status of his people] to rise again; therefore the people of Shang held him in grateful esteem.* 21st year: [The emperor] conferred regular dignities on [the chiefs of] the Quan Yi, Bai Yi, Chi Yi, Xuan Yi, Feng Yi, and Huang Yi. 2

100 5th year: [The emperor] died. *Mourning three years.* **The Emperor Bu Jiang**. First year: The emperor took his position as ruler. 6th year: He attacked Jiuyuan. 35th year: Yin destroyed [the country of] the Pi people. 59th year: [Bu Jiang] abdicated in favor of his younger brother

101 Jiong. **The Emperor Jiong**. First year: The emperor took his position as ruler. 10th year: The emperor Bu Jiang died. *In the age of the Three Dynasties, only Bu Jiang resigned the throne. Truly he had the virtue of a sage.* 18th year: [The emperor] died. *Mourning three years.*

102 **The Emperor Jin**. First year: The emperor took his position as ruler. He resided in Xihe. 4th year: [The emperor] composed the "Tunes of the West." [The lord of] the Kunwu people moved to Xu. 8th year: There was an inauspicious portent in the sky: ten suns rose together. This year [the emperor] died. *Mourning two years.*

103 **The Emperor Kong Jia**. First year: [The emperor] took his position as ruler. He lived in Xihe (West River). He removed [the lord of] Shi-Wei. He had Liu Lei feed the [royal] dragons. 3rd year: The king

104 hunted on Mount Fu. 5th year: He made the "Tunes of the East." 7th year: Liu Lei moved to Luyang. *The king liked to serve ghosts and spirits. He was a man of loose conduct, licentious and disorganized, and the regional lords succumbed to his influence, so that the government of Xia began to decline.*

105 *While he was hunting on Mount Fu in Dongyang, there was a violent wind storm making the sky overcast and dark, so that Kong Jia became confused and lost. He then entered the house of a commoner, as the lady of the house was nursing a child. Someone said, "The emperor has come to see you! It's a lucky day! This child will surely*

7

	045	044	043	042	041	040	039	038	037	036	035	034	033	032	031	
01		畋	**帝**	**帝**	扃	五	殺	臣	年	玄	馮	商	后	是	。	01
02		于	**孔**	**廑**	。	年	其	。	帝	珪	夷	侯	氏	而	**帝**	02
03		萯	**甲**	。	**帝**	陟	君	殷	即	賓	鬬	冥	報	復	**少**	03
04	田	山		元	**扃**	居	綿	侯	位	于	。	死	焉	。	**康**	04
05	于	。		年	。	三	臣	子	。	河	三	于	。	十	。	05
06	東	五		帝	元	年	中	亥	十	。	十	河	元	一	元	06
07	陽	年		即	年	。	葉	賓	二	十	三	。	年	年	年	07
08	萯	作		位	帝	**帝**	衰	于	年	三	年	十	帝	使	帝	08
09	山	東		居	即	**不**	而	有	殷	年	封	七	即	商	即	09
10	天	音		西	位	**降**	上	易	侯	東	昆	年	位	侯	位	10
11	大	。		河	。	。	甲	而	子	狩	吾	陟	居	冥	諸	11
12	風	七		。	十	元	微	淫	亥	于	氏	居	原	治	侯	12
13	晦	年		四	年	年	復	焉	賓	海	子	二	。	河	來	13
14	肓	劉		年	帝	帝	興	有	于	獲	于	年	五	。	朝	14
15	孔	累		作	不	即	故	易	有	大	有	。	年	十	賓	15
16	甲	遷		西	降	位	商	之	易	魚	蘇	**帝**	自	八	虞	16
17	迷	于		音	陟	。	人	君	有	。	。	**芬**	原	年	公	17
18	惑	魯		昆	。	六	報	綿	易	三	三	。	遷	遷	。	18
19	入	陽		吾	三	年	焉	臣	殺	十	十	元	于	于	二	19
20	於	。		氏	代	伐	。	殺	而	三	六	年	老	原	年	20
21	民	王	元	遷	之	九	二	而	放	年	年	帝	丘	。	方	21
22	室	好	年	于	世	苑	十	放	之	商	作	即	。	二	夷	22
23	主	事	即	許	內	。	一	之	。	侯	圜	位	八	十	來	23
24	人	鬼	位	。	禪	三	年	故	十	遷	土	。	年	一	賓	24
25	方	神	居	八	惟	十	命	殷	六	于	。	三	征	年	。	25
26	乳	肆	西	年	不	五	畎	上	年	殷	四	年	于	陟	三	26
27	或	行	河	天	降	年	夷	甲	殷	。	十	九	東	居	年	27
28	曰	淫	廢	有	實	殷	白	微	侯	五	四	夷	海	二	復	28
29	后	亂	豕	祅	有	滅	夷	假	微	十	年	來	及	年	田	29
30	來	諸	韋	孽	聖	皮	赤	師	以	八	陟	御	三	。	稷	30
31	見	侯	氏	十	德	氏	夷	于	河	年	。	。	壽	**帝**	。	31
32	良	化	使	日	。	。	玄	河	之	陟	**帝**	十	得	**杼**	后	32
33	日	之	劉	並	十	五	夷	伯	師	居	**芒**	六	一	。	稷	33
34	也	夏	累	出	八	十	風	以	伐	一	。	年	狐	能	之	34
35	之	政	豢	其	年	九	夷	伐	有	年	元	洛	九	帥	後	35
36	子	始	龍	年	陟	年	黃	有	易	。	年	伯	尾	禹	不	36
37	必	衰	。	陟	居	遜	夷	易	殺	**帝**	帝	用	。	者	窋	37
38			三	居	三	位	。	滅	其	**泄**	即	與	十	也	失	38
39			年	二	年	于	二	之	君	。	位	河	三	故	官	39
40			王	年	。	弟	十	遂	綿	元	以	伯	年	夏	至	40
	105	104	103	102	101	100	099	098	097	096	095	094	093	092	091	

106 *have great good fortune!" But someone else said, "This is more than we can take. This child will surely suffer harm." Kong Jia, hearing them, said, "I, the One Man, will take him as my own son. Who then will harm him?" So he took the child and went home with it.*

107 *When the child grew older, it was [accidentally] killed by an axe, so [the emperor] then made "the Breaking Axes Song." This was [the beginning of] the "Tunes of the East." Among the dragons in Liu Lei's care a female died, and he secretly pickled it and offered [the meat] to the Xia emperor, who liked it.*

108 *But later he had [Liu] hunt for [the missing dragon]. [Liu] was afraid, and went away to Luyang. His descendents became the Fan lineage.* 9th year: [*Di* Kong Jia] died. *Mourning two years.* The *hou* of Yin moved back to Shangqiu. **The Emperor Hao**. First year:

109 The emperor took his position as ruler. He restored the Shi Wei lineage to its state. *As Xia declined, [the lords of] Kunwu and Shi Wei alternated as bo (overlords of the regional lords).* 3rd year: [The emperor] died. Mourning two years. **The Emperor Fa**. First year: The emperor took his position as ruler. The regional lords came as guests at

110 the King's Gate. [Fa] again praised and rewarded those who had merits, convening them at the Shangchi (Imperial Pond). [Delegations of] the various Yi [peoples] offered their [ethnic] dances. 7th year: [The emperor] died. Tai Shan suffered an [earth]quake. **The Emperor Gui [i.e., Jie]**.

111 First year: The emperor took his position as ruler. He dwelt in Zhenxun. 3rd year: He built the Qing Palace. He tore down the Rong Tower. The Quan Yi entered the Qi [area] in rebellion. 6th year: The [chiefs of the] Qizhong *rong* came as guests [in submission). 10th year: The five planets moved in succession; at night

112 stars fell like rain. There was an earthquake. The Yi and Luo [Rivers] ran dry. 11th year: He assembled the regional lords in Reng. [The lord of] You Min fled back home. Following that, [the emperor] destroyed You Min. 13th year: He moved to south of the Yellow River. He began the use of an imperial chariot drawn by human beings

113 14th year: Bian led an army attacking Min Shan. 15th year: Lü, *hou* of Shang, moved to Bo. *[Gui] ordered Bian to attack Shan Min. Shan Min presented two women to Jie, one called Wan and the other Yan.*

114 *The emperor loved the two, although the women bore him no children. He had their names carved on the gems Tiao and Hua: [that on the gem] Tiao was "Wan," [on the gem] Hua was "Yan"; and he sent away his first wife Moxi to Luo. In the Qing Palace*

115 *he decorated the Yao Tower for them to live in. Lady Moxi had intercourse with Yi Yin, for the purpose of making dissension between Yin and Xia.* 17th year: Shang sent Yi Yin to the [Xia] court. 20th year: Yi Yin went back to Shang, and met with Ru

116 Jiu and Ru Fang at the North Gate. 21st year: The Shang army made a punitive expedition against You Luo, and conquered it. After that, [Shang] made a punitive expedition against Jing; Jing fell. 22nd year: Lü, *hou* of Shang, came to court; he was ordered to be imprisoned in the Tower of Xia.

117 23rd year: Lü, *hou* of Shang, was released. After that, the regional lords came as guests to Shang, [acknowledging submission]. 26th year: Shang destroyed Wen. 28th year: Kunwu attacked Shang. Shang assembled the regional lords in Jing Bo.

118 After that [Shang] made a punitive expedition against Wei. The Shang army took Wei. Then they made an expedition against Gu. Zhonggu, the [Xia] chief grand recorder, left [Xia] and fled to Shang. 29th year: The Shang army took Gu. Three suns rose at the same time. Chang, *bo* of Fei, left [Xia] and fled to Shang. In winter, 10th month,

119 they bored through mountains and tunneled through hills, to [let water flow] through to the Yellow River. 30th year: There was a landslide on Mount Qu. [Di Gui] killed his great officer Guan Longfeng. The Shang army made a punitive attack on Kunwu. In the winter, there was a fire in Lingsui. 31st year: From Er, Shang made a punitive attack

120 on the City of Xia, and defeated Kunwu. In a great thunder storm, a battle was fought at Mingtiao, where the Xia army was routed. Jie escaped and fled to Sanzong. The Shang army made a punitive attack on Sanzong, doing battle at Zheng. Jie was captured in Jiaomen, and was banished to Nanchao.

121 *From Yu to Jie there were seventeen reigns. Including when there was a king and when there was not, the total time was 471 years.*

8

		60	59	58	57	56	55	54	53	52	51	50	49	48	47	46	
01	自	夏	鑿	遂	。	鳩			十	中	元	王	帝				01
02	禹	邑	山	征	二	汝			四	星	年	門	即				02
03	至	克	穿	韋	十	方			年	隕	帝	再	位				03
04	桀	昆	陵	商	三	會	飾	后	扁	如	即	保	使	而	既	大	04
05	十	吾	以	師	年	于	瑤	愛	帥	雨	位	墉	豕	使	長	吉	05
06	七	大	通	取	釋	北	臺	二	師	地	居	會	韋	求	為	或	06
07	世	雷	于	韋	商	門	居	女	伐	震	斟	于	氏	之	斧	又	07
08	有	雨	河	遂	侯	。	之	無	岷	伊	鄩	上	復	累	戕	曰	08
09	王	戰	。	征	履	二	末	子	山	洛	。	池	國	懼	乃	不	09
10	與	于	三	顧	諸	十	喜	焉	。	竭	三	諸	。	而	作	勝	10
11	無	鳴	十	太	侯	一	氏	斲	十	。	年	夷	夏	遷	破	也	11
12	王	條	年	史	遂	年	以	其	五	十	築	入	衰	于	斧	之	12
13	用	夏	瞿	令	賓	商	與	名	年	一	傾	舞	昆	魯	之	子	13
14	歲	師	山	終	于	師	伊	於	商	年	宮	。	吾	陽	歌	必	14
15	四	敗	崩	古	商	征	尹	苕	侯	會	毀	七	豕	其	是	有	15
16	百	績	殺	出	。	有	交	華	履	諸	容	年	韋	後	為	殃	16
17	七	桀	其	奔	二	洛	遂	之	遷	侯	臺	陟	相	為	東	孔	17
18	十	出	大	商	十	克	以	玉	于	于	畎	泰	繼	范	音	甲	18
19	一	奔	夫	。	六	之	間	苕	亳	仍	夷	山	為	氏	劉	聞	19
20	年	三	關	二	年	遂	夏	是	。	有	入	震	伯	。	累	之	20
21		朡	龍	十	商	征	十	琬	命	緡	于	**帝**	。	九	所	曰	21
22		商	逄	九	滅	荊	七	華	扁	氏	岐	**癸**	三	年	畜	以	22
23		師	商	年	溫	荊	年	是	伐	逃	以		年	陟	龍	為	23
24		征	師	商	。	降	商	琰	山	歸	叛		陟	居	一	余	24
25		三	征	師	二	。	使	而	民	遂	。		居	二	雌	一	25
26		朡	昆	取	十	二	伊	棄	山	滅	六		二	年	死	人	26
27		戰	吾	顧	八	十	尹	其	民	有	年		年	。	潛	子	27
28		于	冬	三	年	二	來	元	進	緡	歧		。	殷	醢	夫	28
29		郕	聆	日	昆	年	朝	妃	女	。	踵		**帝**	侯	以	誰	29
30		獲	隧	並	吾	商	。	於	于	十	戎		**發**	復	食	殃	30
31		桀	災	出	氏	侯	二	洛	桀	三	來		。	歸	夏	之	31
32		于	。	費	伐	履	十	曰	二	年	賓		元	于	后	乃	32
33		焦	三	伯	商	來	年	妹	人	遷	。		年	商	夏	取	33
34		門	十	昌	商	朝	伊	喜	曰	于	十		帝	丘	后	其	34
35		放	一	出	會	命	尹	於	琬	河	年		即	。	饗	子	35
36		之	年	奔	諸	囚	歸	傾	曰	南	五		位	**帝**	之	以	36
37		于	商	商	侯	履	于	宮	琰	初	星		諸	**昊**	既	歸	37
38		南	自	冬	于	于	商			作	錯		侯	。			38
39		巢	陑	十	景	夏	及			輦	行		賓	元			39
40		。	征	月	亳	臺	汝			。	夜		于	年			40
	121	120	119	118	117	116	115	114	113	112	111	110	109	108	107	106	

122 **Yin-Shang: Cheng Tang, *personal name* Lü**. *Tang had seven names and made nine punitive military campaigns. When he had banished Jie to Nanchao and had returned, there were*

123 *1800 regional lords who came to his court, some being [from so far away that] eight translations [were needed to communicate with them]. [Even the chief of] the Qigong ("wonderful arms") people came in his chariot. All alike extolled "Tian Yi Lü " as Son of Heaven. Three times he declined, but then he did take the position of Son of Heaven. Earlier, in the times of Gao Xin (i.e., the emperor Ku),*

124 *[the emperor] had a wife named Jiandi. At the time of the spring equinox, in the days when the dark birds arrive, she went with the emperor to sacrifice outside the city to pray for a son. She was bathing together with her sister in a stream by the Dark Hill, when a dark bird came holding an egg in its mouth*

125 *and then dropping it. It was of five colors and very beautiful. The two ladies each tried to be the first to get it and cover it with a gem basket. Jiandi got there first and swallowed it. She then became pregnant. [When her time came] her breast split open and she gave birth to Xie. When he grew to manhood he became Yao's minister of instruction,*

126 *and was successful in serving the people, so that he was given the fief of Shang. Thirteen generations later Zhu Gui was born. Zhu Gui had a wife named Fudu, who saw a white vapor penetrating the moon and then felt herself pregnant. [in due time], on an yi day, she bore Tang,*

127 *who was called Tian Yi ("Heaven's Yi"). [His face] was broad below and tapered above, white and bearded. He had a crooked body and a loud voice. He grew to be nine feet tall. His arms had four joints. This was Cheng Tang. When Tang was in Bo he was able to cultivate his virtue.*

128 *When Yi Zhi was about to respond to Tang's summons, he dreamed that he was riding in a boat passing by the sun and moon. Tang then went east as far as Luo, and seeing the altar of the emperor Yao he dropped a jade disc into the water and stood back. Yellow fish leaped up in pairs, and a black*

129 *bird followed him, stopping at the altar, where it turned into a piece of black jade. There was also a black turtle, with red marks forming characters, which said that Jie of Xia lacked moral principles, and that Cheng Tang ought later to attack him. The spirit Taowu*

130 *was seen on Mount Pei. There was a spirit pulling a white wolf with a hook in its mouth into the Shang court. The Power of Metal was about to flourish. Silver flowed out of the mountains. When Tang was about to do Heaven's bidding and banish Jie, he dreamed that he reached the sky and*

131 *licked it. Subsequently he possessed the empire. The men of Shang after that changed the name of the empire to Yin.* 18th year: The king took his position as ruler. He lived in Bo. He for the first time built a building over the Xia alter to the soil. 19th year: There was a great drought. The Di and the Qiang

132 came as guests [in submission]. 20th year: There was a great drought. Jie of Xia died in Ting Shan. The playing of stringed instruments, the singing of songs, and performing of dances were forbidden. 21st year: There was a great drought. Metal money was coined. 22nd year:

133 There was a great drought. 23rd year: There was a great drought. 24th year: There was a great drought. The king prayed in the Mulberry Grove, and it rained. 25th year: He made the "Da Huo" ("Downpour") music. He made his first tour of inspection. He set the rules for offerings [to the court]. 27th year: He moved the Nine Cauldrons to the City of Shang.

134 29th year: He died. **Wai Bing *personal name Sheng***. First year: The king took his position as ruler. He lived in Bo. He appointed Yi Yin chief minister. 2nd year: He died. **Zhong Ren, *personal name Yong***. First year: The king took his position as ruler.

135 He dwelt in Bo. He appointed Yi Yin as his prime minister. 4th year: He died. **Tai Jia, *personal name Zhi***. First year: The king took his position as ruler. He lived in Bo. He appointed Yi Yin chief minister. Yi Yin banished Tai Jia to Tong, and then raised himself [to the position of king]. 7th year:

136 The king escaped from Tong and killed Yi Yin. There was an immense fog for three days; so [the king] then raised to office [Yi Yin's] sons Yi Zhi and Yi Fen, ordering their father's fields and houses to be restored, and equally divided between them. 10th year: [The king] celebrated the Great Xiang rite in the Ancestral Temple.

9

	15	14	13	12	11	10	09	08	07	06	05	04	03	02	01	
01	王	居	邑	大	來										**殷**	01
02	潛	亳	。	旱	賓										**商**	02
03	出	命	二	。	。										**成**	03
04	自	卿	十	二	二	舐	見	鳥	伊	號	成	而	氏	譯	**湯**	04
05	桐	士	九	十	十	之	於	隨	摯	天	功	墜	之	而	**名**	05
06	殺	伊	年	四	年	遂	邳	之	將	乙	於	之	世	來	**履**	06
07	伊	尹	陟	年	大	有	山	止	應	豐	民	五	妃	者		07
08	尹	。	。	大	旱	天	有	於	湯	下	受	色	曰	千		08
09	天	四	**外**	旱	夏	下	神	壇	命	銳	封	甚	簡	八		09
10	大	年	**丙**	王	桀	商	牽	化	夢	上	於	好	狄	百		10
11	霧	陟	**名**	禱	卒	人	白	為	乘	晳	商	二	以	國		11
12	三	。	**勝**	于	于	後	狼	黑	船	而	後	人	春	奇		12
13	日	**太**	。	桑	亭	改	銜	玉	過	有	十	競	分	肱		13
14	乃	**甲**	元	林	山	天	鉤	又	日	髯	三	取	玄	氏		14
15	立	**名**	年	雨	禁	下	而	有	月	句	世	覆	鳥	以		15
16	其	**至**	王	。	弦	之	入	黑	之	身	生	以	至	車		16
17	子	。	即	二	歌	號	商	龜	傍	而	主	玉	之	至		17
18	伊	元	位	十	舞	曰	朝	並	湯	揚	癸	筐	日	乃		18
19	陟	年	居	五	。	殷	金	赤	乃	聲	主	簡	從	同		19
20	伊	王	亳	年	二	。	德	文	東	長	癸	狄	帝	尊		20
21	奮	即	命	作	十	十	將	成	至	九	之	先	祀	天	湯	21
22	命	位	卿	大	一	八	盛	字	於	尺	妃	得	郊	乙	有	22
23	復	居	士	濩	年	年	銀	言	洛	臂	曰	而	禖	履	七	23
24	其	亳	伊	樂	大	王	自	夏	觀	有	扶	吞	與	為	名	24
25	父	命	尹	初	旱	即	山	桀	帝	四	都	之	其	天	而	25
26	之	卿	。	巡	鑄	位	溢	無	堯	肘	見	遂	妹	子	九	26
27	田	士	二	狩	金	居	湯	道	之	是	白	孕	浴	三	征	27
28	宅	伊	年	定	幣	亳	將	成	壇	為	氣	胸	於	讓	放	28
29	而	尹	陟	獻	。	始	奉	湯	沈	成	貫	剖	玄	遂	桀	29
30	中	放	。	令	二	屋	天	遂	璧	湯	月	而	丘	即	於	30
31	分	太	**仲**	。	十	夏	命	當	退	湯	意	生	之	天	南	31
32	之	甲	**壬**	二	二	社	放	代	立	在	感	契	水	子	巢	32
33	。	于	**名**	十	年	。	桀	之	黃	亳	以	長	有	之	而	33
34	十	桐	**庸**	七	大	十	夢	檮	魚	能	乙	為	玄	位	還	34
35	年	乃	。	年	旱	九	及	杌	雙	修	日	堯	鳥	初	諸	35
36	大	自	元	遷	。	年	天	之	踴	其	生	司	銜	高	侯	36
37	饗	立	年	九	二	大	而	神	黑	德	湯	徒	卵	辛	八	37
38	于	。	王	鼎	十	旱										38
39	太	七	即	于	三	氏										39
40	廟	年	位	商	年	羌										40
	136	135	134	133	132	131	130	129	128	127	126	125	124	123	122	

137 For the first time he sacrificed at the Square Numen. 12th year: [The king] died. **Wo Ding**, ***personal name Xun***. First year: The king took his position as ruler. He dwelt in Bo. He gave a charge to Gao Shan as chief minister. 8th year: He instituted sacrifices for Baoheng. 19th year: He died. **Xiao**

138 **Geng**, ***personal name Bian***. First year: The king took his position as ruler. He dwelt in Bo. 5th year: He died. **Xiao Jia**, ***personal name Gao***. First year: The king took his position as ruler. He dwelt in Bo. 17th year: He died. **Yong Ji**, ***personal name Zhou***. First

139 year: The king took his position as ruler. He dwelt in Bo. 12th year: He died. **Tai Wu**, ***personal name Mi***. First year: The king took his position as ruler. He dwelt in Bo. As prime ministers he gave charges to Yi Zhi and Chen Hu. 7th year: A mulberry tree and a stalk of grain grew up in the court.

140 11th year: [The king] charged the shaman Xian to pray to the mountains and streams. 26th year: The western *rong* came as guests [in submission]. The king sent Wang Meng as emissary to them. 31st year: [The king] charged Zhongyan, lord of Bi, to be master of carriages.

141 35th year: Yin carriages were invented. 46th year: There was a great harvest. 58th year: A wall was built for Pugu. 61st year: [The chiefs of] the nine Yi of the east came as guests [in submission]. 75th year: [The king] died.

142 *When Tai Wu met with the mulberry omen, he redirected himself to the cultivation of good conduct. After three years, far away lands respected his shining virtue, and [chiefs of] seventy-six countries, [so far away that they required] repeated translations [to be understood], came [to his court]. The [good] Way of Shang again flourished. In the ancestral temple he was Tai Zong.*

143 **Zhong Ding**, ***personal name Zhuang***. First year: The king took his position as ruler. He moved [the royal residence] from Bo to Xiao, above the Yellow River. 6th year: He made a punitive expedition against the Yi [peoples] of Lan. 9th year: [The king] died. **Wai Ren**, ***personal name Fa***. First year: the king took his position as ruler.

144 He lived in Xiao. The people of Pei and the People of Shen rebelled. 10th year: [The king] died. 12. **Hedan Jia**, ***personal name Zheng***. First year: The king took his position as ruler. He moved from Xiao to Xiang. 3rd year: The lord of Peng vanquished Pei. 4th year: [Hedan Jia] sent a punitive expedition against the Yi of Lan.

145 5th year: The people of Shen entered the Ban Fang [border region]. The lords of Peng and Wei attacked the Ban Fang. The [chief of the] people of Shen came as a guest [in submission]. 9th year: [The king] died. **Zu Yi**, ***personal name Teng***. First year: The king took his position as ruler. From Xiang he moved to

146 Geng. He gave charges to the lords of Peng and of Wei, [recognizing them as lords of their states]. 2nd year: Geng was destroyed [by a flood]. [The king] moved from Geng to Bi. 3rd year: Wu Xian was given a charge as chief minister. 8th year: [Shang] walled [the city of] Bi. 15th year: [The king] gave a charge to Gaoyu, lord of Bin, [recognizing him as lord of his state].

147 19th year: [The king] died. *In the reign of Zu Yi the way of Shang again prospered. His temple name was Zhong Zong.* **Zu Xin**, ***personal name Dan***. First year: The king took his position as ruler. He lived in Bi. 14th year: [The king] died. **Kai Jia**, ***personal name Yu***.

148 First year: The king took his position as ruler. He lived in Bi. 5th year: [The king] died. **Zu Ding**, ***personal name Xin***. First year: The king took his position as ruler. He lived in Bi. 9th year: [The king] died. **Nan Geng**, ***personal name Geng***. First year: The king took his position as ruler.

149 He was living in Bi. 3rd year: He moved to Yan. 6th year: [The king] died. **Yang Jia**, ***personal name He***. First year: The king took his position as ruler. He lived in Yan. 3rd year: He made a punitive expedition west against the *rong* of Dan Shan. 4th year: [The king] died. **Pan Geng**,

150 ***personal name Xun***. First year: The king took his position as ruler. He lived in Yan. 7th year: The lord of Ying came to court. 14th year: From Yan [the king] moved to Beimeng, called Yin. 15th year: The building of the City of Yin was begun. 19th year:

151 An appointment was given to Yayu, recognizing him as lord of Bin. 28th year: [The king] died. **Xiao Xin**, ***personal name Song***. First year: The king took his position as ruler, and dwelt in Yin. 3rd year: The king] died. **Xiao Yi**, ***personal name Lian***. First year: The king took his position as ruler, and dwelt

10

	30	29	28	27	26	25	24	23	22	21	20	19	18	17	16	
01	命	**名**	居	。	十	耿	夷	居	。		。	。	年	**庚**	初	01
02	邠	**旬**	庇	元	九	命	。	囂	**仲**		三	十	王	**名**	祀	02
03	侯	。	。	年	年	彭	五	邳	**丁**		十	一	即	**辨**	方	03
04	亞	元	三	王	陟	伯	年	人	**名**	大	五	年	位	。	明	04
05	圉	年	年	即	。	韋	侁	姺	**莊**	戊	年	命	居	元	。	05
06	。	王	遷	位	祖	伯	人	人	。	遇	作	巫	亳	年	十	06
07	二	即	于	居	乙	。	入	叛	元	祥	寅	咸	。	王	二	07
08	十	位	奄	庇	之	二	于	。	年	桑	車	禱	十	即	年	08
09	八	居	。	。	世	年	班	十	王	側	。	于	二	位	陟	09
10	年	奄	六	五	商	圮	方	年	即	身	四	山	年	居	。	10
11	陟	。	年	年	道	于	彭	陟	位	修	十	川	陟	亳	**沃**	11
12	。	七	陟	陟	復	耿	伯	。	自	行	六	。	。	。	**丁**	12
13	**小**	年	。	。	興	自	韋	**河**	亳	三	年	二	**太**	五	**名**	13
14	**辛**	應	**陽**	**祖**	廟	耿	伯	**亶**	遷	年	大	十	**戊**	年	**絢**	14
15	**名**	侯	**甲**	**丁**	為	遷	伐	**甲**	于	後	有	六	**名**	陟	。	15
16	**頌**	來	**名**	**名**	中	于	班	**名**	囂	遠	年	年	**密**	。	元	16
17	。	朝	**和**	**新**	宗	庇	方	**整**	于	方	。	西	。	**小**	年	17
18	元	。	。	。	。	。	侁	。	河	慕	五	戎	元	**甲**	王	18
19	年	十	元	元	**祖**	三	人	元	上	明	十	來	年	**名**	即	19
20	王	四	年	年	**辛**	年	來	年	。	德	八	賓	王	**高**	位	20
21	即	年	王	王	**名**	命	賓	王	六	重	年	王	即	。	居	21
22	位	自	即	即	**旦**	卿	。	即	年	譯	城	使	位	元	亳	22
23	居	奄	位	位	。	士	九	位	征	而	蒲	王	居	年	命	23
24	殷	遷	居	居	元	巫	年	自	藍	至	姑	孟	亳	王	卿	24
25	。	于	奄	庇	年	賢	陟	囂	夷	者	。	聘	命	即	士	25
26	三	北	。	。	王	。	。	遷	。	七	六	西	卿	位	咎	26
27	年	蒙	三	九	即	八	**祖**	于	九	十	十	戎	士	居	單	27
28	陟	曰	年	年	位	年	**乙**	相	年	六	一	。	伊	亳	。	28
29	。	殷	西	陟	居	城	**名**	。	陟	國	年	三	陟	。	八	29
30	**小**	。	征	。	庇	庇	**滕**	三	。	商	東	十	臣	十	年	30
31	**乙**	十	丹	**南**	。	。	。	年	**外**	道	九	一	扈	七	祠	31
32	**名**	五	山	**庚**	十	十	元	彭	**壬**	復	夷	年	。	年	保	32
33	**斂**	年	戎	**名**	四	五	年	伯	**名**	興	來	命	七	陟	衡	33
34	。	營	。	**更**	年	年	王	克	**發**	廟	賓	費	年	。	。	34
35	元	殷	四	。	陟	命	即	邳	。	為	。	侯	有	**雍**	十	35
36	年	邑	年	元	。	邠	位	。	元	太	七	中	桑	**己**	九	36
37	王	。	陟	年	**開**	侯	自	四	年	宗	十	衍	穀	**名**	年	37
38	即	十	。	王	**甲**	高	相	年	王		五	為	生	**☒**	陟	38
39	位	九	**盤**	即	**名**	圉	遷	征	即		年	車	于	。	。	39
40	居	年	**庚**	位	**踰**	。	于	藍	位		陟	正	朝	元	**小**	40
	151	150	149	148	147	146	145	144	143	142	141	140	139	138	137	

152 in Yin. 6th year: He ordered the heir Wu Ding to live by the Yellow River, and to study with Gan Pan. 10th year: [The king] died. **Wu Ding, *personal name Zhao*.** First year: The king took his position as ruler, and dwelt in Yin. He gave a charge to Gan Pan as chief minister. 3rd

153 year: He dreamed that he sought Fu Yue. He got him [as his minister and adviser]. 6th year: He gave a charge to Fu Yue as chief minister. He visited the school for nourishing the aged. 12th year: He made a sacrifice of gratitude to Shang Jia Wei. 25th year: The king's son Xiao Ji died in the wilderness.

154 29th year: During the *yong* sacrifice in the Great Ancestral Temple, a pheasant appeared. 32nd year: [The Shang army] attacked the Gui Fang, encamping in Jing. 34th year: The royal army vanquished the Gui Fang. [The chiefs of] the Di [people] and the Qiang [people] came [to court] as guests [in submission].

155 43rd year: The royal army destroyed Greater Peng. 50th year: There was a campaign against Shi Wei. [Shi Wei] was vanquished. 59th year: [The king] died. *[The reign of King Wu Ding] was the most benevolent reign in the Yin [Dynasty. He energetically practiced the Way of [ideal] kingship. "He did not dare to be uselessly idle, but admirably brought tranquility to the land of Yin,*

156 *so that in great and small [states alike] there was never any complaint." At this time the empire did not extend beyond the Jiang and the Huang [Rivers] on the east, nor beyond [the lands of] the Di and the Qiang on the west, nor beyond Jing and Man on the south, nor beyond the Shuo Fang on the north. Yet the sounds of praise-songs were heard, and rites that had decayed*

157 *were revived. He was given the temple name Gao Zong.* **Zu Geng, *personal name Yao*.** First year: The king took his position as ruler, and dwelt in Yin. The "Instructions to Gao Zong" was written. 11th year: [The king] died. **Zu Jia, *personal name Zai*.** First year: The king took his position as ruler, and

158 dwelt in Yin. 12th year: He went on a punitive expedition into the western *rong* [region], *and got a cinnabar mine*. In the winter the king returned from the western *rong* [region]. 13th year: [The chiefs of] the western *rong* came as guests [in submission]. A charge was given to Zu Gan as Lord of Bin. 24th year: [The king] reissued Tang's

159 penal code. 27th year: Charges were given to Prince Xiao and Prince Liang. 33rd year: [The king] died. *The king [when young] had lived long in the countryside, and so when he became king he understood the needs of the common people and knew how to protect them and treat them kindly,*

160 *with no disdain for widows and widowers. But by the end of his reign, by making the penal code complex he alienated even those living far away, and the Way of Yin again declined.* **Feng Xin, *personal name Xian*.** First year: The king took his position as ruler, and dwelt in Yin. 4th year: [The king] died. **Geng Ding,**

161 ***personal name Xiao*.** First year: The king took his position [as ruler], and dwelt in Yin. 8th year: [The king] died. **Wu Yi, *personal name Qu*.** 1st year: The king took his position [as ruler], and dwelt in Yin. [The lord of] Bin moved to Zhou near Qi [Shan]. 3rd year: [The king] moved [his residence] from Yin to the north of the He.

162 He confirmed Dan Fu as Duke of Zhou, and gave him the city of Qi. 15th year: [The king] moved from north of the He to Mei. 21st year: Dan Fu, Duke of Zhou, died. 24th year: The Zhou army attacked Cheng, fighting a battle

163 at Bi, and was victorious. 30th year: The Zhou army attacked Yiqu, then captured its lord and returned. 34th year: Ji Li, Duke of Zhou, came to court to pay homage. The King conferred on him 30 *li* [square] of land, ten pairs of gems, and ten horses.

164 35th year: Ji Li, Duke of Zhou, attacked the Gui *rong* of the western tribes. The king hunted [near the confluence of] the He and the Wei Rivers. In a great thunderstorm he was struck by lightening and died. **Wen Ding, *personal name Tuo*.** First year: The king took his position [as king], and dwelt in Yin [as his capital]. 2nd

165 year: Ji Li, Duke of Zhou, attacked the *rong* of Yanjing, but was defeated and routed. 3rd year: The Huan River ceased to flow three times in one day. 4th year: Ji Li, Duke of Zhou, attacked the *rong* of Yuwu, and subdued them. [The king] appointed him *mu shi*.

166 5th year: Zhou built the city of Cheng. 7th year: Ji Li, Duke of Zhou, attacked the Shihu *rong* and subdued them. 11th year: Ji Li, Duke of Zhou, attacked the *rong* of Yitu, and captured three of their chiefs; he came presenting

11

	45	44	43	42	41	40	39	38	37	36	35	34	33	32	31	
01	五	年	十	于	北	**名**		刑	居	復	邦	三	。	年	殷	01
02	年	周	匹	畢	命	**囂**		。	殷	起	至	年	二	夢	。	02
03	周	公	。	克	周	。		二	。	廟	于	王	十	求	六	03
04	作	季	三	之	公	元	不	十	十	號	小	師	九	傅	年	04
05	程	歷	十	。	亶	年	侮	七	二	高	大	滅	年	說	命	05
06	邑	伐	五	三	父	王	鰥	年	年	宗	無	大	肜	得	世	06
07	。	燕	年	十	賜	即	寡	命	征	。	時	彭	祭	之	子	07
08	七	京	周	年	以	位	迨	王	西	**祖**	或	。	太	。	武	08
09	年	之	公	周	岐	居	其	子	戎	**庚**	怨	五	廟	六	丁	09
10	周	戎	季	師	邑	殷	末	囂	得	**名**	是	十	有	年	居	10
11	公	敗	歷	伐	。	。	也	王	一	**曜**	時	年	雉	命	于	11
12	季	績	伐	義	十	八	繁	子	丹	。	輿	征	來	卿	河	12
13	歷	。	西	渠	五	年	刑	良	山	元	地	豕	。	士	學	13
14	伐	三	落	乃	年	陟	以	。	冬	年	東	韋	三	傅	于	14
15	始	年	鬼	獲	自	。	攜	三	王	王	不	克	十	說	甘	15
16	呼	洹	戎	其	河	**武**	遠	十	返	即	過	之	二	視	盤	16
17	之	水	王	君	北	**乙**	殷	三	自	位	江	。	年	學	。	17
18	戎	一	畋	以	遷	**名**	道	年	西	居	黃	五	伐	養	十	18
19	克	日	于	歸	于	**瞿**	復	陟	戎	殷	西	十	鬼	老	年	19
20	之	三	河	。	沬	。	衰	。	。	作	不	九	方	。	陟	20
21	。	絕	渭	三	。	元	。	王	十	高	過	年	次	十	。	21
22	十	。	大	十	二	年	**馮**	舊	三	宗	氐	陟	于	二	**武**	22
23	一	四	雷	四	十	王	**辛**	在	年	之	羌	。	荊	年	**丁**	23
24	年	年	震	年	一	即	**名**	野	西	訓	南	王	。	報	**名**	24
25	周	周	死	周	年	位	**先**	及	戎	。	不	殷	三	祀	**昭**	25
26	公	公	。	公	周	居	。	即	來	十	過	之	十	上	。	26
27	季	季	**文**	季	公	殷	元	位	賓	一	荊	大	四	甲	元	27
28	歷	歷	**丁**	歷	亶	邠	年	知	命	年	蠻	仁	年	微	年	28
29	伐	伐	**名**	來	父	遷	王	小	邠	陟	北	也	王	。	王	29
30	翳	余	**托**	朝	薨	于	即	人	侯	。	不	力	師	二	即	30
31	徒	無	。	王	。	岐	位	之	組	**祖**	過	行	克	十	位	31
32	之	之	元	賜	二	周	居	依	紺	**甲**	朔	王	鬼	五	居	32
33	戎	戎	年	地	十	。	殷	能	。	**名**	方	道	方	年	殷	33
34	獲	克	王	三	四	三	。	保	二	**載**	而	不	氐	王	命	34
35	其	之	即	十	年	年	四	惠	十	。	頌	敢	羌	子	卿	35
36	三	命	位	里	周	自	年	庶	四	元	聲	荒	來	孝	士	36
37	大	為	居	玉	師	殷	陟	民	年	年	作	寧	賓	己	甘	37
38	夫	牧	殷	十	伐	遷	。		重	王	禮	嘉	。	卒	盤	38
39	來	師	。	瑴	程	于	**庚**		作	即	廢	靖	四	于	。	39
40	獻	。	二	馬	戰	河	**丁**		湯	位	而	殷	十	野	三	40
	166	165	164	163	162	161	160	159	158	157	156	155	154	153	152	

167 the victory [to the king]. The king killed Ji Li. 12th year: Phoenixes collected on Qishan [Mountain]. 13th year: [The king] died. *The king congratulated Ji Li for his achievement, and gave him a libation mace, and flavored spirits of black millet; and appointed him the ninth (the highest) rank Lord [of the West].*

168 *But then he confined him in the Hanku ("Cold Storehouse" Prison); and Ji Li died of the harsh treatment. Hence it is said that Wen Ding killed Ji Li.* **Di Yi**, ***personal name Xian***. First year: The king took his position [as ruler], and dwelled in Yin. 2nd year: *The men of Zhou attacked Yin.*

169 3rd year: The king ordered Nan Zhong to oppose the Kunyi on the west, and to wall off the North (Shuofang). In the 6th month there was an earthquake in Zhou. 9th year: [The king] died. **Di Xin**, ***personal name Shou***. First year: The king took his position as ruler, dwelling in Yin. He gave appointments to the lords of Chou,

170 Zhou and Yu. 3rd year: A sparrow produced a hawk. 4th year: [The king] conducted a great hunt in Li. He instituted the punishment of roasting. 5th year, Summer: [the king] had the Nantan tower built. It rained earth in Bo. 6th year: The Lord of the West

171 for the first time performed the *yue* [summer] sacrifice in Bi. 9th year: The [Shang] royal army attacked the You-Su [nation], and returned with Da Ji as captive. [The king] made [for her] the jasper room, and erected the jade gate. 10th year, summer, 6th month: The king hunted in the western borders. 17th year: The Lord of the West

172 attacked the Di. In the winter the king made a pleasure journey in Qi. 21st year, Spring, 1st month: The lords [favoring Zhou] came to the Zhou court [to pay respects]. Bo Yi and Shu Qi left Guzhu and went to Zhou [as subjects]. 22nd year, Winter: [The king] conducted a great hunt in the Wei [valley].

173 23rd year: [The king] imprisoned the Lord of the West in Youli [village]. 29th year: [The king] released the Lord of the West. The lords [favoring Zhou] met the Lord of the West and returned him to [his capital city] Cheng. 30th year, Spring, 3rd month: The Lord of the West led the lords in rendering

174 tribute [to the Shang king]. 31st year: The Lord of the West carried out a military review in Bi, and got Lü Shang as his military commander. 32nd year: There was a conjunction of the Five Planets in Fang. A red crow alighted on the Zhou altar of the soil. The people of Mi invaded Ruan, and the Lord of the West

175 led an army against them. 33rd year: The people of Mi surrendered to the Zhou army. Subsequently they were removed to Cheng. The [Shang] king gave a charge to the Lord of the West, authorizing him to conduct punitive expeditions on his own authority. 34th year: The Zhou army took Ji and Yu.

176 Subsequently it attacked Chong. The people of Chong surrendered. In the winter, 12th month, the Kun Yi invaded Zhou. 35th year: There was a severe famine in Zhou. The Lord of the West moved [his capital] from Cheng to Feng. 36th year, Spring, 1st month: The lords paid respects at the Zhou court.

177 Subsequently [Zhou] attacked the Kun Yi. The Lord of the West had his heir apparent Fa construct [the city of] Hao [as capital]. 37th year: Zhou established [the Hall of] the Circular Moat [in Hao]. 39th year: The [Shang] Great Officer Xin Jia fled to Zhou. 40th year: Zhou

178 built the Ling Tai. The [Shang] king sent Gao Ge to seek for jade in Zhou. 41st year, Spring, 3rd month: Chang, Lord of the West, died. 42nd year: Fa, Lord of the West, received the Cinnibar Writing from Lü Shang. A woman

179 turned into a man. 43rd year [The Lord of the West] held a grand review. There was a landslide on Mount Yao. 44th year: Fa, Lord of the West, attacked Li. 47th year: The [Shang] *nei shi* Xiang Zhi fled to Zhou.

180 48th year: The *yi*-goat was seen. Two suns appeared at once. 51st year, Winter, 11th month, day *wuzi*, the Zhou army crossed at Mengjin and returned. The [Shang] king imprisoned Jizi, and killed Prince Bi Gan. Weizi fled.

181 [Zhou Wu Wang] 11th year: Zhou began its attack on Yin. In the autumn the Zhou army encamped at Xianyuan. In the winter, 12th month, the Zhou army made a sacrifice to Shang Di. The [forces of] the Yong, Shu, Qiang, Mao, Wei, Lu, Peng, and Pu followed the Zhou army to attack Yin.

182 *From Tang's destruction of Xia to Shou there were 29 kings, taking up 496 years.*

12

		60	59	58	57	56	55	54	53	52	51	50	49	48	47	46	
01	。	。	八	化	作	于	遂	伯	貢	。	伯	伯	周	。		捷	01
02	湯	十	年	為	靈	周	伐	帥	。	二	伐	初	侯	三		王	02
03	滅	一	夷	丈	台	遂	崇	師	三	十	翟	禴	邘	年		殺	03
04	夏	年	羊	夫	王	伐	崇	伐	十	三	冬	于	侯	王	而	季	04
05	以	周	見	。	使	昆	人	密	一	年	王	畢	。	命	執	歷	05
06	至	始	二	四	膠	夷	降	。	年	囚	遊	。	三	南	諸	。	06
07	于	伐	日	十	鬲	西	冬	三	西	西	于	九	年	仲	塞	十	07
08	受	殷	並	三	求	伯	十	十	伯	伯	淇	年	有	西	庫	二	08
09	二	秋	出	年	玉	使	二	三	治	于	。	王	雀	拒	季	年	09
10	十	周	。	春	于	世	月	年	兵	羑	二	師	生	昆	歷	有	10
11	九	師	五	大	周	子	昆	密	于	里	十	伐	鸇	夷	困	鳳	11
12	王	次	十	閱	。	發	夷	人	畢	。	一	有	。	城	而	集	12
13	用	于	一	嶢	四	營	侵	降	得	二	年	蘇	四	朔	死	於	13
14	歲	鮮	年	山	十	鎬	周	于	呂	十	春	獲	年	方	因	歧	14
15	四	原	冬	崩	一	。	。	周	尚	九	正	妲	大	夏	謂	山	15
16	百	冬	十	。	年	三	三	師	以	年	月	己	蒐	六	文	。	16
17	九	十	一	四	春	十	十	遂	為	釋	諸	以	于	月	丁	十	17
18	十	有	月	十	三	七	五	遷	師	西	侯	歸	黎	周	殺	三	18
19	六	二	戊	四	月	年	年	于	。	伯	朝	作	作	地	季	年	19
20	年	月	子	年	西	周	周	程	三	諸	周	瓊	炮	震	歷	陟	20
21		周	周	西	伯	作	大	王	十	侯	伯	室	烙	。	。	王	21
22		師	師	伯	昌	辟	飢	錫	二	逆	夷	立	之	九	**帝**	嘉	22
23		有	渡	發	薨	雍	西	命	年	西	叔	玉	刑	年	**乙**	季	23
24		事	孟	伐	。	。	伯	西	五	伯	齊	門	。	陟	**名**	歷	24
25		于	津	黎	四	三	自	伯	星	歸	自	。	五	。	**羕**	之	25
26		上	而	。	十	十	程	得	聚	于	孤	十	年	**帝**	。	功	26
27		帝	還	四	二	九	遷	專	于	程	竹	年	夏	**辛**	元	錫	27
28		庸	王	十	年	年	于	征	房	。	歸	夏	築	**名**	年	之	28
29		蜀	囚	七	西	大	豐	伐	有	三	于	六	南	**受**	王	圭	29
30		羌	箕	年	伯	夫	。	。	赤	十	周	月	單	。	即	瓚	30
31		髳	子	內	發	辛	三	三	烏	年	。	王	之	元	位	秬	31
32		微	殺	史	受	甲	十	十	集	春	二	畋	臺	年	居	鬯	32
33		盧	王	向	丹	出	六	四	于	三	十	于	雨	王	殷	九	33
34		彭	子	摯	書	奔	年	年	周	月	二	西	土	即	。	命	34
35		濮	比	出	于	周	春	周	社	西	年	郊	于	位	二	為	35
36		從	干	奔	呂	。	正	師	密	伯	冬	。	亳	居	年	伯	36
37		周	微	周	尚	四	月	取	人	率	大	十	。	殷	周	既	37
38		師	子	。	有	十	諸	耆	侵	諸	蒐	七	六	命	人		38
39		伐	出	四	女	年	侯	及	阮	侯	于	年	年	九	伐		39
40		殷	奔	十	子	周	朝	邗	西	入	渭	西	西	侯	殷		40
	182	181	180	179	178	177	176	175	174	173	172	171	170	169	168	167	

183 **Zhou**: **Wu Wang of Zhou**, ***personal name Fa***. *In the reign of Gao Xin (Di Ku) there was a consort named Jiang Yuan, who was assisting in a sacrifice in the suburbs of the city, praying for the birth of a son. She saw a giant's footprint and*

184 *stepped in it, and at that moment felt herself being impregnated by a man. Subsequently she did become with child, and gave birth to a son. Thinking the matter unlucky, she abandoned [the baby] in a narrow path [for livestock]; but the sheep and cattle stepped aside and did not tread on it. Also she took it into the middle of a*

185 *mountain forest [intending to leave it there], but [there] she met woodcutters; [and thus could not abandon it]. Also she took it and put it on some cold ice; but a large bird covered it with one wing [to keep it warm]. Jiang Yuan thought this strange, so in the end she accepted [the baby] and nursed him, naming him*

186 *"Qi" ("the abandoned one"). Propping his chin on his hand, he had a strange appearance. When he grew to manhood he became Yao's minister of agriculture, and served the people well. Hou Ji's grandson was Gong Liu, a man of virtue, whom the regional lords all treated with the formal respect due a Son of Heaven.*

187 *Earlier than this, in the reign of Huang Di, a prognostication text said, "In the northwest there will be a king; the time will be a jiazi day; Chang will establish the judgment; Fa will execute the punishment; and Dan will put the Way into effect." Thirteen generations after Gong Liu,*

188 *Ji Li was born. When Ji Li was ten years old, flying dragons were everywhere in [the City of] Yin's Outlands of Mu. This. It seems certain, was a sign of a sage in low estate about to rise. Ji Li's consort was*

189 *Tai Ren, who dreamed that a tall man impregnated her. While urinating in a pigsty she gave birth to Chang. He was Wen Wang of Zhou. With the face of a dragon and the shoulders of a tiger, he grew to be ten feet tall. He had four nipples on his breast. Tai Wang said,*

190 *"The [destiny] that is to make our family line prosper surely lies in Chang!" Ji Li's eldest brother Tai Bo, recognizing that Heaven's Mandate lay with Chang, went off to Yue, never to return, and his younger brother Zhong Yong followed him. So*

191 *Ji Li had the inheritance, passing it on to Chang. Chang became "Lord of the West," and made Feng his capital city. Wen Wang's consort was Tai Si. She dreamed that brambles grew in the Shang court, but her eldest son Fa planted zi-trees in*

192 *the palace grounds, that changed into pines, cedars, yu-oaks and zuo-oaks. She reported this to Wen Wang. Wen Wang gave presents to all of his officials, and together with Fa altogether they acknowledged the auspicious dream. In the last month of autumn, on the day jiazi, a jue-bird with a writing in its beak came to*

193 *Feng [city] leaving it at Chang's door. Chang accepted it with reverence bowing his head to the ground. The essence of the text was this: "Ji Chang is the son of the Azure God; he who destroys Yin is its king Zhou [Xin]." [Chang] was about to go hunting, and the scribe Bian divined about [the prospects]; the divination read, "You will make a great catch;*

194 *it will not be a bear or a grizzly bear. Heaven is sending a great soldier to assist Chang." [The scribe Bian added,] "Your servant's great ancestor the scribe Chou divined about a hunt for Yu, and he got Gao Yao. On that occasion the marks [on the divination shell] were like this." They came to the waters of the Pan Stream, and Lü*

195 *Shang was fishing on the bank. The king dismounted and ran to him, saying with a gesture of reverence, "I have been hoping (wang) for you for seven years, and now at last I see a brilliant [prospect] in this [event]." [Lü] Shang arose and, changing his name, replied, "I, Wang, while fishing got a jade huang-half-disc, the burden of its text [in verse]*

196 *being this: 'The Ji [lineage] has received the Mandate, and Chang will come and make a proposal (ti); he will turn over to you the bells of Luo, and your reward will be in Qi.'" [Lü] Shang went out for a walk, and saw emerge from the Luo [River] a red man, who gave [Lü] Shang a piece of writing: "It is thus commanded: the one who is bidden to assist Chang is you." Wen*

197 *Wang dreamed that the sun and moon were adorning his body, and also that luanyang birds were singing on Mount Qi. Six xun after the first month of spring the five planets came together in Fang. After that there was a phoenix holding a piece of writing in its beak, which wandered into Wen Wang's capital city. The text of the writing*

13

	15	14	13	12	11	10	09	08	07	06	05	04	03	02	01	
01															周	01
02															武	02
03															王	03
04	王	曰	尚	非	豐	闕	季	吾	太	而	之	曰	山	履	名	04
05	夢	姬	釣	熊	置	間	歷	世	任	生	初	棄	林	之	發	05
06	日	受	於	非	于	化	為	當	夢	季	黃	枝	之	當		06
07	月	命	涯	羆	昌	為	嗣	有	長	歷	帝	頤	中	時		07
08	著	昌	王	天	戶	松	以	興	人	季	之	有	會	歆		08
09	其	來	下	遣	昌	柏	及	者	感	歷	世	異	伐	如		09
10	身	提	趨	大	拜	棫	昌	其	己	之	讖	相	林	有		10
11	又	撰	拜	師	稽	柞	昌	在	溲	十	言	長	者	人		11
12	鸞	爾	曰	以	首	以	為	昌	於	年	曰	為	又	道		12
13	鷟	洛	望	佐	受	告	西	乎	豕	飛	西	堯	取	感		13
14	鳴	鈴	公	昌	其	文	伯	季	牢	龍	北	稷	而	已		14
15	於	報	七	臣	文	王	作	歷	而	盈	為	官	置	遂		15
16	吱	在	年	太	要	文	邑	之	生	於	王	有	寒	有		16
17	山	齊	乃	祖	曰	王	于	兄	昌	殷	期	功	冰	身		17
18	孟	尚	今	史	姬	幣	豐	曰	是	之	在	於	上	而		18
19	春	出	見	疇	昌	率	文	太	為	牧	甲	民	大	生		19
20	六	游	光	為	蒼	群	王	伯	周	野	子	后	鳥	男		20
21	旬	見	景	禹	帝	臣	之	知	文	此	昌	稷	以	以	高	21
22	五	赤	于	卜	子	與	妃	天	王	蓋	制	之	一	為	辛	22
23	緯	人	斯	畋	亡	發	曰	命	龍	聖	命	孫	翼	不	氏	23
24	聚	自	尚	得	殷	並	太	在	顏	人	發	曰	籍	祥	之	24
25	房	洛	立	皋	者	拜	姒	昌	虎	在	行	公	覆	棄	世	25
26	後	出	變	陶	紂	吉	夢	適	肩	下	誅	劉	之	之	妃	26
27	有	授	名	其	王	夢	商	越	身	位	旦	有	姜	阨	曰	27
28	鳳	尚	答	兆	將	季	庭	終	長	將	行	德	嫄	巷	姜	28
29	皇	書	曰	類	畋	秋	生	身	十	起	道	諸	以	羊	嫄	29
30	銜	命	望	此	史	之	棘	不	尺	之	及	侯	為	牛	助	30
31	書	曰	釣	至	編	甲	太	反	胸	符	公	皆	異	避	祭	31
32	游	召	得	于	卜	子	子	弟	有	也	劉	以	乃	而	郊	32
33	文	佐	玉	磻	之	赤	發	仲	四	季	之	天	收	不	禖	33
34	王	昌	璜	溪	曰	爵	植	雍	乳	歷	後	子	養	踐	見	34
35	之	者	其	之	將	銜	梓	從	太	之	十	之	焉	又	大	35
36	都	子	文	水	大	書	樹	之	王	妃	三	禮	名	送	人	36
37	書	文	要	呂	獲	及	于	故	曰	曰	世	待	之	之	跡	37
38																38
39																39
40																40
	197	196	195	194	193	192	191	190	189	188	187	186	185	184	183	

198 *was this: "The emperor of Yin is unprincipled, and he oppresses and disorders the world. The august Decree has already moved. Yin will not be able to have it longer; its divine power is far off; the many [supporting] spirits are whistled away. The five planets have gathered in Fang; [their] brightness orders all within the four seas."*

199 *After Wen Wang died, his eldest son Fa succeeded him; this was Wu Wang. Wu Wang had his two front teeth joined together, and had a vacant gaze. When he was about to attack [the Shang king] Zhou [Xin], he got to Mengjin, and eight hundred [allied] regional lords [miraculously] assembled without a time for meeting being set beforehand.*

200 *Some of them said, "Zhou [Xin] should be attacked." But Wu Wang did not follow [this advice]. [Later], when Zhou [Xin] had killed Bi Gan, had put Ji Zi in prison, and when Wei Zi had left him, then [Wu Wang] did attack Zhou [Xin]. As they were crossing [the yellow River] at Mengjin, in mid-stream a white fish jumped into*

201 *the king's boat. The king bent down and took the fish; it was three feet long, and underneath its eyes there were red markings that formed characters, saying that Zhou [Xin] could be attacked. The king copied the text in common script, whereupon the markings on the fish vanished. He then burned the fish to declare [his gratitude] to Heaven.*

202 *Fire descended from Heaven stopping at the king's lodge, flowing into the shape of a red bird. The bird held a stalk of grain in its beak. The stalk of grain was a recognition of the virtue of [Zhou ancestor] Hou Ji. The fire was the fire flowing down from Heaven after the burnt offering of the fish and the announcement to Heaven, responding*

203 *with a sign of good luck. After that, they marched east to attack Zhou [Xin], and were victorious at Muye, their weapons getting no blood on the blades, and the whole world gave its allegiance to [Zhou]. Then Lü Shang was given Qi as his fief. Now that the virtue of Zhou was flourishing, plants and trees grew luxuriantly,*

204 *so that southernwood could be used to build palaces; hence we have the term "southernwood house." [Wu Wang] having possessed the world, he then made the city of Hao his capital.* 12th year: The king led the western tribes and [allied] lords in the attack on Yin, defeating [the Yin] in Muye. The king personally captured Shou

205 in the Tower of Nandan. Then he divided Heaven's Bright [Mandate], setting up Shou's son Lu Fu [as king of Shang]. This was Wu Geng. In the summer, in the fourth month, the king returned to Feng, and sacrificed in the Ancestral Temple. He appointed the Overseers of Yin. Then he hunted in Guan. He composed the Great Martial

206 Music. 13th year: The Lord of Chao came as a guest [acknowledging Zhou sovereignty]. [The king] presented the Yin [conquest to the ancestors] in the Ancestral Temple. Subsequently he enfeoffed all the regional lords. In the autumn there was a great harvest. 14th year: The king became ill. The Duke of Zhou prayed [for him] in a [specially cleared] altar area, and [about this] the "Metal-[bound] Coffer" was written.

207 *15th year: [The chief of] the Sushen people came as guest [to acknowledge Zhou sovereignty]. [The king] for the first time made a tour of inspection of the [Four] Border Mountains. An announcement was made to the cities of Mei. In the winter the Nine Cauldrons were moved to Luo[yang]. 16th year: Ji Zi came to court in homage. In the autumn the royal armies extinguished Pugu. 17th year:*

208 [The king] appointed the heir [Prince] Song in the Eastern Palace [to be his successor]. In the winter, in the 12th month, the king died, at the age of 54 years. **Cheng Wang**, ***personal name Song***.

209 First year: Spring, 1st month: The King took his position [as king]). He appointed as Steward of the Tomb Duke Wen of Zhou, [commanding him] to have charge of all the officers. On day *gengwu* the Duke of Zhou made an announcement to the Regional Lords at the Imperial Gate. In the summer, 6th month, King Wu was buried in Bi. In the autumn, the King was capped.

210 Wu Geng with Yin rebelled. Duke Wen of Zhou left to reside in the east. 2nd year: The people of Yan, the people of Xu, and the Yi-[natives] of the Huai [Valley] invaded Bei in rebellion. In the autumn there was a great [storm] of thunder and lightening, with wind. The King met the Duke of Zhou in the borders [of the royal domain].

211 Afterward they attacked Yin. 3rd year: The royal armies put an end to Yin, and killed [Yin king] Wu Geng, [named] Lu Fu. Yin people were moved to Wey. After that Yan was attacked, put an end to Pugu. 4th year: Spring, 1st month: [The King] for the first time held court in the Ancestral Temple. Summer, 4th month: For the first time

212 [the king performed the rite of] tasting wheat. The royal armies attacked the Huai Yi, and then invaded Yan. 5th year, Spring, 1st month: The King, while in Yan, moved its ruler to Pugu. Summer, 5th month: The King arrived [in Zhou] from Yan. Yin people were moved to [the site of] the city of Luo. After that the boundaries were laid out for

14

	30	29	28	27	26	25	24	23	22	21	20	19	18	17	16	
01	嘗	遂	武	元	命	十	樂	於								01
02	麥	伐	庚	年	王	五	。	南								02
03	王	殷	以	春	世	年	十	單								03
04	師	。	殷	正	子	肅	三	之	蒿	以	火	王	咸	文	又	04
05	伐	三	叛	月	誦	慎	年	臺	堪	吉	自	舟	曰	王	曰	05
06	淮	年	周	王	于	氏	巢	遂	為	也	天	王	紂	既	殷	06
07	夷	王	文	即	東	來	伯	分	宮	遂	止	俯	可	沒	帝	07
08	遂	師	公	位	宮	賓	來	天	室	東	于	取	伐	太	無	08
09	入	滅	出	命	冬	初	賓	之	因	伐	王	魚	矣	子	道	09
10	奄	殷	居	冢	十	狩	荐	明	名	紂	屋	長	武	發	虐	10
11	。	殺	于	宰	有	方	殷	立	蒿	勝	流	三	王	代	亂	11
12	五	武	東	周	二	岳	于	受	室	於	為	尺	不	立	天	12
13	年	庚	。	文	月	誥	太	子	既	牧	赤	目	從	是	下	13
14	春	祿	二	公	王	于	廟	祿	有	野	烏	下	及	為	星	14
15	正	父	年	總	陟	沬	遂	父	天	兵	烏	有	紂	武	命	15
16	月	遷	奄	百	年	邑	大	是	下	不	銜	赤	殺	王	已	16
17	王	殷	人	官	五	冬	封	為	遂	血	穀	文	比	武	移	17
18	在	民	徐	庚	十	遷	諸	武	都	刃	焉	成	干	王	不	18
19	奄	于	人	午	四	九	侯	庚	於	而	穀	字	囚	駢	得	19
20	遷	衛	及	周	。	鼎	秋	夏	鎬	天	者	言	箕	齒	復	20
21	其	遂	淮	公	**成**	于	大	四	十	下	紀	紂	子	望	久	21
22	君	伐	夷	誥	**王**	洛	有	月	二	歸	后	可	微	羊	靈	22
23	于	奄	入	諸	**名**	。	年	王	年	之	稷	伐	子	將	祇	23
24	蒲	滅	于	侯	**誦**	十	。	歸	王	乃	之	王	去	伐	遠	24
25	姑	蒲	邶	于		六	十	于	率	封	德	寫	之	紂	離	25
26	夏	姑	以	皇		年	四	豐	西	呂	火	以	乃	至	百	26
27	五	。	叛	門		箕	年	饗	夷	尚	者	世	伐	於	神	27
28	月	四	秋	夏		子	王	于	諸	於	燔	字	紂	孟	吹	28
29	王	年	大	六		來	有	太	侯	齊	魚	魚	渡	津	去	29
30	至	春	雷	月		朝	疾	廟	伐	周	以	文	孟	八	五	30
31	自	正	電	葬		秋	周	命	殷	德	告	消	津	百	星	31
32	奄	月	以	武		王	文	監	敗	既	天	燔	中	諸	聚	32
33	遷	初	風	王		師	公	殷	之	隆	天	魚	流	侯	房	33
34	殷	朝	王	于		滅	禱	遂	于	草	火	以	白	不	昭	34
35	民	于	逆	畢		蒲	於	狩	坶	木	流	告	魚	期	理	35
36	于	廟	周	秋		姑	壇	于	野	茂	下	天	躍	而	四	36
37	洛	夏	文	王		。	墠	管	王	盛	應	有	入	會	海	37
38	邑	四	公	加		十	作	作	親							38
39	遂	月	于	元		七	金	大	禽							39
40	營	初	郊	服		年	縢	武	受							40
	212	211	210	209	208	207	206	205	204	203	202	201	200	199	198	

213 Cheng Zhou. 6th year: [The King] conducted a great hunt on the south slopes of Mount Qi. 7th year: [In this year] the Duke of Zhou returned the government to the king. In the spring, 2nd month, the King went to Feng. In the 3rd month, Kang Gong of Shao went to Luo and measured the [new] city. On day *jiazi* Duke Wen of Zhou addressed

214 the many officers in Cheng Zhou. After that they walled the Eastern Capital. The King went to the Eastern Capital, and the regional lords came to pay homage. In the winter, the King returned from the Eastern Capital, and established a [new] temple for Gao Yu. 8th year, Spring, 1st month: The King for the first time "mounted the Eastern Steps" and conducted the government in person. [The King] ordered

215 Qin Fu, Lord of Lu, and Ji, Lord of Qi, to move a multitude of Yin [peoples] to Lu. He created the Xiang dance. In the winter, 10th month, the royal armies put an end to Tang, and its people were moved to Du. 9th year, Spring, 1st month: [The King] offered sacrifices in the Great Ancestor Temple, and for the first time used

216 the *zhuo* [music]. The [chief of the] Sushen people came to court in homage. The King had the Lord of Yong grant a charge to [the chief of] the Sushen people. 10th year: The King gave a charge to Tangshu Yu as *hou*. The [chief of the] Yueshang people came to court to do homage. Duke Wen of Zhou left [the court] to reside in Feng. 11th

217 year Spring, 1st month: The King went to Feng. Tangshu [Yu] presented [to the King] a [stalk of] felicitous grain. The King ordered Tangshu to give the grain-[stalk] instead to Duke Wen of Zhou. The King appointed Duke Ping of Zhou to govern the Eastern Capital. 12th year: The royal armies and the army of Yan walled Han.

218 The King granted the Lord of Han a charge [entailing regular dignities at court]. 13th year: The royal armies joined with [the forces of] the lords of Qi and Lu to attack the *rong* hordes. Summer, 6th month: Lu made the Great *di* offering in the temple of the Duke of Zhou. 14th year: The army of Qi invested the city of Qu and conquered it.

219 *After Wu Wang died, when Cheng Wang was young, Dan, Duke of Zhou was regent for seven years, establishing rites and creating [court] music. Spirit birds and phoenixes were seen; the ming bean grew [on the stairs]. So it was that together with Cheng Wang he went to observe the Yellow and Luo [Rivers]. [At the Yellow River] they dropped*

220 *a jade bi-disc in the water. When the rite was finished, the king withdrew and waited. As the sun was setting, a glorious light appeared from everywhere hanging over the river; blue clouds floated in; a blue dragon stood over the altar, holding in its mouth a diagram on a dark colored shell, which it set down and then left. [After a similar] rite*

221 *at the Luo River, there was a similar result. A dark colored turtle and a blue dragon, in an azure brilliance paused at the altar. [The turtle] had on its back a shell on which were carved writings in red markings forming words. The Duke of Zhou, using a writing brush, copied the text in common characters, and when he finished the markings*

222 *[on the turtle] vanished. The turtle then dropped the shell and went away. The words were indications of the rise and fall [of the fortunes of the world] down to the present. Qilin wandered in the [king's] parks, and phoenixes flew about in the [king's] courtyards. The king took a lute and sang:*

223 *"Phoenixes fly about in the Purple Court. What virtue have I, so to move spirit-beings? It's due to the former kings; their kindness is great. It's from their joy that the people feel peace.*

224 [17th year,] Winter: The completion [of the construction of] the City of Luo was announced. 18th year, Spring, 1st month: The King entered the city of Luo, and formally placed the cauldrons there. Phoenixes appeared. Subsequently he offered sacrifice to the River. 19th year: The King made a tour of inspection of the *hou* and *dian* domains, [visiting the sacred] mountains on the [four] borders. Duke Kang of Shao

225 attended him. He returned to Zong Zhou. He confirmed the titles and duties of the many officers. He degraded the Lord of Feng. 21st year: The representations of the application [of the penal laws] were removed [from public display]. Wen Gong of Zhou died in Feng. 22nd year: Duke Wen of Zhou was buried in Bi. 24th

226 year: [The chief of] the Yu-yue came to offer service. 25th year: The King called together a great assembly of the regional lords in the Eastern Capital. All the non-Chinese peoples came to offer service. Winter, 10th month: [The King] returned from the Eastern Capital, and made a great offering in the ancestral temple. 30th year: The Li

227 *rong* came to offer service [in submission]. 33rd year: The King rambled in Juan'e, attended by Duke Kang of Shao. He returned to Zong Zhou. [The king] ordered the royal heir [Prince] Zhao to go to meet [his bride] the daughter [of the lord of Fang]. Qi, Lord of Fang, went back [with them] to Zong Zhou. 34th

15

	45	44	43	42	41	40	39	38	37	36	35	34	33	32	31	
01	戎	四	從	冬						王	年	勺	魯	多	成	01
02	來	年	歸	洛						錫	春	肅	侯	士	周	02
03	賓	於	于	邑						韓	正	慎	禽	于	。	03
04	。	越	宗	告	。	消	于	璧	武	侯	月	氏	父	成	六	04
05	三	來	周	成	鳳	龜	洛	禮	王	命	王	來	齊	周	年	05
06	十	賓	遂	。	凰	隨	亦	畢	沒	。	如	朝	侯	遂	大	06
07	三	。	正	十	翔	甲	如	王	成	十	豐	王	伋	城	蒐	07
08	年	二	百	八	兮	而	之	退	王	三	唐	使	遷	東	于	08
09	王	十	官	年	于	去	玄	俟	少	年	叔	榮	庶	都	岐	09
10	遊	五	黜	春	紫	其	龜	至	周	王	獻	伯	殷	王	陽	10
11	于	年	豐	正	庭	言	青	于	公	師	嘉	錫	于	如	。	11
12	卷	王	侯	月	。	自	龍	日	旦	會	禾	肅	魯	東	七	12
13	阿	大	。	王	余	周	蒼	昃	攝	齊	王	慎	作	都	年	13
14	召	會	二	如	何	公	光	榮	政	侯	命	氏	象	諸	周	14
15	康	諸	十	洛	德	以	止	光	七	魯	唐	命	舞	侯	公	15
16	公	侯	一	邑	兮	迄	于	並	年	侯	叔	。	冬	來	復	16
17	從	于	年	定	以	于	壇	出	制	伐	歸	十	十	朝	政	17
18	歸	東	除	鼎	感	今	背	幕	禮	戎	禾	年	月	冬	于	18
19	于	都	治	鳳	靈	盛	甲	河	作	夏	于	王	王	王	王	19
20	宗	四	象	凰	。	衰	刻	青	樂	六	周	命	師	歸	春	20
21	周	夷	周	見	。	之	書	雲	神	月	文	唐	滅	自	二	21
22	命	來	文	遂	賴	符	赤	浮	烏	魯	公	叔	唐	東	月	22
23	王	賓	公	有	先	麒	文	至	鳳	大	王	虞	遷	都	王	23
24	世	冬	薨	事	王	麟	成	青	凰	禘	命	為	其	立	如	24
25	子	十	于	于	兮	游	字	龍	見	于	周	侯	民	高	豐	25
26	釗	月	豐	河	恩	苑	周	臨	蓂	周	平	越	于	圉	三	26
27	如	歸	。	。	澤	鳳	公	壇	莢	公	公	裳	杜	廟	月	27
28	房	自	二	十	臻	凰	援	銜	生	廟	治	氏	。	。	召	28
29	逆	東	十	九	。	翔	筆	玄	乃	。	東	來	九	八	康	29
30	女	都	二	年	于	庭	以	甲	與	十	都	朝	年	年	公	30
31	房	有	年	王	胥	成	世	之	成	四	。	周	春	春	如	31
32	伯	事	葬	巡	樂	王	文	圖	王	年	十	文	正	正	洛	32
33	祈	于	周	狩	兮	援	寫	坐	觀	齊	二	公	月	月	度	33
34	歸	太	文	侯	民	琴	之	之	于	師	年	出	有	王	邑	34
35	于	廟	公	甸	以	而	書	而	河	圍	王	居	事	初	甲	35
36	宗	。	于	方	寧	歌	成	去	洛	曲	師	于	于	莅	子	36
37	周	三	畢	岳	。	曰	文	禮	沈	城	燕	豐	太	阼	周	37
38	。	十	。	召						克	師	。	廟	親	文	38
39	三	年	二	康						之	城	十	初	政	公	39
40	十	離	十	公						。	韓	一	用	命	誥	40
	227	226	225	224	223	222	221	220	219	218	217	216	215	214	213	

228 year: It rained gold in Xianyang. 37th year, Summer, 4th month, day *yichou*: The King died. **Kang Wang**, ***personal name Zhao***.

229 First year, spring, first month: The king took his position as ruler. He ordered the prime minister Duke Kang of Shao to assume the direction of all the [court] officials. The regional lords came to court [in homage] at the [royal] palace in Feng. 3rd year: [The king] fixed the songs for the [court] music. He performed the auspicious *di* offering to the former king. He publicized the admonitions to the officers in charge of agriculture, and announced them in

230 the ancestral temple. 6th year: Duke Tai of Qi died. 9th year: [The lord of] Tang moved to Jin. He built a palace there that was [too] ornate. The king sent someone to reprove him. 12th year, Summer, 6th month, day *renshen*, the king entered Feng, and gave a charge to the Duke of Bi [as chief minister].

231 In the autumn, Duke Yi of Mao died. 16th year: [The king] gave a charge to Ji, *hou* of Qi, [to be chief minister]. The king made a tour of inspection in the south, as far as Jiujiang ("Nine Rivers') and Lu Shan. 19th year: Qin Fu, *hou* of Lu, died. 21st year: [The lord of Lu] built the Rush

232 Gate [Palace]. 24th year: Kang Gong of Shao died 26th year: Autumn, 9th month, day *jiwei*, the king died. **Zhao Wang**, ***personal name Xia***. First year, Spring, first month: The king took his position as ruler. He restored the institution of displaying representations of the prescribed punishments [on the gate of the palace.

233 6th year: The king gave a charge to Xun Bo. In the winter, 12th month, peach trees and plum trees blossomed. 14th year, Summer, 4th month: The fixed stars were invisible. Autumn, 7th month: The people of Lu killed their lord Zai. 16th year, Summer:

234 [The Zhou armies] attacked Chu. While crossing the Han they met a great *si*. 19th year, Spring: There was a comet in Ziwei. Xin Bo, [who was] Ji Gong, went with the king to attack Chu. The weather was very dark and stormy. Pheasants and hares were all terrified. The Six Armies were lost in the Han [River]. The king died.

235 **Mu Wang**, ***personal name Man***. First year, Spring, first month: The king took his position as ruler. The Zhao Palace was built. Yumi, Lord of Xin, was given a charge. Winter, 10th month, the Zhi Palace was built in Nanzheng (South Zheng). *From Wu Wang to Mu Wang, Zhou controlled the country*

236 *for 100 years. The kings from Mu Wang on made their capital in West Zheng.* 6th year, Spring: Dan, *zi* of Xu, came to court. He was granted a charge as *bo*. 8th year, Spring: The lord of North Tang came to see [the king]. He presented [to the king] a beautiful horse, that] bore Lu'er.

237 9th year: The Spring Palace was built. 11th year: The king charged as *qingshi* Mou Fu, *gong* of Ji. 12th year: Mao Gong Ban, Jing Gong Li, and Feng Gong Gu led armies to support the king and attack the Quan *rong*. In winter,

238 in the 10th month, the king made a tour of inspection to the north, and then campaigned against the Quan *rong*. 13th year, Spring: Ji Gong led a force supporting the king in a western campaign. [They] encamped in Yangyu. Autumn, 7th month: The western *rong* came as guests [in submission]. The *rong* of Xu invaded Luo. Winter, 10th

239 month: Zao Fu served as charioteer for the king, going [back] into Zong Zhou. 14th year: The king led [the forces of] the lord of Chu and attacked the Xu *rong*, defeating them. Summer, 4th month: The king hunted in Junqiu. 5th month: The Fan Palace was built. Autumn, 9th month: The Di people

240 invaded Bi. Winter: The king hunted in the Ping Marsh. The Tiger Pen was built. 15th year: spring, first month: [The chief of] the Liu Kun people came as guest [in submission]. The Chongbi Tower was built. In winter, the king observed the salt marshes. 16th year: Jiu, lord of He, died.

241 The king enfeoffed Zao Fu in Zhao. 17th year: The king campaigned west to Kunlun Hill, and saw Xiwangmu. [Later] that year he/she came to court, and was lodged as a guest in the Zhao Palace. Autumn. 8th month: The *rong* (war prisoners) were transferred to Tai Yuan.

242 *In his expeditions to the north, the king traveled 1000 li through the "Shifting Sands" [country], and another 1000 li through the "heaped Feathers" [country], When he campaigned against the Quan Rong, he captured their five kings and returned east [with them]. In his expeditions to the west, he went as far as [the country where] the green birds cast [their feathers]. In his western expeditions, coming and going over the empire, he traveled 190,000 li.*

16

	60	59	58	57	56	55	54	53	52	51	50	49	48	47	46	
01	**。**	王	侵	月	十	耳	百	。	楚	魏	闕	秋	廟	元	四	01
02	**王**	命	畢	造	月	。	年	**穆**	荊	。	門	毛	。	年	年	02
03	**北**	造	冬	父	王	九	穆	**王**	涉	六	。	懿	六	春	雨	03
04	**征**	父	蒐	御	北	年	王	**名**	漢	年	二	公	年	正	金	04
05	**行**	封	于	王	巡	築	以	**滿**	遇	王	十	薨	齊	月	于	05
06	**流**	于	萍	入	狩	春	下	。	大	錫	四	。	太	王	咸	06
07	**沙**	趙	澤	于	遂	宮	都	元	兕	郇	年	十	公	即	陽	07
08	**千**	。	作	宗	征	。	于	年	。	伯	召	六	薨	位	。	08
09	**里**	十	虎	周	犬	十	西	春	十	命	康	年	。	命	三	09
10	**積**	七	牢	。	戎	一	鄭	正	九	冬	公	錫	九	冢	十	10
11	**羽**	年	。	十	。	年	。	月	年	十	薨	齊	年	宰	七	11
12	**千**	王	十	四	十	王	六	王	春	二	。	侯	唐	召	年	12
13	**里**	西	五	年	三	命	年	即	有	月	二	伋	遷	康	夏	13
14	**征**	征	年	王	年	卿	春	位	星	桃	十	命	于	公	四	14
15	**犬**	昆	春	帥	春	士	徐	作	孛	李	六	王	晉	總	月	15
16	**戎**	侖	正	楚	祭	祭	子	昭	于	華	年	南	作	百	乙	16
17	**取**	丘	月	子	公	公	誕	宮	紫	。	秋	巡	宮	官	丑	17
18	**其**	見	留	伐	帥	謀	來	命	微	十	九	狩	而	諸	王	18
19	**五**	西	昆	徐	師	父	朝	辛	祭	四	月	至	美	侯	陟	19
20	**王**	王	氏	戎	從	。	錫	伯	公	年	己	九	王	朝	。	20
21	**以**	母	來	克	王	十	命	餘	辛	四	未	江	使	于	**康**	21
22	**東**	其	賓	之	西	二	為	靡	伯	月	王	廬	人	豐	**王**	22
23	**西**	年	作	夏	征	年	伯	冬	從	恆	陟	山	讓	宮	**名**	23
24	**征**	西	重	四	次	毛	。	十	王	星	。	。	之	。	**釗**	24
25	**于**	王	璧	月	于	公	八	月	伐	不	**昭**	十	。	三		25
26	**青**	母	臺	王	陽	班	年	築	楚	見	**王**	九	十	年		26
27	**鳥**	來	冬	畋	紆	井	春	祇	天	秋	**名**	年	二	定		27
28	**所**	朝	王	于	秋	公	北	宮	大	七	**瑕**	魯	年	樂		28
29	**解**	賓	觀	軍	七	利	唐	于	曀	月	。	侯	夏	歌		29
30	**西**	于	于	丘	月	逢	之	南	雉	魯	元	禽	六	吉		30
31	**征**	昭	鹽	五	西	公	君	鄭	兔	人	年	父	月	禘		31
32	**還**	宮	澤	月	戎	固	來	。	皆	弒	春	薨	壬	于		32
33	**履**	秋	。	作	來	帥	見	自	震	其	正	。	申	先		33
34	**天**	八	十	范	賓	師	獻	武	喪	君	月	二	王	王		34
35	**下**	月	六	宮	徐	從	一	王	六	宰	王	十	如	申		35
36	**億**	遷	年	秋	戎	王	驪	至	師	。	即	一	豐	戒		36
37	**有**	戎	霍	九	侵	伐	馬	穆	于	十	位	年	錫	農		37
38	**九**	于	侯	月	洛	犬	是	王	漢	六	復	魯	畢	官		38
39	**萬**	太	舊	翟	冬	戎	生	享	王	年	設	築	公	告		39
40	**里**	原	薨	人	十	冬	騄	國	陟	伐	象	茅	命	于		40
	242	241	240	239	238	237	236	235	234	233	232	231	230	229	228	

243 18th year, Spring, first month: The king was residing in the Zhi Palace [in Zong Zhou]. The regional lords came to court [in homage]. 21st year: Wen Gong of Zhai died. 24th year: The king commanded Rong Fu, Recorder of the Left, to write a [historical] record. 35th

244 35th year: The men of Jing invaded Xu. Qian, lord of Mao, led an army defeating the men of Jing at Ji. 37th year: All the armies were mobilized. They went east as far as [the land of] Nine Rivers, [crossing] on bridges of turtles and iguanas piled up. They then attacked Yue, going as far as

245 Yu. The men of Jing came [to court] with tribute [in submission]. 39th year: The king assembled the regional lords on Mount Tu. 45th year: Fei, lord of Lu, died. 51st year: [The king] made the Penal Code of Lü. He gave a charge to the lord of Pu in Feng.

246 55th year: The king died in the Zhi Palace. **Gong Wang, *personal name Yi*.** First year, Spring, first month: The king took his position as ruler. 4th year: The royal army destroyed Mi. 9th year, Spring, first month, *dinghai*: The king

247 had the inner recorder Liang give a charge to Qian, lord of Mao, [to be chief minister]. 12th year: The king died. **Yih Wang, *personal name Jian*.** First year, Spring, first month: The king took his position as ruler. A day dawned twice in Zheng. 7th year: The Western *Rong* encroached on

248 Hao. 13th year: The men of Di encroached on Qi. 15th year: The king moved from Zong Zhou to Huai Village. 17th year: Zhuo, Duke Li of Lu, died. 21st year: The Duke of Guo led a [royal] army north

249 to attack the Quan *rong*, but was badly defeated. 25th year: The king died. *In the reign of Yih Wang, [the king's] daily movements were unscheduled, his announcements and orders were not issued on time, the holder of the [time-]jug was not able to perform his duty, and accordingly the regional lords wandered away from virtue.*

250 **Xiao Wang, *personal name Pifang*.** First year, Spring, first month: The king took his position as ruler. He ordered the lord of Shen to attack the western *rong*. 5th year: [The chiefs of] the western *rong* came to court and presented horses. 7th year, Winter: There was much rain and lightening. The Yangzi and Han Rivers flooded. *This*

251 *year Li Wang was born.* 8th year: For the first time there was pasturing in [the valleys of] the Qian and Wei [Rivers]. 9th year: The king died. **Yi Wang, *personal name Xie*.** First year, Spring, first month: The king took his position as ruler. 2nd year: The men of Shu and the men of Lü came to court and presented red jade.

252 [The king] performed the *bin* rite [of homage] to the He [Yellow River god], using the large mace. 3rd year: The king assembled the regional lords, and boiled Ai Gong of Qi in a cauldron. 6th year: The king went hunting in She Forest, took one rhinoceros, and returned. 7th year: Guo Gong

253 led an army attacking the hordes of Taiyuan, getting as far as Yuquan, and capturing a thousand horses. In the winter, it rained hailstones, as big as whetstones. Xiongqu, lord of Chu, attacked Yong, getting as far as E. 8th year: The king had a fever. The regional lords prayed [for him] to

254 [spirits of] the mountains and streams. The king died. **Li Wang, *personal name Hu*.** First year: The king took his position as ruler. He had the Yi Palace built, and ordered *qingshi* Duke Yi of Yong to direct the consecration of it. The men of Chu came to court and presented turtle shells. 3rd year: The Yi [tribes] of the Huai [valley] encroached on

255 the Luo area. The king ordered Chang Fu, *gong* of Guo, to attack them, but he was unsuccessful. Shan, [who was] Xian Gong of Qi, died. 6th year: Yan, *zi* of Chu, died. 8th year: [The king] began to prosecute people who reviled him. Liang Fu, lord of Rui, cautioned the officials in the court.

256 11th year: The hordes of the west penetrated to Quan Qiu. 12th year: The king fled to Zhi. Men of Zhou surrounded the king's palace, took the child of Duke Mu of Shao, and killed him. 13th year: The king was in Zhi. He, *bo* of Gong, handled

257 the business of the Son of Heaven. 14th year: The Xianyun encroached on the western environs of Zong Zhou. Mu Gong of Shao led an army pursuing the Man [tribes] of Jing as far as Luo. 16th year: Wu Hou of Cai died. Yong, *zi* of Chu, died. 19th

17

	15	14	13	12	11	10	09	08	07	06	05	04	03	02	01	
01	天	一	洛	山	帥	瓊	年	**孝**	伐	鎬	使	。	于	五	。	01
02	子	年	王	川	師	玉	厲	**王**	犬	。	內	五	紂	年	十	02
03	事	西	命	王	伐	賓	王	**名**	戎	十	史	十	荊	荊	八	03
04	。	戎	虢	陟	太	于	生	**辟**	敗	三	良	五	人	人	年	04
05	十	入	公	。	原	河	。	**方**	逋	年	錫	年	來	入	春	05
06	四	于	長	**厲**	之	用	八	。	。	翟	毛	王	貢	徐	正	06
07	年	犬	父	**王**	戎	介	年	元	二	人	伯	陟	。	毛	月	07
08	玁	丘	伐	**名**	至	珪	初	年	十	侵	遷	于	三	伯	王	08
09	狁	。	之	**胡**	于	。	牧	春	五	岐	命	祇	十	遷	居	09
10	侵	十	不	。	俞	三	于	正	年	。	。	宮	九	帥	祇	10
11	宗	二	克	元	泉	年	汧	月	王	十	十	。	年	師	宮	11
12	周	年	齊	年	獲	王	渭	王	陟	五	二	**共**	王	敗	諸	12
13	西	王	獻	春	馬	致	。	即	。	年	年	**王**	會	荊	侯	13
14	鄙	奔	公	正	千	諸	九	位	懿	王	王	**名**	諸	人	來	14
15	召	彘	山	月	匹	侯	年	命	王	自	陟	**繄**	侯	于	朝	15
16	穆	國	薨	王	冬	烹	王	申	之	宗	。	。	于	泲	。	16
17	公	人	。	即	雨	齊	陟	侯	世	周	**懿**	元	塗	。	二	17
18	帥	圍	六	位	雹	哀	。	伐	興	遷	**王**	年	山	三	十	18
19	師	王	年	作	大	公	**夷**	西	居	于	**名**	春	。	十	一	19
20	追	宮	楚	夷	如	于	**王**	戎	無	槐	**堅**	正	四	七	年	20
21	荊	執	子	宮	礪	鼎	**名**	。	節	里	。	月	十	年	祭	21
22	蠻	召	延	命	楚	。	**燮**	五	號	。	元	王	五	大	文	22
23	至	穆	卒	卿	子	六	。	年	令	十	年	即	年	起	公	23
24	于	公	。	士	熊	年	元	西	不	七	春	位	魯	九	薨	24
25	洛	之	八	榮	渠	王	年	戎	時	年	正	。	侯	師	。	25
26	。	子	年	夷	伐	獵	春	來	挈	魯	月	四	濆	東	二	26
27	十	殺	初	公	庸	于	正	獻	壺	厲	王	年	薨	至	十	27
28	六	之	監	落	至	社	月	馬	氏	公	即	王	。	于	四	28
29	年	。	謗	楚	于	林	王	。	不	擢	位	師	五	九	年	29
30	蔡	十	芮	人	鄂	獲	即	七	能	薨	天	滅	十	江	王	30
31	武	三	伯	來	。	犀	位	年	共	。	再	密	一	架	命	31
32	侯	年	良	獻	八	牛	。	冬	其	二	旦	。	年	黿	左	32
33	薨	王	夫	龜	年	一	二	大	職	十	于	九	作	鼉	史	33
34	楚	在	戒	貝	王	以	年	雨	諸	一	鄭	年	呂	以	戎	34
35	子	彘	百	。	有	歸	蜀	電	侯	年	。	春	刑	為	夫	35
36	勇	共	官	三	疾	。	人	江	於	虢	七	正	命	梁	作	36
37	卒	伯	于	年	諸	七	呂	漢	是	公	年	月	甫	遂	記	37
38	。	和	朝	淮	侯	年	人	水	攜	帥	西	丁	侯	伐	。	38
39	十	攝	。	夷	祈	虢	來	。	德	師	戎	亥	于	越	三	39
40	九	行	十	侵	于	公	獻	是	。	北	侵	王	豐	至	十	40
	257	256	255	254	253	252	251	250	249	248	247	246	245	244	243	

258 year: Yi Bo of Cao died. 22nd year: There was a great drought. You Gong of Chen died. 23rd year: There was a great drought. Xi Gong of Song died. 24th year: There was a great drought. Wu Gong of Qii died. 25th

259 year: There was a great drought. Yan, *zi* of Chu, died. 26th year: There was a great drought. The king died in Zhi. Duke Ding of Zhou and Duke Mu of Shao raised up the crown prince Jing and made him king. He, lord of Gong, returned to his state. Then there was heavy

260 rain. *The great drought having lasted a long time, huts and houses all burned. When the Fen King died, divination of the sun was done, and the cracks showed that Li Wang was a calamity. The Duke of Zhou and the Duke of Shao then raised up Crown Prince Jing [to be king]. After that Gong He returned to his own state. He was a man of*

261 *complete virtue: when he was given honor he was not delighted; if he was set aside he was not angry. [After retiring] he wandered to his heart's content atop the hills of Gong.* **Xuan Wang**, ***personal name Jing***.

262 First year, Spring, first month: The king took his position as ruler. Duke Ding of Zhou and Duke Mu of Shao assisted in the government. The tax on fields was restored. War chariots were made. Lord Hui of Yan died. 2nd year: Appointments were given to Huang Fu as Grand Tutor (*Dashi*) and to Xiu Fu as Master of Horse. Lu

263 Shen Gong died. Duke's son Su of Cao killed his lord You Bo Qiang. 3rd year: The king commanded the Great Officer Zhong to attack the *rong* of the west. Shou, Duke Wu of Qi, died. 4th year: The king ordered Jue Fu to go to Han. The lord of Han

264 came to court. 5th year, Summer, 6th month: Yin Ji Fu led an army attacking the Xianyun, proceeding as far as Taiyuan. Autumn, 8th month: Fangshu led an army attacking the Man tribes of Jing. 6th year: Duke Mu of Shao led an army to attack the Huai

265 Yi [tribes]. *The king led an army to attack the hostile peoples of Xu; Huang Fu and Xiu Fu accompanied the king on the expedition; they camped on the Huai River.* Returning from this expedition, the king gave a charge to Duke Mu of Shao. The *rong* of the West killed Zhong of Qin. Shuang, lord of Chu, died.

266 7th year: The king gave a charge to the lord of Shen. The king ordered Zhongshan Fu, lord of Fan, to build a wall around [the capital of] Qi. 8th year: [The king] began the shrine for his father. Duke Wu of Lu came to court [to see the king]. [The king] issued an order naming Xi heir in Lu. 9th year: The king assembled the regional lords

267 in the Eastern Capital. After that he went hunting in Fu. 12th year: Duke Wu of Lu died. The men of Qi killed their lord Wuji, who was Duke Li. They [then] elevated the duke's son Ci [to the position of duke]. 15th year: Li, *hou* of Wey died. The king gave a charge to Guo

268 Wen Gong. 16th year: Jin moved [its capital] to Jiang. 18th year: Yi, *hou* of Cai, died. 21st year: The Lu *gongzi* Bo Yu killed his lord Xi, who was Yi Gong. 22nd year:

269 The king gave a charge to Prince Duo Fu, to live in Luo. 24th year: Ci, Wen Gong of Qi, died. 25th year: There was a great drought. The King prayed in the temple at the edge [of the city]; then it rained. 27th year: , Song Hui

270 Gong Jian died. 28th year: Xun, lord of Chu, died. 29th year: [The king] for the first time did not observe the plowing rite in the Thousand Mou Field. 30th year: There was a hare that gamboled in the capital city Hao. 32nd year: The king's army attacked

271 Lu; he killed Bo Yu, and appointed Xiao Gong Cheng [in his place], [delivering the charge] in the Yi Palace. Xiao, Xi Gong of Chen, died. A horse changed into a man. 33rd year: Duke Cheng of Qi died. The king's army attacked the hostile people of Taiyuan, but was not victorious.

272 37th year: A horse changed into a fox. Lord Xi of Yan died. E, lord of Chu, died. 38th year: The king's army and Lord Mu of Jin attacked the *rong* of Tiao and Ben. The king's army was badly defeated. 39th

18

	30	29	28	27	26	25	24	23	22	21	20	19	18	17	16	
01	三	魯	公	王	文	侯	。	夷	來	慎	元	至	雨	十	年	01
02	十	殺	覸	錫	公	于	七	。	朝	公	年	德	。	五	曹	02
03	七	伯	薨	王	命	東	年	王	。	薨	春	尊	大	年	夷	03
04	年	御	。	子	。	都	王	帥	五	曹	正	之	旱	大	伯	04
05	有	命	二	多	十	遂	錫	師	年	公	月	不	既	旱	薨	05
06	馬	孝	十	父	六	狩	申	伐	夏	子	王	喜	久	楚	。	06
07	化	公	八	命	年	于	伯	徐	六	蘇	即	廢	廬	子	二	07
08	為	稱	年	居	晉	甫	命	戎	月	弒	位	之	舍	嚴	十	08
09	狐	于	楚	洛	遷	。	王	皇	尹	其	周	不	俱	卒	二	09
10	燕	夷	子	。	于	十	命	父	吉	君	定	怒	焚	。	年	10
11	僖	宮	狗	二	絳	二	樊	休	甫	幽	公	逍	會	二	大	11
12	侯	陳	卒	十	。	年	侯	父	帥	伯	召	遙	汾	十	旱	12
13	卒	僖	。	四	十	魯	仲	從	師	彊	穆	得	王	六	陳	13
14	楚	公	二	年	八	武	山	王	伐	。	公	志	崩	年	幽	14
15	子	孝	十	齊	年	公	甫	伐	玁	三	輔	于	卜	大	公	15
16	鄂	薨	九	文	蔡	薨	城	徐	狁	年	政	共	于	旱	薨	16
17	卒	有	年	公	夷	齊	齊	戎	至	王	復	山	太	王	。	17
18	。	馬	初	赤	侯	人	。	次	于	命	田	之	陽	陟	二	18
19	三	化	不	薨	薨	弒	八	于	太	大	賦	首	兆	于	十	19
20	十	為	藉	。	。	其	年	淮	原	夫	作	。	曰	彘	三	20
21	八	人	千	二	二	君	初	。	秋	仲	戎	**宣**	厲	周	年	21
22	年	。	畝	十	十	厲	考	王	八	伐	車	**王**	王	定	大	22
23	王	三	。	五	一	公	室	歸	月	西	燕	**名**	為	公	旱	23
24	師	十	三	年	年	無	魯	自	方	戎	惠	**靖**	祟	召	宋	24
25	及	三	十	大	魯	忌	武	伐	叔	齊	侯		周	穆	僖	25
26	晉	年	年	旱	公	立	公	徐	帥	武	薨		公	公	公	26
27	穆	齊	有	王	子	公	來	錫	師	公	。		召	立	薨	27
28	侯	成	兔	禱	伯	子	朝	召	伐	壽	二		公	太	。	28
29	伐	公	舞	于	御	赤	錫	穆	荊	薨	年		乃	子	二	29
30	條	薨	于	郊	弒	。	魯	公	蠻	。	錫		立	靖	十	30
31	戎	王	鎬	廟	其	十	世	命	。	四	大		太	為	四	31
32	奔	師	京	遂	君	五	子	西	六	年	師		子	王	年	32
33	戎	伐	。	雨	懿	年	戲	戎	年	王	皇		靖	共	大	33
34	王	太	三	。	公	衛	命	殺	召	命	父		共	伯	旱	34
35	師	原	十	二	戲	釐	。	秦	穆	蹶	司		和	和	杞	35
36	敗	之	二	十	。	侯	九	仲	公	父	馬		遂	歸	武	36
37	逋	戎	年	七	二	薨	年	楚	帥	如	休		歸	其	公	37
38	。	不	王	年	十	王	王	子	師	韓	父		國	國	薨	38
39	三	克	師	宋	二	錫	會	霜	伐	韓	命		和	遂	。	39
40	十	。	伐	惠	年	虢	諸	卒	淮	侯	魯		有	大	二	40
	272	271	270	269	268	267	266	265	264	263	262	261	260	259	258	

273 year: The king's army attacked the hostile Jiang people, fighting a battle at Qianmou. The king's army was badly defeated. 40th year: There was a census of the population in Taiyuan. The *rong* destroyed the city of Jiang. The men of Jin defeated the northern *rong* at Fenxi. 41st

274 year: The king's army was defeated in Shen. 43rd year: The king killed the grand officer Du Bo. His son Xishu fled to Jin. Feisheng, Mu Hou of Jin, died. His younger brother Shangshu made himself lord. Chou, the heir, fled.

275 44th year. ***First year of Shangshu of Jin***. 46th year: The king died. **You Wang, *personal name Nie*.**

276 First year, Spring, first month: The king took his position as ruler. Chou, heir of Jin, returned to Jin, and killed Shangshu. The people of Jin elevated Chou [to the position of ruler]; he was Wen Hou. The king gave a charge to the grand tutor Yin Huangfu. 2nd year:

277 ***First year of Wen Hou of Jin***. The Jing, Wei and Luo Rivers ran dry. There was a landslide on Mount Qi. Taxes were increased for the first time. Wen Hou of Jin together with Prince Duofu attacked Ceng, and they subdued it; then [Duo Fu] dwelt on the Hillock of Zheng Fu; he was Huan Gong of Zheng.

278 3rd year: The king took Baosi as concubine. In the winter there was a great storm of lightening and thunder. 4th year: The men of Qin attacked the hostile peoples of the west. Summer, 6th month: there was hoarfrost. Duke Yi of Chen died. 5th year: The king's heir Yijiu fled to Shen. Huangfu

279 made [another] capital in Xiang. 6th year: The king ordered Bo Shi to lead the army to attack the hostile peoples of Liuji. The king's army was defeated and put to flight. The hostile peoples of the west destroyed Gai. Winter, 10th month, first of the month, day *xinmao*: there was a solar eclipse. 7th year: The men of Guo

280 destroyed Jiao. 8th year: The king gave a charge to the Minister of Instruction, Duofu, lord of Zheng. The king designated Bo Fu, the son of Baosi, his heir apparent. 9th year: The lord of Shen sent an embassy to the Xi Rong (hostile peoples of the west) and to [the people of] Ceng. 10th year:

281 The king and the lords made an agreement in the Grand Hall [of the Ancestral Temple]. Autumn, 9th month: peach trees and almond trees bore fruit. The king's army attacked Shen. 11th year, Spring, first month: the sun had a halo. The men of Shen, the men of Ceng, and the Quan *rong* entered Zong Zhou, and killed the king

282 and Huan Gong of Zheng. The Quan *rong* killed Prince Bo Fu, seized Baosi, and returned with her to their homeland. The *hou* of Shen and Lu, the *nan* of Xu and the *zi* of Zheng elevated Yijiu [as Zhou king] in Shen. Han, Duke of Guo, elevated Prnce Yuchen [as king] in Xie.

283 *[After] Wu Wang destroyed Yin, in twenty-four years the cauldrons were placed in the City of Luo. [From then] to [the last year of] You Wang was 257 years. Altogether this was 281 years. From the first year of Wu Wang to [the last year of] You Wang was 292 years.*

284 *After the move east, [the chronicle] begins recording the affairs of Jin; [therefore the words] "the king took his position as ruler" will in all cases be omitted.* ***Jin Wen Hou 11th year***: The king moved [the capital] east to the city of Luo. He gave a charge to Wen Hou. The *hou* of Jin joined with the *hou* of Wey, the *bo* of Zheng, and the *bo* of Qin,

285 with their troops escorting the king in his entry into Cheng Zhou. 12th year: Qin created the western fields for offerings. Duke Xiao of Lu died. Qin and Jin were granted fields in Bin and Qi. 13th year: The men of Qi destroyed Zhu. The king gave a charge as *situ* (minister of instruction)

286 to the *bo*-lord of Zheng. 14th year: *Hou*-lord Qing of Yan died. The men of Zheng destroyed Guo. 15th year: Duke Xiang of Qin led an army attacking the *rong*, and died while with his troops. Duke Dai of Song died. 16th year: *Hou*-lord Ai of Yan

287 died. Zheng moved [its capital] to [the confluence of] the Zhen and Wei [Rivers]. 17th year: Yi, *zi*-lord of Chu, died. 18th year: [The lord of] Zheng killed his great officer Guan Qisi. 20th year: Qin moved [its capital] to [the confluence of] the Qian and Wei [Rivers]. 23rd year:

288 Duke Wu of Wei died. 24th year: The men of Jin destroyed Han. 28th year: Duke Wen of Qin inflicted a great defeat on the *rong* army at [Mount] Qi, and returning [from the campaign] restored [to Qin] the fields east of [Mount] Qi. 31st year: Wen Hou

19

Strip	01–20	21–40	No.
31	九年王師伐姜戎戰于千畝王師敗逋。四十年料	民于太原戎人滅姜邑晉人敗北戎于汾隰。四十	273
32	一年王師敗于申。四十三年王殺大夫杜伯其子	隰叔出奔晉晉穆侯費生薨弟殤叔自立世子仇出	274
33	奔。四十四年。**晉殤叔元年**。四十六年王陟。	**幽王名涅**	275
34	元年春正月王即位晉世子仇歸于晉殺殤叔晉人	立仇是為文侯王錫太師尹氏皇父命。二年。**晉**	276
35	**文侯元年**。涇渭洛竭岐山崩初增賦晉文侯同惠	王子多父伐鄶克之乃居鄭父之丘是為鄭桓公。	277
36	三年王嬖褒姒冬大震電。四年秦人伐西戎夏六	月隕霜陳夷公薨。五年王世子宜臼出奔申皇父	278
37	作都于向。六年王命伯士帥師伐六濟之戎王師	敗逋西戎滅蓋冬十月辛卯朔日有食之。七年虢	279
38	人滅焦。八年王錫司徒鄭伯多父命王立褒姒之	子曰伯服為太子。九年申侯聘西戎及鄫。十年	280
39	春王及諸侯盟于太室秋九月桃杏實王師伐申。	十一年春正月日暈申人鄫人及犬戎入宗周弒王	281
40	及鄭桓公犬戎殺王子伯服執褒姒以歸申侯魯侯	許男鄭子立宜臼于申虢公翰立王子余臣于攜。	282
	武王滅殷二十四年定鼎洛邑至幽王二百五十七	年共二百八十一年自武王至幽王二百九十二年	283
41	自東遷以後始紀晉事王即位皆不書。**晉文侯十**	**一年**王東徙洛邑錫文侯命晉侯會衛侯鄭伯秦伯	284
42	以師從王入于成周。十二年秦作西時魯孝公薨	賜秦晉以邠岐之田。十三年齊人滅祝王錫司徒	285
43	鄭伯命。十四年燕傾侯卒鄭人滅虢。十五年秦	襄公帥師伐戎卒于師宋戴公薨。十六年燕哀侯	286
44	卒鄭遷于溱洧。十七年楚子儀卒。十八年鄭殺	其大夫關其思。二十年秦遷于汧渭。二十三年	287
45	魏武公薨。二十四年晉人滅韓。二十八年秦文	公大敗戎師于岐來歸岐東之田。三十一年文侯	288

289 killed Prince Yuchen in Xie. **33rd year**: Duke Wu of Song died. **34th year**: Qin instituted sacrifices to the Precious Ones of Chen. **35th year**: *Hou*-lord Wen of Jin died. Qin for the first time used the punishment of exterminating an entire clan.

290 **Zhao Hou**. **First year:** [Lord Zhao of] Jin enfeoffed his [father's] younger brother Chengshi in Quwo. 7th year: Pan Fu of Jin murdered his ruler *hou*-lord Zhao, and brought in Chengshi [to make him ruler] but was unsuccessful. *Hou*-lord Xiao, the son of *hou*-lord Zhao, was elevated [to the position of ruler], and the men of Jin killed Pan Fu.

291 **Xiao Hou**. **First year**: The men of Chu encroached on Shen. **4th year**: Duke Zhuang of Wey died. The king's men guarded Shen. **8th year**: Duke Zhuang of Qi died. Huanshu of Quwo in Jin, [personal name] Chengshi, died. His son Shan was raised [to the position of ruler of Quwo]; this was Zhuang Bo.

292 *From this [time the capital of] Jin was in Yi, [so the ruler was] called Yi Hou.* **9th year**: ***First year of Zhuang Bo.*** In Spring there was a great snowstorm. **10th year**: The Di people attacked Yi, getting as far as the outskirts of [the capital of] Jin. Duke Xuan of Song died. Duke Hui of Lu

293 sent Zairang [to the king] to request [permission to use the royal] rites for suburban and ancestral temple [sacrifices]. The king sent Recorder Jue to Lu with an edict stopping it. **15th year**: Zhuang Bo of Quwo in Jin entered [the capital city] Yi, and killed Xiao Hou. The people of Jin drove him out, and set up Xiao Hou's son Que [as successor].

294 This was E Hou. **E Hou Que**, **first year**: There was thunder without clouds. Duke Hui of Lu died. **2nd year**: *Yin Gong of Lu, first year: the Chunqiu begins here. Lu Yin Gong and Zhu Zhuang Gong made a treaty*

295 *in Gumie*. **4th year**, Spring, 2nd month: There was an eclipse of the sun. 3rd month, day *gengxu*: **Ping Wang died**. **5th year**, 10th month: Zhuang Bo rebelled with Quwo, and attacked Yi. The *gongzi* (prince) Wan went to the aid of Yi. Xunshu

296 Zhen pursued him, as far as Jiagu. Yi Hou (i.e., E Hou) burned the standing grain of Quwo, and returned [to Yi]. Yi Hou [later] attacked Quwo, winning a great victory. Wu Gong sued for peace with Yi. [Yi Hou] went as far as Xiang and returned [to Yi]. **6th year**: The king had Guo Gong

297 attack Quwo in Jin. [The circumstances were as follows:] E Hou of Jin had died. Zhuang Bo of Quwo had again attacked Jin. Jin raised Guang, the son of E Hou, [to the position of ruler]. This was Ai Hou. **Ai Hou, first year**: **2nd year**: Zhuang Bo of Quwo died. His son Cheng

298 succeeded him; this was Wu Gong. [Quwo] still had [only] one army. **3rd year**: ***First year of Wu Gong of Quwo***. The men of Rui relied on [their] citadel. The men of Xun, and Dong Bo, all rebelled against Quwo. **First year of Xiaozi Hou**: [The lord of] Quwo

299 captured Ai Hou of Jin. The people of Jin raised [to the rule] the son of Ai Hou, as Xiaozi Hou. Rui Bo Man fled to Wei. **2nd year**: The king's army and the army of Qin besieged [the capital of] Wei, took Rui Bo Man and sent him east. **3rd year**, Winter:

300 The lord of Quwo enticed Xiaozi Hou of Jin [to pay him a visit] and killed him. [The lord of] Quwo of Jin destroyed Xun, taking its territory and giving it to the great officer An of the Yuan lineage. He was [the one now known as] Xunshu. The *rong* people welcomed Rui Bo Wan at the border [of their land]. ***Next year***: The king

301 ordered [the prince of the] Guo-zhong [lineage] to attack Quwo, and set up Min, younger brother of Ai Hou of Jin, as lord of Jin. **Jin Hou Min**, **1st year**. **2nd year**, Spring: Yi (the former Jin capital) was ended. **5th year**: Zhuang Gong of Zheng died. **9th year**, 3rd month,

302 (day) *yiwei*: **Huan Wang died**. **10th year**: Quwo still had (only) one army, differing from Jin. **15th year**, 5th month: Huan Wang was buried. **24th year**: **Zhuang Wang died**. **25th year**, Spring: Qi

303 Huan Gong assembled the regional lords in Beixing, to settle the disturbances in Song. **27th year**: Wu Gong of Quwo put an end to Min, *hou* of Jin, and presented the [captured] treasures to the king. The king appointed **Wu Gong** to be *hou* of Jin, with single army [status].

20

	60	59	58	57	56	55	54	53	52	51	50	49	48	47	46	
01	桓	乙	命	曲	獲	稱	伐	軫	于	是	使	。	孝	昭	殺	01
02	公	未	號	沃	晉	立	晉	追	姑	為	宰	自	侯	侯	王	02
03	會	桓	仲	伯	哀	是	之	之	蔑	鄂	讓	是	元	元	子	03
04	諸	王	伐	誘	侯	為	曲	至	。	侯	請	晉	年	年	余	04
05	侯	陟	曲	晉	晉	武	沃	于	四	。	郊	在	楚	封	臣	05
06	于	。	沃	小	人	公	晉	家	年	鄂	廟	翼	人	其	于	06
07	北	十	立	子	立	尚	鄂	谷	春	侯	之	稱	侵	弟	攜	07
08	杏	年	晉	侯	哀	一	侯	翼	二	郤	禮	翼	申	成	。	08
09	以	曲	哀	殺	侯	軍	卒	侯	月	元	王	侯	。	師	三	09
10	平	沃	侯	之	子	。	曲	焚	日	年	使	。	四	于	十	10
11	宋	尚	弟	晉	為	三	沃	曲	有	無	史	九	年	曲	三	11
12	亂	一	緡	曲	小	年	莊	沃	食	雲	角	年	衛	沃	年	12
13	。	軍	于	沃	子	。	伯	之	之	而	如	。	莊	。	宋	13
14	二	異	翼	滅	侯	曲	復	禾	三	雷	魯	莊	公	七	武	14
15	十	于	為	荀	芮	沃	攻	而	月	魯	諭	伯	卒	年	公	15
16	七	晉	晉	以	伯	武	晉	還	庚	惠	止	元	王	潘	卒	16
17	年	。	侯	其	萬	公	晉	翼	戌	公	之	年	人	父	。	17
18	曲	十	。	地	出	元	立	侯	平	卒	。	。	成	弒	三	18
19	沃	五	侯	賜	奔	年	鄂	伐	王	。	十	春	申	其	十	19
20	武	年	緡	大	魏	。	侯	曲	陟	二	五	大	。	君	四	20
21	公	五	元	夫	。	芮	子	沃	。	年	年	雨	八	昭	年	21
22	滅	月	年	原	二	人	光	大	五	。	晉	雪	年	侯	秦	22
23	晉	葬	。	氏	年	乘	是	捷	年	魯	曲	。	齊	納	作	23
24	侯	桓	二	黯	王	京	為	武	十	隱	沃	十	莊	成	陳	24
25	緡	王	年	是	師	荀	哀	公	月	公	莊	年	公	師	寶	25
26	以	。	春	為	秦	人	侯	請	莊	元	伯	狄	卒	不	祠	26
27	寶	二	滅	荀	師	董	。	成	伯	年	入	人	曲	克	。	27
28	獻	十	翼	叔	圍	伯	哀	于	以	春	翼	伐	沃	立	三	28
29	王	四	。	戎	魏	皆	侯	翼	曲	秋	弒	翼	桓	昭	十	29
30	王	年	五	人	取	叛	元	至	沃	始	孝	至	叔	侯	五	30
31	命	莊	年	逆	芮	曲	年	相	叛	此	侯	于	成	之	年	31
32	武	王	鄭	芮	伯	沃	。	而	伐	。	晉	晉	師	子	文	32
33	公	陟	莊	伯	萬	。	二	還	翼	魯	人	郊	卒	孝	侯	33
34	以	。	公	萬	而	小	年	。	公	隱	逐	宋	子	侯	薨	34
35	一	二	卒	于	東	子	曲	六	子	公	之	宣	鱓	晉	秦	35
36	軍	十	。	郊	之	侯	沃	年	萬	及	立	公	立	人	初	36
37	為	五	九	。	。	元	莊	王	救	邾	孝	薨	是	殺	用	37
38	晉	年	年	明	三	年	伯	使	翼	莊	侯	魯	為	潘	族	38
39	侯	春	三	年	年	曲	卒	虢	荀	公	子	惠	莊	父	刑	39
40	。	齊	月	王	冬	沃	子	公	叔	盟	郤	公	伯	。	。	40
	303	302	301	300	299	298	297	296	295	294	293	292	291	290	289	

289-303: Strip Page 20: Interpretation of Dates with Underline

Strips	Date BCE	Zhou Kings	Jin Lords (red)	QuwoLords
289	748	Ping 23	Wen Hou 33	
	747	24	34	
	746	25	35 dies	
290	745	26	Zhao Hou 1	Chengshi 1
	739	32	7 assassinated	7
291	738	33	Xiao Hou 1	8
	735	36	4	11
	731	40	8	15 dies
292	730	41	9	Zhuang Bo 1
	729	42	10	2
293	724	47	15 killed by ZB	7
294	723	48	E Hou 1	8
	722	49	2 (Chunqiu 1)	9
295	720	51 dies	4	11
	719	Huan 1	5	12
296	718	2	6 dies	13
297	717	3	(Ai Hou 1)[1]	14
	716	4	Ai Hou 2	15 dies
298	715	5	3 (captured)	Wu Gong 1
	709	11	9 = Xiaozi Hou 1	7
299	708	12	2	8
	707	13	3 killed in Quwo	9
300	706	14	(interregnum)[2]	10
	705	15	(Hou Min 1)	11
301	704	16	Hou Min 2	12
	701	19	5	15
	697	23 dies	9	19
302	696	Zhuang 1	10	20
	691	5	15	25
	682	14 dies	24	34
	681	Xi 1	25	35
303	679	3	27 killed by WG	37 (= 27)[3]

According to the *Shiji*, from Wen Hou to Xiaozi Hou there were six generations (inclusive), but from Chengshi to Wu Gong (inclusive) there were three. This seems strange. The *Shiji* and the BA agree that Hou Min was a younger brother of Ai Hou. Ai Hou was captured on a campaign against an ally of Wu Gong, and was killed the next year (Xiaozi Hou's first year) on orders from Wu Gong.

---

[1] Jin first year dates in parentheses at 717 and 705 I take to be implied by the narrative. I have reconstructed the text accordingly, but I am not sure this is correct.

[2] I here call this an "interregnum" year, because Xiaozi Hou was already dead, and the calendar of his successor named in this year by the king would not begin until the following year. Therefore I call this year simply "next year" (*ming nian*).

[3] Having taken the place of Hou Min as *de jure* lord of Jin, Wu Gong of (Jin) Quwo assumed not only Hou Min's title but also his calendar. So even though the current year started as "Wu Gong, 37th year," the next year will be "Wu Gong 28th year." This seems to have been standard procedure.

Comments on Recovered Strip Text

1. These comments assume familiarity with my draft paper for AAS 2006 (Chapter Seven in this book). I have used the procedure explained in that paper, to work out a strip text of the *Zhushu jinian*, as far as I think it can be done. (Indeed, I may well have gone too far.) The *Jinben* text for the last century and a half of its content, following the Three Jin victory over Zhi in 453, must have been in great disorder. There is material that is obviously copied in from other Ji tomb texts in order to give the *Zhushu jinian* more substance, and from 368 on, every year is listed, even if there is nothing to enter for the year. (One can imagine a very long table in the research room in the Jin Dynasty capital, where a mess of strips was being sorted into years, in date boxes around the table. One can suppose that when for political reasons work had to stop, someone made a copy of everything that had been done, just as it was, including boxes which were empty. This copy became the *Jinben.*)

2. There are other equivalent ways in which the text could be arranged. One can imagine a text different from Xun Xu's description of the *Mu Tianzi zhuan* (followed here but extended). It would have the same number of characters or spaces per strip, but on shorter and wider strips, with two columns of half length on each strip. There is some (albeit slight) archaeological evidence for such an arrangement.

3. I mention what concrete evidence I have: illustrations of some bronze reproductions of inscribed bamboo strips, apparently of important documents. (Photographs of objects from the National Palace Museum: adapted from an article printed in the *Traditional Chinese Culture in Taiwan* series, Kwang Hua Publishing Co.; I am looking at an article, "Chinese Bookmaking an Ancient Craft," p. 5, in *The Free China Journal,* January 6, 1996.) They show columns of characters of regular length. In addition to illustrating a short column format, these materials meet an important objection often made to my work, that all texts on bamboo strips so far discovered are in columns of irregular length, in characters of irregular sizes. I am, of course, assuming that the *Zhushu jinian* found in Jixian was in this respect not like these previously discovered objects.

4. I have used italics to indicate (a) a king's personal name when used as part of the title of his reign chronicle; (b) when I am using or adapting *guben* material; (c) when I am composing something I think must have been in the tomb text; and also (d) (sparingly) to call attention to something that requires special attention. I also use italics (e) in the English translation for all subtext matter, and (f) in the Chinese for all embedded subtexts.

5. I use bold font with underline text for all names of rulers when these names function as titles of the rulers' reign chronicles. This applies to both English and Chinese.

6. The letters 'a' and 'b' attached to a strip number specify the top or bottom half of the strip.

Strips 001, 017, 024: These are the only examples of a whole strip given to the names of a ruler used as the title of his chronicle.

003a-014b: I treat this as one unbroken text, as does the *Song shu*. In *Jinben* it is in three pieces, before year one, after year twenty, and after year fifty. (Only when the pieces are joined does the text have a subtext word-count, here 24 half-lines of 17 *zi*. The Jin Dynasty court editors have freely broken and distributed other long subtexts as well as this one. Further, when distributed as in the received *Jinben*, the subtext breaks up two half strips of main text.) Most of the mythological material in these subtexts in *juan* 1 of the *Zhushu jinian* has been copied into Shen Yue's *Song shu*, "Fu Rui Zhi" chapter. (In due course – strip 185 and comment -- I will show that the copying must have been from the *Jinian* to the *Song shu.*)

014b: I repeat "Xianyuan" (in italics). The repetition seems to be needed for sense, and it gives me my word-count. (I delete the last seven *zi* ("[Mingting:] This is the mouth of the present Hanmen Valley.") These words are obviously a Jin note. They are included, however, in the *Song shu* "Fu Rui Zhi" text.)

015b-016b: The subtext begins at 015.39-40. I have deleted 帝王之崩皆曰陟書稱新陟王謂新崩也帝以土德王應地裂而陟 as obviously a Jin insertion, and have supplied '既' "when." The small-character double-column in-text note 大夫歲時朝焉 in the Fan Qin edition should be subtext.

Accordingly I use italics thus: p. 126 last 4 words 'When he was buried' (this being subtext); p. 127, 15b.39 既 ('when', supplied) but not 15b.40 葬 ('buried', given); p. 128, 016, all of lines 1-3 (this being subtext);

and p. 129, column 16, all of characters 25-37 (25-30 大大歲時朝焉 reinterprets Fan Qin as noted above, and 31-37 死七年乃立顓頊 'Seven years after the death [of Huang Di] Zhuan Xu was established [as di]' is supplied from a quotation from Luo Bi's Lu shi, as explained next).

016b.31-37: The *guben* material here comes from the *Lu shi* ("Hou Ji" 6). The "seven years" therein allow determining that Huang Di 50 is supposed to be 2353. The date *gengshen* in main text strip 002b and subtext strip 009b shows that the year totals in the summary lines (121, 182, 283) have to be what they are, and were in the tomb text: 2353 is 100 *zhang* before 453, the date of the Zhao-Han-Wei victory over Zhi Bo that created the Wei state. The day *gengshen* (57) for the first of the 7th month of 2353 is deducible from calendar data for 453, by *zhang-bu* theory. If this had been a forger's work, the seven years would have been in the *Jinben* (or nowhere). These facts, furthermore, show that all relevant parts of the strip text, including the transposed apparent strip-text in Zhou Wu Wang strip 207 altering the length of the Wu Wang reign, were in the text as it left the hands of experts in Wei before the book was buried.

019-020: There could not have been any main entry for "Di Zhi Shao Hao Shi," as found in the *Jinben*. There is no chronicle text in the *Jinben*, only a subtext after the title, prefaced by "Yue an" = "I, Shen Yue, note [the following]." I am assuming that the first 34 *zi* after "Yue an" were an embedded sub-subtext in the introductory subtext for Zhuan Xu, and that Shen removed it and expanded it, using the resulting text as subtext for his own invented main-text entry "Di Zhi Shao Hao Shi"; this I use as sub-subtext (019), but omit its repetition in the sub-subtext. (Shen claimed Shao Hao as his own founding ancestor, as he says in his autobiography at the end of his *Song shu*.) I have used what seemed authentic in Shen Yue's note, inserting it in the Zhuan Xu subtext at a point that seemed right.

023b: The *Wenxian tongkao* (*j*. 250 under Yao) informs me that this Zhi was Di Ku's eldest son, Yao being Zhi's younger brother.

032-046: Subtexts for Yao in *Jinben* are distributed after the title, after year 70, and after Yao's death. They are countable as subtext only when brought together, as I have done. It is possible that the subtext at 032 through 044 (minus the final supplied 既) should precede the opening main text.

042: The Fan Qin text (1.6b) is defective: 其圖以白玉為檢赤上為O泥似黃金. I have used Wang Guowei as in Fang and Wang p. 208 with note.

044-045 The *Song shu* text for Yao ends at 044b, with the words "*Sui rang Shun*." The *guben* material in italics is adapted from Fang and Wang pp. 66-68, items 5 and 6.

048 and 052: Subtexts for Shun are in three lumps, at the beginning, after year 1, and after year 14. I have brought them together here (as they are in the *Song shu*), so that I can count them in 17's and display them on subtext strips. The one after year 14 is much longer than the first two combined, and ends with Shun's abdication in favor of Yu. In year 14 Shun turned over the management of the government to Yu, making this year (or the next) count as the beginning of Xia. Shun 14, 2029 in the *Annals*, would be the first year of the 471 years totaled for Xia in the end-of-Xia summary in strip 121. Wang Guowei and earlier commentators have not noticed this, and always count Xia years from 1989, the first of Yu's *de jure* final eight years (070b), getting 431, or counting only stated reign lengths not including intervals between reigns. Wang suggests (Fang and Wang p. 224) that the totals don't match "because the forger was again assuming the theory that a reign begins only after completion of mourning" 因作偽者復假設喪畢即位之說. Wang is of course right, except that there was no forger. What this reveals is that the "Nivison-Shaughnessy hypothesis" is not new in China, and has been available to chronological thinking so long that no source needs to be given for it; and that the only reason why no chronology scholars in China take it seriously is because none of them takes seriously the possibility that the *Jinben Zhushu jinian* is an authentic ancient text. The "theory" is taken for granted in the *Annals'* account of the Xia (See also p. 9, note 4.).

064b 居三年: At the ends of Xia reigns, the *Jinben* almost always indicates (by *ganzhi sui*-names) a brief interregnum. I think I have shown (*EC* 1990) that these are residues of mourning-completion periods that should each be two years. The tomb text could not have had *sui*-names, but must have indicated the assumed precise length of these interregnums. The most probable wording would be "*ju* 居 *x nian*" (literally, "[then there were] x years of inactivity"; I have translated functionally, "mourning" instead of "inactivity") immediately after the word *zhi* (陟 "died"). I find that these words give word-counts that fit. Since I supply these words, I put them in italics.

072-073: 生性也死命也 (Fang and Wang p. 212) should be simply 生死命也 (072b). (The Jin transcriber apparently had Mencius' Gaozi in his head.) Word count shows that subtext after 五年巡狩會諸侯于涂山 (071a) and at the end of the Yu chronicle belongs together, and that 禹立四十五年 (073a) is subtext, not main text. The 45 years are Shun 14 through 50 and Yu 1 through 8, not counting mourning years for Shun. (Wang Guowei sees "45 years" conflicting with "8th year as more evidence of forgery.)

074-075: The biography of Shu Xi in the *Jin shu* says that Yi (recommended to Heaven by Yu, line 073) tried to usurp Qi's position and Qi killed him. I had assumed that perhaps the first group of Jin editors (280-282) replaced this with what the *Jinben* says, and that the second group (290 ff.) restored it. But perhaps the *guben* alternative text actually comes from another Jixian source. The trouble with the first possibility is that one would have to assume that the first group of editors counted the *zi* they were deleting and carefully composed a substitute text with exactly the same number of *zi*; but there seems to be no evidence that they had this kind of concern for strip text length.

082-083: I assume that the words "*ming nian*" 明年 belong here in the main text rather than (as in all editions) at the beginning of the following long subtext (where "*ming nian*" would hardly make sense). Word count as well as meaning requires this change.

093-094: 13th year of Zhu, BA date 1840, Ming lord of Shang died. There is evidence that the BA date for the succession of Shang Jia Wei of Yin, 1718, is correct. 1840 ought to be Shao Kang 2. Nivison and Shao *Bamboo Annals* will explore the possibility that all BA pre-Shang "Yin" and "Shang" dates are correct.

102 and 110: Like Yin-Shang, the strip count for Xia I reasonably assume to be 60, plus a half strip chronological summary. Di Kong Jia and Di Gui are the only rulers' names each given a half strip when used as reign titles. (This supports my assumption that the Di Gui text was invented, and the Di Kong Jia text was rewritten, at the same time, to cope with the problem of the celestial phenomena of 1576, *Jinben* Di Gui 10, now 1580, but properly Kong Jia 2, originally 1576.) I admit that to get a well-ordered text for Xia I have used at two points *Jinben* text printed as in-text notes (small characters, double columns). Such text is usually excluded from my restored tomb text. The result would have been twelve unused spaces before Di Gui, and eleven unused spaces before Di Kong Jia.

This restriction on in-text notes would have been too strict. (Notice, that while the in-text note at the end of the subtext terminating the chronicle for Tai Wu of Shang is obviously written by a post-discovery hand, still it explicitly tells us something about the tomb text. It would seem that the author(s) of the in-text notes were editing the original text itself. Notice also that first years of Jin lords from Shangshu (Xuan 44) on are in in-text notes, but actually must be original sub-text.) If '能帥禹者也故夏后氏報焉。' is placed (as I do) immediately after the reign title '。帝杼。' (092-093), what would otherwise be twelve unused spaces before Di Kong Jia will be filled; and if '夏衰昆吾豕韋相繼爲伯。' is placed (as I do) immediately after the first year entry for Di Hao (109a), otherwise unused spaces before Di Gui will be filled.

121, 182, and 283: The fact that summary strips 121 and 182 have the second half blank probably indicates that all three summaries were on separate whole strips and were inserted after the rest of the text was written and inscribed; but there is no need to suppose that this was done only after the book came to light in Jin. Strip 182 requires special comment (below).

129: 129.28 成 and 129.30 遂 are lacking in some texts (including Fan Qin).

135: 135.28-29 伊尹 are repeated in all texts I have seen. Perhaps there were repeat marks.

138: In 雍己名伷, the word 伷 is *zhou*, meaning eldest son of the legitimate wife. Yong Ji's position in the received king-list followed here indicates that this is what he was, so this may not be his personal name, but instead may be a comment asserting his legitimacy as king in the main sequence. This would be understandable: oracle inscriptions show that Tai Wu was the main sequence king in this (5th) generation (Keightley *Sources* p. 186 note d). When the order of the two kings was reversed (Chapter Two, VI; and Nivison 1999 and 2002, #7.3.2 through #7.4), the editor doing it could have added "*zhou ye*" to justify the move; this could later have been "corrected" to "*ming zhou*," "personal name Zhou."

142: The subtext for Tai Wu in standard editions has 35 *zi*. I delete particle *zhi* 之 in the phrase "*san nian zhi hou*" ("after three years"), thus reducing the *zi*-count to 17 + 17 *zi*. Also I change the last sentence "*Miao wei Zhong Zong*" to "*Miao wei Tai Zong*," following the double-column small-*zi* note at the end of this subtext, "*Zhushu zuo Tai Zong*."

158a.10-13: I insert 得一丹山 from Fan Qin's in-text note.

167-168: This 2x17 subtext obviously is out of place in the *Jinben*, where it has been put immediately after "The king killed Ji Li," breaking a strip. It must have been farther on after the end of 0167a, ending the Wen Ding chronicle, as I have it.

168: The subtext concludes with the words 文丁殺季歷 "Wen Ding killed Ji Li": These words were quoted out of context by some (perhaps Tang) person, and then were miscopied as 文王殺季歷 "Wen Wang killed Ji Li." Subsequently someone else worked this astonishing mistake into two chapters of some copy of Liu Zhiji's *Shi tong*. Some later editions of the *Shi tong* have continued the error, and even now some critics of the *Zhushu jinian* take seriously the idea that the "original" *Zhushu jinian* revealed that Wen Wang had murdered his own father. Pu Qilong in his 18th-century *Shi tong tong shi* demonstrates that the idea is ridiculous (j. 13, "Yi Gu" and j. 16, "Za Shuo Shang," sections on the *Jizhong Jinian*), merely by close examination of the *Shi tong* text, showing that some unscrupulous hand has deliberately corrupted it. Only someone convinced that the *Jinben* is an outright forgery and that the rich context in it is sheer invention could be deceived by the *Shi tong* quotation. (Fang and Wang, p. 37-38, item 35, do not recognize this as a variant text, even though they do not accept the *Jinben* as authentic.)

168: The date of Ji Li's arrest is said to be year 11 of Wen Ding (Wenwu Ding), = 1114 in the *Jinben* system. How does one interpret this? One theory, "A," has it that one must respect "11th year," but correct (if necessary) the *yuan* date for the reigning king, here "Wen Ding." What was that *yuan* date? (1) We know that Di Xin's true first year was 1086, but his *Annals* first year was 16 years back, at 1102. Before him the *Annals* has Di Yi, 9 years, and Wen Ding, 13 years. So Wen Ding's true first year must be 1086 + 9 + 13, = 1108, and year 11 would be 1098 – impossible: Wen Wang was already king of Zhou at latest by 1099. (2) I have argued that Wen Ding's father king Wu Yi gave his heir Wen Ding his own calendar in 1118. Year 11 would then be 1108. So, on theory A Ji Li must have been arrested in 1108, perhaps dying in prison later. The other theory, "B," is that one does not have to accept the given date for the event no matter what. In this case another factor must be considered: with the re-dating of the conjunction of 1059 back one Jupiter cycle (12 years) to 1071, all late pre-conquest Zhou dates were also moved back 12 years; so one must take the event date "11th year" from 1124 (1102 + 9 + 13), getting 1114, and then reduce by 12, getting 1102.

But theory A has to be wrong, because the record of Ji Li's military actions has him active right up to the year of his death. Theory B, on the other hand, is good, because if Wen Wang had 1099 as a first year, and that year was his post-mourning *yuan*, then his succession year must have been 1101. So Ji Li died in 1102. What was the date, in Chinese terms? If you think Wenwu Ding's reign began in 1108, the year is Wenwu Ding 7, not Wenwu Ding 11. If you think he had a calendar beginning in 1118, for a total of 13 years, then Ji Li's death was not in the Wenwu Ding reign at all.

Could my theory that Wu Yi gave Wenwu Ding a calendar in 1118, dying in 1109, with Wenwu Ding having three more years for a total of 13, still be right? Yes, because I have just proved that *Annals* event dates have no absolute validity but are meaningful only in *Annals* terms. If "Wen Ding 11" is wrong, we cannot then say, "But Wen Ding *something* must be right." E.g., consider the problem of the death date of Wei Gong of Lu. I think I have proved (Nivison 1999 Appendix 1) that he died in 916, which was Gong Wang 2. But the *Annals* says that he died in 918, which in *Annals* terms was Mu Wang 45, a non-date.

The way Shang reigns are re-dated makes it appear that Wen Ding was responsible for Ji Li's death rather than Di Yi. But this is not why Wen Ding's apparent responsibility is noted with surprise as new information by Liu Zhiji; the traditional account (e.g., in *Lü Shi chunqiu*) had Ji Li dying from exhaustion, having worn himself out in serving his people. As noted above, there is also the weird account in some texts of the *Shi tong* that it was Wen Wang rather than Wen Ding who killed Ji Li. This could be imagined only by someone who had never seen or accepted the *Zhushu jinian* (see also p. 171 note 1, and p. 183 under #8.).

The information that Zhou attacked Shang in the second year of Di Yi comes from a quote in *Taiping yulan*. This seems to be the only place where the *Jinben* account of Shang needs to be patched with *guben* material. (I think the date Di Yi 2 is not a *guben* datum at all; the *Taiping yulan* is probably quoting a more complete version of the BA; the Di Yi reign had already been shortened from 19 years to 9 years before the text was buried; if so the original date was Di Yi 12; see next.)

168-169: Shaughnessy (2003.12) has demonstrated convincingly that the words 三年王命南仲西拒昆夷城朔方 refer to an event that happened in Xuan Wang 13 (i.e., in 815, as shown by research which Shaughnessy credits to Ma Chengyuan). He thinks that this indicates that the Jin restorers have misplaced another strip (or half-strip). My reconstruction will not allow this, so I must find a better explanation.

I have argued (Nivison 1999 and 2002, Appendix 2) that Di Yi's actual first year was 1105 (beginning with an *yi* day), for a reign of 19 years, not 9 years as in the BA. And I have shown (*ibid* 2.3 note 3) that the earthquake in Zhou recorded next actually occurred in 1093, which must be Di Yi 13. Therefore at a time, necessarily before the text was buried, when Di Yi still was accorded 19 years, both of these events, the first by error and the second correctly, were entered under year Di Yi 13. At this point, Wen Ding's reign was made to be only three years (as also in the *Wenxian tongkao*). Later, the Warring States chroniclers learned that Wen Ding had 13 years. Not knowing that the first ten were Wu Yi's last ten years (because as I claim in Nivison 1999 and 2002 Appendix 2 Wu Yi gave his heir his own calendar in 1118), the Warring States experts resolved the problem by cutting out the first ten years of Di Yi, so that "12th year" became "2nd year", and "13th year" became "3rd year" (and the year of his death became "9th year" instead of "19th year"). (Some explanation would be needed even if Shaughnessy were right about a strip being misplaced; one would still have to account for an event dated "13th year" getting recorded under "3rd year." But once one has the explanation, one no longer needs to assume a strip was misplaced.)[1]

172-173: Di Xin years 21, 22, and 23 are 1082, 1081, and 1080, counting from 1102. To get absolute dates, one subtracts 12, getting 1070: regional lords favoring Zhou come to the Zhou court (perhaps Chang was 60 *sui* this year); 1069: the Shang king responds to the threat by staging a hunt in the Wei valley, which is the Zhou homeland; and 1068: "the Lord of the West" (Chang, lord of Zhou) is arrested and confined in Youli village. We can infer that a major event in 1068 required the presence of all regional lords, including

---

[1] Central to my argument here is my claim that Di Yi's reign was not 9 years, as in the BA, but was 19 years. I have argued this in detail in Nivison 1999 and 2002, section 7 and Appendix 2. But those monographs have not attracted critical scrutiny, which I need. I will therefore outline the argument herewith, in the hope of provoking attention to what is, after all, a daring claim. The claim is that Wu Yi's 35 years can be got by subtracting 16 years from the BA dates 1159-1125, getting 1143-1109 (then prefixing two years, 1145-1144, for mourning completion) – no surprise there. But I claim that Wenwu Ding's 13 years actually begin in 1118 rather than the expected 1108, and end in 1106 rather than in 1096. If analysis shows this to be true, one must assume that Wu Yi not only identified his heir in 1145 (first day of the post-solstice month being *dingchou*) but made doubly sure of the succession by giving Wenwu Ding his own calendar in 1118. If this is right, it explains why the *Wenxian tongkao* and other secondary sources give "Wen Ding" (or "Tai Ding") only three years. This would require that the Di Yi reign begin in 1105, *zi* month first day *yiyou*, next month first day probably *yimao*. To go on, one must reconstruct the ritual calendar. The inscription launching the 1077 Yi Fang campaign in year 10 implies that the cycle began on 9 September, a *jiaxu* (11) day. But two other inscriptions dated year 3 (hence 1084) imply that the cycle began on 16 October, again a *jiaxu* day. So the cycle has been held at 36 *xun*, causing the first day to move back through the calendar more than five days a year. Taking another jump, way back, we find two inscriptions dated years 7 and 8, implying cycle first days *jiawu* (31). The 8th year inscription is part of a set of seven 10-day routine apotropaic inscriptions, making it datable to 1098, with sacrifice information showing the cycle in the year corresponding to 1098 to have begun on 24 November 1099. So the cycle had been alternating with 36 *xun* and 37 *xun*, keeping the first day moving back an average of only one day in four years. Even at this slow pace, the first day eventually migrated back out of winter into autumn, and from there on the cycle was held at 36 *xun*. This much information gives 1105 as first year – of 19 -- for Di Yi. One might assume 36-37 *xun* alternation prior to 1098-99, back to 1110; in the Shang sacrificial year corresponding to 1110 the cycle first day would be *jiawu* (31), 27 November 1111. (Probably it was 60 days later; see Appendix 4 sections 6 through 8.) 1110 has to be the year of the longest oracle inscription known, *Jia Bian* 2416, 10th month, but with no year date. The occasion was the launching of the campaign against the Yu Fang. (Routine sacrifice inscriptions in the following spring require a cycle beginning on day *jiachen* (41).) By luck there is a fragment in the White collection in Toronto, with a shorter version of the same text, and it bears the date "9th sacrificial year" (Chang Yuzhi p. 246). So year one was 1118.

Chang, in the Shang capital. In a "feudal" system this was how a king controlled his realm: a lord failing to appear for some important event and thus put himself at the mercy of the king would identify himself as a rebel. So what was the event in 1068? *Yi Zhou shu* 21 "Feng Bao" can be dated to 1046 (see p. 239). Again Zhou is hosting friendly lords, pre-conquest, so the Shang calendar is used, and the date in the "Feng Bao" is "23rd year," implying 1068 as the first year of a second Di Xin calendar. A calendar marks the beginning of a reign. I infer that, probably, in 1068 the Shang king (1) assumed the title *di* (37 years after 1105, which was Di Yi 1 – explaining why the *Wenxian tongkao* gives Di Yi 37 years); and (2) perhaps also named his heir Lu Fu *xiao wang*, "junior king" later to be Wu Geng: the first day of 1068 was 1 January, *gengxu* (47). (For 1068 to be the *yuan* of *another* "king" would explain why for a decade at least the 1086 calendar kept on being used.) I find the 1068 calendar confirmed by at least six inscriptions (see Appendix 4, Supplement 1).

175-176 and 181: There is dispute among the commentators about the meaning of the sentence "*Sui qian yu Cheng*" 遂遷于程. Some would take it to say "[Zhou] thereupon moved [its capital] to Cheng" (Di Xin 33 = 1070, less 12 = 1058), and thence to Feng (Di Xin 35 = 1068, less 12 = 1056). These two moves could have marked two announcements of kingship, in 1058 and 1056, resulting in two calendar counts, and two dates for Wen Wang's death, in year nine (*Yi Zhou shu* #25 "Wen zhuan") and year seven (*Shiji* 4 "Zhou Benji"), actually two names for the same year, 1050. Compare Tang of Shang: in Di Gui 15 (strip 113) he moves his capital to Bo; nothing else, but a new calendar is implied. Di Gui's last year 31 is thus Tang 17. This becomes explicit in strip 131, the first year of Tang as king of Shang being "18th year." In the BA for Zhou, however, the count begins (silently again) with the year after Wen Wang's death (Di Xin 41 (strip 178) = 1062, less 12 = actual death date 1050). The count becomes explicit in strip 181, "11th year" (in the received text this is Di Xin 52; '11th year' follows a quote from Yixing in *Tang shu* "Li Zhi."). "12th year" as date of the conquest is thus artificial, created by the 12-year shift of the conjunction date from 1059 back to 1071. The actual year was Wu Wang 10, implied by *Yi Zhou shu* #45 "Wu Jing" and #29 "Bao Dian."

But the meaning approved by CFH (see the long discussion, *juan* 21, pp. 32b-34a) and followed by both Biot and Legge, is (as here) that the just defeated people of Mi "were thereupon moved to Cheng", a city built by Ji Li and apparently the Zhou capital since his time. The fact that 1058 was the year after the conjunction is explanation enough for events such as Wen Wang's death sometimes to be counted from that year. There is good reason (Nivison 1983 pp. 530-531) not to assume an actual calendar beginning in 1058.

182: "Twenty-nine kings" is an error; the text has thirty kings for Shang. Perhaps we might understand the twenty-nine as not including Tang. His death date in the text is 1545, and in Liu Xin as quoted in the *Han shu* (21B) Tang's death year is also the *de jure* first year of his successor Tai Jia; and from 1545 to 1050, the conquest year and therefore the year of death of Shou=Di Xin, is 496 years by inclusive count. But this is not consistent with the summaries for Xia and for Western Zhou; the former, 471 years, covers 2029 through 1559; the latter explicitly begins with Wu Wang counting from the *Jinben* year of Wen Wang's death in the 3rd month, 1062.

The solution to this problem is the fact that in the original true chronology Shang began in 1554, after victory over Xia in 1555; and Di Xin's true *yuan* year was 1086. 496 years from 1555 was 1059, the date of the Shang-terminating and Zhou-heralding conjunction. The next year 1058 was the Zhou Mandate year, and 1058 was in fact the 29th year of Shou = Di Xin. Therefore, in the original form of this summary, 二十九王 was 二十九年, making the text read "from Tang's defeat of Xia until the 29th year of Shou was 496 years." This proves that these dynasty-ending summaries are not post-discovery additions by the Jin court scholars, but were features of all pre-burial stages of the text. (Ironically, 王 is misprinted 年 in the *Guben* of Zhu Youzeng as edited by Wang Guowei, *Guben Zhushu jinian jijiao*, p. 11a. It is impossible to suppose that this was anything but a misprint. No one could have suspected that 受二十九年 is correct.)

Another problem makes this matter interesting. The *Shiji*, "Zhou Benji," says that after having confined Wen Wang for seven years the Shang king released him and *at the same time* granted him authority to take military action without first asking the king's permission. This is impossible to believe, though some scholars have succeeded in believing it. The cause of Sima Qian's confusion must be that the *Annals* chronology still was known, at least in part, and it dates Wen's release to Di Xin 29 (i.e., 1074 minus 12 = 1062, probably the year of release), but Di Xin 29 actually was 1058, the Mandate year; and this too probably still was known.

183-204: This long subtext (the longest) proves that these subtexts were not inserted by Shen Yue, but were copied by Shen into his *Song shu*. In the *Song shu* text, when Hou Ji's mother tries to abandon him in the forest, and can't, because "she encountered wood-cutters" 會伐林者, Shen reads the words as "but it happened that wood-cutters …," apparently thinking that words completing the sentence had been lost in some earlier copying; so he has added the words 荐覆之 "covered him with a grass mat." This has been accepted by Zhao Shaozu (1796), and later by Wang Guowei. But there is nothing corresponding to this in *Shi* Ode 245, which obviously was the subtext author's source; and the idea is senseless anyway, because had the wood-cutters done this rather than rescuing the baby (or by their presence causing its mother to give up her plan to abandon her child) they would have become responsible for its death, instead of causing its survival, which is the point of the story in Ode 245.

197: "Six *xun* after the first month of spring, the five planets came together in Fang" (*Meng chun liu xun wu wei ju Fang* 孟春六旬五緯聚房). This is astronomically impossible. The location of the conjunction of late May 1059 was approximately Yu Gui (Cancer), not Fang (in Scorpio). (The time of year determines the zodiac location of the sun, and a five-planet conjunction must be near enough to the sun to include the inner planets.) For the reason why the original location was changed to Fang (by the Warring States Wei court astrologers), see Chapter Nine, 3.1. The time stated here, however, is approximately right. So an accurate original was modified as little as needed to serve Wei political propaganda.

204-206: "12th year" as conquest date results from moving the conjunction back 12 years; and a "12th year" chronology develops around it, but the relative pacing of events in the BA seems to be accurate (re-dating BA years 12-13-14 to 10-11-12, as in my comment on strips 175-176): conquest year 4th month, victory rites back in Zhou; then appointment of the king's brothers as overseers of Yin, Guanshu 管叔 in the east in Guan (ancestral Shang homeland), Caishu 蔡叔 and Huoshu 霍叔 in the Yin capital area (see *Yi Zhou shu* #48 "Zuo Luo"); then back in the east a royal hunt in Guan demonstrating his triumph. By year's end he is back in Zhou, for formal receptions and formal victory dedications the next year ("13th year" = 11th year). This is followed by formally accepting Shang vassals as Zhou vassals, requiring Wu Wang's presence again in the east, specifically in Guan (*Yi Zhou shu* #38 "Da Kuang," "13th year"), where "Guanshu *ex officio* functioned as Yin Overseer" 管叔自作殷之監. Then after returning home for the last time "a year later, in the 12th month, he died in Hao" ("Zuo Luo" and strip 208, "14th year" = 12th year, as in *Yi Zhou shu* #45 "Wu Jing").

207: This strip, in italics, is the text that Shaughnessy argues was taken from the Cheng chronicle and inserted into the Wu chronicle, lengthening Wu Wang's life by three years. In the Cheng chronicle it would have to be a strip preceding 224 and following 223. Notice that it doesn't quite fit in the Wu chronicle, because there ought to be a blank space between 作金縢 and 十五年.

218 and 225: Italics here call attention to sentences concerning the death of Zhou Gong.

219-223: This subtext praising Zhou Gong needs to be immediately after 夏六月魯大禘于周公廟, recording the last rites for Zhou Gong, which ought to be ending at the end of its line. To make it end the line, one must put the recording of Zhou Gong's death and burial back into years 11-12. (Therefore we can conclude that Zhou Gong died in Cheng 11, which I argue must be 1027.) This will in turn make Shaughnessy's transposed strip text be no longer in strip position. (See the analysis in the preceding chapter.)

222: For the justification for my rewriting the received 迄于秦漢 ("down to Qin and Han") as 以迄于今 ("down to the present"), see Chapter Seven, p. 120. (Others would take the words *Qin Han* as requiring dismissing this entire subtext as fake. A minimum correction is preferable, if a reasonable explanation can be found. We are no longer able to insist that every line in the text must be above suspicion or be crossed out. The transposed strip text as discovered by Shaughnessy has shifted the burden of proof.)

231-232: Kang 19 to end of Kang: in an earlier correct text the Kang chronicle ended at the mid-column break, because Bo Qin's death was actually in Kang 16. Restoring the correct date requires simply deleting 'space *shi jiu nian'* before 'Qin Fu.' The Zhao Wang chronicle then begins at the mid-column break, and was probably in formal mode.

242: This one-line subtext, of main text length, seems designed to fit exactly into this location. This helps confirm the rules of composition I infer and use from the end of the Kang Wang chronicle, in turn derived from examining the text of late Shang events from the second half of strip 160 through the first half of strip 167. (Where the subtexts begin and end allows me to be sure of the word-count of the intervening main text. Note again, that I have moved the subtext for Wen Ding to the end of his chronicle, because if placed where it is in the *Jinben* it would break a strip text.)

261b and following: I am unsure of my reconstruction from here (Xuan Wang) on. The reign titles for Xuan Wang and You Wang may not be in formal mode. Changing this would leave space for more Chinese text. The *Hou Han shu* paraphrases material loosely ascribed to the *Zhushu jinian* for the Xuan Wang reign, some of which is not in the present text. But the text at strip 283, at least, must be one whole strip, and the whole of Western Zhou before 283 is probably 100 strips.

250-1, "*Shi nian Li Wang sheng*": Here I use part of a small-*zi* double-column in-text note. The date is 864, making Li Wang 37 *sui* at death in 828, as Lei Xueqi points out.

275 and 277: 晉殤叔元年……晉文侯元年, in italics as embedded subtext, and note-worthy because Fan and other modern editions have these first-year dates, supplied with *sui*-names, in small-character double-column in-text note format, otherwise normally rejected by me as not part of the tomb text. But they must be in the tomb text, because Du Yu says that Jin dating started with Shangshu, whereas the *Taiping yulan* has "8th year" for Bao Si's son Bo Fu being made heir-apparent, and "10th year" for peaches and almonds fruiting in the 9th month, in both cases like the main text, using the Zhou You Wang year dates (Fang and Wang pp. 62-63). Some have argued that Du Yu is simply wrong here. But it seems possible that he meant to say that Jin exact dating is first *indicated* with Shangshu's first year, given as we give it, while explicit Zhou dating year by year continues through You Wang. One doesn't charge one's source with error if another assumption is at least as possible.

277: Note the word *hui* 惠 before 王子多父, always assumed to be a garble for some king's name. In fact the word as used here is not a name but a verb, with a long-lost meaning "to help" (see Nivison 1996-97 pp. 318-324). Most *Jinben* texts omit *hui* altogether, but the *Yongle Dadian* text of *Shui jing zhu* (quoting the *Jinian*) has it, as do some other texts of *Shui jing zhu* (in quotations); see Fang and Wang pp. 70-71. Word count in my strip text analysis appears to require it. The word 王子 means "prince," and does not need to be preceded by a king's name.

283, Western Zhou summary: The text is obtained by using the summary in *Jinben* and crossing out phrases containing *sui*-names, which could not have been in the strip text composed in Warring States Wei. The meaning is unchanged, unless one quotes only part of it, leaving out a relevant year total, thus: 武王滅殷二十四年定鼎洛邑至幽王二百五十七年, but omitting 共二百八十一年. A possible punctuation of this is 武王滅殷, comma, 二十四年定鼎洛邑 period. 至幽王二百五十七年. And this is ambiguous. If you mentally bracket the words 二十四年定鼎洛邑 (taking "24 years" as part of the "257 years") you have what Pei Yin gives us in his *Shiji jijie*. Hence the widely accepted conquest date 1027, supposedly proved by the authentic "*Guben*" *Zhushu jinian*. Careful analysis of *Jinben* and *Guben* shows that "1027" as conquest date is the result of Pei's confusion, and shows also that he never saw a complete copy of any text, even of the *Jinben*. When he talks about the *Zhushu jinian*, he is probably always quoting or paraphrasing someone else (usually the Western Jin historian Xu Guang, and almost always he says so).

NOTE: It is possible that the *Zhushu jinian* strip bundles (*pian* 篇) were not in 60's but in 30's. If so, then I have here worked out the first 10 of the 13 reported in the *Jin shu* biography of Shu Xi. So could three more 30's have included all of the remaining text to 299 BCE? The fifth 60 above begins at 945, and ends at 679, this being 267 years. If this is two 30's, one 30 is covering (in this case) 133.5 years Three times 133.5 counted from 679 is 679 minus 400.5, = 278.5. This is close enough to 299 (the final date in the *Bamboo Annals*) to justify the conjecture that a *pian* (bundle of strips) did in this case consist of 30 strips. But I suspect that the last part of the *Zhushu jinian* was originally more detailed, so that 30 strips would have covered significantly fewer years. The later bibliographies in the two *Tang shu* describe it as in 14 *juan*. So "14 *pian*" is more likely to have been its original structure.

If my recovery of strip text is correct, it would seem that the most significant difference between the *Jinben* and the *Guben* is that the latter incorporated corrections in the last three or four *pian*, made by the second team of editors/restorers starting in or after 290 CE, including Shu Xi. That group of scholars would have seen this as their primary task, this being where the *Jinben* text is most obviously defective, and obviously the result of work that had been interrupted and had been left unfinished.

And unlike the *Jinben* editors, who were ignoring strip form, the *Guben* group was trying to recover the strip text. (We can know this because the *Jin shu* biography of Shu Xi says that the text they recovered was in 13 *pian*.) If my five sets of 60 are divided into ten *pian*-bundles of 30 *jian* each, however, one finds that each of three of the divisions must be in the middle of a sentence.

One might assume that this is due to inexact copying by the *Jinben* group. At least as likely, the tomb text is what I have proposed above: *pian* of 60 strips each. Shu Xi's group for their own reasons could have decided to turn this into *pian* of 30 strips. Either way, reconstructing a hypothetical 30 strip *pian* text is not difficult. The 3rd 60 becomes *pian* 5 and 6, 5 ending with 居 and 6 beginning with 殷. Solution: in line 147, delete 之 in 祖乙之世, making 殷 end line 151. In line 154, insert 于 before 太廟. The 4th 60 becomes *pian* 7 and 8, 7 ending with 遂營 and 8 beginning with 成周. Solution: delete 祿父 in line 211 (Wu Geng has already been identified in line 205); insert 成王 before 六年 in line213. The 5th 60 becomes *pian* 9 and 10, 9 ending in the middle of a date. Solution: insert personal names of Qi Cheng Gong in line 271, and of Yan Xi Gong in line 272, this makes 三十九年 begin *pian* 10; 王師 after this date is unnecessary and can be deleted.

284-303: New rules apply here and henceforth, and the received *Jinben* text had to be rewritten by me accordingly. In strip 284a the subtext 自東遷以後始紀晉事王即位皆不書 means that the Jin calendar is used and the Zhou calendar is discontinued, starting with Ping Wang. Accordingly, I assume that Zhou kings are to be treated like non-Jin regional lords, often not even named until they die (thus my 平王陟, line 295, rather than simply 王陟). If I am right about this, I have an unexpected solution for an ancient problem about the last Zhou king in the BA, Yin Wang 隱王. This king's name in history is Nan Wang 赧王, and a small-character double-column note after "Yin Wang," perhaps put there by the Western Jin scholars, suggests the explanation that 赧 and 隱 are close together in sound. It is unnecessary to evaluate the phonology. The words 隱王 are not a name but a definite description, "the *yin* king," i.e., "the king one does not mention by name" (隱 as in 隱名 or 隱諱).— in other words, the current Zhou king. The Wei state compilers probably did not even know his name-to-be, would have been expected not to use it had they known it, and could not have used it without violating their rule of not naming an Eastern Zhou king until they recorded his death.

284: I assume also that Eastern Zhou kings' personal names were never given in the tomb text. (If so this is further evidence that post 771 kings were unnamed in the text until they died. "Ping Wang, personal name Yijiu, died" would be weird.). The *Jinben* editors have supplied personal names in in-text notes only for the first five (of twenty-two), through Hui Wang. In line 284 the words 始紀晉事 "[We] first record affairs of Jin" means "we begin using the Jin calendar," and not that only Jin actions are recorded. Everything that happened in China was of some concern to Jin; but it is certainly true that some of the material in the post-771 part of the *Jinben* was not in the tomb text. (I am assuming that this problem does not arise until after strip 303.) I make the date 十一年 explicit by supplying the words 晉文侯 before this date in line 284.

This part of the *jinian* text is especially confusing because it must keep track of the reigns of the two rival ruling lines in Jin. I have taken the line descended from Wen Hou Chou, with capital at Yi, as primary, down to 679 when the Zhou king formally recognized Wu Gong of the Quwo line. I indicate this by putting these year numbers with underline. (Not italics: the Quwo first-year dates are entered as subtext and are therefore in italics.) The next date after strip 303 (not shown) has Wu Gong continuing the calendar of his eliminated rival Jin *hou* Min. The year would have been Wu Gong's 38th and *hou* Min's 28th; so it is called the "28th year" anyway. (In the "Shi'er Zhu Hou Nianbiao" Wu Gong dies in "the 29th year." This was standard practice when one ruler displaced another.)

294-295: Another difficulty in this post-Western Zhou material: In strips 294-295, after the date "2nd year" (of E Hou of Jin, = 722), we read, "First year of Yin Gong of Lu: the *Chunqiu* begins here. Yin Gong of Lu and Zhuang Gong of Zhu made a treaty in Gumie." The first sentence must be subtext, if I include it at all.

Is it likely that this kind of attention would be given to the *Chunqiu* of Lu in the Wei capital ca. 300 BCE? The second is main text, apparently intended as a paraphrase of a line in the *Chunqiu* for the first year of Yin Gong, which says, "3rd month: the Duke and Yifu of Zhulou (or Zhu) made a treaty in Mei (or Mie)." As for Zhuang Gong of Zhulou (or Zhu), he appears under dates 531 (Zhao Gong 11) and 507 (Ding Gong 3, when he was buried). The author of this entry did not know the *Chunqiu* very well, thus we may doubt that he could have been a Jin court scholar; so perhaps the preceding subtext matching the date with the first year of the *Chunqiu* is indeed authentic. (We can perhaps see the paraphrase of the *Chunqiu* entry at Yin Gong 1 as a clumsy attempt by the Wei editors to tie the royal Wei chronicle to the prestige of the Lu chronicle.) I have taken the "*Chunqiu*" subtext from a small-character in-text note, and this makes me uneasy; but the similar and almost immediately preceding in-text note in the received *Jinben* becomes "E Hou Que [of Jin], first year," in my rewriting using Jin dating instead of Zhou dating; and this must be authentic.

296: "Wu Gong" here is not yet Quwo ruler.

297: "Ai Hou first year" stands alone. I assume that the first year has to be named, even if there is no event to record. (For a *wang*, the ritual of chronicle form would provide the event, in the words "*chun zheng yue wang jiwei*."

It is, I suggest, significant that my recovery of strip text ends the last bundle of sixty with an event of basic importance for Jin history. As I review my preceding work, I am reassured that I have it essentially right, because bundles of sixty have historically important final events. Similar reassurance seems to me warranted here, even granted that my work on the last twenty strips has had to be rather creative.

Although the translation for the most part merely adapts Legge, and these comments at the end are mostly comments on structure, not on translation, nonetheless at one notable point I have departed from Legge and follow Biot, in a matter where translation is crucial. On pp. 152-153, in strip *205, for the words "*sui fen tian zhi ming*,..." 遂分天之明 I choose the meaning "Then he divided Heaven's bright [mandate] ..." (Biot: "*Immediatement on partagea le mandate du ciel (la souveraintê) entre le vainqueur et le vaincu.*") Legge here is clumsy and un-startling: "... and entered into the participation of the bright appointment of Heaven," i.e., simply "received" the mandate. (Some argue that the text is a mistake, *fen* 分 for *shou* 受, appealing to the account in the *Shiji*, which has "*shou tian ming ming*" 受天明命. Others take *fen* 分 "divide" as *ban* 頒 "proclaim.") In brief, I am arguing that Wu Wang did *not* "conquer" Shang, but actually cut a deal with the surviving Shang prince.

My argument: Wu Wang had to begin his campaign in mid-winter, in order to have secured his crossing of the Yellow River when the water was lowest, but he had picked 18 April as the "lucky" day for the battle (*jiazi*, Qing Ming Day, etc.). Although the distance from the River to Muye was not great, the long wait had a military logic: luring the Shang into bringing all its forces together, Wu Wang could hope his victory would be decisive. This strategy failed: Lu Fu (Wu Geng) was probably commanding Shang armies in the east. If he had been at Muye, he probably would not have survived the Zhou victory. So Wu Wang "magnanimously" announced that he was allowing Lu Fu to continue the Shang sacrifices as titular king of Shang. But this was simply "cover" for doing what he couldn't avoid: sharing divine legitimacy with the Shang heir.

Chapter Nine

The Bamboo Annals: the Evolution of Its Chronology

(D. S. Nivison 9 August 2006)

To clarify my thinking, I have put together a systematic statement of how I think *Bamboo Annals* chronology evolved during Warring States, including my work in 2006. I had already worked out the exact strip texts for Xia (60 strips), Shang (60 strips) and Western Zhou (100 strips), getting all this from the *Jinben Zhushu jinian.* Earlier reigns (Huang Di through Shun 14) appear to have 60 strips but here the *Jinben* has some serious defects, and for the last two centuries of Jin and Wei to the close in 299 it is very bad. But for the Three Dynasties it is almost perfect.

There were never two distinct original texts of the *Annals*. There was one text, and the first group of Jin court scholars including He Qiao and Xun Xu did a good job with part of it. Their work was cleaned up by the second group including Shu Xi, who removed research aids such as *sui*-names and use of the Eastern Zhou royal calendars, and who went on to try to correct pre-Xia errors and to try to finish what the first group had left undone at the end of the book. They probably filled in information from other tomb materials. In that sense there were two texts (with variants in the course of transmission), but in that sense only.

But there never was a discovered text that gave a different account of the Shang-Zhou transition, as some have supposed in trying to defend their dates for the conquest. The Shu Xi brief biography in the *Jin shu* is sometimes alleged as primary evidence: after all, Shu Xi "was there." But Shu Xi did not write it; he lived and worked three centuries before the *Jin shu* was compiled. Actually the biography is merely a piece of Tang Dynasty hack work, and is such a mess that one cannot trust it for fine points (it confuses Li Wang and You Wang), though one must try to account for what it says. There were, indeed, successive different accounts in earlier stages of the chronicle text in pre-burial Warring States. The following analysis tries to show what those stages were, and how one stage morphed into the next.

1. The 1040 stage (probably correct),[5] selectively:
Yao's reign: 2026-1969 = 58 years (year 58 being the year Yao's son was exiled). Yao dies, 1960.
Xia: 1953-1555 = 399 years (per D. W. Pankenier) ; 1953 = Shun 14 (1959-8, calendar suspended)
Shang: *de jure* 1554-1059 = 496 years (to the Zhou heralding conjunction: DWP)
1058 was the Zhou "Mandate" year, = Wen Wang 42 in his accession calendar (from 1099)
Wu Yi (27th Shang king): 1145/1143-1109 = 2+35 years
Wenwu Ding (28th king): 1118-1109, 1108-1106 = 10+3 years
Di Yi (29th Shang king): 1105-1087, 19 years
Di Xin (30th Shang king): first calendar 1086 (1058 = year 29 = *de jure* first year of Zhou)
Di Xin second calendar 1068 (1040 = year 29 = *de facto* first year of Zhou)
Wen Wang (Chang) of Zhou: 1101/1099-1050 = 2+50 years
1056: new Zhou calendar, probably nominally Wu Wang as king-to-be
The Zhou conquest: 1040 = Wu Wang's 10th (or 17th) year
Wu Wang as lord of Zhou: 1049/1047-1038 = 2+10 = 12 years (*Yi Zhou shu* 45 "Wu Jing")
Wu Wang as king: 1040-1038 = 3 years (*Yi Zhou shu* 29 "Bao Dian")
The Zhou Gong Regency: 1037-1031 = 7 years
Cheng Wang: 1037/1035-1006 = 2+30 years (born 1050 or 1049)
Mu Wang: 956/954-918 = 2+37 years

1.1 The complex calendar situation in the last eight decades of Shang is revealed by a close examination of inscriptions and literary texts. For details see Appendix 4. A key document is *Yi Zhou shu* 21 "Feng Bao": Xi Bo Fa (Wu Wang) is hosting lords of friendly states, cultivating anti-Shang support a few years before the conquest. The propagandist content of this chapter is similar to *Shang shu* 20 "Wei Zi" and

[1] See note at end.

Shang shu 22 "Mu Shi" (both are *jinwen* chapters set in pre-conquest situations). Therefore the event is not a purely Zhou event, so the current Shang calendar is used – the year is "23rd year" – and the day "*gengzi* (37) *shuo*" identifies the day as the first of the *jian zi* 5th month of 1046, which is year 23 in the Shang calendar beginning in 1068. Year 29 (1040) was to be (or perhaps already had been) picked as the year for the conquest campaign; year 29 in the earlier 1086 Di Xin calendar was 1058, the year after the conjunction of 1059, and therefore claimed as the *de jure* first year of Zhou. (For internal use Zhou would use calendars counting from the first years of its own rulers; but for inter-state relations before the conquest one can assume that it used the Shang calendar.)

2. The 1045 stage: Ca. 475-450, someone tried out the new *zhang-bu* system on Zhou conquest dates, assuming 1040 as date of the conquest, campaign events dated in the *jian-yin* calendar. The slight error in the *zhang-bu* system gave him *jiazi* = 1st of the *jian-yin* 3rd month, contrary to the expected late "2nd month." So he reinterpreted dates as in the *jian-zi* calendar, moving all dates back two lunar months (29 + 30 days). This put the battle in the last day of the (*jian-zi*) 2nd month, and the beginning of the campaign in late autumn of 1041. Counting back by 12's, he determined that 1041 was a Chun Huo year (Jupiter in Station 7). This gives the astrological account in *Guoyu* "Zhou Yu" 3.7 (which has the campaign beginning near the end of the *jian-zi* 11th month = *jian-yin* 9th month).

2.1 There is another way to resolve the *jiazi* problem. Begin the campaign in the *jian-yin* 11th = *jian-zi* 1st month, finishing in the next month = *jian-zi* 2nd month, as before. This is the chronology of the "Wu Cheng."

2.1.1 But in what year? Count back from the observed position of Jupiter ca. 545. Since Jupiter's cycle is actually about 11.86 years, a 545-based count will show Jupiter to have been in Chun Huo in 1040, rather than in 1041. If Jupiter was in Chun Huo in 1040, it was due north in 1046, and still in the northern quadrant in 1045 (as in the Yang Liang commentary to *Xunzi* "Ru Xiao," which actually validates 1040, when Jupiter really was in astrological due north, = Xuan Xiao, centered in Xu). Assuming 1045 Xia 11th month as the beginning of the conquest campaign will give *ganzhi* day dates close to the dates in 1041 Xia 9th month (since *ganzhi* day dates in lunar months are similar at five-year intervals and two month intervals).

2.2 Besides being "scientific," 1045 had three advantages:

(a) In the popular mind, Wu Wang had conquered in year 17 (Mandate calendar) and died in year 12 (his own calendar), a seeming contradiction. Switch the dates, by moving conquest and death back 5 years and then moving the death down three. There seem to be vestiges of this having been done by some 1045 partisans, e.g., the death of Bo Qin in Kang 19 instead of the correct Kang 16. (This idea had led me in 1999 to suggest that Shaughnessy's transposed strip was transposed in the late 400's; I now see that this is impossible, because no strip was ever transposed, but only text. Nevertheless, it is possible that this text transposition was done very early.)

(b) In the mind of the Warring States numerologist-"historian," 1045 puts the conquest exactly 100 years after 1145, the succession year of Shang king Wu Yi, and the date when he recognized Dan Fu as the first "Zhou Gong."

(c) The only way to get the conquest in 1045 while keeping Cheng Wang's 30-year calendar beginning at 1035 (and keeping later Zhou dates the same) is to replace the mourning-completion years 1037-1036 by the seven years of the Zhou Gong Regency, making it 1042-1036 instead of 1037-1031, and making 1035-1006 Cheng Wang's *cheng-ren* calendar rather than his post-mourning calendar. This gives greater stature to Zhou Gong, gratifying his admirers in Lu.

2.3. The 1045 system ultimately involved putting Yao 1 back 119 years from 2026 to 2145 (which was 1000 years before the granting by Wu Yi of court recognition to Dan Fu of Zhou). How this was done is an important part of the 1045 scheme, and helps to date its final form. The reign of Yao was important to Zhou-oriented chronology because tradition held that Hou Ji, the Zhou founding ancestor, was Yao's Minister of Agriculture.

(a) The first move was elimination of overlaps. Di Xin's last *de facto* year was his 46th, 1041, impossible if the conquest was 1045. So the *de facto* last Di Xin year replaced the *de jure* last year, back 16 years to the year before Mandate ("Wu Wang") calendar 1, i.e., 1057; thus his first year became 1102 rather than 1086. Other overlaps: Zu Geng's 11 years within Zu Jia's 33; Yang Jia's 4 years within Pan Geng's 28; Zhong Ren's 4 years within Tai Jia's 12. Total 16 + 11 + 4 + 4 = 35, making 1589 Shang 1 (later 1558: v. p. 52).

But there was first the problem of the Di Yi reign, 9 years in the *Annals*, but apparently 19 in fact. I have argued primarily on the basis of oracle inscriptions (a) that Wu Yi gave his heir Wenwu Ding his own calendar in 1118, but died in 1109; and (b) that in this case undoing the overlap was achieved not by back-shifting but by cutting Di Yi from 19 years (1105-1087) to 9 (1095-1087) -- because (with no back-shifting yet) Wu Yi 1 had to be 1145. The nine years then (with Di Xin's reign) was backed 16 to 1111-1103. The Wenwu Ding 13 years had become 1108-1096 instead of 1118-1109, 1108-1106 (Nivison 1999 *SPP* 93 Appendix 2, represented here by Appendix 4; see also the table in section 8 below). So Wenwu Ding was backed 16 to 1124-1112. And the 4-year reign of Feng Xin (= Lin Xin), who predeceased his father Zu Jia, is given his own time in the *Annals*; the 4 years are balanced by dropping 2-year mourning-completions at the beginnings of the Kang Ding and Wu Yi reigns.

(b) Next, in Xia, the post-Xiang mourning interregnum of 2 years was replaced by an invented story of an interregnum of 40 years dominated by Han Zhuo, witnessing the birth and early career of sixth-king Shao Kang. Total added by this invention, 38 years.

(c) Next, Yao's reign of 58 years ending with the exile of his son became 100 years (fitting for a class-A sage king), a total increase of 42 years. 35 + 38 + 42 = 115.

(d) Mourning-completions for Yao, Shun and Yu became 3 years instead of 2, and for Qi of Xia 4 instead of 2. Other Xia mourning-completion interregnums total 1 less than the actual total. (All of this made the *de jure* Xia 1 be 1989, exactly 400 years before 1589.) This brings the total to 119 years (115 + 3 + 2 – 1).

Confirmation: From Huang Di 1 to but not including Zhuan Xu 13 is 100 + 7 (Zuo Che) + 12 = 119. (The "Zhuan Xu calendar" of Zhuan Xu 13th year preserved the date 2287 of the original first year for Huang Di, when Huang Di 1 was moved back 119 years. Later, when mourning periods are dropped, this justification for "13th year" disappears.)

2.3.1 These changes also involved moving the Zhong Kang solar eclipse on the 1st of the *jian-yin* 9th month back from 1876 to 1948, requiring calculations for one 20-*bu* cycle of 1520 years later, based on observations of the sun's positions on the 1st of the *jian-yin* 9th months in years 432-428. Therefore the final 1045 chronology was worked out shortly after that time. (For details, see Nivison and Pang, *EC* 15; and Nivison 1999 and 2002, at 6.2.)

2.4 The 1045 system preserved mourning-completions, necessarily, since 1056 remained Mandate 1 (post-mourning: after the two years allowed for subjects to complete any mourning obligations before acknowledging a new lord). Centennial echoes of 1056 include 956, the succession year of Mu Wang. 656 was the year when Duke Huan of Qi as first of the Five Lords led an alliance to confront Chu, securing Chu's nominal submission to Zhou. 256 was the year when the last Zhou king Nan Wang chose to defy Qin, bringing about Zhou's destruction.

2.4.1 At some time in the 4th century in most chronological thinking mourning-completions were dropped. The total of mourning-completions for Shang after Tai Wu and through Wu Ding had been 31 years. (They were either 2 or 3 years in Shang – 3 would include the predecessor's death year as part of the reign of the successor -- for ritual reasons: a king's *gan* determined his sacrifice day, which could not be later in the same ten-day week than the day of his heir and a king could not have the same *gan* as his predecessor) Since 2145 remained fixed, a gap of 31 years opened up before Shang as a whole. It was filled by the invented reign of the supposed last Xia king Jie = Di Gui, 31 years in the *Jinben.*

2.4.2 Within Shang, the first year of Tai Wu, 5th generation king, was fixed at 1475, which was 100 years after Tang of Shang's kingship declaration in 1575 (the year after the sidereal marvels of 1576). So a gap of 12 years opened before Tai Wu, for four mourning-completions of 3 years each. To fill this gap Tai Wu's successor Yong Ji's post-mourning reign of 12 years was put before Tai Wu and Tai Wu's reign was extended through what had been Yong Ji's tenure, giving Tai Wu 75 years, as in all standard chronologies.

2.4.3 The conjunction marking the beginning of Xia (as discovered by Pankenier) occurred in February of 1953, which was the 14th year of Shun, according to Pankenier, when Shun transferred *de facto* authority to Yu. The extension of chronology backward (to get Yao 1 to be 2145) involved moving this date back one *bu* of 76 years, to 2029, as in the *Jinben*. Pankenier noticed that the date of the conjunction must be Shun 14, because he noticed an echo of the political event of transfer of authority to Yu in the chronicle for Yao: in 2060 = Yao 86, which was the 14th year after Yao abdicated and Shun assumed *de facto* power. At that point Yu is given audience and the use of the Dark Scepter (*Xuan Gui*) symbolizing authority (emblemed in the sky, Pankenier argues, by the configuration of the conjunction of the five visible planets). This was exactly 31 years before the presumably actual event of 2029, re-dated from 1953. The 31 years (the length of the inserted reign of Di Gui) begs for an explanation. The question is open, but I will hazard one, hoping that someone else can do better:

2.4.3.1 I posit two separate changes on 1953, later reconciled:
(1) 1953 becomes 1954, so that Xia is exactly 400 years. Next, undoing of overlaps puts these dates back 31 + 4 years, to 1989 (400 years before 1589). Next, 31 years of mourning completion after Tai Wu are canceled, opening up a 31-year late Xia gap, and Di Gui is invented. (As Pankenier noticed, 1989 to 1953 is 36 years, = 1 + 31 + 4.)
(2) Independently of the above, to get Yao 1 back 119 years from 2026 to 2145, the original Xia 1 (= Yu 1) date 1953 is put back one *bu* (76 years) to 2029, leading to inventing the distinction between *de facto* Yu 1 (2029) and *de jure* Yu 1 (1989, taken from the first set of changes). Then, also from the first set, Di Gui is accepted, pushing 2029 back to 2060, still Shun 14.
(3) Finally, a reconciliation restores 2029 as Shun 14, but invents the story of Yu being given audience in Yao 86 = 2060, thus leaving in place a shadow event that is still Shun 14 in a different sense.

3. The 1050 stage: For propaganda-chronologists in Wei in the late 4th century, received information consisted of the original 1040 chronology, probably still surviving (at least in Song; which surprisingly still knew that the succession year of its founding ancestor Shang Jia Wei was 1718; hence Song picked 1718 minus 2x700 = 318 to declare kingship), and the (modified) 1045 chronology. The Wei experts built into the latter their own system, changing as little as possible.

3.1 Their system they generated by taking 1035 – which was 700 years before 335, when the lord of Wei declared himself king -- as the fief-year of Tangshu Yu, first lord of Wei's parent state Jin. (335 was picked for the declaration so that the first royal calendar year could be 334, an exact century after Wei Si's first year as Wei Wen Hou.) The beginning of Jin had to be a year when Jupiter was in Station 10 (of 12), Da Huo (as in *Guoyu* "Jin Yu" 4). Therefore the Conjunction year 1059 had to be a Station 10 year, it being just 2 x 12 years earlier. The year had been Di Xin 28 *qua* Station 6 year. So Di Xin 28 became the new Station 6 year 1063, four years earlier than 1059, and Di Xin 1 accordingly shifted four years back.

3.2 But the year after the Conjunction had been the Mandate year, and Wen Wang had died in Mandate 9 = 1050. This was impossible for the Wei experts, because (per *Guoyu* "Zhou Yu" 3.7) the conquest year had to be a Chun Huo = Station 7 year, which now had to be 1050. The solution was to move the Conjunction year (and all late pre-conquest Zhou dates) back one Jupiter cycle of 12 years. Hence the conjunction date became 1071 in the *Jinben*. With this move Di Xin 1 became a total of 4 + 12 = 16 years earlier than the original date 1086 – a welcome conclusion, because it agreed with the familiar 1045 system, though for a different reason.

3.2.1 Also with this change, the conquest, in 1050, became Wu Wang 12, since with the conjunction in 1071 Wen Wang's last 9 years became 1070-1062, and Wu Wang 1 became 1061. This too was a welcome conclusion, because in the 1045 scheme too the conquest had been in "year 12," although in a different sense (1045 had been Mandate year 12 ("Wu Wang" year 12) counting from 1056).

3.3 Next for the Wei experts was the problem of accounting for the years after 1050. The concept of 7 + 30 years for Regency plus Cheng Wang was adopted from the 1045 scheme, but Cheng 1 of 30 was taken as the year that had been Cheng Wang's succession year, 1037 (as in the original 1040 scheme, rather than the accession year 1035, used by the 1045 scheme). Thus Regency 1 became 1044.

3.3.1 Three more years were needed, than were provided if Wu Wang died two years after the conquest, i.e., in what was now called Wu 14. The three years were generated by (a) mutilating the Cheng chronicle, putting Zhou Gong's death and burial in Cheng 21-22 instead of 11-12, jumping over the posthumous *di* rite for Zhou Gong in Cheng 13. This had the desired effect (b) of bringing into apparent strip position 40 *zi* or spaces of text that could be fitted (almost) exactly into penultimate position in the Wu chronicle, naming years 15, 16 and 17. (This was Shaughnessy's discovery in *HJAS* 1986, except that only text was moved, indeed no corresponding strip even existed until the Wei experts created one; and the move was the work of Wei Warring States experts, not of Jin Dynasty scholars as Shaughnessy holds.)

3.3.2 But it also had the unfortunate effect (c) of making the sentence recording the *di* rite be no longer the last words on its strip, thus depriving the five-strip encomium narrative subtext for Zhou Gong of its proper location. (The encomium subtext was left where it was, but the preceding strip now ended with an irrelevant sentence. This led the Jin restorers to move the subtext to an impossible location where it would have had to break a strip – providing the clue that led me to the present analysis.) For all this see comments on strips 216-225 in the original Strip Text of the *Bamboo Annals*.

3.4 Two more details in the Wei solution are visible only indirectly in the *Jinben* reconstruction by the He Qiao / Xun Xu group. The aim of the Wei experts was to validate Huicheng Wang's claim to kingship. The full procedure is illustrated in the *Shiji* "Qin Benji": year one, an act or event anticipating kingship (in Qin, it was the performance of a *la* 臘 rite which was the prerogative of a king); year two, a formal declaration; year three, the *yuan* year, beginning at day 1 with the new royal calendar. The *Jinben* at this point is so incomplete that one must fill it in by inference. (The *Shiji* too is defective: see p. 187 note 5.)

3.4.1 The Wei experts apparently appropriated a story for their event/act year one, invented in 320 by Song propagandists to validate Song *jun* Yan's royal calendar as Song Kang Wang beginning in 318. (*Mengzi* 3B5 has Mengzi in Song in 319, asked whether it would be safe for Song to declare kingship.) The story was that the famed "Cauldrons of Zhou" had been lost in the Si River in Song, near the Song city Pengcheng. The *Shiji* "Feng Shan Shu" says that there was a story of such an event so described, supposed to have occurred "115 years before the conquest of the world by Qin," i.e., in 336, which thus must be Wei's event-year. No record is found for declaration-year two, but one can infer that it must be 335, because 334 is known to be Huicheng's *yuan* year as king.

3.4.2 The Jin restorers, however, reached a different conclusion. They did not find a strip telling them that the equivalent of Zhou Xian Wang 34 (i.e., 335) was, in so many words, the year when the lord of Wei declared himself Wang. (This is not surprising: for this part of the Jin-Wei story, much text is missing or mangled.) They needed it badly, and the need led them to a mistake. What they did have was a piece of text that said that in his 36th year the Wei lord changed the *yuan* year, calling the year "year 1" in a new calendar. The *Annals* has this: 三十四年，魏惠成王三十六年，改元稱一年。 The original was probably simply the last part of this, i.e., 三十六年，改元稱一年。 This they interpreted as being the desired declaration statement: "In his 36th year, [our lord] [*declared himself wang, and*] changed the *yuan*, calling this year [his] 'year one'." They then put this not in 334 where it belonged, but in 335, in their notation [Xian Wang] 34th year (三十四年), because that is where they needed it. As a result, their restoration put Wei Huicheng Wang dates back one year (matching the *Shiji*; so it must be right, they thought). And as another result, they gave Huicheng Wang an apparent extra year of life, making his death be year 17 (not 16) in the new calendar (as in *Shiji suoyin* before "Wei Shijia" Ai Wang 1), i.e., counting to 319 taking 335 (not 334) as year 1.

3.4.2.1 327 was 700 years after 1027, "year 18" in the Wei chronology which had made 1044 be Cheng/ Regency year 1. If 320 was the date of the invention of the Si River story by Song, this was 700 years after the real "year 18" counting from 1037, the real Cheng/Regency year 1. (The prediction in *Zuo zhuan* Xuan 3.5 that the *de* 德 of Zhou, giving the cauldrons their weight, would be exhausted at the end of 700 years and generation 30, points to 320, the year after 30th generation Zhou Xian Wang's death in 321.

3.4.2.2 Against this, the 327 date is year 42 of Zhou Xian Wang; and in the *Shiji* year 42 of Nan Wang has another cauldron story, suggesting that "42nd year" was already attached to the cauldron myth in material available to Sima Qian. This would indicate that the dating of the loss of the cauldrons to 1027, qua "year 18" in a 1044 chronology, was already done before Han.

4. One more puzzle: Western Han texts, the *Shang shu* Preface and also the *Shiji* in several places, date the conquest not to a "12th year" (wrong anyway) but to "the 11th year," apparently of Wu Wang (in the "Lu Shijia" this is explicit). The compound error results from a Western Han date convention of using *jian-yin* month names even if the assumed calendar is not *jian-yin*; e.g., if the civil calendar begins with the solstice month, it is called "the 11th month," rather than "1st month." We see this in the "Zhou Benji" account of the conquest campaign: in the 11th year 12th month day *wuwu* (55) the Zhou army crossed the Yellow River; and in the 2nd month (no mention of year: still the 11th year understood) on *jiazi*, was the victory. The Qi and Lu *shijia* chapters have the date "Wu Wang 11th year." "11 year" confirms my analysis, but "Wu Wang" requires an explanation. Apparently the 1056 calendar was nominally for Prince Fa as king-to-be, continuing after Wen Wang's death in 1050 as Wu Wang's calendar in fact.

4.1 Then there are the claims for year 13 as conquest year, picked up in fictitious chapters of the *Shang shu*. The earliest historian to make this claim was Liu Xin (as quoted in *Han shu* 21B pp. 53-54, Guangxu Wang Xianqian (Taiwan Yi-wen photolith) edition). Liu, obviously correcting the *Shiji*, has Wen Wang dying in Mandate year 9 rather than 7, thus moving dates down 2, so that the *Shiji*'s conquest year 11 must be year 13. (Thus Liu Xin like Sima Tan and Sima Qian is fooled by the Han date convention.) Liu satisfies himself that this must be right, because it makes both the Mandate year and the conquest year (per *Guoyu*) be Chun Huo years. Liu's error has in effect been accepted both by Pankenier and by the Three Dynasties Chronology Project.[2]

5. A complete inventory requires mention of the so-called Yin Li chronology, often referred to by Liu Xin. Its conquest year was 1070, which was 25 years earlier than 1045. Its dates for founding events of Shang (Yin) were likewise 25 years back, not from the final stage 1045 dates but from the true dates, i.e., 1554 back 25 to 1579, etc. I have suspected that the 25 years result from moving the first year of Zhou king Li Wang back from 853, the *Jinben* date, to 878, the date one must suppose if one says (like the *Shiji*) that Li Wang reigned 37 years before his exile in 841. (37 years was actually his life-span.) 853 as Li Wang's succession year appears to result from dropping mourning-completions; the date was accepted by the Wei scheme but is not dependent on it.

6. 1040 would have to be year 10, since we know that Wen Wang died in 1050. I know of no statement anywhere in early sources putting the Zhou conquest in year 10. But I am insisting that year 10 is right. We may not have a single sentence asserting that the conquest was in year 10, but we do have two chapters in the *Yi Zhou shu*, one referring to the other and with dates fitting the same year, 1038. Together these imply that the conquest year was Wu Wang's 10th year as lord of Zhou. *Yi Zhou shu* 45 "Wu Jing" is dated simply "12th year," and has Wu Wang experiencing a dream warning him of impending death. Wu Wang's response is to direct that the "Bao Dian" be given to the heir apparent. The "Bao Dian" is *Yi Zhou shu* 29. It contains appropriate advice; and its date is "the King's 3rd year." Furthermore these two texts are independent. Their language is in different styles, of different periods, obviously by different authors. Nobody was trying to set up an inference, an attempt which might call for suspicion.

7. The focus of the foregoing has been the evolution of the chronology in the book we now call the *Zhushu jinian*. To a large extent this implies evolution of text as well, albeit not always precisely. Changes were made not in a text in the modern sense, in which there might be hundreds or thousands of copies, but in a physical entity, consisting of bundles of bamboo strips. There might, of course, be copies elsewhere, whose owners might or might not wish to revise their copies; but we must think of one original, presumably in Daliang in Wei, which started as a copy of another physical entity, a chronicle probably in Lu. It was the book in Lu that got revised making Yao 1 be (in effect) 2145, etc., and it was this book that first had the long subtexts glorifying Zhou traditions. I think we can assume that the Wei specialists began with a copy of the Lu book, and made changes in it for their own purposes. One would expect them to change only what interested them, leaving virtually all of the Lu-Zhou oriented material as it was, if only to avoid the tedious labor of preparing new strips, as far as possible. At least one long subtext, in the Huang Di chronicle,

---

[2] Both the Project and Pankenier accept this Chun Huo theory, and so both put the Zhou conquest in 1046. This is impossible. *Yi Zhou shu* 21 "Feng Bao" is dated "23rd year, *gengzi* (37) *shuo*," not naming the month but in the likely range of time only 1046 5th month fits. The event is interstate (Zhou is hosting friendly lords), making the Shang calendar of 1068 appropriate (see p. 172). *Shang shu* chapters 19 ("Xi Bo Kan Li"), 20 (Wei Zi"), and 22 ("Mu Shi") are like the "Feng Bao" in giving a Warring States perspective on the late pre-conquest scene.

was written or carefully altered by the Wei group. The date in it, year 50, 7th month, day *gengshen*, was important only for Wei. In the Yao chronicle there is another long subtext containing dates. These seem to be based on 2145 as *ji-shou* 紀首 year, which it is in one version of the Lu *zhang-bu* calendar. This must have been Lu work. (This detail is one more proof of the authenticity of the BA.)

7.1 In the BA the rulers of Xia are all called *di*. But there are residues in the text betraying that at one time they were called *wang*. When? Do we see here the work of the Jin editors, copying the *Shiji*? I do not know. (One could strike out the word *di* and replace with *wang*, getting acceptable sense.)

7.2 Much more interesting is the error in the end-of-Shang summary, "29 kings." This almost certainly has to be a "fix" that didn't quite work, made when either in Lu revising or in Wei revising the Mandate year ceased to be "Shou 29th year" as it was in fact ("Shou" 受 being Di Xin's personal name). (But it is at least imaginable that in the Lu *ur*-text there were only 29 Shang kings; Feng Xin aka Lin Xin might have been omitted. Or, perhaps, Wenwu Ding and Di Yi really were the same, Wenwu Di Yi.) In any case, we have here proof (unwelcome to some scholars) that the end-of-dynasty summaries were already in the buried text, and were not added by post-discovery hands. And, of course, this is yet another proof of authenticity.

8. I add here a table showing the complex effect of three changes on years 1118-1086: (1) reducing Di Yi by ten years, undoing the overlapping of the reigns of Wu Yi and Wenwu Ding, and (2) moving Shang kings back sixteen years, undoing the overlapping of Di Xin and Wu Wang (2.3a above; also 3.1-2); and (3) moving late pre-conquest Zhou dates back 12 (3.2). The reduction of Di Yi from 19 to 9 years must have been done very early, before Di Xin 1 ceased to be dated 1086.

The table assumes that Wu Yi's correct dates are 1145/43-1109, read by early chronologists as 1143-1109, then backed 16 years to 1159-1125, as in the BA; and that Zhou Dan Fu's death was in 1127, backed 12 years (with other Zhou dates) to 1139. Thus Ji Li's first year was 1126, backed 12 to 1138. Wen Ding (Wenwu Ding) has two first years, 1118 (calendar given him by his father Wu Yi), and 1108 (his actual succession year). 1108 is then taken as the first year of his 13 years (10 + 3, i.e., 1108-1096), reducing the Di Yi reign from 19 years (1105-1087) to 9 years (1095-1087). The resulting Wen Ding and Di Yi reigns are then backed 16 years: Wen Ding, 1124-1112, and Di Yi, 1111-1103. Ji Li actually died in 1102, i.e., Di Yi 4; but since Zhou dates are backed 12, Ji Li's death date becomes 1114, i.e. Wen Ding 11.

This produces the strange record, of Ji Li in Wen Ding 11 first presenting to the king a victory at court, and the king then killing him. A 34-character subtext gives full details but no explanation: he is first rewarded handsomely, then arrested and imprisoned under such harsh conditions that he dies. It seems unlikely that these two events occurred at the same time. A possible explanation: as in the *Shiji* "Zhou Benji" (where we read that Wen Wang was granted authority to conduct military campaigns at his own discretion – Di Xin 29 in fact = 1058, simultaneously with his being released from seven years captivity in Youli – Di Xin 29 in the BA scheme = 1074, reduced by 12 = 1062), an actual date has gotten confused with a BA date. Wen Ding 11 (BA) = 1114, reduced by 12 = 1102, Ji Li's death date. But Wen Ding 11 counted from true Wen Ding 1 (= 1118) is 1108, Wen Ding's actual succession year, a highly suitable occasion both for Ji Li to dedicate a spectacular victory to his king, and also for the king to respond with lavish gifts, similar to his earlier treatment of Ji Li. (See p. 172, comment on strip 182.)

Explanation of BA date changes, 1118-1086, from year 1 of Wen Ding's first calendar (= Wu Yi 26) through year 19 in Di Yi's original and true calendar, followed by Di Xin 1. (WY = Wu Yi; WD = Wenwu Ding; DY = Di Yi; DX = Di Xin; JL = Ji Li; Chang is Zhou Wen Wang.)

	A	B	C	D	E	F	
1118	WY 26	WD (1) 1	JL 9	WY 26	WD 7	JL 21	1118
1117	27	2	10	27	8	22	1117
1116	28	3	11	28	9	23	1116
1115	29	4	12	29	10	24	1115
1114	30	5	13	30	11	25	1114
1113	31	6	14	31	12	Chang 1	1113
1112	32	7	15	32	13	2	1112
1111	33	8	16	33	DY 1	3	1111
1110	34	9	17	34	2	4	1110
1109	35	10	18	35	3	5	1109
1108		WD (2) 1	19	WD 1	4	6	1108
1107		2	20	2	5	7	1107
1106		3	21	3	6	8	1106
1105		DY 1	22	4	7	9	1105
1104		2	23	5	8	10	1104
1103		3	24	6	9	11	1103
1102		4	25	7	DX 1	12	1102
1101		5	Chang 1	8	2	13	1101
1100		6	2	9	3	14	1100
1099		7	3	10	4	15	1099
1098		8	4	11	5	16	1098
1097		9	5	12	6	17	1097
1096		10	6	13	7	18	1096
1095		11	7	DY 1	8	19	1095
1094		12	8	2	9	20	1094
1093		13 (quake)	9 (quake)	3 (quake)	10	21	1093
1092		14	10	4	11	22	1092
1091		15	11	5	12	23	1091
1090		16	12	6	13	24	1090
1089		17	13	7	14	25	1089
1088		18	14	8	15	26	1088
1087		19	15	9	16	27	1087
1086		DX 1	16	DX 1	17	28	1086

Columns A, B, and C are correct dates. Column D is the result of giving Wenwu Ding his total of 13 years all following Wu Yi's reign, and keeping Di Xin 1 unchanged at 1086, by making Di Yi 11 be Di Yi 1. Column E moves the resulting Shang dates back 16 years. Column F is the result of moving all Zhou dates back 12 years. The BA chronology is the result of combining the changes explained in columns D, E, and F. (So it was Di Yi, not Wenwu Ding, who caused Ji Li's death.) Notice that the Zhou earthquake of 1093 (Chang 9), now in Di Yi 3, was originally in Di Yi 13; the year number '13' is confirmed by the inclusion in Di Yi 3 of military actions taken from Xuan Wang 13, as in the Piji *gui* and other Xuan Wang material. Strip 169 has the following (second half-strip for Di Yi):

三年: 王命南仲西拒昆夷, 城朔方. 夏六月: 周地震.

3rd year: The king commanded Nanzhong to resist the Kun Yi on the west, and to wall the north. Summer, 6th month: There was an earthquake in Zhou.

An earthquake did occur in Zhou in 1093, Chang 9.[3] But Nanzhong was a Xuan Wang era official, and the "walling of the North" was a Xuan Wang era event, datable to Xuan 13 by the Piji *gui*, undated, but dealing with actions in the year following the action in the Guoji Zibo *pan*, dated Xuan 12 (see Appendix 3, inscriptions 48 and 49)[4]. It is hardly conceivable that this editorial mistake could have been made unless at the time it was made the Di Yi chronicle read "13th year: Summer, 6th month: There was an earthquake in Zhou" – "13th year," not "3rd year." (The change to "3rd year" was made when Wu Yi 1 was still 1145.)

The date 1105 for Di Yi 1 shown here, together with Wenwu Ding's having had a calendar of his own during the last ten years of his father Wu Yi's life, is revealed by analysis of late Shang oracle and bronze inscriptions (see Appendix 4, reproducing most of Appendix 2 in Nivison 1999 and 2002).

Another important historical detail is revealed by this analysis. Liu Zhiji had been surprised to learn from the *Zhushu jinian* that Wenwu Ding had caused the death of Ji Li, as in fact the present BA says. Liu's meaning probably was that he had accepted the account of Ji Li's death given in the *Lü shi chunqiu*, i.e., that Ji Li had died because he had worn himself out serving his people. But my analysis seems to show that Wenwu Ding was blameless, and that it is merely BA date shifting that puts Ji Li's death in the Wenwu Ding reign rather than in the Di Yi reign. (The BA account would show that relations between Ji Li and Wenwu Ding were always cordial.) On this matter, consider the words ascribed to Wu Wang (Fa) talking with Zhou Gong (Dan) soon after the Zhou victory in *Yi Zhou shu* #44 "Duo Yi": "Oh, Dan! It has been sixty years since Heaven withheld favor from Yin, since before I, Fa, was born." This conversation must have been in 1040. After Ji Li's death in the Shang "Cold Storehouse" prison in 1102, there probably was never more than a pretense of peace between Zhou and Shang. (Fa was probably born in Di Yi 15 = 1091, dying as Wu Wang in 1038 at 54 *sui*.) Moreover, if we have here a report of an actual conversation, almost certainly Wu Wang would not have thought of his own tenure as the beginning of the legitimacy of Zhou as holder of Heaven's mandate. The "change of Mandate" occurred in the reign of his father; and his father's *de jure* reign began with Wen Wang Chang's accession year 1099, exactly 60 years back.

Note on Section 1: There appears to be a residue of an original correct chronology in the long subtext at the beginning of the Zhou chronicle. Strip 197 says, "Six *xun* after the first month of spring, the five planets came together in Fang 房." Fang is impossible (the conjunction had to be close to the sun, so as to include Mercury; but the sun would not be near Fang until autumn), but "six *xun* after the first month of spring" is almost exact. The *yin* month of 1059 ended with day *yimao* (52), 20 March, in the *xun* (*jia* through *gui*) ending 28 March. Six *xun* plus one day later brings one to 28 May, when the conjunction (actually in Gui 鬼) peaked. The day was *jiazi*, as Pankenier and I noticed in 1981 (he did the math). Most of these long subtexts, however, were not commentaries to the main text chronicle. They were pieces cut from a separate book, then tailored to fit into the chronicle on 17-zi half strips, and then modified further as the chronicle got modified. For example, "Muye" in the subtext just quoted (strip 203) is written 牧野; but in the following chronicle text (strip 204) it is written 坶野.

The Zhou conquest campaign began in the *jian-yin* 11th month = *jian-zi* 1st month, Jupiter at due north, ending at Muye on the next-to-last day, = *jiazi*, of the *jian-yin* 2nd month – all in the same (*jian-zi*) year. The Mandate calendar was 1056-1041 = 16 years (1056 allowed time for subjects to complete outstanding mourning obligations); but dates could also be counted from the Mandate year 1058; the *yuan* year is marked in the BA by change of capital to Feng (1056); this 1056 calendar must have had Wu Wang's name as "junior king."

---

[3] See *Lü shi chunqiu* 6 "Ji Xia" 4 "Zhi Yue," and Nivison 1999 and 2002 section 2.3 with note 3. See also the resume of my argument in note 1 on my comment on strips 168-169 in Chapter Eight.

[4] I am indebted to Prof. E. L. Shaughnessy for calling my attention to the Piji *gui* and to the analysis of Ma Chengyuan on its date. (See Appendix 3, bronze 49 and note.)

A Note on the Legend of the Loss of the Nine Cauldrons in the River Si

(D. S. Nivison, 22 June 2006)

At year Zhou Xian Wang 42, = 327, the *Jinben Zhushu jinian* has the following short entry:九鼎淪泗沒于淵, "The Nine Cauldrons [of Zhou] were lost in the Si [River] and sank in the depths." 700 years earlier, at year 18 of Zhou's second king Cheng Wang, = 1027, the *Jinben* records a public ceremony in Luoyang (Cheng Zhou, the new eastern capital in the middle of the conquered realm), in which these cauldrons were permanently placed there. They were symbols of sovereignty, having been captured from recently conquered Shang, which in turn had captured them from Xia. They had been made by Xia's founder, the great Yu, of metal contributed by the Nine Provinces of archaic China. Or so the legend went.

The *Zuo zhuan*, completed around 310 but containing earlier material of uncertain age, tells (Xuan 3.5) of an (imaginary) incident concerning these cauldrons: A representative of the Zhou king is asked about their size and weight, by the lord of Chu. The response is that the question may not be asked, because the cauldrons embody the "virtue" (de, 德) of Zhou, the basis of Zhou sovereignty, and this has not yet run out. At the time of the original emplacement Cheng Wang had performed a divination getting the response that his dynasty would last 30 generations and 700 years. It is usually assumed that the *Zuo zhuan* story was composed with the loss of the cauldrons in mind; or else the legend was invented with the *Zuo zhuan* story in mind.

It is also usually assumed that when the *Zuo zhuan* contains an account of a divination , that account was composed after the event that the divination predicts. I will argue that this cannot have been something that happened in 327.

There are two other possible applications of the *Zuo zhuan* story.

(1) If Xian Wang was the last king in the 30th generation, terminating the *de jure* tenure of Zhou according to the divination, one could argue that the effective date implied must be the year after his death in 321, i.e., the year 320; and that this must therefore have been the original date given to the story of the loss of the cauldrons. If I am right that the conquest was in 1040 (rather than the *Jinben*'s 1050), and that Cheng Wang's succession year was 1037, in a reign of 2 + 30 years, and if the *Jinben* year number "18th year" for the formal placing of the cauldrons in Luo is nonetheless correct (even though 1027 is a Wei construction, because it depends on counting 18 years from 1044, which is Wei's false date for the first year of Cheng Wang giving him 7 + 30 years), it follows that the originally intended date for the placing of the cauldrons must be 1020, counting 18 from 1037. And of course, the date 700 years later was 320. The story in the *Zuo zhuan* could have been invented in Song, the last major state to declare kingship, in 318.

Possible evidence: the year 1020 would be year 25 in the chronological construction which I ascribe to the experts in chronology in the court of Wei king Xiang Wang (318-296). Their practice was to retain the received dating of major events if they had no reason to change them. In the *Jinben*, Cheng Wang 25 is the date of a great assembly of regional lords in the Zhou capital, just the sort of event most appropriate for the dramatic permanent placing of the cauldrons embodying Zhou legitimacy. All the Wei experts needed to do in changing the date was to delete any mention of the cauldrons in connection with this "25th year" event.

(2) There is another story found near the beginning of the long "Feng Shan Shu" in the *Shiji*. It is a story that the Simas reject; but it invites our examination nonetheless. The story agrees that the cauldrons were lost in the Si River, but says that this happened 115 years before Qin completed its conquest of the rest of China, i.e. 115 years before 221. The date (if by exclusive count, therefore Zhou Xian Wang 33rd year, as in Chen Fengheng 47.21a) would be 336, the year before Wei's declaration of kingship, on my argument.

(One must wonder, why bother about this, 115 years or more later. A possible reason: We may suppose there is, sometime soon after the Qin Conquest, a discussion about the validity, or absurdity, of various portents foretelling the end of Zhou and the beginning of a new world order. The Wei propagandists shortly after 320 had picked up the 320 version of the Si River story, and had claimed that it really happened in 336, justifying the claim made (in 335, I have argued) by the first *wang* in Wei, namely Huicheng Wang, who began his calendar in 334. "How absurd!" someone says. "Look how long it took after that for the Mandate of Heaven to become effective.")

So we can suppose that the Xiang Wang experts finalizing the text of the *Zhushu jinian* ca. 300 plucked the story from 336 and inserted it in 327, honoring the year number "18th year" for the placing of the cauldrons, and fitting their construction of conquest era chronology.

The sequence of events leading to kingship is complete in the record for Qin in the *Shiji* "Qin Benji":

Year 1 in the sequence, something happens as a sign, or is done as a signal, that royalty is imminent; so (326) the Qin ruler has the *la* ceremony performed, appropriate only for a king.

Year 2, there is a declaration at some time during the year (as in Qin Huiwen 13, 325[5]) that henceforth the ruler is to be called *wang*, implying that the next year will begin a new calendar.

Year 3, this year (identified as the year which would have been Huiwen 14, 324) from day 1 is called *yuan nian*, year 1 in a new royal calendar.

I have suggested that the Wei court after the fact made this sequence complete by claiming that the justifying event, in this case the loss of the cauldrons in the Si River, had happened in 336. My chronological arguments (including the present argument) attempt to show that there must have been the required declaration in Wei in year 335. The *Shiji* shows that 334 was a *yuan* year for Wei, though the *Shiji* is mistaken about why this was so; i.e., it supposes that Huicheng Wang had died in 335.

But when did the Si River story come into existence? And who invented it? What evidence there is points to Song, and specifically Yan of Song, succession year 328, *wang* ("Song Kang Wang") as of 318, according to the *Shiji*. We know from the *Mengzi* that Mengzi was in Song on his way to Qi shortly after the death of his royal host "Liang Hui Wang" in 319; and he found (3B5) that the current topic of political argument in Song was whether to "enact royal government" (*xing wang zheng*) and whether the great neighbor states Qi and Chu would attack Song if this were done. So 319 must have been the declaration year for Song. And in the air was the 700 years concept: 318 would be exactly twice 700 years after the succession year of Shang Jia Wei (1718, as dated in the *Jinben*), the Shang and Song founding ancestor.[6] There was no time to spare. In brief, the legend of the loss of the cauldrons must be the "Year One" (invented) event for Song as it moved toward becoming a "kingdom." The intended date was 320.

But why the River Si? This was hundreds of miles from Luoyang, on the way to nowhere, and there was no reason for the Nine *ding* to be transported anywhere. But it was in Song, near the southern boundary between Song and Chu. And there is a more precise location: the "Feng Shan Shu" account has the cauldrons lost "below Pengcheng," a Song city near present Xuzhou on the banks of the Si, at the same time the "Great Hill Altar" (Taiqiu *she*) was lost (nearby, apparently; how, we are not told). This makes sense only if this "altar for the spirits of the land" was the location of a cult maintained in Song for the Zhou kings; if so, there was a double natural destruction, in Song, by land and by water, of sacred objects embodying Zhou authority.

---

[5] The present *Shiji* "Qin Benji" text (and also the "Liu Guo Nianbiao") has the ruler of *Wei* becoming *wang* on day *wuwu* (55) of the 4th month of Qin Huiwen 13. This is a very late text corruption: The *Shiji* "Zhou Benji" at Xian Wang 44, the following (Tang) *Shiji zhengyi* note, the (Northern Song) *Zizhi tongjian* at Zhou Xian Wang 44, and the (Southern Song) *Tong zhi* at Qin Huiwen Jun 13 all have the lord of *Qin* declaring himself *wang* in 325. The *Shiji zhengyi*, furthermore, identifies the *Shiji* "Qin Benji" as its source. And the *Zi Zhi tongjian* and the *Tong zhi* both give the exact month and day. (Perhaps the original text was not "*Wei* 魏 *jun wei wang*" but "*hao*號 *jun wei wang*.")

[6] Exact dates in the Shang remote past were known somewhere in Warring States times, and the obvious place is in Song, whose rulers continued the Shang royal line. Astronomical phenomena (a formation of planets and a meteor shower) recorded in the *Jinben* for 1580 but actually (Pankenier shows) late in 1576 indicate that the *Jinben* date 1575 for the first year of Cheng Tang in his own domain is probably correct. Tang would take the celestial events as signs in his favor, so claiming the next year as his royal Year One. It is even likely that the BA date for the succession year of Shang Jia Wei, 1718, is accurate. It would be 2 x 700 years before the Song ruler began his royal calendar in 318. (And the year 1718 began with a *jia* day, explaining "Shang Jia.")

As for how the *ding* got there, one account (Chen Fengheng loc. cit.) has it that they *fei ru*, "flew into" the waters. The words describe the action of a diver; but flying only a few feet would be marvelous enough for hunks of metal; why blink at hundreds of miles? Objects like the *ding* were numinous. (The *Shiji* says they "shook" of their own accord in 403, when the Zhou king fatally altered the hierarchy of the Zhou order by accepting the division of Jin into Zhao, Han and Wei.)

Furthermore, they are surely entirely mythical. I know of no credible contemporary account at any time, of anyone ever having seen them. The Si River story was perfectly safe: no one would ever effectively contradict it. It was often simply disregarded. The Simas dismiss the story and assume (reasonably) that the Nine Cauldrons were taken to Qin after the surrender of the last Zhou king Nan Wang in 256. Other stories (*Zhan guo ce* and *Shiji*) have them still safe in Luoyang during Nan Wang's reign. And there is an attempt to reconcile these stories, by supposing that the Si River story involved just one of the nine, and that it was only the other eight that Qin appropriated. In 219, the lost cauldron mysteriously made itself visible briefly, and the First Emperor hearing of this (says the "Feng Shan Shu") tried to retrieve it by engaging 1000 divers to hunt for it, in vain. Thus myth engenders more myth.

What interests me most in this little inquiry is the *Jinben* date "18th year" (1027) for the emplacement of the cauldrons. Compare, if you will, the date "10th year" (1035) dating Cheng Wang's giving the fief of Tang to his brother Yu, beginning the state of Jin. Both of the absolute dates in the *Jinben* are wrong. But the date "10th year" is reached by counting back 700 years from 335, important in Wei history as Huicheng Wang's actual royal declaration year, and deducing the consequences. The figure "10" has no other significance. But the year 327 has apparently no importance, being only one of several dates given to the loss of the cauldrons. It is reached by counting forward 700 years from 1027; and given the rest of the Wei experts' chronology the count would not be from 1027 if the year number had not been 18. This shows that "18th year" has independent validity, and so I must use it when I ask, what would the absolute date be if I assume what I know to have been the true date of the conquest (1040), and the implied true succession year (1037) of Cheng Wang. This question pointed me to 320, and thus to the probable importance of Song in the legend of the loss of the cauldrons. It follows logically that if you find my study of this legend persuasive, then I have just given you one more reason to accept 1040 as the date of the Zhou conquest of Shang.[7]

More logic yields the whole picture of the chronological fictions in the *Jinben Zhushu jinian*: If 1035 was the year when Jin began, it was a year when Jupiter was in Da Huo (Station 10), according to the *Guo yu*; therefore 1050 was a Chun Huo (Station 7) year, hence (*Guo yu* again) the year of the conquest. But then, if 1037 was Cheng Wang's first year (as it was), then it must have been merely his first year of *de facto* power, and the seven-year Regency when Cheng was already *de jure* king must have begun in 1044. So 1035 must have been year 10. More: putting the seven-year Regency before Cheng Wang's year 1037 makes Cheng Wang have a 37-year reign beginning in 1044; but if the conquest must be in 1050, three years must be stolen from the Cheng Wang chronicle (as in Chapter Seven); and to avoid having the conquest collide with Wen Wang's death (actually in 1050), the conjunction of 1059 had to be moved back one Jupiter cycle of 12 years to 1071, putting Wen Wang's death in 1062, and creating the date "Wu Wang 12th year" for the conquest. This requires two more things: if the tradition (true) of 100 years from the beginning of Zhou to Mu Wang is to be honored, Mu Wang 1 must become 962, possible only if mourning-completion periods are denied; and for Jupiter to be in station 10 (Da Huo) in 1035, hence also in 1059 and in 1071, four years must be inserted, because these years were actually station 6 years. So together with moving the conjunction back 12 years, this pushes Di Xin's first year, and all Shang dates, back 16 years. The entire chronological fiction we find in the *Annals* is generated by Huicheng Wang choosing 335 to declare himself *wang*. Once one sees this, one can undo the damage step by step and get back to accurate history. Furthermore, it becomes obvious that the *Annals'* chronological fictions are not the mischief of Jin Dynasty court scholars. They are the result of expert Wei state propaganda in the late 4th century BCE.

---

[7] For twelve other reasons, see Ni Dewei (D. S. Nivison), "Wu Wang Ke Shang zhi Riqi," in *Wu Wang ke Shang zhi nian yanjiu*, compiled by Beijing Shifan Daxue Guoxue Yanjiusuo, Beijing: Beijing Shifan Daxue Chubanshe, 1997, 513-532, especially pp.516-523 (and also Chapter One of this book).

Postlude

I am here attempting to communicate appropriately with scholars on both sides of the Pacific Ocean who have studied the problems I address in this book most closely.

These include Shaughnessy and Pankenier on my side of the Pacific, as well as Shao Dongfang; and over yonder, Li Xueqin, who can represent the "Three Dynasties" Project. Shao has an admirable attitude of benevolent skepticism toward my work, an attitude I am trying to cultivate in myself toward him in return. With each of the others my relationship has had difficulties. (In one case this is to say the least an egregious understatement.) Always the difficulties have been intellectually fascinating, and should always have been friendly. When this has not been so, I hold myself to blame. In aiming criticisms with more than necessary vigor I have been driven by the excitement of discovery, not trying to "score," but trying to persuade.

To begin, I must redirect attention to the matter I explore in the second: half of Chapter Seven: the tangle around the date of Zhou Gong's death. I have claimed that the strip Shaughnessy finds to have been given to the Wu Wang chronicle was not an object lifted from the Cheng Wang chronicle but was a text, "invented out of Cheng cloth," so to speak:

The problem is demonstrated again on the next page. But now, I set it up in strip form, to enable me more clearly to point out what it has taught me, and what it can teach you. The central problem is the omitted subtext, strips 219-223: (I have emended in strip 222 "down to Qin and Han" (obviously impossible) to "down to the present.")

219 *After Wu Wang died, when Cheng Wang was young, Dan, Duke of Zhou was regent for seven years, establishing rites and creating [court] music. Spirit birds and phoenixes were seen; the ming bean grew [on the stairs]. So it was that together with Cheng Wang he went to observe the Yellow and Luo [Rivers]. [At the Yellow River] they dropped*

220 *a jade bi-disc in the water. When the rite was finished, the king withdrew and waited. As the sun was setting, a glorious light appeared from everywhere hanging over the river; blue clouds floated in; a blue dragon stood over the altar, holding in its mouth a diagram on a dark colored shell, which it set down and then left. [After a similar] rite*

221 *at the Luo River, there was a similar result. A dark colored turtle and a blue dragon, in an azure brilliance paused at the altar. [The turtle] had on its back a shell on which were carved writings in red markings forming words. The Duke of Zhou, using a writing brush, copied the text in common characters, and when he finished the markings*

222 *[on the turtle] vanished. The turtle then dropped the shell and went away. The words were indications of the rise and fall [of the fortunes of the world] down to the present. Qilin wandered in the [king's] parks, and phoenixes flew about in the [king's] courtyards. The king took a lute and sang:*

223 *"Phoenixes fly about in the Purple Court. What virtue have I, so to move spirit-beings? It's due to the former kings; their kindness is great. It's from their joy that the people feel peace.*

In the BA this has been placed after the record of the cauldron-placing rites in year 18, which in my text ends in mid-strip at 224.27. Having worked out the whole text as far as 679 BCE, recovering the exact form of the text before its discovery in Jin, and finding its total systematic structure, I know that this cannot have been the way the buried text was arranged. The Jin editors have taken similar liberties with the subtexts in the Huang Di and Yao chronicles (breaking these subtexts up and distributing them as if they were ordinary commentary), and also the subtext at the end of the Wen Ding chronicle (moving it to follow what interested them most, i,e,, the death of Ji Li).

In the Cheng Wang chronicle, the Jin editors found the subtext immediately after strip 218, which contains an appropriate sentence, "In summer, 6th month, the Lu state performed a great *di* rite in the *miao* of Zhou Gong." But this sentence does not end the strip. The strip ends with the irrelevant sentence, "In the 14th year, the army of Qi invested Qucheng and conquered it." This seemed to show that the subtext about

Zhou Gong and rituals he performed was out of place. The following shows what was done in Wei, before the *Zhushu jinian* was buried, creating a "virtual strip" which was inserted in the Wu Wang chronicle, and in the process causing the later confusion of the Jin editors about the significance and positioning of the subtext:

The Creation of a "Virtual" Strip

Original Text

216 年春正月王如豐唐叔獻嘉禾王命唐叔歸禾于周文公*周文公薨于豐*王命周平公治東都。十二年

217 *葬周文公于畢*王師燕師城韓王錫韓侯命。十三年王師會齊侯魯侯伐戎*夏六月魯大禘于周公廟*

218 武王沒成王少周公旦攝政七年制禮作樂。。。

222 。。。賴先王兮恩澤臻。于胥樂兮民以寧。

223 。十四年齊師圍曲城克之。*十五年肅慎氏來賓初狩方岳誥于沬邑冬遷九鼎于洛*。*十六年箕子*

224 *來朝秋王師滅蒲姑*。*十七年*冬洛邑告成。十八年春正月王如洛邑定鼎鳳凰見遂有事于河。十

225 九年王巡狩侯甸方岳召康公從歸于宗周遂正百官黜豐侯。二十一年除治象 。二十

Manipulated Text

217 年春正月王如豐唐叔獻嘉禾王命唐叔歸禾于周文公王命周平公治東都。十二年王師燕師城韓

218 王錫韓侯命。十三年王師會齊侯魯侯伐戎*夏六月魯大禘于周公廟*。十四年齊師圍曲城克之。

219 武王沒成王少周公旦攝政七年制禮作樂。。。。

223 。。。賴先王兮恩澤臻。于胥樂兮民以寧。

(unnumbered) *十五年肅慎氏來賓初狩方岳誥于沬邑冬遷九鼎于洛*。*十六年箕子來朝秋王師滅蒲姑*。*十七年*

224 冬洛邑告成。十八年春正月王如洛邑定鼎鳳凰見遂有事于河。十九年王巡狩侯甸方岳召康公

225 從歸于宗周遂正百官黜豐侯。二十一年除治象*周文公薨于豐*。*二十二年葬周文公于畢*。二十

(On strip 225, original and manipulated, see note 6, p. 118.)

The restoration procedure in the Jin court was probably bureaucratized. The strips went first to a committee of transcribers, who produced a copy in current script. Probably it went next to the office that made chronological sense of it by inserting *sui* names for years. (Before this happened, and before Du Yu got to see the text, He Qiao had sequestered the pre-Yao part of it, which must have been in his own office.) Ultimately it got to the main editors whose job was to make sure it all made meaningful sense.

These editors in placing the subtext after year 18 were treating the described rituals as the same ones referred to in the main text involving the placing of the cauldrons. This they could do only if they assumed that Zhou Gong was still alive. So when they saw the text, the manipulation that put the death in year 21 rather than in year 11 had already been done, unless they did it themselves. It could hardly have been done in earlier mechanical stages of processing the discovered material.

It is impossible to believe that they did it themselves. It is just too obvious that the sequence has to have been (1) Zhou Gong's death, (2) his burial, (3) the *di* rite for him. The Jin community of historians must have known this and cared about it, and would have known they couldn't get away with this kind of rewriting of the text. (Perhaps they reasoned that "the Zhou Gong *miao*" in strip 218 was a *miao* for the pre-conquest Zhou rulers who had the title "Zhou Gong.") It is at least imaginable that non-historians in Warring States Daliang, cutting up history for propaganda, didn't care and could get away with it.

Therefore the manipulation must have been done in Daliang, the strip's worth of text thus "liberated" must have been moved in Daliang, and the motive must have been a Warring States Daliang motive. And the move was required if the date of the conquest was to be set at 1050, as it is in the present BA.

For me, this means I was wrong in 2000 to suppose that Shaughnessy's strip move (which I then still accepted) was made in the late 400's as part of a Zhou-oriented revision of chronology. I said this in the monograph republished as Chapter Two, but I have had to rewrite this part of it. I have attached a note admitting as much, because I admire Li Xueqin's model of letting the record of one's own past work stand open for critical examination, as he does, for example, in his *Zhaji*. The manipulation is not likely to have been the work of a Confucian Zhou-Lu-oriented editing of an earlier *jinian* text.

For Li Xueqin and anyone listening to him, the lesson of my "virtual strip" demonstration above is that the BA with achievable fairly simple analysis and reworking gives us a Warring States text, which has for us the earliest available chronology (albeit wrong) of ancient China. Work on chronology cannot ignore it, but must explain it – every single date in it. The Project did not even think of doing this. The Project must, therefore, discard its previous work, all of it, and start over from the beginning.

For Pankenier and Shaughnessy? Both accept Shaughnessy's hypothesis – true -- that a strip's worth of *text* was moved from the Cheng chronicle to the Wu chronicle. Both assume – wrongly -- that this was done by editors in Jin. Both see this as meaning that the chronology of the conquest era was redone at the same time, because giving Wu Wang three more years of life, achieved by inserting this text, is necessary if the conquest is to have the date 1050, its date in the BA. Each sees this as allowing the possibility (and the hope) that the original text as discovered implied the date of the conquest that he favors. They are right about the moving of a piece of text, but they are wrong about when, how and why it was done; and this undermines a large part of their work – just the part that is most important to each of them. Due attention to my "virtual" demonstration on the previous page is going to force each to question his past work.

Not all of that work, however, because Shaughnessy's strip-text discovery and Pankenier's work on conjunctions are invaluable. There is irony here, because my own most important work, since putting the *Jinben Zhushu jinian* back on the table in 1979, has been work exploiting those discoveries by Shaughnessy and Pankenier. Why did they not do this exploiting themselves? Did I grab the ball and run with it, beating them into print?

I did not. Both published in 1986, discoveries they made and that I knew about two years earlier. I did not see the full implications of Pankenier's discoveries until 1988; and before publishing (with Kevin Pang) in 1990 I invited Pankenier to be co-author, thinking it would be unethical not to. He declined, as I foresaw. Accepting would have implied accepting the Nivison-Shaughnessy mourning-completion hypothesis. And accepting that would remove objections to Wang Guowei's analysis of lunar phase terms in *Shang shu* chapters and inscription dates. With Wang reaffirmed, the astrological text in *Guoyu* "Zhou Yu" 3.7 can be shown to be invalid when used for dating the conquest to 1046, as do both Pankenier and the Project.

A part of this persuasion (for both of you) has been the fact that the *Jin shu* biography of Shu Xi says that there were 100 years, not from Wu Wang to Mu Wang (as the BA text says), but from "the receiving of the Mandate" to Mu Wang. That biography is sloppy, with egregious errors; but aside from that, "the receiving of the Mandate" (an expression which does not occur in the BA) is loose in meaning, easily interpretable as referring to the beginning of the reign of the conquering king, exactly as in the BA.

As for Shaughnessy, he was editor of *Early China* at the time the Nivison-Pang article was published. He resisted, and I persisted. (The reasons on both sides were valid, but are of legitimate interest to no one but ourselves.) Happily he got the idea of making the article a "Forum" target. That delighted everybody, including me. We seem now to be close to agreement on many things.

It should be obvious that I could not have written this book, putting together research of three decades, without leaning on the work of others at almost every step. These others include Pankenier, Shaughnessy, and Li Xueqin (whose work is brilliant, even when wrong); and Zhang Peiyu, whose *Xian Qin shi libiao* is always at my elbow. I am grateful.

Note: Both the Zhou-Lu chronology and the Wei chronology (p. 178, 2.2(a)) needed, for different reasons, to have Wu Wang live three years longer than he did. This suggests the following possibility:

The original text was as I give it on p. 190. The text giving the Zhou-Lu chronology simply plucked out the characters that now constitute Strip 207 (the "transposed strip"), leaving everything else in place but combining what is left of what I have called strips 223 and 224 of the original text; there would be an irregular blank space between 'ke zhi' and 'Luo yi'. The Wei editors a century later would have to reconcile this Zhou-Lu text with the original, which I assume still existed. They would assume that what I call the original was a derivative text, and that the present Wu Wang chronicle text (with strip 207) – which they want to show is really the original – requires supposing that there was an intermediate text, i.e., the text I call the "manipulated text," with the material of strip 207 being in the Cheng Wang chronicle, and necessarily in strip position – i.e., they would suppose it had been moved from its strip position in the Wu Wang chronicle, as a strip, to strip position in the Cheng Wang chronicle. They would then see that this assumption has the characters 十四年齊師圍曲城克之 out of place, and that fixing the problem requires moving the texts for Zhou Gong's death and burial to where they are now. So they "correct" the Cheng Wang chronicle accordingly, the result being my "manipulated text." They would rationalize the strange date for the *di* rite at the Zhou Gong *miao* by assuming that this *miao* must have been for all pre-conquest Zhou lords who held the title "Zhou Gong," i.e., Dan Fu and Jili, and perhaps also Chang. (As for what I see as the original text, they would account for this by supposing someone looking at this "intermediate" text thought that the *miao* must be Zhou Gong's alone, and moved the dates of death and burial back to years 11-12, rewriting everything accordingly.)

In fact, the Jin editors too must have supposed the *miao* must be for all earlier "Zhou Gong" lords, thinking that Zhou Gong Dan must have lived to participate in the rites of the "placing of the cauldrons." (This would be why they moved the subtext to its present impossible position.) This account "pardons" everyone, to some extent. But it still requires that the transposition was done *before* the *Zhushu jinian* text was buried, because it still links the weird dating of Zhou Gong's death and burial almost a decade after the di rite with the misplacing of the "transposed strip" text. Death, burial and *di* rite in successive years is the sequence needing no explanation, and the appointment in "year 11" (as in the BA) of "Zhou Ping Gong" as viceroy in the Eastern Capital immediately after Zhou Gong's death is also just what one would expect: Zhou Ping Gong Chen was a younger son of Zhou Wen Gong Dan. He could not have been called "Zhou Ping Gong" until after Dan died. This requires that Zhou Gong's death be in year 11. The Jin scholars might have accepted and (imaginatively) "explained" a received text reading as it does now, but they would not have created such a text by twisting out of shape a received correct original text.

Appendix 1

Sandai Science Survey

(9 Dec '00) -- D. S. Nivison

0. I have in hand a complimentary copy of the "brief text" (*jian ben*, 118 pp; hereafter "*Brief Report*") of the "Research Report" (*Yanjiu Baogao*) of the Xia-Shang-Zhou Dynasties Chronology Project (Xia Shang Zhou Duandai Gongcheng; hereafter "Sandai Project"), subtitled "Report of 1996-2000-Stage Results" (*1996-2000-nian Jieduan Chengguo Baogao*). The publisher is Shijie Tushu Chuban Gongsi 世界圖書出版公司; the publication date is 2000. There is also to be an "Archaeology Report" (*Kaogu Baogao*), and a "Collection of Research Papers" (*Yanjiu Wenji*). The introduction describes the scope of the effort, involving as many as 200 scientists and specialists in sub-fields. It closes by stressing that the results are not the achievement of the final objective of such studies, but do mark "the entry of Three Dynasties chronological studies into a new stage." The editors close (15 October 2000) expressing confidence that on the basis of all the work done future chronological studies will surely be able to achieve conclusions that will be closer and closer to the truth. They express the hope that scholars at home and abroad will offer criticisms and corrections. (See Bibliography at *Xia-Shang-Zhou* ... 2000.)

0.1 This survey omits any pretense to scientific examination of applications of C14, wood ash or human bone dating methods. I am not qualified to discuss them; but I do note with curiosity that I seem to find no such datings (*Brief Report*, pp. 13, 14, 16, 36, 42, 43) that suggest a possibility of Western Zhou dating earlier than 1040 BCE (except for p. 14). Perhaps this is not significant.

0.2 In any case, I will concentrate on astronomical verifications of inscription data and claimed traditional text records that mention or imply astronomical phenomena. These phenomena include lunar eclipses, solar eclipses, conjunctions of the planets, meteor showers, beginnings of lunar months, datings of the winter solstice and related data, positions of Jupiter, and phases of the moon. The last affects the exact dating of over 60 Western Zhou inscribed ritual vessels (pp. 30-35), about which there has been and will continue to be wide disagreement. But my purpose here is only in part to comment on the *Brief Report*. My main objective is to identify and discuss what I see to be the most visible scientific issues in Three Dynasties chronological studies. Right or wrong, readers need to know what I have been thinking.

1. Eclipses

1.1 **Lunar eclipses at the end of the reign of Wu Ding of Shang:** Shang oracle inscriptions believed to be late Wu Ding are discussed in David N. Keightley, *Sources of Shang History* (University of California Press (1978), p. 174, note 19. Keightley finds four, with *ganzhi* for the day, which he dates 1198, 1192, 1189, and 1180. Nivison "The Key to the Chronology of the three Dynasties: the "Modern Text" *Bamboo Annals*" (*Sino-Platonic Papers* 93,1999) 7.6 (p. 18) (and I believe also Shaughnessy) date the last not to 1180 but to 1201, the date of an eclipse with the same *ganzhi*. This puts the latter close to the 1198 eclipse, and the two pieces are from the same excavation pit. It also leaves the 1189 eclipse as the last one in Wu Ding's reign. Eclipses were thought to portend the death of a ruler; and Nivison finds 1189 as the most likely date for the death of Wu Ding. In late Wu Ding inscriptions the king is often ill. The traditional reign length for Wu Ding (22nd Shang king) is 59 years (e.g., in the "Wu Yi" chapter of the *Shang shu*). The Sandai Project accepts this, and also finds Wu Ding's succession year to be 1250 BCE. This is Nivison's date also, but Nivison finds there to have been an initial three years in the calendar for completion of mourning for Wu Ding's father Xiao Yi, followed by a 59-year reign. (The standard view in mainland scholarship seems to be that the three-years mourning institution was invented by the Confucians after 500 BCE.) The *Brief Report* accepts lunar eclipses at 1201, 1198, 1192, and 1189, and adds another at 1181, but judges the last two to be Zu Geng inscriptions (p. 57).

1.1.1 Keightley (who does not accept a 59-year reign for Wu Ding) has argued in conversation with me that he did not choose the 1201 eclipse because it was partial, while the 1180 eclipse was total. This raises a basic point about eclipse records: I hold that all possibly ominous phenomena were recorded at first, and were carried over into permanent records only if they later could be seen as having been ominous; and so some partial or even barely visible ones, or solar eclipses not seen but reported from afar, could be picked up in contemporary records (such as oracle inscriptions), and then get into the permanent record if they turn out to have been significant, even if they were undramatic. Keightley had assumed, as do most scholars, that an eclipse was more likely to be recorded if it was dramatic and frightening. I argue that this amounts to reading back into antiquity a present-day "news-worthiness" conception.

1.2 **The Zhong Kang (Xia Dynasty) solar eclipse:** This consideration is important for the identification of the solar eclipse recorded in the modern text *Bamboo Annals* as in the 9th month of the 5th year of fourth Xia king Zhong Kang. This was identified by Kevin Pang as the ring-form eclipse of 16 October 1876 BCE, fully ring-form only north of the Xia capital but unmistakable there, so the king's court would be expecting a report, which apparently was not forthcoming, so (according to the story) a royal force was sent out to "correct" the responsible border lord. Other scholars (e.g., Zhang Peiyu; also probably the Sandai Project) would rule this eclipse out as not conspicuous enough; but Nivison's historical calculations confirm it: Nivison and Pang, "Astronomical Evidence for the *Bamboo Annals'* Chronicle of Early Xia," *Early China* 15 (1990) pp. 87-95; see also Nivison 1999 and 2002 section 6. Both Zhang and the Sandai Project take the "modern text" *Annals* to be non-authentic, and unusable. The Sandai *Brief Report* (p. 81) says that there was no time earlier than the 14th century BCE when the sun was in Fang at the beginning of the Xia last month of "autumn" (Xia 9th month). But I have checked our figuring and I cannot find an error. Our article located the eclipse in the middle of Fang; this may be wrong; my refiguring locates it at the eastern edge, i.e., at about the longitude of Antares. Perhaps the difficulty is lack of agreement on exactly what space in the lunar zodiac should be called "Fang." For my analysis, see my article "The Origin of the Chinese Lunar Lodge System," in A. F. Aveni, editor, *World Archaeoastronomy* (Cambridge University Press, 1989), The *Report* abandons Fang, and looks only for eclipses on the required date, offering four, in years 2043, 2019, 1970, and 1961. Consequently it has dates for Xia that are far too early. The *Annals* tells us that in the next reign the government was dominated by Han Zhuo (probably already dominant in Zhong Kang's time), who had the king (Xiang) killed. This would justify retaining the eclipse in the records.

1.2.1 It is note-worthy that an exact lunar date of this eclipse is found in the "modern text" *Annals*. If the Nivison-Pang demonstration is valid, it shows that the *Annals* record, though wrong as to the absolute date, was based on an earlier correct record. One consequence is that as far back as early Xia the Chinese conceived the lunar month as beginning with the *shuo* (conjunction of sun and moon, necessary for a solar eclipse), and not with *fei*-day (day of first sighting of the new crescent moon). This is a much debated matter, with (e.g.) Li Xueqin arguing for *shuo*, and Chang Yuzhi arguing for *fei* (See Li Xueqin, *Xia-Shang-Zhou niandaixue zhaji* (Liaoning University Press 1999), p. 92; and Chang Yuzhi, *Yin-Shang lifa yanjiu* (Jilin Wenshi Press, 1998), pp. 318-340.) Nivison's hypothesis that *gan* names of kings were determined by the first days of reigns assumes the rule that lunar months began with *shuo* days; so the success of this hypothesis (e.g., showing that the first day of the reign of Kong Jia of Xia was 17 Feb 1577, *jiazi*) tends to confirm this rule. Objectors will say, a *shuo* is not something that you can see; it has to be calculated; and the early Chinese did not have the exact science to do this. So they just couldn't have taken the *shuo* as beginning a lunar month. I would reply, the conclusion does not follow. All that follows is that they probably would often be wrong. What they did, I argue, was to alternate long (30-day) and short (29-day) months, and occasionally plug in an extra 30-day month, as needed; and even, rarely, a 31-day month (as Chang Yuzhi shows from careful study of oracle inscriptions; but I think she fails to show that there ever were two 29-day months in succession, or less than 29-day months).

1.3 **The lunar eclipse of 1065 BCE**: This is described in *Yi Zhou shu* #23 "Xiao Kai" (see Nivison, 1999 and 2002, 2.4). The "Xiao Kai" chapter has it on day *bingzi* (13) in the (sc. Xia) 1st month, 35th year. Context requires the reign to be that of Zhou Wen Wang, pre-conquest. The eclipse was long, shortly after midnight. The text, presenting Wen Wang's "reflections" addressed to his sons (or officers), opens with a reference to the event prompting him to write: "Heeding the unpredicted lunar eclipse on day *bingzi* of the first month, you should begin planning for the succession" (正月丙子拜望食無時汝開後嗣

諆: I am trying to follow Li Xueqin 2001). A lunar eclipse so described occurred on the night of 12 March, 1065 BCE, making Wen Wang's "1st year" 1099. The *Shiji* and other texts give him a 50-year reign, which would date his death to 1050. Wen Wang is said in the *Annals* to have died 9 years after a conjunction of the five visible planets. This conjunction, in the *Annals* dated 1071, is identified by Pankenier as the conjunction 12 years later, in 1059, so again Wen Wang's death must be 1050; and there are other independent confirmations of this. (Tradition has it that Wen Wang was imprisoned for seven years by the Shang king; by my calculation, again reducing *Annals* dates by 12, this was 1068-62. The text of the chapter has Wen Wang apparently writing back to his court, perhaps fearing for his life.)

1.3.1 Interestingly, the May 2000 draft of the Sandai Project *Brief Report* uses this eclipse datum (3.6.2, p. 40), but the published *Brief Report* has eliminated it. One can see why: The draft at 3.6.2 also uses the *Shiji's* date of Wen Wang's death as being in the 7th year (not 9th) of his "mandate," and the *Shiji's* dating of the conquest as being in the "11th year," taking this as counting from the "Mandate" year ("Zhou Benji"; "*shijia*" chapters put it in the 11th year of Wu Wang rather than in Wen Wang's mandate count). So (the *Report* concludes again) the conquest must be in 1046. The argument is invalid, as I show, 1999 Appendix 4 pp. 38-39. The so-called Xia calendar began the year with the lunar month preceding the month containing the spring equinox. It was early Han convention to use the Xia calendar names of lunar months in any calendar; so if one assumed a calendar that started the year with the winter-solstice lunar month (e.g.), then one would refer to the *second* month of the 11th year as "11th year, 12th month," which is what the *Shiji* does (j. 4, "Zhou Benji"). The *Shiji* appears to have been using a pre-Han source that did not even know about this calendar convention, and that would actually have dated the conquest to 1045. Probably editors of the final version of the *Brief Report* saw this, and "solved" the problem by simply deleting this paragraph. They may have had another reason: "7th year" and "9th year" for Wen Wang's death cannot be reconciled without using the Nivison-Shaughnessy "succession year -- accession year" hypothesis, which the Project's report doesn't accept and avoids discussing. If one does accept it, then the Li Changhao interpretation of lunar phase terms, more or less accepted by the Project (pp. 35-36 and p. 46 (5) 1) turns out to be without foundation, and it at once follows that 1046 cannot be the conquest date. See below.

1.4 **The dawn solar eclipse of 899 BCE**: "In the sky [the day] dawned twice in Zheng" (*tian zai dan yu zheng*). These words occur in the *Bamboo Annals* record of the first year of Zhou king Yih Wang (the 7th king counting from the conquest), in both the debated "modern text" and in an undebated "ancient text" fragment. The consensus now is that this refers to a solar eclipse observed at dawn, or at sunrise, on 21 April 899 BCE. The Sandai Project has endorsed this view. The English astronomer F. R. Stephenson objects, arguing that careful calculations of minute changes in the earth's rotation rate and the moon's period since antiquity show that the eclipse in question began at sunrise hundreds of miles farther east than "Zheng" (probably located about fifty miles east of the Zhou western capital; possibly the site of an observatory) -- perhaps as far east as the western coast of Korea. His calculations are debated. Nivison finds that on quite other evidence he can date the first year of Yih Wang's reign to 899 anyway, without using the eclipse argument. This makes it likely that the text actually means that there was a slight dimming of the very first light of dawn caused by an eclipse far to the east, perhaps noticed only in reflections on high clouds over the Hua Mountains of eastern Shaansi. (See Nivison 1999 and 2002, sections 8.3 and 8.3.1, especially note 10.) It is significant that Yih Wang's reign ended badly; he was succeeded by his uncle Pifang (Xiao Wang), who probably first forced him into virtual exile. One acquaintance (Michel Teboul,, who publishes in French on ancient astronomy) told me in Japan in 1983 that he suspected the phenomenon was the aurora borealis, and not an eclipse at all. But as with the *Yi Zhou shu* lunar eclipse in year 35, the coherence of the astronomical interpretation with other independent evidence for the chronology would seem to be overriding.

1.5 **The early evening lunar eclipse of 783 BCE**: A garbled quotation which could be from the *Bamboo Annals* (i.e., "ancient text") found in the Tang treatise on portents, *Kaiyuan zhan jing*, possibly reads, "In the second year of Shangshu (783) in the sky one evening began twice in Zheng" (*Shangshu er nian tian yi xi zai qi yu zheng*). (Again one suspects that there was an observatory in Zheng.) In this year there was a lunar eclipse beginning at dusk, and Shangshu's reign ended badly. He was a usurping lord of Jin (probably first a regent), who was overthrown and killed in his fourth year. There were two such eclipses in 783. But the link to the *Annals* is merely that this eclipse description occurs in the *Kaiyuan zhanjing* after the description of the Yih Wang eclipse. It is thus not necessary to take it as actually from the *Annals*; and an equally plausible de-garbling would make it an account of an eclipse in the Jin Dynasty. Nivison's reconstruction of the Western Zhou strip text finds no place for this supposed "guben" fragment.

2. Conjunctions and related phenomena:

Dense conjunctions of the planets are very rare, and were thought to herald great political change. Three can be identified prior to 841 BCE (the earliest calendar date that is generally accepted). The Sandai Project discusses the first but pays no attention to the other two, since they are mentioned only in the "modern text" *Bamboo Annals*; and for the other (earliest: 1953 BCE), hinted at in *Mozi* 19, one needs the "modern text" *Annals* to make effective use of it in chronology. Credit for identifying these and showing their importance belongs to Pankenier. (His argument for the Xia conjunction and a review of his earlier work on the other two can be found in his article in *Early China* 9-10, 1983-85.) The three are these:

2.1 **1953 BCE**: A very tight clustering of the five planets in Ying Shi (Aquarius-Pegasus) in February, linked by Pankenier , interpreting a text in *Mozi* chapter 19, with Shun's passing government power to Yu in Shun year 14, = 2029 BCE in the "modern text" *Bamboo Annals*. (2029 is year 1 of 471 in the end-of-Xia summary.) From this Nivison and Pang showed that if one follows Pankenier and takes 1953 as Shun 14, then using *Annals* reign lengths, and positing that the *Annals'* interregnums between reigns, said to be for mourning, ought all to be exactly two years (for completing mourning), one gets the correct date for the solar eclipse in the reign of Zhong Kang. Nivison later extended this method, getting convincing results, e.g., that the first day of the 14th Xia king Kong Jia was 17 February 1577 BCE, a *jiazi* day. The Sandai *Brief Report* takes note of this conjunction (p. 80; no mention of Pankenier) and uses an encyclopedia (*Taiping yulan*) quote from one of the lost Han "apocrypha"; it thus merely has to take the conjunction to be sometime during the reign of Yu. But even with this reasoning its date for the beginning of Xia (2070; p. 86) is much too early.

2.2 **1576 BCE**, November-December: The planets' "*cuo xing*," "moving in succession," which can be taken to be their heliacal risings in rapid succession (so that they were close together); following this "at night stars fell like rain," taken by Pankenier to refer to the annual Geminid meteor shower. The *Annals* date is Di Gui 10 = 1580. These 1576 phenomena show that the first year of Shang must be later, and probably (according to Nivison) shows that 1575, said in the *Annals* to be year 1 of Tang, the Shang conqueror, in his own domain, is an accurate date; i.e., Tang took the stellar display as a sign from Heaven, and declared the next year as his first year (by right) as world ruler. (The Sandai Project's date for the beginning of Shang is approximately 1600; it ignores the 1576 planetary phenomenon.)

2.3 **1059 BCE**, May: A close clustering of the planets in Cancer (closest on 28 May (*jiazi*) according to Pankenier's figures), misdated in the *Annals* to 1071, and located there in lunar lodge Fang, just west of Antares, seven Chinese degrees, in the system found in the Tang *Kaiyuan zhan jing*. (1059 was earlier guessed at by Needham: *Science and Civilisation in China*, vol. 3 (1959), p. 408, note c; but Pankenier's work was independent of Needham's.) From this information one can deduce that the first year of the last Shang king Di Xin was 1086 BCE, confirmable by late Shang oracle inscriptions for the "Ren Fang or Yi Fang campaign showing that Di Xin 10 must be 1077 BCE (contrary to Li Xueqin and the Sandai Project which take Di Xin 1 to be 1075 -- *Brief Report* p. 61; Li, *Zhaji*, pp.245-250). It also follows that the year of death of Wen Wang of Zhou must be 1050, so that the conquest must be within the next dozen years.

[2.3.1 Added 2007: My deduction of 1086 as Di Xin 1: The dating of the 1059 conjunction to 1071 and its relocation from Cancer, i.e., Chun Shou, Jupiter station 6, was probably the work of astrologer-chroniclers in the court of the Wei kingdom around 335-300 BCE. The motive would be to support the claim of kingship by king Huicheng Wang, who had declared his intention in 335. The *Bamboo Annals* makes 1035 (700 years earlier) the date when the Zhou king appointed the first lord of Jin, ancestor state to Wei, and this enfeoffment was known to have been in a year when Jupiter was in Da Huo (Great Fire), station 10. The conjunction was two Jupiter periods earlier, so it had to be said to be in Da Huo too (in "Fang": but Fang is the lunar lodge in the middle of Da Huo). But now, if this year of Di Xin -- call it Year D -- was to continue to be a Chun Shou year, it had to be 4 years earlier, 1063; and Di Xin 1 also must go back 4 years. This made 1062 a Chun Huo (Quail Fire) station 7 year, so that 1050 must be too. But the *Guoyu* text (see below) had spread the idea that the conquest was when Jupiter was in Chun Huo, hence in 1050; and also it was known independently that Wen Wang of Zhou had died in the 9th year of his "Mandate" beginning with the year after the conjunction; and he must have died well before the conquest. The only remedy was to move the conjunction year – now year D+4 -- back one Jupiter cycle of 12 years, to 1071, as in the present text; and this made Di Xin 1 go back another 12 years for a total of 16. The present text's date for Di Xin 1 is 1102. So the true date of Di Xin 1 must be 1086. For the date independently established as 1086 from oracle inscriptions, see below, 4.1.]

2.4 The larger significance of these phenomena is that they show that the "modern text" *Bamboo Annals* is absolutely indispensable for working out the exact chronology of the Three Dynasties. The Sandai Project, by ignoring this text and recent scholarship based on it, had no hope of more than accidental success with a few dates.

3 The Problem of Lunar Phase Terms

3.1 One does not find these terms in Shang materials. Their importance is that they are found in crucial texts recounting events in the year of the Zhou conquest, and they occur systematically in some way in bronze inscription dates that must be interpreted to create, or to check, a chronology of first years of Western Zhou kings. The chronology of Eastern Zhou kings is not problematic; and one rarely sees any lunar phase term in Eastern Zhou era bronze inscriptions other than *chuji* (which may be merely ornamental in these inscriptions).--All of these are dated (if dated at all) in calendars of regional lords.

3.1.1 Terms commonly found in Western Zhou (prior to 770) bronze inscriptions are four: *chuji* 初吉 ("beginning *ji*"), *jishengbo* 既生霸 ("after the birth of the *bo*"), *jiwang* 既望 ("after the full moon"), *jisibo* 既死霸 ("after the death of the *bo*").[1] Other terms found in a few literary texts are these: *zaishengbo* 在生霸 ("at the birth of the *bo*"), *pangsibo* 旁死霸 ("just after death of the *bo*"), *jipangshengbo* 既旁生霸 ("after just after the birth of the *bo*"). I am not sure of "just after" for *pang*, but there is agreement that *pangsibo* follows *jisibo*. There probably were other terms formed analogously.

3.1.2 The meaning of the element *bo* (*po* 魄 in Han) has been debated since antiquity: Liu Xin took 魄 as meaning the unlit part of the lunar disk, and accordingly understood *jishengpo* (his reading) as "full moon," when the unlit part is "born"; others take it as the lighted part., and accordingly take *jishengpo* as equivalent to *fei* 朏, the day of first appearance of the crescent moon. But this assumes that *sheng*, "be born," must refer to the first glimpse. It is just as reasonable to take *po* (*bo*) to be the moon half or more full (i.e., gibbous: the archaic form of the root graph was an egg-shaped figure), with the time from first sighting to half moon being a gestating period, so to speak. (Liu Xin took *jisipo* as *shuo* 朔, the time when the unlit disk begins to "die.")

3.1.3 As for *ji* 吉 in *chuji* 初吉, "beginning *ji*," its common meaning is "good luck," hence the interpretation "lucky day in the first part of the month," by scholars (like Huang Shengzhang, followed by Pankenier) who deny that *chuji* is a lunar phase term at all. But recently in very early Zhou inscriptions (Zhou, not Shang, oracle texts) the term *jiji*, 既吉 "after the *ji*" has been found, effectively refuting this view. Li Xueqin (*Zhaji* pp. 88-104) argues, I think conclusively, that *ji* in *chuji* means *shuo*, the time of conjunction of sun and moon. One must then ask, why *chu*. My own theory (2005-7, not previously published) is that the element *ji* (as in the graph *jie* 結, "a conclusion, tying together" refers to the joining point in time of the passing month and the coming month (or perhaps the binding together, i.e., conjunction, of the sun and moon), and "*chuji*" simply specifies that one is thinking of this point as a beginning rather than as an end. The meaning

---

[1] I have only weak confidence in my reading *bo* for 霸 in inscriptions, written 魄 (normally read *po*) in many literary texts. The normal reading for 霸 is *ba*, when it means "to be or become the ranking *bo* 伯 (chief among the regional lords). Many scholars ignore the problem and always read 霸 as *ba*. All of these words are cognates, based on the archaic word (and pictograph) for moon, *qua* dominant entity in the night sky. (It becomes the graph *bai* 白.)

"good luck" for *ji* could be derivative, based on the custom of regarding the first day of a month as lucky.

3.2 Modern dispute usually rejects Liu Xin's meanings and tries to deduce the meanings from actual usage. There are four main opinions:

(1) The terms name fixed days only, and can be used only in referring to those days. (Different scholars have different lists.) Dong Zuobin held this view, and so now does Liu Qiyi.

(2) In the *Shang shu* the terms name fixed days, *jishengpo*, *jiwang*, and *jisipo* being the first days of the second, third and fourth quarters; in inscriptions they name lunar quarters. (This was the view of Wang Guowei, d. 1927.)

(3) In inscriptions the term *chuji* can be used in reference to any of the first ten days (this is the theory of Huang Shengzhang); *jiwang* is used only for a few days after the full moon; *jishengpo* can be used for any day in the first half of the month; and *jisipo* can be used for any day in the second half of the month (this is the theory of Li Changhao). Variations of this theory: *chuji* just means "lucky day" and can be any day in the month; *jishengpo* and *jisipo* in literary texts name fixed days, but these are earlier days than the first days of the second and fourth quarters.

(4) The terms *chuji*, *jishengpo*, *jiwang*, and *jisipo* name the first days of the four quarters; but the convention in the *Shang shu* is to specify a day within a quarter by naming the first day and then giving the number of the days counting to the day in question, which is named by its *ganzhi*. In inscriptions, however, the convention is to omit the ordinal number of the day in question within that quarter. This is the view Nivison explained in 1983 ("The Dates of Western Chou," *Harvard Journal of Asiatic Studies* 43, pp. 488-489), and Li Xueqin endorsed (arguing that it was Wang Guowei's idea) in 1998 and 1999 (*Zhaji* pp. 130-132).

3.3 The lunar phase terms used in the lost "Wu Cheng" chapter of the *Shang shu* (quoted in part by Liu Xin in his *Shi jing*, "Canon of Generations," incorporated into chapter 21B of Ban Gu's *Han shu*) require that if one thinks the conquest year was 1046, one must adopt a form of the Li Changhao system (taking *jishengpo* and *jisipo* as fixed days, but earlier than the four-quarters system allows). But if one thinks the date was 1045 or 1040, one must adopt the Wang Guowei system, or its modification by Nivison and Li Xueqin. (Liu Xin thought the date was 1122 BCE.) And these choices will be found to dictate or sanction quite different chronologies of the subsequent Western Zhou kings. The Sandai Project *Brief Report* accepts the Li Changhao and Huang Shengzhang system (without naming them: see pp, 35-36, and p. 46); but for *chuji* it apparently accepts the ultra-liberal view that the term can refer to any day in the month so long as it was thought to be a lucky day; thus on p.32, dating bronze inscriptions, #30 Shi Hui *gui*. which has a *chuji* date, is given an absolute date that requires the 20th of the lunar month.

3.4 An important controversy concerning these lunar dating terms, extending also to other aspects of chronology (such as the length of months) is whether there were fixed rules, and how tightly or liberally any rules were applied. Pankenier ("Reflections of the Lunar Aspect on Western Chou Chronology," *T'oung Pao* 1992) appears to think that the use of the terms was so subjective and inexact that bronze inscription internal dates are virtually useless, not just for deriving a chronology with no other aid (anyone ought to agree to that, though many don't), but even for checking and confirming a chronology. Li Xueqin thinks that *chuji* names the *shuo* day, but thinks that identification of that day in a bronze date can stray as much as two days before the correct day. Thus he is willing to date the Shanfu Shan *ding*, first month *chuji gengxu* (47) of the 37th year, to 841, even though the actual *shuo* was *renzi* (49). Nivison would argue that anticipating the correct *shuo* by one day is possible, because (he thinks) it was a standard conception almost always observed that 30-day and 29-day months alternated, and that this was the way *shuo* days were usually identified, though it is not quite true in fact. But he would say that if one's chronology requires supposing that an inscription date is two days early, then one must admit that one's chronology is very doubtful. Nivison and most others of the "four quarters" persuasion argue that fixed rules governed the application of the other lunar terms; e,g., although the precise day of full moon can vary over as much as three days, the use of the term *jiwang* was not a matter of observation and subjective judgment, but was determined by counting days from the day one identified as the *shuo* day (see Nivison, "Standard Time,"2005).

3.5 The case of the Shanfu Shan *ding* points to two other issues of great importance. One is a hypothesis applying (Nivison thinks) to all Three Dynasties chronology. The other is a basic principle of scientific method.

3.5.1 **The 2-yuan hypothesis** (Shaughnessy too accepts this, as applied to Western Zhou): The three-years mourning for one's deceased father was a very old institution, and it normally required a king to wait beyond his succession year (*yuan* year) until his third year (a second *yuan* year) before claiming all of the forms of kingship. Initially years are identified by counting from the succession year. The third year one may call the accession year, and one finds that late in the reign (perhaps after the king's father's chief ministers have passed on) the king will promulgate his own calendar requiring counting from his accession year. In style and decor the Shanfu Shan *ding* is much better dated a half century later than Li (followed by the Sandai Project) dates it. Xuan Wang's accession year would be 825, and the 37th year counting from 825 is 789. The vessel cannot be dated to 791, but it is easily dated in 789, either by supposing that the date is one day early (Shaughnesy's view), or by assuming that at this time the Zhou court was using a calendar beginning the year with the pre-spring-equinox month (Nivison's view). The change from taking 827 as first year to taking 825 as first year appears to have been made in 809. (And it applies to court-oriented inscriptions only, not to provincial ones like the hotly debated "33rd year" date on the Jin Hou Su bell set.) For this reason, different sources can be found to date some events in Xuan Wang's reign two different ways, two years apart. There are many other examples, for other reigns.

3.5.2 **The principle of sufficient explanation**: This cannot be emphasized too strongly: If you have a hypothesis, and you find two pieces of evidence A and B bearing on it, A supporting it and B contradicting it, you cannot simply accept A and say "Since I am taking A as correct and B conflicts with it, B must be wrong, so I will forget about it." This is to argue in a circle. What you must do is find an all-encompassing reasonable explanation that if true shows how the mistake that you are judging B to be could have been made, and that part of your account must be independent of your preference for A. It may show what the truth of A would imply; but it cannot be in effect simply a restatement of your preference for A. And the matter cannot be ignored. Your opponent, favoring B, has an exactly similar obligation.

3.5.2.1 In the case of the Shanfu Shan *ding*, dating it as Li and the Project do involves accepting a part of the *Shiji* account of Li Wang, which has him driven into exile in late 842, which year is implied in the account to be his 37th. (Li Xueqin and the Project, following Li, have to arbitrarily move the 37 years down one year, so as to stretch the definition of *chuji* to allow the Shanfu Shan *ding* in 841.) But the *Shiji's* accounts of events in Wey and in Qi imply that Li Wang's first year could not be earlier than 860. If you accept "37 years," you must offer an *independent explanation* of "not earlier than 860," showing how such a "mistake" could have been made. If you cannot, you have done nothing. Similarly I, taking Li Wang's succession year to be 859, must offer an independent explanation of "37 years" as error. Lei Xueqi did it first, two centuries ago: *The Bamboo Annals* says that Li Wang was born in 864, and we all know that he died in 828, so his life spanned 37 years.[2]

3.5.2.2 Completing the explanation requires showing how the switch from 37-year life to 37-year reign could have been made. I have an account, involving the formulation of the Yin Li chronology, which I would admit is a bold conjecture. (The Yin Li is so called because it identifies 1567, the first year of its 1520-year cycle beginning with the day *jiazi*, as the date of Yi Yin's sacrifice to Tang, 25 years earlier than the correct date; Pankenier has shown that 1554 is the first year of Shang, but the Yin Li year is 1579. So all Yin Li dates have to be 25 years early, down to the generally accepted date 841 as first year of Gong He. The elimination of mourning periods at sometime in the -4th century moved the succession year of Li Wang down to 853, still seen in the "modern text" *Annals*. Moving the date back 25 years to 878 created a 37-year reign through 842.) But one can point to another case like this: Mu Wang's reign is received as 55 years, a figure unquestioned by the Sandai Project, but easily shown to be much too long if one studies the *Bamboo Annals* (though the *Annals* text as it stands also accepts 55 years). Shaughnessy has argued, reasonably from close analysis of the *Annals* text for Zhao Wang, that 55 years is actually the length of Mu Wang's life.

---

[2] More precisely: the birthdate is given in a small-*zi* double-column in-text note. This Nivison has used to propose a restoration of a three-*zi* subtext, "*Li Wang sheng*." See Chapter Eight, strip page 17, strips 250-251, and comment.

4. Intercalation, Solar Seasons, Winter Solstice

There is a long-enduring debate about whether Chinese of the ancient Three Dynasties era adjusted the lunar calendar to the solar year only by adding an occasional lunar month (or sometimes two months) at the end of the year, as "13th month" (and rarely "14th month"). The alternative view is that they had some system for deciding to insert an intercalary month at some point within a year. This can be important in deciding how to interpret a lunar date. E.g., to get the date 1086 as the first year of Di Xin, one must see Di Xin 10 as calling for an intercalary 9th month. Li Xueqin will not allow this possibility.[3] Chen Mengjia did allow it, and Nivison allows it. (Chang Yuzhi also allows intra-year intercalation in the Shang calendar system, and applies the principle to Di Xin; see *Shang dai zhouji zhidu* pp. 286-7.)

4.1 Nivison's view is that occasional instances of "13th month" or "14th month" in dates do not indicate (as most argue) that at the time these inscriptions were made the Chinese had not yet figured out how to decide on when to intercalate within a year. If an intercalation had been missed, and must be made up, or if there were some administrative reason to change the calendar and make the year begin later, the added month or months needed would be placed at the end of the year, because there would be no reason to do anything else (see Appendix 4). The system used was the one that is described in much later historical and commentarial literature. The 365-day normal solar year was divided into 24ths, of 15 or 16 day solar "weather periods" (*jieqi*), and these were grouped into 12 pairs, i.e., solar "months," with the winter solstice being the first day of the second half of the first pair. This day and the middle of each subsequent pair were designated *zhong qi* days (*qi*-center days). The intercalation rule then was that a lunar month must normally contain a *zhong qi* day; if it did not, it was intercalary. It will be found that this rule dictates that the 9th month (Shang calendar) of the year 1077 must be followed by an intercalary 9th month, And the inscriptions for the Ren Fang (Yi Fang) campaign in Di Xin 10 likewise require an intercalary 9th month (making 1086 Di Xin's first year), unless one is willing to suppose four 30-day or 31-day months in succession (the norm has to be alternation of 30 and 29 day months). (D. Nivison, "The Origin of the Chinese Lunar Lodge System," in A. F. Aveni, editor, *World Archaeoastronomy* (Cambridge University Press 1989) pp. 203-218, shows that the 24-part division of the solar year and zodiac must be older even than Shang. The only conceivable reason for it is to serve as a decision procedure for intra-year intercalation.)

4.2 Using the same method, Nivison finds that the year 1098 had an intercalary 3rd month, and the inscriptions thus dated identify the year as the king's 8th; so this reign, which must be Di Yi's, began in 1105. (The Sandai Project date is 1101.) Working out the last example exposes an important problem. The system of solar months with their middle-day *zhong qi* was keyed to the winter solstice day, so one had to know without doubt what that day was. The sun's horizon point of rising is moving very slowly at this time, and the day that is actually the shortest will not be immediately evident; yet it must be identified, with no room for doubt. There came to be technology for doing this, but the system described was in use long before that technology developed. What did the Chinese do? They did what I would do: the winter solstice may be doubtful, but the autumn equinox is not; at that time the sun's point of rising is moving steadily in one direction and relatively rapidly. Once the exact point is determined, one can use it year after year. (If the day is overcast, one can extrapolate from the nearest clear days.) Then one can simply count days to the solstice. But how many days? The distances between the cardinal days (solstices and equinoxes) are actually unequal. But the Chinese have always had a marked systematizing way of conceiving of all of nature. So, four days, centers of four seasons (for them): simply divide the year by four, to the nearest whole number. The result: 91 days from autumn equinox to winter solstice. But the actual interval, in Three Dynasties times, was not 91 days but only 89 days. So we must expect that the Chinese would identify as "*dong zhi*," "winter solstice day," a day that was two days *late.*

4.2.1 This assumption is needed to get the 3rd month intercalation in 1098; and it gives other very important results. One: if the date of the last year of Zhou Gong's 7-year regency at the beginning of Cheng Wang's reign is the year 1036, as the conquest date 1045 probably requires, the year would satisfy lunar dates in the "Shao Gao" chapter of the *Shang shu*, if a "four quarters" interpretation is adopted. In that case, the last

[3] Prof. Li accepts intra-year intercalation for late Shang but denies that it is possible in Di Xin 10 month 9. See Appendix 4, Supplement 3.

month of the year has to be the last month of autumn. This is what I did in my article in *HJAS* in 1983. For this month to be the last in the year is possible, but unlikely. If the conquest date is 1040, then the last year of the Regency will be 1031, and this year will end with what was probably thought to be the month before the winter-solstice month, which is far more likely. The "Luo Gao" chapter says that at the end of the last Regency year, just as he was about to assume full powers, Cheng Wang performed sacrifices, on day *wuchen* (05), a *zheng* sacrifice (winter sacrifice to the royal ancestors) and "*ji sui*," meaning debated. Some take *sui* here to be the name of a "cutting" sacrifice. The more obvious meaning is "year," making the phrase mean that he performed a sacrifice signaling the close of the year and the beginning of the next. The day *wuchen* actually was the day after the winter solstice. But if the solstice day officially recognized was two days after the actual solstice day, Cheng Wang thought he was making the sacrifice "for the year" on the eve of the solstice, obviously appropriate.

4.2.2 Another detail: There was a preference for taking important actions -- making important appointments, on launching campaigns, etc. -- on first days of recognized time periods, e.g., first days of lunar months. A possible choice would naturally be first days of solar "weather periods," *qijie*, dated by counting from the winter solstice.[4] In the conquest year, if 1040, taking the solstice as two days late, and using the lunar dates of events in the "Wu Cheng" chapter of the *Shang shu*, one finds that the campaign starts on one of these first days; the celebration of victory back in the Zhou capital is on another; and the victory day itself, *jiazi* of the (Xia) second month, is on yet another. Moreover, that day -- 18 April -- was the first day of the period called "Qing Ming," and this was the date of the major celebration of the year in honor of ancestors. (And this is true of no other year that can be reasonably proposed as the year of the conquest.) Further, we find in one of the odes in the *Shi jing* (Classic of Poetry) that in one hymn, called (from the first words in it) "Da Ming," the Greater Ming ode, the last line reads as follows -- after an account of the glories of the ancestors, culminating in Wu Wang's victory -- "*Si fa Da Shang, hui zhao Qing Ming*": "Then he attacked Great Shang; this occurred in the morning, Qing Ming Day." The ode appears to be a Qing Ming Day hymn. (I am alone in interpreting the line this way, because I am almost the only person who thinks the victory was in 1040, and probably also the only person who has noticed that the Chinese of this time were dating the solstice two days late.)

5. The Jupiter problem

There are several dates before, during and after the Zhou conquest, when the position of Jupiter -- Sui Xing, "year star" -- must be considered. (Jupiter is called the "year star" because the zodiac is divided into 12 spaces to keep track of the months, and Jupiter moves eastward from one space to the next, approximately and on average, in one solar year. Later, when the five planets are correlated with the so-called "five elements," *wu xing*, Jupiter is called Mu Xing, the Wood Star. The spaces, as successive ideal locations (*ci* 次) of Jupiter, are called "Jupiter stations." These have names, and are defined in two different ways. One way (given us by Liu Xin) divides the zodiac into 12 equal spaces, defined in term of parts of the 28 lunar lodges (*xiu* 宿), which in classical and later times were quite unequal. The other way, yielding very unequal Jupiter stations, assigns seven *xiu* to an approximate fourth of the zodiac, grouped 2 + 3 + 2 as three Jupiter stations. So one can sometimes be unsure what is meant when a Jupiter station is named.

5.1 It must be recognized at the start that ancient interest in Jupiter was astrological not scientific. This fact requires an understanding of some basic Chinese astrological concepts. Astrology is concerned with luck, and maximizing one's luck (and minimizing bad luck) is a matter of expert timing. To keep track of the celestial aspects of timing, the astrologer had a chart, square with an inscribed circle, or better a square plate with a circular plate fixed to it by a peg in the center. The sides were marked with the four cardinal directions. Around the inside edges of the square or around the circle might be inscribed the names of the 28 lunar lodges (*xiu*), seven to a side, grouped, 2 + 3 + 2, into Jupiter stations, whose composition in *xiu* was fixed. And matching them would be the twelve chronograms which are the *zhi* component of the *ganzhi* for a day. The chronograms were arranged in clockwise order (we will see why), whereas the *xiu* were (as one sees them in fact if facing south at night) in counter-clockwise order. In the center of the circular plate (in a

[4] Counting conceptually from the solstice, but actually from the autumn equinox (as explained in Appendix 4).

first class piece of equipment) a peg fixed it to the center of the square, so that it could be rotated. And in the middle of the circle would be drawn a picture of the Big Dipper. The arrangement of the *xiu* was determined thus: If you were to imagine yourself facing due south at midnight at the winter solstice around 2000 BCE the asterisms for the *xiu* that you would be facing must be on the south side of the square, arranged in the order you would see them in the sky. This meant that in the middle of the north side would be the lodge Xu, where the sun would be at the winter solstice. (Look at Nivison 1989, circular diagram p. 209, and precession p. 214.) Xu thus is due north; and it is in the middle of the first chronogram, *zi*. The *xiu* called Xing is due south, and Xing is in the middle of the Jupiter station Chun Huo, Quail Fire. This scheme is tantamount to actually standing facing south at midnight at the winter solstice (2000 BCE), and imagining the lunar zodiac spread out on the horizon, as it would be arranged in the sky at that moment (only part of it, behind your head and below the horizon, would be invisible to you).

5.1.1 What about the Big Dipper? In the sky, it is always pointing with its handle at one part of the zodiac, approximately Scorpio. But the actual Dipper will point at different parts of the imaginary horizon-zodiac at different times. How is that going to work? The moon and planets, each at its own pace, as you view the scene facing south at a fixed hour, say midnight, through the year, appear to move around the zodiac from right to left, west to east, counter-clockwise. The earth too is a planet moving in the same direction as the others around the sun (one doesn't have to know this), so if you use some system for checking the position of the sun against the background stars, the sun will appear to do the same. But this means that if you keep the position of the sun relative to yourself fixed at midnight directly back of you below the horizon, this amounts to your seeing -- at successive midnights -- the background "fixed" stars seeming to move clockwise from left to right. The Big Dipper is part of the scheme of fixed stars, so it will do the same, and its handle -- think of yourself now a god, seeing everything -- will act like the hand on the face of a clock. I am probably describing a universal human conception, and this is probably why "clockwise" is clockwise. This is why the chronograms are arranged in clockwise order: There are twelve of them, and the Dipper points successively to each, in the course of a year; thus they number the (ideal, solar) "months." (The real lunar months are conventionally also numbered with these chronograms, *zi*, *chou*, *yin* ...; but their position on the astrologer's diagram would change from year to year, and they would have to be counted in counter-clockwise fashion, the actual order of the sequence of sun-moon conjunctions.)

5.2 Now, Jupiter: In the picture above, we see that the sun in the course of a year moves in the opposite direction from the direction of the time-keeping Dipper handle in the partly imaginary picture. The ancient astrologers believed, incorrectly, that Jupiter moved in the long run exactly from one station to the next in one year. This suggested keeping track of years by the movement of Jupiter. But also, in early Han it became the practice to count off years using the *ganzhi* system. Earlier than that in Warring States the same system was used but with different names for the several chronograms. The chronograms were ordered in the opposite direction from Jupiter's actual movement. This led to the creation of an imaginary "counter-Jupiter," that in one's astrological mind moved in a clockwise direction, around the circle of chronograms. The "Tian Guan" chapter of the *Shiji* explains exactly how this worked: when real Jupiter, called "Sui" or "Sui Xing," was moving right, into the space corresponding to *chou*, the second chronogram, then counter-Jupiter, called "Tai Sui" or (in the *Shiji*) "Sui Yin" (and confusingly sometimes just "Sui"), was moving left, into *yin*, the third space. (For "right" and "left," think of yourself as standing in the middle of the universe-diagram facing south, so that these real and imaginary events are going on behind you.) Notice, now, that as real Jupiter is moving counter-clockwise through the three chronograms (*chou*, *zi*, *hai*) on the "north" side of the diagram, imaginary Counter-Jupiter will be moving clockwise through the three chronograms (*yin*, *mao*, *chen*) on the "east" side. I will come back to this.

5.3 The Sandai Project has adopted two claimed pieces of evidence for 1046 as conquest date, that turn on the location of the planet Jupiter in 1046.

5.3.1 **First: The Li *gui*:** This is a recently discovered tureen with a brief inscription, apparently made soon after the conquest, with the conquest day *jiazi* as event date. The second sentence, perhaps to be read "*sui ding ke wen su you Shang*," is very difficult and has endured many interpretations in the literature. (For a detailed review of them, see Shaughnessy, *Sources of Western Zhou History* (Berkeley: University of California Press, 1991) pp. 87-105.) The Project has adopted the interpretation of a few scholars, including

Zhang Chenglang (Project *Brief Report* p. 44-45), who takes "*sui*" 歲 as "Jupiter," and the graph I render "*ding*" 鼎 as "*dang*" 當: "Jupiter was in the right place ...." (For the meaning of "the right place" see my discussion of the concept of "*fenye*" 分野 below, 5.5.3.) The remainder then might go, "... [and] we/I were able to report that we would quickly defeat Shang."

5.3.1.1. The first authority named for this interpretation is the late highly respected scholar Yu Xingwu, who is said to have "proposed" (*tichu* 提出) this meaning. Yu's article is found in *Wenwu* 1977 no. 8, pp. 10-12. It is strictly true that Yu did "propose" — that is, mention -- the idea, but only "for reference," as what some others say. Professor Yu's own interpretation, carefully documented with oracle inscription evidence, was to take "*sui*" as "year," and "*ding*" *as zhen* 貞 (or *zheng* 正) giving the phrase the meaning "in the annual divination [ceremony] ...", and he explicitly says that the "Jupiter" interpretation makes the rest "difficult to interpret" (*fei jie* 費解). The *Brief Report* has been carelessly misleading here. Shaughnessy's account leaves one concluding that this bronze text cannot be used as evidence for anything, other than as confirming that the victory was indeed on a *jiazi* day. (Li Xueqin has a brief note on the matter, agreeing with the "Jupiter" interpretation, saying that Yu also "proposed" it, but not as "firmly." See Li, *Zhaji*, pp. 204-5. Li's idea is that the maker of the vessel was a court astrologer who predicted victory and is being rewarded for doing so.)

5.3.1.2. I cannot quite agree with any of these opinions. Yu Xingwu seems to me to be right in reading "*sui ding*" as "in the annual *ding* (*zhen*) rite." But a divination rite may be only formally posing a question, e.g., by announcing an offering, and inviting the recipient spirit to approve or not – the real purpose being to couple the offering with a report; so the rest would go, "we were able to report [to the royal ancestors, ***after*** our victory] that we had quickly defeated the Shang." The day was Qing Ming Day. What could be more appropriate?

5.4 **Second: The *Guoyu***: The main text that all "Jupiter" advocates rely on is in the *Guoyu*, "Zhou Yu" 3 section 7, recounting an advice by "Ling Zhou Jiu" to the Zhou king Jing Wang dated 522, on the casting of some bells. The "science" of tones and the "science" of astrology were intimately related, so the king's musical adviser "Ling" is led to some pertinent ancient history: an astrological account of the skies "when Wu Wang attacked Yin (Shang.)" At that time, "Jupiter was in Chun Huo, the moon was in the Sky Quadriga (Tian Si), the sun was in the Ford at Split Wood (Xi Mu), the *chen* 辰 was at the handle of the (Southern) Dipper (Dou, the 8th lunar lodge), the *xing* 星 was in Tian Yuan, and the positions of the *xing* and the *richen* 日辰 were both in the Northern Corners (Bei Wei)." (I am not quite sure of the meaning of the last two clauses and will deal with them later.)

5.4.1` "When Wu Wang attacked" has to be the day the campaign started, because the text goes on to place the Zhou army before the battle as marshalling at the scene the night before, in the second month; and the sun's location (the Ford at Split Wood) shows that a date is intended that is well before the winter solstice, in early (Chinese) winter or late autumn, necessarily in the preceding year. "The Ford at Split Wood" is defined in the *Erya* classic as "the region of Ji (Basket) and Dou ([Southern] Dipper), which ca. 1000 BCE would be about 223 -255 degrees; but Xi Mu is the name of the 11th Jupiter station, classically defined as Wei (Tail) and Ji, i.e. (ca.1000 BCE) about 214 -233 degrees, thus even farther west. (The solstice point for the sun is of course 270 degees.) Tian Si is defined in the *Erya* as lunar lodge Fang, by my reckoning for 1000 BCE about 196 -203 degrees.

5.4.2 Therefore the date intended must be very near the end of the month -- just as it would be in the "four quarters" interpretation of "Wu Cheng" dates; for the moon moves about 13 degrees a day. The "Wu Cheng" has the campaign starting in the "1st month," on day *guisi* (30), the day after *pangsibo* which one assumes to be the day after *jisibo* beginning the fourth quarter. (Thus if one accepted both the *Guoyu* account and the "Wu Cheng" dates as authentic (disregarding the problem of what year is intended), the two confirm the "four quarters" interpretation of lunar phase terms.) But in late 1047, the pre-solstice month ends on *renyin* (39), by which time the moon, if it had been in Fang on *guisi* day (it wasn't), would be about 100 degrees beyond the implied location of the sun by month's end (the sun moves about 1 degree a day). Therefore if the *Guoyu* text is accepted and taken as identifying the year as 1046, then the "Wu Cheng" dates must be rejected, and then the existence of the supposedly false "Wu Cheng" must be explained.

5.4.3 But probably both the "Wu Cheng" and the *Guoyu* text must be rejected anyway, if 1046 is chosen as conquest year. In late 1047 and early 1046 the months probably begin thus (adjusting to make 30 and 29 day months alternate; but this isn't going to make a difference): *guimao* (40), *guiyou* (10), *renyin* (39: *gumao* (40) = solstice), *renshen* (09), *xinchou* (38), *xinwei* (08), *gengzi* (37) .... The "Wu Cheng" has the campaign starting in a "1st month," and the victory in the "2nd month" (five days counting from *jisibo*, i.e., at the very end of the month, if "four quarters" theory is used). A two-month campaign does not seem allowable in the *Guoyu* scheme, because there is good evidence that at this time the Zhou state was using the "Xia" calendar beginning the year with the pre-spring-equinox month. The "Xia" calendar is what is required by the "Xiao Kai" chapter of the *Yi Zhou shu*, detailing the lunar eclipse of 1065 BCE. And in the "Xia" calendar as applied to 1046, to get a "Xia" 2nd month containing *jiazi* one will need to miss an intercalation at the turn of the year, with months perhaps numbered thus, supposing (with Pankenier, "Reflection" pp. 68-69) that the solstice was mistakenly observed two days *early*: #11 *guiyou* (10) (solstice = *xinchou* (38)), #12 *renyin* (39), #1 *renshen* (09), #2 xinchou (38) .... But then there are two problems: first, as I have argued, the solstice was being systematically observed late, not early; and second, the "1st month" when the campaign begins is long after the solstice, and the *Guoyu* requires that the campaign begins long before the solstice. One might try, then, a four-month campaign, implied in the *Shiji*, beginning in the 11th (solstice) month. This still involves the difficulty of requiring the solstice to be early, still has the moon not in Fang at the start, and still has the date too far before the end of the month for the *Guoyu* account, even if one forgets about the "Wu Cheng." I see no indication that these difficulties have been even noticed by the Sandai Project. It seems obvious that the *Guoyu* text cannot be a record for the beginning of a campaign that achieved a victory in 1046.

5.4.4 There is a tempting way to try using the *Guoyu* text. Take "Jupiter was in Chun Huo" not as a statement about Jupiter as visible planet in the sky at the start of the campaign, but simply as an identification of the year, as being a year when Jupiter was in Chun Huo at the start, and for most of the time. Then one can take the conquest year as 1045, with the campaign starting in late 1046, a "Chun Huo year," even though Jupiter had moved beyond Chun Huo by late autumn. Then the moon will almost be in Fang at the right time, and the "Wu Cheng" dates almost fit, although one will have to suppose a calendar beginning the year with the beginning of the Chinese winter, and not a "Xia" calendar beginning the year three months later with the beginning of spring. The data: late 1046, first month of winter begins *dingmao* (04), 19 Nov; JD 133 9694, *guisi* (30) = 27th (i.e., *jisibo* is the 25th), = 15 Dec, JD 133 9720, sun at 255 = the eastern edge of Dou. But the moon for the day goes about 206 to 219 , beyond the eastern edge of Fang (203). The next month, counting as second month, begins *dingyou* (34) = 19 Dec, so *jiazi* (01) is the 28th, being 15 Jan 1045, the fifth day counting from *jisibo*, which thus is the 24th. This was my date back in 1983; but I had already become convinced that the *Guoyu* text was a construction not a record. My theory then (which I published in English and in Chinese), that the invention was done in the first century BCE, was wrong: it must have been done in the early fifth century BCE. But in any case 1045 as conquest date does not satisfy the *Guoyu* text, though the date is not as obviously hopeless as 1046. I see no other possibilities for using the *Guoyu*.

5.5 **Third: Jupiter "in the north"**: There is a fatal problem that any theory using the *Guoyu* text faces. There is another very different account about the location of Jupiter at the time of the conquest. It must be explained away if the *Guoyu* text is accepted; and likewise if one accepts this other account, then the *Guoyu* account must be explained away. The *Brief Report* contains details that show that its authors were well aware of this account, but they ignore it in their arguments.

5.5.1 This other account has two forms. (1) The "Ru Xiao" chapter (#8) of *Xunzi* says that Wu Wang marching against Shang "faced east to meet Tai Sui" (l. 74). (2) The Yang Liang (Tang Dynasty) commentary to this reads, "Shizi says that when Wu Wang attacked Zhou [Xin, king of Shang], Yu Xin remonstrated, 'When Sui is in the north, one does not attack the north.' Wu Wang did not accept his advice." Shizi's writings are now lost, but there are many Tang and Five Dynasties quotations; his full name was Shi Jiao, and he was a client of Shang Yang (prime minister of Qin executed in 338 BCE).

5.5.2 These two statements are not contradictory, because Tai Sui and Sui are not the same. Together they apply the theory of Jupiter (Sui) and counter-Jupiter (Tai Sui): As the real planet Jupiter (Sui) moves counter-clockwise through the northern chronogram spaces *chou*, *zi*, *hai*, corresponding to winter lunar lodges Dou, Niu, Nu, Xu, Wei, Shi, Bi (*zi* being due north astrologically), the imaginary counter-Jupiter (Tai Sui) moves clockwise through the eastern chronograms *yin, mao, chen* (*mao* being due east). Wu Wang had to march east as far as the crossing of the Yellow River at Mengjin, then northeast toward the Shang capital. In the first part of the march, eastward in a geographical sense, he was "meeting" counter-Jupiter, which was in the "east" in a non-geographical but astrological sense. In the second more dangerous part of his march his enemy was, literally, in the north, which was where the real planet Jupiter was in the astrological sense. In other words, according to Shizi during the conquest campaign Jupiter if in exact north was half way around the zodiac from Jupiter's 1046 zodiac location Chun Huo, which is due south astrologically, and therefore the date must be six years earlier -- impossible: Wen Wang had not yet died -- or six years later, i.e. 1040.

5.5.3 The *Guoyu* text goes on to say that Chun Huo was the "*fenye*" (astrological correlate in the sky) for Zhou, a fact supposed to confirm the Chun Huo account in the *Guoyu*. I know of no instance of "*fenye*" theory earlier than Eastern Zhou; and the correlations are supposed to be geographic as well as political: it is Zhou as centered in its eastern capital at Luoyang that matches Chun Huo. Further, one would expect the simpler "north" theory to be older, and the theory out of which *fenye* theory developed, especially when one considers what astrological "north" means: it is the sun's path in winter, and the midpoint of this "north" is lunar lodge Xu, supposedly the location of midwinter, the winter solstice point. But the precessing winter solstice point could not have been in Xu later than the 19th century BCE, early Xia. So the concept must be very old.

5.5.4 The only scholar I have read who claims to accept the *Guoyu* account and at least tries to cope with the Shizi counter-evidence is Pankenier. He does so in his 1983 Stanford doctoral dissertation "Early Chinese Astronomy and Cosmology: The "Mandate of Heaven" as Epiphany," pp. 241-244. (I have not found anything in Pankenier's later publications.) I am not sure that I understand his argument; it seems to be that "Jupiter was in the north" at the time of the conquest was an idea shared by the Yin Li school of chronology, which dated the conquest to 1070, and the Han apocrypha, and is therefore derivative from Han metaphysics, which he connects with the *Bamboo Annals* having (he thinks) been rewritten *after* the Han to put the conjunction in Fang, i.e., Da Huo, and therefore the "north" idea is not to be entertained as possibly accurate history. But he grants that Shizi and also the Yin Li School are pre-Han; and connecting the conjunction date and place 1071 - Da Huo would mean that the Yin Li conquest date 1070 would have Jupiter at the time in the east, not north. He cites the commentary of the Later Han commentator Gao You on the *Huainanzi*, which like the *Xunzi* says that counter-Jupiter was in the east (so that Jupiter would have to be in the north): Gao You explains that counter-Jupiter was "in *yin*," which would mean that the planet was in *chou*, first chronogram of "north." Pankenier admits that he doesn't know Gao You's source (Gao doesn't give it), but assumes that Gao is linking the *Huainanzi* statement with the Yin Li's date 1070. In this Pankenier is right: in fact Gao was obviously simply applying Liu Xin's erroneous algorithm for locating Jupiter to the Yin Li year 1070, getting the result that Jupiter was in station 12, Xing Ji, in that year. (Jupiter was actually in Chun Huo in 1070.) But none of this shows Shizi's account to be derivative or suspect. (If as I argue the campaign began in January of 1040, at that time Jupiter was in Xu, middle lunar lodge of Jupiter station Xuan Xiao, i.e. in *zi*, in the exact center of the "north" side of an astrologer's diagram.)

5.5.5 If the *Guoyu* account is wrong, how does one explain its existence? Recall that the *Shiji* implies a campaign of four months: Wu Wang crossed the Yellow River on day *wuwu* (55) in the 12th month; so the campaign must have begun in the 11th month, and it ended in the 2nd month (of the next year, though the authors did not understand the dates this way). And recall the lunar eclipse of 1065 BCE, which implies that the Zhou used the "Xia" calendar beginning the year in the *yin* month. The Chinese apparently began to use a system of calculating dates backward and forward by 19-year intervals, "*zhang*," and 76-year *bu*, in the early fifth century BCE. (An astronomer friend of a friend of mine objects that its use began later. But if you use the system called "Yin Li" to deduce dates of first days of *zhang*, supposed not only to be first days of months but also to be winter solstice days, you get accurate dates for both *shuo* and solstices approximately from 579 to 389; and half way between is 484.) Suppose a clever person used this new mathematical toy to check the received dates for the Zhou conquest, and suppose that for him the year was 1040, and the calendar used began the year with the *yin* month. He would find at once that the system -- which is not quite accurate -- made the victory day *jiazi* the 1st of the 3rd month. He would conclude that the right calendar must be the one known as the "Zhou" calendar, beginning the year two months earlier, i.e., 29 + 30 days earlier, restoring the victory to the end of the 2nd month. This would make the campaign begin in the "Xia" 9th month, the last month of autumn. And this is just what the *Guoyu* implies.

5.5.5.1 Further: He believes, as the "Wu Cheng" says, that Wu Wang began marching east on day *guisi* (30), near the end of the month. He is now believing that the campaign began late in 1041. So he uses his knowledge of Jupiter: He thinks, as everyone did at this time, that Jupiter circles the zodiac in 12 years. So he counts down by 12's to his own time, which I assume was the late 470's, and finds that 477 was just 47 12's from 1041. By the end of 477 Jupiter had just reached the end of Chun Huo, which at that time was about 94 to 137 degrees. So he concludes that in late 1041 Jupiter was in Chun Huo.

5.5.5.2 Now he asks, what else was going on in the sky on *guisi* of the Zhou 11th month of 1041? He uses his system to find a month late in 1041 that looks right, as the month that is about to begin when the march starts. What he finds is the month at the end of 1041, beginning on 23 Nov, day *wuxu* (35); but his system applied this far back gives him a two-day error, so that for him this month begins on *bingshen* (33). That looks just about right: *guisi* (30) is three days earlier. So he counts down to his own time by 19's, knowing that although the years are not the first years of *zhang*, they should give lunar months dated the same in relation to the solstice. Counting down thirty 19's, he finds himself looking at the year 471 BCE. Let us suppose this is when he is working. He knows that the *ganzhi* will be different, but the day-count to the end of the year should (he thinks) be the same. So now, to find out what the sky looked like back in 1041 on that *guisi* day, all he has to do, he thinks, is count back three days from the first day, 22 November, of the last month of 471, getting to 19 November. He must now get up very early in the morning on that day, in the dark (when Wu Wang would be getting ready to go), and look. What he sees is the waning moon located about 200 , about to move through the magnificent constellation with Antares, the "King of Heaven," seated in his chariot (Sigma and Tau Scorpii) being drawn westward by his four horses (Beta, Omega, Delta and Pi Scorpii) -- "Tian Si," the Sky Quadriga, i.e., Fang, which in 471 was about 203 -210 degrees. (He knows that the moon moves east about 13 degrees a day; so by the next night it will have passed through Fang.)

5.5.5.3 Not having a time machine, I couldn't just look, as I have my investigator doing. I had to use tables and patience, and a good map of the sky. The tables: Zhang Peiyu, *Zhongguo Xian-Qin Shilibiao*, Jinan: Qi Lu Shushe, 1987; Stahlman, W. D.,and O. Gingerich, *Solar and Planetary Longitudes for years -2500 to+2000 by 10-Day Intervals,* Madison: The University of Wisconsin Press, 1963; Ahnert, P, *Astronimisch-chronologische Tafeln fur Sonne, Mond und Planeten*, Leipzig: Johann Ambrosius Barth, 1960; Shinjo Shinzo (for the Yin Li system), "Shu-sho no Nendai" *Shinagaku* 4.4 (1928), pp. 542-543.

5.5.5.4 What about the sun? It was at 232 degrees on that day (our investigator could tell about where it was, by noting the last stars he could see before dawn, and the first stars he could see after dusk.) This is about 20 degrees beyond Fang, just about at the beginning of lunar lodge Ji; so whether "the Ford at Xi Mu" means Wei and Ji, or Ji and Dou, he can say that that is where the sun was. "The *chen* was in the Dipper's handle" the *Guoyu* says. There are too many meanings given us for "*chen*"; but one, well known, is "the conjunction of the sun and moon," i.e., what happens on the first day of a lunar month. So perhaps this line does not describe the day *guisi*, but identifies the *shuo* at 235 degrees that the investigator had to identify to get back three days to *guisi*, and that puts the *chen* almost at the western tip of the "handle."

5.5.5.5 (Picking up the remaining puzzling statements in the *Guoyu*, perhaps the *xing* is the asterism culminating at dusk, i.e., more or less 90 degrees east of the sun; "*richen*" is (I have supposed) a term referring to the sun as located in the zodiac; and the "Northern Corners" are the zodiac points touched by a square inscribed inside the zodiac circle, i.e., they are the points that divide autumn from winter and winter from spring. The sun's location for the hypothetical investigator, at 232, was at the point that would have been the first "Northern Corner" at the beginning of Zhou. The point 90 degrees east must be in Ying Shi, in the "Northern Palace" but slightly beyond Xuan Xiao, said to be the meaning of "Tian Yuan.")

5.5.6 (I have rejected the two-month campaign given in the "Wu Cheng," even though I accept its lunar dates of days. So how do I explain the existence of a text that used these day dates but cut the campaign from four months to two? It seems to me that the "Wu Cheng" is not an early Zhou text, but was fashioned out of early Zhou materials some time in the fifth century BCE, by someone who discovered just the difficulty that led to the creation of the *Guoyu* text. i.e., the writer found that he could not take the dates to be in the "Xia" calendar because this put the victory at the beginning of month 3. His solution, instead of moving everything back 29 + 30 days, was just to move the victory date back, thus cutting the campaign from four months to two. And since the victory month had to be called "2nd month," the preceding month had to be renamed "1st month.")

5.6 What is the position of the editors of the *Brief Report*? And in particular of Li Xueqin, presumably one of them? They accept the *Guoyu* account, without (as far as I can see) looking at any of the problems it raises. Li Xueqin (*Zhaji* pp. 206-213) defends the *Guoyu* account by arguing that Ling Zhou Jiu was a hereditary officer, "*ling*" being his title, who had duties and family knowledge that would have made it not unlikely that he could have known the astronomical details given in the text. But does Professor Li confront the problem of reconciling lunar phase terms with an application of the *Guoyu* text to 1046? He seems in 1998 (28 March) to endorse the "four quarters" interpretation of the lunar phase terms (implicitly rejected by the *Report*, p. 46), because (*Zhaji* pp. 130-133) he argues (as did I in *Early China* 20 (1995) pp. 187-188) that configuring the introductory accounts in the *Shang shu* chapters "Shao Gao" and "Kang Gao, and the account in the "Luo Gao," leads to the conclusion that the term "*zaishengbo*" names the 7th of the lunar month, thus making *jishengbo* the first day of the second quarter. (I said the 6th or 7th, depending on whether the preceding month was long or short.) But after this (paper dated 25 January 1999) Professor Li has apparently adopted the scheme in the *Brief Report* (e.g., accepting the 3rd and the 5th as *jishengbo* dates, *Zhaji* p. 220). As to the crucial matter of analyzing the implications of the positions of the sun and moon in the *Guoyu* account (which I would argue ought to have driven him to hold his original position), Li argues (pp. 211-212, paper dated 21 January 1999) that the details should be understood (as did Liu Xin and as I do not) as distributed over the course of the campaign rather than referring to the same day. But simply reflect that this campaign at least extended over most of a month, even if only to Mengjin, i.e., 26 days; and the moon must be in Fang at some time during every sidereal lunar cycle of 27 1/3 days.

5.6.1 What about the statement from Shizi that Jupiter was in the north? If one accepts my "principle of sufficient explanation" (which is simply common sense), the Project should have explored this statement with great care, and should have tried to put forward a plausible explanation for it, and adequate reasons for rejecting it, in favor of the "Chun Huo" theory that the Project endorses. But I find nothing. The *Report* (pp. 47-48) explicitly refers to the Shizi evidence. It is plainly set forth in Yu Xingwu's article. (Yu rejects it, arguing that in early Zhou the leaders would have been devoutly respectful of divination; but this does not explain the matter.) If we agree that in 1046 Jupiter was in Chun Huo, astrologically due "south," then Jupiter must have been due "north" in 1040. But the *Report* does not even mention 1040 as a possibility.

Is the confidence of the editors justified, that the labor of the Project over five years does now usher these studies into a "new stage," and that on its foundation future studies can move ever closer to the truth? They must be applauded for inviting criticism. But my fear is that in view of the prestige of the Project, enjoying the weight of the Chinese government, the many ways in which the Project at this "stage" seems to have fixed on wrong directions and indefensible conclusions will have the effect of moving us away from the truth rather than toward it.

(I decided to write this material for Erik Eckholm, *New York Times* science reporter in Beijing in 2000. He wrote the article published in the *Times* on October 10 of that year, on the Project's work and disputes about it. He had interviewed me by telephone, and quoted me in that article; and this led me to correspond with him. At the time Eckholm was thinking of writing a longer and fuller study of the Project's work, and I knew that he would find something like this useful. I have had to revise it. To have published exactly what I originally wrote and sent to Eckholm, correcting myself in footnotes, would have made it too confusing.)

Appendix 2

Material Supporting "Two Approaches to Dating" (Chapter Four)

I. The Reign of Li Wang According to the *Shiji*

A: Evidence for a reign before exile of 37 years, as in the Xia-Shang-Zhou Project's chronology:

"Zhou Benji": 夷王崩, 子厲王胡立. 厲王即位三十年, 好利 .... 諸侯不朝. 三十四年, 王益嚴, 於是國莫敢出言. 三年乃相與畔, 襲厲王; 厲王出奔於彘. "King Yi died, and his son Hu, King Li, became king. [When] King Li had ruled for 30 years he was fond of profit.... The regional lords did not come to court. In the 34th year the king became more severe, ... Thereafter no one in the country dared to speak against him. After three years, they rose together and attacked King Li. King Li fled to Zhi."

34 + 3 = 37; but Sima Qian (or his father) must be misunderstanding his source, which probably meant by the words "厲王即位三十年" that Li Wang was king for 30 years -- including his exile, and not including his initial mourning two years. Actually, Li Wang's life-span was probably 37 years. An original note in the *Bamboo Annals* says he was born in 864. Furthermore, the *Shiji* text continues thus: 厲王太子靜匿召公之家; 國人聞之, 乃圍之. 召公 ... 乃以其子代王太子; 太子竟得脫, "King Li's eldest son Jing was hidden in the household of Duke Shao; the people heard about this and surrounded the place.... Duke Shao ... then substituted his own son for the crown prince, who ultimately escaped." This must put a pre-exile "37 years" in doubt. As Lei Xueqi notices, for the rabble to be so easily deceived into accepting Shao Gong's son for Li Wang's eldest son Prince Jing, both must have been swaddled infants, hardly likely if Li Wang had already been ruling for 37 years.

B: The evidence for a pre-exile reign of not more than 18 years:

"Qi Shijia": 哀公時, 紀侯譖之周; 周烹哀公, 而立其弟靜; 是為胡公. 胡公徙都蒲姑, 而當周夷王之時. 哀公之同母少弟山 ... 殺胡公而自立; 是為獻公... . 九年, 獻公卒, 子武公壽立. 武公九年, 周厲王出奔. "In the time of Duke Ai, Ji Hou made charges against him to Zhou, and [the] Zhou [king] had him boiled in a cauldron, installing his younger brother Jing; he was Duke Hu. Duke Hu moved his capital to Pugu, and was a contemporary of King Yi of Zhou. Duke Ai's younger brother Shan ... killed Duke Hu and made himself duke, as Duke Xian.... In his 9th year Duke Xian died, and his son Shou succeeded him as Duke Wu. In Duke Wu's 9th year King Li of Zhou fled."

Li Wang fled into exile in Zhi in 842, = Wu Gong 9, so Wu Gong 1 = 850, and Xian Gong 1 (of 9) = 859. Therefore Hu Gong was killed in 860, probably still in Yi Wang's reign (as indicated above). The *Bamboo Annals* dates Ai Gong's execution to Yi Wang 3, which would be (in my reconstruction) 865. (Perhaps the unfortunate Ai Gong was accused of supporting the party of the usurping Xiao Wang, who probably did not withdraw -- or get eliminated -- until 864, when Yi Wang finally had an heir. I assume that there were two kings at once, 867-864. My analysis of the *Bamboo Annals* ("modern text") gives me 8 years, 867-860 as Yi Wang's reign, and 2+30 years, 859/857-828, as Li Wang's (*de jure*) reign.)

"Wey Shijia": 頃侯厚賂周夷王, 夷王命衛為侯. 頃侯立十二年卒, 子釐侯立. 釐侯十三年, 周厲王出奔於彘. "Qing Hou gave rich gifts to King Yi of Zhou, who raised the Wey lord's rank to *hou*. When Qing Hou had reigned 12 years he died, being succeeded by his son Xi Hou. In Xi Hou's 13th year King Li of Zhou fled to Zhi."

Xi Hou 13 = 842; so Xi Hou 1 = 854, and Qing Hou 12 = 855. Thus Qing Hou 1 = 866. If Qing Hou's status was raised to "*hou*" by Yi Wang, then Yi Wang was king at least as late as 866.

If one accepts evidence A, one must "explain away" evidence B, and vice versa. The likely explanation eliminating A is obvious: the historian misread his source, and so was led to suppose that "37 years" was Li Wang's pre-exile reign length rather than his life-span. "Explaining away" B would not be easy; for notice that the apparently independent narratives in the two *shijia* chapters support each other. (It is possible that the "Zhou Benji" and the Qi and Wey *shijia* are not the work of the same person.)

II Table Comparing Dates of *Bamboo Annals*, Nivison, and XSZ Project, 900-841

Year	*Bamboo Annals*	Nivison	XSZ Project
900		900 GongWang 18/16,dies	900 Gong Wang 23, dies
899		899 Yih Wang 1 of 27 (eclipse)	899 Yih Wang, 1 of 8 (eclipse)
898		898 mourning	
897		897 Yih, 1 of 25	
896	Gong Wang 12, dies		
895	Yih Wang, 1 of 25		
894			
893			
892			
891			891 Xiao Wang 1 of 6
890			
889			
888			
887			
886			
885			885 Yi Wang 1 of 8
884			
883		883 Yih 17/15 exiled to Huaili	
882		882 Pifang (= Xiao) 1 of 15	
881		in power?	
880			
879			
878			
877			877 Li Wang 1 of 37 (through
876			Gong He 1)
875			
874			
873		873 Yih 27/25, deposed (?)	
872		872 Xiao Wang 1 of 5 (+ 4 = 9)	
871			
870	Xiao Wang 1 of 9		
869			
868		868 Yih dies (?)	
867		867 Yi Wang 1 of 8 (Xiao 6)	
866			
865			
864	Xiao 7, Li Wang born	864 Yi 4 (Xiao 9), Li born (life	
863		37 *sui* through 828)	
862			
861	Yi Wang 1 of 8		
860		860 Yi dies	
859		859 Li Wang, mourning	
858		mourning	
857		857 Li Wang, 1 of 30 (to Xuan	
856		Wang 1 = 827)	
855			
854			
853	Li Wang 1		
852			
851			
850			
849			
848			
847			
846			
845			
844		844 Li 16/14, 21 *sui* = year 1	
843			
842	Li Wang 12, flees to Zhi	842 Li 18/16 = year 3; flees to Zhi	
841	Gong He 1 of 14	841 Gong He 1 of 14	Gong He 1, = Li 37, flees

III Explanation of Table in II (Nivison's system is obtained primarily by explaining the "modern text" *Bamboo Annals* (BA) system. Inscription dates are used only to *test* the result.)

1. Assume that originally all kings after Mu Wang who directly succeeded their own fathers began their reigns with two years of mourning, which were dropped, in a revised chronology sometime in the 4th century BCE. There are five such kings: Gong, Yih, Li, Xuan, and You. Gong Wang's reign in the BA is 907-896, 12 years. Therefore assume that originally it began 2 x 5 years earlier, in 917. (The second *yuan* (which here would be 915) is used late in a reign.)

2. Assume that the "double dawn" in the BA account of Yih Wang's year 1 was the eclipse of 21 April 899, in his succession year. (Tentatively only, because of Stephenson's reservations.) This makes Gong's dates 917/915-900, 2 + 16 years. We need an explanation for 16 being reduced to 12 in the BA, and for 895 as Yih 1. (Gong Wang's reign is 12 years also in *Wenxian tongkao, j.* 250.)

3. The BA has entries for years 1-3, 6-8 for Yi Wang So assume he did have 8 years and look for an explanation for the missing years 4-5.

4. Xuan Wang's date 827 is established; assume that after dropping of mourning intervals it was reduced by 2 x 2 to 823, but has been corrected. This accounts for 853, BA first year for Li Wang. 853 is down 2 x 3 = 6, from 859/857-828, 2 + 30 years. Hence "*Li Wang ji wei sanshi nian*" 厲王即位三十年, misunderstood in the *Shiji.*

5. Therefore: Gong, 917/915-900; Yih, 899/897-873 (25 years, in almost all sources); Xiao, 872-868, 5 years; Yi, 867-860, 8 years; Li, 859/857-828 (etc.). Why only 5 for Xiao, not 9 as in the BA?

6. Because the BA 's Xiao 7-8, = 864-863, are the missing years 4-5, = 864-863, in the actual Yi reign. Yi Wang's son and heir Prince Hu = Li Wang was born in 864. After the restoration of Yi Wang (Xiao was his great uncle), Xiao apparently held on for 4 years, 867-864, giving up once Yi Wang had an heir. The BA gives him those 4 years (which have become 865-862), pushing earlier reigns back, reducing Gong Wang from (2 +) 16 to 12, and raising Yih Wang year 1 from 899 to 903, down 2 x 4 to 895. ***This triple explanation seems to be the only one possible; so this analysis must be correct.*** (Contra Stephenson, the sunrise eclipse must not have been so far east that it or its effects could not have been reported to the Zhou capital.)

The XSZ Project: derives its dates almost entirely from inscriptions -- impossible: there are too many different ways of interpreting their dates. The exception is 899, which the Project takes as the date of the "double dawn" (in both "modern text" and "ancient text" of the *Annals*), taken as a sunrise eclipse -- ignoring Stephenson, apparently.

1. The Project does not recognize the "modern text" *Bamboo Annals.* Nor does it even consider the theory of post-mourning reign counts (for which there is much independent evidence; see IV). Thus it commits the "safe evidence" fallacy, of ignoring evidence deemed unsafe, even when one's own theory would fail if that evidence were to be true.

2. Thus it cannot handle high-numbered bronze inscriptions that belong in the later years of Xuan Wang, when the post-mourning *yuan* 825 was used -- notably, the 37-year Shanfu Shan *ding* (date 789, counting from post-mourning *yuan* 825). This bronze is therefore put in Li Wang's reign, which the *Shiji*, in the "Zhou Benji," says was 37 years down to Li Wang's being driven into exile at the end of 842. (But lunar phase problems then force taking the 37th year as the first year of Gong He.) **So Yi Wang's reign ended in 878, the Project supposes.**

3. But the Project in doing this discounts a much discussed contradiction in the *Shiji.* The "Qi Shijia" (*Shiji* 32) says that Ai Gong was denounced and boiled alive (the corrected BA date: Yi 3 = 865), being replaced by a younger brother, Hu Gong, who "was a contemporary of Yi Wang," and who was in turn assassinated by a still younger brother, who then -- i.e., as of the next calendar year -- became Xian Gong, reigning 9 years. Xian Gong's successor was Wu Gong, in whose 9th year, = 842, Li Wang fled into exile.

So probably Yi Wang was still alive at some time in 860, probably his last year. This is supported by the "Wey Shijia" (*Shiji* 37), which says that Qing Hou of Wey gained the favor of Yi Wang (who raised his feudal status); Qing Hou reigned 12 years, and in the 13th year of his successor Xi Hou, Li Wang of Zhou fled. **This implies that Yi Wang was still king at sometime between 866 and 855 -- long after 878.**

4. The double thrust of the "*shijia*" evidence is especially impressive. This evidence can't be dismissed as false without explanation; and none is attempted (or imaginable). On the other hand, the 37 year reign given Li Wang in the "Zhou Benji" is easily explained as error: Li Wang's life-span has gotten confused with his reign before exile. One must always honor *the principle of total evidence*, which demands that *prima facie* evidence that is rejected *must be explained*. It is never enough merely to find a reason for accepting evidence that one prefers.

IV. The 2-*yuan* Hypothesis -- A Summary of the Evidence

The hypothesis is that down to the end of Western Zhou (771), the normal practice was for a reign of record to begin with the year following the new king's completion of mourning for his deceased father (at least in all cases where the predecessor-king was the father of the new king). In Western Zhou, this meant that the first two years of a king's actual reign were not counted in his recorded reign length. In inscriptions, dates during the reign were counted from the actual succession year at first; later in the reign (probably after the death or retirement of his father's chief ministers) the king's post-mourning first year was used. Thus in Xuan Wang's reign the *yuan* year was 827 until 809; after that it was 825, at least for non-provincial texts. I proposed the hypothesis at the Metropolitan Museum conference "The Great Bronze Age of China" in 1980, and it was endorsed and refined by Shaughnessy in his *Sources of Western Zhou History* in 1991. The following list of evidence is not complete:

A: Evidence Independent of the "Modern Text" *Bamboo Annals* (*BA*)

1. The *Shiji*, *shijia* chapters, fixing the date of Xuan Wang 1 in relation to the reigns of regional lords: In most cases the date so fixed is 827. But the "Chen Shijia" determines the date to be 825. (N&S p. 7)

2. Dates for certain events in the reign of Xuan Wang as given in *Hou Han shu* are two years less than the dates for those events in the *Shiji*. (N&S p. 6) [I now see reason to doubt this. – DSN 2007]

3. The date "**12th year** 6th month, *gengwu* (07), *fei*" in the authentic "Bi Ming" chapter of the *Shang shu* (see *Han shu* 21B; a Kang Wang date) cannot be in the same calendar as the date "**25th year**, 8th month, *jiwang*, *jiashen* (21)" in the Xiao Yu *ding* inscription (the text implies that the time is Kang Wang's reign; and no disagreements about the meaning of "*jiwang*" are involved). It is necessary to assume that the latter date is in a calendar beginning two years later than the calendar required by the "Bi Ming" date. My analysis, adapted from Shaughnessy, *Sources* pp. 244-5:

Year/ yuan:	Reign Years 1005	1003 /	Months 1	2	3	4	5	6	7	8	9	10	11	12	13
994h	12	10					36	05	35	04	34	03	33	03	32
993z	13	11	02	31	01	30	60	29	59	28	58	27	57	26	
992z	14	12	56	26	55	25	54	24	53	23	52	22	51	21	50
991z	15	13	20	50	19	49	18	48	17	47	16	46	15	45	
990z	16	14	14	44	14	43	13	42	12	41	11	40	10	39	09
989z	17	15	38	08	37	07	37	06	36	05	35	04	34	03	
988z	18	16	33	02	32	01	31	60	30	60	29	59	28	58	27
987c	19	17	57	26	56	25	55	24	54	23	53	23	52	22	
986z	20	18	51	21	50	20	49	19	48	18	47	17	46	16	45
985c	21	19	15	44	14	43	13	42	12	41	11	40	10	40	
984c	22	20	09	39	08	38	07	37	06	36	05	35	04	34	04
983c	23	21	33	03	32	02	31	01	30	60	29	59	28	58	
982c	24	22	28	57	27	56	26	55	25	54	24	53	23	52	22
981y	25	23	51	21	51	20	50	19	49	18	48	17	47	16	
980c	26	24	46	15	45	14	44	13	43	12	42	11	41	10	40
979yr	27	25	09	39	08	38	08	37	07	36i	06				

Ganzhi day numbers in italics are altered by one day from days calculated by Zhang Peiyu, in order to regularize alternation of long and short months. The table assumes an intercalation every other year, to change the beginning of the year from winter (in 994) to spring (in 979); but there are other ways in which this might have been done. For the meanings of my notations "994h" (etc.) see the table of dated inscriptions (below). "*36i*" in the line for "979yr" means that I take this "8th" month to be intercalary 7th (Zhang's 10th; see p. 13, note 1, below). The next month counts as 8th, beginning *jisi* (06), after a long month; so *jiwang* day is *jiashen* (21), the 16th, as required.

4. The reign of Wen Wang of Zhou is implied to be 52 years in the *Lü-shi chunqiu* (when an error in that text is corrected; see Nivison 1999 and 2002, 2.3 note 3); but in the *Shiji* and in the "Wu Yi" chapter of the *Shang shu* it is 50 years. (50 years is also implied in *Yi Zhou shu* "Xiao Kai.")

5. The *Gongyang zhuan* (Wen Gong 9, i.e., 618 BCE) says that a king or lord does not formally claim his title until his 3rd year, after completing mourning.

6. The He *zun* inscription, apparently describing an address by Cheng Wang on the occasion of the founding of Luoyang in the 7th year of the Regency, names the year "5th year."

B: Evidence from the "Modern Text" *Bamboo Annals*

7. The BA gives both the 5th year and the 7th year as the date of the founding of Luoyang.

8. Like the *Shiji*, the BA several times has dates in Xuan Wang's reign two years higher than corresponding dates in the *Hou Han shu* (which probably is quoting the "ancient text," *guben*, of the *Annals*). [As above, I now have reservations about this. See note p.216.]

9. Like the (corrected) *Lü shi Chunqiu* (Nivison 1999 and 2002 above), the BA gives Wen Wang a 52-year reign.

10. The BA chronicle for Xia has brief interregnums between reigns, the most often occurring number being two years. The first gap is said to be for completion of mourning. When the BA is corrected making all of these interregnums exactly two years, and (following Pankenier) the conjunction of 1953 is matched with Shun's granting authority to Yu in Shun 14, then the solar eclipse in year 5 of Zhong Kang is correctly dated to 16 October 1876, and the first day of the reign of Kong Jia is 17 Feb 1577, a *jiazi* day. Further, 1555, the last year of Xia (according to Pankenier) turns out to be the last year of Fa, the BA*'s* next-to-last ruler, showing (with other evidence) that Di Gui ("Jie") is imaginary. (Nivison 1999 and 2002, 6.3 ff.)

11. The foregoing implies that *gan* names of kings are determined by the first days of their reigns. Apply this principle to the BA reigns for Shang kings, assuming that a king's last year counts in his calendar only if he lives through more than half of it (so that the date gap is either 2 or 3 years), and assuming that if the succession year yields a *gan* that is the same as that of the predeceasing king, then the post-mourning year determines the *gan*. Then one has an explanation why in all accounts the reign of Tai Wu is extended to an impossible 75 years, and why, in all accounts, Yong Ji precedes him, whereas the oracle inscriptions show that Yong Ji followed Tai Wu. (Nivison 1999 and 2002, Section 7.)

12. If one assumes that mourning completion years were dropped from the last three Western Zhou reigns (the last two later being corrected), giving Li Wang 30 years *de jure* after mourning (the probable correct interpretation of the source the *Shiji* "Zhou Benji" must have been using; see I), then Li Wang's first year becomes 853, the BA*'s* date.

C: Other Important Evidence Involving Bronze Inscriptions

13. When the 2-*yuan* hypothesis is used to analyze and correct the BA, the resulting dates for Mu Wang (2 + 37 years, 956/4-918, instead of 55 years, 962-908) are confirmed by bronze inscription dates.

14. When 825 is recognized as a second *yuan* for Xuan Wang, then high numbered inscriptions such as the 37-year Shanfu Shan *ding* are datable in late Xuan, as stylistically they must be.

15 Using the 2-*yuan* hypothesis, one can date in Gong Wang's reign inscriptions mentioning Gong Wang as reigning king (5th year Qiu Wei *ding*; 15th year Jue Cao *ding*), using the 4-quarters analysis of lunar phase terms of Wang Guowei (now shown to be correct, by the Jin Hou Su Bell Set inscription; see "Ni and Xia 2001", and VI).

V. Zhou Conquest Date: Jupiter; *yuexiang*; Death of Wen Wang; Campaign Events

1. The two texts on Jupiter's position at the time of the conquest of Shang:

Guoyu 國語, "Zhou Yu" 周語 3.7: 昔武王伐殷, 歲在鶉火, 月在天駟, 日在析木之津, 辰在斗柄, 星在天黿. "Long ago, when King Wu attacked Yin [-Shang], Jupiter was in Quail Fire, the moon was in the Sky Quadriga, the sun was in the Ford at Split Wood, the *chen* was in the Dipper's Handle, and the *xing* (star(s) [culminating at dusk]) was in the Sky Turtle." (The meanings of the words "*chen*" and "*xing*" are debated. "Quail Fire" is Jupiter station 7 (of 12) in the Chinese zodiac, and Jupiter was thought to move around the zodiac in exactly 12 years. "Sky Quadriga" is lunar lodge Fang, ancient breadth 7 degrees clockwise from Antares. The "Ford" (across the Milky Way) at "Split Wood" locates the sun as in late autumn or early winter, supposedly at the beginning of Wu's campaign.)

Xunzi 荀子,"Ru Xiao" 儒效: 武王之誅紂也, 行之以兵忌, 東面而迎太歲. "When King Wu punished Zhou [Xin of Shang], he marched against him on an unlucky day for war, facing east confronting Counter-Jupiter." Commentary (Yang Liang 楊諒): 尸子曰, 武王伐紂, 魚辛諫曰, 歲在北方, 不北征. 武王不從. "Shizi says, "When King Wu attacked Zhou [Xin], Yu Xin protested, saying, 'When Jupiter is in the north, one does not attack northward.' King Wu did not accept his advice." (In Chinese astrology, imaginary Counter-Jupiter (Tai Sui or Sui Yin) moves clockwise through the "eastern" quadrant as actual Jupiter (Sui Xing or Mu Xing) moves counter-clockwise through the "northern" quadrant. To attack Shang, the Zhou army had first to march east, then turning north across the Yellow River.)

2. The two *yuexiang* 月相 theories that are most often accepted at present:

Approximate Four Quarters (Wang Guowei 王國維 (d. 1927) and similar theories): *chuji* 初吉, 1st; *jishengbo* 既生霸, 7th (after a long month) or 8th; *jiwang* 既望, 16th or 17th; *jisipo* 既死霸, 24th or 25th. (A day is called "*chuji*" if it is *chuji* or any day to but not including the next *yuexiang* day; and so also for other *yuexiang;* Nivison 1983 [revised in Chapter One 1.4.11.1].

Xia-Shang-Zhou (XSZ) Project (similar to Li Changhao 黎昌顥, pub. 1981): *chuji*, 1st through 10th; *jishengbo*, *fei* (2nd or 3rd) up to *jiwang*; *jiwang*, apparent full moon, probably 16th-17th or 17th-18th; *jisibo*, any later day. (Project, *Brief Report* of October 2000, pp. 35-36)

3. Death date of Wen Wang: The BA dates his reign 1113-1062, the last nine years being the nine years following the conjunction of five planets, actually in 1059. This conjunction is dated 12 years early, in 1071. Therefore Wen Wang died in 1050. (There are many supporting proofs.)

4. "Wu Cheng" dates of campaign events: 1st month, day *guisi* (30), following *pangsibo* (which is the day after *jisibo*), Wu Wang begins his march; 2nd month, day *wuwu* (55), Yellow River crossed; 2nd month, *jiazi* (01), being 5 days (inclusive) after *jisibo*, victory at Muye; 4th month, day *gengxu* (47), being 6 days inclusive after *jipangshengbo* (which is three days after *jishengbo*) victory rites in Zhou begin. The *Shiji* ("Zhou Benji") does not use *yuexiang* terms, but is consistent with this account, except that it has the river crossing on day *wuwu* in the 12th month (= Zhou 2nd month), thus (probably correctly) extending the campaign over two more months. [For the chronology of the conquest campaign illustrating *yuexiang* terms, see Chapter One, 1.4.11.1, in this book.]

The conquest must have been within a dozen years after Wen Wang's death. 1046 was the only such year when Jupiter was in Quail Fire. So (it is argued) if one accepts the *Guoyu* text, 1046 must be the date. But the "Wu Cheng" day dates and *yuexiang* dates fit 1046 only if the correct *yuexiang* theory is the one adopted by the XSZ Project: the Project takes the 1st month of 1046 as long, beginning with day *guiyu* (10), so *guisi* (30) would be the 21st, and *jisibo* would be the 19th; and in the 2nd month (short) *jisibo* would be the 18th.

The Jin Hou Su *bianzhong* inscription, however, when correctly dated (to late795, as in Nivison and Shaughnessy, *Zhongguoshi Yanjiu* 2001.1, p. 5) shows that a Wang Guowei-type theory is the correct one (see VI). The implication of the Jin Hou Su inscription therefore is this: if the *yuexiang* dates in the "Wu Cheng" are accepted, the *Guoyu* text must be either rejected along with 1046 as conquest date, or not interpreted as implying that date. And in any case, if the *Guoyu* text is accepted as authentic, a plausible explanation must be offered for the existence of the *Xunzi* account; i.e., it must somehow be "explained away." It cannot be ignored. The Jin Hou Su bell set, found in 1992-3, consists of 16 bells, and its long inscription, concerning a campaign east by Xian Hou Su of Jin and the Zhou king, in "the king's 33rd year," is continuous through the set. For translation and illustrations, with coverage of the voluminous literature in Chinese, see Jaehoon Shim, "The Jin Hou Su *Bianzhong* Inscription and Its Significance," *Early China* 22 (1997), pp. 43-75.

VI. The Chronology of the Jin Hou Su *bianzhong* Inscription

The dating involves a problem that has baffled all Chinese investigators. The bells' style is late Western Zhou, and the date "king's 33rd year" thus points to Xuan Wang, traditionally accepted dates 827-782. But Hou Su, identifiable as Jin Xian Hou, is dated in the *Shiji* to Xuan 6-16 (822-812), his successor being Mu Hou, Xuan 17-43 (811-785). The XSZ Project therefore has put the inscription in Li Wang's reign (giving Li Wang 37 years before his exile -- surely wrong), supposing the campaign to have occurred before Su became lord of Jin. The Nivison-Shaughnessy solution: the *Shiji* (and all other early texts) have reversed Xian Hou and Mu Hou, as shown by the sequence of Jin lords. The *zhao-mu* rule (for shrine locations in the ancestral temple) requires that *zhao* and *mu* ancestors be in alternating generations. But the received sequence is Xian Hou, Mu Hou, Shangshu, Wen Hou, Zhao Hou; and Shangshu, a usurper and brother of the preceding lord, doesn't count. When the order is corrected, Mu Hou is Xuan 6-32 (822-796) and Xian Hou Su is Xuan 33-43 (795-785). This correction is shown to be beyond doubt by the resulting re-dating of events. See the last page of Nivison and Shaughnessy in *Zhongguoshi Yanjiu* 2001.1: e.g., the Tiao-rong campaign is dated to year 38 in the *Annals*, and to year 36 in the *Hou Han shu.* [But see note at end.]

Year	Xuan Wang Reign Year 827 *yuan*	825 *yuan*	Jin Hou Su Reign year	Historical Events
795	33	31	1	King's expedition to East and South begins
794	34	32	2	King attacks Lu
793	35	33	3	
792	36	34	4	
791	37	35	5	
790	38	36	6	King and Jin (Mu) Xian Hou attack Tiao-rong
789	39	37	7	Jin Wen Hou Chou born
788	40	38	8	
787	41	39	9	Battle at Qian-mou
786	42	40	10	Jin prince Chengshi born
785	43	41	11	Xian Hou Su dies, Wen Hou Chou 5 *sui*

Notice the corrected dates for the births of the princes, Chou in 789 and Chengshi in 786, who are named for the military events at the times of their conceptions in the two preceding years 790 and 787. When the dates of the births, by error given to Mu Hou in the *Shiji*, are correctly given to Xian Hou, and Xian Hou's reign of 11 years is made to follow Mu Hou, then the implied dates for the Tiao-rong and Qian-mou campaigns are exactly as given us in the *Hou Han shu* and the "modern text" *Bamboo Annals*.

So "the king's 33rd year" must be 795 (this being a provincial inscription, the 2-*yuan* rule is not applicable). But there is a second problem: the *yuexiang* terms in the text fit the year 794, not 795. The solution to this is probably that the year date is Zhou, but the month and day dates are in the local Jin calendar. Other late Xuan inscriptions show that at this time the Zhou court calendar began the year with the first month of spring. If we assume that the local Jin calendar began the year with the first month of winter, then the Jin "1st month" will be the Zhou 10th month, in a year that is still the Zhou year 33.

But there is a third problem: The text has two dates in month 2; first -- at the end of bell 1 -- we find "*jiwang*, *guimao* (40), then -- the first words in bell 2 -- "*jisibo*, *renyin* (39). So there is a mistake in the text. How should it be corrected? A royal reward ceremony is described on *chuji wuyin* (15) in month 6, the most probable date being the first of the month (following Zhang Peiyu, *Zhongguo Xian-Qin shi li biao*, first 5 months of 794):

Day	01	02	03	04	05	06	07	08	09	10	11	12	13	14	15	16	17	18	19	20	21	22	23	24	25	26	27	28	29	30
Month																														
2	16	17	18	19	20	21	22	23	24	25	26	27	28	29	30	31	32	33	34	35	36	37	38	***39***	***40***	41	42	43	44	45
3	46	47	48	49	50	51	52	53	54	55	56	57	58	59	60	01	02	03	04	05	06	07	08	09	10	11	12	13	14	
4	15	16	17	18	19	20	21	22	23	24	25	26	27	28	29	30	31	32	33	34	35	36	37	38	39	40	41	42	43	44
5	45	46	47	48	49	50	51	52	53	54	55	56	57	58	59	60	01	02	03	04	05	06	07	08	09	10	11	12	13	14
6	***15***																													

The XSZ Project chooses to suppose that "*guimao*" (40) in month 2 is a mistake for "*xinmao*" (28) -- impossible, for once the inscription year is correctly determined, *xinmao* in this month has to be the 13th, which is much too early to be a *jiwang* day. (Supposing *guisi* (30) would give the 15th, still two days too early in a long month.) So the only solution (Ma Chengyuan's) is to conclude that the inscriber lost track of the sequence of days in moving from bell 1 to bell 2, and we should have "*jiwang*, *renyin*," and "*jisibo*, *guimao*." Thus the Wang Guowei system is validated.

[Reservations (November 2007) on the use of the *Hou Han shu* to support the two-*yuan* hypothesis: The relevant material may be found in Fang and Wang pp. 56-58 (1981 edition) or pp. 59-61 (2005 edition). The trouble is that all of the evidence for discrepancies of two years between *Hou Han shu* dates and BA dates comes from one paragraph in the *Hou Han shu*, which can be read in different ways. Further, one has to assume that Fan Ye had at hand a BA text with Xuan Wang event dates based on the accession *yuan* 825, and it is doubtful that the Jixian tomb contained such a text.

The evidence (Fang and Wang #32 ff in the chapter on Zhou): "When Xuan Wang became king, in his 4th year he had Qin Zhong attack the *rong*, and they killed him. So the king ordered Qin Zhong's son Zhuang Gong, with 7000 men, to attack the *rong*, smashing them. With this there was a bit of respite." And (#34) "27 years later the king dispatched troops to attack the *rong* of Taiyuan without success." Other military actions are dated (#36) "5 years later," (#37) "2 years later," (#38) "Next year," and (#39) "10 years later." I.e., all these dates are dependent on what "27 years" is counted from. The BA dates the initial order to Xuan 3 rather than to Xuan 4, but probably this is merely a difference in calendars; a campaign ordered in the *zi* month in the Zhou capital would be in at the beginning of Zhou year four, but only at the end of year three for the BA. An important matter is the date of Qin Zhong's death; in the BA it is in Xuan 6. In the *Hou Han shu* the only date we have is Xuan 4, when the campaign began, and to get the difference of two years in all these dates one has to count from Xuan 4. I have not been able to induce my co-author Shaughnessy to share my doubt (which occurred to me, unfortunately, only after we had published on the Jin Hou Su bell set). In his recent book (*RECT* 2006 p. 213) he speculates that the tomb text of the BA gave Xuan Wang only 44 years, with intra-reign events dated from 825. One noteworthy detail seems to support Shaughnessy: The bell set is dated "33rd year," but that date probably refers to the year before the main action of the campaign, for the following month and day dates fit Xuan 34, which is 794 counted from 827. For some time the Jin and Zhou forces separate after reaching the east. As Shaughnessy points out, it seems likely that it was then that Xuan Wang took action in Lu, executing Bo Yu, who had assassinated his predecessor Yih Gong in 897, and setting up Xiao Gong Cheng instead. But in the BA this action is dated Xuan 32, not Xuan 34. This does suggest that the date "Xuan 32" is counted from the succession *yuan* 825. This argument is perhaps weakened by the fact that (as Wang Guowei notes) the *Guoyu* "Zhou Yu" also dates this action to Xuan 32. But even if we suppose the Jin editors used the *Guoyu* to correct the discovered *Annals* text by changing "34th year" to "32nd year," the *Guoyu* itself is evidence for 825 having been a second "first year" for Xuan Wang.]

Western Zhou Chronology in the "Modern Text" *Bamboo Annals*
Derivation of *Annals* Dates from True Dates

Diagram One: Conquest to Zhao Wang

Top Lines: Proposed Original Dates; Bottom Lines: "Modern Text" *Bamboo Annals* Dates

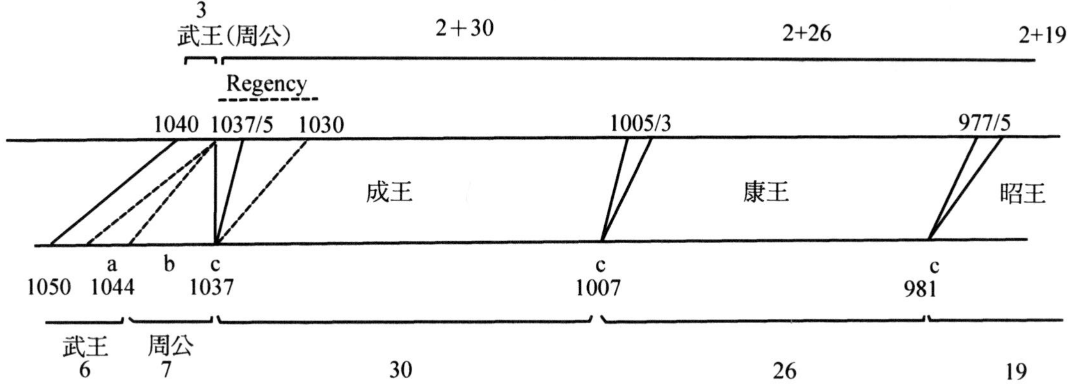

a: Strip text move (proposed by Shaughnessy) gives Wu Wang 3 more years; with the 7-year Regency shift, Conquest is re-dated 1040 to 1050.
b: Regency changed from 7 years beginning with Cheng's succession to 7 years preceding; succession year reconceived as the first year of his majority.
c: Mourning periods are eliminated, shifting 1st years back cumulatively; thus 1005/3 becomes 1007, etc.

Diagram Two: Zhao Wang to Gong Wang

Top Line: Original Dates. Zhao 2+19 years, 977/5-957; Mu 2+37 years, 956/4-918.

Bottom Line: BA Dates. By denying mourning periods for 3 earlier kings and 5 later ones (who succeeded their fathers), Mu Wang's reign is stretched from 2+37 years to 55 years (as generally in later texts).

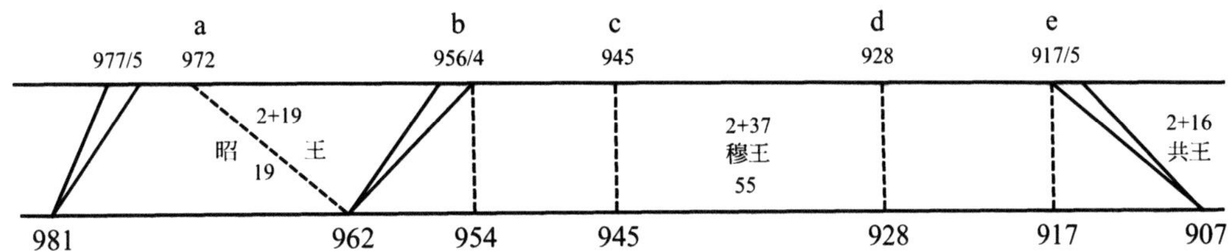

a: Mu Wang's birth date shifted down 10 years (2 x 5), makes his life-span appear to be his reign-length (55 years).
b: Elimination of mourning periods moves 956 to 962; event dates are kept the same by adding 6 to the year number and inserting blank years 2-5. Proof: the Shi Ju *gui* inscription, 3rd year, 4th month, featuring the construction of a new palace; and the *Annals* date for the "Spring Palace," 9th year.
c: Centennial of the Conquest (retained, probably from a Zhou-Lu chronicle, which moved the Regency back only 5 years, making it the 7 years before 1035; without a transposed 3-year strip text, this dated the conquest to 1045).
d: Date of launching of the Chu campaign (Mu 35 in the *Annals*) under Mao Qian; confirmed as 928 (Mu 29) by the Ban *gui* inscription, 1st of 8th month (1st of month being appropriate for launching date).
e: *Annals*-implied date of 1st year of Lu Li Gong (actually 915, coincident with "1st year" of Gong Wang; the *Annals* implies 917, wrong "1st year." (It has Li Gong's predecessor Wei Gong dying in year 45 = 918.)

Diagram Three: Gong Wang to Li Wang

The top line of I represents actual dates; I shows the effect of giving Xiao Wang alone the four years that were probably concurrent with the first four years of Yi Wang. The bottom line of II shows the effect of dropping mourning periods while keeping the absolute dates -- namely 864-3 -- of what had been Yi Wang 4-5. These two years become Xiao Wang 7-8, while Yi Wang 4-5 become blank.

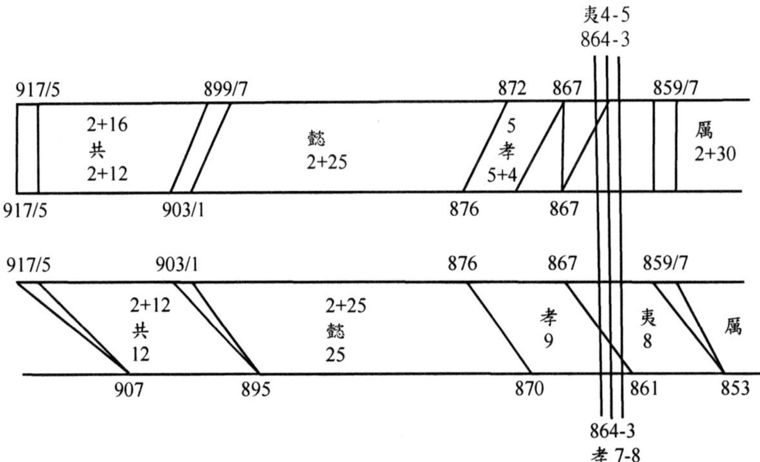

Xiao Wang probably claimed still to be king until Yi Wang's heir Prince Hu (later Li Wang) was born in 864. Thus his reign seemed to be 9 years rather than 5. The *Annals* gives him the added 4 years, but leaves Mu Wang's death date unchanged (in I above). So Gong Wang's reign in the end becomes 12 years only.

Diagram Four: Li Wang to You Wang

a, b, c: Deletion of mourning periods shifts dates of Li Wang and following rulers down.
d, e: Correct dates for Gong He and Xuan Wang are later restored.

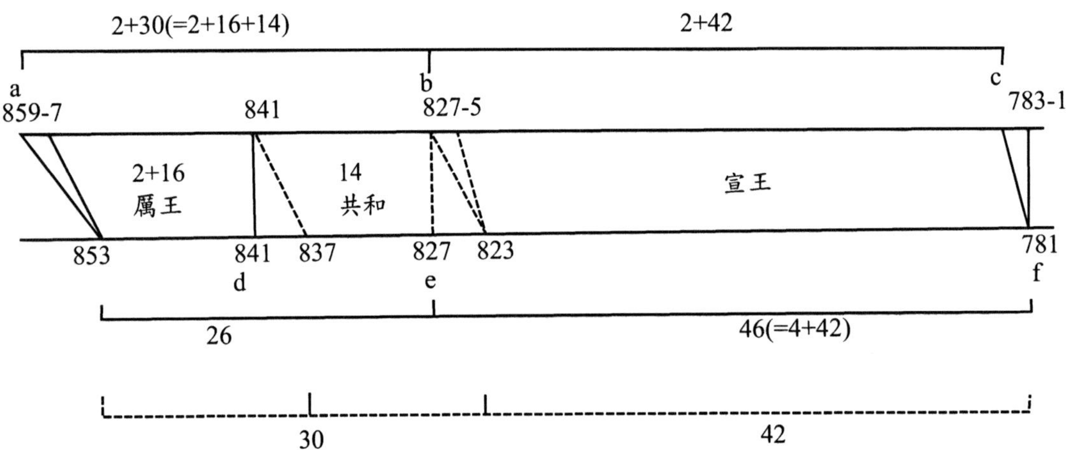

f: In the *Annals*, You Wang's chronicle has an entry for each of the 11 years, 781-771. So it is unlikely that the first two years were mourning years, normally deleted. The Shi Hong *gui* inscription, with a complete 1st year date, resembles the Mao Gong *ding* inscription in wording. The latter has no date, but in content seems to be a first year inscription. And both of these in wording resemble the "Wen Hou zhi Ming" chapter of the *Shang shu*, which is the text of a "charge" to Wen Hou of Jin by Ping Wang in 770. The Shi Hong *gui's* date does not fit 781, but does fit 783. So Xuan Wang probably actually died in 784, making 783-2 mourning years. [There are interesting reasons for doubting this theory. The problem bears watching. See Appendix 3, comment on Bronze 63, Shi Hong *gui*.]

Appendix 3

Proposed Absolute Dates for Fully Dated Bronzes (2007)

(Revision of dates in Nivison 1999 and 2002)
(These dates are far from certain, and are often different from my first attempts in 1983. Problems are addressed in my notes. With two exceptions, only inscriptions with complete dates are included.)

"2/8" (e.g.) introducing the second item, the Shi Ju *gui gai*, indicates that this inscription is number 8 in Zhu Fenghan 朱鳳瀚 and Zhang Rongming 張榮明, editors, *Xi Zhou zhu wang niandai yanjiu* 西周諸王年代研究 (Guizhou Renming Chubanshe, 1998) pp. 438-512.

After the name of the vessel (e.g., "Xiao Yu *ding*") the year and month appear (e.g., 25/8).

A, B, C, D are the four lunar quarters, in the following system:
(1) After a long (30-day) month, A = 1st through 6th, B = 7th through 15th, C = 16th through 23rd, D = 24th on;
(2) After a short (29-day) month, A = 1st through 7th, B = 8th through 16th, C = 17th through 24th, D = 25th on.

The date after the ruler's name is the *yuan* year (first year) in the applicable calendar. The next date is the proposed year of the inscription. Lower case letters h, z, c, y designate the proposed year of the inscription as beginning with the *hai* (pre-solstice) month, the *zi* (winter solstice) month, the *chou* (post-solstice) month, or the *yin* (pre-equinox) month.

Numbers in parentheses are *ganzhi*; the next to last column gives the month number in Zhang Peiyu's tables and the ***ganzhi*** for the first day of that month, in Zhang's tables. A following number in square brackets is my proposed ***ganji*** for the day, if different from Zhang's.

r after the proposed year for the inscription indicates that I calculate this year to have had an intercalary month before the month of the inscription.
In '[r13]' the '13' is not a Zhang Peiyu month number, but simply means that I assume the year to have ended with a 13th month.
* indicates that my year-date agrees with Shaughnessy, *Sources*, Appendix Two. (But sometimes he offers an option when I do not; and sometimes we agree on the year but not on the month and day.)
! indicates a year-dating that would be rejected by Shaughnessy.
+ indicates a listing not in DSN 1983. (But very often I have changed dates proposed in 1983 listings.)

1	Xiao Yu *ding*,	25/8 C(21)	Kang	1003	979yr	11(06)	16th*
2/8	Shi Ju *gui gai*	3/4 B(58)	Mu	956	954c	4(44)	15th*
3/1	Geng Ying *ding*,	22/4 C(46)	Mu	956	935z	4(24)	23rd*
4	Lu (?Xian) *gui*	24/9 C(27)	Mu	956	933z	9(9)	19th*+
5/7	Qiu Wei *gui*,	27/3 B(35)	Mu	956	930z	3(26)	10th*
6	Ban *gui*	(29)/8 A(11)	Mu	956	928z	8(11)	1st+
7/12	Hu gui *gai*	30/4 A(11)	Mu	956	927z	4(07)	5th+
8/2	Xian *gui*,	34/5 C(55)	Mu	954	921z	5(32)	24th+
9/14	Qiu Wei *he*,	3/3 B(39)	Gong	917	915c	4(27)	13th*

10/3 Qiu Wei *ding* I, 5/1 A(47) Gong 917 913c 2(47) 1st*

11/16 Qi Sheng Lu *yi*, 8/12 A(24) Gong 917 910c 909.1(24) 1st*+

12/4 Qiu Wei *ding* II, 9/1 D(17) Gong 917 909c 2(53) 25th*

13/9 Zou *gui*, 12/3 C(27) Gong 917 906c 4(05) 23rd*

14/5 Que Cao *ding* II, 15/5 B(19) Gong 915 901z 5(06) 14th*

15/11 Shi Hu *gui*, 1/6 C(11) Yih 899 899z 6(53) 19th*

16/55 Hu *ding*, 1/6 C(12) Yih 899 899z 6(53) 20th* [r13]

17/15 Wu *fangyi*, 2/2 A(24) Yih 899 898c 3(19) 6th*

18/6 Yi *zhi*, 2/3 A(52) Yih 899 898c 4(49) 4th*

19/29 Xing *hu* 13/9 A(15) Yih 899 887z 9(12) 4th!

20/13 Taishi Cuo *gui*, 12/1 C(31) Yih 897 886z 1(11) 21st* [r13]

21/62 Wang *gui*, 13/6 A(35) Yih 897 885c 7(32) 4th*

22/17 Xiu *pan* 20/1 C(11) Yih 897 878z 1(55) 17th*

23/27 Mu *gui*, 7/13 B(51) Xiao 872 866h 12(39) 13th*

24/58 Shi Yu *gui*, 3/3 A(11) Yi 867 865z 3(08) 4th!

25/57 Shi Chen *ding*, 3/3 A(11) Yi 867 865z 3(08) 4th!

26/18 Shi Shi *gui* I, 1/4 B(51) Yi 865 865z 4(37) 15th*

27/21 Jian *gui*, 5/3 A(27) Yi 867 863z 3(26) 2nd! [r13]

28/59 Da *xu gai* 3/5 B(39) Yi 865 863z 5(25) 15th+

29/28 Xing *xu*, 4/2 B(35) Yi 865 862c 3(21) 15th*

30/60 San Ji *xu*, 4/8 A(24) Yi 865 862c 9(17)[18] 7th* [r13]

31/19 Shi Shi *gui* II, 5/9 B(19) Yi 865 861c 10(11) 9th* [r13]

32/61 Bo Shifu *ding*, 6/8 A(06) Yi 865 860y 10(05) 2nd*

33/20 Wang Chen *gui*, 2/3 A(27) Li 859 858c 4(27) 1st! [r13]

34/30 Ni *zhong*, 1/3 B(57) Li 857 857y 5(51)[50] 8th*

35/24 Shi Dui *gui* I, 1/5 A(51) Li 857 857y 7(50) 2nd*

36 Shi Fufu *xu*, 1/6 A(24) Li 857 857y 8(19) 6th*

37/48 Zheng Ji *xu* 1/6 A(24) Li 857 857y 8(19) 6th+

38/22 Shi Li *gui*, 11/9 A(24) Li 857 847c 10(20) 5th*

39/26 Da *gui*, 12/3 B(24) Li 857 846c 4(17) 8th*

40/37 Da *ding*, 15/3 D(24) Li 857 843y 5(59) 26th*

41/25 Shi Dui *gui* II, 3/2 A(24) Li 844 842c 3(25)[24] 1st!

42/47 Shi Hui *gui*, 1/1 A(24) Gong He 841 841y 3(19) 6th*

43/10 Wuji *gui*, 13/1 A(39) Gong He 841 829c 2(39) 1st!

44/33 Ke *xu*, 18/12 A(27) Li 844 827c 13(23) 5th!

45/34 Bo Ke *hu* 16/7 B(32) Gong He 841 826c 8(18) 15th!

46/43 Song *ding*, 3/5 D(11) Xuan 827 825z 5(45) 27th*

47/51 Xi Jia *pan*, 5/3 D(27) Xuan 827 823z 3(04) 24th*

48/52 Guoji Zibo *pan*, 12/1 A(24) Xuan 827 816z 1(25)[24] 1st*

49 Piji *gui* (13)/9 A(45) Xuan 827 815z 9(44) 2nd+

50/31 Ke *zhong*, 16/9 A(27) Xuan 827 812h 8(28)[27] 1st*

51/ Wu Hu *ding* 18/13 B(23) Xuan 827 810h 12(15) 9th+

52/40 Zou *ding*, 19/4 C(28) Xuan 827 809h 3(13) 16th*+

53/38 Ci *ding*, 17/12 B(52) Xuan 825 809hr 12(39)[38] 15th*

54/35 Bo Ju Sheng *hu*, 26/10 A(16) Xuan 825 800y 12(16) 1st*

55/49 Huan *pan*, 28/5 C(27) Xuan 825 798y 7(07) 21st*

56/46 Yi *gui*, 27[29]/1 C(24) Xuan 825 797y 3(4) 21st!

57/41 Ge You Cong *ding*, 32/3 A(29) Xuan 827 796y 5(26) 4th!

58/53 Jin Hou Su *zhong*,.33/1[12] B(55) Xuan 827 795h 12(47) 9th*+

59/50 Bo Kuifu *xu*, 33/8 D(28) Xuan 825 793y 10(07)[06] 23rd*

60/42 Shanfu Shan *ding*, 37/1 A(47) Xuan 825 789y 3(47) 1st*

61 Qiu *ding* I 42/5 B(52) Xuan 825 784c 6(46) 7th*+

62 Qiu *ding* II 43/6 B(24) Xuan 825 783c 7(10) 15th*+

63/56 Shi Hong *gui*, 1/2 C(27) You 783 783c 3(12) 16th!

64 Shi Mou *gui*, 1/9 C(24) You 783 783cr 11(08) 17th*

65/23 X *gui*, 2/1 A(24) You 781 780c 2(25)[24] 1st*

66/54 Zha *zhong*, 3/4 A(51) You 781 779c 5(48) 4th*

Notes on Inscription Dates:

(Nivison and Shaughnessy are in approximate agreement on Western Zhou chronology and on the meanings of lunar phase terms in inscriptions and in the *Shang shu*. They agree on the dates of these bronze texts in 80% of all cases. I dated many of these bronzes incorrectly in my first article on chronology in 1983.)

1. Xiao Yu *ding*: KB 12 (62) 682. The year 979 was a 13-month year, probably with the 10th month intercalary, making it intercalary 7th, if the civil year began with the *yin* month.[1] I assume that this month began with *jihai* (36) rather than with *gengzi* (37), so that the next month, counting as 8th and beginning with *jisi* (06) follows a long month, making *jiwang* day *jiashen* (21) the 16th. The initial day-date in the inscription is not legible, but it can be deduced from text near the end, saying that the next day was *yiyou* (22). (Compare with this Shaughnessy's careful analysis, Shaughnessy 1991 pp. 24-245, showing how this inscription supports the "2 *yuan*" hypothesis. The Three Dynasties Project avoids the Xiao Yu *ding*.)

2. Shi Ju *gui gai*: KB 19 (100) 304. The inscription has the king visiting the "new *gong* 宮" on the middle day of the middle month of spring. The date 954 is the accession date of Mu Wang, so he is done with mourning restraints. The year is designated "9th year" in the BA, counting from the incorrect *yuan* 962. The BA says "The Spring Palace was built." This confirms the date of the inscription, and also shows that BA dates in the Mu Wang chronicle must be counted from 962 rather than from 956 (or 954). For another demonstration of this point, see #6 Ban *gui*. (This is one important matter on which Shaughnessy and I do not agree. I have added the Ban *gui* for this reason, even though its date is incomplete.)

3. Geng Ying *ding*: KB 16 (80) 78. Others sometimes date this to Kang Wang. One would use his accession *yuan* 1003; the date implied, 982, seems early but may be possible.

4. Lu *gui*: Recently (ca. 2005) acquired by the Chinese National Museum. For text and analysis see Wang Guanying, "Lu *gui* Kaoshi," *Zhongguo Lishi Wenwu* 2006.3, pp. 4-6. Shaughnessy 2006 uses it, together with the Qiu Wei *gui*, the Hu *gui gai*, and the Xian *gui*, to confirm the *yuan* 956 for Mu Wang. (I am unsure of the pronunciation of the name rendered here "Lu." Others render it "Xian".)

5. Qiu Wei *gui*: *Wenwu* 1976.5 p. 27. Three other dated Qiu Wei vessels belong in the Gong Wang reign. The received incorrect reign length of 55 years for Mu Wang (instead of 39 years, 956-918) has led to misdating of all these bronzes; the natural assumption has been that Mu Wang and Gong Wang dates would separate the Qiu Wei *gui* by too many years from the others, which have low year numbers, 3, 5, and 9, hence must be in another reign. (The Three Dynasties Project never questions the traditional reign length of 55 years. The correct reign length of 2 + 37 years can be deduced from the "2 *yuan*" hypothesis together with the BA. The Project ignores both.)

6. Ban *gui*: Chen Mengjia, "Xi Zhou Tongqi Duandai" *Kaogu Xuebao* 9 (1955) p. 70. The date in the inscription does not include the year, but we can get it from the BA: it dates the expedition led by Mao Ban's son Mao Qian, described in the inscription, to the "35th year" and the "37th year" (a campaign to the southeast three years long). Counting from 962, one obtains the year 928 (Mu Wang 29) for the launching of the campaign, which is when the account in the inscription begins. This makes day *jiaxu* (11) the first of the 8th month; and the first of the month is appropriate for the beginning of such a campaign. (If one were to count from the correct *yuan* 956, as some would insist, one would get 922 as year 35. For month 8 one would have to assume a *chou* or a *hai* calendar (getting the 5th, 6th, or 7th); but the Mu Wang court seems to have been using a *zi* calendar at this time.)

---

[1] Whether intra-year intercalation was practiced prior to Chunqiu times is debated, but need not be. The system of 24 solar weather periods was a decision procedure for determining the need for an intercalary month short of the end of the year; and that system is older than Shang (though the present names for the periods may not be) -- see D. S. Nivison, "The Origin of the Chinese Lunar Lodge System," A. F. Aveni, ed., *World Archaeoastronomy* (Cambridge, England: Cambridge University Press, 1989) pp. 203-218. Intra-year intercalation was not always done, but the method was available; I have identified a number of instances in late Shang (pp. 232, 236, 245-247, 255-260).

7. Hu *gui gai*: *Kaogu yu Wenwu* 1997.3, pp. 78-79.

8. Xian *gui*: The preceding month is short, so the 24th is the last day of *jiwang*. This is the only Mu Wang bronze I know of dated on Mu Wang's accession *yuan* 954. In accord with Shaughnessy's amendment to the "2 *yuan*" hypothesis, the accession *yuan* comes into use only late in the reign.

9. Qiu Wei *he*: KB 49 (supplement 11) 256.

10. The 5th-year Qiu Wei *ding* names Gong Wang, probably as reigning king. (KB 49 (supplement 11) 262)

11. Qi Sheng Lu *yi gai*: Shaughnessy 1991 pp. 50-51 and 284; *Kaogu yu Wenwu* 1984.5.

12. 9th year Qiu Wei *ding*: KB 49 (supplement 11) 267

13. Zou *gui*: KB 21 (122) 520.

14. The 15th-year Que Cao *ding* names Gong Wang as reigning king. (KB 20 (107) 383)

15. Shi Hu *gui*: KB 19 (104) 353.

16. Hu *ding*: KB 23 (135) 113

17. Wu *fangyi*: KB 19 (105) 370

18. Yi *zhi*: KB 21 (114) 449

19. Xing *hu*: KB 50 (supplement 15) 383. The date 887 is probably wrong. In 1999 I dated it 815; in 1991 Shaughnessy dated it 903; in 2002 I dated it 845. There is a "San Nian Xing *hu*" with an incomplete date, which Shirakawa may have confused with this "Shisan Nian" vessel: his illustration of the "San Nian" (p. 385) appears to be the same as Zhu and Zhang #29 "Shisan Nian." There is a major disagreement between Shaughnessy and Lothar von Falkenhausen on the dating of the Wei Bo Xing vessels and the Shi Qiang *pan* by Xing's father. Shaughnessy with most of the field puts the Shi Qiang *pan* in the reign of Gong Wang, the last named king in its very long inscription being Mu Wang. Falkenhausen, however, argues that Xiao Wang, who was Gong Wang's brother, was not merely rescuing the dynasty from his less than competent nephew Yih Wang, but was actually challenging the legitimacy of Kong Wang, so that any text under Xiao Wang's aegis would not be able to mention Gong Wang or Yih Wang, and in using the word "wang" would be referring to Xiao Wang. To my own unpracticed eye these two *hu* do look like Xuan Wang era *hu*. For more on this puzzle, see L. von Falkenhausen's excellent book (2006, pp. 56-64) and Shaughnessy's careful review (2007, pp. 1129-1132).

20. Taishi Cuo *gui*: KB 22 (126) 38

21. Wang *gui*: KB 22 (129) 67

22. Xiu *pan*: KB 25 (146) 296

23. Mu *gui*: KB 19 (104) 361

24. Shi Yu *gui*: KB 22 (124) 9. Location Shi Lu Gong; the guarantor is Sima Gong; compare #25, 27, 29.

25. Shi Chen *ding*: KB 22 (125) 18. Location Shi Lu Gong; the guarantor is Sima Gong; compare #24, 27, 29.

26. Shi Shi *gui* I: KB 25 (140) 229. The 1st-year Shi Shi *gui* uses the accession calendar anachronistically, probably because it was made at the same time as the 3rd-year vessel. (I find it necessary to assume an

accession calendar for Yi Wang, even though it appears not to be reflected in the chronology of the *Bamboo Annals*. This must mean that Yi Wang's father Yih Wang actually lived until 868, although exiled to Huaili (I assume) by his uncle Pifang = Xiao Wang (my dates for Xiao: 872-868).

27. Jian *gui*: KB 22 (127) 55. Location, Shi Lu Gong. The guarantor is Sima Gong; compare #24, 25, 29.

28. Da *xu gai*: *Wenwu* 1990.7, p. 33

29. Xing *xu*: KB 50 (supplement 15) 379. Location Shi Lu Gong. The guarantor is Sima Gong and the recorder is Shi Nian; compare #24, 25, 27.

30. San Ji *xu*: KB 48 (supplement 4) 201. "San" vessels with the same date: San Bo Jufu *ding*; San Ji *gui*. (Ferguson 589a)

31. Shi Shi *gui* II: KB 25 (141) 236

32. Bo Shifu *ding* or Shi Bo Shifu *ding*: (Ferguson 894b) Hand copy only; see Zhu and Zhang #61.

33. Wang chen *gui*: *Wenwu* 1980.5, 63-66. Shaughnessy dates this to 898, but is forced to make the day the 9th, in my view not acceptable for A (*chuji*). (He does not allow a mourning period after Yi Wang. His date 898 for the Wang Chen *gui* assumes the year began with the *zi* month; but his dating the Wu *fangyi* to 898 assumes the year began with the *chou* month.)

34. Ni *zhong*: *Kaogu yu Wenwu* 1981.1

35. Shi Dui *gui* I: KB 31 (187) 751

36. Shu Fufu *xu*: KB 29 (174) 562

37. Zheng Ji *xu*: *Mingwen xuan* 402; *Kaogu* 1965.9 Plate 2

38. Shi Li *gui*: KB 31 (189) 767

39. Da *gui*: KB 29 (175) 571

40. Da *ding*: KB 29 (176) 584

41. Shi Dui *gui* II: The 3rd-year Shi Dui *gui* and the 1st-year Shi Dui *gui* use different calendars, yet they must be in the same reign, because in the 3rd-year inscription the king quotes his own order in the 1st-year inscription. This is a problem that has puzzled everyone. The accession calendar hypothesis does not solve the problem. The only other possibility is a coming-of-age calendar, starting in 844. Li Wang was born in 864. The *Annals* (in-text note) date of his birth, Xiao 7, must be counted from the *Annals* date for Xiao 1, and not from the true date for Xiao 1, *contra* Shaughnessy, *Sources* p. 283; 864 as birth-date makes Li Wang's life 37 years, explaining the mistaken idea (*Shiji*, "Zhou Benji") that his pre-exile reign was 37 years.

42. Shi Hui *gui*: KB 31 (186) 740

43. Wuji *gui*: KB 22 (128) 62. The pure *wa-wen* style of this *gui* can be as early as Mu Wang, and some doubt that it can be as late as this. But Wuji appears to be a first cousin of Shanfu Ke (both dedicate vessels to "Grandfather Li Ji"; see the Xiao Ke *ding*, with a 23rd year date). Possibly Wuji is the Wuji who became Duke Li of Qi (824-816). The ornateness of the Ke vessels shows that Ke was very wealthy.

44. Ke *xu*: Dating this bronze is a problem that has vexed me and others. I take the Ke to be Bo Ke in the Bo Ke *hu*. Here Ke formally acknowledges (to the "*tianzi*," i.e., to legal authority; the just deceased Li Wang is implied by use of 844 as *yuan*) the duly registered receipt of a band of servants (or slaves). This

I assume is a gift from Gong He (see next), who is, I assume, in the process of closing down his capital residence, about to retire to his domain in Wei. KB 28 (166) 485.

45. Bo Ke *hu*: The text, acknowledging a gift of servants (I assume these are the subject of the Ke *xu* inscription), shows that Gong He is still respected as head of state, even though the year must be 826, the year after Xuan Wang's *de jure* succession. (The maker, Bo Ke, expresses his gratitude for "the friendship of *Tian you wang bo*" 天佑王伯, i.e., "the lord functioning as king, assisted by Heaven.") It is not surprising that Gong He had not completely withdrawn; Xuan Wang was almost certainly still a minor, with his father's protectors in the Fen valley, who would be moving slowly and carefully. KB 28 (170) 525.

46. Song *ding*: other "Song" bronzes with this date: Song *hu*; Song *gui*. KB 24 (137) 165

47. Xi Jia *pan*: KB 32 (191) 785

48. Guoji Zibo *pan*: KB 32 (193) 800

49. Piji *gui*: The year is not given, but Ma Chengyuan has convincingly argued that the military action is the same one in which Guoji Zibo figures, but later, in the next year (Shaughnessy 2003, citing Ma Chengyuan, *Shang-Zhou qingtongqi mingwen xuan* (1988) p. 310 note 1).

50. Ke *zhong*: KB 28 (171) 531

51. Wu Hu *ding*: See Zhu and Zhang p, 512.

52. X *ding*: *Mingwen xuan* 423.

53. Ci *ding*: Another "Ci" vessel, the Ci *gui*, has the same date. There was a mid-year change of *yuan* from 827 to 825 in 809 (perhaps marking completion of mourning for Gong He); so an intercalation (converting the year to a *zi* year) between month 3 (= 4) for the X *ding*, and month 12, for the Ci *ding*, is not surprising. KB 49 (supplement 11) 280.

54. Bo Ju Sheng *hu*: KB 27 (159) 417.

55. Huan *pan*: KB 29 (177) 590.

56. Yi *gui*: KB 28 (169) 520. The year date "*ershi qi*" (27) appears to have been corrected after firing to "*ershi jiu*" (29).

57. Ge You Cong *ding* (cauldron of Ge, Squire of You): KB 29 (180) 627. You 攸 was a small statelet southwest of Lu. The calendar used for the year is the Xuan Wang succession calendar rather than the Zhou court's accession calendar. The year date in the text is uncertain, however, and perhaps should be read "31st year" (= 797). If so, then the solution may be like that for the Jin Hou Su *bianzhong*: You "3rd month" of 796 = Zhou 12th month of 797: 797.1 = (28), (29) = 2nd.

58. Jin Hou Su *bianzhong*: The calendar used for the year is the Xuan Wang succession calendar counting from 827, because this is a bronze from a regional state. The Zhou court at this time apparently was using a calendar beginning the year with the *yin* month; but Jin, I assume, had a calendar beginning the year earlier, with the *hai* month. The result is that the Jin "1st month" in the year approximately corresponding to 794 is the Zhou "10th month" in its year approximately corresponding to 795 (hence the date is still in the Zhou "33rd year"); the month would be the 12th (pre-solstice), in a *zi* calendar. (Jaehoon Shim, "The Jin Hou Su *bianzhong* Inscription and Its Significance," *Early China* 22 (1997) pp. 43-75.)

59. Bo Kuifu *xu*: *Wenwu* 1979.11, pp. 16-20. The day, "23rd," ought to be *jiwang* and not *jisipo*. The use may be carelessly irregular (*jisipo* is written merely "*jisi*.") Properly the day should be gengwu (07), but the syzygy was at 00.21, so jisi (06) is a reasonable correction. The brief text doesn't indicate any court business.

60. Shanfu Shan *ding*: KB 26 (154) 357.

61. Qiu *ding* I: (Xia Hanyi 2003.5) "Qiu" perhaps should be "Lai."

62. Qiu *ding* II: (Xia Hanyi 2003.5) "Qiu" perhaps should be "Lai."

63. Shi Hong 訇 *gui* or Shi Xun 旬 (= 詢) *gui*: KB 31 (183) 710. For the dating, see D. S. Nivison, "The Authenticity of the Mao Gung *ting* Inscription," in F. David Bulbeck and Noel Barnard, editors, *Ancient Chinese and Southeast Asian Bronze Age Cultures* (Taipei: SMC Publishing, Inc., 1996-7) pp. 311-341. DSN admits uncertainty: Others would put this inscription in the reign of Gong Wang: the year would have to be 917, assuming a *zi* calendar, first day of month 2 being *guiyu* (10), making the date the 18th. But throughout most of Gong Wang's reign a *chou* calendar was being used; and the language in the inscription is almost the same as in the Mao Gong *ding*, which must be late Western Zhou. (One would even be tempted to guess that the two were written or edited by the same court scribe.) On the other hand, the date 783 requires supposing that Xuan Wang had a reign of only 2 + 42 years rather than 46 years as given by tradition. And also required is supposing that the 43rd year Qiu *ding* (Qiu *ding* II above) though having a Xuan Wang date is actually dated in the mourning period for Xuan Wang. This would be so interesting that the possibility ought not to be brushed aside yet.

64. Shi Mou *gui*: KB 26 (152) 344.

65. X *gui*: KB 31 (185) 733.

66. Zha *zhong*: KB 33 (198) 898.

01 小盂鼎	23 牧簋	45 伯克壺
02 師遽簋蓋	24 師艅簋	46 頌鼎
03 庚嬴鼎	25 師晨鼎	47 兮甲盤
04 親簋	26 師旋簋 (I)	48 虢季子伯盤
05 裘衛簋	27 諫簋	49 不基簋
06 班簋	28 达盨蓋	50 克鍾
07 虎簋蓋	29 㾜盨	51 吳虎鼎
08 鮮簋	30 散季盨	52 䞈鼎
09 裘衛盉	31 師旋簋 (II)	53 此鼎
10 裘衛鼎 I	32 史伯碩父鼎	54 番匊生壺
11 齊生魯方彝蓋	33 王臣簋	55 寰盤
12 裘衛鼎 II	34 逆鍾	56 伊簋
13 走簋	35 師兌簋 (I)	57 鬲攸從鼎
14 趞曹鼎 II	36 叔專父	58 晉侯蘇編鍾
15 師虎簋	37 鄭季盨	59 伯窺父盨
16 曶鼎	38 師嫠簋	60 善夫山鼎
17 吳方彝	39 大簋	61 逑鼎 (I)
18 趩觶	40 大鼎	62 逑鼎 (II)
19 㾜壺	41 師兌簋 (II)	63 師訇簋
20 大師虘簋	42 師獸簋	64 師類簋
21 望簋	43 無㠱簋	65 鄸簋
22 休盤	44 克盨	66 柞鍾

Inscribed Objects in Appendix 4 Supplement 1:

Biji *you* #1 (2nd year), #2 (4th year), #3 (6th year) 𠨘其卣

Hu shang bo gu 虎上膊骨

Xiaochen Yi *jia* 小臣邑斝

Sui Cha *you* 巂臿卣

Shu Ling *yi* 戍鈴彝

Zai Hu *jiao* 宰 椃 角

Si *yi* 肆彝

Qin Zi *fang ding* 寢孳方鼎

Fan (?) *fang ding* 瓶方鼎

Appendix 4

The Late Shang Ritual Cycle: The Yi Fang Campaign Inscriptions (and What They Imply)

The date 1086 as first year for Di Xin can be deduced from the *Bamboo Annals* (which has the date 1102) and data from the *Guoyu*. But independently of this, the late Shang Yi Fang campaign inscriptions make the date 1086 indisputable. The *Bamboo Annals* is wrong, however, in giving Di Yi only nine years (1111-1103) instead of nineteen (1105-1087); and wrong again in giving Wen Ding (Wenwu Ding) thirteen years (1124-1112) instead of three years (1108-1106). Wenwu Ding's first ten years were nominal only, being actually the last ten years (1118-1109) of Wu Yi's 2+35 years (1145/43-1109).

Late Shang ritual inscriptions are necessary for ascertaining these dates. The oracle bone inscriptions for the Yi Fang campaign make it possible to assign absolute dates to events in the late Shang ritual cycle, as worked out by Dong Zuobin and Shima Kunio. Others who have done interesting and important work include Chen Mengjia, Xu Jinxiong, Chang Yuzhi, Xu Fengxian and Li Xueqin. This ritual cycle was a schedule for five rituals for all of the deceased Shang kings. It consisted of three series, taken together normally of 36 *xun* (earlier, sometimes only 35), often 37. The cycle averaged less than a solar year, so over time the first day of the cycle became earlier and earlier. I try to find how it worked over sixty-six years, from 1111 to 1046.

There are bronze inscriptions as well as bone inscriptions for this time. In Supplement 1 I try to work out the absolute dates of these inscriptions important for my argument.

The Yi Fang inscriptions also allow a recovery of the *zhang* intercalation cycle for the first 20 years of Di Xin's reign. Projecting this back through time, one can confirm key dates, including 1189 as death date for the 22nd Shang king Wu Ding. This I do in Supplement 2. (The Project's date is 1192.)

A late Shang chronology different from mine has been worked out by Li Xueqin and Xu Fengxian, and adopted by the Xia-Shang-Zhou Chronology Project. In Supplement 3 I will examine this system, explaining a mistake (by Shima Kunio) on which it is based. I add my construction of the cycle for Di Xin 1 through 12.

1. The sacrificial year (*si*) can be described as ideally 36 *xun* (10-day periods) alternating with 37 *xun* years. A typical inscription was made on the last day (*gui* day) of a *xun*, announcing the sacrifice(s) for the next day. Therefore it is convenient to key the system to *jia* kings (the *gan* name determined the sacrifice day in a 10-day *xun*). There were five sacrifices: *ji*, *zai* and *xie*, in successive *xun* for all kings, in the first third of the sacrificial year; *yong*, in the second third, and *yi*, in the last third. In a normal 36-*xun* sacrificial year, the *ji* series had 13 *xun*, so that the final *xie* rite for Zu Jia occurred in the *xun* before the *yong* series began. Each of the three series began with a common ceremonial (*gongdian*) for all recipients of sacrifice. To make a 37-*xun* cycle-year, one *xun* would be inserted after a *gongdian*, or added at the end of the *yi* series. To make a 35-*xun* cycle probably the last *xun* of the *yong* series would be dropped. The entire *jia* schedule can be reconstructed from charts at pp. 57, 59 and 60 of Shima, *Kenkyu*; and the entire schedule of primary sacrifice days (*ji*, *yong*, *yi*) for all kings and consorts in any third of the year is given in a diagram, p. 101 (also p. 534) in Shima, *Kenkyu,* adapted below. There is disagreement as to which series, *ji*, *yong*, or *yi*, was conceived as starting the ritual year, Shima (whom I follow, not with confidence) taking it to be the *ji* series (see Chang 1987, pp. 186-91). But the most important seems to be the last in a sequence: the *xie* in the *ji* series *ji*, *zai*, *xie*; and the *yi* in the main cycle, *ji-zai-xie*, *yong*, *yi*. Xu Fengxian (pp. 28-29) takes the yi series as first, beginning in the 4th month, sometimes the 3rd or 5th.

The important question not yet settled is how to map this schema out on correct absolute dates over so-called Period Five of the shell and bone inscriptions. One must do this if one is to obtain chronological information from this material. It is this that I attempt to do here. There are two competing systems. One is that of Li Xueqin (1999, based on work by Xu Fengxian), adopted by the Three Dynasties Project (2000), and presented (slightly modified) in a recent book (2006) by Xu Fengxian. The other is mine, first published in 1999, based on work by E. Shaughnessy, D. Pankenier and me in 1982, but apparently ignored in China. The essential difference is the date assigned to the inscriptions for the Yi Fang campaign.

1.1 Below is Shima's full description of the ritual cycle, based on analysis of hundreds of *gui*-day inscriptions. (It was the practice on the last day of a *xun*, i.e., *gui*-day, for the king to ritually "clear the air" by performing a divination rite assuring that no misfortune would occur during the next *xun*, at the same time stating what rites were scheduled for the next day, which was of course a *jia*-day.) First, I give a table of the schedule for each series, for all kings before Di Yi, with consorts.

In adapting Shima Kunio's work, I have coded consorts' names: the name is *bi* plus the *gan* of the column she is in, preceded by the column letter and row number of her king. E.g., 'I2' in column G = *geng* column, row 3, means "Shi Ren Bi Geng," Shi Ren being the king in column I (= *ren*) row 2. Her rites are on *geng*-day in the third *xun* of each series. In the *ji* series, however, consorts apparently did not receive a *ji* ritual but did receive *zai* and *xie* rites.

J gui	I ren	H xin	G geng	F ji	E wu	D ding	C bing	B yi	A Jia	Day / *xun*
									Gong dian	1
Shi Gui	Shi Ren					Bao Ding	Bao Bing	Bao Yi	Shang Jia	2
			I2			Da Ding		Da Yi		3
	G4	A4	Da Geng		D3		B3 Bu Bing		J2 Da Jia	4
	E5			Yong Ji	Da Wu				Xiao Jia	5
D6	Bu Ren			D6		Zhong Ding				6
	H7	Zu Xin		B7				Zu Yi	Qian Jia	7
			H7 Nan D8 Geng	D8		Zu Ding			H7 Wo Jia	8
		Xiao Xin	Pan Geng						D8 Yang Jia	9
D10		D10	B10 Zu Geng	B10 Zu Ji		Wu Ding		Xiao Yi		10
		D11			D10 A11	Kang Ding			Zu Jia	11
D12					B12	Wenwu Ding		Wu Yi		12

Last day of a *xun* = ritual cycle *xun* number + zero; the above is the order in any 12-*xun* set, *ji, yong,* or *yi*.

1.2. For the sacrificial schedule for Jia kings, and the way *ji*, *zai* and *xie* sacrifices were compounded in late Shang, see Shima, *Kenkyu*, pp. 56-61. (Names of kings are here the ones encountered in inscriptions; Qian Jia = Hedan Jia; Qiang Jia = Wo Jia = Kai Jia; Xiang Jia = Yang Jia.)

Xun 1	*ji gongdian*		
Xun 2	*Ji* Shang Jia		
Xun 3		*Zai* Shang Jia	
Xun 4	*Ji* Da Jia		*Xie* Shang Jia
Xun 5	*Ji* Xiao Jia	*Zai* Da Jia	
Xun 6		*Zai* Xiao Jia	*Xie* Da Jia
Xun 7	*Ji* Qian Jia		*Xie* Xiao Jia
Xun 8	*Ji* Qiang Jia (= Wo Jia)	*Zai* Qian Jia	
Xun 9	*Ji* Xiang Jia (= Yang Jia)	*Zai* Qiang Jia	*Xie* Qian Jia
Xun 10		*Zai* Xiang Jia	*Xie* Qiang Jia
Xun 11	*Ji* Zu Jia		*Xie* Xiang Jia
Xun 12		*Zai* Zu Jia	
Xun 13			*Xie* Zu Jia
Xun 14	*yong gongdian*		
Xun 15	*Yong* Shang Jia		
Xun 16			
Xun 17	*Yong* Da Jia		

Xun 18	*Yong* Xiao Jia
Xun 19	
Xun 20	*Yong* Qian Jia
Xun 21	*Yong* Qiang Jia
Xun 22	*Yong* Xiang Jia
Xun 23	
Xun 24	*Yong* Zu Jia
Xun 25	
Xun 26	*yi gongdian*
Xun 27	*Yi* Shang Jia
Xun 28	
Xun 29	*Yi* Da Jia
Xun 30	*Yi* Xiao Jia
Xun 31	
Xun 32	*Yi* Qian Jia
Xun 33	*Yi* Qiang Jia
Xun 34	*Yi* Xiang Jia
Xun 35	
Xun 36	*Yi* Zu Jia

Cycles of 35 *xun* must often have been used in times earlier than considered here. (There is one instance in 1080-79.) Cycles of 37 *xun* were needed to alternate with 36 *xun* cycles to average 365 days per year, but this was not always done, e.g., between 1093 and 1077, so that during this time the first day of the cycle moved back from late November to early September. I believe that Di Yi began a calendar for his heir (who became Di Xin) in 1086, and died a few years later, probably in 1082. His successor Zhou Xin (Shou) then revised the calendar, moving the first month from the *hai* month to the *chou* month (where it had been under Wu Yi) by adding two months at the end of the year, and after the end of mourning he resumed the practice of alternating 36 and 37 *xun* cycles (see section 8) until the cycle first day moved from *jiaxu* (11) to *jiazi* (01), whereupon (in 1068) he began a new calendar, declaring himself "Di Xin," and probably naming his heir Lu Fu "junior king" (*xiao wang*)[1], to be known as Wu Geng. (The year 1068 began with a *geng* day.) The resulting *jian chou* calendar may have lasted to the end of Shang. It has always been thought to have been the standard Shang calendar.

I hesitate to venture descriptions of these rites (or sacrifices). Some, perhaps all, must have been public events; e.g., a date in an inscription can sometimes be given as (or include) "*yong* 肜-day," "*yi* 翌-day," or "*xie* 劦-5day," apparently without need for further identification. There is some evidence that some or all of them involved robed public processions, perhaps like the frequent *matsuri* in Kyoto. (There are divinations revealing anxiety about rain that might disrupt such an event and spoil the robes.) An example is part of the long inscription (see section 6) that begins the campaign against the Yu Fang (*Jia-bian* 2416; Shima, *Sorui*, 518.4): "Let it be on [this] day of the robed *yi* rite that we march forth." (*hui yi yi ri bu* 惠衣翌日步). All I can claim to know are the names, and the standard sequence.

2. First I will give my own analysis. One must begin with a set of related inscriptions supplying enough detail to identify the year, the reign, and for at least one inscription recording a sacrifice the year, month and day within the reign. Probably the only such set is the set of over seventy to over 100 inscriptions (depending on what one includes) that record the daily progress of the eastern campaign against the Yi Fang (or Ren Fang) centered in the Huai valley area, in years 10-11 of a king who must be Di Xin. (A convenient list is given in Chen Mengjia 1956 pp. 301-304.). One of these inscriptions is dated 10th year 12th month day *jiawu* (31); the next is dated 1st month [*ding*]*you* (34). Thus they require that year 10 ended with either *jiawu* (31), *yiwei* (32) or *bingshen* (33). There are also two which are dated 10th year 9th month *jiawu* (31) and 9th month *guihai* (60). Taken together, these imply that year 10 contained an intercalary 9th month, if one

[1] Wu Ding's originally designated heir Zu Ji received cult as "*xiao wang* Fu Ji" in the reign of Kang Ding (Shima *Sorui* p. 549c, *Nan Ming* 631). The myth, repeated in the *Bamboo Annals*, that Wu Ding disowned his eldest son is due to an ancient misunderstanding of *Shang shu* chapter 18 "Gao Zong Yong Ri" as "the day of the *yong* by Gao Zong" rather than "the day of the *yong* for Gao Zong" (Nivison, "The King and the Bird," unpublished paper for AAS, 1984).

assumes a regular alternation of long and short months:

12th month: (02) – (31), (03) – (32), or (04) – (33)
11th month: (33) – (01), (34) – (02), or (35) – (03)
10th month: (03) – (32), (04) – (33), or (05) – (34)
9th month: (34) – (02), (35) – (03), or (36) – (04): Must contain (60); does not contain (31)
9th month: (04) – (33), (05) – (34), or (06) – (35): Must contain (31); does not contain (60)

One can see from this that the second-up 9th month above, containing *guihai* (60), must be intercalary 9th month. Dong Zuobin and Chen Mengjia agree, presumably through the same simple reasoning.

2.1 The only such year in late Shang is 1077 BCE, interpreted as taking the winter solstice month as last month, which ended with day *yiwei* (32), i.e. the middle choice above. That the year must have an intercalary 9th month is seen clearly from the inscriptions (data from Chen Mengjia 1956 pp. 301-302) that name the year, together with intervening inscriptions where the year is implied but not stated; here, month lengths assume the year is 1077 BCE, as in Zhang Peiyu (1987).

Year	Month	Day	Month length	
10	9	*jiawu* (31)	05-34 (30 days)	(*zai* for Shang Jia)
	9	*guihai* (60)	35-03 (29 days)	(intercalary)
	10	*guiyou* (10)	04-33 (30 days)	
10	10	*jiawu* (31)		
	11	*guimao* (40)	34-02 (29 days)	
	11	*guichou* (50)		
	11	*guihai* (60)		
	12	*jisi* (06)	03-32 (30 days)	
	12	*guiyou* (10)		
	12	*guiwei* (20)		
	12	*guisi* (30)		
10	12	*jiawu* (31)		(*yong* [for Shang Jia])
[11]	01	[*ding*]*you*(34)	33-01 (29 days)	

The autumn equinox day, 2 Oct, JD 132 8324, was day *dingyou* (34), *qi*-center at the end of the first "9th" lunar month; therefore the next lunar month that I call "9th," of 29 days, contained no *qi*-center, and must be intercalary, if the rule stated in later literature is applied (and in this material it gives consistent results).[2]

2.2 This is a powerful result. The Chinese of this time assumed that the seasons are equal in number of days, dividing the solar year by four, to the nearest whole number. It seems that they determined the dates of the solstices and equinoxes (midpoints of the seasons), together with the dates of all other *qi*-center days, by counting not from the winter solstice (the formal concept), but from the autumn equinox. This must be so, because the interval from the autumn equinox to the true winter solstice is not an expected 91 days but only 89 or 88 days; so if they had counted from the true winter solstice they would have gotten the autumn equinox two or three days *early*; but here they got it exactly right. It follows that whenever we have a date problem where the winter solstice date must be assumed, we must take the recognized solstice to be a day which is two or three days *late*. This can be of crucial importance in determining late Shang and early Zhou absolute dates, including notably the date (1040) of the Zhou conquest, as I showed in Chapter One.[3]

---

[2] A *qi*-center is the middle day of a solar month (twelfth of the solar year, 30 or 31 days); the recognized solstice and equinox days are *qi*-centers. (This concept is not astronomically exact, as I explain in 2.2.)

[3] If the 24 *qi*-periods are set by counting days from the autumn equinox (even if formally from the assumed winter solstice), then the Muye victory day *jiazi* of (*jian yin*) month 2 in 1040 is Qing Ming Day, as in *Shi*, "Da Ming." This is why the Li *gui* says "in the cauldron rite for the year (*sui ding*) we were able to inform [the royal ancestors] that we had vanquished the Shang" (*ke wen su you Shang*). Qing Ming day was the primary day for veneration of ancestors, therefore the appropriate day for the king's diviner to report his victory to his predecessors.

2.3 Very different are the conclusions of Prof. Li Xueqin (1999) and the Three Dynasties Project (2000), recently (2006) defended in part by Xu Fengxian. In an article in his *Zhaji* (1999, pp. 245-250) Prof. Li picks the year 1066, so that Di Xin 1 becomes 1075 (the Three Dynasties Project's date), and argues that the *ganzhi* day count in months 9 through 12 in 1066 has been set aside temporarily for (military) convenience, using instead a so-called "*yi jia shi gui*" system, taking each month as beginning with a *jia* day and containing exactly three ten-day *xun*. Prof. Li also proposes that the year-end inscription dated "10th year 12th month *jiawu* (31), *yong*" (for Shang Jia) must be a mistake, the correct date being 11th year 1st month. (This is required by the "*yi jia shi gui*" scheme.) Thus he is not forced to find a year ending with *jiawu* (31), *yiwei* (32), or *bingshen* (33), which would have eliminated 1066 and forced the choice of 1077. Xu Fengxian has wisely doubted the "*yi jia shi gui*" idea, but retains the year 1066. Xu also assumes that the opening inscription dated *zai* for Shang Jia on *jiawu* (31) in the 9th month is an error, the month really being the 8th. I will deal with this theory more fully in Supplement 3.

2.4 Intra-year intercalation is not a problem. The Chinese were already before the Shang Dynasty using a division of the year into equal 24ths (Nivison 1989). This can only be to provide a basis for the *qi*-center scheme for tracking the moon, so as to decide when to plug in an extra lunar month as needed at any time of year. It is a mistake to assume (as most scholars do) that a "13th month" must imply that intra-year intercalation was not being done. The Chinese added a "13th month" (or sometimes inserted an extra 6th month) to mend or alter the calendar. They used the *qi*-center rule otherwise. (Sometimes they used both methods of intercalation at once; for examples, see Supplement 2 below.)

3. The inscription recording the launching of the Yi Fang campaign is *HJ* 36482, dated "day *jiawu* (31) ... 9th month, coincident with the *zai* sacrifice to Shang Jia, in the 10th *si* (year)." These inscriptions confirm the reconstruction (e.g., in Shima, *Kenkyu*) of the ritual cycle: the interval from Shang Jia *zai* to Shang Jia *yong* is exactly 12 *xun*, as it should be. Further, since we know the absolute date of the autumn equinox in this year, the data determine the date of the inscription to be 29 September 1077 BCE, JD 132 8321, and imply that the ritual cycle in this year began (with the first, i.e., *gongdian* 工典 sacrifice of the *ji* 祭 series) on 9 September, JD 132 8301, a *jiaxu* (11) day.

3.1 Thus year one in this royal calendar is 1086 BCE. This is just what I expected. As I have explained (e.g., in Chapter Nine), if the date of the Zhou conquest of Shang is 1040, and was later thought to be 1045, that rethinking implied that the last year of Di Xin could not be 1041. I think that the solution must have been to reason that the last year of Shang must really have been the year preceding the first year of Zhou in the *de jure* (or *zheng tong*) sense, the first year of the Mandate calendar, 1056. Making 1057 be the year that 1041 had been for Di Xin meant moving the reign back 16 years. But the date we now find in the BA for Di Xin 1 is 1102. So to find the true Di Xin 1 we must count down 16 years from 1102, and this is 1086. This should be no surprise: once the fief year of Tangshu Yu was set at 1035, exactly 700 years before Wei Huicheng Wang declared himself king in 335, then if one continues to suppose (with the *Guoyu*) that his fief year was a year when Jupiter was in Da Huo, Station 10, and supposes (again with the *Guoyu*) that the conquest year was a year when Jupiter was in Chun Huo, Station 7, one can again deduce, quite independently, that Di Xin 1 must have been set back 16 years, so that the true year must be 1086. (See Chapter Nine, 3.1 and 3.2. The actual conjunction year 1059 (2x12 before 1035), Jupiter station 6, becomes station 10, so the station 6 year goes back 4; but if Wen Wang died 9 years after the conjunction (*Yi Zhou shu* "Wen chuan"), he would be dying in the conquest year; therefore the conjunction year had to be moved back one 12-year Jupiter cycle to 1071, as in the *Bamboo Annals*; the total back-shift is 16.)

There is yet another independent confirmation that 1086 is right. The *Shiji* tells us something quite unbelievable: that in the very same year when the Shang king released Wen Wang from seven years' detention in Youli, he gave Wen Wang the authority to undertake punitive military campaigns at his own discretion. The year claimed to be when Zhou received this authority was the year after the conjunction changing the Mandate, i.e., 1058, which I (counting from 1086) must call Di Xin 29. But for the *Annals*, Di Xin 29 is the year when Wen was released from Youli. This is probably the source of the *Shiji* authors' confusion: probably both of these bits of data were still available in Western Han.

And perhaps one more semi-proof: The end-of-Shang summary in the *Annals* says that from Tang's destruction of Xia to Shou (i.e., Di Xin), 29 kings, took up 496 years. But in the *Annals* there are 30 Shang kings, not 29. The text must originally have had the word *nian*, year, instead of *wang*, king. Then it would read, from Tang's destruction of Xia until the 29th year of Shou was 496 years. This is exactly right, if the first year of Di Xin was 1086. The "29th year of Shou" counting from 1086 is 1058, the Zhou "Mandate" year, which (as Pankenier has shown) was exactly 496 years after the beginning of Shang in 1554.

3.2 There is, however, a lot of literature on this matter, and most scholars (other than perhaps Shaughnessy) would not support me. Consider Xu Fengxian: She has a table, year after year, and the first ten years of Di Xin are assumed to be 1075-1066 (pp. 162-172). And she has a list (pp. 85-86; no table, because she has no exact dates) of inscriptions dated years 2 through 10, which she assigns to Di Yi, because they don't fit into her dates for Di Xin. (In seeing these as belonging to one reign, she follows *Heji* in part.) She has found much more material than I had, and I use it gratefully. Working out my own contrasting analysis has taught me much. I have deduced the data in columns 3 through 8:

1: Year / lunar month	2: Day (*ganzhi*) and Rite	3: Rite, Cycle Day	4: Cycle 1st day+ month	5: Year 1st month	6: Julian Day of rite	7: Date of rite (lunar)	8: Date of rite (Julian)
2/4 [4]	(21) *yong* Shang Jia	141	(01) 11	*hai*	132 5051	2.4.27	3 Mar 1085
3/6 [5]	(31) *yong* Qiang Jia	201	(11) 11	*hai*	132 5621	3.6.14	9 May 1084
3/6	(41) *yong* Yang Jia	211	(11) 11	*hai*	132 5631	3.6.24	19 Mar 1084
3/7	(01) *yong* Zu Jia	231	(11) 11	*hai*	132 5651	3.7.15	8 Je 1084
3/8	(21) *yi* gongdian	251	(11) 11	*hai*	132 5671	3.8.5	28 Je 1084
3/8	(31) *yi* Shang Jia	261	(11) 11	*hai*	132 5681	3.8.15	8 Jy 1084
3/11 [6]	(11) *ji gongdian*	001	(11) 11	*hai*	132 5781	3.11.26	16 Oct 1084
3/12	(21) ji Shang Jia	011	(11) 11	*hai*	132 5791	3.12.7	26 Oct 1084
3/12	(31) zai Shang Jia	021	(11) 11	*hai*	132 5801	3.12.17	5 Nov 1084
3/12	(41) *ji* Da Jia						
	zai Shang Jia	031	(11) 11	*hai*	132 5811	3.12.27	15 Nov 1084
4/1	(51) *ji* Xiao Jia						
	zai Da Jia	041	(11) 11	*hai*	132 5821	4.1.7	25 Nov 1084
4/7 [7]	(51) *yong* Yang Jia	211	(21) 1	*zi*	131 9101	4.7.21	3 Jy 1102
4/[4] [8]	(31) *yong* Shang Jia	141	(11) 11	*hai*	132 5921	4.4.19	5 Mar 1083
5/9 [9]	(41) *yi* Shang Jia	261	(21) 1	*zi*	131 9511	5.9.17	16 Aug 1101
6?/12 [10]	(21) *yi* Zu Jia	351	(31) 1	*hai*	132 0691	8.12.16	9 Nov 1098
7/5 [11]	(21) *zai* Zu Jia	111	(31) 1	*hai*	132 0091	7.5.6	18 Mar 1099
7/5	(31) *xie* Zu Jia	121	(31) 1	*hai*	132 0101	7.5.16	28 Mar 1099
7/5	(41) *yong gongdian*	131	(31) 1	*hai*	132 0111	7.5.26	7 Apr 1099
7/6	(51) *yong* Shang Jia	141	(31) 1	*hai*	132 0121	7.6.6	17 Apr 1099
8/2 [12]	(11) *ji* Xiao Jia						

[4] *HJ* 37836. This confirms my guess that the cycle beginning 17 Oct 1086 had 37 *xun*.

[5] *HJ* 35756 and *HJ* 37838 (includes 3.6 though 3.8).

[6] *HJ* 37840 and *HJ* 35529 (includes 3.11 through 4.1).

[7] *HJ* 37839; reign of Di Yi, not Di Xin.

[8] *HJ* 37841

[9] *HJ* 37844; this inscription (Di Yi) has required me to amend my chronology (Nivison 1999 and 2002), changing the cycle 1st day from *jiaxu* (11) to *jiashen* (21). This cycle must have 36 *xun* rather than 37, and the preceding cycle must have 37 *xun* rather than 36; also, since year 4 is a *jian zi* year, and year 5 is also a *jian zi* year, the intercalation due in the middle of year 5 must have been omitted.

[10] *HJ* 37845; all that remains of the year number is a down-stroke to the right which could be part of a 6 or part of an 8. The data fit Yi Wang 8 but no possible year 6.

[11] *HJ* 35422 etc

[12] *Ying* 2503 etc. I analyze this set of inscriptions below. "2nd month" dates the act of divining, not the scheduled rite, which was on the next day (first day of the following month, as in column 7).

	zai Da Jia	041	(31) 1	*hai*	132 0381	8.3.1	3 Jan 1098
8/3	(21) *zai* Xiao Jia						
	xie Da Jia	051	(31) 1	*hai*	132 0391	8.3.11	13 Jan 1098
8/3	(31) *ji* Qian Jia						
	xie Xiao Jia	061	(31) 1	*hai*	132 0401	8.3.21	23 Jan 1098
8/3	(41) *ji* Qiang Jia						
	zai Qian Jia	071	(31) 1	*hai*	132 0411	8.i3.1	3 Feb 1098
8/3	(51) *ji* Yang Jia						
	zai Qiang Jia						
	xie Qian Jia	081	(31) 1	*hai*	132 0421	8.i3.11	12 Feb 1098
8/4? [13]	(01) *zai Yang Jia*						
	xie Qiang Jia	091	(31) 1	*hai*	132 0431	8.i3.21	22 Feb 1098
8/[4]	(11) [*ji*] Zu Jia						
	xie Yang Jia	101	(31) 1	*hai*	132 0441	8.4.2	4 Mar 1098
8/7 [14]	(41) *yong* Qian Jia	191	(31)	*chou*	131 5851	8.7.19	8 Aug 1111
9/10 [15]	(04) *yi* Da Ding	274	(31) 2	*chou*	131 6294	9.10.18	26 Oct 1110
[10]/3 [16]	(21) *ji* Xiao Jia						
	zai Da Jia	041	(41) 2	*chou*	131 6431	10.3.7	11 Mar 1109
[10/5] [17]	(41) *xie* Zu Jia	121	(41)	*chou*	131 6511	10.5.28	30 May 1109
2/5 [18]	(41) *yong* Shang Jia	141	(21)	*chou*	131 7231	2.5.10	20 May 1107

The hope was that here are specimens from each year, 2 through 10, in one reign. But the later the starting month, the earlier must be the date, because over time the starting date of the "annual" cycle, which averages less than a solar year, must become earlier and earlier. These inscriptions actually, I think, are distributed through the last four reigns of Shang. The 2nd and 3rd year dates with starting day (01) and (11) in month 11 belong in the reign of Di Xin; so also two of the 4th-year dates, with starting day (11). The other 4th-year specimen, starting in month 1 on day (21), belongs in 1102, in Di Yi's reign. Di Yi also can claim the 5th-year inscription with cycle beginning on day (21) in month 1.

The "6th-year" inscription does not fit in any year 6. The year date in the fragment has only a down-stroke to right, which could be part of a 6 or part of an 8, and it does fit in Di Yi 8. All of the 7's and almost all of the 8's are Di Yi's. (For the remaining ones in years 9 and 10, the last year 8, and Xu's "year 2" assigned to Wenwu Ding – all *jian chou* -- see sections 6 and 8 below).

4. But first, a quite different objection comes from Chang Yuzhi. She accepts Shang intra-year intercalation. But she argues, with much data from inscriptions of all kinds, that in Shang and earlier the Chinese were conceiving of the lunar month as beginning with *fei* 朏, the day of the moon's first appearance 月出 low in the western sky at evening, and that they were not thinking of the month as beginning with the *shuo* 朔 day, when the moon meets 月逆 the sun (an event we cannot see; see Chang 1998 pp. 322-340).

4.1 This is a challenge I must meet. In my analysis of the Yi Fang inscriptions, I am using Zhang Peiyu, who gives me each lunar month calculated as beginning with the *shuo*. More than that, throughout this book I am assuming *shuo* dates as the first days of lunar months, notably in my account of *gan* names of kings as determined by the first days of their reigns, i.e., as determined by the first days of the first lunar months of their reigns. The consistency of my results, for Shang Jia Wei and Kong Jia through all thirty of the Shang kings, counts against Chang's argument. But that is not enough. I must look at her reasoning.

---

[13] I will argue that the month number is (or should be) 3, not 4.

[14] *HJ* 37847, 37872

[15] *HJ* 36511 (*Jia bian* 2416)

[16] *Hou Shang* 18.6

[17] *Hou Shang* 18.7.

[18] *HJ* 35427 + 37837

First, she points out correctly that the Chinese of the time did not have an astronomical science enabling them to calculate the exact day of the invisible *shuo* event; second, the word "*shuo*" is not found until late Western Zhou; and third, *jiagu* inscriptions show that sometimes the length of a lunar month was taken to be longer or shorter than a system of calculation would lead one to expect; so they must have been relying on subjective observation. I would reply, point one, a science of calculation is not needed; one could estimate the time of the invisible *shuo* by simple observations at other times in the month. (Nor would one need a correct astronomical explanation of what one looks at. One could simply be trying to make consistent sense of what one sees in the sky, as a panorama of moving spots of light.) One would often not get it just right; but this takes care of point three. As for point two, the word *run* for intercalation is not found until Eastern Zhou; so the non-occurrence of "*shuo*" is irrelevant. I use the words "sunrise" and "sunset" without your being justified in supposing that I have a pre-Copernican concept of the heavens.

5. Another inscription, *HJ* 37852, anticipates trouble with the Yi Fang, and is dated "*yihai* (12) ... 2nd month, coincident with the *yong* for Zu Yi, in the 9th *si*." This fixes the date as 20 March 1078 BCE, JD 132 7762, and implies that the current ritual cycle began 10 Sept 1079, JD 132 7571, a *jiazi* (01) day, with the civil year again (as in 2.1 above) beginning with the post-solstice month. To get this date, I assume that the 1079 (Di Xin 8) *yong* series was cut to 11 *xun*, because after the end of mourning Di Yi had to be added to the ritual calendar. The effect was to put *yong* sacrifices in the *xun* after Zu Jia into the *yi gongdian xun*, and Di Yi (necessarily coming in the *xun* after Wu Yi and Wenwu Ding) into the *yi* Shang Jia *xun*, making his rites coincident with the *yi* for Bao Yi (and so also for all series). Too many "former kings" were crowding into the cycle. The Fan *fang ding* (Supplement 1) shows that in 1065 Di Yi's *yong* was coincident with the *yi* for Bao Yi, with no deleted *xun*; so this assignment was permanent.

5.1 Two other inscriptions, however (*Xu-bian* 1.5.1, i.e., *HJ* 37840), are dated *guiyou* (10), 11th month, and *guiwei* (20), 12th month, 3rd *si*, and still give *jiaxu* (11) as the first day of the *ji* series, which must be 16 October 1084, JD 132 5781. If this date is in the 11th month in 1084, the civil year began with the *hai* (pre-solstice) month, which was 19 Nov - 18 Dec. It follows that from 1084 until 1079 the cycle was kept at an average of 36 *xun*, and (with one exception) began with *jiaxu*, so that the first day of the cycle moved back 21 days every four years; and that at some time between these dates the beginning of the civil year was moved forward two months, probably by adding two months at the end of a year. This was probably done at the end of Di Xin 5 (1082), which probably was the year of Di Yi's death (see 5.1.1). The *Xiaochen* Yi *jia* (Akatsuka #4, see Supplement 1) shows that a *jian chou* calendar was in use in Di Xin 6 (1081).

5.1.1 Huangfu Mi (*Taiping yulan* 83 citing *Di wang shiji*) says Di Yi reigned 37 years. This total (see 6.2 below) requires counting 1118-1109 and 1108-1106 (Wenwu Ding), 1105-1087 (Wenwu Ding renamed Di Yi), and 1086-1082, assuming the 1086 calendar to have been created by Di Yi for his heir Shou. (1086 began with a *jiazi* day.) Wenwu Ding / Di Yi had after Wu Yi's death altered the calendar from *jian chou* to *jian hai* by omitting intercalations in 1106 and 1101. Shou seems at once to have restored the *jian chou* calendar after Di Yi died, by adding two months at the end of 1082. He took the title Di Xin 37 years after 1105 (when Wenwu Ding had taken the title Di Yi), with a new calendar, in 1068 (proved in Supplement 1).

5.2 One of the longest sets of ten-day inscriptions is #2503 in Li, Qi and Allan, 1985, composing fragments in several earlier publications. (Note – as Xu Jinxiong has pointed out -- that the month dates the diviner's action on *gui*-day, not the *jia*-day sacrifices; here, in (1) *jiaxu* will turn out to be the first day of month 3, if I have the date correct.):

(1) *Guiyou* (10) ... 2nd month. *Jiaxu* (11), *ji* for Xiao Jia, etc.; the king's 8th *si*.
(2) *Guiwei* (20) ... 3rd month. *Jiashen* (21), *zai* for Xiao Jia, etc.
(3) *Guisi* (30) ... 3rd month. *Jiawu* (31), *ji* for Qian Jia, etc.
(4) *Guimao* (40) ... 3rd month. *Jiachen* (41), *ji* for Qiang Jia, etc.
(5) *Guichou* (50) ...3rd month. *Jiayin* (51), *ji* for Xiang Jia,etc.
(6) *Guihai* (60) ... ? month. *Jiazi* (01), *zai* for Xiang Jia, etc.
(7) *Guiyou* (10) ... ? month. *Jiaxu*, *ji* for Zu Jia, etc.

In a hand copy in an earlier collection, the month number in the next-to-last is rendered "4"; but it is actually doubtful.[19] If one believes, as I do, that months were almost never allowed to run to 31 days, this "8th *si*" probably contained an intercalary third month. I now try again, experimentally, the later rule that a month lacking a *qi*-center is intercalary, together with the hypothesis that *qi* divisions were determined by counting 15-day or 16-day periods from an observed autumn equinox, making the officially recognized winter solstice two days late. The inscription data determine that the current cycle began on *jiawu* (31), so it must be in a calendar other than the one beginning in 1086.

5.3 But it is also implied that the first day of the cycle must fall in the first month of the civil year; so the date must be earlier than the date of any such inscription examined so far. Why? 1084 12th month had the cycle first day at *jiaxu* (11). The above 7-*xun* set has the cycle first day at *jiawu* (31). To move it forward to *jiaxu* (11), @ 2 years / *xun* = 2 x 4, required eight years. 1084.12 is almost 1083. The target year has at least 20 days as "3rd month," so the first day of the cycle followed in that year cannot be more than 10 days into the first month. We need to account for 40 days, less two. 38 days @ 5.25/year is about seven years; so we should count 7, then 8, back from 1083, to get the year of the 7-*xun* set. The year to study is 1098.

The options are (a) a 31-day month covering lines 2 though 5 in the set, or (b) an intercalation covering lines 5 through 7, if line 6 will allow it. But (a) is not possible: Zhang Peiyu's tables show that neither 1098 nor any year close to it has what could be a "3rd month" beginning with *jiashen* or anything close to it.[20] (If the "3rd month" actually began with *jiaxu* (11), as I will argue, there would have to be at least 41 days in the month, hardly a serious possibility.) But 1098 did have an intercalary month that would be intercalary 2nd or 3rd, if the civil year began with the *hai* month.[21]

My *qi*-center table in Supplement 2 to this appendix points to 1098: note the intercalation in the "1080" row for the beginning of 1079, and then count back 19 years. This will show there was no other intercalary month at this time of year until 19 years (1 *zhang*) before or after 1098. I conclude that if scientific examination of #2503 reveals a "4th month" in what corresponds to line 6, then the

---

[19] So much is resting on this doubt that I have searched for other possibilities, but I find none, given the constraint that the cycle must begin with *jiawu* (31) in the first month. That Xu Jinxiong is correct in holding that the month date dates only the *gui*-day act of divination and not necessarily also the following (*jia*-day or later) scheduled rites is shown by the following (*Zhui-he* 21*, a fragment covering seven successive *gui*-day divinations, taken from Shima 1958 p. 62): "….*Guisi* (30), 4th month, coincident with *yong* for Shi Gui; *yiwei* (32), *yong* for Da Yi. *Guimao* (40), 5th month; *jiachen* (41), *yong* for Da Jia…." This *says* that "4th month" applies to *guisi* (30), and does not rule out the possibility that the 5th month started with *jiawu* (31) or *yiwei* (32). A similar point can be made about the month date at the end of a royal verification, i.e., it dates the act of verification, and not necessarily all of its content. The following is from *HJ* 10976 (Chang Yuzhi 1998 p. 290): "Crack on *xinwei* (08), Zheng certifying: Next month, the 8th. [month], Di (God) will command [much] rain…. On *dingyou* (34) it rained, continuing to *jiayin* (51), a total of 18 days. 9th month." This does not show that what was counted as "8th month" could have been at most 25 days, i.e., *renshen* (09) through *bingshen* (33), because we have no way of knowing what month day *dingyou* (34) was in, except by assuming that the 8th month was of normal length, which would put day *dinyou* (34) in the 8th month, not the 9th. (Indeed, that this is a verification of rain predicted in the 8th month suggests that *dingyou* must be well before the end of that month. What this example does show is that whatever day (*shuo* or *fei*) ordinarily counted as the first day of a month, in this case that day – the first day of the 9th – probably had to be determined by calculation, not observation, because probably it was raining at the time.) *(When I fail to find *HJ* numbers for *jiagu* I use abbreviations as in Keightley, *Sources* 229-231.)

[20] One might be tempted by 1079, an "8th year" with a 3rd month (zi calendar) beginning with *jiashen* (21). But the calendar at this time seems to require the *chou* month as first month with *jiaxu* (11) as cycle first day.

[21] Zhang Peiyu 1987 has *xinwei* (08) as winter solstice day in the *zi* month of 1098, which would normally be read two days late as day *guiyou* (10), counting 91 days from the observed autumn equinox. Stahlman and Gingerich 1963 implies *gengwu* (07) rather than *xinwei* (08), which suggests *renshen* (09) as the day the Chinese would pick, but also indicates that the true count was 88 days in this year rather than the normal 89, so that counting 91 days would identify *guiyou* (10) anyway. To fit the data to the #2503 set, we must suppose that Zhang's 4th month was made to begin with *guiyou* (10) rather than with *jiaxu* (11) (to be expected anyway, if they were trying to maintain a regular alternation of long and short months), thus making the preceding month short. Then there are two possibilities: (1) the Chinese may have taken *renshen* (09) as the solstice day, getting *guimao* at the end of the next month as the next *qi*-center, making that month unproblematically "3rd month," the following month then being intercalary; or (2) they may have remained undecided about the solstice day and tentatively called the next month "3rd month," concluding at the end of it that it did not have the expected *qi*-center, hence the designation "3rd month" must be continued for another lunar cycle.

inscriber made a mistake.[22]

For 1098, Zhang Peiyu 1987 gives the actual solstice as *xinwei* (08), 31 Dec (1099), so the recognized solstice (hence a *qi*-center) would be 2 Jan, *guiyou* (10), which was the last day of the lunar month. (I am assuming with Xu Jinxiong that the month date applies only to the crack, not to the scheduled rites thereafter.) Minor adjustments in Zhang then will imply two "3rd" months, one of which must be intercalary. Therefore, again, the civil year is starting with the *hai* month. And if this year is the eighth, then the first year must be 1105 (as I knew it must; for argument and the importance of this, see end note).

5.4 Further, it happens that we have a 7th *si* set of inscriptions, which is consistent with this "8th *si*" set and has the same cycle first day, jiawu (31). See the table at 3.2, and notice that in month 5 of year 7 there are three *jia* days, *jiashen* (22), *jiawu* (31), and *jiachen* (41). If the 8th year set is interpreted as having a 31-day month *jiashen* (21) through *jiayin* (51), then those 8th year *jia* days must be the first and last days of the 3rd month. This is incompatible with the *jia* days included in month 5 of the 7th year set, and would require that the two sets be in different reigns. But the estimate putting the 8th year set approximately in 1098 also implies that the 7th year set should be dated about the same time.

6. One might plot the ritual calendar experimentally for seven years: cycle first day, civil year first month, and *xun* in the cycle:

1099-8	*jiawu*	(31)	*hai*	36, 37
1097-6	*jiachen*	(41)	*hai*	36, 37
1095-4	*jiayin*	(51)	*hai*	36, 37
1093	*jiazi*	(01)	*hai*	36

By that time it would be evident that keeping the cycle beginning in the first month of the civil year, even when that month is moved back to the first month of winter, is impossible (for when 36 *xun* and 37 *xun* cycles alternate the cycle first day still moves back one day every four years). So the calendar masters gave up, and probably let the ritual year run at 36 *xun* through 1086, keeping the first ritual day *jiazi*. Then they ran a 37-*xun* ritual year, raising the first day to *jiaxu*, where it remained (with exceptions as noted) through 1077. Thus the beginning of the ritual year rapidly moved back from early winter to early autumn. Probably from 1092 on the term "*si*" was thought of as just meaning "year" in the ordinary sense. But working back from 1099 is not as simple.

6.1 The few extant inscriptions of the campaign against the Yu Fang fit the years 1110-1109; and (if one counts back alternating 36-*xun* and 37-*xun* years) one would expect the cycle for these years to begin with *jiawu* (31 and *jiachen* (41). A well-argued view (Chen Mengjia 1956 p. 310) is that Yu was located near Qinyang, about 150 miles southwest of Anyang.[23] The opening inscription (*Jia-bian* 2416 (*HJ* 36511), the longest one known) is dated "day *dingmao* (04)…10th month, coincident with the *yi* for Da Ding." The *yi* for Da Ding (son of Tang, father of Da Jia, i.e., Tai Jia) is on day 274, so the cycle began on day *jiawu* (31). Routine sacrifice inscriptions in the following spring require a ritual year beginning on a *jiachen* (41) day. The last known inscription for the campaign, on an animal skull, has the king in the autumn on a hunt in Yu

---

[22] Inscriptions on oracle materials were sometimes at first painted, and inscribed later. The inscriber could have forgotten that here "2nd month" refers only to the cracking on *guiyou*, and that *guiyou* was the last day of the month. Line 7 for *guiyou* (10) has to be 4th month, and so would be a line 8 for *guiwei* (20) and a line 9 for *guisi* (30). If the last were on a separate bone, the inscriber could easily have concluded that the painted "3" ought to have another line making it "4".

[23] "Yu Fang" could simply refer to a border people located beyond Yu. Chen Mengjia is uncommitted about the relative date, putting both the Yi Fang campaign and the Yu Fang campaign in the "Yi-Xin era." Li Xueqin (1959) dated the Yi Fang campaign in Di Yi's reign but now (*Zhaji*) assigns it to Di Xin; in his earlier work, however, he dated the Yu Fang campaign later than the Yi Fang campaign and assigned it to Di Xin. My own primary reason for dating it earlier is my hypothesis that since the average length of the ritual cycle was shorter than a solar year, over a long time its beginning date in the year would become earlier and earlier. "10th month" for the *yi* for Da Ding (day 274 in the cycle) indicates a beginning day for the cycle which was four and a half months *later* than the beginning day required in the Yi Fang set, so it is evidence for a much *earlier* year for the Yu Fang event.

Fang territory, a standard way of marking a victory. If Di Xin's calendar actually began in 1086, whereas the *Bamboo Annals* dates it to 1102, late Shang dates are being back-dated 16 years. The *Annals'* date for the death of Wu Yi is 1125; so it must actually have been in 1109. The *Annals* record says that Wu Yi died in a thunderstorm during a hunt "in the He - Wei area," apparently late in the year. This would be one or two hundred miles farther west, but an appropriate location for a triumphal hunt.

6.2 Wu Yi's dates are 1105/43-1109, 2+35 years. Are the two years for these inscriptions then Wu Yi 34-35? *Jia-bian* 2416 has no year date. But fragment #1908 in the White collection (see Chang 1987 p. 246) is a shorter version of the same text, and it is dated "9th *si*." Therefore I conclude that late in his reign Wu Yi began a new calendar for his heir Wenwu Ding, in 1118. The *Annals'* thirteen years for "Wen Ding" ought to be, then, 1118-1106; and the three years assigned to him in other chronologies must be 1108-1106. In 1105 Wenwu Ding perhaps changed his title to "Di Yi," starting a new calendar. (There are late Shang inscriptions referring to "Wenwu Di Yi.") In any case, the year 1105 began with an *yi* day, which would account for the name Di Yi of the reigning king. The *zi* month first day was *yiyou* (22). The *Annals* gives Di Yi only nine years, probably because Warring States editors could not accept a ten-year overlap of the Wu Yi and Wenwu Ding reigns; so they cut ten years out of the 19-year "Di Yi" reign (1105-1087), making it 1095-1087, backed 16 years to 1111-1103. (For clarification and confirmation of this see Chapter Nine section 8 in this book, with table; also the "Note" at the end of this Appendix.)

6.3 But years 1108-1106 do not fit a simple projection back to 1110, cycle first day jiawu (31). One would expect Wenwu Ding 2, 1107, to have *jiayin* (51) as cycle first day, but Xu Fengxian's material (p. 86) shows me it must be *jiashen* (21). If so, Wenwu Ding, as soon as he assumed control, must have altered the ritual calendar by running four 35-*xun* cycles, omitting the *xun* between *yong* Zu Jia and *yi gongdian*, not yet needed, because he was still alive, and his father was being mourned. The result was what I show in section 8. The civil calendar must have been altered to match (by omitting intercalations): Di Yi 4-5 were *jian zi* years; Di Yi 7-8 were *jian hai* years. Wu Yi's calendar thus had been *jian chou*. The date of *Jia-bian* 2416, "10th month," turns out to be 26 October 1110, in month 11 in Zhang Peiyu's ables.

7. Some chronologies (e.g., *Di Wang Shiji*) give "Di Yi" 37 years. This figure probably has a basis: I have inferred that there was another "*di*" inauguration in 1068.[24] The 23rd year of a calendar beginning in 1068 would be 1046. *Yi Zhou shu* 21 "Feng Bao" has Wu Wang and Zhou Gong receiving lords from other states, in a situation that is obviously late pre-conquest, on the first (*shuo*) of the month (not named), called day *gengzi* (37), in the "23rd year."[25] There are only two late pre-conquest years containing months beginning with *gengzi*: 1046 and 1041. If 1068 began a new year count, moreover, this would help to explain why no inscriptions for Di Xin's era have been discovered with year dates much higher than 20. If 1068 was the year of a second "*di*" inaugural, it was picked, and perhaps groomed, for the event. 1105-4 had been *jiazi* years in the cycle. To make 1068-7 *jiazi* years, Di Xin would have to resume alternating 36-*xun* and 37-*xun* cycles by letting the cycle beginning 9 Sep 1077 run 37 *xun*. I tentatively assume that he did this, and kept on doing it. I have at least five inscriptions dated on 1068 as *yuan*. But at the same time, I have found at least three convincingly dated later than 1068, using 1086 as *yuan*.

8. Below is my tentative table of cycle dates from 1111 through 1046. Asterisks * mark dates (** for implied first-year dates) arguably confirmed by inscriptions or texts:

Year	*ganzhi si* 1st day	Reign/year			JD#[26] *si* 1st day	Date of *si* 1st day	*xun*
1111*	31	Wu Yi	(33)	8*	131 5661	31 Jan 1111	36[27]
1110*	31		(34)	9*	6021	26 Jan 1110	37
1109*	41		(35)	10*	6391	31 Jan 1109	35[28]

[24] On the importance of the year 1068, see Chapter Eight, strips 172-173 and comments. But notice also that if Di Yi actually died in 1082 and is identical with Wenwu *ding*, then the tenure of "Wenwu Di Yi" was 1118-1082, 37 years.

[25] There are mistranslations of this text implying that the event was post-conquest, treating "23rd year" as a garble.

[26] For JD numbers, use Stahlman and Gingerich (1963); for the *ganzhi*, divide by 60 and subtract 10 or add 50.

[27] Years 8, 9 and 10 are (I am supposing) in Wenwu Ding's first calendar beginning in 1118 (given him by his father).

[28] The sequence of 35 *xun* cycles is required by *HJ* 35427 + *HJ* 37837 as quoted by Xu, p. 86, implying *jiashen* (21) cycle 1st day in Wenwu Ding 2. The *HJ* reproduction, however, is not clear enough for me to read all of it. Also, she gives *HJ* 37398 as dated "10th *si*, 9th month, *yong*" (*ibid*), an animal skull inscription, which confirms that the calendar

1108**	31	Wenwu Ding	1**(11)		6741	15 Jan 1108	35
1107*	21		2* (12)		7091	31 Dec 1108	35
1106	11		3 (13)		7441	16 Dec 1107	35
1105**	01	"Di Yi"	1**		7791	1 Dec 1106	36
1104	01		2		8151	25 Nov 1105	37
1103	11		3		8521	30 Nov 1104	37
1102*	21		4*		8891	5 Dec 1103	36
1101*	21		5*		9251	30 Nov 1102	36
1100	21		6		9611	24 Nov 1101	37
1099*	31		7*		9981	29 Nov 1100	36
1098*	31		8*		132 0341	24 Nov 1099	37
1097	41		9		0711	29 Nov 1098	36
1096	41		10		1071	23 Nov 1097	37
1095	51		11		1441	28 Nov 1096	36
1094	51		12		1801	23 Nov 1095	37
1093*	01		13*		2171	28 Nov 1094	36
1092	01		14		2531	22 Nov 1093	36
1091*	01		15*		2891	17 Nov 1092	36
1090	01		16		3251	12 Nov 1091	36
1089	01		17		3611	7 Nov 1090	36
1088	01		18		3971	2 Nov 1089	36
1087	01		19		4331	27 Oct 1088	36
1086**	01	Zhou Xin		1**	4691	22 Oct 1087	36
1085*	01			2*	5051	17 Oct 1086	37
	11				5421	21 Oct 1085	36
1084*	11			3*	5781	16 Oct 1084	36
1083*	11			4*	6141	12 Oct 1083	36
1082	11			5	6501	06 Oct 1082	36
1081*	11			6*	6861	30 Sep 1081	36
1080*	11			7*	7221	25 Sep 1080	35
1079*	01			8*	7571	10 Sep 1079	37[29]
1078*	11			9*	7941	15 Sep 1078	36
1077*	11			10*	8301	09 Sep 1077	37
1076*	21			11*	8671	14 Sep 1076	36
1075	21			12	9031	09 Sep 1075	37
1074	31			13	9401	14 Sep 1074	36
1073	31			14	9761	08 Sep 1073	37
1072	41			15	133 0131	13 Sep 1072	36
1071	41			16	0491	08 Sep 1071	37
1070	51			17	0861	13 Sep 1070	36
1069	51			18	1221	07 Sep 1069	37
1068**	01	Di Xin	1**	19	1591	12 Sep 1068	36
1067*	01	(=Zhou Xin)	2*	20*	1951	07 Sep 1067	37
1066*	11		3*	21*	2321	12 Sep 1066	36
1065*	11		4*	22*	2681	06 Sep 1065	37
1064	21		5	23	3051	11 Sep 1064	36
1063*	21		6*	24	3411	06 Sep 1063	37
1062	31		7	25	3781	11 Sep 1062	37
1061	41		8	26	4151	15 Sep 1061	37
1060*	51		9*	27	4521	20 Sep 1060	37
1059*	01		10	28*	4891	25 Sep 1059	37
1058*	11		11	29*	5261	30 Sep 1058	37
1057	21		12	.	5631	04 Oct 1057	37
1056	31		13	.	6001	09 Oct 1056	37
1055	41		14	.	6371	14 Oct 1055	37
1054	51		15		6741	19 Oct 1054	37
1053	01		16		7111	23 Oct 1053	37
1052	11		17		7481	28 Oct 1052	37
1051	21		18		7851	02 Nov 1051	37
1050	31		19		8221	07 Nov 1050	36
1049*	31		20*		8581	01 Nov 1049	37
1048	41		21		8951	06 Nov 1048	36
1047	41		22		9311	01 Nov 1047	37
1046*	51		23*		9681	06 Nov 1046	36

1040** (End of Shang; asterisks indicate inscriptions or other evidence.)

---

in 1109 was *jian chou*, as in 3.2 above. (Akatsuka p. 651 and Chang 1987 p. 249; see my Appendix 4, Supplement 1.)

[29] See p.257 note 45.

Supplement 1: Late Shang Bronze Inscriptions (and others), with Dates

I examine first an inscription on an animal skull, a trophy from a hunt closing the Yu Fang campaign, which I have dated to 1110-1109. *HJ* 37398 is a large fold-out illustration; see also Akatsuka p. 651 (no analysis) and Chang 1987 p. 249 (a clear hand copy of the readable part of the text): ... *zai jiu yue, wei wang shi si yong ri, wang lai zheng Yu Fang bo [Yan],* ".... in the 9th month, the king's 10th *si, yong* day, the king returning from campaign against Yu Fang lord [Yan]."

For 1109 the applicable *si* first day was 31 January, JD 131 6391. The *jian chou* 9th month began *jiaxu* (11), 28 August, JD 131 6601, which was day 211 in the cycle, first day of *xun* 22, *yong* for Xiang Jia. This shows that there must have been four 35-*xun* cycles beginning in 1109, with matching alterations in the civil calendar shifting from *jian chou* to *jian zi* and then *jian hai*, by 1099-1098. If we instead project a *jian hai* calendar and alternating 36-37 *xun* cycles back from 1099 to 1110, there would be no *yong* day. (This argument is probable only, depending on assuming a first-of-month date.)

Akatsuka #1, p. 615: Biji *you* #1, date 2nd year, *bingchen* (53), 1st month, coinciding with the *yong* for Bi Bing, consort of Da Yi (r. 1554-1543). There are two more Biji vessels, dated 4th year and 6th year.

The *yong* for Bi Bing is the 3rd day of the 4th *xun* of the *yong* series. This day is the 17th *xun* in the cycle. Therefore the day should be day 163 in the cycle. If this day is *bingchen* (53), the cycle must begin with *jiaxu* (11). (163 – (2 x 60) = day 43, which must also be *bingchen* (53); so day 1 = *jiaxu* (11).)

If the *yuan* is 1086, year 2 is 1085, the first day of the *ji* series being *jiaxu* (11). But this yields a date in the (*yin*) 2nd month. This shows the applicable first day of the cycle must be earlier, and the *yuan* later.

Year 2 (*yuan* 1068) would be 1067. The applicable *si* 1st day is 12 Sep 1068, = JD 133 1591, a *jiazi* (01) day, not a *jiaxu* (11) day. For the date of the 2nd year Biji you to fit, I must shift the empty *xun* after the *yong* for Zu Jia back, making it an intercalary *xun* before the Biji *you*'s date in the cycle, perhaps between *yong gongdian* and *yong* Shang Jia. This will make the date the 173rd day, JD 133 1763, a *bingchen* day, 3 March 1067, the 14th day of the *yin* month, therefore "1st month."[30]

Hu shang bo (upper fore-limb of a tiger), 3rd year 10th month day *xinyou* (58), *xie* day:

3rd year (*yuan* 1068) =1066, cycle first day JD 133 2321, 12 September. 1066 had 13 months, with an intercalary 7th month (*zi* calendar), so "10th month" (*yin* calendar) is Zhang Peiyu's 13th month, 1st = *guisi* (30); *xinyou* (58) was the 28th, = 28 Dec 1066, JD 133 2428, the 108th day in the cycle, therefore the 8th day in the 11th *xun*. This was *xie*-day for Xiao Xin, also for Wu Ding Bi Xin (the *ji* rite was for males only).

Akatsuka #2, p. 631: Biji *you* #2, 4th year: The date is *yisi* (42), 4th month, 4th year, *yi* day – but for whom?

1068 as *yuan*; 4th year 1065. The applicable first day of the cycle is *jiaxu* (11), 12 September 1066, JD 133 2321. The (*yin* calendar) 4th month of 1065 begins with *gengyin* (27), 25 May, this being JD 133 2577. Day *yisi* (42) is 15 days later, so it is JD 133 2592, which must be day 272 in the cycle (JD 133 2321 to JD 133 2592, inclusive count), the second day in *xun* 28. This is the 3rd *xun* in the *yi* series, following the *xun* containing the *yi* for Shang Jia; so its second day is the *yi* for Da Yi (Tai Yi). The date is 9 June 1065.

Da Yi is the dynastic founder Cheng Tang. The inscription announces rituals honoring "Wenwu Di Yi," probably another name for the king's father. I assume that in 1068 Zhou Xin took the title *di* and named his son Lu Fu "junior king" (*xiao wang*) with the cult name-to-be Wu Geng. (1068 began with a *geng* day.)

Akatsuka #3, p. 636: Biji *you* #3, 6th year: The date is day *yihai* (12), 6th month, 6th year, *yi* day.

---

[30] This change will also make the *yong* for Di Yi coincide with the *yi* for Bao Yi, as expected (see Fan *fang ding* below).

Again I try 1068 as *yuan*. The year then is 1063, and the applicable *si* 1st day is 11 September 1064, JD 133 3051. Zhang Peiyu's 8th month, presumably *yin* calendar 6th month, does not have *yihai*.

But the year was a 13-month year. The solstice was *jiaxu* (11), which would be observed two days late, as *bingzi* (13). This would produce an intercalary 5th month (*zi*-calendar), making ZPY's 9th count as the *yin* 6th, *dingwei* (44) through *bingzi* (13), so *yihai* (12) was its next-to-last day, 28 August, JD 133 3402.

Akatsuka #4, p. 648, *Xiaochen* Yi *jia*: Date, "*guisi* (30), the king gave *Xiaochen* Yi 10 strings of cowries, which he used to make for his mother Gui a precious *yi* vessel. The king's 6th *si*, *yong* day, in the 4th month.

I assume that *guisi* (30) is picked because Yi's mother has a *gui* name, and that "*yong* day" is the *jia* day after "*yong* night," preceding the scheduled *yong* for a *jia* king. Qiang Jia looks possible: his *yong* is day 201 in the cycle, and if day 201 is (31), then day 1 is (11), indicating a Di Xin date in his first calendar. The year would be 1081, applicable cycle first day would be 6 October 1082, JD 132 6501, day 201 being JD 132 6701, 23 April 1081. Zhang's tables make the date the first day of *zi* calendar month 5, hence the 1st of (*chou*) month 4. Most bronzes assume a *jian yin* calendar. When one does not, as here, it is probably using the official calendar. If so, Di Xin's 1086 calendar had shifted from *jian hai* to *jian chou* by 1081.

Yinxu West #1713 (Xu pp. 48-49), a bronze dedication text, date *renshen* (09), 6th month, 7th *si*, *yi* day.

This is in Di Xin's 1086 calendar, hence 1080. Zhang Peiyu month 8 is *jian yin* month 6. The first *jia* day in this month is *jiazi* (01); in my table (below) for Di Xin years 1-12, this is *yi* day for Xiao Jia; the following *ren* day is *yi* for Da Wu Bi Ren. The date: 25 July 1080.

Akatsuka #7, p. 660: Sui Cha *you*: Complete date, *dingsi* (54) … 9th month, the king's 9th *si*, *xie* day.

Try 1086 as *yuan*; 9th si is 1078, applicable first day of the cycle is 15 September, JD 132 7941. *Dingsi* (54) then is day 4 of *xun* 5 which is the *xie* for Da Ding, day 44 in the cycle, therefore JD 132 7984, which is 28 October (*per* Stahlman & Gingerich). Zhang's tables tell us that this is the 15th of the 11th month, *zi* calendar, so 9th month in a *yin* calendar.

Akatsuka #8, p. 664: Shu Ling *yi*, 10th year: Complete date, "*jiyou* (46) … 9th month, the king's 10th year, *xie* day 5, "on the way east."

The last words suggest that this 10th year 9th month *xie* day is one *xun* after the *zai* for Shang Jia when the Yi Fang campaign started. The *xie* day should therefore be 9 October 1077, making the date *jiyou* (46) be 14 October. (Xu p. 176 interprets the date as "15th year." The same error is made in dating the Zai Hu *jiao* to year 25 instead of year 20, pp. 82-83. The Shu Ling *yi* confirms that "25th year" is a mistake.)

Akatsuka #9, p. 665: Zai Hu *jiao*: "Day *gengshen* (57). The King was in East Jian. The King came, with me attending. He gave me five strings of cowries. I am using them to make for my father Ding a precious *yi* vessel. 6th month, the King's 20th *si*, *yi*[-day] plus 5."

There is an illustration on p. 83 of Xu's book. She interprets the date as "25th year," apparently taking "*you wu*" (+ 5) as going with "*nian si yi*" (20th year of *yi* sacrifice) rather than with "*yi*[-day].". The Project's *Brief Report* (p. 58) does the same, without naming the vessel, simply saying that there is one dated "25th year." Akatsuka gets it right (p. 666). "25th year" was also Dong Zuobin's view (Xu p. 109).

Five days before *gengshen* (57) is *yimao* 乙卯 (52), which is of course the *yi* 翊 day. An *yi* 翊 day on an *yi* 乙 day was apparently lucky. We see this in the 4th-year Biji *you* (Xu p. 46 text, p. 47 illustration): "coincident with *yi-yi* 乙翊 day." (The date in this Biji vessel is *yisi* 乙巳 (42)… 4th month, the king's 4th *si*, *yi* 翊 day.) This is why Zai Hu phrases his date the way he does, instead of just calling it *gengshen*.

But what is the absolute date? In my table pp. 239-40 as it was in Nivison 2002 pp. 272-273, alternating 36- and 37-*xun* cycles after 1078, year 20=1049 (*yuan* 1068) applicable cycle first day was *jiawu* (31), 8

September 1050, JD 133 8161. The *yi* for Bao Yi is day 262. If this is *yimao* (52), the cycle first day must be *jiawu* (31), as I had figured. Day 262 counting beginning with JD 133 8161 would be JD 133 8422, which is 26 May 1049, the 29th of lunar month 6 in Zhang Peiyu's tables, so *gengshen* is in Zhang's 7th month. Zhang gives *wuzi* (25) as the winter solstice day, which I take (adding 2) as *gengyin* (27). This is the 1st of Zhang's month 2, so Zhang's month 1 is intercalary month 11, and his month 7 is *jian zi* month 6. This seems to satisfy the date in the Zai Hu *jiao*, but it does not, for the following (surprising) reason:

Xu's book provides *jiagu* material on 20th year inscriptions at pp. 104-106 in her Chapter Five. There are two long series of *jia* days, one of them (Xu's section #4)[31] for the king's movements from place to place in the east, the other (#3)[32] for rites in the ritual calendar. They are incompatible: e.g., in the former (#4), month 6 has *jia* days *jiachen* (41), *jiayin* (51), and *jiazi* (01); but in the latter (#3), month 6 has *jiawu* (31), *jiachen* (41, and *jiayin* (51). The former (which turns out to be earlier) extends from 20th year month 5 through 21st year month 2; the latter is shorter but richer, months 6 to 9, with scheduled sacrifices. In both, every month has three *jia* days, with no two-*jia*-day months. Being incompatible, they must be in different reign-calendars. My analysis for late Shang provides only two possibilities long enough: the calendar beginning with 1086, and the calendar beginning with 1068. (The 1086 calendar runs past 1068.)

For my analysis – for the *whole* of late Shang -- to meet this (absolutely crucial) test, the two sequences *must* fit into my two calendars, *and they do*. The earlier "20th year" is 1067, when the king was moving about in or near a place named by a complex character, top half with disputed reconstruction, bottom half a *hewen* of *wu* 五 above *you* 酉.[33] The later "20th year" is 1049, and it seems to have exactly what is needed for the Zai Hu *jiao*: 6th month last *jia*-day *jiayin* (51), *yi* for Shang Jia; and of course the next day is *yimao* (52), *yi* for Bao Yi. But the sequence must be *jian chou*, standard for *jiagu* after 1081, making the vessel date *jian yin*, not *jian zi*. Also, this later 20th year sequence shows an "intercalary" *xun* before *yi* Shang Jia. For day 262 to be *yi* Bao Yi, the normally empty *xun* 25 after *yong* Zu Jia must be omitted.

But there must be a major correction for the 20th year sequence putting *yi* Shang Jia in *jian chou* month 6, two months *later* than *jian zi* month 5. I conclude, then, that all six 36-*xun* cycles from 1062 through 1051 must be 37 *xun* instead, perhaps each with the extra *xun* before *yi* Shang Jia. (The motive probably was to move the first day of the cycle forward to where it had been in earlier years.) There would be then altogether exactly six more *xun* before the Zai Hu *jiao yi*-day date. It would still be the *yi* day after the *yi* for Shang Jia, but would be 60 days later, not 26 May but 25 July, last day of *jian yin* month 5; so *gengshen* is 30 July 1049, the 5th day in *jian yin* month 6.

Akatsuka #10, p. 668: Si *yi*, also called the *Wuchen yi*, 20th year: The complete date is day *wuchen* (05), 11th month, 20th year, "xie day, coinciding with Bi Wu, consort of Wu Yi."

Here 1086 is *yuan* year. The date is 1067 (disregarding *yuan* 1068). Ladies don't get *ji* rites, so the *xie* for Bi Wu is in the same *xun* as the *xie* for Zu Jia, which is *xun* 13. Thus the day is day 125, requiring a *si* beginning with *jiazi* (01), as expected for 1067.

The applicable *si* first day is 7 September 1067, JD 133 1951. Day 125 is JD 133 2075, 9 January 1066, which is the first day of the *jian yin* 12th month of 1067.

But the Si *yi* itself says "11th month (though this is disputed). The text ends with the key information "one pig": a pig was offered in sacrifice. This detail shows that this bronze vessel is a *minjian* product; the maker is probably using the popular calendar taking the month as beginning with *fei*-day, when the new moon is first seen, second or third of the month if one is counting beginning with the *shuo*, as Zhang Peiyu and I do. So probably for the maker *wuchen* is late in the 11th month rather than the first day of the 12th month.

---

[31] Qian 2.14.4; Qian 2.14.1 + Qian 4.28.1 = HJ 37863; HJ 36856 (as in Xu p. 105).

[32] Qian 3.28.4 + Xu 6.1.8 + Xu 6.5.2 = HJ 37867 (as in Xu p. 104).

[33] Prof. Li points to Sun Yirang's noting that a character in *Shuowen* is like this place name except that it has *kou* 口 below instead of *you* 酉. Xu Shen writes that it should be pronounced like *xie* 寫. Prof. Li further concludes that the place was probably near Ju 莒 on the southern border of ancient Qi in the Shandong area (*Zhaji* pp. 59-60).

Qin Zi *fang ding*: date *jiazi* (01), 12th month, *xie* for Zu Jia, 20th year.

Li Xueqin (*Zhaji* p. 48) points to this *ding* in his analysis of the Si *yi*. They must be in the same *xun*, but it seems I must argue that the Qin Zi *fang ding* must be in the previous (*yin* 11th) month (since *wuchen* was the first of the month), even though called "12th month." Perhaps this is the solution: the maker is using the *chou* calendar, in use in *jiagu* - material on the subject-matter of this appendix, from 1081 on.

Fan *fang ding*, 22nd year, 5th month *yiwei* (32), *yong* Wenwu Di Yi (Xu Fengxian p. 156):

The *yuan* is 1086. Year 22 is 1065. The applicable cycle first day is 12 September 1066, which is JD 133 2321, a *jiaxu* (11) day. The *yi* for Bao Yi is day 262, which must be JD 133 2582, an *yiwei* (32) day, 30 May 1065. This is the 6th of Zhang Peiyu's 6th month, so in the 5th month in a *jian chou* calendar. See section 5 on p. 236, where I argue that the *yi* for Bao Yi became the regular *yong* day for Di Yi. In 1079, when I assumed Di Yi's place in the cycle was first being fixed after completion of mourning for him, it was necessary to delete the *xun* between *yong* Zu Jia and *yi Gongdian* to make *yong* Di Yi coincide with *yi* Bao Yi; but later the deletion was not necessary; the Bao Yi date in any series had apparently become standard as the date for the preceding series sacrifice for Di Yi.

Xu Fengxian (Chapter 5: pp. 103-124) discusses six "20th year" inscriptions, four *jiagu*, two bronzes. To these I have added a seventh, the bronze Zai Hu *jiao* (which for her is "25th year"). I have just examined the bronzes, and two of the *jiagu* (in my analysis of the Zai Hu *jiao*). The other two *jiagu* are her #1 and #2, pp. 103-104. I think both can be dated to 1049; but they present a few problems.

Xu #1, *HJ* 37868: This is a routine ten-day fragment, the day date missing except for the expected "*jia*." The rest is "2nd month ... *xie*-day for Zu Jia, 20th year."

The *xie* for Zu Jia is in *xun* 13, hence day 121. If the date is 1049, the cycle begins on a *jiawu* (31) day, so day 121 (= 60n + 1) must also be *jiawu* (31). The effective cycle first day (section 8) is JD 133 8221, which is 7 November 1050; *xie*-day for Zu Jia therefore is JD 133 8341 (6 March 1049), *jiawu* (31), which is the 7th of Zhang Peiyu's 4rd month, therefore (one would think) *jian chou* 3nd month. But as I observed in discussing the Zai Hu *jiao*, properly this year began with an intercalary month which would have to be intercalary 11th. Thus Zhang's 4th month must properly be *jian chou* 2nd month. *HJ* 37867 (Xu #3 pp. 30-31 and 104) covering months 6 to 9 requires that month 6 contain *jiawu* (31) *yi gongdian*, and *jiayin* (51) *yi* Shang Jia (the *xun* beginning *jiachen* (41) being irregular or "intercalary"). For this to be so, one must assume that the normal inactive *xun* between *yong* Zu Jia and *yi gongdian* is omitted.

Xu #2, *HJ* 37864 and (same text) *HJ* 37865: "[*Gui*]*hai* (60), the king cracking and authenticating: 'Wine offerings and *yong*-day rites from [Shang Jia to] all consorts, with robed ceremonial.' No troubles [from the bone. The king read the crack] and said, 'Good fortune!' [This is] in the 3rd month, the king's 20th *si*."

I assume that a text of this kind does not name a king's sacrifice day, but the words "*yong* day" indicate it must be an appropriate date within the *yong* series, and since the cracking was on *guihai* (60) the rituals are to occur on the next day, *jiazi* (01). If the date is 1049, Zhang's 5th month is *jian chou* 3rd month, being days *wuwu* (55) through *bingxu* (23). The first *jia*-day of this month is *jiazi* (01), unassigned. The preceding *jia*-day *jiayin* (51), in month 2, is *yong*-day for Shang Jia.

After presenting the "20th year" texts, Xu reviews scholarship puzzling about there being so many texts thus dated. Some have argued that the character I translate "20th" is sometimes a form of the character *yue* "to say," hence "to decree" (*ling*); or even *yuan*, "1st." I doubt that these suggestions would have been made if a way had been seen to date all the inscriptions to a "20th" year. And it seems to me that the number of known texts dated to a specific year is so small that seven having "20th year" is not statistically troubling. (All of them belong either in 1067 or in 1049.)

Supplement 2: The First Twenty years of Di Xin: *Qi*-Centers and Intercalary Months

I present here a table of *qi*-centers, in years 1086 through 1067, the first 20 years of Di Xin. Each dated line plots *qi*-centers beginning with the Julian Day number for the autumn equinox for the year. The *qi*-centers are identified by adding intervals from the autumn equinox day number, according to the system I have used on p. 21 when analyzing the Zhou conquest campaign (as in *Huainanzi*, "Tian Wen"): 31, 30, 30 (= 91, winter solstice); 31, 30, 30 (= 91, spring equinox); 31, 31, 30 (= 92, summer solstice); 31, 30, 30 (= 91, autumn equinox). I could have counted out a similar system from summer solstice days, with the same properties but with some one-day changes.

That this is the system the Chinese of late Shang and early Zhou actually used is shown by the fact that they consistently got the winter solstice two days late. (Once in four or five years it would be three days late. Counting from a correct observed spring equinox date would have yielded a correct winter solstice day.) Therefore I have assumed that when, approximately every four years, their day count was one day short before the next autumn equinox, they must (when applying the system correctly) have accepted the extra day and then restarted the count with the following true autumn equinox day.

The *qi*-center system is a solar system, so the *qi*-center dates occur near the beginning of each of the twelve months in the modern calendar. The exact day, as given by Zhang Peiyu, *Xian Qin Shilibiao,* is in line three for each year, in the column for the month. Above the day of the month, and below the Julian date, is the numerical value for the *ganzhi* for the day. (After the first column, only the last four digits of the Julian number are given.)

Note that from 1086 through 1068 is 19 years, the length of a *zhang*. (I am tempted to guess the Chinese had noticed the *zhang* regularity as early as this. The discovery is thought to be six centuries later.). As I should expect if I have added correctly, the 19 years contain seven intercalary months, and the next year begins the cycle anew, as here: the intercalary month in the top line occurs at the same point in the year as in the bottom line. (Similarly, there must be an intercalation at or near the beginning of the 19th year before 1079, i.e., in 1098, as found above; see the "1080" row.)

I have begun each displayed "year" with the autumn equinox month, because I think that this is the way the Chinese of the time identified *qi*-center days. Consequently the displayed intercalations are in years 1085 through 1066. Month numbers assume a *zi* calendar. Actually (I believe) the Di Xin court was using a *hai* calendar through 1084 and probably longer, and had shifted to a *chou* calendar by 1081.

Each intercalation is indicated by the pair (in bold italics underlined) of *qi*-center days before and after the intercalary month.

"1086" row, intercalation after month 7 of 1085: Month 7 of 1085 ends with (22) and thus contains *qi*-center (21); the next *qi*-center is (52), beginning a month; so the intervening lunar month (23 – (51) is intercalary month 7.

"1083" row, intercalation after month 4 of 1082: Month 4 of 1082 ends with (06), and so contains *qi*-center (05); the next *qi*-center is (36), beginning a lunar month, so the intervening month (07) – (35) is intercalary month 4.

"1080" row, intercalation after month 1 of 1079: Month 1 of 1079 ends with (50), a *qi*-center; the next month but one begins with *qi*-center (21); so the intervening month is intercalary month 1.

"1077" row, intercalation after month 9 of 1077: Day *dingyou* (34) (Oct 2, 1077, sun at 180 degrees, autumn equinox) is a *qi*-center; the next *qi*-center is *wuchen* (05) (Nov 2); therefore the intervening lunar month *wuxu* (35) through *bingyin* (03) (Oct 3- Oct 31), lacking a *qi*-center, is intercalary.

"1075" row, intercalation after month 5 of 1074: Month 5 of 1074 ends with *qi*-center (18), and the next *qi*-center (49) begins the next month but one; so the intervening month (19) – (48) is intercalary month 5.

"1072" row, intercalation after month 4 of 1071: Month 4 of 1071 ends with (02), a *qi*-center; and *qi*-center (33) begins the next month but one; so the intervening month (03) – (32) is intercalary month 4.

"1069" row, intercalation after month 11 of 1069: Month 11 of 1069 ends with *qi*-center (47) and the next month but one begins with the next *qi*-center (17); so the intervening month (48) – (16) is intercalary month 11.

"1067" row, intercalation after month 7 of 1066: Month 7 of 1066 ends with *qi*-center (01) and the next month but one begins with the next *qi*-center ((32), so the intervening month (02) – (31) is intercalary month 7.

		Oct	Nov	Dec	Jan	Feb	Mar	Apr	May	June	July	Aug	Sep	Oct
		10	11	12	1	2	3	4	5	6	7	8	9	10
1086	Oct 3, 132	5037,	5068,	5098,	5128,	5159,	5189,	5219,	5250,	5281,	*5311,*	*5342,*	5372	
		47	18	48	18	49	19	49	20	51	21	52	22	
		3	3	3	2'85	2	3	2	3	3	3	3	2	
1085	Oct 2, 132	5402,	5433,	5463,	5493,	5524,	5554,	5584,	5615,	5646,	5676,	5707,	5737,	5767
		52	23	53	23	54	24	54	25	56	26	57	27	57
		2	2	2	1'84	1	3	2	3	3	3	3	2	2
1084	Oct 3, 132	5768,	5799,	5829,	5859,	5890,	5920,	5950,	5981,	6012,	6042,	6073,	6103	
		58	29	59	29	60	30	60	31	02	32	03	33	
		3	3	3	2'83	2	4	3	4	4	4	4	3	
1083	Oct 3, 132	6133,	6164,	6194,	6224,	6255,	6285,	*6315,*	*6346*,	6377,	6407,	6438,	6468	
		03	34	04	34	05	35	05	36	07	37	08	38	
		3	3	3	2'82	2	4	3	4	4	4	4	3	
1082	Oct 3, 132	6498,	6529,	6559,	6589,	6620,	6650,	6680,	6711,	6742,	6772,	6803,	6833	
		08	39	09	39	10	40	10	41	12	42	13	43	
		3	3	3	2'81	2	3	2	3	3	3	3	2	
1081	Oct 2, 132	6863,	6894,	6924,	6954,	6985,	7015,	7045,	7076,	7107,	7137,	7168,	7198,	7228
		13	44	14	44	15	45	15	46	17	47	18	48	18
		2	2	2	1'80	1	3	2	3	3	3	3	2	2
1080	Oct 3, 132	7229,	7260,	7290,	*7320,*	*7351*,	7381,	7411,	7442,	7473,	7503,	7534,	7564	
		19	50	20	50	21	51	21	52	23	53	24	54	
		3	3	3	2'79	2	4	3	4	4	4	4	3	
1079	Oct 3, 132	7594,	7625,	7655,	7685,	7716,	7746,	7776,	7807,	7838,	7868,	7899,	7929	
		24	55	25	55	26	56	26	57	28	58	29	59	
		3	3	3	2'78	2	4	3	4	4	4	4	3	
1078	Oct 3, 132	7959,	7990,	8020,	8050,	8081,	8111,	8141,	8172,	8203,	8233,	8264,	8294	
		29	60	30	60	31	01	31	02	33	03	34	04	
		3	3	3	2'77	2	3	2	3	3	3	3	2	
1077	Oct 2, 132	*8324,*	*8355,*	8385,	8415,	8446,	8476,	8506,	8537,	8568,	8598,	8629,	8659	
		34	05	35	05	36	06	36	07	38	08	39	09	
		2	2	2	1'76	1	3	2	3	3	3	3	2	
1076	Oct 2, 132	8689.	8720,	8750,	8780,	8811,	8841,	8871,	8902,	8933,	8963,	8994,	9024,	9054
		39	10	40	10	41	11	41	12	43	13	44	14	44
		2	2	2	1'75	1	3	2	3	3	3	3	2	2
1075	Oct 3, 132	9055,	9086,	9116,	9146,	9177,	9207,	9237,	*9268,*	*9299*,	9329,	9360,	9390,	
		45	16	46	16	47	17	47	18	49	19	50	20	
		3	3	3	2'74	2	4	3	4	4	4	4	3	
1074	Oct 3, 132	9420,	9451,	9481,	9511,	9542,	9572.	9602,	9633,	9664,	9694,	9725,	9755,	
		50	21	51	21	52	22	52	23	54	24	55	25	
		3	3	3	2'73	2	3	2	3	3	3	3	2	
1073	Oct 2, 132	9785,	9816,	9846,	9876,	9907,	9937,	9967,	9998,	0029,	0059,	0090,	0120,	
		55	26	56	26	57	27	57	28	59	29	60	30	
		2	2	2	1'72	1	3	2	3	3	3	3	2	
1072	Oct 2, 133	0150,	0181,	0211,	0241,	0272,	0302,	*0332,*	*0363*,	0394,	0424,	0455,	0485,	0515
		60	31	01	31	02	32	02	33	04	34	05	35	05
		2	2	2	1'71	1	3	2	3	3	3	3	2	2
1071	Oct 3, 133	0516,	0547,	0577,	0607,	0638,	0668,	0698,	0729,	0760,	0790,	0821,	0851	
		06	37	07	37	08	38	08	39	10	40	11	41	
		3	3	3	2'70	2	4	3	4	4	4	4	3	
1070	Oct 3, 133	0881,	0912,	0942,	0972,	1003,	1033,	1063,	1094,	1125,	1155,	1186,	1216	
		11	42	12	42	13	43	13	44	15	45	16	46	
		3	3	3	2'69	2	3	2	3	3	3	3	2	
1069	Oct 2, 133	1246,	*1277,*	*1307*,	1337,	1368,	1398,	1428,	1459,	1490,	1520,	1551,	1581	
		16	47	17	47	18	48	18	49	20	50	21	51	
		2	2	2	1'68	1	3	2	3	3	3	3	2	
1068	Oct 2, 133	1611,	1642,	1672,	1702,	1733,	1763,	1793,	1824,	1855,	1885,	1916,	1946,	1976
		21	52	22	52	23	53	23	54	25	55	26	56	26
		2	2	2	1'67	1	3	2	3	3	3	3	2	2
1067	Oct 3, 133	1977,	2008,	2038,	2068,	2099,	2129,	2159,	2190,	2221,	*2251,*	*2282*,	2312	
		27	58	28	58	29	59	29	60	31	01	32	02	
		3	3	3	2'66	2	4	3	4	4	4	4	3	

I used this table to confirm 1098 as the "8th year" in the #2305 set, by counting back 19 years from 1079. For another example, consider that 3 x 19 = 57, and 2 x 31 = 62. The *ganzhi* for first days of lunar months are nearly repeated at 31-year intervals, exactly repeated at 62-year intervals, and almost repeated at 5-year intervals; and 57 + 5 = 62. 1071 + (2 x 57) = 1185. This suggests that 1185 ought to have an intercalation in mid-spring, as does 1071 (in the 1072 row). Chang Yuzhi (1998 pp. 307-308, #13) displays a set from *Heji* (*HJ* 11545) implying (in my analysis below) an intercalary 4th month. Bin is the diviner.

For 1185, Zhang Peiyu gives *yiwei* (32) as winter solstice in the *zi* month but Stahlman and Gingerich give (31); I would argue that the Chinese (counting 182 days from the summer solstice: 4 July 1186, JD 128 8421 to 2 January 1185, JD 128 8603) identified the winter solstice as two days late, at *bingshen* (33). The essential data from the fragment are these: 2nd month has *guihai* (60); 3rd month has *guiyou* (10); 5th month has *guimao* (40) and *guichou* (50). Parentheses around a number mean that the number represents the corresponding *ganzhi*. Filling in:

1	*zi* month:	(06) – (35)	(winter solstice *qi*-center (33); add 31)
2	*chou* month:	(36) – (05)	(*qi*-center (04); add 30); "(60), 2nd month"
3	*yin* month	(06) – (35)	(*qi*-center (34); add 30); "(10), 3rd month"
4	*mao* month	(36) – (04)	(*qi*-center (04); add 31)
i4	(intercalary)	(05) – (34)	(no *qi*-center)
5	*chen* month	(35) – (03)	(*qi*-center (35); add 31); "(40), 5th month"; "(50), 5th month"

The intercalary month is April 3 through May 2. In 1071 (in my table) it is also April 3 through May 2.

My analysis is not quite the same as Chang's, of course, but the date 1185 is probably consistent with Bin as diviner. I invite her to study it. (Chang would have to be at least open-minded about the *shuo* vs. *fei* problem.) Bin is a Period I (late Wu Ding) diviner; I date Wu Ding's death (this book, pp. 46 and 49) to 1189. This makes 1188 Zu Geng's succession year, and because that year began with a *ding* day, which was Wu Ding's day and so had to be avoided, Zu Geng's *gan* was determined by his accession year, in this case 1185: the *zi* month first day *jisi* (06) provided the *gan* for Wu Ding's heir Zu Ji ("*xiao wang*," junior king), chief mourner, with substitute king Zu Geng taking the next day.

Chang Yuzhi (1998, pp. 312-313) has another, #17 (*HJ* 26643), which I think I have been able to date exactly, using the same method. #17 is more difficult, and more interesting, because the date must be 1188, Zu Geng's succession year. Wu Ding had had a long reign: tradition gives him 59 years, and I give him three more at the beginning for completion of mourning. Oracle inscriptions late in his reign reveal that he was a sick man. The last few years were probably disorganized enough so that an intercalation had been missed, making 1188 begin with the *hai* month, and there was catching-up to be done. Chang has shown that #17 cannot be explained without assuming either two intercalary months or one intercalary month plus an extra-long 31-day month, all in the middle of one year (p. 314); I find I need two intercalary months. My analysis starts from 1074 (showing an intercalation between May and June), counting back 2 x 57 years. The data: *guiwei* (20), 6th month; *guichou* (50), 6th month; *guihai* (60), 6th month; *guiyou* (10), *guisi* (30), *guimao* (40); then *guichou* (50), 7th month; then *guisi* (30). The diviners are Xiong, Da and Chu, all active in the Zu Geng – Zu Jia era. Zhang Peiyu gives *jimao* (16) as the solstice; for me, it must be *xinsi* (18), JD 128 7508, 2 January. My analysis (the year is *jian hai*; ZPY's month 1 is DSN's month 2):

ZPY:	1 (54)	DSN: 2	(54) – (23)	(winter solstice *qi*-center (18); add 31)
	2 (24)	3	(24) – (52)	(*qi*-center (49); add 30)
	3 (54)	4	(53) – (22)	(*qi*-center (19); add 30)
	4 (23)	5	(23) – (51)	(*qi*-center (49); add 31)
	5 (52)	6	(52) – (21)	(*qi*-center (20); add 31); "(20), 6th month"
	6 (22)	i6	(22) – (50)	(lacks *qi*-center) "(50), 6th month"
	7 (51)	i6	(51) – (20)	(*qi*-center (51); add 30); "(60), 6th month"; "(10)"
	8 (20)	7	(21) – (50)	(*qi*-center (21); add 31); "(30)"; "(40)"; "(50), 7th month"
	9 (50)	8	(51) – (19)	(*qi*-center (52); add 30)
	10 (19)	9	(20) – (48)	(*qi*-center (22); add 30); "(30)"

I have followed Zhang Peiyu's *biao* as far as possible, while obeying the inscriptiion's instructions (three consecutive months numbered '6'; and putting *guichou* (50) in month 7), making long and short months alternate, and heeding the requirements of the *qi*-center system (as applied in Chapter One, p. 21). The year had thirteen lunar months. ZPY's 11, 12, 13 begin (49), (19), (49); one would expect (50), (19), (49). None of my 1st-day changes is more than one day. The first month 6 simply follows "month 5"; the second keeps the number '6' because it lacks a *qi*-center day, so is a normal intercalary month; the third converts the year from *jian hai* to *jian zi*. By following ZPY less closely I could have made the third month 6 lack a *qi*-center, with the second month 6 being the intercalation converting the year to a *jian zi* year. But it is surely right as I have it: the first day of *wu* month 7, *jiashen* (21), was JD 128 7691, = 4 July 1188, sun at 90, summer solstice, and Xia Zhi in the *qi* system. Thus the calendar is here made accurate to the day.

How did "primitive" Chinese astronomy and calendar science attain this degree of accuracy? The *qi*-center system as I have understood and applied it makes good sense, but without a formal rule for what we call "leap years" (and allowing perhaps deliberately a "standard time" winter solstice which was two days late), it is not accurate, and had to be corrected every few years by systematic observations. We can assume they did not have the technology for sufficiently exact time-keeping to minutes and seconds, but without that there are ways of identifying the solstices and equinoxes with high probability. The winter solstice would not do, even though the *qi* centers were formally marked off by counting from the conventionally identified Dong Zhi, because to use a gnomon-like instrument confidently one would want to compare days before and after, making corrections in one's first approximations; and anyway the weather might be bad. But once the "Dong Zhi" had been decided, the counting began at once, with Dong Zhi as day one. So "Dong Zhi" had to be identified by count from an earlier day. The obvious choices are the summer solstice and the autumn equinox, counting 91 days (365 divided by four to the nearest whole number) between the "cardinal points." (The intervals in days from the true winter solstice are, usually, 90, 95, 91, 89. The spring equinox was not used: allowing a standard 92 days to the summer solstice, it would have given a more or less accurate winter solstice rather than one two days late.)

The simplest method would be to focus on the summer solstice, with plenty of time to compare days and *xun* before and after, and then to count 2 times 91, checking on the autumn equinox along the way (their interval 91 days from summer solstice to autumn equinox is about right.) This is the focus to be expected. As Chang Yuzhi has shown (I take this up below), month 7, the *wu* month, was the first month in the Shang agricultural year; so Xia Zhi was "new year's day" for the Shang farmer.

Especially interesting to me is the measure of confirmation my analysis of Chang's #17 above gives to my death date 1189 for Wu Ding, because I deduced this date years ago, following completely different lines of argument. One line of argument began with my establishing the chronology of Xia, discovering that the first day of the reign of 14th king Kong Jia was a *jiazi* day. This indicated that *gan* names of kings, notably including Shang kings, must have been determined by the first days of their reigns. In this way I eventually worked out a "best explanation" chronology (necessarily tentative) for the whole of Shang, including Wu Ding. A second independent line of argument works back from my date 1086 for Di Xin. That date had been moved back in the *Annals* 16 years to 1102. There was a further back-shift in the Zu Geng and Zu Jia reigns: I found that Zu Jia's supposed 33 years had actually included Zu Geng's 11 years, i.e., when Zu Jia usurped the succession he claimed Zu Geng's calendar as his own. (Compare the year count of Wu Gong of (Quwo) Jin, after he eliminated the rival line of Jin lords in 679.) Traditionalist *zheng tong* chronology could not accept this, so Zu Geng's first year was moved back another 11 years. Therefore his first year in the *Annals*, 1215, must be reduced by 16 + 11 years to get the true date 1188.

Most scholars have agreed that a cluster of *jiagu* records of lunar eclipses ca. 1200-1180 must resolve the matter of Wu Ding's death date. D. N. Keightley (*Sources* 1978 p. 174 n. 19) lists four, 1198, 1192, 1189, and 1180, and he chooses the last. (But the data giving 1180 really refers, I think, to a partial eclipse in 1201; so 1189 is last.) The PRC Xia-Shang-Zhou Chronology Project chooses 1192, making Wu Ding's first year (of 59) be 1250. My choice is 1189, making Wu Ding's accession year be 1247 and his succession year 1250 (beginning with a *ding* day). The Nivison-Shaughnessy accession year hypothesis is rejected in China (too hastily, after inadequate study, Zhu and Zhang 1998 p. 424), and my *gan* hypothesis seems to have been ignored altogether. These two theories are used and implied in all of my work on the Shang. So the foregoing 1188 analysis confirms them.

Dating *HJ* 26643 (Chang's #17) to 1188, which had been my succession year of Zu Geng, and finding that the information in *HJ* 26643 does fit a king's first year, thus tends to confirm two of my theories which have been rejected or ignored by others, but which I have maintained are essential for Three Dynasties chronological research, as well as for research on the *Bamboo Annals* (*Jinben Zhushu jinian*). It tends also, of course, to confirm strongly my judgment that the reign lengths in the so-called "Modern Text" *Bamboo Annals* are usually correct. This judgment has been basic in my work on the chronology of both Xia and Shang. (The PRC Project has never given the "Modern Text" *Annals* serious attention, nor has Keightley.)

To complete my argument, I will offer an analysis of the last five years of Wu Ding's reign, 1193-1189.

Chang Yuzhi, In her book *Yin Shang lifa yanjiu*, pp. 400-422, argues from well selected agricultural inscriptions that the first month in the Shang calendar was the *wu* month, containing the summer solstice. If this is right without an important quaification, most of my work on Shang chronology is wrong.

I think that her argument for the *wu* month being the first month in these texts is decisive. But there is overwhelming evidence that in most other kinds of texts the first month of the Shang year was the *winter* solstice month, or one month before or one or two months after that. My argument that the first day of a reign determines the king's *gan* (and his sacrifice day) is consistent, and accounts for the evidence. That argument assumes that a reign begins at the beginning of a year, and it assumes also that the beginning of a year is almost always the *hai, zi or chou* (sometimes *yin*) month.

My argument for 1086 being the first year of the reign of Di Xin has several independent proofs, one of which is the collection of Yi Fang campaign inscriptions, which takes the ninth month as the month of the autumn equinox. (The equinox happens to be at the end of the 9th month, so a second (intercalary) 9th month is required.) This implies that the first month in the calendar being used was the *chou* month. A major military campaign, moreover, most appropriately would begin at the end of the growing season, as this one does.

Or consider the rainfall prediction and verification on pp. 290-291 of Chang's 1998 book (#23): "Crack on *xinwei* (08), Zheng certifying: next month, the 8th, Di will command much rain. Certifying: next month, the 8th, Di will not command much rain. (Verification:) On *dingyou* (34) it rained, until *jiayin* (51), 18 days. 9th month." (As I observed, "9th month" dates the act of verifying, not the content of the verification.) If month 1 were the *wu* month, months 8 and 9 would be the *chou* and *yin* months, in the winter dry season when rain was not expected or needed. But if the first month was the *zi* month, then months 8 and 9 would be the months of middle and late summer, when drought would be disastrous.

I am forced to the conclusion that the Shang used two different calendars, one for routine agricultural schedules on the one hand, and another for political, military and most other matters on the other hand. The conclusion ought to have been not that *the* Shang calendar was a *wu* calendar, but that *a* Shang calendar was a *wu* calendar. The Shang divination system or systems used at least two radically different calendars, with first months a half year apart. (This is surely amazing.)

As final proof of this, I call attention to the cluster of inscriptions dating lunar eclipses near the end of the reign of Wu Ding. My date for his death is 1189. One of the inscriptions dating lunar eclipses contains not only the *ganzhi* for the day, but also gives the number of the preceding month: it is "*shi san yue*" (13th month), implying that the eclipse occurred in the following first month. This information has made it possible to date the eclipse to 27 December 1192[34], necessarily the middle of a lunar month, which thus must be the zi month. So the zi month in this case must be the first month of the year.

This is as required by my *qi*-center argument confirming that 1188 must be the succession year of Zu Geng. Furthermore, a *qi-center* analysis of the relevant late Wu Ding inscriptions leads to an explanation why Zu Geng's reign began with a year taking the *hai* month as first month.

---

[34] D. N.Keightley, *Sources of Shang History*, Berkeley: University of California Press (1978), p. 174, n. 19.

I will now analyze years approximately corresponding to 1193-1189 (Zhang Peiyu, *Xian Qin shilibiao*, p. 27):

1193: solstice (50) taken to be (52); apparently the Chinese took the interval from (observed) autumn equinox to (deduced) winter solstice to be one fourth of the year; but it is actually two (or three) days less.

For ZPY, 1193 has 13 months. First days are as follows:
(23) (52) (22) (52) (21) (51) (21) (50) (20) (49) (18) (48) (17)

ZPY's first month does not contain (52). (52) is the first day of ZPY's 2nd month. ZPY's last month of 1194 ends with (22). Therefore ZPY's first month of 1193 cannot contain a *qi*-center, and must be intercalary. So it cannot be the first month, but must be intercalary first month, which must follow the first month; thus year 1193 must have begun with the *hai* month at the end of ZPY's 1194. It contained an intercalation, so it was a 13-month year, but it ended one month short. Day (17) above began the next year.

For ZPY, 1192 has 12 months, first days as follows:
(47) (16) (46) (16) (45) (15) (44) (14) (43) (13) (42) (12)

The last month above, beginning with (12), contained *gui*-days (20), (30), and (40). These days are put in "month 13" in two inscriptions recording the eclipse of 27 December 1192. (The inscriptions: *Jinzhang* 594 and *Ku-Fang* 1595.) Therefore 1192 must have begun with ZPY's last month of 1193, and was a 13-month year, in Wu Ding's calendar.

But ZPY's next year 1191 actually was (astronomically) a 13-month year, as ZPY shows. Its first days:
(41) (11) (40) (10) (39) (09) (38) (08) (38) (07) (37) (06) (36)

The eclipse occurred "in 7 days (inclusive), between (56) and (57)," obviously counting the "7 days" beginning with (50), in the month *after* the "13th month." ((41) *jiachen* was 12 December 1192. From (41) to (56) is 15 days; 15 days from Dec 12 is Dec 27, 1192.) Having given 13 months to both 1193 and 1192, not surprisingly the Chinese did not also take 1191 as a 13-month year. So the intercalation was omitted.

Therefore 1190 began with ZPY's 13th month of 1191, and ended with ZPY's 11th month of 1190. ZPY's first days for 1190, a 12-month year:
(05) (35) (04) (34) (03) (33) (02) (32) (01) (31) (01) (30)

So also with ZPY's 1189: it began with ZPY's 12th month of 1190 and ended with ZPY's 11th month of 1189. ZPY's first days of months in 1189[35]:
(60) (29) (59) (28) (58) (27) (56) (26) (55) (25) (55) (25)

Therefore the *hai* month of 1189 beginning with (25) became the first month of 1188, the first year of Zu Geng. My previously worked out analysis of Chang's #17 (on pp. 312-314) is consistent with this: #17 (*HJ* 26643) turned out to be dated 1188. I had found myself required to take ZPY's first day of 1188, (54), as the first day of the *second* month of the year corresponding to 1188.[36]

---

[35] Keightley (ibid.) dates the lunar eclipse of 1189 to 25 October; no month was given in the inscription.

[36] Xu Fengxian (letter of 24 June 2008) has offered me thought-provoking advice on matters in this appendix and supplement. She points out that in Chinese classical literature mapping the year into *qi*-periods always begins with the winter solstice, not the autumn equinox; and that the technical problem of determining the winter solstice day is easier than determining the autumn equinox day. She is right. But (1) in the 11th century, the Chinese' crude technology, plus the ritual need to be able to say, "Today is the solstice day," with no possibility of changing the decision later, required them to have some rule for locating a "solstice day" (in any weather) by counting from an earlier date. And (2) for this reason which day – winter solstice or autumn equinox -- was easier to pinpoint correctly is irrelevant. But the question is interesting. It redirected my attention from the autumn equinox to the summer solstice, as the probable base date for counting. I am studying the problem. (The *zhang-bu* count from summer solstice to autumn equinox is approximately correct.) Meanwhile, throughout this book I have left in place my assumption that the base date for counting was the autumn equinox. The important point is that the "standard time" winter solstice was apparently two days late.

Supplement 3: The Project's Chronology for Di Xin

Through Zhang Lidong, I recently learned about Xu Fengxian's book (2006), *Shang mo zhouji sipu heli yanjiu* (Research on the dating of the ritual cycle in late Shang). This is exactly the problem I have been working on here. I had wondered where to find the reasoning behind the Project's position. One finds it in Xu's book, but discussion between Xu and Prof. Li had been going on for years, as seen in Li's article in his *Zhaji* (pp. 245-250), "Another Discussion about the Ritual Calendar for Di Xin Years 1 through 11" (*Zai shuo Di Xin yuan zhi shiyi si sipu*). Reading Xu's book led me to revise my work, making corrections and additions. But our results are completely different; at most one of us can be right.

The problem for all of us is to reconcile the Yi Fang campaign set in years 10-11 with two texts dated "year 9," which seem to be chronologically tied together, one being explicitly on the impending conflict with the Yi Fang. In section 3 above, I wrote, "Another inscription, *HJ* 37852, anticipates trouble with the Yi Fang, and is dated '*yihai* (12) ... 2nd month, coincident with the *yong* for Zu Yi, in the 9th *si*.'" Before this one in Xu's book is *Ming* 61, a fragment in two parts, first "Guichou (50) ... divining: Now ... Lady ... has ...." Then (above, so possibly later in time) "Childbirth not good. 1st month, coincident with *yong* night for Xiao Jia, 9th *si*." ("*yong* night" is the night *before*, not after, *yong* day).

The *yong* night for Xiao Jia in the ritual schedule is exactly 22 days before the *yong* for Zu Yi, and *guichou* (50) is exactly 22 days before *yihai* (12). So it might seem obvious that Shima Kunio must be right (*Kenkyu* p. 141) in saying that the two parts of *Ming* 61 are a unit, in which the day date *guizhou* (50) dates both lower and upper pieces.[37] If this is accepted, it follows that to get the two rites into month 1 and month 2, one must interpret the Yi Fang set so as to put the two 9th month dates, "*jiawu* (31), *zai* for Shang Jia" and later "*guihai* (60)" at the beginning and end of the *same* 9th month, with no intercalary month. Any other choice will put the *Ming* 61 ritual date in month 2, contrary to what the fragment explicitly says. To Shima, understandably followed by Xu and Prof. Li, this proves that there is no intercalary 9th month implied in the Yi Fang set. So Xu and Li do not even pause to look at the year 1077 in Zhang Peiyu's *Shili Biao,* and choose 1066 as Di Xin 10, making 1075 Di Xin 1.

That the Yi Fang set can seem to fit at all in 1066 is surprising, but the fit is hardly comfortable. One must assume four long months in succession, one of which would be a 31-day month. One must also say that the *yong* date at the end of the year, "10th year 12th month *jiawu* (31) *yong*" is a mistake and that "*jiawu* (31) *yong*" should be in the 1st month of year 11. (That solves the problem of finding a year ending with jiawu (31), *yiwei* (32), or *bingshen* (33).) Xu goes farther and says that "9th month" for the *zai* for Shang Jia is an error for "8th month." Xu is reassured by being able to date the "2nd-year Biji *you*" in 1074; this I assume is what Li is saying when in a note in his *Zhaji* article he says that Xu shows that 1074 is Di Xin 2.

If this is wrong, Shima Kunio has made a mistake. The mistake: "Childbirth not good" (i.e., the child turned out to be a girl) shows that the subject of the whole set, including the lower part or parts from which we have only a few words, was concern about the sex of an expected birth of a royal consort's child. There would be no point in resorting to divination about this when the lady was already in labor. So the top portion, which is complete, is not the negative component of a positive-negative *duizhen* pair of *trial* statements (or questions, as some would still insist). The statement is a *report*, terminating the whole story, certified by a date to a specific *yong* "night" (because the birth occurred at night), functioning as the *verification* of a *previous* trial statement (complete with *zhen* and *ganzhi* day-date). This must have been coupled with a royal prediction, which a "good" birth would have falsified. For a sadly amusing example, see Keightley's 1978 book, figure 12 (*Bing Bian* 247.1). I adapt Keightley's translation (using *pinyin*):

> Crack on *jiashen* (21), Que divined: (Charge:) "Fu Hao's childbearing will be good." (Prognostigation:) The king, reading the cracks, said, "If it be a *ding* day childbearing, it will be good. If it be a *geng* day childbearing, it will be extremely auspicious." (Verification:) On the 31st day, *jiayin* (51), she gave birth. It was not good. It was a girl.

---

[37] Xu p. 54 cites Shima *Kenkyu* p. 141, and adds that Xu Jinxiong, Chang Yuzhi and Li Xueqin all agree with Shima.

(There is a similar negative "charge" and "verification.") Keightley's example is from Period I, in a very different style, but it illustrates the basic idea. The obvious inference is that the date *guichou* (50) dates what was done three or more *xun earlier* than the birth event.

If so, the only reason for dating *Ming* 61 to the month before *HJ* 37852 *and in the same year* is that the date in *Ming* 61 is explicitly "9th *si*." (The Menzies collection *Yinxu buci* (*Ming*) was published in 1917; there can be no way to argue that *Ming* 61 and *HJ* 37852 were found together.) For Xu and Li the same year for both would seem inescapable, because they have never considered the possibility that there could be another Di Xin calendar. They have not, because their analysis showed them Di Xin's reign was 1075-1047, only 29 years, whereas for me it was 1086-1041, a total of 46 years. Moreover, they think they have a late Shang bronze dated "25th *si*" (Project *Brief Report* p. 58; Xu pp. 82-83, *Zai* Hu *jiao*). (The correct date is "day *gengshen* (57), 20th *si*, *yi*-day plus 5"; see Akatsuka p. 666). Thus they do not have to ask (as I must) why we have no Di Xin inscriptions dated in the higher 20's, 30's, and low 40's.

Ming 61 belongs in Di Xin's second calendar. The 9th *si* assuming *yuan* 1068 would be 1060. The applicable first day of the cycle would be 15 September 1061, JD 133 4151, day *jiachen* (41). The "*yong* night" for Xiao Jia was the night before the *yong* day, hence day 170 in the cycle. The date then is JD 133 4320, which was 3 March 1060, day *guisi* (30). This day was 40 days *after guichou* (50). The interval is nearly the same as in Keightley's example.

I have independent reasons, from the literary record, for my dating of late Shang, and the Project has none, for its dating (except for *Guoyu* "Zhou Yu" 3.7, which I show in Appendix 1 is a 5th century BCE invention). My independent reasons rest directly or indirectly on the "Modern Text" *Bamboo Annals*, and the Project will have none of that. The *Annals* question is going to have to be settled, probably, before there can be agreement on anything else.

Meanwhile, reflect on this: In his 1959 book *Yin Dai Dili Jianlun* pp. 37-41 Li accepts the *jiagu* that for me dictate an intercalary 9th month in Di Xin 10 (pp. 37-38), but states flatly that in Yin and Western Zhou there was only end-of-year intercalation (p. 41). In his *Zhaji*, he has come to accept intra-year intercalation, but has found other reasons to reject an intercalary 9th month in Di Xin 10. (In 1959, he had thought that the campaign was in Di Yi's reign, but he has changed his mind on that.)

Why? He inspects Shang bronzes judged to be in Di Xin's reign, with dates between 2 and 10, and looks at the 2nd year Biji *you*. It can be dated in 1074, and in other years. He chooses 1074, probably because he thinks he can squeeze the Yi Fang set for year 10 into 1066, but only if he does not allow an intercalary 9th month in Di Xin 10. Placing Ming 61 immediately before *HJ* 37852 forces this step. Perhaps I would have done the same, had I not already gone my own way, seeing the need and justification for a second Di Xin calendar, before *Ming* 61 came to my attention. (Perhaps I would now even be defending the Project's chronology, instead of "tearing it to pieces"!)

As things stand, I am able to date all the Di Xin inscriptions I can find, either in the 1086 calendar or in the 1068 calendar. I find that most of the bronzes take the *yin* month as first month. One thing I have not been able to explain with complete confidence is why there are several inscriptions using 1086 as *yuan*, dated in years after 1068. The matter needs watching, but perhaps no explanation is needed. There was no change of king; Zhou Xin, king of the 1086 calendar, was still king, called "Di Xin" from 1068 on. The 1068 calendar I assume was nominally for Wu Geng as "junior king"; this calendar existed and could be used at once. It was, and probably in time became the only one used. It was used in 1049 in the Zai Hu *jiao* and in ten-day sacrifice *jia-gu* inscriptions, and in 1046 in the *Yi Zhou shu* "Feng Bao" for inter-state relations. The real king was still Di Xin.

Appendix 4: the Late Shang Ritual Cycle

Note: My account of the chronology of the last eight decades of Shang is complex and not conventional. I summarize it here, together with my main reasons for proposing it.

Wu Yi died in 1109. (Here I reduce the *Annals* date 1125 by 16.) He had reigned for 2+35 years, given as 35 years in the *Annals*. But inscriptions for the Yu Fang campaign indicate that he died in "year 10." So if I have dated them correctly, Wu Yi must have declared a new calendar, presumably for his son and heir to be Wenwu Ding, beginning 1118.

The Di Yi reign calendar began in 1105, a year beginning with an *yi*-day. Therefore Wenwu Ding's 13 years in the *Annals* were 10 (1118-1109) + 3 (1108-1106).

The *Annals'* 9-year reign for Di Yi is wrong. Pre-burial *Annals* editing changed 19 years to 9 years; i.e., the Wei state editors would not cut Wu Yi 10 years short, and would not admit overlapping reigns. Yet they knew 13 years was right. So instead of giving Wenwu Ding only 3 years as do other chronologies, they gave him 13, and cut out the first 10 years of Di Yi. Therefore *Annals* Di Yi dates "3rd year" and :9th year" ought to be "13th year" and "19th year." The length of Di Yi's reign was 19 years.

Di Xin's first year was 1086 (not 1075, the Project's date). Di Xin already had his *gan* ("Xin" probably as of 1106). 1086 began with a *jiazi* day. So he was probably appointed king in this year, Di Yi living on, perhaps to 1082.

Di Xin began a second calendar in 1068, probably only then calling himself "*di*." This calendar was probably conceived, however, as for Di Xin's heir Lu Fu – to be "Wu Geng" (1068 began with a *geng*-day). For Di Xin's activities as *wang*, the 1086 calendar continued to be used.

Some proofs:

I put the Yu Fang campaign this early because the average length of the ritual cycle was slightly less than a solar year, so the later in the year the first day of the current cycle is, the earlier must be the absolute date. Also my dating seems confirmed by an adjusted analysis of the chronology of events in the *Annals*: the Yu Fang campaign is not mentioned, but an inscription indicates that it ended with a triumphal hunt, which I date late summer or autumn 1109, and the *Annals* says that Wu Yi died from being struck by lightening during a hunt, date 1125, corrected to 1109.

For Di Yi year 1, 1105 fits. 1086 as Di Xin 1 is virtually certain, and so is 1106 as Wenwu Ding 3 (or 13), his accession year if Wu Yi died in 1109. The strongest proof is the events dated Di Yi 3: an earthquake in Zhou (confirmable as in 1093, from *Lü shi chunqiu*); and "Nanzhong" ordered to "oppose the Kun Yi" (same as the Xianyun), "and wall off the north." Nanzhong was actually one of Zhou Xuan Wang's military commanders. His activity was part of a campaign datable by inscriptions to 815, Xuan 13.[38] At the time this mistake was made, "Di Yi 3" must have been "Di Yi 13." If so, there is an explanation for the myth that "Wen Wang produced Wu Wang in [his] 15th year": the year (not "his") was Di Yi 15 = 1091. The *Annals* says Wu Wang died having lived 54 years, and one can prove independently that he died in 1038.

The Yi Fang campaign set of *jiagu* requires as 10th year a year with an intercalary 9th month, ending with *jiawu* (31), *yiwei* (32), or *bingshen* (33), roughly in the middle of the first half of the eleventh century. The only possible year is 1077, making 1086 be Di Xin 1. The Project had the bad luck of starting with data and mis-data which made this seem impossible. So from the start the Project missed not only the right date to match with a ritual cycle date, but also missed an invaluable clue, connecting *qi*-centers with intercalary months, showing that the *zhang* system was applicable even as far back as late Shang. Instead of mapping out a tentative chronology with intercalary months in place, and then testing it with inscriptions, the Project scholars tried to begin with inscriptions and use them to identify intercalations, with no supporting intercalation theory.

---

[38] Ma Chengyuan, 1988, p. 310 n. 1; I am indebted to Prof. E. L. Shaughnessy for this reference. The bronzes are the Guoji Zibo *pan* and the Piji *gui*, #48 and #49 on p.225 above.

I was luckier, through sheer ignorance avoiding *Ming* 61 and what Shima Kunio does with it. So I was led directly to a 46-year reign for Di Xin, 1086-1041. This forced me to see that there had to be a second Di Xin calendar. Where did it begin? There were two clues. There was the later tradition that Di Yi had 37 years. I knew that Di Yi 1 was 1105. Perhaps the unknown calendar was a "*dì*" calendar beginning 37 years later: 1068. The second clue was *Yi Zhou shu* "Feng Bao"; and to use this all I had to do was not to let myself be scared off by Pankenier's misunderstanding of it.[39] This chapter presents a gathering in Zhou of pro-Zhou lords well before the conquest. Its date is incomplete: 23rd year, *gengzi shuo,* month missing. The only year in the likely time-span with a month beginning with *gengzi* was 1046 (5th *jian zi* month), and if this was year 23, year 1 must be 1068.[40]

Identifying 1077 as Di Xin 10, with an intercalary 9th month, led me to notice that the *zhang* theory, together with the concept that an intercalary month is a month lacking a *qi*-center, was working. Moreover, in 1077 the sans-*qi*-center intercalary 9th month was the month immediately following the autumn equinox day, which is a *qi*-center day in intercalation theory. So the Chinese of the time, treating the seasons (if only for convenience) as equal in length (which they are not) were mapping out the solar year into *qi*-periods by counting days from a correctly identified autumn equinox day, and consequently were getting a conventional winter solstice day two days late. This led immediately to a conclusive proof that 1040 was the conquest year, and much later to a reconfirmation of 1188 as Zu Geng's succession year, showing me that my strategy for recovering all of Shang chronology – to the day -- had been on target.

The last thing I noticed was that if the Shang calendar was being used for late Shang inter-state relations (as in the "Feng Pao"), then the Shang date for the conquest might be significant. The Zhou *de jure* year 1 was 1058, the year after the great conjunction, and year 29 in the 1086 calendar. The Zhou *de facto* year 1, i.e., the year of the conquest itself, was 1040, which was year 29 in the 1068 calendar. So Zhou "lucky date" strategy becomes clear: first the year was chosen – year 29, but in the current calendar – then (of course) *jiazi* had to be the day. But which *jiazi*? It recurs every 60 days. A simple check showed them that if the choice were *jian yin* month 2, the *jiazi* day would be Qing Ming Day. Obviously this must be Heaven's will. No wonder Wu Wang refused to listen to Yu Xin's warning.

We may be tempted to smile, but we should not. Having Heaven's will be obvious to your forces and your allies would be only marginally more important than having it be obvious to your hapless opponents. This was how great battles could be won.

(I leave open the problem of identifying "Wenwu Di Yi." It could be that there were two kings named "Wenwu," father: Wenwu Ding, and son: Wenwu Yi; the latter being recognized as "*dì*" posthumously in 1068, when his son Zhou Xin assumed the title "*dì*" for himself. Or possibly there was only one "Wenwu" king, given the *gan* name *ding* at the beginning of Wu Yi's reign, but declaring himself "*dì*" in 1105 (first day *yiyou*) and so receiving cult on a *ding* day or on an *yi* day – a problem perhaps needing resolution by divination. There are many examples of rites addressed (when?) to "Wenwu Ding" announced on a *bing* day (next day being *ding*), and also a few addressed to "Wenwu Di" performed on an *yi* day (Shima, *Sorui* 537.2-3). If there was only one "Wenwu" king, the 37 years assigned to him could be not just the interval between *yuan* 1105 and *yuan* 1068, but also this king's actual reign-span through different calendars, 1118-1082, if I am not absurd in suggesting 1082 as his year of death.)

Addendum: To persons I name in gratitude on p. 5, I add Prof. Jeffrey K. Riegel, who several years ago left Berkeley to relocate in Australia, perhaps forgetting that I still have his copy of Akatsuka. I couldn't have done Appendix 4 without it. Jeff has given me much good advice over many years -- DSN April 2009.

[39] Pankenier *BSOAS* lv (1992) 3 P.499; *EC* 7(1981-2(=1983)) P.35; also Shaughnessy, *EC* 11-12(1985-87) pp. 53-54.

[40] The existence of the 1068 calendar is, I think, proved conclusively by *HJ* 37867 (Xu Fengxian 2006 p. 104), taken together with the Zai Hu *jiao* (when correctly read "20th year, *yi* plus 5"), as explained above pp.243-4.

Di Xin 1 through 12 (1086-1075)

1086 Di Xin 1	Jia Rite Days	Royal Ancestor
2 (*zi*) 01[41] 12/21	01 *ji* 11 *ji* 21 *ji*	Qian Jia Qiang Jia Xiang Jia
3 31 1/20	31 41 *ji* 51	 Zu Jia
4 60 2/18	01 11 *yong* 21 *yong*	 *Gong Dian* Shang Jia
5 30 3/20	31 41 *yong* 51 *yong*	 Da Jia Xiao Jia
6 60 4/19	01 11 *yong* 21 *yong*	 Qian Jia Qiang Jia
7 29 5/18	31 *yong* 41 51 *yong*	Xiang Jia Zu Jia
8 59 6/17	01 11 *yi* 21 *yi*	 *Gongdian* Shang Jia
9 29 7/17	31 41 *yi* 51 *yi*	 Da Jia Xiao Jia
10 58 8/15	01 11 *yi* 21 *yi*	 Qian Jia Qiang Jia
11 28 9/14	31 *yi* 41 51 *yi*	Xiang Jia Zu Jia
12 57 10/13	01 *ji* 11 *ji* 21	*Gongdian* [37] Shang Jia
1 (*hai*) 26 11/11	31 *ji* 41 *ji* 51	Da Jia Xiao Jia
Left Column:: upper left is civil calendar lunar month;	upper right is *ganzhi* for first day of the lunar month;	lower left is Julian month and day corresponding to lunar month first day.

1085 Di Xin 2	Jia Rite Days	Royal Ancestor
2 (*zi*) 56 12/11	01 *ji* 11 *ji* 21 *ji*	Qian Jia Qiang Jia Xiang Jia
3 25 1/9	31 41 *ji* 51	 Zu Jia
4 55 2/8	01 11 *yong* 21 *yong*	 *Gongdian* Shang Jia*[42]
5 24 3/8	31 41 *yong* 51 *yong*	 Da Jia Xiao Jia
6 54 4/7	01 11 *yong* 21 *yong*	 Qian Jia Qiang Jia
7 23 5/6	31 *yong* 41 51 *yong*	Xiang Jia Zu Jia
8 53 6/5	01 11 *yi* 21 *yi*	 *Gongdian* Shang Jia
i8 23 7/5	31 41 *yi* 51 *yi*	 Da Jia Xiao Jia
9 52 8/3	01 11 *yi* 21 *yi*	 Qian Jia Qiang Jia
10 22 9/2	31 *yi* 41 51 *yi*	Xiang Jia Zu Jia
11 52 10/2	 01 11 *ji*	 (extra *xun*) *Gongdian* [36]
12 21 10/31	21 *ji* 31 41 *ji*	Shang Jia Da Jia
1 51 11/30	51 *ji* 01 11 *ji*	Xiao Jia Qian Jia

[41] Di Xin's first day (*zi* month) was *jiazi* (01). This suggests that the date was picked, as would be the case if he were given a calendar by his father Di Yi, still living.

[42] *HJ* 37836; shows *jian hai* calendar in use here. (Asterisk *, here and later, marks a date with an inscription.)

1084 Di Xin 3	Jia Rite Days	Royal Ancestor
2 (*zi*) 20 12/29	21 *ji* 31 *ji* 41	Qiang Jia Xiang Jia
3 49 1/27	51 *ji* 01 11	Zu Jia
4 19 2/26	21 *yong* 31 *yong* 41	*Gongdian* Shang Jia
5 48 3/27	51 *yong* 01 *yong* 11	Da Jia Xiao Jia
6 18 4/26	21 *yong* 31 *yong* 41 *yong*	Qian Jia Qiang Jia*[43] Xiang Jia*
7 47 5/25	51 01 *yong* 11	 Zu Jia*
8 17 6/24	21 *yi* 31 *yi* 41	*Gongdian** Shang Jia*
9 46 7/23	51 *yi* 01 *yi* 11	Da Jia Xiao Jia
10 16 8/22	21 *yi* 31 *yi* 41 *yi*	Qian Jia Qiang Jia Xiang Jia
11 46 9/21	51 01 *yi* 11 *ji*	 Zu Jia *Gongdian**[44] [36]
12 15 10/20	21 *ji* 31 *zai* 41 *ji*	Shang Jia* Shang Jia* Da Jia*
1 45 11/19	51 *ji* 01 11 *ji*	Xiao Jia* Qian Jia

1083 Di Xin 4	Jia Rite Days	Royal Ancestor
2 (*zi*) 15 12/19	21 *ji* 31 *ji* 41	Qiang Jia Xiang Jia
3 44 1/17	51 *ji* 01 11	Zu Jia
4 13 2/15	21 *yong* 31 *yong* 41	*Gongdian* Shang Jia
5 43 3/17	51 *yong* 01 *yong* 11	Da Jia Xiao Jia
6 12 4/15	21 *yong* 31 *yong* 41 *yong*	Qian Jia Qiang Jia Xiang Jia
7 42 5/15	51 01 *yong*	 Zu Jia
8 11 6/13	11 21 *yi* 31 *yi*	 *Gongdian* Shang Jia
9 40 7/12	41 51 *yi* 01 *yi*	 Da Jia Xiao Jia
10 10 8/11	11 21 *yi* 31 *yi*	 Qian Jia Qiang Jia
11 40 9/10	41 *yi* 51 01 *yi*	Xiang Jia Zu Jia
12 10 10/10	11 *ji* 21 *ji* 31	*Gongdian* [36] Shang Jia
1 39 11/8	41 *ji* 51 *ji* 01	Da Jia Xiao Jia

[43] *HJ* 35736, 37836

[44] *HJ* 37840, 35529. This sequence, specifying "11th month" and "12th month in successive xun, the first two events in the cycle, makes it virtually impossible to assign any other absolute date.

1082 [45] Di Xin 5	Jia Rite Days	Royal Ancestor
2 (*zi*) 09 12/8	11 *ji* 21 *ji* 31 *ji*	Qian Jia Quang Jia Xiang Jia
3 39 1/7	41 51 *ji* 01	 Zu Jia
4 08 2/5	11 21 *yong* 31 *yong*	 *Gongdian* Shang Jia
5 38 3/7	41 51 *yong* 01 *yong*	 Da Jia Xiao Jia
i5 07 4/5	11 21 *yong* 31 *yong*	 Qian Jia Qiang Jia
6 36 5/4	41 *yong* 51 01 *yong*	Xiang Jia Zu Jia
7 05 6/2	11 21 *yi* 31 *yi*	 *Gongdian* Shang Jia
8 35 7/8	41 51 *yi* 01 *yi*	 Da Jia Xiao Jia
9 04 7/31	11 21 *yi* 31 *yi*	 Qian Jia Qiang Jia
10 34 8/30	41 *yi* 51 01 *yi*	Xiang Jia Zu Jia
11 04 9/29	11 *ji* 21 *ji* 31	*Gongdian* [36] Shang Jia
12 33 10/38	41 *ji* 51 *ji* 01	Da Jia Xiao Jia
13 03 11/27	11 *ji* 21 *ji* 31 *ji*	Qian Jia Qiang Jia Xiang Jia

1081 Di Xin 6	Jia Rite Days	Royal Ancestor
14 (*zi*) 33 12/27	41 51 *ji* 01	 Zu Jia
1 03 1/26	11 21 *yong* 31 *yong*	 *Gongdian* Shang Jia
2 32 2/24	41 51 *yong* 01 *yong*	 Da Jia Xiao Jia
3 02 3/25	11 21 *yong*	 Qian Jia
4 31 4/23	31 *yong* 41 *yong* 51	Qiang Jia*[46] Xiang Jia
5 60 5/22	01 *yong* 11 21 *yi*	Zu Jia *Gongdian*
6 29 6/20	31 *yi* 41 51 *yi*	Shang Jia Da Jia
7 59 7/20	01 *yi* 11 21 *yi*	Xiao Jia Qian Jia
8 28 8/18	31 *yi* 41 *yi* 51	Qiang Jia Xiang Jia
9 58 9/17	01 *yi* 11 *ji* 21 *ji*	Zu Jia *Gongdian* [36] Shang Jia
10 27 10/16	31 41 *ji* 51 *ji*	 Da Jia Xiao Jia
11 57 11/15	01 11 *ji* 21 *ji*	 Qian Jia Qiang Jia

[45] Di Yi must have died in this year, his 37th (from 1118). *HJ* 37852 requires the *yong* Qian Jia *xun* in 1078 (Di Xin 9) to be in the 2nd month, in a cycle beginning with *jiazi*. This in turn requires that the *xun* between *yong* Zu Jia and *yi Gongdian* be omitted. The effect was to make Di Yi's *yong* coincide with the *yi* for Bao *yi*, thus placing Di Yi in the ritual calendar, which I assume had to be done when mourning was completed.

[46] Akatsuka #4, *Xiaochen* Yi *jia*, shows that this rite as dated counted as the 1st of month 4; therefore the calendar was *jian chou* by this time. The probable cause of the change was Di Yi's death.

1080 Di Xin 7	Jia Days	Rite	Royal Ancestor
12 (*zi*) 27	31 41 51	*ji* *ji*	Xiang Jia Zu Jia
1 57 1/14	01 11 21	 *yong*	 *Gongdian*
2 26 2/12	31 41 51	*yong* *yong*	Shang Jia Da Jia
3 56 3/14	01 11 21	*yong* *yong*	Xiao Jia Qian Jia
4 25 4/12	31 41 51	*yong* *yong*	Qiang Jia Xiang Jia
5 55 5/12	01 11 21	*yong* *yi*	Zu Jia *Gongdian*
6 24 6/10	31 41 51	*yi* *yi*	Shang Jia Da Jia
7 53 7/9	01 11 21	*yi* *yi*	Xiao Jia*[48] Qian Jia
8 23 8/8	31 41 51	*yi* *yi*	Qiang Jia Xiang Jia
9 52 9/6	01 11 21	*yi* *ji* *ji*	Zu Jia *Gongdian* [35] Shang Jia
10 22 10/6	 31 41	 *ji*	 Da Jia
11 51 11/4	51 01 11	*ji* *ji*	Xiao Jia Qian Jia

1079 Di Xin 8	Jia Days	Rite	Royal Ancestor
12 (*zi*) 21 12/4	21 31 41	*ji* *ji*	Qiang Jia Xiang Jia
1 51 1/4	51 01 11	*ji*	Zu Jia
i1 21 2/2	21 31 41	*yong* *yong*	*Gongdian* Shang Jia
2 50 3/3	51 01 11	*yong* *yong*	Da Jia Xiao Jia
3 20 4/2	21 31 41	*yong* *yong* *yong*	Qian Jia Qiang Jia Xiang Jia
4 49 5/1	51 01 11	 *yong* *yi*	 Zu Jia[47] *Gongdian*
5 19 5/31	21 31 41	*yi* *yi*	Shang Jia Da Jia
6 48 6/29	51 01 11	*yi* *yi*	Xiao Jia Qian Jia
7 17 7/28	21 31 41	*yi* *yi*	Qiang Jia Xiang Jia
8 47 8/27	51 01 11	*yi* *ji* *ji*	Zu Jia *Gongdian* [37] Shang Jia
9 16 9/25	21 31 41	 *ji* *ji*	 Da Jia Xiao Jia
10 46 10/25	51 01 11	 *ji* *ji*	 Qian Jia Qiang Jia
11 15 11/23	21 31 41	*ji* *ji*	Xiang Jia Zu Jia

[47] Omitting the *xun* after *yong* Zu Jia and before *yi Gongdian* made this cycle only 35 *xun* (as required by *HJ* 37852, Di Xin 9, 2nd month). This made the *yong* for Di Yi (probably recently dead) coincide with the *yi* for Bao Yi, where it remained. (Supplement 1, Fan *fang ding*, *yong* for Di Yi, 22nd year 5th month *yiwei* (32) in 1065.)

[48] *Yinxu West* #1713 (see Supplement 1) is dated *renshen* (09), 7th *si*, month 6, *yi* day. The date fits 1080, *renshen* in the *yi* Xiao Jia *xun*, assuming a *jian yin* calendar, commonly used in bronze inscriptions. The *yi* rite is for Da Wu Bi Ren.

1078 Di Xin 9	Jia Rite Days	Royal Ancestor
12 (*zi*) 45 12/23	51 01 11 *yong*	 *Gongdian*
1 15 1/22	21 *yong* 31 41 *yong*	Shang Jia Da Jia
2 44 2/20	51 *yong* 01 11 *yong*	Xiao Jia Qian Jia*[49]
3 14 3/22	21 *yong* 31 *yong* 41	Qiang Jia Xiang Jia
4 44 4/21	51 *yong* 01 11 *yi*	Zu Jia *Gongdian*
5 13 5/20	21 *yi* 31 41 *yi*	Shang Jia Da Jia
6 43 6/19	51 *yi* 01 11 *yi*	Xiao Jia Qian Jia
7 12 7/18	21 *yi* 31 *yi*	Qiang Jia Xiang Jia
8 41 8/16	41 51 *yi* 01	 Zu Jia (extra *xun*)
9 11 9/15	11 *ji* 21 *ji* 31	Gongdian [36] Shang Jia
10 40 10/14	41 *ji* 51 *ji* 01	Da Jia Xiao Jia*[51]
11 10 11/13	11 *ji* 21 *ji* 31 *ji*	Qian Jia Qiang Jia Xiang Jia

1077 Di Xin 10	Jia Rite Days	Royal Ancestor
12 (*zi*) 39 12/12	41 51 *ji* 01	 Zu Jia
1 09 1/11	11 21 *yong* 31 *yong*	 *Gongdian* Shang Jia
2 38 2/9	41 51 *yong* 01 *yong*	 Da Jia Xiao Jia
3 08 3/10	11 21 *yong* 31 *yong*	 Qian Jia Qiang Jia
4 38 4/9	41 *yong* 51 01 *yong*	Xiang Jia Zu Jia
5 07 5/8	11 21 *yi* 31 *yi*	 *Gongdian* Shang Jia
6 37 6/7	41 51 *yi* 01 *yi*	 Da Jia Xiao Jia
7 06 7/6	11 21 *yi* 31 *yi*	 Qian Jia Qiang Jia
8 36 8/5	41 *yi* 51 01 *yi*	Xiang Jia Zu Jia
9 05 9/3	11 *ji* 21 *ji* 31 *zai*	*Gongdian* [37] Shang Jia Shang Jia*[50]
i9 35 10/3	41 *ji* 51 *ji* 01	Da Jia* Xiao Jia
10 04 11/1	11 *ji* 21 *ji* 31 *ji*	Qian Jia Qiang Jia Xiang Jia
11 34 12/1	41 51 *ji* 01	 Zu Jia

[49] *HJ* 37852 is dated "*yihai* (12) … 2nd month, coincident with *yong* for Zu Yi" (the day after the *yong* for Qian Jia), "in the 9th *si*." A cycle beginning with *jiazi* (01) is implied.

[50] Qian 3.27.6 + 4.18.1; Shima *Kenkyu* p. 141; *guihai* (60) is also in the "9th month" (i.e., intercalary 9th; Chen 1956 p. 301). Day *dingyou* (34) was the autumn equinox, making the following month intercalary.

[51] Akatsuka #7 *Sui* Cha *you*, *dingsi* (54), 9th month, 9th year, *xie* day: the *xie* for Da Ding is three days after the *ji* for Xiao Jia. (9th month: the inscription assumes a *jian yin* calendar.)

1076 Di Xin 11	Jia Rite Days	Royal Ancestor
12 (*zi*) 03 12/30	11 21 *yong* 31 *yong*	 *Gongdian* Shang Jia*[52]
1 33 1/29	41 51 *yong* 01 *yong*	 Da Jia Xiao Jia
2 02 2/27	11 21 *yong* 31 *yong*	 Qian Jia Qiang Jia
3 32 3/29	41 *yong* 51	Xiang Jia
4 01 4/27	01 *yong* 11 21 *yi*	Zu Jia *Gongdian*
5 31 5/27	31 *yi* 41 51 *yi*	Shang Jia Da Jia
6 01 6/26	01 *yi* 11 21 *yi*	Xiao Jia Qian Jia
7 30 7/25	31 *yi* 41 *yi* 51	Qiang Jia Xiang Jia
8 60 8/24	01 *yi* 11 21 *ji*	Zu Jia (extra *xun*) Gongdian [36]
9 29 9/22	31 *ji* 41 51 *ji*	Shang Jia Da Jia
10 59 10/22	01 *ji* 11 21 *ji*	Xiao Jia Qian Jia
11 28 11/20	31 *ji* 41 *ji* 51	Qiang Jia Xiang Jia

1075 Di Xin 12	Jia Rite Days	Royal Ancestor
12 (*zi*) 58 12/20	01 *ji* 11 21	Zu Jia
1 27 1/18	31 *yong* 41 *yong* 51	*Gongdian* *Shang Jia*
2 57 2/17	01 *yong* 11 *yong* 21	Da Jia Xiao Jia
3 26 3/18	31 *yong* 41 *yong* 51 *yong*	Qian Jia Qiang Jia Xiang Jia
4 56 4/17	01 11 *yong* 21	 Zu Jia
5 25 5/16	31 *yi* 41 *yi* 51	*Gongdian* Shang Jia
6 55 6/15	01 *yi* 11 *yi* 21	Da Jia Xiao Jia
7 24 7/14	31 *yi* 41 *yi* 51 *yi*	Qian Jia Qiang Jia Xiang Jia
8 54 8/13	01 11 *yi* 21 *ji*	 Zu Jia *Gongdian* [37]
9 24 9/12	31 *ji* 41 51 *ji*	Shang Jia Da Jia
10 53 10/11	01 *ji* 11 21 *ji*	Xiao Jia Qian Jia
11 23 11/10	31 *ji* 41 *ji* 51	Qiang Jia Xiang Jia

[52] *Kufang* 1672, *Jinzhang* 574; Shima *Kenkyu* p. 141; Chen 1956 p. 302. The system of Xu and Li puts this *jiawu* (31) *yong* in the first month of 1065 (Xu 2006 p. 172; Li *Zhaji* p. 249). The explicit date "10th year, *yong*, 12th month, *jiawu*" is assumed to be an error.

Bibliography
and abbreviations

AAS: Association for Asian Studies.

Ahnert, Paul, *Astronimisch-chronologische Tafeln fur Sonne, Mond und Planeten*, Leipzig: Johann Ambrosius Barth, 1960.

Akatsuka, Kiyoshi 赤塚忠, *Chugoku Kodai no Shukyo to Bunka: In Ocho no Saishi* 中國古代の宗教と文化: 殷王朝の祭祀 (*Religion and Culture in Ancient China: A Study of the Rituals of the Yin Dynasty*), Tokyo: Kadokawa Shoten 角川書店, 1977.

Allan, Sarah, review of Shaughnessy, *Sources of Western Zhou History*, in *Bulletin of the School of Oriental and African Studies*, lv.3, 1992, pp. 585-587.

Allan, Sarah, translator, "China Launches an Ambitious Multi-year Xia Shang Zhou Chronology Project," *Early China News* vol. 9, 1996, pp. 1, 10-14. (Exactly what document is being translated is not stated, but it is clearly an official government document of some kind. Eight "leaders" are named, who are to be "in charge of the funds, examining and approving work plans, holding hearings for periodic reports, and providing directions for research work," reporting to the State Council and meeting with the Council annually. State Councilors Li Tieying and Song Jian are to be "supervisors of the project." All of this was initiated by Song Jian on the 29th of September, 1995. A meeting sponsored by Li Tieying and Song Jian December 21 1995 named four "chief scientists," Li Xueqin, Qiu Shihua, Li Boqian and Xi Zezong, who would jointly chair the project. The project was to be organized into nine detailed "research tasks" with named scholars in charge of each.)

Allan, Sarah: see Li Xueqin.

A. F. Aveni (ed.), *World Archaeoastronomy.* Cambridge: Cambridge University Press (1989).

BA: "Modern Text" *Bamboo Annals* ("Jinben" *Zhushu jinian*).

Biot, Edouard, 1841 (Decembre) "Tchou-chou-ki-nien," (Part I) *Journal Asiatique*, PP. 537-578.1842 (Mai) "Tchou-chou-ki-nien," (Part II) *Journal Asiatique,* pp. 381-431.

Brief Report: see *Xia-Shang-Zhou Duandai Gongcheng ... 2000.*

Brooks, E. Bruce, and A. Taeko Brooks, *The Original Analects: Saayings of Confucius and His Successors.* New York: Columbia University Press, 1998.

BSOAS: *Bulletin of the School of Oriental and African Studies.*

Chang Yuzhi, 常玉芝, *Shang dai zhouji zhidu* 商代周祭制度, Zhongguo Kexue Chubanshe, 1987.

Chang Yuzhi, *Yin-Shang lifa yanjiu* 殷商曆法研究, Jilin Wenshi Press, 1998.

Chavannes, Édouard, *Les Mémoires Historiques de Se-ma Ts'ien,* 5 vols., Paris: Ernest Leroux, 1895-1905 (rpr. Adrien Maisonneuve, 1967-1969)

CFH: (used for the following).

Chen Fengheng 陳逢衡, *Zhushu jinian jizheng* 竹書紀年集證, 50 *juan*, Yiluxian 裛露軒 edition,1813.

Chen Li 陳力, "Jinben *Zhushu jinian* yanjiu" 今本竹書紀年研究, in *Sichuan Daxue Xuebao congkan* 四川大學學報叢刊 28 (1985). (This is included in Shao 1998 pp. 386-410, and in *Jinben lunji* pp. 143-171; most of it is translated into English in "Fresh Evidence" below.)

Chen Li, "Jinben Zhushu jinian di Shiliao Jiazhi" 今本竹書紀年的史料價值: excerpt from the above in Zhu and Zhang, pp. 237-238.

Chen Li, "Fresh Evidence for the Authenticity of *Jinben Zhushu Jinian*," (*Social Sciences in China* 1993.3, October, vol. 14 no. 3. This is a partial translation (by Chen Tifang) of Chen Li, "Jinben *Zhushu jinian* Yanjiu," *Sichuan Daxue Xuebao Congkan* no. 28. For the Chinese original text of Chen's article, see *Jinben lunji* pp. 143-171, or Shao 1998 pp. 386-410.

Chen Li, "Jin- Guben *Zhushu Jinian* zhi San Dai Jinian ji Xiangguan Wenti" 今古本竹書紀年之三代 積年及相關 問題, *Sichuan Daxue Xuebao* 1997 no. 4, p. 80 (included in *Jinben Lunji* pp. 219-235).

Chen Mengjia 陳夢家, "Xi Zhou Tongqi Duandai" 西周銅器斷代, 1: *Kaogu xuebao* 1955.9 (pp. 137-175); 2: ibid 1955.10 (pp. 69-142); 3: ibid 1956.1 (pp. 65-114); 4: ibid 1956.2 (pp. 85-94); 5: ibid 1956.3 (pp. 105-127); 6: ibid 1956.4 (pp. 85-122).

Chen Mengjia, *Yin xu buci zongshu* 殷虛卜辭綜述, Peking: Kexue Chubanshe, 1956.

Chen Mengjia, *Liu guo jinian* 六國紀年, Shanghai：Xuexi Chubanshe 學習出版社, 1955.

"Chinese Bookmaking an Ancient Craft," Los Angeles: *The Free China Journal,* vol. xiii no. 1, Jan 6, 1996, p. 5. (This has an illustration of two Warring States era bamboo pieces modeled in bronze, "photos courtesy of the National Palace Museum." The characters are of uniform size and the columns are of uniform length.)

Creel, Herrlee G., *Studies in Early Chinese Culture (First Series)*, Wakefield, Massachusetts: The Murray Printing Company, facsimile reprint of 1948 original published by the American Council of Learned Societies, 1938 (especially xvii-xxii).

Cullen, Christopher, "The Birthday of the Old Man of Jiang County and other Puzzles: Work in Progress on Liu Xin's *Canon of the Ages*," *Asia Major* (Third Series, Volume xiv, Part 2 (2001), pp. 27-60.

Debnicki, Aleksy, *The Chu-shu-chi-nian as a Source to the Social History of Ancient China*, Warszawa, 1956 (reviewed by J. Průšek).

EC: *Early China.*

Eckholm, Erik, "In China, Ancient History Kindles Modern Doubts," The *New York Times* (International section), Friday, November 10, 2000, p. A3.

Falkenhausen, Lothar von, *Chinese Society in the Age of Confucius (1000-250 BC): The Archaeological Evidence*, Los Angeles: Cotsen Institute of Archaeology, University of California, Los Angeles, 2006.

Fan Qin 范欽 (1506-1585): see *Zhushu jinian.*

Fang Shanzhu (Pang Sunjoo 方善柱), "Xi Zhou Niandaixue shang di jige Wenti" 西周年代學上的幾個問題, *Dalu Zazhi* 51.1 (1975.7), pp. 15-23.

Fang Shanzhu, excerpt from the above in Zhu and Zhang, pp 125-126.

Fang Shiming 方詩銘、Wang Xiuling 王修齡, *Guben Zhushu jinian jizheng* 古本竹書紀年輯證, Shanghai: Shanghai Guji Chubanshe 上海古籍出版社, 1981; revised edition, 2005.

Fang Shiming, "Guan yu Wang Guowei di *Zhushu jiian* Liang Shu" 關於王國維的竹書紀年兩書, included in Wu Ze 吳澤, ed., *Wang Guowei xueshu yanjiu lunji* 王國維學術研究論集 vol. 2, Shanghai: Huadong Shifan Daxue Chubanshe 華東師範大學出版社, 1987.

Fang Shiming, "Zhushu jinian Guben Sanyi ji Jinben Yuanliu Kao" 竹書紀年古本散佚及今本源流考,

included in Yin Da 尹達, ed., *Jinian Gu Jiegang Xiansheng xueshu lunwenji* 紀念顧頡剛先生學術論文集 vol. 2，Chengdu： Ba Shu Shushe 巴蜀書社, 1990.

Fan Xiangyong 范祥雍, *Guben Zhushu jinian jiaoding bu* 古本竹書紀年校訂補, Shanghai：Shanghai Renmin Chubanshe, 1957.

Fan Xiangyong, "Guan yu *Guben Zhushu jinian* di Wangyi Niandai" 關於古本竹書紀年的亡佚年代，*Wenshi* 文史 25 (1985).

Fang Xuanling 房玄齡 and others, *Jin shu* 晉書, Beijing: Zhonghua Shuju, 1974.

Fu Sinian 傅斯年, "Zhou Dong-Feng yu Yin Yi-Min" 周東封與殷遺民, *Zhongyang Yanjiuyuan Lishi Yuyan Yanjiusuo Jikan* vol. 4, no. 3 (1936), pp. 233-239.

Fukaisen 福開森 (John C. Ferguson, compiler), *Lidai zhulu jijin mu* 歷代3著録吉金目 ("Catalog of the Recorded Bronzes of Successive Dynasties"), Shanghai, 1939 rpr Tokyo: Daian, 1967.

Gu Yanwu 顧炎武, *Rizhi lu* 日知錄 *juan* 5, "San Nian Sang" 三年喪 (28th section (out of 49 sections in the chapter))

Han shu 漢書, 21B, quoting Liu Xin 劉歆 (pp. 48b-49a in Wang Xianqian, *Han shu bu zhu* (Guangxu 26 = 1900), Taipei Yiwen Yinshuguan photolith).

Hawkes, David, *Ch'u Tz'u: the Songs of the South, an ancient Chinese anthology*, Oxford: The Clarendon Press, 1959.

He Yunzhong 何允中: see *Zhushu jinian*.

HJ: (used for the following).

HJAS: *Harvard Journal Of Asian Studies*.

Heji: Guo Moruo, 郭沫若 Chief Compiler; Hu Houxuan, 胡厚宣 General Editor and Compiler, *Jiaguwen Heji*, 甲骨刎文合集 13 *juan*, Beijing: Zhonghua Shuju, 1982.

Hessler, Peter, *Oracle Bones: A Journey Between China's, Past and Present*, New York: HarperCollins Publishers, 2006.

Hu Shi 胡適, *Zhongguo zhexueshi dagang* 中國哲學史大綱, Commercial Press, 1919

Hu Shi, "Sannian Sangfu di Zhujian Tuixing" 三年喪服的逐漸推行, *Wuhan Daxue Wenzhe Jikan* vol. 1, no. 2 (1930), pp. 405-414.

Hu Shi, "Shuo Ru 說儒," *Zhongyang Yanjiuyuan Lishi Yuyan Yanjiusuo Jikan* vol. 4,no. 3 (1936), pp. 244-246.

Huang Shengzhang 黄盛璋, "Cong Tongqi Ming Ke Shilun Xi Zhou Lifa Ruogan Wenti" 从铜器名刻试论西周历法若干问题. *Yazhou Wenming Luncong* 亚洲文明論从(Huang Shengzhang, chief compiler), Chengdu, 1986, pp. 11-32. (Surveys opinions and conclusions; argues against the 4-quareters theory of lunar phase terms.)

j: *juan*.

JD: Julian Day number.

Jia-bian: For this, and other commonly used short titles of collections of *jiagu*, see Keightley, *Sources* (1978) pp. 229-231 and Shima Kunio, *Inkyo bokuji sorui* 1977 ed., p. 589.

Jiabian: See Keightley *Sources* 1978 pp. 229-31 at *Chia-pien.*

Jian bao: see p. 81.

Jiang Zudi 蔣祖棣, "Xi Zhou Niandai Yanjiu zhi Yiwen: dui 'Xia Shang Zhou Duandai Gongcheng' Fangfalun de Piping" 西周年代研究之疑問： 對'夏商周斷代工程'方法論的批評, in *Su Bai Xiansheng Bajhi Huadan Jinian Wenji* 宿白先生八秩華誕紀念文集, Beijing: Wenwu Chubanshe (2002), vol. 1, pp 89-108. Reprinted in *Gushi Kao* 9 (2003), pp. 75-94. This issue of *Gushi kao* contains three other related articles by Jiang Zudi critical of the Three Dynasties Project, two of which were submitted to *Zhongguo Wenwubao* and rejected.

Jinben Lunji: abbr. Shao and Ni 2002.

Jinzhang: See Keightley ibid at *Chin-chang.*

Jin shu jiaozhu 晉書斠注, commentary to *Jinshu* by Liu Chenggan 劉承幹 and Wu Shijian 吳士鑑, Beijing 1928; reprint by Yiwen Yinshuguan, Taipei.

Kaiyuan zhanjing 開元占經: see Qutan Xida.

Kaoding: *Yi Xiaoxiao Zhai kaoding Zhushu jinian* 亦囂囂齋考訂竹書紀年: see Lei Xueqi, *Zhushu jinian* 6 *juan*, with attachments.

Keightley, David N., "The *Bamboo Annals* and Shang-Chou Chronology,"*Harvard Journal of Asiatic Studies* 38.2, 1978.

Keightley, D. N., *Sources of Shang History*, Berkeley: University of California Press (1978). (See *Jiabian.*)

Knapp, Keith N., "The *Ru* Reinterpretation of *Xiao*," *Early China* 20 (1995), pp. 195-222, especially pp. 209-213.

Knoblock, John, and Jeffrey Riegel, *The Annals of Lü Buwei* 吕氏春秋: *a Complete Translation and Study*, Stanford: Stanford University Press, 2000.

Kufang: See Keightley ibid at *K'u-fang.*

Legge, James, *The Chinese Classics*. 5 vols. Hong Kong: Hong Kong University Press, 1960.

Legge, J., *The Chinese Classics*, volume III: *The Shoo King, or Book of Historical Documents*. London: Henry Froude, 1865.

Legge, J., *The Annals of the Bamboo Books*, included in Legge, *The Shoo King*, Prolegomena, 105-183.

Lei Xueqi 雷學淇, *Zhushu jinian yizheng* 竹書紀年義證, 40 *juan*. Preface dated 1810. Rpr. Taipei: Yiwen Yinshuguan 藝文印書館, 1976.

Lei Xueqi, *Kaoding Zhushu jinian* 考訂竹書紀年, Jianshentang edition with supplements 潤身堂補刊本, 1883.

Lei Xueqi, *Zhushu jinian* 6 *juan*, with attachments: *Pian wu* 辨誤 1 *juan*; *kaozheng* 考證 1 *juan*; *Nianbiao* 年表 2 *juan*; *Li fa tian xiang tu* 厤法天象圖, 1 *juan*; *Di xing du yi tu* 地形都邑圖, 1 *juan*; *Shixi minghao tu* 世系名號圖, 2 *juan*. Edition: Tongxhou Lei Shi Yixiaoxiao Zhai *Kaoding Zhushu jinian* 通州雷氏亦囂囂齋考訂竹書紀年.

Li, Changhao 黎昌顥, ed., *Zhongguo Tianwenxue Shi* 中國天文學史, Beijing: Kexue chubanshe, 1981. Cited in Pankenier, *T'oung Pao* 2002 p. 41, with translation of relevant material on lunar phase dates pp. 51-55.

Li, Feng, *Landscape and Power in Early China: The Crisis and Fall of the Western Zhou, 1045-771 BC*, Cambridge University Press, 2006; Appendix 3: *The* Bamboo Annals *and issues of the chronology of King You's reign*, pp. 347-354.

Li Xueqin 李學勤, *Yin Dai Dili Jianlun* 殷代地理簡論, Beijing: Kexue Chubanshe, 1959.

Li Xueqin, with Qi Wenxin 齊文心 and Ailan 艾蘭 (Sarah Allan), *Yinguo suo Zang Jiagu Ji* 英國所藏甲骨集 (*Oracle Bone Collections in Great Britain*), Zhonghua Shuju, 1985.

Li Xueqin, "*Guben Zhushu jinian* yu Xia Dai Shi" 古本竹書紀年與夏代史, included in Tian Changwu 田昌五, ed., *Hua Xia Wenming* 華夏文明, Beijing: Beijing Daxue Chubanshe, 1987.

Li Xueqin, with Sarah Allan (Ailan), "Xian gui di Chubu Yanjiu" 鮮簋的初步研究, in *Ou-Zhou suo Zang Zhongguo Qingtongqi Yizhu* 歐洲所藏中國青銅器遺珠 (*Chinese Bronzes: a Selection from European Collections*), Wenwu Chubanshe 1995, pp. 419-422, with Plates 108 A and B.

Li Xueqin, *Xia Shang Zhou niandaixue zhaji* 夏商周年代學札記, Shenyang 瀋陽: Liaoning Daxue Chubanshe 遼寧大學出版社, 1999 (abbr. *Zhaji*).

Li Xueqin, "'Xiao Kai' Que Ji Yueshi" 小開確記月食, in *Qingzhu Wang Zhihua Jiaoshou bashi sui lunwenji* 慶祝王之化教授八十歲論文集, Shanghai: Huafeng 華奉 Shifan Daxue Chubanshe, 2001 (1999), pp. 94-96.

Li Xueqin, "Yueji, Chuji, Jiji" 月吉 初吉 既吉, in *Zhaji* pp. 88-96 (1997).

Li Xueqin, "Li *gui* Ming yu Sui Xing" 利簋銘與歲星, in *Zhaji* pp. 204-205 (1998).

Li Xueqin, "Ling Zhoujiu yu Wu Wang Fa Yin Tianxiang" 伶州鳩與武王伐殷天象, in *Zhaji* pp. 206-213 (1999).

Li Xueqin, "Shi Shuo Xuan Wang Zaonian Liri" 試說宣王早年曆日 in *Zhaji* pp. 220-223 (1999).

Li Xueqin, "Di Xin Yuan zhi Shiyi Si Sipu di Buchong yu Jianyan" 帝辛元至十一祀祀譜的补充與檢驗, in *Zhaji* pp.230-239.

Li Xueqin, "Zai Shuo Di Xin Yuan zhi Shiyi Si Sipu" 再說帝辛元至十一祀祀譜, in Zhaji pp. 245-250.

Lin Chunpu 林春溥, *Zhushu jinian buzheng* 竹書紀年補證, 4 *juan*, included in Yang Jialuo 楊家駱, compiler, *Zhushu jinian ba zhong* 竹書紀年八種, Taipei: Shijie Shuju, 1963.

Lin Chunpu, *Gu shi jinian* 古史紀年, included in Lin, *Zhubo Shanfang shiwu zhong* 竹柏山房十五種, 1837.

Liu Dianjue 劉殿爵 (D. C. Lau)、Chen Fangzheng 陳方正, eds., *Zhushu jinian zhuzi suoyin* 竹書紀年逐字索引, Hong Kong: Commercial Press, 1998. (English title: Concordance to the Zhushu jinian: The ICS Ancient Chinesse Texts Concordance Series, Historical Works No. 13, The Chinese University of Hong Kong Institute of Chinese Studies.)

Lau, D. C., *Confucius: The Analects*, Penguin Books, Harmondsworth, 1984 (1979).

Liu Zhiji: see Pu Qilong.

Loewe, Michael, ed., *Early Chinese Texts: A Bibliographical Guide*; Berkeley: The Society for the Study of Early China, and The Institute of East Asian Studies, University of California, 1993.

Luo Bi 羅泌，*Lu shi* 路史，included in *Wenyuange Siku quanshu* 文淵閣四庫全書 (photolithographic edition), vol. 383, Taipei: Taiwan Commercial Press，1986.

M (or *Ming*): James M. Menzies (明義士), *Yin xu buci* 殷虛卜辭, edited by Xu Jinxiong 許進雄, Toronto 1972, 1977; Shanghai 1917. (Keightley ibid.)

Ma Chengyuan 馬承源, compiler, *Shang-Zhou qingtongqi mingwen xuan* 商周青銅器銘文選, Wenwu Chubanshe 1998.

Mencius; Translated and with an introduction by D. C. Lau. Harmondsworth: Penguin Books, Ltd., 1970 (rpr. 1983).

Metcalf, Peter, and Richard Huntington, *Celebrations of death: the anthropology of mortuary ritual.* Second edition, Cambridge: Cambridge University Press, 1991.

MH: Chavannes, *Mémoires Historiques.*

Minjian lun Sandai 民間論三代: *Gushi Kao* 古史考 9 (2003), Hainan Chubanshe. Part One (of three) is titled "Mian Dui Mian di Duihua" 面對面的對話 pp. 1-238. This consists of sixteen articles on or related to the Three Dynasties Project. The second article, giving the title to the whole, is by Zhang Lidong 張立東: "Mian Dui Mian di Duihua" – 'Xia Shang Zhou Duandai Gongcheng' di Meiguo zhi Lü" 面對面的對話 –夏商周斷代工程的美國之旅, dated 24 May 2002, the day it was first published in the Beijing newsprint weekly *Zhongguo Wenwubao.*

Needham, Joseph, with the collaboration of Wang Ling, *Science and Civilization in China* vol, 3, *Mathematics and the Sciences of the Heavens and the Earth*, Cambridge: Cambridge University Press, 1959.

Nivison, D. S., "The Dates of Western Chou," *Harvard Journal of Asiatic Studies* 43 (1983) pp. 518-524. (This article is largely superseded by Nivison's later work. But some of it is important, notably: (1) the "two *yuan*" hypothesis; (2) the validity of much of the Jinben *Zhushu jinian* (*Bamboo Annals*); (3) the basic correctness of Wang Guowei's interpretation of *yuexiang* terms in dates.)

Nivison, D. S., "1040 as the Date of the Zhou Conquest" (Research Note), *Early China* 8 (1982-83, published in 1984), pp. 70-78. (DSN has now concluded that 1040 is the correct date, but the argument in this article is partly wrong.)

Nivison, D. S., "The King and the Bird: a Possible Genuine Shang Literary Text and Its Echoes in Later Philosophy and Religion" (unpublished; presented at the annual meeting of the Society for the Study of Early China, held concurrently with the 36th Annual Meeting of the Association for Asian Studies, Washington DC, 24 March 1984). The paper argues that the "Gao Zong Yong Ri" chapter of the Shang shu was misunderstood in Warring States China as describing a rite *by* Gao Zong (= Wu Ding) rather than *for* him. Wu Ding was already dead; therefore the "Zu Ji" in the story is Wu Ding's heir, alive and well in the reign of Zu Geng, substitute king while Zu Ji functioned as chief mourner. The fact that Zu Ji never became king (Zu Jia usurped the succession) led to the myth that Wu Ding had disinherited his filial son Zu Ji (= "Xiao Ji"), angered by his courageous criticism. The *Bamboo Annals* accepts the myth in part, but muddles it, making "Xiao Ji" die before the "Yong Ri" incident.

Nivison, D. S., "*Guoyu* Wu Wang ke Yin Tianxiang Bianwei," *Guwenzi Yanjiu* 12 (1985), pp. 445-461. (This article tries to show that the text in *Guoyu* "Zhou Yu" 3.7, describing the astrological aspects of the heavens when Wu Wang's conquest campaign began, was composed and inserted into the Guoyu in early Han after the compilation of the *Shiji.* This hypothesis is wrong (as shown, e.g., by Li Xueqin, *Zhaji* p. 210). Nivison's present view is that the *Guoyu* astrological text was invented and calculated in the 5th century BCE, and was incorporated into the *Guoyu* when it was first compiled, in the late 4th century.)

Nivison, D. S., "A New Study of Xiaotun Yinxu Wenzi Jiabian 2416" (in English and in Chinese, presented at the International Conference on Shang Culture, Anyang, PRC, September 1987; revised 2007). (Unpublished; translates and tries to date the longest Oracle Bone inscription so far discovered.)

Nivison, D. S., "A Telltale Mistake in the *Lü shi chunqiu*: the Earthquake Supposedly in the Eighth Year of

Wen Wang of Zhou" (unpublished conference paper, Boulder, University of Colorado, annual meeting of the Western Branch of the American Oriental Society, October, 1989). The paper agrees with a note by Kong Chao to *Yi Zhou shu* "Zuo Luo," that the word *sui* 歲 in a date means "next year," implying that the date in the *Lü shi chunqiu* ought to have been "ninth year" rather than "eighth year," and that Wen Wang's total reign was 52 years rather than "51 years" as stated in *Lü shi chunqiu* 6 "Ji Xia" 4 "Zhi Yue." The earthquake is dated in the *Bamboo Annals* to 1109 BCE, correctable to 1093 (by subtracting 16).

Nivison, D. S., "The Origin of the Chinese Lunar Lodge System," in A. F. Aveni (ed.), *World Archaeoastronomy.* Cambridge: Cambridge University Press (1989), pp. 203-218.

Nivison, D. S., "The "Question" Question," *Early China* 14 (1989) pp. 115-125. (Translated as "Wen "Wen"," in *Guoji Hanxue Congshu* 3 (2007) pp. 139-148, Taipei: Lexue Shuju. (Argues, supporting Keightley and Serruys, that in almost all cases *jiagu* divination texts are not questions but trial statements.)

Nivison, D. S., and Kevin. D. Pang, "Astronomical Evidence for the *Bamboo Annals'* Chronicle of Early Xia." *Early China* 15 (1990), pp. 87-95. Forum: "Response," pp. 151-172. (Combines work by Pankenier, Pang and Nivison to establish an exact chronology of Xia from 1953 to 1876 BCE.)

Nivison, D. S., "*Chu shu chi nien* 竹書紀年," in Michael Loewe, ed. *Early Chinese Texts: A Bibliographical Guide*. Berkeley: The Society for the Study of Early China and the Institute of East Asian Studies, University of California, Berkeley, 1993.

Nivison, D. S., "An Interpretation of the "Shao Gao"," *Early China* 20 (1995), pp. 177-193. (Finds evidence in the "Shao Gao" chapter of the *Shang shu* for the "four quarters" interpretation of lunar phase (*yuexiang*) terms in dates.)

Nivison, D. S. (edited by Bryan Van Norden), *The Ways of Confucianism: Investigations in Chinese Philosophy,* (Chicago and La Salle: Open Court, 1996). (The book has now been translated into Chinese, by Zhou Chicheng, see Ni Dewei 2006.)

Nivison, D. S., ""Virtue" in Bone and Bronze," included in Nivison (edited by Bryan Van Norden), *The Ways of Confucianism,* pp. 17-23. (This was the first of three "Walter Y. Evans-Wentz" Lectures at Stanford in February, 1980. For a Chinese translation, see Ni Dewei 2006, pp. 21-36.)

Nivison, D. S., "The Authenticity of the Mao Gong *ding* Inscription," in F. David Bulbeck and Noel Barnard (eds.), *Ancient Chinese and Southeast Asian Bronze Age Cultures.* Taipei: SMC Publishing, Inc. (1996-97), pp. 311-344.

Ni Dewei 倪德衛 (Nivison, D. S.), "Wu Wang Ke Shang zhi Riqi" 武王克商之日期, in Beijing Shefan Daxue Guoxue Yanjiusuo (Compilers), *Wu Wang Ke Shang zhi Nian Yanjiu.* Peking: Beijing Shefan Daxue Chubanshe (1997), pp. 513-532.

Ni Dewei (Nivison, D. S.), "Ke Shang yihou Xi Zhou Zhu Wang zhi Nianli" 克商以後西周諸王之年曆, in Zhu Fenghan 朱風瀚 and Zhang Yingming 張X明 (eds.), *Xi Zhou Zhu Wang Niandai Yanjiu.* Guizhou: Guizhou Renmin Chubanshe (1998), pp. 380-387.

Nivison, D. S., "The Key to the Chronology of the Three Dynasties: The "Modern Text" *Bamboo Annals*," *Sino-Platonic Papers* 93 (January 1999) pp. 1-68.

Nivison, D. S., "The Chronology of the Three Dynasties," in Patrick Suppes, Julius Moravcsik, and Henry Mendell, eds. *Ancient and Medieval Traditions in the Exact Sciences: Essays in Memory of Wilbur Knorr.* (Stanford: CSLI Publications, 2000), pp. 203-227.

Nivison, D. S., "Zhang Peiyu on the *Dayan Li yi* and the *Jinben Zhushu jinian*," accepted for publication by *Lishi Yanjiu* pending translation, 3 June 2000.

Ni Dewei 倪德衛、Xia Hanyi 夏含夷, "Jin Hou di Shixi ji qi dui Zhongguo Gudai Jinian di Yiyi" 晉侯的世系及其對中國古代紀年的意義, *Zhongguo Shi Yanjiu* 中國史研究, 2001.1 pp. 3-10.

Nivison, D. S., and Edward L. Shaughnessy, The Jin Hou Su Bells Inscription and Its Implications for the Chronology of Early China," *Early China* 25 (2000: actually 2002) pp. 29-48).

Nivison, D. S., "Mengzi as Philosopher of History," in Alan K. L. Chan, ed., *Mencius: Contexts and Interpretations*, Honolulu: University of Hawai'i Press, 2002, pp. 282-304.

Ni Dewei (David Nivison), translated by Shao Dongfang 邵東方, "San Dai niandaixue zhi guanjian: *Jinben Zhushu jinian*" 三代紀年之關鍵: "今本"竹書紀年, *Jingxue Yanjiu Luncong* 經學研究論叢 10 (pp. 223-309), Taipei: Taiwan Xuesheng Shuju, 2002. (This is a revision as well as translation of Nivison 1999.)

Nivison, D. S., "The Xia-Shang-Zhou Chronology Project: Two Approaches to Dating," *The Journal of East Asian Archaeology*, vol. 4.1-4 (pp. 359-366), 2002. (This is Nivison's paper presented in the panel on the Three Dynasties Chronology Project, at the 2002 annual meeting of AAS in Washington, DC. The paper is included in the present book as Chapter Four. For a Chinese translation, see Ni Dewei 2006, pp. 21-36.)

Nivison, 2002: Shao Dongfang's translation of Ni Dewei (Nivison 1999).

Ni Dewei 2003 (Nivison, 2002 AAS paper), translated by Xu Fengxian (q.v.), "Xia, Shang, Zhou Duandai Gongcheng: Queding Niandai di Liang Zhong Tujing" 夏商周斷代工程：確定年代的兩種途徑，*Zhongguo Wenzhe Yanjiu Tongxun* 13.4 (Dec. 2003), Nangang: Zhongyang Yanjiuyuan Zhongguo Wenzhe Yanjiusuo. (Dr. Xu's translation has also been published in the PRC.)

Nivison, D. S., "Huang Di to Zhi Bo: a Problem in Historical Epistemology"; unpublished paper for the annual meeting of the Western Branch, American Oriental Society, University of California in Berkeley, 10 October 2003.

Nivison, D. S., "Standard Time," in Martin R. Jones and Nancy Cartwright (eds.), *Idealization XII: Correcting the Model. Idealization and Abstraction in the Sciences (Poznań Studies in the Philosophy of the Sciences and the Humanities*, vol. 86), pp. 219-231. Amsterdam/New York, NY: Rodopi, 2005.

Ni Dewei (Nivison, D. S., edited by Bryan Van Norden, *The Ways of Confucianism*, 1996), translated by Zhou Chicheng 周炽成, *Ru Jia zhi Dao: Zhongguo Zhexue zhi Tantao* 儒家之道：中国哲学之探讨, Nanjing: Jiangsu Renmin Chubanshe, 2006.

Nivison, D. S., and Shao Dongfang, *The Bamboo Annals*. (Expected publication 2008)

Pankenier, David W., "Astronomical Dates in Shang and Western Zhou, *Early China* 7 (1981-2; actually published 1983), pp. 2-37.

Pankenier, D. W., "*Mozi* and the Dates of Xia,Shang and Zhou: A Research Note." *Early China* 9-10 (1983-85), pp. 175-183. (A Chinese translation of Pankenier's article is included in *Jinben lunji*. pp. 297-303: "Mozi yu Xia Shang Zhou di Niandai – *Zhushu jinian* Yanjiu Zhaji.")

Pankenier, D. W., "The Metempsychosis in the Moon," *Bulletin of the Museum of Far Eastern Antiquities* 58 (1986), pp. 149-159.

Pankenier, D. W., Forum criticism of Nivison and Pang, *Early China* 15 (1990), pp. 117-132.

Pankenier, D. W., "The *Bamboo Annals* Revisited: Problems of Method in Using the Chronicle as a Source for the Chronology of Early Zhou," *Bulletin of the School of Oriental and African Studies* Vol. LV, Parts 2 & 3, 1992.

Pankenier, D. W., "Reflections of the Lunar Aspect on Western Chou Chronology," *Toung Pao* lxxviii, 1992.

Pankenier, D. W. (Ban Dawei 班大为), *Zhongguo shanggu shishi jiebi: tianwen Gaoguxue yanjiu* 中国上古史实揭秘秘 -- 天文考古學研究, Shanghai: Shanghai Guji Chubanshe, 2008. (Contains translations by Xu Fengxian of all of Pankenier's articles above except *EC* 1990, plus six more, dated 1995-2004; several of the ones included are highly critical of Nivison, but apparently contain no references to Nivison's post-1992 work, in which Pankenier's criticisms are either accepted or effectively refuted.)

Pines, Y., "Intellectual Change in the Chunqiu Period: the Reliability of the Speeches in the *Zuo zhuan* as Sources of Chunqiu Intellectual History." *Early China* 22 (1997), pp. 77-132.

Pu Qilong 浦起龍, *Shi tong tong shi* 史通通釋. (The *Shi tong* by the early 8th century historian and critic Liu Zhiji 劉知幾, with commentary by Pu; Pu was a *jinshi* of 1730, born 1679.)

Qian Mu 錢穆, *Xian Qin zhu zi xinian* 先秦諸子繫年, Hong Kong: Hong Kong Daxue Chubanshe，1956.

Qian Mu, "Guben Zhushu jinian jijiao Buzheng" 古本竹書紀年輯校補正, included in Yang Jialuo 楊家駱, ed., Zhushu jinian ba zhong, Taipei: Shijie Shuju, 1963.

Qutan Xida 瞿曇悉達 (Gautama Siddhartha, fl. 713-741), *Kaiyuan zhanjing* 開元占經 in reprint (1973) of Wenyuange manuscript *Siku quanshu zhenben* Collection #4, vols. 172-181, Taipei: Commercial Press.

RECT: Shaughnessy, *Rewriting Early Chinese Texts.*

Report: see *Brief Report.*

Shang shu da zhuan, by Fu Sheng 伏勝, commentary by Zheng Xuan 鄭玄; edited text Shang shu da zhuan jijiao 尚書大傳輯校 by Chen Shouqi 陳壽祺; included in Congshu jicheng 叢書集成, First series, Shanghai Commercial Press 1937.

Shao Dongfang 邵東方, *Cui Shu (1740-1816): his life, scholarship, and rediscovery*; Doctoral dissertation in History, University of Hawaii, May 1994.

Shao Dongfang, "Cong Sixiang Qingxiang he Zhushu Tili Tan *Jinben Zhushu jinian* di Zhenwei Wenti" 從思想傾向和著述體例談今本竹書紀年的真偽問題, *Zhongguo Zhexueshi* 中國哲學史 1998.3; included in Shao 2005 pp. 1-36.

Shao Dongfang, *Cui Shu yu Chongguo xueshushi yanjiu* 崔述與中國學術史研究, Beijing: Renmin Chubanshe, 1998.

Shao Dongfang, "*Jinben Zhushu jinian* zhu Wenti Kaolun -- yu Chen Li Xiansheng Shangque" 今本竹書紀年諸問題考論 -- 與陳力先生商榷, included in Shao, 1998 pp.293-385; and (reduced and edited) in Shao and Ni 2002 pp. 173-217.

Shao Dongfang, "*Jinben Zhushu jinian* Zhou Wu Wang, Cheng Wang Jipu Pailie Wenti Zai Fenxi" 今本竹書紀年周武王、成王紀譜排列問題再分析, *Zhongguo Shi Yanjiu* 中國史研究 2000.1; included in Shao and Ni 2002 pp. 101-120, and in Shao 2005 pp. 1-36.

Shao Dongfang, "Liu Dianjue deng Dianjiao *Jizhong jinian cunzhen* Bian Wu Ju Li" 劉殿爵等點校汲冢紀年存真辨誤舉例, *Jingxue Yanjiu Luncong* 11, 2002; included in Shao 2005 pp. 60-75.

Shao Dongfang, "Jin Gongzi Chonger Fan Guo Ji He Kao" 晉公子重耳返國濟河詩問考 (in Shao 2005 pp. 76-89).

Shao Dongfang, *Wenxian kaoshi yu lishi tanyan* 文獻考釋與歷史探研 (Textual criticism and historical inquiry), Guilin: Guangxi Shifan Daxue Chubanshe, 2005.

Shao Dongfang 邵東方 and Ni Dewei 倪德衛 (David S. Nivison), eds., *Jinben Zhushu Jinian Lunji* 今本竹書紀年論集 (Studies on the Modern Text of the Bamboo Annals), Taipei: Tonsan Press, 2002. This book contains fifteen articles, by ten authors. There are two prefaces (dated 2001), by Shao (pp. v-xiii) and Nivison (pp. xv-xxii). These prefaces are published separately in *Lishi: Lilun yu Piping* (History: Theory and Criticism), 2 (2001), Taipei: Tonsan Press. One of the articles is by Nivison: "Lun Jinben Zhushu jinian di Lishi Jiazhi" ("On the Historical Value of the 'Modern Text' of the *Bamboo Annals*") pp. 41-82; this is mainly the part on Western Zhou, in Nivison as translated by Shao, "San Dai Niandaixue zhi Guanjian" (2002).

Xia Hanyi 夏含夷 (Shaughnessy, Edward), "Ye Tan Wu Wang di Zunian -- Jian Lun *Jinben Zhushu jinian* di zhenwei" 也談武王的卒年 -- 兼論今本竹書紀年的真偽, *Wen Shi* 文史 29 (1985).

Shaughnessy, Edward. L., "On the Authenticity of the *Bamboo Annals*," *Harvard Journal of Asiatic Studies* 46.1 (1986).

Shaughnessy, E. L., "The 'Current' *Bamboo Annals* and the Date of the Zhou Conquest of Shang," *Early China* 11-12 1985-1987.

Shaughnessy, E. L., *Sources of Western Zhou History: Inscribed Bronze Vessels*. Berkeley: University of California Press, 1991.

Shaughnessy, E. L., "*Shang shu* 尚書 (*Shu ching* 書經)," pp. 376-389, in Michael Loewe, ed. *Early Chinese Texts: A Bibiographical Guide*. Berkeley: The Society for the Study of Early China and the Institute of East Asian Studies, University of California, Berkeley, 1993.

Shaughnessy, E. L., "*I Chou shu* 逸周書," pp. 229-233, in Michael Loewe, ed. *Early Chinese Texts,* 1993.

Xia Hanyi, "*Zhushu jinian* yu Zhou Wu Wang Ke Shang di Niandai" 竹書紀年與周武王克商的年代, *Wen Shi* 38 (1994).

Shaughnessy, E. L., *Before Confucius* Albany: State University of New York Press, 1997.

Xia Hanyi, *Wen gu zhi xin lu: Shang Zhou wenhuashi guanjian* 溫故知新錄: 商周文化史管見, Taipei: Daoxiang Chubanshe 導向出版社, 1997.

Shaughnessy, E. L., "The Editing and Editions of the *Bamboo Annals,*" paper presented in a workshop on the Xia-Shang-Zhou Chronology Project at the University of Chicago, April 13, 2002.

Xia Hanyi, "Sishier nian sishisan nian Yu Qiu ding de niandai" 四十二年四十三年虞逑鼎的年代, *Zhongguo Lishi Wenwu* 2003.5, pp. 49-52 (逑: maybe 來 is phonetic, = "Lai").

Xia Hanyi, "'Zhushu jinian' Cuo Jian San Zhong" 竹書紀年錯簡三證 (typescript dated 2003.12.17).

Xia Hanyi, *Gushi yiguan* 古史異觀, Shanghai: Shanghai Guji Chubanshe, 2005. This is a collection of many of Shaughnessy's articles written by him in Chinese (a few were translated). Especially valuable for BA studies are tables at the end of the book matching BA texts with quotations, arranged by quoting sources, Xu Guang, Li Daoyuan, et al.

Shaughnessy, E. L., *Rewriting Early Chinese Texts*, Albany: State University of New York Press, 2006.

Shaughnessy, E. L., "Texts Lost in Texts: Recovering the "Zhai Gong" Chapter of the Yi Zhou shu," (in Essays celebrating the 60th birthday of Christoph Harbsmeier pp. 31-47, photocopy received Oct 2006), pp. 31-47.

Xia Hanyi, "You 42 Nian, 43 Nian 'Qiu *ding'* Tan Zhou Xuan Wang Zai Wei, Tongqi Mingwen Yuexiang he 'Xia Shang Zhou Duandai Gongcheng' zhu Wenti" 由42年, 43年 '逑鼎'談周宣王在位, 銅器銘文月相和 '夏商周斷代工程'諸問題: 21 pp. (typescript in Chinese received October 2006).

Xia Hanyi, "Cong 'X *gui'* Kan Zhou Mu Wang Zai Wei Nian Shu ji Niandai Wenti 從 'X簋'看周穆王在位年數及年代問題, *Zhongguo Lishi Wenwu* 2006.3, pp. 4-10. ('X *gui'*: I have guessed that this should be "Lu *gui*"; the name appears to be a combination of 彔 and 見; Shaughnessy 2006.7 renders it "Xian *gui*.")

Shaughnessy, E. L., "Chronologies of Ancient China," Hong Kong Baptist University Golden Lecture Series, 7 November 2006, typescript, 25 pp.

Shaughnessy, E. L., Review of Falkenhausen 2006, *Journal of Asian Studies* 66.4 (November 2007), pp. 1129-1132.

Shen Yue 沈約, *Song shu* 宋書, Beijing: Zhonghua Shuju, 1974.

Shim, Jaehoon, "The Jin Hou Su *Bianzhong* Inscription and Its Significance," *Early China* 22 (1997), pp. 43-75.

Shima Kunio, *In-kyo Bokuji Kenkyu* 殷墟卜辭研究, Tokyo: Kyuko Shoin, 1958.

Shima Kunio 島邦男, *In-kyo bokuji sorui* 殷墟卜辭綜類, Tokyo: Kyuko Shoin 汲古書院, 1977 (1967).

Shinjo Shinzo 新城新藏, "Shu-Sho no Nendai" 周初の年代, *Shinagaku* 4.4 (Showa 3.4 = April 1928), pp. 1-150.

Shirakawa Shizuka 白川靜, *Kimbun Tsushaku* 金文通釋, *Hakutsuru Bijutsukanshi* 白鶴美術館誌, Kobe, 1962-.

Sima Qian 司馬遷, *Shiji* 史記, Beijing: Zhonghua Shuju, 1959.

Sivin, Nathan, *Cosmos and Computation in Early Chinese Mathematical Astronomy*, Leiden: E. J. Brill, 1969.

SPP: *Sino-Platonic Papers*, an occasional publication edited by Victor Mair, University of Pennsylvania, at first published photographically, now published electronically "on line."

Stahlman, W. D.,and O. Gingerich, *Solar and Planetary Longitudes for years -2500 to+2000 by 10-Day Intervals,* Madison: The University of Wisconsin Press, 1963.

Stephenson, F. R., "A Re-investigation of the "Double Dawn" Event Recorded in the *Bamboo Annals*," *Quarterly Journal of the Royal Astronomical Society* 33 (1992), pp. 91-98.

Stephenson, F. R., and M. A. Houlden, *Atlas of historical eclipse maps: East Asia, 1500 BC – AD 1900*, Cambridge: Cambridge University Press, 1986.

Wang Guowei 王國維, *Jinben Zhushu jinian shuzheng* 今本竹書紀年疏證, included in Yang Jialuo, ed., *Zhushu jian ba zhong.*

Wang Guowei, *Guben Zhushu jinian jijiao* 古本竹書紀年輯校, included in Yang Jialuo, ed., *Zhushu jinian ba zhong*, Taipei: Shijie Shuju, 1963.

Wang Guowei, *Guantang ji lin* 觀堂集林, Taipei: Zhonghua Shuju, 1959.

Wang Guowei, "Shengbo Sibo Kao" 生霸死霸考, included in *Guantang jilin*, *j.* 1.

White: Hsu Jinxiong, ed., *Oracle Bones from the White and other Collections*, listed by Keightley *Sources* 1978 as forthcoming, used by Chang 1987 with short title "Huaite" 懷特.

Wu Guan 吳琯 (Ming Dynasty), editor, *Zhushu jinian* 竹書紀年, included in *Gujin yi shi* 古今逸史.

Wu Wang Ke Shang zhi Nian Yanjiu 武王克商之年研究, compiled by Beijing Shifan Daxue 北京師範大學, Guoxue Yanjiusuo 國學研究所, Beijing: Beijing Shifan Daxue Chubanshe, 1997.

Xia Hanyi 夏含夷: see Shaughnessy, E. L.

Xia-Shang-Zhou duandai gongcheng: 1996-2000 nian jieduan chengguo baogao (jian ben) 夏商周斷代工程：1996－2000年階段成果報告 (簡本), Beijing: Shijie Tushu Chuban Gongsi, 2000.

Xia-Shang-Zhou duandai gongcheng jianbao (*Bulletin of the Xia-Shang-Zhou Genealogy Project*): no. 1, 2 April 1996; no. 100, 15 October 2000 (and more).

Xu Fengxian 徐鳳先 2003, see Nivison 2003 above.

Xu Fengxian, *Shang Mo Zhouji Sipu Heli Yanjiu* 商末周祭祀譜合曆研究, Beijing: Shijie Tushu Chuban Gongsi, 2006.

Xu Wenjing 徐文靖，*Zhushu jinian tongjian* 竹書紀年統箋 (Qing, Qianlong 15 (1750) edition), Taipei: Yiwen Yinshuguan photolithographic edition, 1966.

Xu Zhentao 徐振韬 and Jiang Yaotiao 蒋窈窕, *Wu xing juhe yu Xia Shang Zhou niandai yanjiu* 五星聚合与夏商周年代研究; Beijing: Shijie Tushu Chuban Gongsi, 2006.

Yang Chaoming 楊朝明, "*Jinben Zhushu jinian* bing fei Wei Shu Shuo" 今本竹書紀年并非偽書說, Qi Lu Xuekan 齊魯學刊, 1997.6. (In *Jinben lunji* pp. 305-320.)

Yang Chaoming, "Shen Yue yu *Jinben Zhushu jinian*" 沈約與今本竹書紀年, *Shixueshi Yanjiu* 史學史研究, 1999.4. (In *Jinben lunji* pp. 321-342.)

Yang Jialuo 楊家駱, ed. *Zhushu jinian ba zhong* 竹書紀年八種, Taipei：Shijie Shuju, 1963.

Yang Kuan 楊寬, *Zhanguo shi* 戰國史, (revised and expanded), Shanghai: Shanghai Renmin Chubanshe, 1998.

Yang Ximei 楊希枚, "Mengzi Teng Wen-Gong Pian San-nian Sang Gushi di Fenxi" 孟子滕文公篇三年喪故事的分析, in Yang Ximei, *Xian-Qin wenhuashi lunji* 先秦文化史論集, Beijing: Zhongguo Shehui Kexue Chubanshe, 1995, pp. 402-432. (Originally this appeared in *Shihuo Yuekan* 1.3 (1971) pp. 1-17.) Knapp (*Early China* 20 p. 213 note 54) locates this in *Shihuo Yuekan* 食貨月刊 1.3 (June 1977), pp. 135-152.

Yong Rong 永瑢 and others, *Siku quanshu zongmu* 四庫全書總目, Beijing: Zhonghua Shuju Photolithographic edition, 1965.

Yu Xingwu 于省吾, "Li *gui* Mingwen Kaoshi" 利簋銘文考釋, *Wenwu* 1977.8 pp. 10-12.

Zhaji: see Li Xueqin 1999.

Zhang Lidong 張立東: see *Minjian Lun Sandai* 民間論三代.

ZPY: used for the following.

Zhang, Peiyu 張培瑜, *Zhongguo Xian-Qin Shi Libiao* 中國先秦史曆表, Ji'nan 濟南: Qi-Lu Shushe 齊魯書社, 1987.

Zhang Peiyu, Forum criticism of Nivison and Pang, *Early China* 15 (1990), pp. 133-150.

Zhang, Peiyu, "*Dayan liyi* yu *Jinben Zhushu jinian*, 大衍曆議與今本竹書紀年, *Lishi Yanjiu* 歷史研究, 1999.3.

Zhang Xuecheng (1738-1801), *Zhang shi yi shu*, 30 + 18 + 2 *juan*, published by Liu Chenggan, Wuxing: Jiayetang, 1922.

Zhao Shaozu 趙紹祖, *Jiaobu Zhushu jinian* 校補竹書紀年, Gumozhai 古墨齋 edition, 1796.

Zheng Huisheng 郑慧生 (Henan Daxue Dept. of History), "Xiao Ji di Cunzai yu Zu Ji Buci di Youwu" 孝己的存在与祖己卜辞的有无, 14 pp., 1986 (paper for the International Conference on Shang History, Anyang, 1987).

Zhongguo Wenwubao 中國文物報, article by Liu Xing 劉星, "Quexi di Duihua: Xia Shang Zhou Duandai Gongcheng yinqi di Haiwai Xueshu Taolun Jishi " 缺席的對話：夏商周斷代工程引起的海外學術討論紀實, June 6, 2001 (a long article presenting or quoting the views of about a dozen U. S. and English scholars on the Three Dynasties Project).

Zhongguo Wenwubao, May 24, 2002, article by Zhang Lidong on the U. S. visit (AAS and University of Chicago) by Li Xueqin, Zhang Changshou, Qiu Shihua and Zhang Peiyu: see *Minjian lun Sandai.*

Zhongguo Wenwubao, Su Hui 蘇輝 (Editor), "Meiguo zhi Xing Dawen – guanyu "Xia Shang Zhou Duandai Gongcheng" 美國之行答問 – 關於"夏商周斷代工程"," *Zhongguo Wenwubao*, August 16, 2002, no. 5. (A response to the article by Zhang Lidong, May 24, 2002: Li Xueqin, Qiu Shihua, Zhang Changshou and Zhang Peiyu answering questions put by the editors).

Zhu Fenghan 朱風瀚 and Zhang Rongming 張榮明, compilers, *Xi Zhou zhu Wang Niandai Yanjiu* 西周諸王年代研究, Guiyang: Guizhou renmin Chubanshe, 1998.

Zhu Xizu 朱希祖, *Jizhong shukao* 汲冢書考, Beijing: Zhinghua Shuju, 1960.

Zhu Youzeng 朱右曾, *Jizhong Jinian cunzhen* 汲冢紀年存真, Guiyanzhai 歸硯齋 edition, included in Gu Tinglong, 顧廷龍, ed. *Xuxiu Siku quanshu* 續修四庫全書 vol. 336, Shanghai: Shanghai Guji Chubanshe, 1995.

Zhushu jinian 竹書紀年, edited by Fan Qin 范欽 (1506-1585), included in *Tianyi Ge* 天一閣 (Ming Dynasty; photolithographic reprint in *Sibu Congkan*, Commercial Press)

Zhushu jinian, print by He Yunzhong 何允中 (Ming Dynasty), edited by Zhang Suichen 張遂辰,included in *Han Wei Congshu* 漢魏叢書.

Zhushu jinian, included (with *Mu Tianzi zhuan* 穆天子傳) in *Jizhong xuanshu* 汲冢選書, edited by Zhong Xing 鍾惺 (1574-1624).

Abbreviations

(not including short titles)

AAS	Association for Asian Studies
BA	*Jinben Zhushu jinian* ("Modern Text" *Bamboo Annals*)
BMFEA	*Bulletin of the Museum of Far Eastern Antiquities*
Brief Report	*Brief Report* See Bibliography: *Xia-Shang-Zhou ... 2000*
BSOAS	*Bulletin of the School of Oriental and African Studies*
CFH	See Bibliography, Chen Fengheng
CSLI	Center for the Study of Language and Information, Stanford University
EC	*Early China*
HJ	*Jiaguwen heji*
HJAS	*Harvard Journal of Asiatic Studies*
j.	*juan*
JAS	*Journal of Asian Studies*
JAOS	*Journal of the American Oriental Society*
JEAA	*Journal of East Asian Archaeology*
Jia-bian	*Xiaotun jia-bian**
Jian ben	*Brief Report*: see Bibliography, *Xia-Shang-Zhou ... 2000*
JD	Julian Day number
Jinben lunji	*Jinben Zhushu jinian lunji* (Shao and Nivison eds.)
KB	See Bibliography, Shirakawa Shizuka, *Kimbun Tsushaku*
MH	See Bibliography, Chavannes
N&S	Nivison and Shaughnessy
N 2002	Nivison 1999 translated by Shao Dongfang 2002
RECT	E. L. Shaughnessy, *Rewriting early Chinese texts*
Report	Same as *Brief Report*
SPP	*Sino-Platonic Papers*
XSZ	Xia-Shang-Zhou
*Xu-bian**	
Zhaji	Li Xueqin, *Xia Shang Zhou niandaixue zhaji*
Zhui-he*	
ZPY	Zhang Peiyu, *Xian Qin shi li biao*

* For this and other abbreviations of titles of collections of *jiagu* inscriptions, see Keightley, *Sources*, pp. 229-231.

Index

Columns in the restored strip text, pp. 126-165, are indicated by *, and pages are not given.

THE SIXTY-DAY "*GANZHI*" CYCLE

		甲	乙	丙	丁	戊	己	庚	辛	壬	癸
Gan:		**jia**	**yi**	**bing**	**ding**	**wu**	**ji**	**geng**	**xin**	**ren**	**gui**
		1	**2**	**3**	**4**	**5**	**6**	**7**	**8**	**9**	**10**
***Zhi*:**											
子 zi	1	01		13		25		37		49	
丑 chou	2		02		14		26		38		50
寅 yin	3	51		03		15		27		39	
卯 mao	4		52		04		16		28		40
辰 chen	5	41		53		05		17		29	
巳 si	6		42		54		06		18		30
午 wu	7	31		43		55		07		19	
未 wei	8		32		44		56		08		20
申 shen	9	21		33		45		57		09	
酉 you	10		22		34		46		58		10
戌 xu	11	11		23		35		47		59	
亥 hai	12		12		24		36		48		60

E.g., "*jiazi*" is "01"; "*yichou*" is "02"; etc. Naming days, the system has probably been in continuous use since pre-Shang times. In the Han Dynasty it came to be used to name years as well; and it is so used in the present text of the BA. E.g., the year 1051 BCE is "*gengyin*" (27). The *ganzhi* for any day can be obtained from the Julian Day number, by dividing by 60 and subtracting 10 from the remainder. If the remainder is 10 or less, add 50 to the remainder. (Julian Day numbers may be obtained from Stahlman and Gingerich.) In tables, when space does not allow using the day-name, I put the number in parentheses: (01) for *jiazi*, etc.